CONTENTS

PREFACE

Because the world is always changing, a new edition of this book is necessary every two years. Since the last edition, the world's economy has suffered a huge blow resulting in an alarming rise in unemployment figures worldwide and a dramatic collapse in the value of sterling. This book has been around for so long that I can remember the last major recession at the beginning of the 1990s. Ironically, that crisis seemed to create more opportunities for casual and temporary work because employers did not want to commit to taking on more permanent staff.

In these troubled times, the idea of fleeing to a new place with potentially new opportunities and a stronger currency might appeal more than ever. If job prospects are dire at home, why hang around to become depressed? Travel can transport you to a new universe where credit crunches don't seem to matter so much. If you are convinced that finding work at home will be next to impossible, one idea is to broaden your horizons and your skills elsewhere, by working in a Rocky Mountain ski resort or temping in an Australian city. Volunteering or interning may also prove a worthwhile investment in enhancing future career prospects, perhaps a placement teaching in a school in the Andes, or joining a marine research project in Madagascar.

Nowadays, working abroad has become such a mainstream idea that it has spawned scores of websites, been featured on primetime television and is serviced by a huge infrastructure for those who want to combine work and travel. This book has grown up with the travel industry and takes account of all those shortcuts to fixing up work abroad that now exist. The inclusion in its pages of hundreds if not thousands of potential employers, mediating agencies and useful internet sites sometimes makes me feel like a walking database.

Yet the swashbuckling kind of traveller who is prepared to carve out his or her own adventures is also alive and well and using this book to navigate. For this fourteenth edition of *Work Your Way Around the World* my network of informants included a new graduate who exchanged Spanish for English lessons in Santiago Chile until he was in a position to land a teaching contract at a prestigious English institute, a New Zealander who has found casual work from Buenos Aires to Stockholm, an Irish woman who ignored the discouraging recruitment and visa info from Disneyworld and spent a terrific year in Florida, a man no longer in the first flush of youth who has worked in exotic places like Mali and Mauritania, and is now in a small city south of Beijing as an English teacher, saving some of his salary for his next adventure, a young English woman who used an agency to fix up an internship in a video production company in Sydney, and a school leaver who busked in Paris and Seville and is now exchanging a few hours of work a day in order to stay free at a lakeside hostel in Guatemala. Almost with one voice, these travellers urge people whatever their backgrounds to give it a go and expose themselves to the unexpected friendliness and generosity of foreign residents and fellow travellers.

Anybody who occasionally feels the call of the road, the spirit of adventure flicker will, I hope, enjoy reading this book and dreaming. My aim has been to make the information in these 404 pages as concrete and up-to-the-minute as possible, to cut all the vague generalities and waffle. But amongst all the specific contact addresses, websites and realistic practical advice, the stories of working travellers are interwoven to inspire and encourage. This book is written to renew optimism and spark the imagination of all potential travellers.

Susan Griffith
Cambridge
July 2009

ACKNOWLEDGEMENTS

I never get tired of meeting and hearing from those intrepid travellers who are out there, sometimes living the life of Reilly, sometimes living on the edge. Their stories always enliven (and justify) my struggle to keep this book as up to date as possible. This new revised edition of *Work Your Way Around the World* would not have been possible without the help of hundreds of travellers who have generously shared their information over the years. Some have been writing to me over several editions, and their loyalty is greatly appreciated.

I would especially like to thank all those travellers who have crouched over keyboards in remote corners of the world and even (occasionally) bought a stamp to communicate with me since the last edition was prepared two years ago. All their pearls of travelling wisdom have been enthusiastically received and have been distilled into the pages that follow. My warmest thanks are owed to the following:

Jonathan Alderman, Rachel Beebe, Doug Burgess, Richard Ferguson, Tom Grundy, Catherine Howard, Bradwell Jackson, Paul Jones, Anna Ling, Barry O'Leary, Fiona Passey, Laura Rich, Emily Sloane, Holly Tate and Julia Wilson.

While every effort has been made to ensure that the information contained in this book was accurate at the time of going to press, some details are bound to change within the lifetime of this edition. Wages, exchange rates and government policies are particularly susceptible to fluctuations, and the ones quoted here are intended merely as a guide.

If in the course of your travels you come across something which might be of interest to readers of the next edition, please write to Susan Griffith at Vacation-Work/Crimson Publishing, Westminster House, Kew Road, Richmond, Surrey, TW9 2ND or email her at s.griffith@ntlworld.com (she promises to reply). This book depends very much on up-to-date reports from travellers who have worked their way. The best contributions will be rewarded with a free copy of the next edition or any other Vacation-Work title (listed at the end of this book).

INTRODUCTION

LIVING THE DREAM

The idea of going all the way around the world holds more than a touch of romance. From the early heroic navigators like Ferdinand Magellan to the fictional traveller Phileas Fogg, circumnavigators of our planet have always captured the imagination of adventurous souls. More recently Michael Palin's globetrotting television series and award-winning travel blogs like twoguysaroundtheworld.com attract huge audiences, perhaps because so many of us relish a chance to imagine ourselves – impossibly ambitious as it sounds – as round-the-world explorers.

Nothing can compare with the joy of the open road. The sense of possibility and adventure brings feelings of exhilaration, long submerged in the workaday routines of home. Cheap air travel has opened up parts of the globe once reserved for the seriously affluent. When travelling in far-flung corners of the world, you can escape the demands of modern life in the Western world, the chores, the clutter, the technology. Whatever your stage of life, travelling spontaneously means you have the freedom to choose from an infinite spectrum of possibilities. Those who have experienced independent travel normally catch the bug and long to visit more places, see more wonders and spend a longer time abroad. Today trekking in the hinterland of Rio de Janeiro or diving in the Philippines can be within the grasp of ordinary folk. The longing might stem from a fascination left over from childhood with an exotic destination like Madagascar or Patagonia. The motivation might come from a friend's reminiscences or a television travelogue or a personal passion for a certain culture or natural habitat. At some point a vague idea begins to crystallise into an actual possibility.

That is the point at which the purple prose of brochure-speak must be interrupted by hard-headed planning. The first question is always: how can I afford such a trip? Magellan had the backing of the King and Queen of Spain, Phileas Fogg was a gentleman of independent means and Michael Palin could call on the resources of the BBC. How can ordinary people possibly move their dreams on to reality? The conventional means to an exciting end is to work and save hard. A grim spell of working overtime and denying yourself a social life is one route to being able to join a safari in Tanzania, a watersport instructor's course on the Mediterranean or a bungee jump in New Zealand. But what if it were possible to skip this stage and head off towards the horizon sooner than that? Instead of trying to finance the expensive trips advertised in glossy travel brochures, what about trying to find alternative ways of experiencing those same places at a fraction of the cost?

The catchy phrase 'work your way around the world' may contain the answer to the thorny question of funding. Picking up bits and pieces of work along the way can go a long way to reducing the cost. Even if it is unrealistic to expect to walk into highly paid jobs in Beijing or Berlin (though they do exist), other informal ways exist of offsetting the cost of travel. Work-for-keep arrangements on a New Zealand farm or Costa Rican eco-lodge will mean that you have to save far less than if you booked a long-haul package holiday to those destinations – in some cases little more than the cost of the flight.

Short of emigrating or marrying a native, working abroad is an excellent way to experience a foreign culture from the inside. The plucky Briton who spends a few months on a Queensland outback station will have a different tale to tell about Australia from the one who serves behind the bar in a Sydney pub. Yet both will experience the exhilaration of doing something completely unfamiliar in an alien setting.

Anyone with a taste for adventure and a modicum of nerve has the potential for exploring far-flung corners of the globe on very little money. In an ideal world, it would be possible to register with an international employment agency and wait to be assigned to a glamorous job as an underwater model in the Caribbean, history co-ordinator for a European tour company or snowboard instructor in the Rockies. But jobs abroad, like jobs at home, must be ferreted out. The hundreds of pages that follow will help you to do just that.

THE DECISION TO GO

For many, deciding to get up and go is the biggest stumbling-block. Often the hardest step is fixing a departure date. Once you have bought a ticket, explained to your friends and family that you are off to see the world (they will either be envious or disapproving) and packed away your possessions, the rest seems to look after itself. Inevitably first-time travellers suffer some separation anxieties and pre-departure blues as they contemplate leaving behind the comfortable routines of home. But these are usually much worse in anticipation than in retrospect. As long as you have enough motivation, together with some money and a copy of this book, you are all set to have a great time abroad.

Either you follow your first impulse and opt for an immediate change of scenery, or you plan a job and a route in advance. On the one hand people use working as a means to an end; they work in order to fund further travelling. Other people look upon a job abroad as an end in itself, a way to explore other cultures, a means of satisfying their curiosity about whether there is any truth in the clichés about other nationalities. Often it is the best way to shake off the boredom which comes with routine. One contributor to this book felt quite liberated when she decided to drop everything – her 'cushy secretarial job, Debenhams account card, stiletto heels' – and embark on a working holiday around Europe. Another finally kicked over the traces of what he described as the 'office job from Hell' when he went off to Thailand to teach English.

When you are wondering whether you are the right sort to work abroad, do not imagine you are a special case. It is not only students, school-leavers and people on the dole who enjoy the chance to travel and work, but also a large number of people with a profession, craft or trade which they were happy to abandon temporarily. We have heard from a man who left the Met Office to pick grapes in Pauillac, a sixth former teaching in Nepal, a mechanical engineer crewing on yachts in the South Pacific, a fire poi busker in Spain, a bicycle courier who got a job as a sports coach at a prep school in Kenya, a nurse who busked in Norway and another who worked on a sheep station in Australia, an Australian teacher who became a nanny in Istanbul, a Scottish lawyer who worked as a chalet girl in a French ski resort, a German tourism trainee who planted trees in Canada, a chartered surveyor who took more than two years off from his job to work his way around the world and a journalist and tour operator couple who picked up casual jobs to fund their 'Stuff Mammon World Tour' and ended up living quite comfortably in Hong Kong. All were motivated not by a desire to earn money but by a craving for new and different experiences, and a conviction that not all events which make up one's life need to be career-furthering or 'success'-oriented.

PREPARATION

It is not the Mr Micawbers of this world who succeed at getting jobs. (Mr Micawber is the character in Charles Dickens's *David Copperfield* who is famous for living in hopeful expectation without taking any practical steps to bring about a successful outcome.) If you sit around as he did 'waiting for something to turn up' you will soon find yourself penniless with no prospects for replenishing your travel funds. If you wait in idleness at home or if you sit in your hostel all day worrying about your dwindling euros or pesos, hesitating and dithering because you are convinced the situation is hopeless or that you lack the necessary documents to work, you will get absolutely nowhere.

Every successful venture combines periodic flights of fancy with methodical planning. The majority of us lack the courage (or the recklessness) just to get up and go. And any homework you do ahead of time will benefit you later, if only because it will give you more confidence. But it is important to strike a good balance between slavishly following a predetermined itinerary which might prevent you from grasping opportunities as they arise and setting off with no idea of what you're looking for. Many travel converts regret their initial decision to buy an air ticket with a fixed return date.

For many people, a shortage of money is the main obstacle. It is the rare individual who trusts to fate and sets off with next to nothing. Other people wait until they have substantial savings before they dare leave home which gives them the enviable freedom to work only when they want to.

SOMETIMES PENURY ACTS AS A SPUR TO ACTION AS IT DID IN THE CASE OF ROGER BLAKE:
I left home with a substantial amount in savings. But they are long gone and for 18 months I have only been living off whatever I make locally. I have been down to just $50 more times than I'd care to remember. But somehow I always seem to come right. When I hear fellow travellers grumbling and sick with worry that they are down to $500, I cannot help but exclaim that they should enjoy it. In other words, when you've got it, flaunt it! Enjoy! There are those (usually with a few hundred dollars in the bank) who are 'looking for work' and those (including myself) who are looking for work. When your funds are REALLY low you WILL find a job, believe me.

Anyone embarking on an extended trip will have to have a certain amount of capital to buy tickets, visas, insurance (see below), etc. But it is amazing how a little can go a long way if you are willing to take a wide variety of casual jobs en route and willing to weather the financial doldrums. Stephen Psallidas had £40 one December and four months later (most of which was spent working as a waiter in Paris) he had £1,600 for a planned year in Australia.

Money

It is of course always a good idea to have an emergency fund in reserve if possible, or at least access to money from home should you run into difficulties (see section on 'Transferring Money' in *In Extremis* at the end of this book). How much you decide to set aside before leaving will depend on whether or not you have a gambling streak. But even gamblers should take only sensible risks. If you don't have much cash, it's probably advisable to have a return ticket. For example, if you decide to crew on a yacht from the Mediterranean and don't have much money, you could buy a very cheap last minute return flight to Rhodes or the Canaries. If you succeed and waste the return half of your charter, wonderful; if not, you will have had a few weeks in the sun – disappointing perhaps but not desperate.

Attitudes to saving vary too. Some people relish the planning stages while saving for a trip. Others find saving over a long period depressing and start to long for those clubbing nights and meals out of which they have been deprived. When Xuela Edwards returned after two years of working her way around Europe, she tried to hang on to the travelling mentality which makes it much easier to save money: '*My advice is to consider your home country in the same way as others. It makes you more resourceful. Try to avoid the car loans and high living that usually make up home life. I'm sure that the reason bulb workers in Holland for example save so much money is because they live in tents (which I admit would be tricky at home).'*

Mike Tunnicliffe spent more on his world travels than he intended but didn't regret it: '*Originally, I intended to finance my year with casual work and return to England having spent only the price of my ticket. In the end, I delved far deeper into my life's savings than I had intended to do, but I was fortunate in having savings on which to draw, and I made the conscious decision to enjoy my year while I had the chance. In other words, fun now, pay later.*'

Once you are resolved to travel, set a realistic target amount to save and then go for it wholeheartedly. Don't get just any job, get one which is either highly paid (easier said than done of course) or one which offers as much overtime as you want. Dedicated working travellers consider a 70-hour week quite tolerable which will have the additional advantage of leaving you too shattered to conduct an expensive social life. If you have collected some assets before setting off, you are luckier than most. Property owners can arrange for the rental money to follow them at regular intervals.

The average budget of a travelling student is about £25–£30 a day though many survive in countries like Laos and Bolivia on half that. Whatever the size of your travelling fund, you should plan to access your money from three sources: cash, credit cards and travellers' cheques. Travellers' cheques are safer than cash, though they cost an extra 1% or 2%. They are a useful standby if you happen to find yourself stranded in a place without an ATM. American Express have monopolised the market and their cheques are sold by most banks. Try to avoid frequent transactions since suitable banks outside big cities are not always easy to find and encashing them can incur a service charge. The website moneyfacts.co.uk carries a comparative list of commission charged by the main providers (search for 'Travel Money').

The most straightforward way to access money abroad is by using your bank debit card in hole-in-the-wall ATMs. There is usually a minimum fee for a withdrawal so you should get larger amounts out at one time than you would at home. Read the fine print on those boring leaflets that come with your debit card because it may be that your bank will gouge you with various loading fees, withdrawal fees and transaction fees. For example the transaction fee for withdrawing foreign currency abroad or paying at point-of-sale with a standard Maestro card is 2.65% in addition to the ordinary exchange rate disadvantage, plus cash machine withdrawals cost 2.25% of the sterling transaction. In everyday language this means that a withdrawal from a hole-in-the-wall can cost £4–£5. The Point of Sale charge is a more reasonable 75 pence. If you are going to be abroad for a considerable period drawing on funds in your home account, it would be worth shopping around for the best deal which is at present offered in the UK by the Nationwide Building Society. Until June 2009, their FlexAccount debit card permitted free withdrawals. However that now applies only to Europe; outside Europe there is a 1% charge, which is still cheaper than most.

The Post Office sells a Travel Money Card which is a prepaid, reloadable card that can be used like a debit card at ATMs and most shops but is not linked to your bank account. You can purchase it online and load it with sterling, euros or US dollars. Be aware that the exchange rate and transaction fees may not be better than the rival methods. Similarly the Travellers Cashcard (iceplc.com), part of MasterCard, and Travelex's Cash Passport (travelex.co.uk) operate the same way, but charge steep exchange rates.

It is always advisable to keep a small amount of cash handy. Sterling is fine for many countries but US dollars are preferred in much of the world such as Latin America and Israel. The easiest way to look up the exchange rate of any world currency when planning your travels is to check on the internet (e.g. xe.net/ucc) or to look at the Monday edition of the *Financial Times.* Most banks require a few days' notice to obtain a foreign currency for you. Marks & Spencer's *Travel Money* offers favourable exchange rates with no commission or handling charges on currency or travellers' cheques. Furthermore these can be ordered online and posted to your home. The Post Office and Thomas Cook also offer decent rates.

A credit card is useful for many purposes, provided you will not be tempted to abuse it. A credit card can be invaluable in an emergency and handy for showing at borders where the officials frown on penniless tourists, as Roger Blake discovered when he tried to leave Australia on a one-way ticket:

> ***On my world travels, I'm usually prepared to be challenged, by having printed bank statements (of borrowed money) at the ready. However, having never been asked before I didn't bother this time and, sods law, at Melbourne airport they weren't happy about allowing me to leave on a one-way ticket to New Zealand without proof of 'sufficient funds'. I pointed out that it states on my NZ work visa 'outward passage waived' but they were having none of it. I only had about $400 in my pocket. But fortunately I have generous 'credit' available on my credit card. I was able to log onto my account via the internet and that was enough to persuade them to let me through...eventually, just one day short of a year to the day after I arrived.***

From London to La Paz there are crooks lurking, ready to pounce upon the unsuspecting traveller. Theft takes many forms, from the highly trained gangs of gypsy children who artfully pick pockets all over Europe to violent attacks on the streets of American cities. Even more depressing is the theft which takes place by other travellers in youth hostels or on beaches. Risks can be reduced by carrying your wealth in several places including a comfortable money belt worn inside your clothing, steering clear of seedy or crowded areas, avoiding counting your money in public and moderating your intake of alcohol. If you are mugged, and have an insurance policy which covers cash, you must obtain a police report (often for a fee) to stand any chance of recouping part of your loss.

While you are busy saving money to reach your desired target, you should be thinking of other ways in which to prepare yourself, including health, what to take and which contacts and skills you might cultivate.

Baggage

While aiming to travel as light as possible (leave the hair products behind) you should consider the advantage of taking certain extra pieces of equipment. For example many working travellers consider the extra weight of a tent and sleeping bag worthwhile in view of the independence and flexibility it gives them if they are offered work by a farmer who cannot provide accommodation. A comfortable pair of shoes is essential, since a job hunt abroad often involves a lot of pavement pounding.

Mobile phones are now *de rigueur* for any job hunt on the road (see section below on 'Staying in Touch' for advice). Other items that can be packed that might be useful for a specific money-making project include a penny whistle or guitar for busking, a jacket and tie for getting work as an English teacher or data inputter, a pair of gloves (fingerless, rubber, as appropriate) for cold-weather fruit-picking, and so on. Leave at home anything of value (monetary or sentimental). The general rule is stick to the bare essentials (including a Swiss army knife – but not in your hand luggage if you're flying or it will be confiscated at security). One travelling tip is to carry dental floss, useful not only for your teeth but as strong twine for mending backpacks, hanging up laundry, etc. You might allow yourself the odd (lightweight) luxury, such as an iPod (though theft will be a worry and recharging a hassle), short-wave radio or a jar of peanut butter. If you have prearranged a job, you can always post some belongings on ahead.

Good maps and guides always enhance one's enjoyment of a trip. If you are going to be based in a major city, buy a map ahead of time. Plan to visit the famous map and travel shop Edward Stanford Ltd with branches in Bristol and Manchester as well as the mother-store in Covent Garden, London, whose searchable catalogue is online at stanfords.co.uk. Also recommended is Daunt Books for Travellers (83 Marylebone High Street, London W1; dauntbooks.co.uk and four other branches in London) which stock fiction and travel writing alongside guide books and maps. The Map Shop in Worcestershire (☎ 0800 085 4080/01684 593146; themapshop.co.uk) and Maps Worldwide in Wiltshire (01225 707004; mapsworldwide.co.uk) both do an extensive mail order business in specialised maps, guide books and GPS equipment.

Dozens of travel specialists throughout North America exist from the Globe Corner Bookstore in Harvard Square, Boston (globecorner.com) to Get Lost Books in San Francisco (getlostbooks.com) and Wanderlust in Vancouver.

Insurance

Extensive information about health issues for travellers is given at the end of the next chapter about Travel. One of the keys to avoiding medical disaster is to have adequate insurance cover. All travellers must face the possibility of an accident befalling them abroad. In countries like India, Turkey and Venezuela, the rate of road traffic accidents can be as much as twenty times greater than in the UK. Research carried out by the Foreign and Commonwealth Office revealed that more than a quarter of travellers aged 16–34 do not purchase travel insurance, which means that about three million people are taking a serious risk.

Given the limitations of state-provided reciprocal health cover (i.e. that it covers only emergencies), you should certainly take out comprehensive private cover which will cover extras like loss of baggage and, more importantly, emergency repatriation. Every enterprise in the travel business is delighted to sell you insurance because of the commission earned. Shopping around can save you money. Ring several insurance companies with your specifications and compare prices. If you are going abroad to work, you are expected to inform your insurer ahead of time (which is often impossible). Many policies will be invalidated if you injure yourself at work, e.g. put out your back while picking plums or cut yourself in a restaurant kitchen. Normal travel policies may not cover volunteer jobs either unless specified on the policy.

Many companies charge less, though you will have to decide whether you are satisfied with their level of cover. Most offer a standard rate that covers medical emergencies and a premium rate that covers personal baggage, cancellation, etc. If you are not planning to visit North America, the premiums will be much less expensive. Some companies to consider are listed here. Expect to pay roughly £25 per month for basic backpacker cover and £30–£40 for more extensive cover.

Club Direct: West Sussex; ☎ 0800 083 2466; clubdirect.com; work abroad is included provided it does not involve using heavy machinery.

Columbus Direct: ☎ 0870 033 9988; columbusdirect.com; one of the giants in the field of travel insurance affiliated with Rough Guides; from £220 for twelve months worldwide cover.

Coverworks Direct: Cheshire; ☎ 01270 625431; coverworksdirect.com Policy specially designed for working holidays in Australia and New Zealand; in 2009 had a special offer of including a free working holiday visa for Australia with a 12-month worldwide policy costing £289.

Direct Travel Insurance: ☎ 0845 605 2700; direct-travel.co.uk; consistently among the cheapest, e.g. 12 months worldwide minimalist cover starting at £131.

Downunder Worldwide Travel Insurance: London W2; ☎ 0800 393908; duinsure.com; can be extended while you're on the road.
Endsleigh Insurance: ☎ 0800 028 3571; 12 months of backpacker basic cover costs £335, £402 for comprehensive cover; maximum age 35.
gosure.com: ☎ 0845 222 0020; gosure.com; explorer one-year policies for 18–34 year olds cost £216 with no baggage cover, £240 with baggage cover.
MRL Insurance: Surrey; ☎ 0845 676 0691; mrlinsurance.co.uk.
Navigator Travel Insurance Services Ltd Manchester; 0161 973 6435; navigatortravel.co.uk.

If you do have to make a claim, you may be unpleasantly surprised by the amount of the settlement eventually paid. Loss adjusters have ways of making calculations which prove that you are entitled to less than you think. The golden rule is to amass as much documentation as possible to support your claim, most importantly a police report.

Recommended US insurers for extended stays abroad are International SOS Assistance Inc (☎ 1 800 523 8930; internationalsos.com) which is used by the Peace Corps and is designed for people working in remote areas. A firm which specialises in providing insurance for Americans living overseas is Wallach & Company (☎ 1 800 237 6615; wallach.com).

Security

Travel inevitably involves balancing risks and navigating through hazards real or imagined. The Foreign and Commonwealth Office of the UK government runs a regular and updated service; you can check fco.gov.uk/travel or ring the Travel Advice Unit on 0845 850 2829 (£0.04 per minute) though the advisors will tell you nothing more than is on the website which gives frequently updated and detailed risk assessments of any trouble spots, including civil unrest, terrorism and crime. The FCO promotes a 'Know Before You Go' campaign to raise awareness among backpackers and independent travellers of potential risks and dangers and how to guard against them, principally by taking out a water-tight insurance policy. The same emphasis can be detected on the FCO site aimed specifically at younger travellers: gogapyear.co.uk.

The site travellingalone.co.uk features articles on various topics of interest to the potentially nervous lone traveller. A couple of specialist organisations put on courses to prepare clients for potential dangers and problems on a world trip or gap year. Needless to say, these are normally aimed at naïve 18-year-olds whose parents are paying for the course, though they are open to anyone willing to pay the fee of £150–£350. The main providers are Safetrek in Devon (☎ 01884 839704; safetrek.co.uk), Planet Wise near Oxford (☎ 0870 2000 220; PlanetWise.net) which runs one-day travel safety and awareness courses for £160, and Objective Gap Safety (☎ 01788 899029; objectivegapyear.com) whose one-day courses in London cost £150.

Qualifications

These sensible precautions of purchasing maps, buying insurance, finding out about malaria, etc. are relatively straightforward and easy. Other specific ways of preparing yourself, such as studying a language, learning to sail or dive, cook or drive, or taking up a fitness programme, are a different kettle of fish. But the traveller who has a definite commitment may well consider embarking on a self-improvement scheme before setting off. Among the most useful qualifications you can acquire are a certificate in Teaching English as a Foreign Language (see chapter *Teaching English*) and a knowledge of sailing or diving (see *Tourism* chapter for the address of a course which also offers job placement).

It is a good idea to take documentary evidence of any qualifications you have earned. Also take along a sheaf of references, both character and work-related, if possible, all on headed notepaper. It is difficult to arrange for these to be sent once you're on the road. An even smarter move is to scan these documents before you depart and email them to yourself. That way you can access them from any internet café around the world. It is a good idea to prepare your CV at the same time. When it comes time to apply for a job abroad, you'll have the template on the computer and can just tinker with it according to the vacancy you're going for.

Language

Having even a limited knowledge of a foreign language is especially valuable for the job-seeker. Evening language classes offered by local authorities usually follow the academic year and are aimed at hobby learners. Intensive courses offered privately are much more expensive. If you are really dedicated, consider using a self-study programme with books and tapes, distance learning course or broadcast language course, though discipline is required to make progress. Although many people have been turning to the web to teach them a language, many conventional teach-yourself courses are still on the market, for example the *Take Off in...* series from OUP (askoxford.com/languages) available as mp3 downloads, the BBC (bbc.co.uk/languages), Linguaphone (☎ 0800 136973; linguaphone.co.uk) and Audioforum (audioforum.com). Linguaphone recommends half an hour of study a day for three months to master the basics of a language. Even if you don't make much headway with the course at home, take the tapes and books with you since you will have more incentive to learn once you are immersed in a language.

A more enjoyable way of learning a language (and normally a more successful one) is by speaking it with the natives. The cheapest way to do this is to link up with a native speaker living in your local area, possibly by putting an ad in a local paper or making contact through a local English language school. Numerous organisations offer 'in-country' language courses, though these tend to be expensive. CESA Languages Abroad in Cornwall (☎ 01209 211800; cesalanguages.com) and Language Courses Abroad Ltd (☎ 01509 211612; languagesabroad.co.uk) offer the chance to learn languages on location. Edinburgh-based Caledonia Languages Abroad (☎ 0131 621 7721; caledonialanguages.co.uk) offers language courses worldwide and in Latin America combines language courses with volunteer placements. An effective US-based search engine for locating courses is provided by the Institute of International Education on iiepassport.org. Alternatives are abroadlanguages.com and worldwide.edu.

Another possibility is to forgo structured lessons and simply live with a family, which has the further advantage of allowing you to become known in a community which might lead to job openings later. Some tourist offices and private agencies arrange paying guest stays, also known as homestays, which are designed for people wishing to learn or improve language skills in the context of family life.

BASED ON HIS YEARS OF LIVING ON THREE CONTINENTS, TILL BRUCKNER THINKS THAT LEARNING THE LANGUAGE IS PIVOTAL:

Learning the local language will not only help you find a job on the spot, it also makes life abroad so much more rewarding. As an extra bonus, you'll find work easier to come by when you return home too. The first thing I do when I arrive somewhere now is to get myself language lessons. The teacher will have met many other foreigners, have local connections and speak some English. In other words, he or she is the natural starting point on your job hunt. If you make clear that you can only continue paying for your lessons if you find a way of earning some money, you've found a highly motivated ally in your search for work.

Making Contacts

The importance of knowing people, not necessarily in high places but on the spot, is stressed by many of our contributors. Some people are lucky enough to have family and friends scattered around the world in positions to offer advice or even employment. Others must create their own contacts by exploiting less obvious connections.

Dick Bird, who spent over a year travelling around South America, light-heartedly anticipates how this works:

> ***In Bolivia we hope to start practising another survival technique known as 'having some addresses'. The procedure is quite simple. Before leaving one's country of origin, inform everyone you know from your immediate family to the most casual acquaintance, that you are about to leave for South America. With only a little cajoling they might volunteer the address of somebody they once met on the platform of Clapham Junction or some other tenuous connection who went out to South America to seek their fortunes. You then present your worthy self on the unsuspecting emigré's doorstep and announce that you have been in close and recent communication with their nearest and dearest. Although you won't necessarily be welcomed with open arms, the chances are they will be eager for your company and conversation. Furthermore these contacts are often useful for finding work: doing odd jobs, farming, tutoring people they know, etc.***

With the rise of Facebook, international connections are easier to establish than ever. Maybe you dimly recall that someone you went to primary school with moved to New Zealand or Tenerife and you could re-establish contact. By joining online communities and travel forums, you can make virtual friends and find advice from around the world. Some enterprising and imaginative bloggers have benefited from sharing their stories, pictures and videos and attracted offers of hospitality and even sponsorship. For example, the two Americans who set up twoguysaroundtheworld.com won Lonely Planet's Travel Blogger Award in 2009 and their website has contributed to their ability to go round the world on a limited budget.

One way of developing contacts is to join a travel club such as the Globetrotters Club (BCM/Roving, London WC1N 3XX; globetrotters.co.uk) for £15 a year. The Club has no office and so correspondence addressed to the above box office address is answered by volunteers. Members receive a bi-monthly travel newsletter and a list of members, many of whom are willing to extend hospitality to other globetrotters and possibly to advise them on local employment prospects.

Servas International is an organisation begun by an American Quaker, which runs a worldwide programme of free hospitality exchanges for travellers, to further world peace and understanding. Normally you don't stay with one host for more than a couple of days. To become a Servas traveller or host in the UK, contact Servas Britain (☎ 020 8444 7778; servasbritain.u-net.com) who can forward your enquiry to your area co-ordinator. Before a traveller can be given a list of hosts, he or she must pay a fee of £25 (£35 for couples) and be interviewed by a coordinator. Servas US is in California (☎ 707 825 1714; usservas.org) and is linked to couchsurfing (see below). There is a joining fee of US$85 and a refundable deposit of $25 for host lists in up to five countries. Prices are reduced if you agree also to be a host as well as a traveller.

Hospitality exchange organisations can make travel both interesting and cheap. The one with the highest profile is the wonderfully named couchsurfing.com. Like so many internet-based projects, the system depends on users' feedback, which means that you can check on a potential host's profile in advance and be fairly sure that dodgy hosts will be outed straightaway.

Bradwell Jackson had been mulling over the possibility of travelling the world for about a decade before he finally gave up his drug abuse counselling job in the US to take off for an indeterminate period of time. On his earlier travels he had discovered the benefits of joining Servas and two other free accommodation networks Global Freeloaders (globalfreeloaders.com) and the Hospitality Club (hospitalityclub.org) which has a special area for hitch-hikers. His first destination was Mexico where to his delight he found English teaching work at the first place he happened to enquire in Mexico City:

> ***I really must say right away that Servas is not simply for freeloading in people's homes. However, once you take the plunge and commit to wandering the earth, things just start to fall into place. If you belong to clubs such as Global Freeloaders, Hospitality Club, or any of the other homestay organisations, don't be surprised if the family you stay with invites you for an extended stay. The first such family I stayed with in Mexico invited me to stay for six months. All they asked is that I help with the costs of the food they prepared for me and hot water I used.***

Bradwell has continued his couchsurfing travels in some unlikely locations. He left Mauritania at the beginning of 2008 and stayed with a host in Bamako, Mali who offered to let him stay for two months in exchange for two hours of English lessons a day. His host was a wealthy man who gave Brad all his meals, internet access, laundry and so on. He commented that *'once one lands into a dream situation like this, you are apt to feel a bit guilty, and such hospitality takes time to get used to. Still, I am certainly not complaining'.*

When you register with the Hospitality Club, Global Freeloaders, place2stay.net or the Couchsurfing Project (couchsurfing.com), all of which are completely free, you agree to host the occasional visitor in your home in order to earn the right to stay with other members worldwide.

Other hospitality clubs and exchanges are worth investigating. Women Welcome Women World Wide (☎ 01494 465441; womenwelcomewomen.org.uk) enables women of different countries to visit one another. There is no set subscription, but the minimum donation requested is £35/$67, which covers the cost of the membership list and three newsletters in which members may publish announcements. There are currently 2,500 members (aged 16–80+) in 83 countries.

Travelling Alone or in Company

Many travellers emphasise the benefits of travelling alone, especially the chance to make friends with the locals more easily. Most are surprised that loneliness is hardly an issue, since there are always congenial companions to be found in travellers' hostels, harbourside pubs, language classes, etc. some of whom even team up with each other if they happen to be heading in the same direction. If you are anxious about the trials and traumas of being on your own, try a short trip and see how you like it.

Women can travel solo just as enjoyably as men, as Woden Teachout discovered when she was 24:

> ***I'm female, American and like to travel alone. I have travelled with friends on occasion which is definitely more 'fun' but it lacks the perilous sense of possibility and adventure that I love most about travelling. Whatever situations you get yourself into when you are on your own, you have to get out of. I have been terribly frightened: I spent the night of my 21st birthday huddled in a cellar hole in downtown Malmo, Sweden, wet and shivering, knowing that a local rapist had claimed three victims within the fortnight. But by the same token, the glorious moments, the stick-out-your-thumb-and-be-glad-for-whatever-is-going-to-happen-next moments, the feelings of triumph and absolute freedom, are uniquely yours.***

You have to be fairly lucky to have a friend who is both willing and available when you are ready to embark on a working trip. If you don't have a suitable companion and are convinced you need one, you can search on appropriate internet forums like Lonely Planet's Thorntree, backpackers.com with a 'Travel Buddies' forum, companions2travel.co.uk or (if appropriate) gapyear.com, any of which might turn up a like-minded companion. Start your search for a companion well in advance of your proposed departure date so there will be a chance to get to know the person a bit before the trip.

There are also a few agencies in the US which try to match up compatible travel companions for an annual or a one-off fee, for example TravelChums (travelchums.com).

Staying in Touch

Fixing yourself up with a web-based email account before leaving home is now virtually compulsory. This allows you to keep in touch with and receive messages from home and also with friends met on the road.

Roaming charges for mobiles can cost an arm and a leg. Contact your mobile phone company to check on coverage; if not you may need to take it into a shop to have the phone 'unlocked'. Also check what deals your provider offers, which can be spectacularly complex. Vodafone's 'Passport' is a free tariff option available with any handset, which allows you to make calls at your home tariff after paying a 75p connection fee. It is available in most of Europe, Australia, New Zealand and Japan but not North America (abroad.vodafone.co.uk).

If you are going to be on the move a lot, you might want to invest in a gadget that can charge your mobile and iPod using solar power: the Solio charger (solio.com) retails from about £40.

Warn friends not to call your UK mobile while you are away; you will be paying for all incoming calls from abroad. If you are staying in one country for more than a few weeks and use your phone a lot, consider getting either a cheap local mobile phone or a local Sim card for your UK mobile.

Even better, ensure your UK contacts have the special access codes available for low cost dialling to your destination. One of the most often recommended discount companies (for people phoning abroad from the UK) is telediscount.co.uk in the UK which offers unbeatable prices: in many cases you can make an international call at local rates.

A plethora of companies in the UK and US sell pre-paid calling cards intended to simplify international phoning. You credit your card account with an amount of your choice (normally starting at £10 or £20), or buy a card for $10 or $20. You are given an access code which can be used from any phone. Lonely Planet, the travel publisher, has an easy-to-use communications card called eKit which offers low cost calls, voice mail and email (lonelyplanet.ekit.com). A company called 0044 (0044.co.uk) sells foreign Sim cards which allow you to take your mobile with you and call at local rates while you're away. Their global Sim card costs £20 compared to £30 from GoSim (gosim.com).

More and more travellers send digital photos home electronically and set up their own website or blog (i.e. web log) to share their travel tales with family and friends. Lots of companies will help you create your own blog, for example blogger.com/start (which is free) while the photo and video sharing site http://community.webshots.com is designed for people to upload their photos (free for storing up to 1,000 photos). Another recommended site for starting your own blog or following the travel blogs of others is http://blogs.bootsnall.com.

Clearly there are advantages to such easy communication, though there are also travellers out there who spend an inordinate amount of time tracking down and inhabiting cybercafés instead of looking around the country and meeting locals in the old-fashioned, strike-up-a-conversation way. Danny Jacobson from Madison is also ambivalent about its virtues (and committed his thoughts to paper): *'I've met loads of travellers using e-mail to meet people online, to keep in touch with people they've met travelling, to find out information about a place and to publish their own adventures. It all seems to be making the world an incredibly small place. Myself, I admit I've spent a fair share of money on e-mail and rely on it at times quite a bit. I worry that it is getting easier and easier to do everything from a sitting position.'*

It would be a shame if email deprived long-term travellers of arriving at a poste restante address and having the pleasure (sweeter because it has been deferred) of reading their mail.

RED TAPE

Passports and Work Permits

A ten-year UK passport costs £72 for 32 pages and £85 for 48 pages, and should be processed by the Identity and Passport Service within three weeks. The one-week fast track application procedure costs £97 and an existing passport can be renewed within one day if it is done in person at a passport office but only if you have made a prior appointment by ringing 0300 222 0000 and pay the premium fee of £123. Passport office addresses are listed on passport application forms available from main post offices. All relevant information can be found on the website ips.gov.uk.

Most countries will want to see that your passport has at least 90 days to run beyond your proposed stay. If your passport is lost or stolen while travelling, contact first the police then your nearest consulate. Obtaining replacement travel documents is easier if you have a record of the passport number and its date and place of issue, so keep these in a separate place, preferably a photocopy of the title page scanned and stored in your email account.

The free reciprocity of labour within the European Union means that the red tape has been simplified (though not done away with completely). As will become clear as you read further in this book, work permits outside the EU are not readily available to ordinary mortals. (As a rule of thumb, the word visa applies to entering, visiting and exiting a country, whereas permits are for longer stays including working.) To be eligible for a work permit, you must invariably have an employer or sponsoring company willing to apply to the immigration authorities on your behalf months in advance of the job's starting date, while you are in your home country. This is usually a next-to-impossible feat unless you are a high ranking nuclear physicist, a foreign correspondent or are participating in an organised exchange programme where the red tape is taken care of by your sponsoring organisation. Wherever possible, we have mentioned such possibilities throughout this book. For general information about visas, see the next chapter.

Once you are installed in a country, be aware that any enemy you make who knows that your legal position is dodgy will be tempted to tip off the authorities. For example if you are trying to freelance as a guide and are resented by local operators, you may find yourself in trouble.

Bureaucracy at Large

Having your papers in order is a recurring problem for the working traveller. Andrew Winwood thinks that this book underestimates the difficulties: '*I wish that you would be honest about immigration, obtaining the proper visas, etc. But having said that, I wouldn't have had the nerve to go in the first place if I'd known how hard it would be.*'

It is easy to understand why every country in the world has immigration policies that are principally job protection schemes for their own nationals. Nevertheless it can be frustrating to encounter bureaucratic hassles if you merely intend to teach English for a month or work on a farm, and there are really no local candidates available. In all the countries with which we deal, we have tried to set out as clearly as possible the official position regarding visas and work and/or residence permits for both EU and non-EU readers.

If you are cautious by nature you may be very reluctant to transgress the regulations. People in this category will feel happier if they can arrange things through official channels, such as approved exchange organisations or agencies which arrange permits. Other travellers are prepared to throw caution to the winds and echo Helen Welch's view that 'government bureaucracy is the same anywhere, i.e. notoriously slow; by the time the system discovers that you are an alien you can be long gone'. This is more serious in some countries and in certain circumstances than in others, and we have tried to give some idea in this book of the enthusiasm with which the immigration laws are enforced from country to country and the probable outcome for employer and employee if the rules are broken. The authorities will usually turn a blind eye in areas where there is a labour shortage and enforce the letter of the law when there is a glut of unemployed foreign workers. If you do land an unofficial job (helping a Greek islander build a taverna, picking kiwifruit in New Zealand, doing odd jobs at an orphanage in central Africa) try to be as discreet as possible. Noisy boasting has been the downfall of many a traveller who has attracted unwelcome attention. It is always important to be as sensitive as possible to local customs and expectations.

Whenever you pass through immigration at airports with only a tourist visa, never let on that you intend anything other than sightseeing. Do not use the word 'work' or even 'volunteer'. If the authorities are suspicious they may search your luggage so do not carry anything as incriminating as was found in the bag of a Mexican man arriving at Manchester airport in March 2009; he was carrying a good luck card for his 'new life in the UK' and was promptly deported the next day.

GETTING A JOB BEFORE YOU GO

The subsequent chapters contain a great deal of advice and a number of useful web addresses and phone numbers for people wishing to fix up a job before they leave home. If you have ever worked for a firm with branches abroad (e.g. Starbucks, Manpower, even McDonalds) it may be worth contacting sister branches abroad about prospects. There are lots of 'easy' ways to break into the world of working travellers, for instance working on an American summer camp, joining a two-week volunteer project on the Continent or going on a kibbutz, all of which can be fixed up beforehand through obvious channels. Inevitably these will introduce you to an international circle of travellers whose experiences will entertain, instruct and inspire the novice traveller.

Professional or skilled people have a chance of prearranging a job. For example nurses, plumbers, architects, motor mechanics, piano tuners, teachers, divers, hairdressers, secretaries and computer programmers can sometimes find work abroad within their profession by answering online adverts or scouring specialist journals, by writing direct to hospitals, schools and businesses abroad, and by registering with the appropriate professional association or recruitment agency.

But the majority of people who dream about working their way around the world do not have a professional or trade qualification. Many will be students who are on the way to becoming qualified, but are impatient to broaden their horizons before graduation. The main requirement seems to be perseverance. Dennis Bricault sent off 137 letters in order to fix up a summer job as a volunteer at an alpine youth hostel.

ROB ABBLETT RECOUNTS HOW DOGGEDNESS WORKED IN HIS FAVOUR:
Armed with a couple of addresses of Corsican clementine farmers, I hounded them mercilessly over the years with my requests for work. The organic fruit farm wouldn't employ me on any terms and seemed a bit miffed when I phoned them. My present employer would throw my letters straight into the waste-paper basket. By pure chance one of them escaped his attention and got through to the sleeping partner who happened to have had an English nanny and spoke excellent English. He persuaded my boss to employ me on condition that he accepted full responsibility for kicking me off the orchard if I turned out to be like the last Brit who worked here many years ago. Apparently I have been an exemplary worker and have been wined and dined over the Christmas period with many a banquet.

Several editions ago, a reader and traveller expressed his longing for a miraculous network of information for working travellers:

> ***Wouldn't it be great if someone set up a scheme, whereby people could forward correspondence to an exchange of some kind, for people to swap addresses of places they've worked abroad. For example someone planning to work in Nice could write to some agency to obtain the address of another traveller who could tell him what the manager's like or if the chef is an axe-wielding homicidal maniac or that the accommodation is a hole in the bottom of the local coal mine. This would enable working travellers to avoid the rip-off places; also it might save them turning up in places where the work potential is zero.***

The scheme which Stephen thought was a pipedream just a few years ago now has a name, the internet. Somewhere on the web, you can probably find out that the axe-wielding chef has been replaced by a Quaker and that the coal mine has been tastefully refurbished.

Employment Agencies

Adverts that offer glamorous jobs and high wages abroad should be treated with scepticism. They are often placed by one-man companies who are in fact selling printed bumph about jobs on cruise ships, in the United States or whatever, which will not get you much closer to any dream job, whatever their ads promise (e.g. 'Earn up to £400 a week in Japan' or 'Would you like to work on a luxury cruise ship?'). A not infrequent con is to charge people for regular job listings and contacts in their chosen destination, which may consist of adverts lifted from newspapers or addresses from the *Yellow Pages* long out of date.

By law UK employment agencies (and those in many other countries) are not permitted to charge job-seekers an upfront fee. They make their money from the company or organisation seeking staff. Every so often a bogus agency will place false recruitment advertisements in the tabloid press charging a 'registration fee' or a compulsory charge for extra services. They then disappear without trace. Some operate as clubs offering members certain services such as translating and circulating CVs. Travellers should be cautious of job offers found online. At the time of writing in 2009, an individual had been arrested in England after registering as a bogus 'family' on an au pair matching website and was asking applicants to transfer funds in advance of arrival.

There are of course reputable international recruitment agencies in Britain, the USA and elsewhere, many of them operating solely online. Specialist agencies for qualified personnel can be very useful, for example agencies for financial and IT vacancies with branches worldwide. Agencies with a range of specialities from disc jockeys for international hotels to English teachers for language schools abroad are mentioned in the relevant chapters which follow.

Do not neglect EURES, the state-run employment service within Europe which helps unskilled workers to find seasonal jobs in other member states as well as professional job-seekers.

International Placement Organisations

Established organisations that assist students and other young people to work abroad are invaluable for guiding people through the red tape problems and for providing a soft landing for first time travellers:

BUNAC: 16 Bowling Green Lane, London EC1R 0QH; ☎ 020 7251 3472; bunac.org; a student club (annual membership £5) which helps students and in some programmes non-students to work abroad; has a choice of programmes in the United States, Canada, Australia, New Zealand, South Africa, Ghana, Costa Rica, Peru, Cambodia and China; programme fees usually include an arrival orientation course, UK and in-country support, accommodation and food.

BUNAC USA: PO Box 430, Southbury, CT 06488; ☎ 203 264 0901; outgoing programmes for Americans to France, Ireland, Australia, New Zealand and Canada.

Global Choices: Barkat House, 22 St Olav's Court, Canada Water, Lower Road, London SE16 2XB; ☎ 020 7394 7319; info@globalchoices.co.uk; voluntary work, internships, practical training and work experience worldwide from 2 weeks to 18 months; placements are arranged for a fee in many fields in Australia, USA, India, Argentina, Brazil, Spain, Greece, Singapore and others.

IST Plus Ltd: Rosedale House, Rosedale Road, Richmond, Surrey TW9 2SZ; ☎ 020 8939 9057; info@istplus.com; istplus.com; partner agency of the Council for International Educational Exchange in the US; working programmes for Britons in the USA, Australia, New Zealand, Thailand and China; Americans who want to join a teaching programme in Chile, China, Korea, Spain or Thailand should contact CIEE, 300 Fore Street, Portland, ME 04101; ☎ 207 553 5047; ciee.org/teach.

Working Abroad/InterExchange Inc: 161 Sixth Avenue, New York, NY 10013; ☎ 212 924 0446; workingabroad.org; various work, au pairing and volunteer programmes in Australia, New Zealand, Spain, France, Germany, Netherlands, Costa Rica, Peru, Chile, Argentina, Ghana, South Africa, Namibia, Thailand and India.

OVC South Africa: with 22 offices throughout the country (ovc.co.za) can organise work placements in the UK, USA, Canada and book kibbutz volunteer placements in Israel as well as many other programmes in Asia and the Antipodes.

CCUSA: 1st Floor North, Devon House, 171/177 Great Portland St, London W1W 5PQ; ☎ 020 7637 0779; ccusa.com; offices also in Leeds and Musselburgh in the UK and HQ in Sausalito California; work Experience programmes in the US (general and summer camps) and Australia/New Zealand plus summer camp counselling in Canada, Russia and Croatia, and volunteering in Latin America.

Twin Training and Travel Ltd: 67–71 Lewisham High Street, London, SE13 5JX; ☎ 0800 804 8380 or 020 8297 3251; workabroad@twinuk.com; workandvolunteer.com; work experience in Europe and volunteer programmes in three continents.

Youth exchange organisations and commercial agencies offer packages which help their nationals to take advantage of the work permit rules. For example Travel CUTS in Canada operates the SWAP programme (swap.ca) which sends Canadian students to work in many countries. A large number of approved work abroad programmes operate for Canadian young people from Latvia to Italy (listed on the Canadian government's site international.gc.ca/experience).

Australians might also like to contact exchange agencies that facilitate job placements abroad, for example studentplacement.org.au.

Rita Hoek is one person who decided to participate in an organised programme, the Work and Travel Australia programme offered by Travel Active based in Venray, Netherlands:

> ***Though I'm not suggesting these programmes are perfect for everybody's specific plans, it's been of great help to me. You join a discount-group airfare (cheaper and easier), they help with getting a visa and most programmes provide a first week of accommodation, assistance in getting a tax file number and opening a bank account, a service to forward your mail, general information about work and travelling and heaps more. If you don't want to feel completely lost at the airport while travelling for the first time (as I was), I can surely recommend it.***

Another Dutch organisation of possible interest is JoHo (joho.org) whose goal is to set up as many support centres worldwide as possible to deal with work, travel and international cooperation. They are always looking for new partners, including backpackers' hostels, volunteer projects, and so on.

IAESTE is the abbreviation for the International Association for the Exchange of Students for Technical Experience. It provides international course-related vacation training for thousands of university-level students in 80 member countries. Placements are available in engineering, science, agriculture, architecture and related fields. British undergraduates should apply directly to IAESTE UK at the British Council (iaeste.org.uk). The US affiliate is the Association for International Practical Training or AIPT (☎ 410 997 3069; aipt.org) which can make long- and short-term placements of graduates and young professionals as well as college students in related fields.

In the US, several agencies offer a range of programmes for varying fees. AIDE (aideabroad.org), formerly the Alliance Abroad Group, arranges a variety of overseas placements including work placements in Australia, teaching in Spain, China and several South American countries, and volunteer placements in a range of countries.

Useful Sources of Information

Websites and reference books, directories of jobs and specialist journals can all be useful. Publications covering specific countries or specific kinds of work (e.g. *Teaching English Abroad* or *Living, Studying and Working in Italy*) are mentioned in the relevant chapters. Of general interest are:

Summer Jobs Worldwide: (Crimson Publishing, £12.99); published each autumn.

Your Gap Year: (Crimson, 6th edition 2010; £12.99); covers all the specialist placement organisations with first-hand accounts, as well as extensive county-by-country advice on how to wing it on your year off.

Prospects: prospects.ac.uk; official UK graduates' career website, links to 'Jobs Abroad'.

Transitions Abroad: transitionsabroad.com; maintains great online resources for volunteering and working, even though the printed magazine has ceased publication.

Verge Magazine: Canada; vergemagazine.ca; quarterly magazine covering work, volunteering and adventure abroad; annual subscription rate abroad is $25.

A host of commercial websites promises to provide free online recruitment services for travellers. These include the admirable Jobs Abroad Bulletin (jobsabroadbulletin.co.uk), a free monthly e-bulletin on working abroad and gap years; seasonworkers.com, natives.co.uk (originally for ski resort work but has now branched out); anyworkanywhere.com, jobsmonkey.com (especially for North America), and so on. Everywhere you look on the internet potentially useful links can be found. Travel Tree (traveltree.co.uk) is a directory aimed at people looking for educational travel, gap year ideas, internships, volunteering, etc. JobSlave.com was launched as a network of recruitment sites aimed at the youth market covering everything from bar jobs in Sydney to banking jobs in London. It comprises findaGapjob.com, findaStudentjob.com, findaGraduatejob.com and findaSkiResortjob.com.

A surprising number of company home pages feature an icon you can click to find out about jobs; often to be found under the heading 'About Us'. Elsewhere on the web, committed individuals around the world manage non-commercial sites on everything from kibbutzim to bar-tending.

Advertisements

If you are thinking of advertising your interest in working abroad, try to be as specific as possible. While surfing the net you will often come across postings along the lines of 'Looking for no-skills job anywhere. Please help me' which seems worse than hopeless. For a good example of a reader not targeting his self-advertisement carefully enough, see Fergus Cooney's story in the chapter on *Teaching English*. An increasing number of foreign newspapers can be read online making it much easier to reply to job advertisements as soon as they appear than in the old days when you had to track down a hard copy in a library or embassy reading room. Nevertheless any potential employer is likely to look askance at someone in Dudley or Kirkcaldy who answers an ad for someone to start immediately in a pub on Corfu or a fruit farm in Western Australia.

Web forums can be goldmines. Annelies Van der Plas has used the Dutch travellers' forum wereldwijzer.nl to good effect more than once. The advert she placed was very general:

> ***Instead of waiting and looking on wereldwijzer.nl, we placed an advertisement there ourselves. I was enthusiastic about this forum, because I had got my job on the Greek island of Kos this way. The advertisement was something like this: 'Two hard-working students are looking for a job abroad for July and August'. Our first response was from a man from a campsite where they all walk naked (don't know the English word for it). As you can imagine we waited for other responses. The second response was from a Dutch woman also from a campsite in France. The job was to entertain the children on the campsite and help the owners with cleaning, preparing the barbecue and serving dinner. At first we were a little sceptical, but we looked at their homepage and searched for information and experiences about the campsite. Our contact (Jane) told us that it's not really a party job, but instead you would be part of 'the family'. By this she meant that people at the campsite eat (almost) every night on one long table together. You really get to know the people. This is the thing that persuaded us to take the job. Another plus was that Jane gave us the e-mail address of a girl who worked there before. She told us what we could expect, which was helpful. Within one or two weeks we received our train tickets in the post (worth about €200 each). Also I received a phonecall from Jane; we talked about some practical things and fun stuff, like horse riding (she was very glad that for the first time one of her employees liked horses). The best thing to do before you accept a job abroad is to search the internet for experiences, which is what we did.***

Two of the most useful sites are the free community noticeboards gumtree and Craigslist; the latter started in San Francisco in 1995 but has spread to 570 cities from Auckland to Buenos Aires, Moscow to Cairo. With notification of about half a million new job ads a month, it is probably the biggest job board in the world, as well as carrying accommodation listings and everything else. It also lists many unpaid jobs and internships.

GETTING A JOB ON ARRIVAL

For those who leave home without something fixed up, a lot of initiative will be needed. Many travellers find it easier to locate casual work in country areas rather than cities, and outside the student holiday periods (although just before Christmas is a good time, when staff turnover is high). But it is possible in cities too, on building sites, in restaurants and in factories. If you go for the jobs which are least appealing, e.g. an orderly in a hospital for the criminally insane, a loo attendant, doing a street promotion dressed as a koala or a hamburger, a pylon painter, assistant in a battery chicken farm, charity collector, dog meat factory worker, or just plain dogsbodies, the chances are you will be taken on sooner rather than later.

It always helps to have a neat appearance in order to dissociate yourself from the image of the hobo or hippy. Keenness and persistence are essential. Even if a prospective employer turns you down at first, ask again since it is human nature to want to reward keenness and he or she may decide that an extra staff member could be useful after all. Polite pestering pays off. For example, if your requests for work down on the docks produce nothing one day, you must return the next day. After a week your face will be familiar and your eagerness and availability known to potential employers. If nothing seems to be materialising, volunteer to help mend nets (thereby adding a new skill to the ones you can offer) and if an opening does eventually arise, you will be the obvious choice. If you want a job teaching English in a school but there appear to be no openings, volunteer to assist with a class one day a week for no pay and if you prove yourself competent, you will have an excellent chance of filling any vacancy which does occur. So patience and persistence should become your watchwords, and before long you will belong to the fraternity of experienced, worldly-wise travellers who can maintain themselves on the road for extended periods.

Despite her tender years when she first started travelling and fending for herself, Carisa Fey had learned the value of quiet observation: '*My motto was and still is watch the people that do the job you want and then copy them. So my first few days in London I spent walking through the city watching people. After I found out what the businesswomen wore, I went to the shops and bought as cheaply as possible a very neat suit and the right kinds of accessories.*'

You may follow the advice in this book to go to Avignon in France in August, for example, to pick plums or to resorts along the Ocean Road in Australia to get bar work. When you arrive you may be disappointed to learn that the harvest was unusually early or the resort has already hired enough staff. But your informant may go on to say that if you wait two weeks you can pick grapes or if you travel to the next reef island, there is a shortage of dining room staff. In other words, one thing leads to another once you are on the track.

A certain amount of bravado is a good, even a necessary, thing. If you must exaggerate the amount of experience you have had or the time you intend to stay in order to get a chance to do a job, then so be it. There is little room for shyness and self-effacement in the enterprise of working your way around the world. (On the other hand, bluffing is not recommended if it might result in danger, for example if you pretend to have more sailing experience than you really do for a transatlantic crossing.)

AFTER CIRCUMNAVIGATING THE GLOBE AND WORKING IN A NUMBER OF COUNTRIES DAVID COOKSLEY COMMENTS:

All the information and contacts in the world are absolutely useless unless you make a personal approach to the particular situation. You must be resourceful and never retiring. If I were the manager of a large company which needed self-motivating sales people, I'd hire all the contributors to Work Your Way Around the World since they have the ability to communicate with anyone anywhere in any language.

Meeting People

The most worthwhile source of information is without question your fellow travellers, met in hostels, Irish pubs, etc. Other travellers can be surprisingly generous with their information and assistance. Hostel staff may be well versed in the local opportunities for casual jobs. Of course hostels are also the best places for working travellers to stay. Bookings at hostels worldwide can be made on hostelbookers.com, hostels.com, hostels.net and hostelworld.com. The original Youth Hostels federation is now called Hostelling International (hihostels.com) and consists of 4,000 hostels in 80 countries. Membership costs only £9.95 for those under 26 (☎ 01629 592700 in the UK; yha.org.uk).

If you have a particular hobby or interest, ask if there is a local club, where you will meet like-minded people; join local cyclists, cavers, environmental activists, train spotters, jazz buffs – the more obscure the more welcome you are likely to be. Join language courses, find out if the English language bookshop has a useful notice board and perhaps even attend the functions of the English language church, where you are likely to meet the expatriate community or be offered free advice by the vicar. Marta Eleniak introduced herself to the local Polish club, since she has a Polish surname and a fondness for the country, to ask if she could put up a notice asking for accommodation. The kindly soul to whom she was speaking told her not to worry about it; she'd find her a place to move into the next day. She has come to the conclusion that learning to be a 'fog-horn' is an invaluable characteristic.

TILL BRUCKNER HAS (RELUCTANTLY) BEEN PERSUADED THAT HOBNOBBING WITH THE RICH AND POWERFUL CAN BE THE KEY TO JOB SUCCESS:
The one lesson I have failed to learn over and over again is the value of socialising. In Bolivia, I shoved a pamphlet advertising myself as a trekking guide under the doors of dozens of agencies without ever getting a reply. It just doesn't work that way. Nobody will ever bother to ring you if they don't know you. A week before I left, I met an old Bolivian friend and when I told him that I'd been unable to find work, he said he couldn't believe it because his cousin had an agency and needed a German speaker. In the Sudan, I sent off my CV to all major NGOs offering myself as an unpaid volunteer. All I got was two negative replies. A week before I left (again) I went to a social event at a foreign embassy where I got talking with the head of a big charity. She told me about the problems they had with writing endless reports. I asked her why she hadn't replied to my application and it turned out she'd never seen it. The moral of the story is that in some countries the best place to start looking for a job is down the pub, especially the sort of pub where well-off locals and expats hang out. I absolutely loathe exactly that kind of establishment but you might well hit the jackpot in there. You're unlikely to get hired by someone poor after all.

If your contacts can't offer you a real job they might know of a 'pseudo job' or 'non-job' which can keep you afloat: guarding their yacht, doing odd jobs around their property, babysitting, typing, teaching the children English, or just staying for free. These neatly avoid the issue of work permits, too, since they are arranged on an entirely unofficial and personal basis. Human contacts are usually stronger than red tape.

Chance

When you first set off, the possibility of being a sheep-catcher in the Australian outback or an English tutor in Turkey may never have crossed your mind. Chance is a fine thing and is one of the traveller's greatest allies. Brigitte Albrech had saved up leave from her job in the German tourist industry to go on holiday in Mexico. While there, she became friendly with some Québecois who invited her to join them as tree planters in Western Canada, and she never made it back to her job.

There will be times when you will be amazed by the lucky chain of events which led you into a certain situation. 'Being in the right place at the right time' would have made a suitable subtitle to this book, though of course there are steps you can take to put yourself in the right place. Here are some examples of how luck, often in combination with initiative, has resulted in travellers finding paid work:

- Mark Kilburn took up busking in a small Dutch town and was eventually asked to play a few nights a week in a nearby pub for a fee.
- Stuart Britton was befriended by a fisherman in a dusty little town in Mexico and was soon tutoring some of the fisherman's friends and acquaintances (and living in his house).
- While standing in a post office queue in the south of France, Brian Williams overheard the word *boulot* (which he knew to mean odd job) and *cerises*. He tapped the lady on the shoulder and offered his cherry picking expertise. After an unsuccessful search for the address she had given him, he finally asked directions of someone who offered him a job in their orchard instead.
- On a flight to Reykjavik, Caroline Nicholls happened to sit next to the wife of the managing director of a large fish-packing cooperative in Iceland who told her they were short of staff.

- After finishing his summer stint as a camp counsellor in the US, Mark Kinder decided to try one parachute jump. He enjoyed it so much that he learned how to pack parachutes and was able to fund himself at the aerodrome for months afterwards.
- While looking for work on a boat in Antibes, Tom Morton found a job as a goatherd for six weeks in the mountains near Monte Carlo.
- Dominic Fitzgibbon mentioned to his landlady in Rome that he intended to leave soon for Greece since he had been unable to find a job locally in six weeks of looking. She decided he was far too nice to become a washer-up in a taverna and arranged for him to work as a hall porter at a friend's hotel.
- A Gowing was a little startled to wake up one evening in Frankfurt station to find a middle-aged women staring down at him. She offered him the chance of working with her travelling fun-fair.
- While getting her jabs for Africa at a clinic in Gibraltar, Mary Hall (a nurse cycling across Europe) noticed a door marked 'District Nurses', barged in and the following week had moved in as a live-in private nurse for a failing old lady.
- While shopping in a supermarket in Cyprus, Rhona Stannage noticed a local man with a trolley full of wine and beer, and assumed it could not be for his own consumption. She approached him, ascertained that he ran a restaurant and a day or two later was employed as a waitress.
- Connie Paraskeva shared a taxi in Bangkok with an American nurse who told her about a vacancy in a refugee camp.

The examples could be multiplied *ad infinitum* of how travellers, by keeping their ears open and by making their willingness to help obvious, have fallen into work. One of the keys to success is total flexibility. Within ten minutes of a chance conversation with a family sharing her breakfast table in an Amsterdam hotel, Caroline Langdon had paid her bill, packed her bags and was off to Portugal with them as their mother's help.

Of course there is always such a thing as bad luck too. You may have received all sorts of inside information about a job on a Greek island, a vineyard or in a ski resort. But if a terrorist attack has decimated tourism or if there was a late frost which killed off the grapes or if the snowfalls are late arriving for the ski season, there will be far fewer jobs and your information may prove useless. Unpredictability is built into the kinds of jobs which travellers do.

Design

You cannot rely on luck alone; you will have to create your own luck at times. You may have to spend many hours surfing the internet, or apply to 20 hotels before one will accept you or you may have to inform 20 acquaintances of your general plans before one gives you the address of a useful contact.

You must check notice boards and newspaper advertisements, register with agencies and most important of all use the unselective 'walk-in-and-ask' method, just like job-seekers anywhere. Two important tools for an on-the-spot job hunt are the *Yellow Pages* and a phone. When Mary Hall was starting her job search in Switzerland, a friend gave her an odd piece of advice which she claims works, to smile while speaking on the phone. Some people say that all initial approaches are best made by telephone since refusals are less demoralising than in person and you need not worry about the scruffiness of your wardrobe.

One old hand, Alan Corrie, describes his approach: 'The town of Annecy in the French Alps looked great so I found a fairly cheap hostel and got down to getting organised. This meant I was doing the rounds of the agencies, employment office, notice boards and cafés for a few days. After a matter of minutes in a town, I begin to sprout plastic bags full of maps, plans, lists, addresses and scraps of advice from people I have met on the road.' Alan sounds unusually cheerful and optimistic about job-hunting and the result is that he worked in Europe for the better part of a decade. Our working wanderers have displayed remarkable initiative and found their jobs in a great variety of ways:

- Waiter in Northern Cyprus: I arranged my job by writing direct to the restaurant after seeing a two-minute clip on a BBC travel programme. Rita wrote back and offered me a job.
- Farmhand on a Danish farm: I placed an advert in *Landsbladet*, the farmers' magazine, and chose one from four replies.
- Au pair to a family in Helsinki: I found work as a nanny in Finland simply by placing advertisement cards in a few playgroups.
- Teacher at a language school in southern Italy: We used the *Yellow Pages* in a Sicilian post office and from our 30 speculative applications received four job offers without so much as an interview.
- Winery guide in Spain: I composed a modest and polite letter and sent it to an address copied from one of my father's wine labels. I was astonished at their favourable reply. Several years later the same contributor wrote to say, I sent a copy of the page in your book where I am mentioned to prospective employers in Australia, and I was offered a job on a vineyard near Melbourne.
- Factory assistant in Ghana: I asked the local Amnesty International representative for any leads.

Implicit in all these stories is that you must take positive action.

REWARDS AND RISKS

The Delights

The rewards of travelling are mostly self-evident: the interesting characters and lifestyles you are sure to meet, the wealth of anecdotes you will collect with which you can regale your grandchildren and photos with which you can bore your friends, a feeling of achievement, an increased self-reliance and maturity, learning to budget, a better perspective on your own country and your own habits, a good sun tan... the list could continue. Stephen Psallidas summed up his views on travelling:

> ***Meeting people from all over the world gives you a more tolerant attitude to other nationalities, races, etc. More importantly you learn to tolerate yourself, to learn more about your strengths and weaknesses. While we're on the clichés, you definitely 'find yourself, man'.***

One traveller came back from a stint of working on the Continent feeling a part of Europe rather than just an Englishman. (Perhaps some Eurocrat should be subsidising this book.) Sometimes travels abroad change the direction of your life. After working his way around the world in many low-paid and exploitative jobs, Ken Smith decided to specialise in studying employment law. After deciding to cycle through Africa on an extended holiday, Mary Hall changed her career and ended up working for aid organisations in Africa and the Middle East.

One of the best aspects of the travelling life is that you are a free and unfettered agent. Albert Schweizer might have been thinking of the working traveller instead of equatorial Africans when he wrote: '*He works well under certain circumstances so long as the circumstances require it. He is not idle, but he is a free man, hence he is always a casual worker.*'

The Dangers

Of course things can go desperately wrong. As the number of young people backpacking to remote corners whether on gap years or otherwise has risen, it is inevitable that accidents will occur and will be widely reported. So if a young man slips down a waterfall in Costa Rica or a British girl is killed by a freak accident with a high voltage cable in Ecuador or a bus carrying overlanding travellers is held up by armed bandits in the Andes, the world hears about it. On the other hand if a student dies of a drug overdose or is killed on his bicycle in his hometown, this is not reported nationally.

A much less remote possibility than murder or kidnapping is that you might be robbed or lose your luggage or become involved in a traffic accident. You may get sick or lonely, or fed up, have a demoralising run of bad luck or fail to find a job, and begin to run out of money (if this is the case, consult the chapter *In Extremis*).

Many unofficial jobs carry with them an element of insecurity. You may not be protected by employment legislation and may not be in a position to negotiate with the boss. Often the work may be available to travellers like you because the conditions are unacceptable to a stable local population (or because the place is too remote to have a local population). If you have cultivated the right attitude, you will not hesitate to drift on to a new situation if the old one should become undesirable for any reason.

Much is now said about 'socially responsible tourism' and perhaps working travellers who put up with dreadful employers are doing both their host community and other travellers a disservice. Stephen Psallidas's advice (based on his own experience of exploitative Greek bosses) is not to put up with it: '*My advice when you are mistreated or your employer acts unprofessionally is to shout back when they shout at you. If things don't improve threaten to walk out and then do so. You will be doing a favour to future working travellers, and you will almost certainly be able to find something else if you try hard enough.*'

Even when a planned working holiday does not work out successfully, the experience will be far more memorable than just staying at home. This view is held by Stephen Hands who didn't regret his decision to go abroad to look for work (although it didn't work out) but he did regret boasting to all his friends that he was off for an indefinite period to see the world. After writing pages about her dodgy and difficult jobs in Australia, Emma Dunnage concluded with a typical paradox: 'But we did have the best time of our lives'.

Though travelling itself is seldom boring, a job which you find to help out your finances along the way may well be. True 'working holidays' are rare: one example is to exchange your labour for a free trip with an outback Australian camping tour operator (see *Australia* chapter). But in many cases, the expression 'working holiday' is an oxymoron (like 'cruel kindness'). Jobs are jobs wherever you do them. David Anderson, who found himself working on an isolated Danish farm where he didn't feel at home in any way, recommends taking (a) your time to decide to accept a job, (b) a copy of *War and Peace* and (c) enough money to facilitate leaving if necessary. The best policy is to leave home only after you have the reserves to be able to work when you want to.

ONE OF THE UNEXPECTED DRAWBACKS OF BECOMING A GLOBAL CITIZEN WAS IDENTIFIED BY CARISA FEY:

One of the blessings and the curses of travelling a lot is that your best friends live all over the world. Good, because you always have an excuse to go and visit a foreign country. But bad because you usually never have more than one close friend nearby.

Coming Home

Kristin Moen thinks that there should be a big warning at the beginning of *Work Your Way Around the World:* WHEN YOU FIRST START TO TRAVEL THERE IS NO WAY YOU CAN STOP! Correspondents have variously called travel an illness and an addiction. Once you set off you will probably come across a few restless souls for whom the idea of settling down is anathema and for whom the word 'vagabondage' was invented. But these are the exceptions.

In the majority of cases, homesickness eventually sets in, and the longing for a pint of bitter, a bacon sandwich, a baseball game, Radio 4, green fields, Marks & Spencer or Mum's home cooking will get the better of you. Or perhaps duty intervenes as in the case of Michael Tunison: '*I had planned to go on to South America this summer, but I had to return home under emergency circumstances. Not one, but two of my best friends were getting married. What is a poor globe-trotter to do with people rather inconsiderately going on with their lives when he isn't even there? But after a year it was actually quite nice to have a chance to organise my things and repack for further adventures.*'

Settling back will be difficult especially if you have not been able to set aside some money for 'The Return'. As soon as he left Asia en route back from Australia, Riwan Hafiz began to feel depressed and when he arrived at Heathrow wanted to put a blanket over his head. It can be a wretched feeling after some glorious adventures to find yourself with nothing to start over on. Life at home may seem dull and routine at first, while the outlook of your friends and family can strike you as narrow and limited. If you have been round the world between school and further study, you may find it difficult to bridge the gulf between you and your stay-at-home peers who may feel a little threatened or belittled by your experiences. If you have spent time in developing countries the reverse culture shock may be acute, as Chris Miksovsky from Colorado discovered:

> ***Memories of the trip already come racing back at the oddest of times. A few days after returning to the US, I went to a large grocery store with my mother. It was overwhelming. Rows and rows of colours and logos all screaming to get your attention. I wandered over to the popcorn display and stood dumbfounded by the variety: buttered, lite, generic, Redenbacker, Paul Newman's au naturel, from single serving sachet through economy family popcorn-orgy size. I counted over 25 unique offerings... of popcorn.***

But it passes. The reverse culture shock normally wears off soon enough and you will begin to feel reintegrated in your group of friends, your job or course.

People often wonder whether a long spell of travelling or living abroad will damage their future job prospects. According to numerous surveys on graduate employment, most employers are sympathetic to people who defer entry to the labour market. In the majority of cases, travel seems to be considered an advantage, something that makes you stand out from the crowd. Marcus Scrace found that even in his profession of chartered surveying, employers looked favourably on someone who had had the get-up-and-go to work his way around the world. Naturally it helps if you can present your experiences positively, if only to prevent the potential employer from imagining you out of your skull on a beach in Goa for 12 months. Your travels must be presented constructively and not as an extended doss. Stephen Psallidas, who returned after three years on the road, is convinced that he would never have got a good job (as Projects Manager in Computer Education) before he left. Not that he gained any relevant experience on his travels but he had learned how to be persistent and pester employers for an interview.

Some hostility is probably inevitable especially when the job market is shrinking making employers more conservative. Jane Thomas knew that it would be tough finding a job when she got back to England, but she didn't know how tough. Some interviewers did express their concern and suspicion that she would want to take off again (which at that time was exactly what she did want to do). But she also found that she could adapt the short-term jobs she had done in the US and Australia to fit whatever job she was trying to get. In some cases the jobs you have found abroad are a positive boost to your 'real life' prospects, as in the case of Michael Tunison from Michigan:

> ***Newspaper work was exactly what I thought I was leaving behind by globetrotting. I'd temporarily sacrificed (I believed) my career as a journalist. The last place I thought I'd be working was at a daily in Mexico. But things never work out as planned and before I knew it I was the managing editor's assistant and a month or so later the managing editor of the paper's weekend editions. How ironic. By taking a step my newspaper friends believed to be an irresponsible career move, I was soon years ahead of where I'd have been following the old safe route back home.***

If travelling requires a much greater investment of energy than staying at home, it will reward the effort many times over.

A HOST OF TRAVELLERS HAVE MENTIONED HOW MUCH THEY VALUE THEIR COLLECTION OF MEMORIES. SINCE WE HAVE BEEN GUIDED BY THE EXPERIENCES OF ORDINARY TRAVELLERS THROUGHOUT THE WRITING OF THIS BOOK, LET ONE OF THEIR NUMBER, STEVE HENDRY, END THE INTRODUCTION:

I left home with about £100 and no return ticket. I spent two years in Israel, three years in Thailand, one year in Japan. I have lived in the sun for years, with Arabs on the seashore and with wealthy Japanese. If I can do it, you can too. I've learned so very much. Travelling is 100% fun and educational. What are you waiting for?

TRAVEL

Unscripted travel provides a chance to shed the clutter and flee the routines of modern student or workaday life, to indulge in the unalloyed pleasure of choosing one or more destinations from among an infinite number of possibilities. The travel shelves of bookshops are dense with names to conjure with: Karakoram, Kilimanjaro, Kalimantan, Bali, Cali and Mali. And of course Paris, Prague and Pennsylvania are not to be sniffed at either. Some people take time out to embark on a particular journey they have long dreamed of, to set off on journeys that range from straightforward backpacking to expeditions to organised adventure trips. The choices can be overwhelming: will it be trekking in the hinterland of Rio de Janeiro or finding the perfect beach on a Thai island?

Canvassing the options for exciting travel at bargain prices is an endlessly fascinating pastime. The price of flying has fallen substantially in real terms over the past two decades and it is quite possible that we are currently experiencing the heyday of flying. Fares will gradually creep up as anxiety about environmental degradation takes hold and governments begin to impose higher taxes and more restrictions. The increase of Air Passenger Duty in the UK from November 2009 so that the range will be £11–£55 per flight is indicative, and due to rise to £12–£85 in 2010.

There follow some general guidelines for finding bargains in train, coach, ship and air travel. More detailed information on specific destinations can be found in travel guides from Lonely Planet and Rough Guides. The amount of travel information on the internet is staggering and this chapter cannot hope to tap its resources. There are websites on everything from sleeping in airports (sleepinginairports.net) to sharing lifts across North America (erideshare.com). Many sites have pages of intriguing links; to name just one, try bugeurope.com ('BUG' stands for Backpackers' Ultimate Guide).

Air

Scheduled airfares are best avoided. They are primarily designed for airline accountants and businessmen on expense accounts. You should be looking at no-frills flying, cheap charters and last minute discounted tickets. Air travel within individual countries and continents is not always subject to this choice, though some special deals are available.

For longhaul flights, especially to Asia, Australasia and most recently Latin America, discounted tickets are available in plenty. Hundreds of travel websites compete with high street travel agencies to offer the lowest fares. Because of their enormous turnover and sophisticated computer systems, agencies like STA can sometimes offer the best deals.

Check adverts in the travel press like the Saturday *Independent* and in the London free magazine *TNT*. Phone a few outfits to find the baseline fare and then try to find better on the internet. A good start when browsing the internet is flightfind.co.uk or cheapflights.co.uk. The monolithic sites like opodo.com, travelocity.com, expedia.co.uk and lastminute.com are worth checking but do not always come up with the best deals. When users log onto their destination, they must provide specific dates which makes the process of comparing fares, times and airlines time-consuming. Less well known search engines like ticketstoworld.com may come up with cheaper options on airlines like Aeroflot and Etihad.

The price of round-the-world (RTW) tickets has remained fairly consistent over the past few years, though taxes and fuel surcharges have leapt up. You shouldn't count on getting much change from £1,000 even for the most limited route. Check roundtheworldflights.com (0844 844 2540) or Travel Nation in Hove, Sussex (☎ 01273 718025; travel-nation.co.uk) for ideas. RTW fares start at £629 for four stops departing London between April and June (plus taxes of

£350–£650 depending on stops) and have a maximum validity of one year. The cheapest fares involve one or more gaps which you must cover overland. The most amazing RTW fare on offer at the time of writing was with Air New Zealand (available through Travelmood): London – Los Angeles – Auckland – Hong Kong – London for £599 including tax.

The typical RTW deal imposes a mileage limit of 28,000 miles so you will have to make some careful calculations. Another tip for finding the cheapest available fares is to tap into the expat community of the country to which you would like to fly. For example the cheapest flights from Toronto to Korea are probably found among the many travel agencies to be found in the city's 'Little Korea' district on Bloor Street West.

Flying on obscure airlines like Romania's Tarom or Asian carriers like EVA Airways is guaranteed to be more interesting than flying on Air Canada or British Airways. When Sarah Spiller fell in love with Sri Lanka after joining a turtle conservation project and persuaded her husband that they should buy a holiday house there, she made several trips on Sri Lankan Airlines and felt that she was already on holiday the minute she stepped aboard. Some of the principal agencies specialising in longhaul travel are listed here. All of these offer a wide choice of fares including RTW. Telephone bookings are possible, though these agencies are often so busy that it can be difficult to get through. Although STA specialise in deals for students and under-26s, they can assist anybody.

STA Travel: About 40 branches in the UK and hundreds more worldwide; offer low cost flights, accommodation, insurance, car hire, round-the-world tickets, overland travel, adventure tours, ski, and gap year travel; for bookings and enquiries call STA Travel on ☎ 0871 230 0040 or log on at statravel.co.uk to find fares and check availability; you can request a quote by email or make an appointment at your nearest branch.

Trailfinders Ltd: 194 Kensington High St, London W8 7RG; ☎ 0845 058 5858 worldwide; ☎ 0845 050 5940 Europe; trailfinders.com; 22 branches in UK cities plus Ireland and Australia.

Flight Centre: Branches around the UK; ☎ 0870 499 0040; flightcentre.co.uk.

Journey Latin America: 12–13 Heathfield Terrace, Chiswick, London W4 4JE; ☎ 020 8747 3108; journeylatinamerica.co.uk; a fully-bonded tour operator which specialises in tailor-made holidays and group tours to all of Latin America; one of the best flight deals at the time of writing was to Mexico City or Panama for about £400 and to Caracas for £475.

Marco Polo Travel: 24A Park St, Bristol BS1 5JA; ☎ 0117 929 4123; marcopolotravel.co.uk; discounted airfares worldwide.

North South Travel: Moulsham Mill Centre, Parkway, Chelmsford, Essex CM2 7PX; ☎ 01245 608291; northsouthtravel.co.uk; discount travel agency that donates all its profits to projects in the developing world.

South American Experience: Welby House, 96 Wilton Road, London SW1V 1DW; ☎ 0845 277 3366; southamericanexperience.co.uk. Latin American specialist with good customer service.

Travelbag: 3–5 High St, Alton, Hants GU34 1TL; ☎ 0871 703 4700; travelbag.co.uk; 8 other UK branches; originally Australia & New Zealand specialist.

Travelmood: London office 214 Edgware Road, London W2 1DH; ☎ 0800 011 1945; travelmood.com; now part of TUI.

It is sometimes worth paying more for flexibility if you are not sure that you won't want to change your itinerary. Roger Blake was pleased with the round-the-world ticket he bought from STA that took in Johannesburg, Australia and South America. But once he embarked he wanted to stay in Africa longer than he had anticipated and wanted to alter the onward flight dates:

> ***That is the biggest problem of having an air ticket. I had planned for six months in Africa but I've already spent five months in only three countries. I have been into the British Airways office here in Kampala to try my verbal skills but have been told the 12-month period of validity is non-negotiable. How stupid I was to presume I would get a refund when it states clearly on the back of the ticket that they may be able to offer refunds/credit. A lesson for me and a warning to future 'work your wayers' to check before they buy whether or not the ticket is refundable/extendable.***

In the US, check the discount flight listings in the back of the travel sections of the *New York Times* and *Los Angeles Times*. Discounted tickets are available online from Air Treks in San Francisco (☎ 1 877 247 8735; AirTreks.com) which specialises in multi-stop and round-the-world fares. By far the cheapest airfares from the US to Europe, Mexico, the Caribbean and Hawaii are available to people who are flexible about departure dates and destinations, and are prepared to travel on a standby basis. The passenger chooses a block of possible dates (up to a four-day 'window') and preferred destinations. A company like Airtech (airtech.com) then tries to match these requirements with empty airline seats being released at knock-down prices. Lately availability of transatlantic flights has decreased using this method.

From the UK to Europe it is generally cheaper to fly on an off-peak no-frills flight out of Stansted, Luton or regional airport than it is to go by rail or bus. Almost all bookings with Easyjet, Ryanair, Bmibaby, Jet2 at Leeds and so on are made online. No-frills flying has been available in North America for some time, especially through Southwest Airlines based in Dallas (southwest.com) and has recently been expanding with the expansion of little-known airlines serving obscure cities, like Direct Air (visitdirecdtair.com) and Allegiant Air (allegiantair.com). Southwest were advertising a one-way fare of $113 including taxes between Philadelphia and Los Angeles (spring 2009).

This style of flying has spread to the continent and discount airlines have proliferated like Germanwings in Germany and Wizz Air in Poland at wizzair.com. To check which discount airlines operate to which European destinations, log on to flycheapo.com. The idea has spread to Australia with Richard Branson's Virgin Blue (virginblue.com.au) and Jetstar (jetstar.com) and to Canada with airlines like WestJet offering cheap domestic flights.

Driving

In some countries you might decide to buy a cheap car and hope that it lasts long enough for you to see the country. This works especially well in Australia as described by a blogger at http://blog.tickettotheworld.co.uk in 2008:

> ***We bought a Toyota Hi-Ace pop top camper van in Sydney from another backpacker in the Kings Cross Car Market for $4500. It was 24 years old and had done approx. 300,000km at the time but looked in great condition. It also came with a huge mosquito tent, table, chairs, a barbeque and all cooking utensils, saucepans, etc. There was a fridge and hob/grill inside the van and enough room for two people to sleep. With our new purchase and all paperwork sorted out, we drove anti-clockwise all the way around Australia. Driving 40,000km around Australia was a true adventure, and one I will never forget. The best thing about it – we sold our camper for $4,250 losing only $250! What a bargain.***

A camper van also gives great flexibility in Britain and Europe, especially if you are interested in chasing fruit harvests. Anna Ling and her friend Andy bought a van in England for £900 in preparation for travels to no fixed destination in Europe in 2008. They stayed in it while saving for their trip packing eggs in Somerset and then while picking grapes in the Champagne region. Of course a camper van incurs expenses in insurance, repairs and fuel.

An informal camper van market takes place daily in London on York Way at Market Road, N7 near the Caledonian Road tube station. You might also check ads in *Auto Trader, Exchange & Mart* and *LOOT* or if starting in London on gumtree.com, London's online community.

Hitch-hiking

Over the past generation, hitch-hiking has fallen by the wayside (so to speak), and is practised now by only a few diehards, even though it is not only the best travel bargain around, but the most rewarding as well. This may be because young travellers and students are generally more affluent and also because of a heightened sense of paranoia (though the dangers remain infinitesimal). However there are still enough people out there interested to support a number of websites including hitchhikers.org which has an up-to-date ride board. Many shared lifts these days are fixed up via online marketplaces ahead of time, sometimes referred to as digital hitch-hiking. A similar online rideshare community is PickupPal.com which is strong in North America. Another interesting website is digihitch.com with relevant articles and forums.

Hitch-hiking is also good for the environment. As long ago as 1998, a UK government report was published to promote car-sharing. One of the suggested measures was to introduce hitch-hiker pick-up zones at motorway junctions which would be brightly lit and possibly equipped with closed circuit TVs. Special hitching spots in the Netherlands are called *liftershalte*. By following a few rules the risks of hitch-hiking can be minimised. Never accept a lift from a driver who seems drunk, drowsy or suspicious. Women should try not to hitch alone. A small dose of paranoia is not a bad thing.

Train and Coach

The Thomas Cook *Overseas Timetable* is the bible for overland travellers outside Europe; within Europe, consult the up-to-date *European Timetable*, both for £15.99 but discounted on thomascooktimetables.com. One of the wonders of the internet is the site maintained by the 'Man in Seat 61' (seat61.com) which carries masses of information about overland train travel and tickets. Rail passes are generally not much use to job-seeking travellers since they benefit people who want to do a great deal of travelling.

Coaches and/or shared taxis serve almost every community you are ever likely to want to visit. In the developing world, the price per kilometre is vanishingly small and sometimes comes with complimentary food and kung fu videos.

One of the most interesting revolutions in youth travel has been the explosion of backpackers' bus services which are hop-on hop-off coach services following prescribed routes. These can be found in New Zealand, Australia, South Africa (BazBus), Ireland, Scotland, England and the continent. Generally they are not really cheap enough to serve as a job-seeker's preferred mode of transport. For example a Flexitrip pass on Busabout Europe (☎ 020 7950 1661; busabout.com) costs £289 and allows six stops within the whole operating season May to October; many other permutations are available.

For travel on the Eurolines coach network, see the section on Europe below.

Bicycle

CYCLING IS NOT ONLY HEALTHY AND FREE, IT CAN SIMPLIFY THE BUSINESS OF FINDING WORK, AS ADAM COOK DISCOVERED IN FRANCE:
Looking for work by bicycle is one of the very best methods as it allows you free unlimited travel far from the big towns and the competition. You can so easily visit the small villages and farms, some of which are off the beaten track.

In addition, employers may realise that people who have been cycling for a while are at least moderately fit and may choose them for the job, ahead of the flabbier vehicle-bound competition. In many parts of the world you will also become an object of fascination, which can only aid your job-finding chances. If you do decide to travel extensively by bicycle, you might consider joining the Cyclists' Touring Club based in Guildford (☎ 0844 736 8450; ctc.org.uk) which provides free technical, legal and touring information to members as well as third party insurance; membership costs £12 if you are a student under 26, £36 otherwise.

EUROPE

The European landmass is one of the most expensive areas of the world to traverse. One of the cheapest ways is to pre-arrange a shared lift. Ride-sharing can be fixed up via websites as mentioned above or by community agencies, often called 'Allostop' where you may have to make a contribution to the driver's expenses, e.g.€50 for Amsterdam to Warsaw. There are dozens of lift-sharing outlets across Europe, especially in Germany, where there are Citynetz offices in Berlin, Düsseldorf, Freiburg, Hamburg, Munich, etc. Most require you to register which is free in some cases or costs €10–€20 in others. In most cases you will have to pay 3–4 Eurocents per kilometre you want to travel. In France, look for Allostop (allostop.net), and in Belgium Taxistop/ Eurostop (taxistop.be). Matches can seldom be made straightaway, so this system is of interest to those who can plan ahead.

The explosion of competition on European air routes has seen some amazingly low fares, though taxes and add-ons make it almost impossible to spend less than £50 on a return flight. As well as checking Ryanair and easyjet, don't forget foreign no-frills carriers like Transavia in the Netherlands and Norwegian Air Shuttle.

Eurolines is the group name for 32 independent coach operators serving 500 destinations in all European countries from Ireland to Romania. Return fares start at £45 for London-Amsterdam if booked a week in advance. Bookings can be made online at eurolines.co.uk or by phoning 08717 818181. So called 'funfares' mean that some off-season fares from the UK are even lower, e.g. £15 one way to Brussels, Amsterdam and Dublin.

For smaller independent coach operators, check advertisements in London magazines like *TNT*. For example Poltours (☎ 020 8810 5625) links the UK with many cities in Poland; one-way fares start at around £60, return £95 with a slight reduction for students.

NORTH AMERICA

Incredibly, the price of flying across the Atlantic has been steadily decreasing over the past decade, though with rising taxes, it is difficult to find much for less than £250. Competition is fiercest and therefore prices lowest on the main routes between London and New York and Los Angeles/ San Francisco. In many cases, summer fares will be twice as high as winter ones. One-way fares are also available to eastern seaboard cities like Washington and Boston.

The USA and Canada share the longest common frontier in the world, which gives some idea of the potential problems and expense of getting around. You may want to consider Driveaway (see *United States* chapter) and also bus and air travel which are both cheaper than in Europe. Hitch-hiking in the USA is often unnerving and sometimes fraught with danger, danger not only from crazy drivers but also from the law, especially where 'No Hitch-hiking' signs abound. It is a more reasonable proposition in Canada. Ride-sharing makes more sense on this continent.

Greyhound still markets their various bus passes lasting 7, 15, 30 or 60 days, costing US$340–$850 (discoverypass.com). Promotional advance purchase fares of $99 for any trip within the USA are good value. Megabus (megabus.com) is expanding its network in North America and recently started operating between New York and Toronto as well as Chicago-Detroit and connecting routes. The earlier you book online, the better the bargain, e.g. $1 for New York to Washington.

Other forms of transport in the USA are probably more expensive but may have their own attractions, such as the trips run by Green Tortoise (494 Broadway, San Francisco, California 94133; ☎ 800 867 8647; greentortoise.com) which use vehicles converted to sleep about 35 people and which make interesting detours and stopovers. Attempts to revive long-distance train travel in the US have not been terribly successful and several grand old routes are threatened with closure. Amtrak (☎ 1 800 872 7245; amtrak.com) offers limited rail passes such as 7 days in 21 around California for $159 or the whole network starting at $389 for eight journeys within 15 days.

LATIN AMERICA

In the low seasons of January to May and October-November, you can get from London to South America on a cheap one way ticket, though this is rarely the best way to do it because international tickets bought out there are very expensive. Having a return ticket makes it much easier to cross borders. Open-dated returns are available as are open jaw tickets (where you fly into one point and back from another).

A fully bonded operator that specialises in travel to and around this area of the world is Journey Latin America mentioned above; they consistently offer the lowest fares and the most expertise. Another advantage is that they deal exclusively with Latin America and hence are the best source of up-to-date travel information. A plethora of airpasses is also available which can be cheaper if bought at the same time as your transatlantic ticket. Another specialist in the field is South American Experience. Taxes are levied on international flights within South America: the cheapest way to fly from one capital to another (assuming you have plenty of time) is to take a domestic flight (within, say, Brazil), cross the border by land and then buy another domestic ticket (within, say, Peru). The alternatives include the remnants of a British-built railway system and the ubiquitous bus, both of which are extremely cheap and interesting. A rough estimate of the price of bus travel in South America is $2 for every hour of travel.

Among the most reliable travel guides to the continent is the warhorse *South American Handbook* published annually by Footprint Handbooks (2009, £22.50). For information on travel in Latin America join South American Explorers. They maintain clubhouses in Lima, Cusco, Quito and Buenos Aires (saexplorers.org); membership costs $60, $90 per couple. In addition to travel information they have also developed extensive databases of volunteering and teaching jobs for members to access.

AFRICA

Flights to Cairo are advertised from £250 return, while the special offers to Nairobi start as low as £350 return. A specialist agency is the Africa Travel Centre (150 Southampton Row, London WC1B 5AL; ☎ 0845 450 1520; africatravel.co.uk). Melhart Travel in Manchester (☎ 0870 787 4467; melharttravel.com) specialises in Southern Africa. A return flight to Johannesburg or Cape Town in the low season (April-June) can be found for less than £400.

The overland routes are fraught with difficulties, and careful research must be done before setting off via the Sahara or through the Sudan. Jennifer McKibben, who spent some time in East Africa, recommends trying to negotiate a cheap seat in one of the overland expedition vehicles which are so much in evidence in that part of the world, assuming 'half their number have stormed off the bus or truck, unable to bear each other any longer'.

ASIA

Most travellers take advantage of the competitive discount flight market from London to Asian destinations. Crystal Travel (☎ 0800 368 0300; crystaltravel.co.uk) sets out a clear choice of cheap flights when searched. For example the cheapest quoted return price London to Mumbai is less than £300 including tax on India's emerging airlines, Jet Airways and Kingfisher.

Once you're installed in Asia, travel is highly affordable. The railways of the Indian subcontinent are a fascinating social phenomenon and also dirt cheap. Throughout Asia, airfares are not expensive, particularly around the discount triangle of Bangkok, Hong Kong and Singapore. For example no-frills discount carriers like Air Asia offer cheap low season fares on popular routes such as Bangkok-Phnom Penh (though beware of restricted baggage allowances). Recently Tiger Airways (tigerairways.com) which is based in Singapore has been expanding its low-cost Ryanair-type services to Australia, India and China. The notable exception to the generalisation about cheap public transport in Asia is Japan.

Travel within the People's Republic of China can initially be exasperating as you struggle with the inscrutable bureaucracy and the utterly incomprehensible nature of stations and airports (where little allowance is made for those who do not understand Chinese characters). But like most things in the East, once you come to terms with the people and their way of life, travelling once more becomes a pleasurable experience.

With upheavals in Russia, the Trans-Siberian rail journey is not as cheap as it used to be. Specialist travel agents can arrange the Trans-Siberian trip for you, for instance the excellent travel company *Regent Holidays* (☎ 0870 499 0911; regent-holidays.co.uk) which pioneered tourism in Cuba, Eastern Europe and Central Asia.

For lesser known routes such as the Silk Route Railway through Kazakhstan and China, you will have to put it together yourself, possibly with the help of seat61.com mentioned above. If you are already in China, you can simply organise the ticket and visas yourself as Barry O'Leary did:

> ***I had discovered that if you book the Trans-Siberian on your own and don't pay for an agency to rip you off and organise everything yourself it's actually really cheap. Sure you have some hassle getting visas for China, Mongolia and Russia but isn't that all part of the fun? The total cost to get from Beijing to Moscow with three visas was only about £250, not bad for six days on a train and some tasty meat and celery stuff.***

Tom Grundy did the trip more recently starting in Tallinn and ending in Hong Kong for less than £300; see his globalcitizen.co.uk/adventures/transsiberian/costs.html for some useful tips.

AUSTRALASIA

Since 2008, European passport holders outside Australia can apply online for eVisitor status free of charge which will allow them to enter Australia as tourists staying no more than three months. For longer stays or for people from outside the eligible list of nations, an Electronic Travel Authority (ETA) must be obtained via a private agency like Visas Australia or the Australian Immigration Department's website (eta.immi.gov.au) which will incur a fee of A$20.

Per mile, the flight to the Antipodes is cheaper than most. Emirates Air or JAL often turn out to be the cheapest, although Qantas has been competing strongly of late with promotional fares of less than £600 return to Sydney available through specialists like Austravel (☎ 0800 988 4676; austravel.com).

Your transport problems are by no means over when you land in Perth or Sydney because of the vast distances and you will have to give some thought to how you intend to get around. Richard Branson's Virgin Blue (virginblue.com.au) has some good deals and his Pacific Blue flies across the Tasman to New Zealand for one-way fares starting at A$70 (carry-on baggage only). Compare also the no-frills domestic airline Jetstar (jetstar.com.au), a subsidiary of Qantas and Regional Express (rex.com.au) which sells a one-month pass to backpackers for A$499 and two months for A$949, valid on its network which covers the south-east corner of Australia, stretching from Coober Pedy to Brisbane.

If you plan a major tour of Australia you might consider purchasing a Greyhound coach pass although they are expensive. The all-Australia pass valid for 12 months costs an astronomical A$2,700. If you just want to get from one coast to another as quickly as possible, point-to-point tickets, e.g. Sydney-Adelaide (22 hours for A$150) are the best idea. Students and backpackers are eligible for the Rail Explorer Pass which gives six months of unlimited travel on the *Ghan*, the *Indian Pacific* and the *Overland* for A$590 plus fuel surcharges ☎ +61 8 8213 4592; (gsr.com.au/backpackers).

A multiplicity of private operators has sprung up to serve the backpacking market such as Oz Experience (which has a reputation as a party bus) and Wayward Bus. The hop-on hop-off service in New Zealand is the Magic Travellers Network (☎ +64 9 358 5600; magicbus.co.nz) which picks up from hostels around New Zealand. Writing from New South Wales, Geertje Korf passed on the following warning: '*A guy I met from Canada arrived here on a bus whose driver had promised him guaranteed work for up to $100 a day. He paid $70 for transport from Sydney and had the impression that he would be taken to an orchard, shown where to pitch his tent, etc. But instead the driver simply dropped him off at the job centre. He could have saved money by just catching the ordinary bus and walking.*'

Having your own transport is a great advantage when job-hunting in Australia. Some places have second-hand cars and camper vans for sale which they will buy back at the end of your stay, for example Boomerang Cars in Adelaide, 261 Currie St ☎ 0414 882559; boomerangcars.com.au) or Travellers Auto Barn in Sydney, Melbourne, Brisbane, Cairns, Perth and Darwin (travellers-autobarn.com). Expect to pay $2,000+ for an old car (like a gas-guzzling Ford Falcon) and more for a camper van. Car hire is expensive, but occasionally 'relocations' are available, i.e. hire cars that need to be returned to their depots. Just pick up the *Yellow Pages* and phone through the rental companies and ask for relocation deals, which is exactly what Roger Blake did when he wanted to travel from Adelaide to Melbourne:

> ***The Great Ocean Road is renowned as one of the most scenic drives in the world and I was determined not to see it from a tour bus window. I phoned a hundred and one rental companies looking for a relocation (taking a vehicle back to its state depot due to one-way rental demands). I got***

lucky because they desperately needed one to leave the next day. Only a $1 per day rental and so desperate that they even gave me a $100 for fuel. So I spent the following three days on my own in a flash 4/5 berth Mercedes-Benz motorhome on the spectacular Great Ocean Road along the coast of Victoria. The whole drive is dangerously scenic. And the cost to me? A whopping A$63!

Apollo Motorhomes lists the $1-a-day campervan relocations it has available on its website apollocamper.com.au/reloc.aspx (☎ 1800 777779). The best places to start are Cairns, Darwin, Adelaide and Broome where drivers are given up to $750 worth of fuel in addition. Many vehicles need repositioning from Christchurch back to Auckland and often the ferry fee is thrown in.

Backpackers' hostels are a good bet for finding drivers going your way, provided you are able to wait for a suitable ride. Try also the lift-sharing forum on backpackingaround.com.au.

Once in New Zealand it is difficult to imagine a country more favourable to hitch-hikers and budget travellers with a network of cheap and cheerful hostels and mountain huts for 'trampers'. Camping on beaches, fields and in woodlands is generally permitted. Tranzscenic railways has some low season deals on the South Island (☎ 0800 872467; tranzscenic.co.nz).

TRAVELLERS' HEALTH

No matter what country you are heading for, you should obtain the Department of Health leaflet T7.1 *Health Advice for Travellers* (updated May 2006). This leaflet should be available from any post office or doctor's surgery. Alternatively you can request a free copy on the Health Literature Line ☎ 0870 155 5455 or read it online at dh.gov.uk, which also has country-by-country details.

The old E111 certificate of entitlement to medical treatment within Europe has been superseded by the European Health Insurance Card (EHIC) which covers short stays. If you plan to work abroad for up to a year, you should also apply for form E101 from HMRC, Charity, Assets and Residence, Room BP1301, Benton Park View, Newcastle upon Tyne NE98 1ZZ, to prove that you are paying compulsory tax and contributions in the UK. See nhs.uk/Movingabroad/Pages/Workingabroad.aspx for details.

If you have a pre-existing medical condition it's important to anticipate what you might require in a crisis. Ask your GP or specialist support group for advice before you leave. Under extreme climatic conditions chronic or pre-existing conditions can be aggravated. Try to ascertain how easy it will be to access medicines on your trip, whether you'll be able to carry emergency supplies with you and how far you will be from specialist help. Always carry medications in their original containers and as a precaution you might carry a note from your doctor with an explanation of the drugs you're carrying and the relevant facts of your medical history. This could also include details of any allergies, for example an intolerance of penicillin. This might be of use if you are involved in an accident or medical emergency.

Any visits beyond the developed world, particularly to tropical climates, require careful preparation. You will face the risk of contracting malaria or water-borne diseases like giardiasis. You will need to provide your medical practitioner with precise details about where you intend to travel. Visit a travel medical centre at least a month before departure because some immunisations like those for yellow fever must be given well in advance. Expert medical advice is widely available on how to avoid tropical illness, so you should take advantage of modern medicine to protect yourself. And be prepared to pay for the necessary inoculations which are not normally covered by the NHS. It is always worth asking at your own surgery since if they are able to give good advice (and the internet has made that possible for any doctor worth his or her salt), the injections may be considerably cheaper than at a private specialist clinic where you are likely to pay between £30 and £50 per vaccine.

Specialist Advice

Increasingly, people are carrying out their own health research on the internet; check for example fitfortravel.scot.nhs.uk, tmb.ie and travelhealth.co.uk. The website of the World Health Organization, who.int/ith, has some information including a listing of the very few countries in which certain vaccinations are a requirement of entry.

A company that has become one of the most authoritative sources of travellers' health information in Britain is MASTA (enquiries@masta.org; masta-travel-health.com). It maintains a database of the latest disease situation for all countries and the latest recommendations for the prevention of tropical and other diseases. This advice is provided via a personalised Health Brief based on your destinations and nature of your trip, which is emailed to you from their website for £3.99. MASTA's network of travel clinics administers inoculations and sells medical kits and other specialist equipment like water purifiers, mosquito nets and repellents.

Private specialist clinics abound in London but are thin on the ground elsewhere. A worldwide searchable listing of specialist travel clinics is maintained by the International Society of Travel Medicine (istm.org) though many countries are not included.

The Hospital for Tropical Diseases in central London (Mortimer Market Building, Capper Street, Tottenham Court Road, WC1E 6AU) offers appointments at its Travel Clinic (☎ 020 7388 9600) and operates an automated Travellers Healthline Advisory Service on ☎ 020 7950 7799 (thehtd.org) which charges 50p a minute (average phone call lasts about seven minutes).

Other travel clinics include Nomad Travel Clinics in several London locations including Victoria (☎ 020 7823 5823; nomadtravel.co.uk) and also in Bristol, Manchester and Southampton. They offer walk-in appointments though you may have to wait at busy times. The Royal Free Travel Health Centre at the Royal Free Hospital on Pond St in London (☎ 020 7830 2885; travelclinicroyalfree.com) is a well-regarded private clinic, and the Trailfinders Travel Clinic (194 Kensington High St; ☎ 020 7983 3999; trailfinders.com) is long-established. Several online shops compete for travellers' custom, among them Travelpharm (☎ 01395 233771; travelpharm.com) which carries an extensive range of mosquito nets, anti-malaria drugs, water purification equipment and travel accessories. The website carries lots of health information.

For routine travellers' complaints, it is worth looking at a general guide to travel medicine such as *Bugs, Bites and Bowels* by Dr Jane Wilson Howarth (Cadogan, £9.99). Travel health books all emphasise the necessity of avoiding tap water in developing countries and can recommend ways to purify your drinking water by filtering, boiling or chemical additives (iodine is more reliable than chlorine).

Americans seeking general travel health advice should ring the Center for Disease Control & Prevention Hotline in Atlanta on ☎ 1 877 394 8747; cdc.gov. CDC issues travel announcements for international travellers rated from mild to extreme, i.e. minimal risk to a recommendation that non-essential travel be completely avoided.

For advice on protecting your sexual health, Marie Stopes International (☎ 0845 300 8090; mariestopes.org.uk) is helpful. The government's free booklet *Drugs Abroad* and the National Drugs Helpline (☎ 0800 776600) can give information on drugs laws abroad.

Malaria

Malaria is undoubtedly the greatest danger posed by visits to many tropical areas. The disease has been making a comeback in many parts of the world, due to the resistance of certain strains of mosquito to the pesticides and preventative medications that have been so extensively relied upon in the past. Because of increasing resistance, it is important to consult a specialist service as above. You can become better informed by looking at specialist websites such as hpa.org.uk/infections/topics_az/malaria/default.htm or preventingmalaria.info. You need to obtain the best information available to help you devise the most appropriate strategy for protection in the areas you intend to visit. Research indicates for example that the statistical chance of being bitten by a malarial mosquito in Thailand is once a year, but in Sierra Leone it rises to once a night. Start your research early since some courses of malaria prophylaxis need to be started up to three weeks before departure. It is always a good idea to find out in advance if you are going to suffer any side effects as well.

Falciparum malaria is potentially fatal. On average between 2,000 and 2,500 travellers return to the UK with malaria every year, and between ten and twenty will die. The two main drugs can be obtained over the counter: chloroquine and proguanil (brand name Paludrine). In regions resistant to these drugs, you will have to take both or a third line of defence such as mefloquine (brand name Lariam) available only on prescription. Because of possible side effects it is important that your doctor be able to vary the level of toxicity to match the risks prevalent in your destination. A relatively new (and expensive) drug called Malarone is used as an alternative to mefloquine or doxycycline, and is recommended for short trips to highly chloroquine-resistant areas. New drugs are being developed all the time and sometimes there is a time lag before they are licensed in the UK or USA. For example in her gap year in Madagascar, Karen Hedges twice contracted (non-dangerous) malaria but was quickly treated with an effective drug called Coartem, expensive by local standards, and not yet licensed in the UK.

Unfortunately these prophylactic medications are not foolproof, and even those who have scrupulously swallowed their pills before and after their trip as well as during it have been known to contract the disease. It is therefore essential to take mechanical precautions against mosquitoes. If possible, screen the windows and sleep under a permethrin-impregnated mosquito net since the offending mosquitoes feed between dusk and dawn. (Practise putting your mosquito net up before leaving home since some are tricky to assemble.) If you don't have a net, cover your limbs at nightfall with light-coloured garments, apply insect repellent with the active ingredient DEET and sleep with a fan on to keep the air moving. Try to keep your room free of the insects too by using mosquito coils, vaporisers, etc.

DEET is strong (not to say toxic) enough to last many hours. Wrist and ankle bands impregnated with the chemical are available and easy to use. Cover your limbs as night falls (6pm on the equator). Wearing fine silk clothes discourages bites and keep the repellent topped up.

Prevention is vastly preferable to cure. It is a difficult disease to treat, particularly in its advanced stages. If you suffer a fever up to twelve months after returning home from a malarial zone, visit your doctor and mention your travels, even if you suspect it might just be flu.

FORMALITIES AT BORDERS

Whichever mode of transport you choose, there are a number of formalities that must be tackled before you set off, to ensure that your journey is not fraught with an unexpected range of disasters. Heightened security everywhere means that more time must be set aside for airports and borders.

Visas

Outside the Schengen area of Europe in which border controls have been largely abolished for EU nationals, you can't continue in one direction for very long before you are impeded by border guards demanding to see your papers. After 9/11, immigration and security checks are tighter than ever before and many countries have imposed visa restrictions, particularly on North Americans in retaliation for all the new restrictions the US has implemented. Embassy websites are the best source of information or you can check online information posted by visa agencies. For example CIBT in London (uk.cibt.com) allows you to search visa requirements and costs for UK nationals visiting any country, and also shows their massive handling charges for applying on your behalf.

Non-Europeans should be careful not to overstay the 90-day limit on their Schengen visa. If it is picked up on departure, you will be liable for a huge fine, as New Zealander Richard Ferguson discovered in September 2008:

> ***After staying in Faliraki longer than I really wanted to, I finally had a ticket out of ChavLand. I had heard about the 90-day rule, but when I'd left Portugal after five months the year before, no worries. I had overstayed in Greece by 22 days which I learned when the Greek guy at the airport started yellin' at me: 'Pay 600 Euro cash or 4 years no Europe it will be!' So I paid the 600 euros. Stupid when I could have gone on a boat to Turkey and back in one day with a fresh stamp in my passport.***

Getting visas is a headache anywhere, and most travellers feel happier obtaining them in their home country. Set aside a chunk of your travel budget to cover the costs because many cost £30–£40 or more, including India, China, Vietnam and Armenia. Requirements for American travellers are completely different. In general, last-minute applications can incur a much higher fee, for example a Russian visa costs £115 if applied for seven days in advance, but £210 for the express two-day processing. If you do not want to pin yourself down to entry dates, you may decide to apply for visas as you travel for example from a neighbouring country, which in many cases is cheaper, though may cause delays.

If you intend to cross a great many borders, especially on an overland trip through Africa, ensure that you have all the relevant documentation and that your passport contains as many blank pages as frontiers which you intend to cross. Travellers have been turned back purely because the border guard refused to use a page with another stamp on it. Details of work permit regulations and so on can be found in the country chapters in this book.

Always reply simply and politely to any questions asked by immigration or customs officials. Roger Blake has a word of warning:

> ***Arriving in New Zealand was not really a problem other than a strange encounter with a customs officer: 'Are you bringing drugs into the country?' 'No!' 'Do you take drugs?' 'NO!' I reply. She asks 'Why not?' This is the kind of carefully planned (and corrupt) trap for would-be's that you occasionally come across. Anyway, no worries on my part.***

Money

On arrival at a border, you may be asked to prove that a) you have enough to support yourself for the duration of your proposed stay, and b) that you have the means to leave the country without undermining the economy by engaging in unauthorised activities (e.g. working, changing money on the black market, smuggling, etc.). The authorities are more likely to take an interest in a scruffy impecunious looking backpacker. Sometimes border personnel wish to see proof of absurdly large sums such as $1,000 for each month of your proposed stay. Remember that well-dressed travellers who carry suitcases rather than rucksacks will be challenged less often. Because Michel Falardeau was travelling on one-way tickets without all that much money, he wore a business suit whenever he was due to meet an immigration official, and this worked for him on his round-the-world trip. You can get away with having less money if you have an onward ticket, and the names and addresses of residents whom you intend to visit.

Find out beforehand whether there is a departure tax. For example to fly out of Hong Kong you must pay HK$120 (over £10) at the airport, Ecuador US$40 and so on. This can be an unexpected nuisance or a total disaster. Information about transferring emergency funds from home is given in the chapter *In Extremis* at the end of this book.

WORKING A PASSAGE

Many people setting out on their world travels assume, not unreasonably, that a large chunk of their savings must inevitably be swallowed up by airlines, railways and shipping companies. With a little advance planning, a fair amount of bravado and a dose of good fortune you can follow the example of thousands of travellers who have successfully voyaged around the globe keeping costs to a minimum.

Hitch-hiking is one way of crossing landmasses (see 'Travel') though it has fallen so out of favour with the 21st century traveller that alternatives must be found. Fortunately, if you are serious about travelling free or cheaply, there are several methods of working a passage by land or sea.

SEA

Cruise Liners

The luxury cruise liner business has been booming for at least a decade. More British holidaymakers go on cruises than take skiing holidays. Over a thousand liners sail the world's oceans at present, with many new ships on order through 2012. These megaliners or resort ships operate on a vast scale, like floating cities, and require a full range of staff. An estimated 13.2 million people took a cruise in 2008, an astonishing statistic. Most recruitment takes place through agents or 'concessionaires', all of whom say that they are looking only for qualified and experienced staff. But in many cases it is sufficient to be over 21 and have an extrovert personality and plenty of stamina for the very long hours of work on board.

Job-seekers with no experience or specialised skills should be wary of agencies that invite them to pay a fee to circulate their CV online. The privately maintained site cruisejunkie.com includes a link to a no-frills page of cruise-related resources, which includes lists of cruise lines and concessionaires. Another list of links can be found on the subscription site cruisejobfinder.com ($12.95 for a month).

Many cruise lines have special recruitment sites or pages that will set out how you should apply, e.g. Disney's site dcljobs.com has information about its concessionaires worldwide. For the giant Royal Caribbean, which carries about a quarter of all cruise passengers, go to royalcaribbean.co.uk or http://jobs.rccl.com; for Regent Seven Seas Cruises log on to rssc.com/employment and for Princess Cruises, check out http://employment.princess.com/employment/index.html.

According to Jane Roberts, who crossed the Atlantic from Venezuela to Estonia as a cruise line croupier, not all employees are experienced professionals:

> ***I worked in the casino department of four different cruise ships and met many people doing jobs as waiters, bar tenders, stewards and stewardesses. These jobs are very easy to come by. In fact 80% of all crew members are people who have never done that particular job in their lives. The turn-over of staff is high, even when people sign year-long contracts. It is difficult to live and work with the same people 24 hours a day. Crew don't get days off, perhaps just the odd breakfast or lunch off once a month. Patience levels have to be extremely high, since people who take holidays on cruise ships seem to think that they own the damn ship. Having to be sickeningly nice can take its toll very quickly.***

Contract lengths (some as short as four months) and conditions vary from ship to ship. Typically, crew are contracted for nine months and then get six weeks holiday. Wages are usually US$500–$750 a month, which is not much for working 12–14 hour days, sometimes seven days a week. Jobs which attract tips are the worst paid.

A list of agents around the world can be found at cruiselinesjobs.com/eng/recruitment. Some agencies in the UK that advertise for cruise line staff, often with a minimum of several years experience, include Cast-a-way (tel/fax 01204 655504; cast-a-way.co.uk) and Cruise Service Center Ltd, c/o Palme & Associates in Cornwall (☎ 01872 242566; cruiseservicecenter.com). Others can be found on the continent such as International Cruise Management Agency in Norway (icma.no) and International Service in France (internationalservices.fr). Anyone already in Florida might be able to arrange interviews with the cruise lines or their concessionaires.

The correct visa for working at sea in US waters is a C-1/D Crewman transit visa which is granted only after you have a job contract. Recently it has become necessary to undergo a face-to-face interview at the US Embassy before gaining this visa.

Private Yachts

People who sail the seas for pleasure are always hiring and sometimes firing crew members. If you display a reasonable level of common sense, vigour and amiability, and take the trouble to observe yachting etiquette, you should find it possible to persuade a yachtsman that you will be an asset to his crew. It should be stressed that inexperienced crew are almost never paid; in fact most skippers expect some contribution towards expenses; US$25 a day is a standard starting fee for food, drink, fuel, harbour fees, etc. Safety is of paramount importance as has been highlighted by several recent tragedies at sea. One of the best sources of information for cruising yachtsmen and women and aspiring crew is noonsite.com.

After crewing from Tonga to New Zealand and then on to Australia, Gerhard Flaig summed up the pros and cons of ocean sailing:

> ***It definitely is adventurous to sail on the ocean. You usually meet dolphins, whales, fish and birds. You get in close touch with nature to see and feel the waves and to see wonderful sunsets. You learn about sailing, meteorology, navigation. But there are also drawbacks. Maybe you get seasick, that's no fun. Then you have to deal with pouring rain and heavy storms. You have to get up in the middle of the night for the watch. The boat is wobbling all the time so that makes every little job more difficult, even going to the toilet. Maybe there is no wind at all for days and then it's frustrating not to move and to be far away from land. If you are willing to deal with all that then a sailing trip can be most rewarding.***

Obviously, it is much easier to become a crew member if you have some experience. But there are opportunities for people who lack experience at sea, and it is unwise to exaggerate your skills. Once you have worked on one yacht it will be much easier to get on the next one. The yachting world is a small one. The more experience you have, the more favourable arrangements you will be able to negotiate. Also, your chances are better of having a financial contribution waived if you are prepared to crew on unpopular routes, for example crossing the Atlantic west to east is much tougher than vice versa. If you are embarking on a serious round-the-world-on-a-shoestring venture, read a yachting book such as the RYA's training publication *Competent Crew* (£9.99) which contains invaluable information on technical sea terms and the basics of navigation. If you demonstrate to a skipper that you take safety seriously enough to have learned a little about the procedures and if you are clean and sober, sensible and polite, you are probably well on your way to filling a crewing vacancy.

Even better would be to sign up for a sailing course (and take your certificate with you). The first level, Competent Crew, can be reached in a five-day course at any Royal Yachting Association recognised centre for about £500. Anyone who is a confident cook, carpenter, electrician, mechanic or sewing machine operator (for sail-mending) may be able to market those skills too.

Crew and skippers must obtain a STCW 95 (Standards of Training, Certification and Watchkeeping for Seafarers; stcw.org), which is evidence of basic safety training.

It might not be much more expensive to undertake a sail training course abroad, for instance in Croatia with Activity Yachting (☎ 01243 641304; activityyachting.com) where at the end of a week's hands-on sailing, you should have earned the International Certificate of Competence (ICC).

Several firms specialise in preparing people for a career in sailing or watersports such as the UK Sailing Academy in West Cowes on the Isle of Wight PO31 7PQ (☎ 01983 294941; uksa.org) and Flying Fish also in Cowes (☎ 0871 250 2500; flyingfishonline.com) both of which offer a follow-up careers service. If these courses are too expensive, go down to your nearest marina and offer to do some hard and tedious maintenance work, sanding, painting, varnishing or scraping barnacles from the hull, in exchange for sailing tuition. Later you can aim for an easier life looking after a boat for an absent skipper by living onboard and checking anchors and bilges. It is a good idea to buy a log book in which you can enter all relevant experience and voyages, and be sure to ask the captains of boats you have been on for a letter of reference.

As one skipper comments, 'A beginner ceases to be a passenger if he or she can tie half a dozen knots and hitches, knows how to read the lights of various kinds of ships and boats at night, and isn't permanently seasick.' Sometimes the arrangement is halfway between working and hitching a lift. There may not be much actual work to do but you could make cups of coffee, sand deck chairs, play Scrabble with the captain's wife or help look after the children of a cruising family. Some solo women sailors concentrate on job-hunting on cruisers sailed by retired couples for the sake of their security.

If you are planning your trip a long way in advance and have relevant experience, scour the classified columns of *Yachting Monthly*, *Yachting World* or *Practical Boat Owner*, though advertisers are likely to require a substantial payment or contribution towards expenses on your part. Increasingly skippers use the internet to find paying crew. Sites that promise to match crew with captains include floatplan.com/crew.htm, which carries details of actual vacancies, for example from March 2009, 'Amateur crew wanted to cruise Turkey and Greek Aegean islands'. A certain number of listings contain a lonely hearts element: 'Mexico and Beyond – Attractive fit slender female crew member wanted for Mexico, South Pacific and beyond. Seeking a smart, stable woman, who loves adventure, cruising, has a sense of humour and a good heart. Romance a possibility, but as we will be short-handed most of the time, the passion for sailing and a life of adventure is the crucial element.' Women should be warned that the yachting world is notoriously sexist. Even in a world where Ellen McArthur is a household name, it is often assumed that women aboard yachts are there to cook.

Crewing agencies in Britain, France, Denmark, the West Indies, United States and elsewhere match yacht captains with crew. These are mostly of use to professional experienced sailors. A list of yachting employment agencies that recruit catering staff is available from the cordon bleu cookery school Tante Marie at tantemarie.co.uk/forms/Yachting_Agencies.doc. The site yachtandcrew.com has links to crew agencies worldwide.

The Cruising Association (CA House, 1 Northey St, Limehouse Basin, London E14 8BT; ☎ 020 7537 2828; cruising.org.uk/cahouse/crewing.shtml) runs a crewing service to put skippers in touch with unpaid crew. Meetings are held on the first Thursday of the month at 7pm between February and May for this purpose (though phone to confirm). They claim to offer a variety of sailing (including two or three week cruises to the Mediterranean and transatlantic passages) to suit virtually every level of experience. The service is free to CA members; otherwise the annual fee is £20, £30 a couple.

Among the online crew recruitment services based in the UK is the Global Crew Network (☎ 07773 361959; globalcrewnetwork.com) which specialises in crew recruitment for superyachts, luxury motor and sailing yachts worldwide. Another matching service is operated by Crewseekers near Southampton (tel/fax 01489 578319; info@crewseekers.co.uk). Their membership charges are £60 for six months, £85 for a year; joint members may be added for an extra £15/£25. Their web pages (crewseekers.co.uk) are updated daily showing the latest boats worldwide requiring crew.

Alternatives include:

Crew Network Worldwide: crewnetwork.com; crewing offices in Antibes, Palma de Mallorca, Newport, Fort Lauderdale, San Diego, Auckland, St Maarten and Viareggio.

Reliance Yacht Management: Farnborough, Hampshire; ☎ 01252 378239; info@reliance-yachts.com.

Crewfile.com: sailingcrew.blogspot.com; crewing positions with visible email addresses; one advertiser at the time of writing intends to be sailing the world until 2010 and estimates that crewmembers will need only about $200 a month for food and expenses.

Concentrations of crewing agencies can be found in yachting honeypots such as Antibes and Fort Lauderdale. The main crewing agencies in Antibes are housed in La Galerie du Port, 8 boulevard d'Aguillon, 06600 Antibes. For example try contacting Luxury Yachts (luxyachts.com). In these places you will also find crew houses, and accommodation favoured by yachties. The sites jf-recruiting.com and workonaboat.com/crew-houses carry yacht crew accommodation listings.

Once you're abroad, there is always a chance of tracking down your own sailing adventures. Frank Schiller split expenses with the New Zealand couple who took him (a complete sailing novice) aboard their yacht bound for Tonga and he ended up spending four very affordable months at sea. Always be sure to discuss the details of payment before setting sail. Many captains will ask you to pay a bond (say $500) for a long journey. Captains are responsible for making sure their crew can get back to their country of origin after the voyage is finished.

Whenever you end up finding a yacht to crew on, you may be letting yourself in for discomfort and danger, not to mention boredom, especially if you find yourself painting the boat in dock for the umpteenth time. Yachts require a surprising amount of maintenance. Offshore sailing is a risky business and you should be sure that the skipper to whom you have entrusted your life is a veteran sailor. A well-used but well-kept boat is a good sign.

Make sure before you leave the safety of dry land that your personality and politics do not clash with that of the captain. Quickly tiring of Gibraltar, Nicola Sarjeant and her Dutch boyfriend decided to join the hordes of people looking for a working passage on a yacht:

> ***We asked around from boat to boat but most people weren't interested or wanted experienced people. We also put up a note in a shop in the harbour. This was answered by an Englishman who wanted a couple to help him crew to the Canaries and on to the West Indies. We had to contribute to food and expenses as well as do two four-hour watches per day. We also scrubbed and painted the bottom of the yacht. Because we were inexperienced we weren't paid which at the time seemed the best deal going in Gibraltar as there were many experienced people looking for crewing positions. I must caution anybody considering this kind of thing to think seriously about whether they can get along with the other people on the boat for a period of several weeks without throwing someone overboard. It turned out the captain had wanted a couple because he assumed a woman would cook dinner, wash dishes, etc. By the time we reached Gran Canaria (after three weeks because we made so many stops) the four of us were at each other's throats. My boyfriend and I hopped off (penniless). The trip had turned out to be quite expensive, though we saw islands I wouldn't otherwise have seen (Madeira in particular) and we got to learn a little about sailing. However the***

> ***sailing is mostly quite boring (a yacht is very slow moving) and when you don't like the people, a lot of the fun goes out of the trip.***

Charming the Captain

In every marina and harbour there are people planning and preparing for long trips. There may be requests for crew posted on harbour notice boards, in yacht clubs or chandlery shops from Marina Bay in Gibraltar to Rushcutter's Bay in Sydney. Or you may have to approach skippers on spec. The most straightforward (and usually the most successful) method is to head for the nearest yacht marina and ask captains directly. To locate the yacht basin in an unfamiliar town, simply ask at your hotel or the tourist office. The harbour water supply or dinghy dock is usually a good place to meet yachties. One sailor looking for a berth in Thailand found that he had to swim out to the anchored yachts to knock on their hulls, which culminated in a free ride to Malaysia.

Since many of the yachts moored are used for local pleasure sailing only, concentrate on the yachts with foreign flags. Some travellers contend that boat-owners appreciate a straightforward approach: 'Good morning. I'd like to work for you.' Others think that this might catch captains off guard, and that it is better to approach the question in a more roundabout fashion. Many British, North American and Australian travellers are working their way around by cleaning boats and then participating as crew members as a means of alleviating travel expenses to their next destination. If you are not afraid to ask, your options can be greatly increased.

A yacht is a home, so an unwelcome intrusion on board is as bad as entering a house uninvited. The accepted phrase is 'permission to board?' Once on board, behave as politely and as deferentially as you would in any stranger's home. Once you get to know both the boat and its owner, you can find ways to make yourself useful, whether washing up or scraping barnacles from the hull. You are then more likely to be offered a berth when the yacht finally sails.

This is one time when it is *not* a good idea to exaggerate your qualifications, since skippers who find out that they have been misled will be justifiably furious and, at worst, it could be life-endangering. Britons will probably do better with yachts sailing the British flag, and women often have an edge if only because of their relative novelty in a world dominated by men.

Women sailors encounter special problems and in fact are usually trying *not* to charm the captain to excess. Mirjam Koppelaars, who responded to a notice posted by a yachtsman in Gibraltar, spells out the problems:

> ***I must put some words of warning, especially for the female sailors. Most captains who are actively looking for crew are not really interested in finding competent crew, but in finding female company for day – and nighttime. Be aware of this and think it over before boarding a boat. Elise from Norway and I sailed with this extremely peculiar captain and a third crew member (Simon from England) over to the Canary Islands. I shouldn't complain too much about it, since we were one of the only boats which actually made this trip without any damage that year, but anyway, we were all three very glad that we could jump over to another boat in Las Palmas.***

Crewing in the Mediterranean

The standard pattern is for a traveller to get a job on a yacht for the summer charter season on the Mediterranean and then sail with the same yacht or power boat (the latter are generally more boring) to the Americas or (very occasionally) South Africa. Hundreds of boats descend on Gibraltar in the spring, many of which will be ready for a crew change. Hundreds more leave each autumn from the French Riviera, the Costa del Sol, the Canary Islands, etc. The annual ARC (Atlantic Rally for Cruisers) from the Canaries (departing the last Sunday in November in order to reach the West Indies for Christmas) is a convoy for the cautious more than a race, so this is an excellent time to be in Gran Canaria looking for a boat especially if you are willing to contribute $25 a day for the three week crossing. Gran Canaria is the last traditional victualling stop before the Atlantic crossing; the contemplation of thousands of miles of Atlantic Ocean often encourages owners and skippers to take on extra crew.

As mentioned, yacht crew placement agencies are concentrated in Antibes. For example the Crew Network Worldwide with its HQ in Florida has an office in the south of France (antibes@crewnetwork.com) plus an affiliate in Mallorca called YachtHelp. These agencies are mainly attempting to fill professional vacancies and do not want to be inundated with applications from unsuitable candidates. Competition for jobs on luxury yachts and super yachts is so acute that some candidates enrol in specialist training courses. In Mallorca, contact the international yacht crew agency Fred Dovaston SL in Puerto Portals (☎ 971 677 375; yachtjob.com) which also has a crew consultant in Gibraltar.

When Richard Ferguson checked out Palma de Mallorca in the summer of 2008, he found the scene discouraging:

> ***Palma is THE place to try to get a job on a superyacht. But everyone knows this so nowadays there are heaps and heaps and heaps of Kiwis, Aussies, Saffas and Brits trying their luck. All have their STCW (standard course) but few have any experience which is really what the yachts are after. It seemed that the most demand was for stewardesses (boys need not apply), engineers and chefs. If you do land a job you can get well paid.***

More job-seekers have gravitated to Europe because of the strength of the euro, which might account for the recent mobs of job-seekers.

Crewing from the Caribbean

Yachts arrive in the Caribbean in the autumn (October to December) and leave again in April and May before the hurricane season begins (the official date is June 1st though plenty of boats stay around until July). A multitude of yachts gathers at the biggest end-of-season event, Antigua Race Week (end of April/beginning of May), which affords excellent opportunities to arrange a berth to Venezuela, Europe or the South Pacific. If you have accumulated experience during the season you should have little difficulty in finding a passage back to the Mediterranean or the UK.

According to Paul Crabb, Antigua is by far the most promising place to look for a crewing position. Now a professional sailor, he is an advocate of spending time in the yachties' bar and demonstrating what good company you are without drinking to excess. Paul was lucky enough to get day work on a yacht belonging to Richard Wright, the late ex-keyboard player for Pink Floyd. Other good places to look for a lift are Barbados between November and February and St Lucia at the beginning of December. Barbados is traditionally the place transatlantic vessels arrive, though vessels participating in the ARC often end up at Rodney Bay Marina on St Lucia in the first two weeks of December which makes this an ideal time and place to search for a crew position. After the long Atlantic crossing many skippers and crew are desperate to get away from each other.

Another excellent place to head is the Yacht Haven Marina in St Thomas, US Virgin Islands. Hanging around the Bridge pub and the yacht supply stores should result in contact with skippers. Also try Trinidad at Carnival time in February. This is the largest gathering of cruisers in the Caribbean and therefore offers some extraordinarily good crewing opportunities.

General tips for inspiring confidence in skippers include dressing neatly, telling the skipper that you meet immigration requirements (and if you don't have an onward ticket, offer to leave an equivalent deposit), showing your health insurance certificate, reassuring him that you are not carrying any illegal substances (inviting him to search your luggage if he would like), and finally if possible showing a reference from another skipper.

Crewing from the Americas

Apart from introducing yourself to boat-owners at the docks, the primary ways to find a crewing position in the US are by registering with a crewing agency, staying in a crew house where you are likely to hear of forthcoming vacancies, answering an advert in the yachting press or hanging around at a yachting supply store, some of which have notice boards.

If intending to sign up with a crewing agency, it is virtually essential to do so in person. At that time you can enquire about visas, though you are likely to be told that it is permissible to join the crew of a foreign-registered yacht on a tourist visa provided you don't cruise in US waters for longer than 29 days (whereupon you should have a B-1 business visa).

A number of crewing agencies are located in Fort Lauderdale, the yachting capital of Florida. The website of Floyd's Hostel and Crew House (floridahostel.com/placement.html) carries a list of about ten local agencies with which it is possible to register in person and in some cases for a job-seeker's fee of $25–$75. Experienced crew often bypass the agencies and simply ask captains directly. Chefs/cooks are especially in demand.

Yachts sail from the west coast of North America to Hawaii, Tahiti and beyond in April/May or September/October. In the autumn there are several organised gatherings of 'yachties' in California which provide an excellent chance to fix up a crewing position. As well as running relevant classified adverts, the monthly yachting magazine *Latitude 38* (15 Locust Ave, Mill Valley, CA 94941; ☎ 415 383 8200; latitude38.com) compiles a Mexico Only Crew List in early September, and also hosts a spring crew list party in March. Women job-seekers are advised by *Latitude 38* to ask as many pertinent (but not impertinent) questions as possible about the duties (strictly sailing) which they will be expected to perform.

Ports along Baja California (the long Mexican peninsula) are surprisingly popular because skippers want to avoid the high mooring fees of California to the north. It has been estimated that there are as many as 400 foreign yachts moored in La Paz at any one time, a Baja town 22 hours by bus from Tijuana.

Further south, Panama is an excellent place to find a passage especially in March but any time between January and May. Apparently there are always a few sailboats stranded there for lack of crew. The vast continent of South America may afford possibilities. Between May and August, hundreds of yachts congregate in Puerto la Cruz and Cumaná in Venezuela to avoid the hurricanes in the Caribbean.

Crewing in the South Pacific

AFTER SEVERAL EXHAUSTING BUT LUCRATIVE MONTHS OF FRUIT-PICKING IN AUSTRALIA AND NEW ZEALAND, FRANK SCHILLER FROM GERMANY WAS ALL SET TO FULFIL ONE OF HIS DREAMS:

I was hellbent on scoring a ride on an ocean-going yacht for any Pacific destination – after all I'd read alluring stories of Joseph Conrad and Jack London. In June I stood in front of a 4-Square shop window in Russell in New Zealand's Bay of Islands when by pure chance a notice was put up by the shop keeper:

'Crew wanted for Tonga.' Less than an hour later I found myself sailing across the bay back to Opua. After a week of doing odd jobs on the boat I was en route to Nukualofa. Pure magic. All this despite never having set foot on a yacht before, once more stressing the theme of your book that nothing's impossible!

Since the New Zealand owners had two kids, they needed someone to give them a hand. In no time I was doing night watches, taking sights with the sextant (the skipper taught me a few lessons on navigation which I was very keen on), cooking and washing up and most important of all – I became 'Uncle Frankie' to the kids. If you get along well with everyone on board, there are no worries going sailing in a matchbox. (But if there are hassles – no escape, even on a 100 footer.) Yachting, in fact, can be a very rewarding and adventurous thing to embark on.

The best season to ask around in Fiji, Samoa, Tonga, etc. is July to October when most boats leave to sail to Hawaii or New Zealand. Suva, the capital of Fiji, and Papeete in Tahiti are hubs of much yachting activity in the South Pacific. Try the Royal Suva Yacht Club or the much smaller Tradewinds Marina (Suva). In New Zealand the best places by far to find crewing jobs are Opua in the Bay of Islands and Whangarei where the boats are close together and the people all know one another. Although the Westhaven Marina in Auckland Harbour is one of the biggest in the southern hemisphere, it can be more difficult to meet the right people because of the anonymity of a big city. You might try the Auckland office of the crewing agency Crew Network at Westhaven (☎ 09 302 0178; newzealand@crewnetwork.com).

Crewing from Other Countries

Many yachts travelling around Africa lose their crew in Cape Town and need new crew for the onward journey. Durban Yacht Club is recommended though sailing from Cape Town to Durban against the ocean currents is a joyless endeavour. Yachts leave the East African coast for the Seychelles in January or February and for Madagascar and South Africa in August/September. Visit the yacht clubs in Dar es Salaam and Mombasa. The best time to try in South-East Asia is September/October. West of Sri Lanka there are crewing opportunities each spring to the Red Sea, Mauritius, the Seychelles and East Africa.

In fact the possibilities are infinite for people without a fixed timetable. For example the author of this book met by chance a charming sailor in a post office in Cochin, South India and could have crewed across the Indian Ocean to Dar es Salaam had it not been for the tyranny of publisher's deadlines (alas).

LAND

If you possess a heavy goods vehicle (HGV) or passenger carrying vehicle (PCV) licence, you will have a distinct advantage wherever you go. These are costly in money and time to acquire, but open opportunities throughout the world. Anyone interested should compare costs, e.g. it is much cheaper and easier to obtain in New Zealand than in the UK. Most training centres will assess how much tuition you will need before trying the test, often 15–25 hours (at approximately £30–£35 an hour). People with enough mechanical knowledge to make running repairs to their vehicle are especially in demand.

Overland Tours

If you do have or are willing to train for one of the specialist licences and have some knowledge of mechanics, you may be eligible to work as an expedition driver. Competent tour leaders are greatly in demand by the many overland companies and youth travel specialists which advertise their tours and occasionally their vacancies in magazines like *TNT*. Look also in the glossy magazine for independent travellers *Wanderlust* (sold in Borders) which carries occasional relevant ads in its Jobshop column (wanderlust.co.uk/job-shop).

Leaders have to contend with vehicle breakdowns, border crossings, and the trip whinger (usually the one with a calculator). It is always an advantage and sometimes a requirement to have been on one of the tours of the company you want to work for.

Autumn is the time when recruitment tends to take place. Here is a selected list of overland operators some of whose websites include information on tour leader and/or driver recruitment. All UK employers are looking for staff who have the right to work in the UK/EU. For more companies, see the directory of tour operators maintained by Overland Expedition Resources (go-overland.com). Specialist companies which operate only in one region (e.g. Africa, Latin America) are mentioned in the relevant chapters.

Dragoman: ☎ 01728 862255; recruitment@dragoman.co.uk; dragoman.co.uk; have a good reputation and look for leader drivers over 25 willing to train for the PCV licence in their workshops (if they don't already have one); minimum commitment of two years for expeditions to Africa, Asia, South and Central America.

Exodus: London SW12; exodus.co.uk; suitable candidates (aged 25+) for leader positions in Africa, Asia and the Americas can acquire the appropriate licence during the months of training; knowledge of Italian, Spanish, French or Japanese highly valued.

Explore Worldwide: Farnborough, Hants; explore.co.uk/about-explore/jobs; Europe's largest adventure tour operator employing 300 tour leaders for Europe, Africa, Asia and the Americas; must have first aid certificate and preferably a second language; must be UK resident and over 25; training given (refundable bond of £250).

Imaginative Traveller: imaginative-traveller.com; tour leaders for at least 12 months for Middle East, China, Thailand, Vietnam, etc.

Kumuka Expeditions: London W8; humanresources@kumuka.com; kumuka.co.uk; looking for qualified diesel mechanics with a PCV or HGV licence to be drivers; tour leaders (minimum age 23) chosen according to experience and personality.

Tucan Travel: London W3; 020 8896 6700; tucantravel.com and its sister company Budget Expeditions for 18–35 year olds to South America, Europe, Egypt, China, India and Southeast Asia.

The pay on a training trip will be low, about £100 per week. Incidental expenses such as visas, passports, air tickets, etc. are paid for. Your company will also pay your food kitty contributions and will cover any compulsory money changes that may exist en route. Although it is hard work, it is undoubtedly an interesting and exciting job. Once you are a full expedition leader, you will be paid at a higher rate and have a chance of earning bonuses. Brett Archer from New Zealand enjoyed his stint of working for an African overland company though found it a little daunting to have 18 people dependent on him in such circumstances.

Expeditions

One romantic idea for working your way around the world is to become part of an expedition venturing into the more remote and unspoiled parts of the world from Tierra del Fuego to Irian

Jaya. It would be nice if you could be invited to join a party of latter-day explorers in exchange for some menial duty such as portering or cooking. However expedition organisers and leaders nowadays demand that participants have some special skills or expertise to contribute beyond mere eagerness. For example an advert for people needed on an Arctic expedition included among its volunteer requirements a post-doctoral archaeologist, an electronics officer for proton magnetometer maintenance and an antenna theorist. One suspects that they weren't inundated with applications.

The Royal Geographical Society (1 Kensington Gore, London SW7 2AR) encourages and assists many British expeditions. Occasionally there are requests from expedition leaders for specialists with either scientific or medical skills, preferably with past expedition experience, and for this a register of personnel is maintained. The RGS is now allied with the Institute of British Geographers (IBG) and keeps files of expedition reports that might be of assistance to expedition planners. Raleigh International is a UK-based charity which aims to develop young people aged 17–25 by offering them the chance to undertake demanding environmental and community projects on expeditions overseas (see section on 'Gap Year and Career Break Placements' in the *Volunteering* chapter). They have an ongoing need for more experienced individuals (25+) to join expedition teams as self-funding staff, e.g. project manager, accountant, doctor, nurse, engineer, photographer, builder, trek leader and communications expert.

World Challenge Expeditions (High Wycombe; ☎ 01494 427600; world-challenge.co.uk) takes on expedition leaders to supervise school expeditions to developing countries. Trips take place in the summer and the minimum commitment is three or six weeks. Applicants must have a national qualification such as summer Mountain Leader or Walking Group Leader plus some experience of working with young people and preferably of travelling in the developing world. Remuneration is negotiable but at least all expenses will be covered.

When joining any expedition you are unlikely to escape a financial liability, for most expeditions levy a fee from each participant. Sponsorship, and the amount of it, from companies, trusts and other sources will depend upon the aims of the expedition and the benefits to the donor. And once the money and equipment are forthcoming the expedition then has obligations to its sponsors and forfeits much of its freedom. Raising sponsorship, a job with which all expedition members should help, is probably the biggest headache of all and involves endless letter-writing and the visiting, cap in hand, of dozens of commercial establishments and other possible sources of income.

AIR COURIERS

Changes in the international system of document delivery mean that the role of the air courier has disappeared. No longer do international courier companies give heavily subsidised flights to members of the public to physically accompany bags of time-sensitive documents on long haul flights. So to find out how to spend as little as possible on flights, check out the previous chapter on Travel.

ENTERPRISE

You don't have to spend eight hours a day washing dishes or stripping a strawberry patch in order to earn money abroad. Many travellers have found or made opportunities to go into business for themselves, exchanging steady wage packets for less predictable sources of income. The people who have succeeded in this type of work tend to have a large degree of initiative, determination and often creativity; they have identified some local need and go on to exploit it.

Often they find themselves on the borderline of the law. If you paint the sun setting over a harbour you are an artist; sell the painting to someone who stops to admire it and you may, in law, become a street trader requiring a permit. If you wash motorists' windscreens at traffic lights, you might be doing them a service, but the police might consider you an obstruction. At worst you will find yourself being moved on, though a few exceptions have been noted in the country chapters.

IMPORT/EXPORT

With experience, travellers come to know what items can be bought cheaply in one country and profitably sold in another. Wherever something is exorbitantly priced, it is possible to sell informally to local people or fellow tourists at a profit. But as the world shrinks and trade barriers dissolve, the possibilities are becoming fewer. After his extensive travels in Turkey and Asia, the American Tim Leffel (now publisher of an online travel magazine *Perceptive Travel*) concluded: *'The enterprise opportunities seem to be vanishing faster than you can say "free trade". There weren't many things in high demand that you could buy cheaper in the US or across a neighbouring border, at least where we were, unless you were dealing in big-ticket electronics. Bringing things back, of course, is a different story.'*

On the other hand niches can always be found. For example, a Derbyshire man realised that Germans in the town twinned with his loved British goods including the obvious things like tea and marmalade. He went over with a supply of Union Jack beach towels and sold them at the local market in a very short time. Or a Scottish woman had T-shirts printed up with Gaelic motifs and sold them at the Canadian Highland Games. Past readers have recommended carrying around cigarette papers which are expensive in Scandinavia, for example, and hard to obtain in Greece, Brazil, etc. Ian McArthur planned to take about 500 packets to Goa where he'd heard that the selling price was five times higher than in Britain. Travellers in the Far East (Bangkok, Hong Kong and Japan) have been known to stock up on the newest play station games (which are often a third the price they are in the UK) with a view to selling them discreetly at home. Only a buff would be able to make this work, since only certain UK computers are 'chipped up' (adapted) to cope with import games.

Some travellers think it's worthwhile to load up on bronze trinkets, alpaca sweaters, jade jewelry, rosewood boxes, sisal baskets from Kenya, Tibetan woollens, Turkish carpets or anything else which they know are more expensive or unobtainable elsewhere. Before engaging in this sort of activity you'll have to master the art of haggling, which involves patience and good humour. Usually it is difficult to make much of a profit on one-off trips abroad. Also, you should be thoroughly acquainted with customs regulations as well as the market back home.

Do not believe every foreign trader who promises vast profits in your home country, for example selling Tahitian pearls or Sri Lankan sapphires, or who assures you that you will have no difficulty at customs. In fact do not believe any of them. Almost invariably they are inventing a story in order to make a bulk sale. No consumer protection is available to their gulls. Bangkok seems to be the capital of smooth-talking swindlers. A warning notice in a Bangkok hostel, which reads 'These people are vicious and evil and all they say is lies' was written by a German who parted with

US$1,100 for '$3,000 plus' of sapphires, only to be told by his 'guaranteed buyer' (an unwitting jeweller in Sydney) that their true value was $250.

Yet there is a host of travellers successfully selling exotica as Kristen Moen reports: *'I was in Corfu selling jewelry I had bought in India, Nepal, Thailand and China. Quite a lot of my friends do similar things. When they come home from Asia and South America they sell jewelry and other things and they make almost enough money to finance their trip. Of course you have to be careful when you buy so you don't get cheated but you learn along the way.'*

Currency Exchange

In countries where there is a soft currency, i.e. one that cannot officially be used to buy dollars or sterling, or where the government attaches an unjustifiably high value to its currency, a black market often develops. Tempting as the rewards might be, you should be aware of the pitfalls. The black market attracts shady characters who regularly cheat even the canniest travellers, making them regret their greed. Favourite ploys include handing the tourist an envelope full of shredded newspaper or one large denomination bill wrapped cleverly around a wad of lower bills, or pretending to spot a policeman and then vanishing after taking your dollars but before giving you your pesos, rupees, shillings, etc.

To guard against such an outcome, always avoid trading on the street especially after dark. Familiarise yourself with the appearance of all denominations of currency and take along a friend to assist you.

Second-hand Gear

Outside the consumer societies of the West, there is a fluctuating demand for gadgets and gewgaws, and various items we take for granted can be sold or traded. T-shirts with Western slogans have had spells of popularity in different places, though in most cases a local entrepreneur will have latched on to this market. Even if you don't get cash, you might trade for goods and services or an interesting souvenir. Writing in *Rough News*, the newsletter from Rough Guides, Justyn Evans from Milton Keynes described what he observed on an overland trip through Africa:

> ***We stopped in Nakuru in Kenya to do some shopping. One young vendor, trying to sell hand-painted cards, showed some unusual initiative. When I turned down his request to buy something, he asked if I had anything to trade. Jokingly I pulled my biro from a back pocket. Eagerly he tested it and offered me a card in return. While travelling around Kenya I had lots of requests to trade. On more than one occasion I could have walked away wearing only my underwear. Everyone wanted something I was wearing. When it comes to pens, however, most people are picky. Your standard biro just won't do any more, 'clicky' pens are the in thing. Watches are also popular. I had more offers for my watch than anything else and I wished I'd taken an old one with me.***

Elfed Guyatt from Wales thinks that Sweden is a particularly promising destination for any would-be entrepreneurs:

> ***In the weekend market stalls people just set up their own table and sell off all sorts of odds and ends. The prices are incredibly high compared to Britain for certain things. You should make 500% profit on selling things like medals, caps, British and American books in subjects that interest the Swedes, in fact anything that looks different and not easily available in their country. They do like showing off possessions here. Souvenirs of London or Shakespeare go well. I saw a very cheap, small brass Big Ben table bell sell for £12.50 and an old battered cricket bat went for £25.***

SPOTTING LOCAL OPPORTUNITIES

The opportunities for finding eager customers on whatever doorstep you find yourself are endless and we can only give some idea of the remarkable range of ways to earn money by using your initiative and your imagination. If you see a gap in the market, try to fill it. For example Stephen Psallidas toyed seriously with the idea of buying a bicycle in the tomato-growing capital of Queensland in order to hire it out to job-seeking tomato pickers since at the time Bowen was, if not a one-horse town, a one-bicycle town. After getting to know the Greek island of Levkas fairly well, Camilla Lambert hired a jeep at weekends and took three paying passengers out for a day's excursion. One Englishman acquired a chain saw in Spain and made a killing by hiring himself out to farmers to prune their olive trees. A Canadian who was having trouble being hired by a language school in a provincial city in Taiwan set up his own English immersion social club which easily covered his costs in the two months he ran it. You just need to exploit any manual or artistic or public relations skill you already have or which you have cultivated for the purpose.

Homemade Handicrafts

A number of people have successfully supported themselves abroad by selling home-made jewellery and other items on the street. Once you master a skill you can move around with it, perhaps following the festival circuit around Europe or wherever mobs of people gather. Careful preparations can pay dividends; for example Jennifer Tong picked up shells from a beach near Eilat and invested £5 in a pair of pliers and some wire, clips and beads when she was in Israel. With these materials she made simple earrings which were bought for £2 a pair on the Greek Islands. Even more simply, Amy Ignatow collected smooth pebbles in Israel, decorated them with a permanent pen and sold them on the street in Jerusalem for £3 each. Steve Pringle sold earrings in Madrid which he had made from a stock of cheap imitation diamonds he had brought over from London. Braided or knotted friendship bracelets are popular in travellers' resorts and can usually be sold for a few quid and take no more than 15 minutes to make. You have to find something that doesn't require too much time, which Emma Hoare failed to do while on her gap year:

> ***In the south of France I met up with a girl I had been previously travelling with, and decided to make money by selling bags that we'd sewn. We went on to Spain and quickly discovered that sitting in little pensione rooms stitching minuscule beads onto cheap, flimsy fabric was a recipe for mental deterioration and, at times, uncontrollable hysteria. Then I decided that I had put too much effort into my bags to sell them. They were my little works of art and I was damned if I was going to let some horrible young tourist have it for a fiver and then leave it on the floor in a club somewhere (see what I mean about mental deterioration?).***

It is worth looking out for cheap and unusual raw materials such as beads from Morocco, shells from Papua New Guinea or bamboo from Crete. An aspiring sculptress who makes copper wire sculptures found that business was slow at the beginning of the Edinburgh Festival but hotted up, allowing her to fund several months of post-Festival travels. Needless to say, you have to be good at what you do for this to be effective.

If you can draw, knit, sew, sculpt or work with wood or leather then you may be able to produce something that people want to buy in holiday resorts. The skill of drawing henna tattoos or braiding hair with beads or 'hair wraps' can make a lot of money. All you need for the latter is the expertise, some cheap multi-coloured beads and thread with which to tie off the ends. The weather will have an obvious effect on success or failure as Nicole Gluckstern from San Francisco found at the Edinburgh Fringe Festival: *'For cash I did hair wraps. But due to a number of circum-*

stances (closure of the traditional place for setting up called the Mound, inconvenient show time right in the middle of the best selling part of the day and incessant rain), I did not even break even, although I made enough to cover most of my expenses and only spent about $200 of my own money in three weeks, not too bad for a fantastic time.'

International sporting fixtures are a good bet too so creative craftsmen and women might think about heading for South Africa for the World Cup in 2010. A Canadian whom Roger Blake met on his travels in Africa had made $500 painting flags on faces during one World Cup.

Beaches and Mobs

You should learn to look on any crowd of people as a potential market for what you have to sell. People emerging from a club are often grateful for a hotdog or sandwich or skiers queuing for a lift might appreciate some chocolate. If you loiter in a place where people regularly emerge from a remote place, as at the end of treks in Nepal or New Zealand, you could probably sell some interesting food and drink of which they have been deprived. Stephen Psallidas decided to become a portable off-licence with a view to selling wine to the devotees who flock to see Jim Morrison's grave in Paris. Unfortunately this was not a popular idea with the local cannabis sellers and he ended up drinking the wine himself.

Sunbathers on a wide unspoilt beach may be longing for a cold bottle of beer, sun tan lotion, a donut, or a few pre-stamped postcards and a ballpoint pen, and won't mind paying over the odds for them (especially if you have printed up your own postcards from your travel photos). Choose your beach carefully: if a beach is already swarming with cold drinks salesmen (as is the case along much of the French and Spanish Mediterranean), you're unlikely to be welcomed by potential customers. If a beach has none, selling may well be forbidden, as one reader discovered at Sydney's Bondi Beach, when the beach inspector chased them off after a few minutes.

If a crowd is scheduled to gather for a special occasion, think of the things they may need. Enterprising mechanics might consider taking their tools and some spare parts to a tourist mecca like Oktoberfest, then set up in the car park to fix and adjust the thousands of travel-weary vans and cars which assemble there. The award for the most original salesman should go to the person who spotted an unruly crowd waiting for the arrival of an unpopular Canadian Prime Minister in Sudbury, Ontario. He got hold of some eggs and sold them for use as missiles. Another situation which could be exploited is the refusal to allow scantily clad tourists into some European churches: renting out a pair of trousers would be a valuable service. If you have the right product, you can sell to a wider market. One traveller earned his way in South America by selling peanut butter he'd made himself from local peanuts to American tourists outside the archaeological sites of Colombia. Ski bums regularly make pocket money by delivering croissants from the local bakery to self-catering holiday-makers. Tessa Shaw picked snails at night by the River Ardèche in southern France and then set up a stall in the market at Carpentras. She found that Fridays were particularly profitable, since restaurateurs and shopkeepers drove down from Paris to buy stock for the weekend.

BASED ON HIS TRAVELS ALAN HADEN EMAILED WITH A SUGGESTION FOR ADDING A STRING TO YOUR MONEY-SPINNING BOW:

Having been inspired by your book to work abroad, I felt that it might be of use for others to learn the skills of Palmistry or Tarot. These intuitive divination methods will allow a traveller to make plenty

of money anywhere in the world. If you're a good palm reader and stuck for cash, just head down to the local tourist area or festival/market place and you'll find it easy to make a bundle of cash for your efforts. After arranging a job abroad, I used my skills to earn extra cash by charging £5–£10 for a quick 5-minute reading.

Writing and the Media

A few lucky people manage to subsidise their journeys abroad by selling articles or photographs based on their travels. There are two main markets for your creative work: local English language publications abroad, and newspapers and magazines in your home country. A trip to Northern Queensland might not seem newsworthy to you when you're there, but Frank Schiller sold an account of his trip to a German magazine for several hundred dollars. You can find out about local publications by studying news-stands when you are abroad.

It is very difficult for unpublished authors to have an article accepted by the mainstream travel press; the travel magazine *Wanderlust* receives so many submissions that the editors cannot read them all (see their 'Guidelines for Writers' at wanderlust.co.uk/writing-guidelines). In-flight magazines of foreign airlines sometimes buy freelance pieces. Enterprising journalists have also set up sites on the worldwide web and have funded it or made a profit through sponsorship.

If you have already published, take along a cuttings book. Before you go abroad, it is a good idea to study the market, to get an idea of what editors are looking for. English language publications, whether print or online, might buy something from you.

All magazines that accept freelance travel writing will be looking for a fresh view and new angle. Feel free to use the first person singular in a travel article. Describe interesting or curious incidents which, while not being of earth-shaking significance, help to brighten up the story. Quote the people you met on the trip: the innkeeper, the museum guard, as well as giving practical information on how to get there, what to see, where to stay and where to eat. Everything should be delivered in a light, readable manner. According to one experienced freelancer, sex really does sell abroad as at home, as do accounts of people coming through tragedies.

If at all possible, persuade an editor to give you a commission before you leave, as Tim Leffel did:

> *I had a few assignments set up before I left New Jersey as a travel writer and have started to sell a few other things from the trip now that I'm back. I've already made over $1,400 from various pieces, though none of the cheques were in hand until after my return. It's not something to do for quick money: 'quick' in an editor's mind means 'less than a year'. I've met lots of would-be writers and photographers who hit me up for advice on financing their travels, having not done the most basic research steps it takes to even get started. In my opinion, you must be someone who has something to say and be good at marketing it to even cover your costs, much less make a profit. I do make a profit now and then, but that's because of a trade publication I've written for for a few years (they pay me good money to review swank hotels).*

Illustrated travel articles are best of all. Editors are usually less interested in arty effects than in photos that tell a story.

English language newspapers around the world are a real source of potential casual work from Japan to Eastern Europe, Mexico City to Bangkok. You can track down the ones with a web presence via the Kidon Media site (kidon.com/media-link/english.php) and the internet Public Library (ipl.org/div/news), from the *Phnom Penh Post* to the *St Petersburg Times.* Many of the people working on these papers had never been inside a newsroom before. Business experience might well be appreciated in this context. Anyone who can get a job as a proofreader and show themselves competent will quickly advance to copy-editor or even reporter. Editors may not want to hire globetrotters, but staff turnover is often so high that they don't have much choice. Till Bruckner who wrote some freelance pieces for the *Bolivia Times* recommends making sure you will be paid for the work accepted.

International firms with branches abroad are less glamorous employers of writing skills, but they may need someone to edit their newsletter or brochures. You can offer to correct the English of museum labels, menus or travel brochures. You might get a free meal in exchange for your grammatical expertise (though you may unwittingly be depriving future travellers of a source of amusement). When Carisa Fey translated into her native German the menu of an exclusive restaurant in the Mexican resort of Puerto Vallarta she was paid in margaritas. One of the most remarkable literary coups was reported in the papers some years ago. A student called Daniel Wilson sent his CV and an example of his verse to the president of Kiribati asking if he would like him to become the poet-in-residence. To his astonishment, he had a reply inviting him to occupy a beach hut and become their national poet for a time.

You do not necessarily have to be sensational; the local paper in Windsor, Ontario might like to print the opinions of a visitor from Windsor, Berkshire about its fair city. Till Bruckner sent a good tip for would-be journalists: *'In most developing countries there are a few dozen Peace Corps volunteers. If you contact their local rag back in the US over email, they will more likely than not be interested in a short feature on what Local John is doing in Uzbekistan. An 800 word piece with photo should net $80–$130. Worked fine for me in Georgia.'*

All you readers who imagine that the ideal job would be to write a travel guide should pay attention to the following description by Woden Teachout who spent one summer researching Ireland for the well-known *Let's Go* series:

> ***I got lucky and was hired by Harvard Student Agency (which hires only students) to update their chapter on Ireland. They gave me $600 for air travel and $40 a day for expenses and profit. It was a mixed blessing. I spent most of each day visiting local historical societies and talking to all the Mrs O'Learys who run B&Bs, checking their bathrooms for cleanliness and trying to figure out how to vary descriptions of fluffy white bedrooms. At night I would run around to three or four pubs, trying to encapsulate each atmosphere in a good one-liner and then back to the hostel to write up the day's work. When you're writing a guidebook you can never quite relax, since you are always evaluating in your head. And since you have a fixed itinerary, you are not as free to follow the whims of chance and circumstance. It was definitely nice to get paid to travel, and go to places I otherwise would have missed, but on the whole it felt like indentured servitude.***

Because so many people are now blogging about their travels, some of them extremely entertainingly, it is becoming even harder for publishers to find a market for travel writing in print. Travellers' Tales (travellerstales.org) offers (expensive) short courses in travel writing and photography taught by working journalists/photographers in Morocco and Spain as well as the UK. A cheaper way to acquire some of this practical wisdom would be to look at Lonely Planet's *Guide to Travel Writing* (£10.99).

Photography

There are a number of online photo libraries in the UK such as istockphoto.com pay a royalty of 20% to the photographer on fees the website earns by selling your photo. Another major digital library is alamy.com, though the charge it makes to certain categories of user is next to nothing, so photographers cannot expect to earn much.

Even if you have no particular skill with a camera or pen you may be able to profit from being in the right place at the right time. Earl Young has strong opinions on the subject: *'Anyone who fails to carry a camera in foreign countries is a fool. What if an international incident happens to take place in the street in front of you one day and you don't happen to be carrying your camera?'*

Of course nowadays newsworthy events are captured instantly by someone with a mobile phone. If you do get a photo of a terrorist attack or any newsworthy event, don't waste a second contacting the news wire services; Reuters, Agence France Presse and Associated Press have offices or representatives in most capital cities. If your photograph is the one that's syndicated in newspapers worldwide, you need not work your way any further.

Although digital photography has brought about a revolution, there will always be tourists who will not have the necessary equipment with which to capture a key moment. With the right gadgetry it is possible to set yourself up as a portrait photographer on beaches, near monuments, where people try an adventure activity like parascending for the first time and so on. If potential customers like the image you show them on your digital camera, you can go ahead and print it out and sell it to them.

Another place to set yourself up as a freelance photographer is at a place that specialises in hosting weddings of holidaying couples. Certain places (and not just Las Vegas) become popular with couples looking for something different from the village church. Long-time working travellers Nicola and Peter Dickinson found just such a place on Rhodes where they tied the knot themselves and dream of returning as a freelance photographer and painter.

Busking

If you can play an instrument, sing, tap dance, juggle, conjure, draw caricatures or act, you may be able to earn money on the streets. Most successful buskers say that musical talent is less important than the spot you choose and the way you collect. You can ask a few backpackers at your hostel to stand and watch and look enthusiastic about your act and in return buy them a beer or two. Passers-by are more likely to stop to watch if there is already a crowd gathered.

To busk, you need the tools of your trade, perhaps an accomplice to collect money and an audience. A favourable climate helps, though some of the most successful buskers we have heard from have played in Northern Europe in mid-winter. One of the keys to success (in addition to talent) is originality. We have had reports from opposite ends of the world (Sweden and Northern Queensland) that kilted bagpipe-playing buskers are always a hit. Most international buskers say that people abroad (especially in Scandinavia, Germany, Switzerland and Spain) are more generous than in Britain, that there is less trouble with being moved on and it is not too difficult to keep yourself by busking around the cafés of Europe. Anna Ling has worked up a short fire poi show, i.e. twirling a rope with two lit ends that makes a pattern in the darkness. Ahead of her performances in Seville, Granada, Paris, etc. in the summer of 2008, she checked out which pavement cafés allowed enough space for her routine. When her accomplice circulated with a hat, the vast majority of diners gave a coin. You need a great deal of confidence in your abilities, to go abroad specifically to busk; it may be better to regard performing as a possible way of subsidising a holiday.

Festivals and other large gatherings of merry-makers are potentially lucrative; bear in mind that the more potential a position has, the greater the competition is liable to be for it. Guitarist-cum-TEFL teacher Fergus Cooney found that competition can be acute, even at ordinary times:

> ***Please don't ever write a 'Guide to Busking'. We travelling folk would soon be out of business. It's bad enough as it is. For example this year 40 accordion players from Romania swamped Montpellier and killed busking for the rest of us.***

Regulations about street performing vary from country to country, but in general you will be tolerated if you are causing no obstruction or other harm. Often you are supposed to obtain a municipal licence; ask at a youth information bureau or become an expert by attending a busking festival, listed at buskercentral.com/calendar.php. You may even find that busking leads to better things. It is said that Eric Clapton, Simon & Garfunkel and Pierce Brosnan all started their careers as buskers. Work-your-wayer Mark Kilburn was offered a job playing guitar in a night club in Holland on the basis of his street performances, Armin Birrer was encouraged by a film writer who heard him to try for a job as a film extra in Melbourne, and Kev Vincent was invited to leave the streets of San Tropez behind to entertain on a millionaire's gin palace.

Artists

An artist who paints local scenes or copies local post cards can do well in holiday resorts. If you can draw a reasonable likeness you could set yourself up as a street portraitist. Two friends Belinda and Pandora found it fairly easy to make money in both Britain and the Continent especially among holiday-makers. Belinda used unlined brown paper bought in an industrial roll and oil pastels or children's crayons. You can also use driftwood or smooth pebbles. It is awkward to carry around two chairs with you so she relied on borrowing them from an adjacent café or church hall. Artistically you shouldn't be over-scrupulous; when a disappointed subject asked 'Do I really look that old?' Belinda didn't hesitate to erase a few wrinkles.

Apparently boat owners are a particularly vain bunch and will often jump at the chance to have their vessel immortalised on canvas, so loiter around yacht marinas with your sketchbook. Stephen Psallidas noticed a trend in Mykonos for tavernas, banks and other public buildings to display paintings of themselves. Face painting is a portable skill and there is money to be made from organising children's parties wherever there is an expat community. Even if you can't make any money from your artistic endeavours, you may bring pleasure to the locals.

Film Extras

If you like the idea of mingling with the stars in Hollywood for a few days and being well paid for it – forget it. In most international film studios even extras belong to trade unions which exclude outsiders. When a film is being shot on location you may have the opportunity of helping to fill out a crowd scene – in fact the accepted term is 'crowd artist' – but it is a matter of luck coming across these, though your chances are better in some places than others. The picturesque streets of old Budapest together with the relatively lower shooting costs make it a favourite location (in fact the author once spotted an off-duty Ben Kingsley in a restaurant in Budapest).

In the massive Asian film industry, film-makers actively seek out Caucasian faces, especially to be villains, dupes or dissolutes. Agents for film companies usually look for their supernumerary staff among the budget hotels of Bombay, Bangkok, Hong Kong, Cairo, etc. knowing that they will find plenty of travellers only too willing to spend one or two days hanging around a film set in exchange for a few rupees or dollars. In fact by local standards the wage is generous.

Film-making

Never mind just being a film extra... Aspiring film-makers might want to consider choosing a foreign location, as Outlook Productions did a few summers ago. Hannah Adcock and some friends (all twenty-somethings) had set up a semi-professional production company with a strong theatrical background, specialising in Greek tragedy and Shakespeare. Plans for making a film adaptation of Shakespeare's *Twelfth Night* had been discussed over a long period but it wasn't until the director and producer visited the Greek island of Patmos that they realised Patmos *was* the Illyria of their dreams (the magical island where all the action in *Twelfth Night* takes place). The island was so perfect that even one of *Twelfth Night's* more inconsequential lines took on a deeper meaning, 'prithee foolish Greek, depart from me'!

DIRECTOR OF PHOTOGRAPHY AND 'WARDROBE MISTRESS' HANNAH ADCOCK DESCRIBES THE INS AND OUTS OF ORGANISING ONE OF THE MOST ENTERPRISING AND GLAMOROUS WORKING HOLIDAYS IMAGINABLE:

The company felt confident that they could sell the film, either to digital TV channels, educational institutions, even to a distributor, because Twelfth Night is a well known play, school children have to study it, and everyone will be so glad it is not Kenneth Branagh that they might just go out and buy it. The company failed to extract funding from organisations such as the Arts Council but it did attract private investors: people who had come to theatrical shows, liked what they saw and believed in the company. It is a really good idea if you are a theatre/production company to keep a mailing list of people who appreciate your work. However, private investment only goes so far when you are making a digital feature film. Paying wages was out of the question so cast and crew were invited to 'profit share'. This way all cast and crew rise or fall on the success or failure of the production, which is a huge risk but a good incentive to work hard!

The whole project took more than three years from idea to wrap. This included such necessary phases as location searching, formulating a shooting script, attracting finance, finding cast, crew and equipment, researching markets and organising post-production. The company let cast and crew make their own accommodation arrangements. This was fine but actors who are asked to work at 6am and have forgotten their breakfast will be difficult. The company also underestimated certain logistical difficulties, for example how to transport costumes and how much will this cost. The key seems to be a painful attention to detail.

The Director notified island officials about filming plans but they never replied. As long as the company didn't obstruct the public or tell them to move, red tape wasn't an issue. Once you have researched and then bought suitable equipment don't forget that it can (and will) break down. If possible have contingency plans since if you are miles from anywhere this is difficult. We had a dead mic for a week and had to fall back on post-production dubbing for some close-ups/medium close-ups.

In conclusion this is a great way to get into a tough sector (and not just by making the tea). You should get respect for initiative, but this is not a guaranteed money spinner.

Another way to gain experience in the competitive film, video, and multi-media production industry is to undertake unpaid work experience. If you want to do this abroad, you may have to resign yourself to enlisting the help (for a fee) of a mediating agency. In 2009, Holly Tate spent three months working for Pedestrian TV, a media company in Sydney, on a placement that was fixed up (for a fee of £800) by Intern Options (internoptions.com). She thought it was a great experience:

> *The office is really small, everyone gets on well and it's a pretty fun place to work. I think I've been really lucky. Since I arrived I've learnt a lot of things, like editing, which I'd never done before. They've included me in lots of production meetings and creative brainstorming sessions for new projects, which has been invaluable experience for when I apply for jobs back home.*

ODD JOBS

If you can't or don't want to get a steady job you could consider offering your services as an odd job person. Small towns are probably a better bet than big cities because people are more trusting and word gets around faster. The best areas to look for odd jobs and household maintenance jobs are in expatriate enclaves abroad (especially on the Mediterranean or in Mexico). Fellow backpackers might also need your services if you can cut hair, do tattoos, or fix bicycles. Brian Williams from North Wales, travelling with his partner Adrienne Robinson and their three year old son, found his skills as a mechanic in demand wherever he went, including Fiji, New Zealand and Australia. If your sphere of expertise is domestic, you can often find a market for housework and ironing. Hand deliver a little printed notice in the neighbourhood where you're based and see what happens.

Painters and decorators can always pick up work. Michael Cooley from British Columbia spent some time in northern California where he was offered a job just because he was wearing his painters' whites in town. It is a good policy to suggest a specific job when you are on the doorstep, rather than just to ask vaguely if there is anything to be done. Householders are more likely to respond favourably if you tactfully suggest that their garden is not devoid of weeds, or that the hinges on the gate could be brought into the twenty-first century. You should never underestimate the laziness of other people: in summer lawns need mowing, garages need cleaning, cars need washing, and in winter snow needs clearing. If you propose to specialise in something like window cleaning you should invest in some basic equipment: people prefer to hire a window cleaner who has his own bucket, chamois and ladder.

Susan and Eric Beney took a break from travelling with their daughters overland to Australia to spend a while on the small Greek island of Halki. They arrived in April, before the tourist rush, and there was no evidence of any work around. But they successfully created a job from scratch:

> ***The beach was a terrible mess with rubbish washed up in the winter storms, so we set ourselves the task of cleaning it up and asked the Mayor for rubbish bags. After we had been here for five weeks and our funds were sadly depleted, Eric was asked if he would like the job of 'port cleaner'. This job entailed sweeping the harbour and cleaning the streets three days a week and cleaning the loos daily. The job hadn't been done for a month so was quite a task in the beginning but I helped Eric get the loos to a reasonable standard and after that the job was quite a nice little number with plenty of time off. The pay was more than £100 a month and of course it has endeared Eric to the locals, none of whom would do such a job. Apparently a council allowance is made for this job so it could be worthwhile searching out the local Mayor and offering your services. Even the police are happy about it or turn a blind eye. Because we have now been here a while Eric has also done lots of other odd jobs for people as there is very little spare labour on the Island (or the locals are too lazy!).***

BUSINESS AND INDUSTRY

This book does not set out to advise job-seekers who are looking for professional posts. The European employment service (EURES) and a raft of recruitment sites and careers databases like eurograduate.com address the needs of those who are looking for skilled jobs. Information about cross-border applications is widely available and there are firms which advise on just that (e.g. labourmobility.com).

Although work in offices, mines, shops and factories is not seasonal in the way that work in orchards and hotels is, there are plenty of casual opportunities. You might be needed in a shop during the pre-Christmas rush, or in a swimming pool firm before the summer, or on an Easter-egg production line in February/March. Just as Russia and the former Eastern bloc countries allowed energetic individuals in the 1990s to flourish if they could spot an emerging business opportunity, that mantle has passed to China which has been rushing pell mell towards commercial expansion. Westerners with specific skills to offer such as in financial services, consultancy, IT and telecommunications may still be able to find opportunities in trade and joint ventures. According to a recent estimate, some 600,000 foreigners are living and working in the country. For specific guidance, look at the book *Live and Work in China* (Crimson Publishing, 2008, £14.99).

Remote Working

One notable work-abroad trend has been for more and more people to carry on an online business from anywhere in the world. Graphic designers, copy-editors and short-traders have all succeeded in doing business through their computers. Websites with telling names like laptophobo.com and NuNomad.com appeal to the market addressed by an article in *Business Week*:

> ***Do you ever wish you could win the lottery, chuck the rat race, and take off to explore the world? Heck – who hasn't? These days, however, there's a group of independent-minded, techno-savvy entrepreneurs who are turning that dream into a reality. They call themselves New Nomads, and they've transformed work-at-home into work-anywhere-you-damn-well-please.***

One such peripatetic businessman is Charlie Wetherall originally from Montana who attributes his current lifestyle to having read *Work Your Way Around the World*, which he describes on his website runawaytrader.com:

> ***I was reflecting today about how I got into this runaway mode in the first place and recalled that I can blame Susan Griffith for some of it. Her book offered a glimmer of hope that – someday – I could scrape up enough courage to escape the drudgery of my own existence and see some of the world. I never gave up on the idea of flitting about the globe and inventing a way to pay for that extravagance as I traveled. Now we can do business, that is, make a living, from practically anywhere on the planet. Sure, you may choose an occupation like ditch-digger or a police officer that requires your local presence, but you can also pick an income-producing gig that can be performed from anywhere on the world. All you have to do is figure out what you're good at, and take it on the road – and get paid for it. Simple as that. Thanks to wireless and other advanced computer technologies, it's now possible to make money buying and selling stocks as I do from almost anywhere in America, and anywhere in the world. As for me, it's strictly pay as you go. If I make money day trading, I go, and keep going. If I don't, I'm marooned. It's as simple as that. I want to know if I can day trade at basecamp on Mount Everest (that's a trip I'm scheduling for spring). I know I can get to all these exotic places. But can I whip out my laptop and make a trade from wherever 'there' is?***

Shops

Even monolingual people may find shop work outside the English-speaking world by approaching shopkeepers who sell primarily to tourists. You could present yourself to a carpet merchant in a coastal Turkish town or to an electronics shop in a Japanese shopping precinct favoured by American tourists and offer to sell (initially) on commission. Not only will your fluency in English be an asset but your enthusiasm about the product for sale may inspire confidence in your compatriots. Make sure the percentage you are given is worthwhile; the range will be 2%-20% depending on the value of the goods (lower for electronic goods and higher for cheap souvenirs).

Mystery shopping is something that might allow you to earn some extra cash, but not a living. Mystery shopping agencies send individuals who fit the appropriate demographic to visit shops, restaurants, car dealers, banks, etc. as anonymous shoppers, in order to report back objectively on customer service. Further information can be found on the website borntoloaf.co.uk. Bare International (bareinternational.com) even claims to carry out mystery shops on airlines. No specific experience is required. The company has offices in the US, Belgium, Brazil, India and China but makes use of 'mystery evaluators' in the UK as well. Shoppers of all different profiles are needed so anyone over 18 can sign up. The promised pay range is £10–£40 an hour, but on the whole, this is not the way to make your fortune.

Commercial and Secretarial

Students and recent graduates in business, management science, marketing, accounting, finance, computer applications or economics may be interested in an organisation run by a global student network based in 90 countries. AIESEC – a French acronym for the International Association for Students of Economics and Management (aiesec.co.uk) can organise placements in any of its member countries, aimed at giving participants an insight into living and working in another culture.

A number of commercial companies charge candidates a hefty fee for arranging a work experience placement in a foreign business, usually with the primary aim of allowing the foreigner to improve his or her knowledge of the local language in a working environment. Twin Work and Volunteer Abroad in London (☎ 020 8297 3251; workabroad@twinuk.com) runs a work experience/internship programme in several European countries, as does Interspeak in Cheshire (interspeak.co.uk).

Trained secretaries who are fluent in a European language should be able to arrange work within the EU. Most major European cities have a British Chamber of Commerce where it may be possible to deposit your CV for inspection by local businesses, or the Chamber of Commerce may run a website on which your request for work can be posted. It will normally be necessary to join the Chamber before you will be offered this service.

Specialist cross-border employment agencies can help the highly qualified. Multilingual Europe Ltd is an online job board that specialises in the recruitment of contract multilingual customer service, sales and marketing, IT and finance in Europe (multilingualvacancies.com).

GAMBLING

Well used by a practised operator, a pack of cards, a backgammon board or set of poker dice are a possible source of extra income. When Peter Stonemann was living in Copenhagen he noticed people gathered at the wall of Hallands Kirke where they offered to play fast games of chess for bets of 20 kroner. Poker, bridge and backgammon are widely played for money throughout the world; if you become proficient there is every reason to use your skills for profit. The great thing about poker and backgammon is that they are comparatively simple games in which at every stage there is a mathematically correct play. The vast majority of players in amateur schools never take the trouble to learn the percentages. If you do, and so long as you keep out of the professional games, you will win.

The 'Three Card Trick' or 'Spot the Lady' requires a definite element of dexterity but with regular practice you will become competent in a few weeks and can confidently invite customers to place their money on the Lady which hopefully is never the card they choose.

Rolling two dice for someone and getting them to bet on what number will come up is another possible ruse. The possible numbers are 2 to 12 so the odds about any one number appear to be 10/1. In fact they range from 35/1 for a 2 or 12 to 5/1 for a 7. Actually it is better to get the pigeon to roll the dice and let you bet on 6's 7's and 8's (6/1, 5/1, 6/1) and keep him paying out at 10/1 until he can stand it no longer.

Another ploy which can be used to advantage is to fleece a con-man. It never fails but has its dangerous side and it works like this. All over the world you will find pool halls, pubs or arcades where sharks try to induce mugs to play pool, darts or some other game for money. You put on your best clothes and go into one of these alone and quietly play by yourself – obviously you are not very good and the con-artist soon spots you as a possible touch. He invites you to play. But con-men, like the rest of us, are greedy; they don't want just to take $1 off you; they want the lot and they aim to do this by letting you think you are a match for them and even raise your hopes that you may win some money. To do this they will always lose the first and probably the second game. You take the money and leave – and make sure you know where the exit is.

Amazingly the big operators in Las Vegas and Atlantic City in the US and the Gold Coast in Australia can also be taken for a few dollars on the same principle. Always looking to get new punters into their gaming palaces they subsidise day tours or return trips to their gleaming portals in the desert or by the sea. The fare (subsidised) may be $5 and when you get there they give you free food and possibly even some chips, say $20 worth, to play the tables or the machines. Cash these in and you are a day older with all expenses paid.

EU EMPLOYMENT AND TAX

According to Article 8a of the Maastricht Treaty, every citizen of the European Union has the right to travel, reside and work in any member state. The only reason for refusing entry is on grounds of public security and public health. But this does not mean that all the red tape and attendant hassles have been done away with.

In January 2007, Romania and Bulgaria joined the European Union. Together with the ten accession countries that joined in May 2004 (Cyprus, Czech Republic, Estonia, Hungary, Latvia, Lithuania, Malta, Poland, Slovakia and Slovenia), this brings the total to 27 member countries. Regulations affecting the free movement of labour in and out of these new members differ but in most cases reciprocal transitional controls have been implemented for up to a maximum of seven years before full mobility of labour will be allowed. Note that the free reciprocity of labour extends to countries of the European Economic Area (EEA), which includes Iceland, Liechtenstein and Norway. Old member states have pretty well abolished the necessity for EU nationals to acquire a residence permit after three months. Usually some sort of registration process is necessary but the paperwork in most countries has been simplified.

Despite the fact that the system does not always work perfectly, a lot of labour does move freely over national borders. In fact about 2% of the resident population in the EU is living in a different member state from the one to which they belong. Some Americans may have access to the EU if they are fortunate enough to be of Irish or Italian descent and can prove that they have a grandparent of either nationality, in which case they can obtain dual nationality. From the European traveller's point of view there are many bureaucratic advantages to the EU. The free European Health Insurance Card (EHIC) means that citizens will automatically receive free or subsidised health care.

NATIONAL EMPLOYMENT SERVICES IN THE EU

Every EU country possesses a network of employment offices similar to the UK's Jobcentre Plus, details of which are given in the individual country chapters. Although EU legislation requires national employment services to treat applicants from other member states in exactly the same way as their own citizens, it is impossible to prevent a certain amount of bias from entering the system. An employer is allowed to turn down an applicant who does not speak enough of the language to perform his job adequately for obvious reasons.

No amount of positive legislation will change the attitude of the official of the Amsterdam employment office who said 'How can we help the English to find work? We do not have enough jobs for our own people' or of the French ANPE (Jobcentre) employee who told Noel Kirkpatrick that he would prefer to give a job to any Moroccan or Algerian because of their fluent French, rather than someone from Britain. The computerised, pan-European job information network EURES (EURopean Employment Service) is accessible through Jobcentre Plus offices around the UK and all national employment services in Europe. Throughout Europe hundreds of specially trained Euroadvisers can advise on vacancies within Europe, of which about a million are registered with EURES at any one time in 20 languages. It is also possible to access the EURES database online via the EURES portal http://ec.europa.eu/eures to check current vacancies from Iceland to Greece. Other urls will lead you to the same information such as eurosummerjobs.com.

Vacancies are usually for six months or longer, and are often in hotels and catering, personal services or for skilled, semi-skilled and (increasingly) managerial jobs. Naturally, language skills are very often a requirement. A random sample of job vacancies might include a nursery nurse for Finland, welders and chefs for Germany, a loom turner for Ireland and catering staff for a Spanish theme park. EURES can be used free by employers. If you are already abroad, make an appointment with the local Euroadviser or you might ring them from home since they should have a lot of local knowledge and will be able to communicate in English.

If you are a national of a European Economic Area country working in another member state, you will be covered by European Social Security regulations. Information can be read online at dwp.gov.uk/international.

EU EXCHANGES

The aim of the EU's Leonardo da Vinci programme is to improve the quality of vocational training systems and their capacity for innovation. It grants students and recent graduates 75% or even full funding to undertake overseas work placements of between 3 and 12 months (for students) or between 2 and 12 months (recent graduates). Applications for Leonardo funding must be submitted by organisations, not individuals. Details are available from the ECOTEC, acting as the Leonardo UK National Agency in Birmingham (☎ 0845 199 2929; leonardo@ecotec.com). Another provider of the Leonardo programme is Twin Work and Volunteer in London (workandvolunteer.com) who offer fully funded ten week placements in Europe which include language training and a vocational internship.

High flyers who would like to work for the European Commission as administrators, translators, secretaries, etc. must compete in open competitions; the Brussels office of the European Personnel Selection department (+33 2-299 3131) can provide information or you can find out about short-term *stages* from the Traineeships Office (http://ec.europa.eu/stages). The Commission does not offer any work placements or summer jobs other than the three and five-month *stagiaire* positions in Brussels or Luxembourg for university graduates of all nationalities. Applications must be submitted online not later than the end of August for positions starting in March, and mid-February for positions starting in October.

CLAIMING JOBSEEKER'S ALLOWANCE IN EUROPE

Not many people know that it is possible to claim Jobseeker's Allowance in other EU countries. But of course the bureaucracy is not easy to negotiate. JSA is an entitlement that has to be 'bought' by paying a certain number of contributions into a country's unemployment insurance organisation. In Britain these contributions are represented by Class 1 National Insurance contributions. Other EU countries have similar systems, and contributions paid in one country can be taken into account when building up entitlement to unemployment benefit in another.

Any EU national who has been registered unemployed for at least four weeks in the UK and is entitled to receive the UK allowance can arrange to receive it for up to three months, paid at the UK rate, while looking for work elsewhere in the EU. Applicants should inform their local Jobcentre Plus in Britain of their intention to look for work abroad at least six weeks before departure. It is helpful if you have a precise departure date and a definite destination, preferably with an address. While transferring benefits sounds good in theory, you should not expect to be handed a cheque on the day of arrival. The process can be long and painful so it is very important that you have enough money to tide you over. It can take months before you see any of your benefits in hard cash.

ELIGIBILITY REQUIREMENTS FOR UNEMPLOYMENT BENEFIT IN EEA COUNTRIES

COUNTRY	NAME OF UNEMPLOYMENT BENEFIT	QUALIFYING CONDITIONS
Austria	*Arbeitslosengeld*	At least 52 weeks (or 26 weeks if under the age of 25) in preceding 104 weeks
Belgium	*Allocations de chômage*	Between 75 days employment in last 10 months and 600 days employment in last 36 months, depending on age
Denmark	*Dagpenge*	Membership of an unemployment fund during the last 12 months and have worked for 52 weeks within the past 3 years (see workindenmark.dk)
Finland	*Työttömyysavustus*	At least 26 weeks in preceding 24 months
France	*Allocation d'assurance chômage* (also known as ASSEDIC)	Must be out of work or legitimately dismissed; must be capable of work and less than 60 years old, plus must have paid 3 months UB insurance in the last 12 months
Germany	*Arbeitslosengeld*	At least one year of insurable employment during the previous 2 years
Gibraltar	Unemployment benefit	At least 30 paid contributions in the last 52 weeks
Greece	*Epidoma anergias*	At least 125 days of work during the 14 months preceding job loss
Iceland	*Tryggingastofnun*	425 hours in preceding 12 months
Ireland	*Unemployment benefit*	39 weeks paid insurance plus 48 contributions paid/credited in the year preceding the benefit year
Italy	*Indennita ordinaria*	One year during the previous 2 years; must also have been registered for at least 2 years with an unemployment insurance scheme
Luxembourg	*Allocations de chômage*	At least 26 weeks in the previous 12 months
Netherlands	*Werkloosheidswet* (also known as WW)	26 weeks in the previous 39 weeks
Norway	*Arbeidsledighetstrygd*	Must have earned at least 100,000 kroner in previous year
Spain	*Prestación por Desempleo*	At least 12 months employment within previous 6 years
Sweden	*Dagpenning*	At least 80 days spread over 5 months in preceding 12 months
United Kingdom	Job-seeker's allowance (flat rate)	Contributions must have been paid in one of the 2 tax years on which the claim is based amounting to at least 25 times the minimum contribution (i.e. 25 × £95)

The UK and Ireland differ from most other EU countries in paying a flat rate of job-seeker's allowance. In the UK this is currently £60.50 per week for claimaints over 25, £47.95 for 18–24 year olds. Other member countries base their rates of unemployment benefit on a percentage of the wage most recently earned by the applicant, varying from 30.3% (plus a small daily allowance) in France to a maximum of 90% in Denmark.

In order to claim you must:

- Have become unemployed in that country through no fault of your own.
- Be both fit and available to work.
- Possess documentary proof of your last job and (normally) a residence permit.
- Be registered as unemployed with the employment office.
- Have paid sufficient contributions into unemployment insurance organisations in the EU.

In all countries it is essential to register as unemployed with the national employment service, normally within seven days, before claiming from the unemployment insurance fund. If you need to have a period of work in another EU country taken into account to make you eligible for unemployment benefit you will need to provide proof of the contributions you paid there on form E301 which you should obtain from the unemployment insurance organisation of the country where you paid the contributions. If you do not have this form to hand when you apply for unemployment benefit the office at which you are claiming can obtain it for you, but this may lead to a delay in processing your application.

TAX

There really isn't any such thing as legal tax-free income whatever an agency or employer promises. The only people who are not liable to pay any tax are those who earn less than the personal allowance (whatever that may be). However there are ways to minimise tax. The traveller who works for less than the full tax year will generally find himself having too much tax deducted at source and, if so, it should be possible to reclaim some of it via the local tax authority.

If you are working on a longer-term basis abroad, your UK tax liability depends on whether you are classed as 'resident', 'ordinarily resident' or 'domiciled' in the UK. Working travellers are normally considered domiciled in the UK even if they are away for more than a year. You should be exempt from UK tax if you are out of the country for a complete tax year (6 April to 5 April) though you are allowed to spend up to 62 days (i.e. one-sixth) of the tax year back in England without it affecting your tax position. Anyone who is present in the UK for more than 182 days during a particular tax year will be treated as resident with no exceptions. HM Revenue & Customs has overhauled the system, and as of April 2009, the document HMRC6 'Residence, Domicile and the Remittance Basis' replaced the old IR20 'Residents and Non-Residents: Liability to Tax in the UK '.

To have any chance of minimising your tax, keep all pay slips, receipts and financial documents in case you need to plead your case at a later date. If your tax status abroad is not completely legitimate, you will be taxed in the UK as Jamie Masters found to his cost after nine months of English teaching in Crete:

> ***I didn't know that if you are working abroad for less than a year, you are liable to be taxed in Britain, and had cheerfully let the tax people know that I was working in Greece. The rules state that the tax you pay in Greece can be transferred to England to offset the tax you owe at home. But I didn't pay any tax in Greece (just bribes). Stupid, stupid. I should have just told the tax man that I was travelling. Rule number one: if you're working illegally, deny everything.***

In many countries where you can work legitimately (e.g. EU countries) your employer will expect you to clarify your tax position with the local tax office at the beginning of your work period. This can be to your advantage, for example in Denmark where, unless you obtain a tax card (*skattekort*), you will be put on the Danish equivalent of an emergency code and 62% of your earnings will be automatically deducted at source. Glyn Evans who picked apples in Denmark returned several times to the local Radhus to complain about the excessive tax, and finally obtained a *skattekort* entitling him to a taxation rate of 31%. Nowadays, the Danes offer significant tax concessions to foreign seasonal workers (see *Scandinavia* chapter). Germany is another country where it is customary for foreign workers to register at the tax office (*Finanzamt*).

When you have finished a job your employer should give you a form which will state the amount of tax he or she has taken from your wages. If this is not forthcoming, you should collect your pay slips. Even a scruffy piece of paper may be sufficient proof of your having paid tax if it states the dates you worked and the amount of tax deducted, and is signed by your employer. If your employer won't give you any written proof at all, the odds are that he has been pocketing the money he has deducted, in which case there is no point in trying to reclaim it from the tax office!

You then take this evidence to the local tax office and fill in a tax rebate form. On this form you will have to state that you will not be working in that country again during the tax year, and give the date of your departure. You may be asked to surrender your residence and/or work permit to prevent you from simply moving to another town and getting a new job or you may have to show your return ticket to prove that you are leaving. Bureaucratic delays often mean that your refund will have to be posted to you abroad. It can take weeks, and frequently months, for your claim to be processed. You therefore need to be sure that you will be at the address you give them for some length of time; if you are not sure of your future movements, give the address of a relative or friend.

Some countries, e.g. Germany, Denmark and the US, stipulate that you are not allowed to reclaim any tax until the end of the tax year. The rule in Germany as in Britain is that you must have resided in Germany for at least six months of the tax year in order to qualify for a rebate. One way of making the whole process easier is to use a specialist agency. The company Taxback.com which was originally Irish now has 23 offices around the world including in the UK, Australia and the US. It specialises in claiming rebates for clients who have worked abroad. In the UK it can be found at 277–281 Oxford St, London W1C 2DL (020 7659 9188; uk@taxback.com).

Part 1
Work Your Way

TOURISM
THE COUNTRYSIDE
TEACHING ENGLISH
CHILDCARE
VOLUNTEERING

TOURISM

A staggering 19 million jobs in the European Union are travel and tourism-related which represents nearly 13% of the workforce. The tourist industry, like agriculture, is a mainstay of the traveller-cum-worker. The seasonal nature of hotel and restaurant work discourages a stable working population, and so hotel proprietors often rely on foreign labour during the busy season. Also, many tourist destinations are in remote places where there *is* no local pool of labour. For this reason travellers have ended up working in hotels in some of the most beautiful corners of the world from the South Island of New Zealand to Lapland.

AGENCIES AND WEBSITES

People with a background in hotels and catering may be able to fix up overseas contracts while still in the UK. EURES, the European Employment Service, registers quite a few foreign vacancies in the tourist industry (particularly in France and Italy) via Jobcentre Plus. Specialist agencies will be of interest to qualified hotel staff including chefs, hotel receptionists and restaurant staff.

Specialist recruitment websites can be invaluable. One of the best is seasonworkers.com, a site that has been designed to help people find a summer job, outdoor sports job, gap year project or ski resort job quickly and easily. Dozens of other sites may prove useful such as seasonal-jobs.com (formerly voovs.com) and resortjobs.co.uk (part of natives.co.uk).

Two US-based sites coolworks.com and jobmonkey.com are especially recommended for seasonal jobs in the tourist industry. The UK agency Jobs in the Alps (jobs-in-the-alps.co.uk) places young Britons in French and Swiss hotels for a summer or winter season. The application deadline for summer jobs (minimum three months) is April 15th.The independent travellers' monthly magazine *Wanderlust* has a Jobshop column which advertises vacancies with adventure travel companies, e.g. as cycle or hill-walking tour leaders.

Wherever there is a demand for jobs, there will be an agency charging clients to make the necessary arrangements. Air-Pro Working Holidays in Wembley (☎ 0845 259 3243; air-pro.co.uk) arranges for sun-worshipping party types to find work in Tenerife, Magaluf, Ibiza and the other usual suspects. Punters pay £68 to register and from £370 for an 'option fee' to have a job and accommodation found for them.

HOTELS AND RESTAURANTS

If you secure a hotel job without speaking the language of the country and lacking relevant experience, you will probably be placed at the bottom of the pecking order, e.g. in the laundry or washing dishes. Some hotels might confuse you by using fancy terms for menial jobs, for example 'valet runner' for collector-of-dirty-laundry or 'kitchen porter' for pot-washer. Reception and bar jobs are usually the most sought after and highly paid. However the lowly jobs have their saving graces. The usual hours of chamber staff (7am–2pm) allow plenty of free time.

Even the job of dish-washer, stereotyped as the most lowly of all jobs with visions of the down and out George Orwell as a plongeur washing dishes in a Paris café, should not be dismissed too easily. Nick Langley enjoyed life far more as a dish-washer in Munich than as a civil servant in Britain.

Many people thrive on the animated atmosphere and on kitchen conviviality. Nick Langley maintains that once you're established you'll gain more respect by shouting back if unreasonable demands are made, but adds the proviso, 'but not at the powerful head cook, please!' Heated tempers usually cool down after a couple of beers at the end of a shift.

The earlier you decide to apply for seasonal hotel work the better are your chances. Hotels in a country such as Switzerland recruit months before the summer season, and it is advisable to apply to as many hotel addresses as possible by March, preferably in their own language. Even though English holds sway in many resorts – an ad on cyprusjobs.com was recently spotted from an employer asking for 'good knowledge of spoke and written english' – a knowledge of more than one language is an immense asset for work in Europe. If you have an interest in working in a particular country, get a list of hotels and contact the largest ones (e.g. the ones with over 100 rooms) and then apply in the language of the country. Mass emailing of your CV will be much less effective than applying in writing or in person.

On the other hand you might not be able to plan so far ahead, or you may have no luck with written applications, so it will be necessary to look for a hotel job once you've arrived in a foreign country. All but the most desperate hoteliers are far more willing to consider a candidate who is standing there in the flesh than one who writes a letter out of the blue. One job-seeker recommends showing up bright and early (about 8am) to impress prospective employers. Perseverance is necessary when you're asking door to door at hotels. One of our contributors was repeatedly rejected by hotels in Amsterdam on the grounds that she was too late in the summer (i.e. August). Her last hope was the Hilton Hotel and she thought she might as well give it a try since it might be her only chance to see the inside of a Hilton. She was amazed when she was hired instantly as a chambermaid. It also might be necessary to return to the same hotel several times if you think there's a glimmer of hope.

KATHRYN HALLIWELL DESCRIBED HER JOB HUNT IN LES GETS IN THE HAUTE SAVOIE OF FRANCE:

I had to ask from hotel to hotel for three days before finding the job, and experienced what I have come to know through experience and others' reports is the normal way to hire a casual worker. The boss told me blankly that he had no work. As I was leaving he said, what sort of work? I told him anything. He said I could come back the next day in case something came up. I did and was told he was out, come again tomorrow. I eventually did get the job and realised he had just been testing my attitude as he had every other employee when they first applied.

When going door to door, try to get past the receptionist to ask the manager personally. If you are offered a position (either in person or in writing) try to get a signed contract setting out clearly the hours, salary and conditions of work. If this is not possible, you should at least discuss these issues with the boss.

Colm Murphy took a two-year leave of absence from his job in the airline industry of Ireland to work his way around Australia and New Zealand. He describes how it doesn't pay to be a wallflower in this business:

> ***You have got to sell yourself. Nobody else is going to get you your first job, only your skills, experience and references and most importantly the first impression you make. The manager or human resources person who interviews you has to have a gut instinct that you will be honest and hard-working. When you get a trial or a job, it is very important to have a good attitude and create that vital first impression with work colleagues, management and, most importantly, the customers.***

Only in a handful of cases can agencies and leisure groups place people without any expertise in foreign hotels; however wages in these cases are normally negligible.

Catering Jobs

Hotels represent just one aspect of the tourist trade, and there are many more interesting venues for cooking and serving, including luxury yachts, holiday ranches, safari camps and ski chalets. (For information about working on cruise liners, see chapter *Working a Passage*.) People with some training in catering will find it much easier to work their way around the world than the rest of us. The serious traveller might even consider enrolling in a catering course before embarking on his or her journey. One of the most interesting opportunities spotted recently was with a small British tour operator who was looking for a cook to work at a wilderness lodge in Northern Mongolia: no wage was to be paid but flights and expenses would be covered (4thworldadventure.com).

Of course, there are opportunities for the unskilled. You might find a job cooking hamburgers in a fast food chain, bearing in mind that the Oxford English Dictionary includes the coinage 'Mcjob' to refer to any form of dead-end, low-paid employment. Pay is low, hours unreliable or inconvenient and the attitude to discipline more worthy of school children. When you are applying for jobs like this, which are not seasonal, you should stress that you intend to work for an indefinite period, make a career of fast food catering, etc. In fact staff turnover is usually very high. This will also aid your case when you are obliged to badger them to give you extra hours.

A good way of gaining initial experience is to get a kitchen job with a large organisation in Britain such as Butlins (owned by the Bourne Leisure Group; bournejobs.co.uk) or PGL Adventure in Ross-on-Wye (☎ 0870 401 4411; recruitment@pgl.co.uk; pgl.co.uk/recruitment). Since they have so many vacancies, they offer to train candidates and pay them about £400 a month. PGL also have holiday centres abroad in France and Spain where staff are given accommodation, meals, uniform and return transport to the resort.

OTHER OPPORTUNITIES WITHIN TOURISM

Your average big-spending pampered tourist, so often ridiculed by budget travellers, indirectly provides great scope for employment. He wants to eat ice cream on the beach or croissants in his ski chalet, so you might be the one providing this service. He would be most distressed if he got dripped on in his hotel bed, so you may get hired to tar the roof before the season begins. He doesn't want to be pestered by his children, so you spend the day teaching them how to swim or draw at a holiday camp. He is not happy unless he goes home with a genuine sachet of Ardèche lavender or a Texan 10-gallon hat sold to him by a charming souvenir shop assistant, who will be you. He needs to be entertained so you get a job in an amusement arcade, the local pub or windsurfing school. And so it could continue. The point is that casual jobs proliferate in tourist centres.

Of course there are also many opportunities at the budget end of tourism, in travellers' hostels and so on.

DUSTIE HICKEY DESCRIBES THE WAY SHE WENT ABOUT GETTING A JOB IN THE AVIGNON YOUTH HOSTEL WHICH IS TYPICAL:

I checked out all the hostels in Avignon and had help to write a letter in French. Then I telephoned because I did not get a reply. The hostels could not promise me any work till they met me. Before I left the farm in Brittany where I was working, I telephoned again to remind them I was on my way. When I arrived the hostel I'd chosen was very busy. For free B & B, I just had to keep the dormitory clean, but I pitched in and helped with cleaning, laundry, breakfast, etc. The manager was pleased and gave me a little money. At the end of July the paid assistant left so I was given her job, and eventually I had a room to myself.

Several large Italian companies based on the continent recruit numbers of so-called 'animators', i.e. people to organise and lead the entertainment and sports programmes for adults or children in holiday resorts. For example the Italian company Time Out Tourist Service places international staff in resorts in Greece, Spain, Tunisia, Egypt, etc. Obviously there is a strong preference for good linguists as well as those with the right personalities. For further information contact one of their offices or ring them on +347 4099150 (timeoutourism.com). Another company is the Greek-based Agency Remarc (sunseafun.com) which sends animators and entertainers to resorts mainly in Greece and Cyprus and a few others. More companies are listed in the chapter on Italy.

Not many working travellers will be able to face selling timeshare properties but any who are interested should look at timesharestaff.com and royalrecruitment.com.

Pubs and Clubs

Bars and clubs should not be omitted from your list of likely employers. Caroline Scott bought the club magazine *Mixmag* in the winter and contacted a number of Ibiza clubs, one of which hired her for the summer season. If you want to job-hunt after arrival, you might consider carrying a set of 'black and whites' (black trousers/skirt and white shirt) in case you pick up a job as a bartender or waiter. If you have no experience, it can be worthwhile volunteering to work at your local pub before you leave home for a week or two and then ask for a reference.

Once you are abroad, ask at English-style pubs which are found from the Costa del Sol to the Zamalek district of Cairo, from Santa Monica California to Austrian ski resorts and try to exploit the British connection. Irish people are at an even greater advantage since there are Irish bars and pubs around the world from Molly Malone's in Paris to Irish Village in Dubai. In ordinary bars on the Continent you may be expected to be proficient in the prevailing language, although exceptions are made, particularly in the case of glamorous-looking applicants and in Scandinavia where so many locals speak English. Women (especially blonde ones) can find jobs from Amsterdam to Hong Kong, but should be sure that they can distinguish between bars and brothels.

Places like the Canaries, Ibiza, Corfu, Rhodes and the Caribbean islands are bursting at the seams with clubs of one kind or another. As long as you investigate the establishments in the place you want to work before accepting a job, you should not encounter too many unpleasant surprises. Handing out promotional leaflets for bars and clubs (known as 'PR-ing') is a job which travellers frequently do, especially in Spain.

Special Events

Great bursts of tourist activity take place around major events. For example 15,000 volunteers will be needed for the World Cup in South Africa in 2010 (worldcup2010southafrica.org.uk). Normally volunteers have to be over 18, be resident in the host city and preferably have experience in sport or volunteering. Applications will be accepted online a year or less in advance. No wage is paid and perks are few in many of these world events since the organisers know that there will be no shortage of eager participants.

On a smaller scale, annual arts festivals and sporting events, trade fairs and World Fairs are all useful providers of casual employment possibilities, both during and before or after when facilities are set up and then dismantled. It is not possible for an event such as Oktoberfest in Munich (held every year in late September) to host over 6 million visitors without a great deal of extra labour being enlisted to prepare the 560,000 barbecued chickens, 346,000 pairs of sausages and to dispense the 1,000,000 gallons of beer consumed. The main problem is finding affordable accommodation during these peak-time events.

Sometimes recruitment for major events is contracted out to employment agencies such as Adecco, which is the chosen partner of the Cirque du Soleil. Richard Ferguson commented that the last (13th) edition should have included a recommendation of doing casual work with this French-Canadian touring entertainment. He worked for the Cirque when it came to Auckland, and he would have followed it to Australia except he had to complete a course:

> ***I was an usher, and they also employ people for selling tickets, merchandise, food and beverage and for the VIP tent. The work is not hard and you can have a great time and get to know a lot of the 'stars' as it were (as long as you don't become a 'groupie' and get star struck).***

TOUR OPERATORS

Acting as a tour guide, representative or courier for a tour operator is one way of combining work with travel. In most cases employers want staff who will stay at least for the whole summer season April to October inclusive. The peak recruitment time is the preceding autumn, though strong candidates can be interviewed much later. Knowledge of a European language is always requested, though it is unusual for reps in Greece or Portugal to speak those languages. Debbie Harrison was taken aback at the ease with which she got a season's work as a rep in Greece without relevant experience or qualifications. Personality and maturity seem to be what count most and a commitment to the company, and possibly also to tourism as a career. By all accounts interviews can be fairly gruelling as they try to weed out the candidates who will crack under the pressure of holidaymakers' complaints and problems.

Considering the rigours and pressures of the job of package tour company representative, wages are low, though of course accommodation is provided. Often wages are paid into a bank account at home. Employers usually expect their reps to supplement meagre wages by accepting commissions from restaurants, shops, car hire firms, etc. not to mention tips from clients.

A qualification in childcare is highly marketable in this sphere since more and more tour operators are attempting to woo families. In the first instance, search the internet and see which tour operator's style suits you. Most big companies devote some of their web pages to recruitment, some with online application facilities. The giant companies TUI and Thomas Cook have swallowed up a number of others and have centralised recruitment systems, mainly done online:

TUI UK & Ireland: tuitraveljobs.co.uk and shgjobs.co.uk; includes First Choice, Thomson and many other brands, employing more than 19,000 people worldwide.

Thomas Cook: thomascookvacancies.co.uk; the Thomas Cook Group employs 31,000 people for various brands; hires large numbers of beach villa reps, creche reps, resort reps and transfer reps.

Other sizeable tour operators include:

Club Med: International Recruitment, Lyon, France; clubmedjobs.com; range of staff (who must be able to speak French) to work as GO's (*Gentils Organisateurs*) for their upmarket holiday villages in Europe and North Africa. As well as general hotel and catering staff, they require sports instructors, children's reps, hostesses, shop staff and tour guides.

Mark Warner Ltd: Resorts Recruitment Department, London W8; ☎ 08717 033955 or 0844 884 3770 for childcare positions; markwarner-recruitment.co.uk; runs Beach Resorts in Corsica, Italy, Sardinia, Portugal, Greece, the Red Sea and Indian Ocean for which it employs hotel managers, customer service officers, childcare staff, chefs, bar and waiting staff, watersports, tennis and aerobics instructors, pool attendants, health and beauty staff, maintenance/drivers and night watchmen; all staff must be 18 or over and can apply any time throughout the year; the wages run from £50–£250 per week;

benefits include use of watersports facilities, accommodation, meals, travel, medical insurance and the potential for winter work at their ski chalet hotels in Europe.

Monarch/Cosmos: monarch.co.uk/jobs; holiday consultants, operations assistants, children's reps, etc. for the Mediterranean and beyond.

Working in Africa, Asia and Latin America as an adventure tour leader is discussed in the chapter *Working a Passage: Overland Tours.* A list of special interest and activity tour operators (to whom people with specialist skills can apply) is available from AITO, the Association of Independent Tour Operators (aito.co.uk). In the US, consult the *Specialty Travel Index* (specialtytravel.com); the directory is issued twice a year at a cost of $10 in the US, $25 abroad.

A number of companies specialise in tours for school children, both British and American. For example the London office of the American Council for International Studies (AIFS UK, London SW7; ☎ 020 7590 7474; tm_dept@acis.com; acis.com/tmapplication) is looking for 100 clever linguists to become tour managers to lead groups of American high school students around Europe. A student group tour operator that takes on group leaders and couriers in the UK is Halsbury Travel Ltd in Nottingham (☎ 0115 940 4303; halsbury.com) who take on 100 group leaders, 50 couriers and in winter 100 ski reps.

Contiki (contiki.co.uk/jobs) specialises in coach tours for clients aged 18–35 and hires EU nationals and those with UK work visas as tour managers and coach drivers. Applications can be made online or by post by candidates with independent travel experience who are able to join a 60-day European training programme. Another youth-oriented European tour operator is Busabout (London SW1; ☎ 020 7950 1661; recruitment@busabout.com) which posts full recruitment information on its website (busabout.com/Work-for-Us). Both Contiki and Busabout charge £200 as a training bond.

Campsite Couriers

A different kind of courier is needed by the large camping holiday operators. British camping holiday firms (addresses below) hire large numbers of people to remain on one campsite on the Continent for several months. The Holidaybreak Group alone recruits up to 2,000 campsite couriers and children's couriers. The courier's job is to clean the tents and mobile homes between visitors, greet customers and deal with difficulties (particularly illness or car breakdowns) and introduce holidaymakers to the attractions of the area or even arrange and host social functions and amuse the children. All of this will be rewarded with on average £100–£125 a week (though some companies pay less) in addition to free tent accommodation. Many companies offer half-season contracts March/April to mid-July and mid-July to the end of September.

Setting up and dismantling the campsites in March/April and September (known as *montage* and *démontage*) is often done by a separate team. The work is hard but the language requirements are nil. The company Brad Europe Ltd (bradeurope.com) provides a linen hire service to over 300 campsites throughout France, Italy, Spain, Holland, Germany and Austria, so hires drivers and laundry operatives to work for four to six months.

Some camping holiday and tour operators based in Britain are as follows (with the European countries in which they are active):

Canvas Holidays: Dunfermline, Scotland; ☎ 01383 629012; canvasholidaysrecruitment.com; mainly France but also Germany, Austria, Switzerland, Italy, Luxembourg, Netherlands and Spain.

Club Cantabrica Holidays Ltd: St. Albans, Herts; ☎ 01727 866177; cantabrica.co.uk; France, Austria and Spain (including Majorca); summer and winter positions.

Eurocamp: Overseas Recruitment Department (Ref WW/09); ☎ 01606 787525; holidaybreakjobs.com; up to 1,500 staff for 200 campsites in most European countries; applications accepted from October; interviews held in Hartford, Cheshire over the winter; average wage £131 a week (2009).

Siblu Holidays: Recruitment Team, Hemel Hempstead; ☎ 01442 293230; recruitment@siblu.com; park reps and children's courier staff for France, Spain and Italy.

Keycamp Holidays: Overseas Recruitment Department, Northwich, Cheshire; ☎ 01606 787525; holidaybreakjobs.com; operate in most European countries.

Vacansoleil: Eindhoven, Netherlands (☎ 31 040 8447748; camping-jobs@vacansoleil.com). Application form for seasonal work is available online vacansoleil.com. Supply summer staff to campsites around France, Spain, Italy, Denmark, Belgium and Holland.

Be warned that an offer of a job may be more tentative than it seems, as Karen Martin describes:

> ***Before we left in May, we had both been interviewed for the job of campsite courier. We got the jobs and signed the contracts, and our rough start date was the 7th of July. They did not make the position clear that an offer 'subject to terms and conditions' means that it is possible that a week before the start date you can be told that there is no longer a job due to lack of customers, which is what happened to us. We really felt let down.***

Successful couriers make the job look easy, but it does demand a lot of hard work and patience. Occasionally it is very hard to keep up the happy, smiling, never-ruffled courier look, but most seem to end up enjoying the job. Alison Cooper described her job with Eurocamp on a site in Corsica as immensely enjoyable, though it was not as easy as the clients thought:

> ***Living on a campsite in high season had one or two drawbacks: the toilets and showers were dirty, with constant queues, the water was freezing cold, the campsite was very very noisy and if you're unfortunate enough to have your tent in sunlight, it turns into a tropical greenhouse. Of course we did get difficult customers who complained for a variety of reasons: they wanted to be nearer to the beach, off the main road, in a cooler tent with more grass around it, etc. etc. But mostly our customers were friendly and we soon discovered that the friendlier we were to them, the cleaner they left their tents.***
>
> ***I found it difficult at first to get used to living, eating, working and socialising with the other two couriers 24 hours a day. But we all got on quite well and had a good time, unlike at a neighbouring campsite where the couriers hated each other. Our campsite had a swimming pool and direct beach access, though nightlife was limited. The one disco did get very repetitive.***

Caroline Nicholls' problems at a campsite in Brittany included frequent power failures, blocked loos and leaking tents: '*Every time there was a steady downpour, one of the tents developed an indoor lake, due to the unfortunate angle at which we had pitched it. I would appear, mop in hand, with cries of "I don't understand. This has never happened before." Working as a courier would be a good grounding for an acting career.*'

The big companies interview hundreds of candidates and have filled many posts by the end of January. But there is a very high dropout rate (over 50%) and vacancies are filled from a reserve list, so it is worth ringing around the companies as late as April for cancellations. Despite keen competition, anyone who has studied a European language and has an outgoing personality stands a good chance if he or she applies early and widely enough.

Activity Holidays

Many specialist tour companies employ leaders for their clients (children and/or adults) who want a walking, cycling, watersports holiday, etc. Companies that operate in only one country are included in the country chapters.

Acorn Adventure Ltd: West Midlands; ☎ 0121 504 2066; acorn-jobs.co.uk; require 300 seasonal staff including catering, maintenance and admin as well as qualified canoeing, climbing, hillwalking, kayaking, sailing and windsurfing instructors to work in centres in the UK, France and Italy.

In2actionLtd: 11 York Avenue, Cowes, Isle of Wight PO32 6QY; recruitment Department; ☎ 01983 297607; recruitment@in2action.co.uk; action Team members lead children in a range of sports and acitivities, in resorts from Turkey to Mexico.

King's Camps: Sheffield; ☎ 0845 643 5280; kcjobs.org/holiday-jobs; recruit children's activity couriers on behalf of Eurocamp and Keycamp for France, Spain and Italy.

PGL Travel: Ross-on-Wye, Herefordshire; ☎ 0870 401 4411; recruitment@pgl.co.uk; pgl.co.uk/recruitment; recruit for about 2,500 seasonal vacancies at their holiday centres throughout Britain plus France and Spain; they publish on their website and in a brochure their requirements for activity instructors as well as group leaders, catering and support staff.

Ramblers' Holidays Ltd: Welwyn Garden City, Herts; ☎ 01707 331133; mandyd@ramblersholidays.co.uk; tour leaders (preferably mature people) needed for programme of walking holidays worldwide.

Sunsail International: Portsmouth; ☎ 02392 334600; recruitment@tuiactivity.com; sunsail.com/hr; now part of TUI, this is the office that recruits for the activity sector including JCA, Skibound and Travelbound; employs about 1,000 staff for their flotilla and bareboat sailing holidays and watersports hotels in the Mediterranean, especially Greece and Turkey; from March to October, positions are available as flotilla skippers, hostesses, diesel engineers, qualified dinghy, yacht and windsurfing instructors, receptionists, chefs, bar staff and qualified nannies.

Village Camps: Recruitment Office, Nyon, Switzerland; ☎ +41 22 990 9405; personnel@villagecamps.ch; qualified and experienced staff needed to join international teams at spring, summer and autumn residential and day camps in Switzerland, Austria, Holland, France and England; vacancies for activity specialists, language teachers and nurses; room and board, accident/liability insurance and an expense allowance are provided; staff must be at least 21 to apply; visit villagecamps.com/personnel for application details.

Any competent sailor, canoeist, diver, climber, rider, etc. should have no difficulty marketing their skills abroad. If you would like to do a watersports course with a view to working abroad, you might be interested in one of the instructors' courses offered by Flying Fish on the Isle of Wight (☎ 0871 250 2500; flyingfishonline.com). They offer training as instructors in windsurfing, diving, dinghy sailing and yachting. A typical six-week sailing instructor course in Greece will cost about £2,675 all-inclusive though shorter courses are cheaper. The website allows access to water sport job vacancies around the world.

Diving resorts around the world from the Red Sea to the Great Barrier Reef are staffed by people who started out as recreational divers with the basic PADI (Professional Association of Diving Instructors) Open Water Diver qualification. The PADI website (padi.com) has an Employment Bulletin Board for paid-up PADI professionals, divided according to region of the world (USA, Asia/Pacific, Europe and so on). Dive centres in exotic locations around the world accept trainee divers willing to work in exchange for living expenses and dive training. To take two examples, Hurricane Divers in Playa Santa Cruz (Oaxaca, Mexico; hurricanedivers.com) operate a three-month Divemaster Internship programme for anyone over 18 who is willing to spend long hours taking bookings, filling tanks and cleaning toilets. In Thailand Mermaid's Dive Centre in Pattaya is allied to an internship programme called Learn in Asia Dive Internships Co. Ltd (pjscuba@gmail.com; learn-in-asia.com).

WINTER RESORTS

Ski resort work is by no means confined to the Alps. Skiing centres can be found in Finnish Lapland and Argentine Patagonia, from the dormant volcanoes of North America to the active ones of New Zealand. And there are dozens of ski resorts in North America, in addition to the most famous ones such as Whistler and Banff in the Canadian Rockies, or Aspen and Vail in Colorado.

Winter tourism offers some variations on the usual theme of hotels and catering. Staff are needed to operate the ski tows and lifts, to be in charge of chalets, to patrol the slopes, to file, wax and mend hired skis, to groom and shovel snow, and of course to instruct would-be skiers. The season in the European Alps lasts from about Christmas until late April/early May. Between Christmas and the New Year is a terrifically busy time as is the middle two weeks of February during half-term. If you are lucky you might get a kitchen or dining room job in an establishment which does not serve lunch (since all the guests are out on the slopes). This means that you might have up to six hours free in the middle of the day for skiing, though three to four hours is more usual. However the hours in some large ski resort hotels are the same as in any hotel, i.e. eight to ten hours split up inconveniently throughout the day, and you should be prepared to have only one day off per week for skiing. Because jobs in ski resorts are so popular among the travelling community, wages can be low, though you should get the statutory minimum in Switzerland. Many employees are (or become) avid skiers and in their view it is recompense enough to have easy access to the slopes during their time off.

Either you can try to fix up a job with a British-based ski tour company before you leave (which has more security but lower wages and tends to isolate you in an English-speaking ghetto), or you can look for work on the spot.

Ski Holiday Companies

In the spring preceding the winter season in which you want to work, contact ski tour companies to find out their application procedures and interview timetable. Most of the recruitment takes place online and the websites of most major ski tour operators feature a 'Recruitment' icon. Most companies are looking for resort representatives (who will need language skills), chalet staff (described below), cleaners, qualified cooks, odd jobbers and ski guides/instructors. An increasing number of companies are offering nanny and creche facilities, so this is a further possibility for women and men with a childcare background. A certain number of staff have been hired by mid-June, though there are always vacancies until the beginning of the season and during it as well.

Specialist ski recruitment websites can be extremely helpful. The superb Natives.co.uk posts current vacancies on behalf of a selection of the major operators and also includes detailed resort descriptions and links to seasonal workers' email addresses. Try also Season Workers (seasonworkers.com) and Free Radicals (freeradicals.co.uk) which describe themselves as one-stop shops for recruitment of winter staff for Europe and North America. The smaller Ski Staff (skistaff.co.uk) specialises in placing staff with British ski tour operators in France.

Another way of fixing up a job in advance is to go through the agency Jobs in the Alps (info@jobs-in-the-alps.co.uk). They recruit about 250 staff for various positions in winter resorts especially in Switzerland, for which good German or French is usually required. You must arrange to be interviewed, usually in London, by the end of September and be prepared to sign a contract for the whole season, four months in the winter December–April. Wages are about £500 a month net for a five-day week; candidates must have EU nationality.

Here are some of the major UK companies. Some have a limited number of vacancies which they can fill from a list of people who have worked for them during the summer season or have been personally recommended by former employees, so you should not be too disappointed if you are initially unsuccessful.

Inghams Travel: London SW15; ☎ 020 8780 4400 or 020 8780 8803; inghams.co.uk/general_pages/job.html; 450 chalet, chalet hotel or bar work for winter season in France, Italy, Austria, Switzerland and Bulgaria; perks include free ski pass, ski and boot hire, meals, accommodation and return travel from the UK.

Crystal Holidays: ☎ 0845 055 0258; jobsinwinter.co.uk/crystal; 1,500 resort reps and chalet/hotel staff for 140 ski resorts in Europe (especially France, Austria and Italy) and North America (visa required).

Equity Travel: Brighton; ☎ 01273 648273; equity.co.uk/employment; recruits chefs, housekeeping and waiting staff, handymen, night porters, plongeurs and bar staff (EU nationality essential) as well as ski reps and tour reps for its sizeable operation in Austria, France and Italy.

Esprit Holidays Ltd: Fleet, Hants; ☎ 01252 618318; recruitment@esprit-holidays.co.uk; vacancies for resort managers, hotel managers, chalet controllers, resort reps, chalet chefs and host/cooks, chalet and hotel assistants, nannies and alpine rangers to work in resorts in France, Austria and Italy.

First Choice/Skibound: Crawley, W Sussex; 0870 750 1204; overseas.recruitment@firstchoice.co.uk; 750 winter staff from EU employed in France, Italy, Austria, etc.

NBV Leisure Ltd: Bromley, Kent; ☎ 0870 220 2148; nbvleisure.com/recruitment.html; catered chalet summer and winter holidays in France and Austria.

Neilson Overseas: Brighton; neilson.co.uk/jobs.aspx; part of Thomas Cook Group; resorts in Andorra, Austria, Bulgaria, Canada, France and Italy among others.

Powder Byrne: London; ☎ 020 8246 5342; powderbyrne.com; upmarket company operating in Switzerland, France, Italy and Austria. Also recruit staff for summer resorts programme in Greece, Tunisia, etc.

Simply Ski: Part of TUI group; shgjobs.co.uk; chalet and other staff needed in Austria, France and Switzerland.

Skibound: skibound.co.uk; snow sports holidays for school parties; owned by TUI.

Skiworld: London W6; ☎ 0870 420 5914/3; recruitment@skiworld.ltd.uk; skiworld.ltd.uk; catered chalet and hotel holidays in France, Austria, Switzerland, Canada, USA and others.

Supertravel Ski: London SE1; ☎ 020 7962 1369; skijobs@lotusgroup.co.uk; supertravel.co.uk/jobs.asp; takes on winter staff for France and Austria; all applicants must hold an EU passport and have an NI number.

You can find other ski company addresses by consulting ski guide books, magazines and travel agents. Another good idea is to attend the Metro Ski & Snowboard Show held each October at Olympia in London where some ski companies hand out job descriptions and applications. This is attended by natives.co.uk who also host their own Job Fair in Hammersmith in November.

The wages paid by most tour operators are fairly dire, though they are on top of bed, board and a ski pass. One of the excuses given for the low pay is that staff can supplement their wages with tips, something that made Susan Beney and her husband uncomfortable when they worked for Le Ski in France:

> ***We did make good tips which became our spending money, so no tips, no treats. Being Aussies (with joint UK nationality), it goes against the grain to expect tips. And then you find yourself judging guests by how much they tip you – horrible way to be. We worked long hours six days a week, and were probably a bit too conscientious due to our age (we have just become grandparents). It's still a good way to experience a season in the Alps, but just be prepared to be overworked and underpaid. Listen to the young folk who have got the work down to a fine art and really know how to cut corners since they are there to ski and socialise.***

Applying on the Spot

The best time to look is at the end of the preceding winter season though this has the disadvantage of committing you a long way in advance. The next best time is the first fortnight in September when the summer season is finishing and there are still plenty of foreign workers around who will have helpful advice. The final possibility is to turn up in the month before the season begins when you will be faced with many refusals. In November you will be told you're too early because everything's closed, in December you're too late because all the jobs are spoken for. If you miss out on landing a job before the season, it could be worth trying again in early January, since workers tend to disappear after the holidays.

EVERY NEGATIVE EXPERIENCE IS COUNTER-BALANCED BY OTHERS LIKE MARY JELLIFFE'S ACCOUNT OF OPPORTUNITIES IN THE FRENCH RESORT OF MÉRIBEL:

At the beginning of the season there were many 'ski bums' looking for work in Méribel. Many found something. People earned money by clearing snow, cleaning, babysitting, etc. You do need some money to support yourself while looking for work but if you are determined enough, I'm sure you'll get something eventually. One group of ski bums organised a weekly slalom race from which they were able to make a living. Another set up a video service; another made and sold boxer shorts for £10 a pair.

Chalet Staff

The number of chalets in the Alps has hugely increased over the past decade with the biggest areas of expansion being Méribel, Courchevel and Val d'Isère in France, Verbier in Switzerland and St Anton in Austria. Chalet clients are looked after by a chalet girl or (increasingly) chalet boy. The chalet host does everything (sometimes as part of a team) from cooking first-class meals for the ten or so guests to clearing the snow from the footpath (or delegating that job). She is responsible for keeping the chalet clean, preparing breakfast, packed lunches, tea and dinner, providing ice and advice, and generally keeping everybody happy. Fifteen-hour days are standard.

Although this sounds an impossible regimen, many chalet girls manage to fit in several hours of skiing in the middle of each day. The standards of cookery skills required vary from company to company depending on the degree of luxury (i.e. the price) of the holidays. Whereas some advertise good home cooking, others offer cordon bleu cookery every night of the week (except the one night which the chalet girl has off). In most cases, you will have to cook a trial meal for the tour company before being accepted for the job or at least submit detailed menu plans. Eighteen-year-old Dan Hanfling baked a creditable cake for his interview and was pleased to be offered a chalet job. But on arriving in the Alps, he learned that chalet staff in their first season are not always assigned their own chalet, but are expected to service a number of them by carrying supplies, cleaning toilets, etc. This job was a lot less glamorous than he had imagined, and he returned to England after just a few weeks (to the consternation of his parents who had booked a Christmas holiday in the same resort).

Ski Instructors

To become a fully-fledged ski instructor, qualified to work in foreign ski schools, costs a great deal of time and money. Freelance or 'black' instructors – those who tout in bars offering a few hours of instruction in return for pocket money – are persecuted by the authorities in most alpine resorts. The main legitimate opportunities for British skiers without paper qualifications are as instructors for school parties or as ski guides/ski rangers.

If you are interested in qualifying as an instructor, contact the British Association of Snowsport Instructors or BASI in Grantown-on-Spey (☎ 01479 861403; basi.org.uk). BASI courses take place throughout the season and also on the glacier in the summer. Most instructors teach from two to six hours a day depending on demand, and are expected to participate in the evening entertainment programme.

Several private companies have introduced ski and snowsport instructors' courses in Canada, New Zealand, Argentina and the Alps, particularly targeting the gap year market. Be warned that these are very expensive, typically £6,000+ for a 12-week course.

SKI RESORTS AROUND THE WORLD

FRANCE	SWITZERLAND	AUSTRIA	ITALY
Chamonix	Davos	Kitzbühel	Cortina d'Ampezzo
Les Contamines	St.Moritz	Söll	Courmayeur
Val d'Isère	Zermatt	Lech	Sestriere
Courchevel	Gstaad	Badgastein	Bormio
Méribel	Klosters	St Anton	Campitello
St Christoph	Villars	Mayrhofen	Canazei
Flaine	Wengen & Mürren	Kaprun	Livigno
Avoriaz	Crans-Montana	Alpbach	Abetone
Les Arcs	Kandersteg	Brand	Corvara
La Plagne	Adelboden	Kirchberg	Selva
Tignes	Verbier	St Johann	Sauze d'Oulx
Montgenèvre	Grindelwald	Solden	Asiago
	Arosa	Obergurgl	S Stefano di Cadore
	Saas Fee	Zell am See	Alleghi
SPAIN	**GERMANY**	**NORWAY**	**SCOTLAND**
Sol y Nieve	Garmisch-	Voss	Aviemore
Formigal	Partenkirchen	Geilo	Glenshee (Glenisla)
Cerler	Oberstdorf	Telemark	Carrbridge
	Berchtesgaden	Lillehammer	Glencoe
		Gausdal	
		Synnfjell	
ANDORRA	**FINNISH LAPLAND**		
Arinsal	Levi		
Soldeu	Ylläs		
Pas de la Casa			
NEW ZEALAND	**AUSTRALIA**	**CANADA**	**USA**
Queenstown	Falls Creek (VIC)	Whistler/Blackcomb Banff	Aspen, Colorado
Coronet Peak	Mount Hotham	Lake Louise	Copper Mountain
Mount Hutt	Mount Buffalo	Sunshine Village	Steamboat Springs
Mount Ruapehu	Mount Buller	Fernie	Ottawa Vail
		Hidden Valley	Breckenridge
Bulgaria	Thredbo (NSW)	Blue Mountain	Alpine Meadows, CA
Borovets	Perisher	Mont Tremblant	Lake Tahoe
	Mount Field (Tas)	Mont Sainte-Anne	Mt Batchelor, OR
Romania	Ben Lomond		Mount Hood
Poiana Brasov			Aleyska, AK
			Park City, UT
			Sun Valley, ID
			Jackson Hole, WY
			Big Mountain, MO
			Waterville Valley, NH
			Stowe, VT

THE COUNTRYSIDE

HARVESTING

Itinerant workers have traditionally travelled hundreds of miles to gather in the fruits of the land, from the tiny blueberry to the mighty watermelon. It might even be possible to pick your way around the world, by following the seasons and the ripening crops. The old-style gypsies, who roamed over Europe picking fruit as they went, have been joined by both nomadic young people and large numbers of East Europeans looking to earn western wages.

Living and working in rural areas is a more authentic way of experiencing an alien culture compared to working in tourism. It is easy to see why farms, vineyards and orchards play such a large part in the chapters that follow, since harvests provide so much scope for people working their way around the world.

Although the problem of work permits does dog the footsteps of fruit pickers abroad, there is always a good chance that the urgency of the farmers' needs will overrule the impulse to follow the regulations.

The availability of harvesting work for travellers in Europe has been reduced by the large numbers of Romanians, Poles, Albanians, etc. now roaming every corner of Europe earning wages far in excess of what then can earn at home.

Where to look for work

The vast majority of this kind of work is found only after meeting the farmers face-to-face either well in advance of the busy season or once it's underway and the growers are desperate if they don't have enough labour. However, in a few isolated cases, specialist agencies try to match up farmers and travelling harvesters. While in Holland Karen Martin made contact with a Dutch company called Appellation Controlée (apcon.nl) set up by two ex-travellers who wanted to help people find work on farms offering good pay and conditions in France. It was after paying the agency registration fee that she and her boyfriend Paul were assigned to jobs in the Loire Valley (see chapter on France). An agency in Australia called Grunt Labour Services specialises in harvesting work (see *Australia* chapter).

As usual the internet can play a key role. Check fruitfuljobs.com and pickingjobs.com which publicise vacancies in harvests which are perennially short of workers such as in the berry harvests of Scotland, cherry picking on the South Island of New Zealand and the massive fruit harvests of Victoria, Australia. There are some country-specific sites as well such as seasonalwork.co.nz.

State-run employment offices are worth a try, especially in France and Australia. After visiting the French equivalent of a Jobcentre and also a private agency in Epernay, at the beginning of September 2008, Anna Ling and her boyfriend Andy were given a list of phone numbers of potential farm employers. Preparing for a marathon of phoning, they bought a local phone card but struck lucky on their very first call. They visited the vineyard in Champagne, were interviewed in the home of the wine-grower and told to come back when the harvest started, which was September 20th. They were not so lucky with following up this harvest. In their search for apple picking work south of Epernay and near Bordeaux, they followed up every imaginable lead only to hit a series of brick walls. You win a few, lose a few.

Asking around in backpacker hostels, campsites and local pubs is often successful, though not always; Jon Loop says this is great for people who are good at meeting prospective employers in pubs, unlike him who just gets drunk and falls over. If you are in a densely farmed area, it might even be worth trying to visit farmers personally. Farm hands and people already picking in the fields will be able to offer advice as well. You may want to consider hiring or borrowing a bicycle, moped or car for a day of concentrated job-hunting.

One of the job-seeker's best allies is a very detailed map. Helpful locals can then point out their suggestions on a map rather than give verbal instructions (possibly in a language you barely know). An excellent reference book for prospective grape-pickers is Hugh Johnson's *World Atlas of Wine* (published by Mitchell Beazley, 2007/8 edition, £35) which includes splendidly detailed maps of wine-producing regions from Corsica to California. It is of course much too heavy and expensive to carry around, though you could perhaps take a few good photocopies of the regions you plan to try. Alternatively, get a list of vineyards from the regional tourist offices or wine producers' association and write to (or visit) the proprietors, asking for work. Detailed maps can be downloaded from the internet.

Technique

Picking fruit may not be as easy as it sounds. If you are part of a large team you may be expected to work at the same speed as the most experienced picker, which can be both exhausting and discouraging. Be assured that your speed will quickly improve with experience, a fact you will need to hang on to for the first few days if you are being paid according to the quantity you pick, known as piece work, which is how the vast majority of picking jobs are paid. When Andrew Walford was tempted to feel envious of the people who could fill seven or eight bins of apples a day in Shepparton, Australia, he consoled himself that, even if his record was only five, at least he wasn't as eccentric as they were. Rather than succumb to feelings of inferiority, watch their technique closely. There are often external limitations to the amount you can earn. Sometimes picking is called off in bad weather. Sometimes you are forced to take some days off while the next crop ripens fully or because the price on the market has dropped. Be prepared to amuse (and finance) yourself on idle days.

Informal competitions can enliven the tedium. Alan Corrie describes his fellow tomato-picker on a farm near Auch in the Gascony region of southern France, with undisguised admiration:

> ***In August I was taken on by a farmer to join his contracted Moroccan worker picking tomatoes. This is paid by the crate, and iron discipline and single-minded determination are needed to breach the fifty crates barrier per ten-hour day, and get in amongst the good earnings. When my first half century had been verified, I was punching the air in triumphant salute. The next day, toying with extremis, fifty-three was achieved, and I had the distinct feeling while unloading at the depot that the workers there were nudging one another and confiding 'c'est lui, mon dieu, comme une tempète dans les tomates!'***
>
> ***Ahmed, meanwhile, was touching seventy crates a day. Any day now, I reasoned, we'd be on a par, sending the boss off to buy a calculator and to order extra crates. This was not to be however. I had peaked. Desperation set in; the crates were becoming bigger, tomatoes always lying awkwardly, the heat blistering; I began to flounder, drained and dejected in the low forties. My colleague when I last asked him was turning in a cool eighty a day, which if you knew anything about tomato picking I would not ask you to believe. You would have to see it for yourself. I'm thinking of giving guided tours of the scene of his campaign for knowing seasonal workers and afficionados: 'Yup,' I'll nod my head – greyhaired as it now is after the experience – in the direction of a little altar-like structure, 'I was there, seen it wi' m'own eyes. I swear it, them little rascals wuz up'n jumpin' in that thaar bucket of his.' Anyway, good luck to him. It was with some relief that I was transferred to the shady plum groves across the road.***

During August in the South of France the only equipment you'll need is a sun hat. But if you are planning to pick apples in British Columbia or olives in the Greek winter, you will need warm clothing, waterproofs and possibly also rubber boots for muddy fields and gloves for wet fruit. Gloves can also be useful if you are picking fruit which has been sprayed with an insecticide that irritates cuts or stains your hands an unsightly colour. If it is too awkward to pick wearing gloves, you can tape up your hands with surgical tape to prevent blistering.

FARMING

Not all casual work in rural areas revolves around fruit and vegetable harvests. There are a lot of miscellaneous seasonal jobs created by the agricultural industry, from castrating maize to crutching sheep, from scaring birds away from cherry orchards to herding goats (something which seems to reduce most novices to tears), from weeding olive groves to spraying banana plantations. There is always the chance of work if you knock on farmers' doors.

Many farms, especially in Europe, are relatively small family-run businesses, and the farmer may not need to look any further than his or her own family for labour. But often farmers are looking for one able-bodied assistant over the summer months, and if you are fortunate to be that one, you will probably be treated as a member of the family, sharing their meals and their outings. It is more important to be able to communicate with the farmer than if you are hired as a fruit picker, since the instructions given to farm hands are more complicated. It also helps to have some tractor-driving or other farm experience or at least an aptitude for machinery.

Even if the work you are given is tedious, this might be exactly what you want, as was the case with Joseph Tame who spent a few weeks working on an organic farm in Switzerland one spring: *'The type of work can at times be tremendously repetitive (such as the four hours a day every day spent scraping cow shit from the yard!). Yet in this repetitiveness you have a freedom, a freedom of the mind that enables you to mull over any thoughts or feelings that in England would be swept aside by the stress of everyday life. Here I have all the time in the world; and in this world, time is not money.'*

AS SO MUCH DEPENDS ON THE GENEROSITY OF THE HOSTS, KAREN MARTIN AND PAUL ANSELL WERE LUCKY AT THEIR MAIZE AND APPLE FARM IN FRANCE:

It is, I imagine, like many farms out in the sticks, but the wife is happy to drive us to the supermarket or train station if you fancy going to big places like Angers or Saumur. They have given us loads of fresh fruit, washed our clothes, given us lots of their very good (very strong) drink, let us use their internet and even lent us money when we first arrived.

Advertising and the Internet

Placing an advert in the national farmers' journal is especially worthwhile for people who have had some relevant experience. Gary Tennant placed the following advert in the Danish farmers' weekly *Landsbladet* and elicited four offers: *'23 year old Englishman now in Denmark would like farm work. Have been working on a kibbutz (4 months) in the fields and tractor work. Just finished gardening work in England and want to try different farming. Telephone 06191679, ask for Gary.'*

Targeting small rural newspapers can also pay dividends partly because it will almost certainly be a novelty. Ken Smith noticed a small ad in the *Oamaru Mail* in New Zealand: 'Young German man seeks farm work. Has tractor experience and good work habits.' The scope of replies would be greater from New Zealand's national farming paper *Farm News* whose website allows free access to its classified ads (farmnews.co.nz).

Range of Opportunities

Many long-term itinerant workers meet up with people who are interested in alternative lifestyles which may include organic farming or goat cheese production as a way of earning a living. In rural areas, a polite request for room and board in exchange for half a day's work often succeeds. Rob Abblett has worked on farms all over the world from Mexico to Malawi, Sweden to Salt Spring Island, Canada. He simply gathers lists of contacts from organisations like the ones listed in this section and gets in touch with the ones that sound appealing:

> ***I've visited, worked and had many varied experiences on over 30 communes around the world. I like them because they are so varied and full of interesting people, usually with alternative ideas, beliefs, but also because I almost always find someone that I can really connect with, for sometimes I need to be with like-minded folk.***

Tree nurseries are often a good source of casual work and in some countries (especially Canada) tree planting is a job often done by nomadic types. Without any formal training in agriculture, it is possible to get some preliminary experience. A few European countries have programmes whereby young people spend a month or two assisting on a farm, e.g. Norway and Switzerland. A farming background is not necessary for participating in these schemes, though of course it always helps.

It is not impossible to find work on farms and ranches that have diversified to accept paying visitors. This is particularly popular in the United States (where guest ranches are called 'dude ranches') and Australia. These establishments need both domestic and outdoor assistants to lead guests on trail rides, show them places or events of local interest, etc.

Volunteering your labour on a farm in exchange for bed and board is an excellent way to gain agricultural experience at the same time as a cultural exchange. The site helpx.net provides contact details free of charge for farms and properties looking for helpers, mainly in Australia and New Zealand but expanding in Europe and worldwide. It is also worth having a look at the site workaway.info run from Spain which has up-to-date rural job listings worldwide which potential work-for-keep volunteers can access by paying a fee of €15.

Equestrian and Other Rural Work

The International Exchange Program (IEP) is a scheme by which partner organisations in Britain, Ireland, Australia, New Zealand and the USA co-operate to offer work placements and rural exchanges to qualified candidates. They offer 300–400 agricultural, equine, horticultural and winemaking placements of varying lengths and also act as a recruitment agency making permanent and relief placements in the equestrian and agricultural industries. Equestrian staff require a suitable background. One year of practical experience is usually needed for all placements, though additional training is often available. Placements as nannies or general farm assistants may not require experience. The organisations to contact for information are:

IEP-UK: Rutland, UK; ☎ 0845 347 9105; ws@iepuk.com; iepuk.com; equine staff agency and co-ordinator of international agricultural exchanges.

TEP Pty Ltd Australia: ☎ 02 4587 9770; tepeople.com.au; deal exclusively with placing equestrian and thoroughbred staff.

Communicating for Agriculture Educational Programs: Fergus Falls, MN, USA; ☎ 218 739 3241; caep.org; as well as arranging incoming programme, places US candidates aged 18–30 with at least two years of practical experience in agricultural, horticultural, equine or wine-making positions in many countries from Sweden to South Africa.

Experienced grooms, riding instructors and stable staff may consider registering with a specialist agency such as Career Grooms in London (☎ 020 7289 6385; careergrooms.co.uk). Equipeople is an Irish company that supplies staff to the horse sector in Ireland and abroad (equipeoplestaff.com), and the internet employment site based in Florida, Equistaff (equistaff.com), has an international clientele.

Other agencies advertise in the specialist press, for example *Horse and Hound*. Stable staff and lightweight riders are needed for work on studs and in racing establishments around the world. For those who like horses but lack experience, becoming a volunteer at a riding stable might be the answer, which can be arranged in some countries through the WWOOF exchange.

WWOOF

CANADIAN LEONA BALDWIN AND PARTNER DECIDED TO GO DOWN THIS ROUTE TO FIX UP A WORK-FOR-KEEP PLACEMENT AT A TREKKING CENTRE IN NEW ZEALAND:

From the Bay of Islands to Invercargill, WWOOFing opportunities were advertised everywhere, at Yoga retreats, ski resorts, cattle farms and horse trekking centres. Our preference was for the latter. Ever since my 'My Little Pony' days of youth, dazzled by storybook images of unicorns and Black Beauty, I had loved horses. As it transpired, it was destined to be a love affair from afar. My first riding experience at the age of ten had found me clinging helplessly to the saddle and then face down in the snow. The best thing you can do in those circumstances is get right back on. But I hadn't, and now 15 years later, I decided to make amends.

Luckily, our first choice in horse trekking farms had a vacancy for two WWOOFers, and we were invited to come and stay in the scenic Ruapehu district. Soon after arrival I found myself in the paddock ready to confront the four-legged demons of my past. And there they stood, 14 pairs of ears pricked up, eyes wild, muscles taut and ready for action. My knees went weak. As I reached up over my head to attach the rope to its neck, heart in my throat, I took a step and to my great surprise, it moved obediently behind me. I was in control!

With growing fears of unsustainable farming methods and genetically modified foods, the organic farming movement is attracting an ever-growing following around the world, from Toulouse to Turkey (to Prince Charles's Highgrove). Organic farms everywhere take on volunteers to help them minimise or abolish the use of chemicals and heavy machinery. There are various co-ordinating bodies, many of which go under the name of WWOOF.

WWOOF stands for World Wide Opportunities on Organic Farms, changed from Willing Workers on Organic Farms, with an eye to the sensitivities of immigration officers around the world who always bridle at the word 'work'. (If the topic arises at immigration, avoid the word 'working'; it is preferable to present yourself as a student of organic farming who is planning an educational farm visit or a cultural exchange.)

The International WWOOF Association (IWA) has a global website wwoofinternational.org with links to both the national organisations in the countries that have a WWOOF co-ordinator and to those which do not, known as WWOOF Independents. Each national group is autonomous with its own aims, system, fees and rules. Most prefer applicants to have gained some experience on an organic farm in their own country first, though this is not essential. WWOOF is an exchange: in return for your help on organic farms, gardens and homesteads, you receive meals, a place to sleep and a practical insight into organic growing. The work-for-keep exchange is a simple one that can be immensely satisfying. Visitors are expected to work around six hours per day in return for free accommodation and can stay from a few days to many months depending on whether or not they click with the owners and, of course, how much work needs to be done.

If you want to WWOOF in countries that have their own WWOOF organisation like Italy or Korea, it is necessary to join the national WWOOF organisation before you can obtain addresses of their member properties. This usually costs €15 or €20 per year. At present there are more than 40 countries with their own WWOOF co-ordinators from Canada to Kazakhstan, Austria to Australia, many of which are mentioned in the following chapters of this book with the price of joining.

To obtain the addresses of properties in all the left-over countries, It is necessary to purchase the WWOOF Independents list which contains multiple addresses in Norway, Poland, South Africa, etc., but only one or two in countries like Slovenia and Panama. Access to the list by internet can be obtained by paying the joining fee of £15 online (wwoof.org/independents.asp).

Mike Tunnicliffe joined the long-established WWOOF New Zealand to avoid work permit hassles and his experience is typical of WWOOFers' in other countries: *'My second choice of farm was a marvellous experience. For 15 days I earned no money but neither did I spend any, and I enjoyed life on the farm as part of the family. There is a wide variety of WWOOF farms and I thoroughly recommend the scheme to anyone who isn't desperate to earn money.'*

Before arranging a longish stay on an organic farm, consider whether or not you will find such an environment congenial. Many organic farmers are non-smoking vegetarians and living conditions may be primitive by some people's standards. Although positive experiences are typical, Craig Ashworth expressed reservations about WWOOF, based on his experiences in New Zealand, and claims that a proportion of WWOOF hosts are 'quite wacky'. (See *Denmark* chapter for a first-hand account of total incompatibility in this context.) Bear in mind that the work you are given to do may not always be very salubrious: for example Armin Birrer, who has spent time on organic farms in many countries, claims that the weirdest job he ever did was to spend a day in New Zealand picking worms out of a pile of rabbit dung to be used to soften the soil around some melon plants. With such a loose network of individuals around the world, the system is bound to be hit and miss. Danny Jacobson was willing to take that gamble and on the whole was happy with his WWOOF experiences in South Australia:

> ***One was an organic fig/garlic farm and the other a vineyard. Both were great though the farmers can be really bizarre and sometimes anal about how things are done. On the fig farm, the lady even gave us grades according to how we'd done that day and it was pretty annoying. Still it was really beautiful and the work was good. On the vineyard, the guy was very nice and extremely enthusiastic about making the best wine in the world.***

Communities

Many communities (formerly called communes) welcome foreign visitors and willingly exchange hospitality for work. Although not all the work is agricultural, much of it is. Some are radical or esoteric in their practices so find out as much as you can before planning to visit. The majority are vegetarian. The details and possible fees must be established on a case-by-case basis. The following resources are relevant:

Diggers and Dreamers: The Guide to Communal Living: Published by Edge of Time, BCM Edge, London WC1N 3XX; ☎ 0800 083 0451; edgeoftime.co.uk; the 2008/9 edition (£14.50) contains an updated listing of communities in the UK.

Eurotopia: Directory of Intentional Communities and Ecovillages in Europe: eurotopia.de; english version not updated since 2005; lists 336 international communities in 23 countries (mainly Europe and the UK); €20.

Communities: USA; http://directory.ic.org; *The Communities Directory* (new edition September 2009); lists 1,000 communities mainly in the US and some abroad including eco-villages, rural land trusts, co-housing groups, kibbutzim, student co-ops, organic farms, monasteries, urban artist collectives, etc.; many of the listings can be consulted online.

Agricultural Exchanges

The international equestrian exchange IEP described above is also open to other categories of agricultural worker. In addition, opportunities exist worldwide for young people aged between 18 and 30 who have good practical farming experience. AgriVenture (run by the International Agricultural Exchange Association) arranges agricultural/horticultural placements for British and European participants in the USA, Canada, Australia, New Zealand and Japan. Placements in the USA and Canada begin in February and April and last for seven or nine months. Placements for Australia and New Zealand run throughout the year and last for four to 12 months. Placements in Japan begin in April and last four to twelve months. They also offer a Workabout programme whereby you have short-term placements as you travel round Australia, New Zealand and Canada. There are also several round-the-world itineraries which depart in the autumn to the southern hemisphere for six to seven months followed by another six to seven months in the northern hemisphere. Participants pay between £2,030 and £4,500 which includes airline tickets, visas, insurance, orientation seminar and work placements, living and working with an approved hosting enterprise.Trainees are then paid a realistic wage. Details from the IAEA in Wisbech, Cambridgeshire (☎ 01945 450999; agriventure.net).

TEACHING ENGLISH

This chapter used to begin with a quotation from a traveller-turned-professional-EFL-teacher, Dick Bird:

> ***It is extremely difficult for anyone whose mother tongue is English to starve in an inhabited place, since there are always people who will pay good money to watch you display a talent as basic as talking. Throughout the world, native speakers of English are at a premium.***

But this rosy view of the traveller's prospects must now be moderated somewhat. Although the English language is still the language which millions of people around the world want to learn, finding work as an English teacher is not as easy as many people assume. Furthermore there is a worrying trend even for people with a qualification to have difficulty. The number of both public and private institutes turning out certified TEFL teachers has greatly increased in the past ten years, creating a glut of teachers all chasing the same jobs, especially in the major cities of Europe.

Having sounded that warning note, it must be said that there are still areas of the world where the boom in English language learning seems to know no bounds, from Ecuador to China, Poland to Vietnam. In cowboy schools and back-street agencies, being a native speaker and dressing neatly are sometimes sufficient qualifications to get a job. But for more stable teaching jobs in recognised language schools, you will have to sign a contract (minimum three months, usually nine) and have some kind of qualification which ranges from a university degree to a certificate in education with a specialisation in English Language Teaching (the term now preferred to Teaching English as a Foreign Language or TEFL).

One of the best sources of information about the whole topic of English teaching (if I may be permitted to say so) is the 2009 edition of *Teaching English Abroad* by Susan Griffith (Crimson Publishing, £14.99). This chapter can only provide the most general introduction to such topics as TEFL training and recruitment; for specific information about individual countries, see the country chapters.

ELT TRAINING

The only way to outrival the competition and make the job hunt (not to mention the job itself) easier is to do a training course. The British Council website is a good starting place for information: britishcouncil.org/teacherrecruitment-tefl-qualifications.htm.

There are two standard recognised qualifications that will improve your range of job options by an order of magnitude. The best known is the Certificate in English Language Teaching to Adults (CELTA) administered and awarded by the University of Cambridge ESOL Examinations (☎ 01223 553355; cambridgeesol.org/teaching). The other is the Certificate in TESOL (Teaching English to Speakers of Other Languages) offered by Trinity College London (☎ 020 7820 6100; tesol@trinitycollege.co.uk; trinitycollege.co.uk). Both are intensive and expensive, averaging £850–£950. These courses involve at least 100 hours of rigorous training with a practical emphasis (full-time for four weeks or part-time over several months). Although there are no fixed prerequisites apart from a suitable level of language awareness, not everyone who applies is accepted. And almost no one finds these intensive courses a breeze. Fergus Cooney says that on his CELTA course, they barely had time for a coffee during the day and that several trainees broke down in tears during breaks, himself (almost) included.

For people confused by the number of training courses jostling for attention in the marketplace, the language and teacher training consultancy Cactus (cactusteachers.com) can provide advice free of charge.

A list of centres in the UK and abroad offering the Cambridge CELTA is available from Cambridge Assessment, which oversees the ESOL exams mentioned above; they are all linked from their website as well. In addition to the centres throughout the UK, Cambridge CELTA courses are offered at more than 250 overseas centres from the Middle East to Queensland, including ten in the US and 30 in Australia and New Zealand.

A number of centres offer short introductory courses in TEFL, which vary enormously in quality and price. These may be less challenging and the qualification not widely recognised, but this did not deter the self-confessedly unacademic Roger Blake who felt that he benefited greatly from a short TEFL course:

> ***Of the many things that I have achieved over the past few years, one of the most significant must be my certificate in TEFL. Partly inspired during a backpacker style holiday to New York where I saw a subway advertisement asking for English teachers, I followed it up and did a crash weekend course with i-to-i. To my surprise I enjoyed it so much that I then did their language awareness module by home study to improve my understanding and ability to teach. (It is worth noting that i-to-i's courses are aimed at casual would-be teachers not career professionals.) Not being the academic sort, I amazed myself in completing 40 hours but it was worth it. Since then I have been particularly keen to get off on my travels.***

Short courses are sometimes marketed as preparatory programmes for more serious courses. Others are just as intensive as the Cambridge and Trinity courses. Among the best known are:

EF English First Teacher Training: 26 Wilbraham Road, Fallowfield, Manchester M14 6JX; ☎ 0161 256 1400; englishfirst.com; 4-week EF Certificate course offered monthly in Manchester and occasionally other locations; cost £575 (this course is subsidised, with successful trainees guaranteed teaching posts in China, Indonesia or Russia) or £875 for those who do not wish to commit to working for EF.

i-to-i: Leeds; ☎ 0871 423 9941; onlinetefl.com; intensive TEFL weekend courses at venues in UK/Eire cities for £190; an optional 20-hour home-study grammar module can be added for an extra £40; online TEFL courses (40, 60 or 100 hours) also available from any location worldwide; prices for online courses are £175, £210 and £335 respectively.

Saxoncourt Teacher Training: London W1; ☎ 020 7499 8533; saxoncourt.com; subsidised one-week introductory TEFL course throughout the year for positions in China, Japan and Taiwan.

TEFL Time: West Sussex; ☎ 020 7558 8721; tefltime.com; weekend courses affiliated with the volunteer placement agency Travellers Worldwide; course fee £189.

TEFL Training: Witney, Oxfordshire; ☎ 01993 891121; tefltraining.co.uk; 20-hour practical and intensive weekend seminars in cities around the UK; £210.

Other centres for American readers to consider apart from CELTA ones are Transworld Schools in San Francisco (☎ 1 888 588 8335/ 415 928 2835; transworldschools.com) and the School of Teaching English as a Second Language in Seattle (☎ 206 781 8607; schooloftesl.com) which offer their own four-week Certificate courses. TEFL International (teflinternational.org.uk) is an expanding company offering its own 120-hour PELT certificate (Practical English Language Teaching) and TESOL Certificate franchised courses in dozens of locations (Thailand, China, Costa Rica, Seville, Seoul, etc.). Prices vary but are normally $1,690 plus accommodation.

What English Teaching Involves

It is difficult to generalise about what work you will actually be required to do. At one extreme your job will be to listen to Korean businessmen reading English novels aloud to correct their pronunciation. At the other extreme you may have a gruelling schedule of lesson preparation and teaching recalcitrant adolescents. Whatever the teaching you find, things probably won't go as smoothly as you would wish.

BARRY O'LEARY HAS TAUGHT ENGLISH IN THAILAND, AUSTRALIA, ECUADOR, BRAZIL AND NOW SPAIN. HE DESCRIBES HIS JOB IN QUITO:

The teaching varied. In one school I was responsible for conversation classes. I had no guidance with the type of lessons they wanted so had to use resources from my course, the internet and my imagination. In every lesson a local teacher was there to help with any language barriers. The working conditions were very relaxed, no lesson plans or meetings, I was just given a timetable and left to get on with it. As long as the students were smiling, I was seen to be a good teacher.

I was lucky enough to find an apartment with an Ecuadorian family through an advertisement in an internet café. I made enough money to pay for my rent, food and some social activities and even managed to travel a bit with my last pay packet – and the dollars went much further in Peru.

The students were all great, the teenagers tending to be cheeky, a few times they changed the theme of the lessons to 'Make the teacher dance like a fool' before they did any work, but this was all part of the fun. It was a very relaxed atmosphere most of the time. I really enjoyed working with local teachers and they were all very open and friendly and interested in my life in England since many of them had never left Ecuador.

Native speaker teachers are nearly always employed to stimulate conversation rather than to teach grammar. Yet a basic knowledge of English grammar is a great asset when pupils come to ask awkward questions. The book *English Grammar in Use* by Raymond Murphy is recommended for its clear explanations and accompanying student exercises.

The teaching of young children is a booming area of TEFL from Portugal to Taiwan, and usually involves repetitive drills, sing-songs, puzzles and games. Intermediate learners can be difficult, since they will have reached a plateau and may be discouraged. Adults are usually well motivated though may be inhibited about speaking. Teaching professionals and business people is almost always well paid. Only 18 himself, Sam James had to teach a variety of age groups in Barcelona during his gap year and, despite the problems, ended up enjoying it:

> *The children I taught were fairly unruly and noisy. The teenagers were, as ever, pretty uninterested in learning, though if one struck on something they enjoyed they would work much better. Activities based on the lyrics of songs seemed to be good. They had a tendency to select answers at random in multiple choice exercises. On the other hand they were only ever loud rather than very rude or disobedient. The young children (8–12) were harder work. They tended to understand selectively, acting confused if they didn't like an instruction. Part of the problem was that the class was far too long (three hours) for children of that age and their concentration and behaviour tended to tail off as the time passed.*

Most schools practise the direct method (total immersion in English) so not knowing the language shouldn't prevent you from getting a job. Some employers may provide nothing more than a scratched blackboard and will expect you to dive in using the 'chalk and talk' method. Brochures picked up from tourist offices or airlines can be a useful peg on which to hang a lesson.

FINDING A JOB

Teaching jobs are either fixed up from home or sought out on location. Obviously it is less nerve-racking to have everything sorted out before you leave home, but this option is usually available only to the qualified. It also has the disadvantage that you don't know what you're letting yourself in for.

In Advance

Everywhere you look on the internet, potentially useful links can be found for job-seeking English teachers. Hundreds of websites are devoted to EFL/ESL jobs, many in Asia. Most of them have links to Dave Sperling's ESL Café (eslcafe.com). 'Dave' provides a mind-boggling but well-organised amount of material for the future or current teacher including accounts of people's experiences of teaching abroad (but bear in mind that these are the opinions of individuals). It is possible at Dave's ESL café to post a message offering your services, but it is important to be fairly specific as Fergus Cooney discovered:

> ***I posted a message simply stating 'Qualified teacher seeking job'. Within two days I was inundated with many dozens of replies requesting my CV and, more surprisingly with job offers everywhere, although the majority were from Korea, Taiwan and China. 'Jackpot' I thought (I have since realised that many schools/agents must have an automatic reply system which e-mails those who advertise in the way I did). I quickly began sifting through them, but not as quickly as they kept arriving in my inbox. Before a few more days had passed, I had become utterly confused and had forgotten which school was which, so I deleted them all, got a new e-mail address and posted a second, more specific message on Dave's.***

Here is a list of some of the key recruitment sites:

TEFL.com: Popular vehicle for schools around the world to publicise vacancies
englishjobmaze.com: Majority of jobs in China and Korea
eslbase.com
tefl.net
eslteachersboard.com
tefllogue.com

Other websites that are country specific e.g. ohayosensei.com (jobs in Japan) and ajarn.com (teaching in Thailand) are listed in the relevant country chapters. The major language school chains hire substantial numbers of teachers, many of whom will have graduated from in-house training courses. Among the major employers of EFL teachers are Berlitz (berlitz.com), EF English First (mentioned above), International House (ihworld.com), Language Link in London (languagelink.co.uk), Linguarama (linguarama.com), Saxoncourt (saxoncourt.com) and Wall Street Institute International (wallstreetinstitute.com).

Scope for untrained but eager volunteers exists for those willing to pay an agency to place them in a language teaching situation abroad, for example by many of the gap year agencies listed in the chapter on Volunteering. IST Plus (☎ 020 8939 9057; istplus.com) sends graduate volunteers to teach English in China and Thailand, for a fee.

The British Council (10 Spring Gardens, London SW1A 2BN; ☎ 020 7389 4596; assistants@britishcouncil.org) administers language assistant placements to help local teachers of English in many countries from France to Venezuela. Applicants for assistant posts must normally be aged 20–30, native English speakers, with at least two years of university-level education in the language of the destination country. Application forms are available from October; the deadline is December of the preceding academic year.

North American Organisations

A selection of key programmes and organisations in the US includes:

WorldTeach Inc.: Harvard University; ☎ 617 495 5527/ 800 4-TEACH-0; worldteach.org; private, non-profit organisation which places several hundred volunteers as teachers of EFL or ESL in countries which request assistance; provides college graduates with one-year contracts to American Samoa, Bangladesh, Costa Rica, Ecuador, Namibia, Kenya, the Marshall Islands, China, Venezuela, Chile, Pohnpei, Mongolia, Rwanda, South Africa and Guyana; 8-week summer programmes in Bulgaria, China, Costa Rica, Ecuador, Poland, Namibia and South Africa; many participants pay a volunteer contribution ranging from $500 to $7,990, but several new programmes are fully funded by the host country.

Educators Abroad Ltd: Surrey; ☎ 01737 768254; educatorsabroad.org; manages and operates the ELTAP (English Language Teaching Assistant Program; eltap.org) which sends volunteer teachers to 26 countries on all continents; placements last 4–10 weeks throughout the year and the programme fee is $2,300–$4,200 plus travel; placement fee on application; accommodation and board provided by host schools.

Global Crossroad: Irving, Texas; ☎ 1 866 387 7816; globalcrossroad.com: Volunteer teaching and internships in 23 countries; paid teaching in China (1–12 months); placement fees from $799 for China, but more typically $1,399 for Peru.

LanguageCorps: Stow, Massachusetts; ☎ 877 216 3267 or 978 562 2100; languagecorps.com; intensive on-site TESOL training and guaranteed job in many countries in Asia, Europe and Latin America. Fees $1,695–$3,995.

On the Spot

Jobs in any field are difficult to get without an interview and English teaching is no different. In almost all cases (especially in Europe) it is more effective to go to your preferred destination, CV in hand, and call on language schools and companies. The director of the Mainz branch of a chain of language schools is just one language school director who has emphasised the importance of applying locally:

> ***Schools like ours cannot under normal operating circumstances hire someone unseen merely on the basis of his/her resumé and photo. Moreover, when the need for a teacher arises, usually that vacancy must be filled within a matter of days which, for people applying from abroad, is a physical impossibility. I would suggest that an applicant should arrange for a face-to-face interview and make him/herself available at a moment's notice. Of course, I do appreciate the compromising situation to which anyone in need of employment would thus be exposed. Regrettably, I know of no other method.***

When looking for work at private language schools, it is helpful if you can claim some qualifications, though you will seldom be asked to provide proof of same. If you have a degree (in any subject), take along the proof. In countries from Mexico to Japan, travelling teachers have stressed the importance of dressing smartly, having a respectable briefcase and a typed CV.

Consult the British Council in your destination, and trawl the internet and the *Yellow Pages* (print or online) in order to draw up a list of addresses where you can ask for work. Business schools often need teachers of commercial English. Read the adverts in the English language papers. Visit centres where foreigners study the local language and check the notice board or befriend the secretary.

An alternative to working for a language school is to set yourself up as a freelance private tutor. While undercutting the fees charged by the big schools, you can still earn more than as a contract teacher. Normally you will have to be fairly well established in a place before you can attempt to support yourself by private teaching, preferably with some decent premises in which to give lessons (either private or group) and with a telephone. Bear in mind the disadvantages of working for yourself, viz. frequent last-minute cancellations by clients, unpaid travelling time (if you teach in clients' homes or offices), no social security and an absence of professional support and teaching materials. To succeed, you will have to promote yourself unashamedly. Try posting eye-catching bilingual notices all around town (especially the prosperous areas) or even leafletting door to door. You can be more selective, and concentrate on relevant notice boards. If you are less interested in making money than integrating with a culture, exchanging conversation for board and lodging may be an appealing possibility, which usually relies on having a network of contacts.

A recent posting on Lonely Planet's Thorntree messageboard confirms that setting yourself up as an English tutor can work:

> ***Back in December I posted a message asking people if they thought it was possible to get short-term jobs abroad or if it was a good idea to make tutoring flyers to put up around town. Both were ideas to supplement the money I already had saved and to have some new adventures/meet locals while travelling. I got a ton of negative responses telling me those ideas wouldn't work, etc. etc. Just wanted to post back on here 6 months later that it IS possible and my friend and I just did it. We got teaching jobs in Egypt that paid fairly well, without having work permits, without having TEFL, and the classes were for business professionals and thus were short terms (5 weeks). Also, we put up tutoring flyers all over Cairo and made a decent amount of money doing private tutoring. So to anyone who has any travel/working goals, don't let the lame negative people crush your dream or tell you it's not possible.***

CHILDCARE

The terms au pair, mother's help and nanny are often applied rather loosely, since all are primarily live-in jobs concerned with looking after children. Nannies normally have some formal training and take full charge of the children. Mother's helps work full-time and undertake general housework and/or cooking as well as childcare. Au pairs are supposed to work for no more than 30 hours a week and are expected to learn a foreign language while living with a family.

One of the great advantages of these live-in positions generally is that demand is so great that they are relatively easy to get (at least for women). Occasionally, young men can find live-in jobs, and slowly the number of families and therefore agencies willing to entertain the possibility of having a male au pair is increasing. Au pairs can often benefit from legislation which exempts them from work permit requirements.

The standard length of stay is for one academic year, typically September to June. Summer stays can also be arranged to coincide with the school holidays. The advantage of a summer placement is that the au pair will accompany the family to their holiday destination at the seaside or in the mountains; the disadvantage is that the children will be your responsibility for more hours than they would be if they were at school, and also most language classes will close for the summer. Make enquiries as early as possible, since there is a shortage of summer-only positions.

Anyone interested in finding out about all aspects of live-in childcare should consult the fifth edition of *The Au Pair & Nanny's Guide to Working Abroad* (Crimson Publishing, £12.95).

PROS AND CONS

The term au pair means 'on equal terms' and often the terminology 'hostess' and 'hospitality' is used rather than employer/employee. Therefore the success of the arrangement depends more than usual on whether individuals hit it off, so there is always an element of risk when living in a family of strangers. The Council of Europe guidelines stipulate that au pairs should be aged 18–27 (though these limits are flexible), should be expected to work about five hours a day, five days per week plus a couple of evenings of babysitting, must be given a private room and full board, health insurance, opportunities to learn the language and pocket money.

Once you have arrived in the family, it is important to clarify immediately what your hours and duties will be, which day you will be paid, whether you can expect a rise and how much notice either party must give if they wish to terminate the arrangement. This gets everyone off to a business-like start. But no matter how well-defined your duties are, there are bound to be occasions when your extra services will be taken for granted. It may seem that your time is not your own. Kathryn Halliwell worked for a family in Vancouver, Canada for a year and describes this problem: *'A live-in job is a very committed one. It is extremely difficult to say no when the employers ring at 6pm to say they can't be home for another two hours. Children don't consider a nanny as an employee and tension develops if a child can't understand why you won't take him swimming on your day off.'*

At one extreme you have the family (with one well-behaved child) who invites you along on skiing trips with them and asks you to do a mere 24 hours of child-minding and light housework a week. On the other hand you might be treated like a kitchen skivvy by the mother, and like a concubine by the father, while at the same time trying to look after their four spoiled brats. So it is advisable to find out as much as possible about the family before accepting the job. If you do not like the sound of the situation at the beginning you should insist that the agency offer any available alternatives.

Different national temperaments and mores can cause problems. In conservative families in countries like Turkey, southern Italy or even the US, it is unacceptable for young women to go out alone at night, so your social life may be very restricted.

ON THE OTHER HAND, GILLIAN FORSYTH'S EXPERIENCE WHEN SHE AU PAIRED IN BAVARIA WAS A GREAT SUCCESS:

I had no official day off or free time but was treated as a member of the family. Wherever they went I went too. I found this much more interesting than being treated as an employee as I really got to know the country and the people. In the evenings I did not have to sit in my room, but chatted with the family. Three years later we still keep in close contact and I have been skiing with them twice since, on an au pair/friend basis.

If you do not have a friendly arrangement with your family, it is easy to feel lonely and cut off in a foreign country. Many au pairs make friends at their language classes. Some agencies issue lists of other au pairs in the vicinity. Despite all the possible problems, au pairing does provide an easy and often enjoyable introduction to living and travelling abroad. A family placement is a safe and stable environment for young, under-confident and impecunious people who want to work abroad.

Pay and Duties

The standard pocket money paid to au pairs in Europe nowadays is €260–€300 a month which with a strong euro represents a reasonable income in addition to room and board. In Switzerland, au pairs earn (by law) £400–£450 a month, and statutory minimums are also high in Belgium and Austria (€450 per month for 20 hours a week).

Nannying can be an excellent passport to spending a season in a summer or winter resort for those with a qualification or experience. Most large tour and campsite holiday operators like Mark Warner, Thomas Cook and TUI Holidays (addresses in *Tourism* chapter) employ nannies with qualifications or experience in childcare to look after the children of holidaymakers. Companies that specialise in arranging summer and winter holidays for families, such as Esprit Holidays, employ a considerable number of childcare staff as well as other employees for their summer programme in the Alps (☎ 01252 618318; recruitment@esprit-holidays.co.uk).

Most au pairs' duties revolve around the children. For some, taking sole responsibility for a child can be fairly alarming. You should be prepared to handle a few emergencies (for example sick or lost children) as well as the usual excursions to the park or collecting them from school. The agency questionnaire will ask you in detail what experience you have had with children and whether you are willing to look after newborn infants, etc.

APPLYING

Many au pair agencies now operate only as online matching services. The old-fashioned one-woman agency still exists. However they are allowed to charge a modest fee (until recently £40 + VAT) and only on acceptance. With these restrictions in place, It is impossible for agencies to make a profit and as a result agencies which at one time sent many British girls abroad are now concentrating almost exclusively on placing foreign girls with paying client families in the UK.

If you are already abroad, check in the local English language newspaper or visit an au pair agency office in the country where you are (addresses provided in country chapters). Many European agencies charge a substantial fee of €200+ which they claim is necessary to guarantee a minimum quality of service.

Other ways of hearing about openings are to check the notice boards at the local English-speaking churches or ask the head teacher of a junior school if she/he knows of any families wanting an au pair. One tip for finding babysitting jobs in resorts is to introduce yourself to the *portière* or receptionist on the desk of good hotels and ask them to refer guests looking for a babysitter to you, possibly offering them a small commission. With more suspicion around these days, informal arrangements like this are less likely to succeed; some potential clients might be reassured if you have good references and, assuming you have worked in the past through an agency who has applied on your behalf, a CRB (Criminal Records Bureau) check; further details at crb.gov.uk.

The Internet

Cyberspace buzzes with an exchange of information about live-in childcare. Finding agency details is very easy with several clicks of a mouse. Au pair placement was something that was always done by telephone and correspondence rather than requiring a face-to-face interview, so it is an activity that is well suited to an online database. Among the most popular sites are aupair-agency.com, greataupair.com, findaupair.com, au-pair-box.com and aupair-world.net (German-based), aupairconnect.com (US-based), aupair-select.com and aupairs.co.uk. With nearly 20,000 registered au pairs and nannies and nearly 4,000 vacancies, GreatAuPair claims to be the largest agency.

Internet agencies enable families and applicants to engage in DIY arrangements. They invite prospective au pairs to register their details, including age, nationality, relevant experience and in many cases a photo, to be uploaded onto a website which then becomes accessible to registered families. The families then make contact with suitable au pairs after paying an introduction fee to the web-based agency. Registration is invariably free for the job-seeker.

One problem identified by the traditional agencies is that this method makes it very difficult to carry out any effective screening of either party. On the other hand, the same could be said for sits vac advertising in the conventional way (see below). If relying on the internet it is essential to ascertain exactly the nature of the situation and the expectations of your new employer. Work out in your mind what you will do in the event the arrangement does not work out; if the agency is simply a database-provider, they will be able to offer no back-up. Jean-Marc Cressini, director of the French agency Oliver Twist, thinks that this book '*should really warn applicants about free websites, as we have just been informed by Interpol that some girls have paid large amounts of money to families who do not exist. A person pretending to be a family has been arrested in England for asking applicants for large bank transfers*'. You should be suspicious of any individual or company that asks for money upfront, and certainly not a family.

Agencies in the UK

Arguably there is too little regulation in the world of au pair agencies, and things can go wrong in even the most tightly controlled programmes. Many leading au pair agencies and youth exchange organisations in Europe belong to IAPA, the International Au Pair Association, an international body trying to regulate the industry. The IAPA website iapa.org has clear links to its member agencies around the world.

Agencies that specialise in one country are mentioned in the country chapters. The following UK au pair and/or nanny agencies all deal with a number of European countries:

Angels International Au Pairs Agency: Bournemouth; ☎ 01202 571065; aupair1.com; France and other European countries; £75 administration fee.

Au Pair Agency Bournemouth: 45 Strouden Road, Bournemouth BH9 1QL; ☎ 01202 532600; andrea.rose@virgin.net.

Au Pair Connections: Southampton; ☎ 01489 780438; aupairconnections.co.uk; France, Spain, Italy, Austria.

Care Agency: Abingdon, Oxfordshire; ☎ 01235 525115; aupairbix.co.uk; France, Germany, Spain, Italy.

Childcare International Ltd: Trafalgar House, Grenville Place, London NW7 3SA; ☎ 0800 652 0020 or 020 8906 3116; childint.co.uk; separate divisions for Europe, Canada, Australia and New Zealand.

Childcare Solution & Worldnet UK: ☎ 01444 453566; worldnetuk.com or thechildcaresolution.com; au pairs placed in Italy, France, Germany, Spain, Norway and Finland. Childcare USA, seasonal nannies in European resorts and other Work Abroad placements.

Edgware & Solihull Au Pair & Nanny Agency: Hertfordshire; ☎ 01923 289737; theaupair-shop.com; Europe and the USA.

Janet White Agency: Leeds; ☎ 0113 266 6507; janetwhite.com: Europe, Canada and the US.

Jolaine Agency: Barnet, Herts EN5 3AN; ☎ 020 8449 1334; jolaine@talktalk.net; placements in Italy and Spain as well as the UK; Fee of £40 + VAT.

Nanny & Au Pair Connection: Bolton; ☎ 0845 166 2216; info@aupairs-nannies.co.uk; aupairs-nannies.co.uk; partnered with 22 agents abroad including in Belgium, France, Spain, Portugal, Switzerland, Austria, Germany, Greece, Turkey and USA.

Quick Help Agency: London; ☎ 020 7794 8666; quickhelp.co.uk; mainly Austria, France and Germany.

Total Nannies: Surrey; ☎ 020 8542 3067; totalnannies.com; so-called cultural exchange programme by which female candidates are placed with professional families mainly in Italy but also in Germany, Switzerland and the USA.

Agencies Worldwide

Many North Americans are eager to learn the language and absorb the culture of European countries, and indeed some do become au pairs, though the term is not universally recognised in the US and Canada. The red tape is more difficult for them, especially in certain countries like Italy and Spain, however they are rarely prohibited from spending six months or a year working with families. Agencies that can help include:

Globetrotters Education Consulting: Ontario: ☎ 416 565 4420; laura@globetrotterseducation.ca; globetrotterseducation.ca; vacancies possible in Spain, Italy, France, UK, Norway and Germany; placement fee $500.

InterExchange/Working Abroad: New York; ☎ 212 924 0446 or 1 800 597 3675; workingabroad.org; send au pairs to France, Germany, Netherlands and Spain; fees from $500–$600 for au pair placement.

Au pairing is very popular among South Africans especially in the Netherlands for obvious linguistic reasons (since Afrikaans is based on the Dutch that the Boers took to southern Africa). A specialist agency in Johannesburg is Au Pair in Holland (aupairinholland.co.za) or try JCR Cultural Exchange (jcr.co.za).

Agencies in New Zealand and Australia include the Brisbane-based online agency globalnannies.com and Nannies Abroad Ltd./International Working Holidays in Auckland (☎ +64 9 416 5337; iwh.co.nz/nanniesabroad.co.nz) which places New Zealanders in au pair and live-in language-assistance positions in France, Germany and Italy and nannies in Canada.

VOLUNTEERING

Volunteering can open doors in exotic places that would otherwise be out-of-reach. Everyone should be aware that volunteering almost always costs the volunteer money, sometimes substantial sums. Yet the cost will be much less than a mere tourist would pay. For example volunteering to take part in a marine survey can be a very economical way to visit an expensive or exclusive destination like the Seychelles. You won't get the first class amenities but you will get to see the same things the tourists are paying a much higher price to see. Similarly, joining a voluntary scheme on a lion reserve in Zimbabwe will allow you to have more exposure to the animals than the tourists who have paid five times as much.

Many volunteer schemes are open to all nationalities and often avoid work permit hassles. By participating in a project such as building a community centre in a Turkish village, looking after orphaned refugee children or just helping out at a youth hostel, you have the unique opportunity to live and work in a remote community, and the chance to meet up with like-minded people from many countries who can point you towards new job prospects. You may be able to improve or acquire a language skill and to learn something of the customs of the society in which you are volunteering. You will also gain practical experience, for instance in the fields of construction, archaeology or social welfare which will stand you in good stead when applying for paid jobs elsewhere.

Volunteers with no medical, technical or other relevant background and with no knowledge of the local language inevitably find it difficult to make a concrete difference to the lives of others. They learn the hard though valuable lesson that the giving of aid is a messy and complicated business, and that quite often they benefit from the experience far more than those they aim to help.

Most fixing organisations charge volunteers to cover the cost of recruiting, screening, interviewing, pre-departure orientation, insurance, etc. on top of travel, food and lodging. Many of these are profit-making companies though some do give a proportion of the fees paid by volunteers to support the projects with which they're linked. If you are thinking of signing up with a company or organisation with which you are not familiar, it is a wise precaution to carry out some investigations and if possible check with former volunteers. Be sure that you are aware whether the agency is a charity/non-profit or a commercial enterprise and ask for a breakdown of the costs.

In any case it is worth giving careful thought to whether or not you need to go through a mediating organisation. After chunks of time spent working and travelling in Latin America and having fixed up a teaching placement in Africa that turned out not to be as it was described by the placement agency, Till Bruckner knows his mind on this question:

> ***It strikes me as weird to collect volunteers from Britain who have to pay a fee plus their airfares to teach the children of the better-off in universities. In a country with poverty on that scale, there's more useful things you can do with £500 to help people in need. If you want fun, go elsewhere. If you want to help, put the £500 in an Oxfam charity box. I can see that some people might appreciate organisational support if they want to volunteer, but except in very restrictive countries (like Sudan), it's not really necessary. I met two girls in Bolivia who had just walked into a home for street kids and volunteered there and then. They got free board and lodging and all they did was talk to the kids and play with them since nobody ever did that. Those girls really did something valuable there. But if they had found themselves not able to contribute anything they would have had the freedom to walk out on the spot.***

After participating in several prearranged voluntary projects in the United States, Catherine Brewin did not resent the fee she had paid to Involvement Volunteers:

> ***The whole business of paying to do voluntary work is a bit hard to swallow. But having looked into the matter quite a bit, it does seem to be the norm. While it may be a bit unfair (who knows***

how much profit or loss these voluntary organisations make or how worthy their projects?), most people I've met did seem to feel good about the experience. The group I was with did raise the odd comment about it all, but did not seem unduly concerned. However I should mention that most were around 18 years old and their parents were paying some if not all the costs.

The tsunami disaster of Boxing Day 2004 focused minds on helping in an emergency in an unprecedented way. The outpourings of financial help from around the world were reinforced by an upsurge in the number of people wanting to donate their time to help. As with all emergency relief work, skilled and experienced professionals are in demand while well-meaning amateurs potentially just get in the way. In the immediate aftermath, relief workers with professional skills were needed, many of whom were recruited via United Nations Volunteers (unv.org). A host of NGOs is still working on reconstruction projects in Sri Lanka and Thailand which willing volunteers can join.

SOURCES OF INFORMATION

Worldwide Volunteering based in Somerset (☎ 01935 825588; wwv.org.uk) has developed an authoritative online search-and-match database of volunteering opportunities for 16–35 year olds. As well as being a web-based resource of voluntary opportunities worldwide, another provider Workingabroad.com (also based in Somerset as it happens) will prepare a personalised report after you complete a detailed request form; the fee is £29/$52 by email, £36/$65 by post (tel/fax 01935 864458; victoria.McNeil@workingabroad.com).

The World Service Enquiry of the respected charity Christians Abroad (London SW9; ☎ 0870 770 3274; wse.org.uk) provides information and advice to people of any faith or none who are thinking of working overseas, and sells a handful of titles on working and volunteering in development.

The revolution in information technology has made it easier for the individual to become acquainted with the amazing range of possibilities. One of the best web-based directories is traveltree.co.uk. It covers gap year ideas and volunteering opportunities worldwide as well as internships and educational travel. *Transitions Abroad* magazine maintains great online resources for volunteering (transitionsabroad.com). The best of the websites have a multitude of links to organisations big and small that can make use of volunteers. For example idealist.org is a US-based easily searchable site that will take you to the great monolithic charities like the Peace Corps as well as to small grassroots organisations. It lists 20,000 non-profit and community organisations in 150 countries.

Non-profit Ecoteer based in Plymouth (☎ 01752 702247; ecoteer.com) is a database of more than 150 projects worldwide that need volunteers and are willing to provide food and accommodation at no, or at little, cost. Ecoteer provides contact information to members who pay £10 to join.

The travellers' organisation Your Safe Planet has also become involved with volunteering. Its modus operandi is to connect clients (membership fee £45) with a reliable local person at your destination who can advise on local volunteering projects that are free and ethical (☎ 0141 416 4622; yoursafeplanet.com).

PROS AND CONS

Bear in mind that volunteer work, especially in the developing world, can be not only tough and character-building but also disillusioning (see Mary Hall's description of her year at a Uganda clinic in the *Africa* chapter). And just as the working traveller must be alert to exploitation in paid jobs, so he or she should be careful in voluntary situations as well. Occasionally eager young volunteers are forced to conclude that the people in charge of the organisation charge volunteers well in excess of essential running costs. Fortunately the experiences of one volunteer in Africa are rare: he claims to have discovered that the community development projects described in the literature from an organisation in Sierra Leone did not exist and furthermore the director had previously jumped bail from Freetown CID. If you are in any doubt about an organisation you are considering working for, ask for the names of one or two past volunteers whom you can contact for an informal reference. Any worthy organisation should be happy to oblige.

Disillusionment can be a problem for even the most privileged volunteers working for the most respectable charities. When Danny Jacobson visited Bulgaria, he found the country stuffed full of Peace Corps volunteers:

> ***I had always envisioned Peace Corps volunteers to be off in Third World countries living in huts, repairing trees and teaching English to tribal children. In fact, in Bulgaria they all had sly apartments, decent salaries and an average of about 20 hours a week to commit to the cause. Everything from toothpaste to toilet paper was provided and twice a year they were all carted out to some fancy hotel to practise the language and bond. Pretty much everyone we met had a similar story: they joined to try to make a difference and were now left disenchanted and feeling useless. Since the Peace Corps is pretty relaxed about assigning duties – basically you are dropped off in a town and left to your own resources with no supervision – Chris had to start teaching English and later worked with a couple of guys to help build mountain huts and maintain hiking trails. Everyone was pessimistic because it seemed to take forever to get anything done.***

Morale might well be higher in other countries.

GAP YEAR AND CAREER BREAK PLACEMENTS

Far more students have been taking a year out to volunteer, work and travel between school and university than used to be the case, though the credit crunch and talk of rising tuition fees may put the brakes on that trend. Many organisations attempt to make it possible for school-leavers as well as older people taking a gap year to undertake useful unpaid work abroad for between three and 12 months. Normally anyone can join a project provided they can pay the programme fees. All volunteers are asked to fundraise substantial sums, such as £2500–£3500 for three months. This is a brief listing of the major specialist organisations; for more information see my books *Your Gap Year* (Crimson, 2010, £12.99) or *Gap Years for Grown-ups* (2008, £12.99). The website gapyear.com can also be useful. Note that the market in career breaks is growing very fast and has given rise to a couple of specialist websites, notably thecareerbreaksite.com.

Most of the organisations listed here are founder members of the Year Out Group (☎ 01380 816696; yearoutgroup.org) which was formed to promote well-structured gap year programmes and now has 37 members:

Africa & Asia Venture: ☎ 01380 729009; aventure.co.uk; voluntary teaching and sports coaching placements last 5 weeks to 5 months for students and graduates aged 18–24 in Africa, Asia and Mexico.

Cactus Volunteers Abroad: Brighton; ☎ 0845 130 4775; volunteer@cactuslanguage.com; volunteers-abroad.com; wide range of volunteer and language placements (especially in Latin America) and shorter volunteer holidays.

Changing Worlds: Surrey; 01883 340960; changingworlds.co.uk; voluntary placements in schools, orphanages, conservation projects, etc. in Ghana, Honduras, India, Latvia and Thailand, plus paid and voluntary jobs in hotels and farms in Australia and New Zealand.

Global Vision International (GVI): St Albans; ☎ 01727 250250; gvi.co.uk; 150+ conservation and humanitarian projects and internships throughout Africa, Latin America, Asia and the USA.

Global Volunteer Network: Lower Hutt, New Zealand; +64 4 569 9080; volunteer.org.nz; volunteer projects including English teaching, environmental work, animal welfare, health and sanitation and cultural homestays in Asia, Africa, Latin America, Alaska and New Zealand.

Global Volunteer Projects: Newcastle; ☎ 0191 222 0404; globalvolunteerprojects.org; unpaid work experience projects in medical fields, journalism, teaching, etc. in Ghana, Tanzania, China, India, Cambodia and Mexico.

Greenforce: London SW6; ☎ 020 7384 3343; greenforce.org; one-time specialist in environmental expeditions, Greenforce now offers a range of gap year and adventure programmes in ten countries; trekforce at same address.

i-to-i: Leeds; ☎ 0800 011 1156; i-to-i.com; large commercial company now owned by First Choice Holidays; TEFL and conservation placements in Latin America, Africa, Russia and Asia; 500 projects in 22 countries.

Lattitude: Reading; ☎ 0118 959 4914; lattitude.org.uk; formerly GAP Activity Projects; posts are for between four and eleven months (six is average) and most cost £1,500–£1,800 plus airfares and insurance, while board, lodging and (sometimes) pocket money are provided.

Madventurer: Newcastle-upon-Tyne; ☎ 0845 121 1996; madventurer.com; combined development projects and adventurous overland travel in Peru, Ecuador, Ghana, Tanzania, Kenya, Uganda, South Africa, Fiji, Vanuatu, India, Vietnam and Thailand.

MondoChallenge: Newbury; ☎ 01635 45556; mondochallenge.org; volunteers to help with teaching and business development programmes in Africa, Asia and South America; from £1,400 for 3 months.

Original Volunteers: Norwich; ☎ 0800 345 7582; low-cost volunteering opportunities worldwide to clients who join the programme for £195 per year.

Outreach International: Somerset; ☎ 01458 274957; outreachinternational.co.uk; tries to match the interests and skills of individual volunteers with selected projects in Mexico, Cambodia, Ecuador including the Galapagos Islands, Costa Rica and Sri Lanka; volunteers might teach English, computer or art skills, work with street children or in orphanages, help to conserve sea turtles, etc. for 3–6 months.

Oyster Worldwide: East Sussex; ☎ 0800 980 9516 or 01892 770771; oysterworldwide.com; gap year placement organisation offering paid work in mountain resorts in Canada (Quebec and the Rockies) and volunteer projects in Brazil (Rio or Sao Paulo), in Chilean Patagonia, Nepal, Romania, Zambia and Tanzania.

Personal Overseas Development: Cheltenham; ☎ 01242 250901; thepodsite.co.uk; range of teaching, conservation and social work projects in Peru, Belize, Tanzania, Thailand, Cambodia and Nepal; sample prices £495 for unlimited period working in dog and cat care in Thailand.

Projects Abroad: Sussex; ☎ 01903 708300; info@projects-abroad.co.uk; about 4,000 people are recruited annually as English language teaching assistants, business interns, conservation volunteers and in other fields; 22 destination countries include Moldova, Togo and Bolivia.

Project Trust: Isle of Coll, Scotland; ☎ 01879 230444; info@projecttrust.org.uk; educational charity that sends British school-leavers aged 17–19 overseas for a year to 22 countries; fund-raising target for 2009 is £4,660.

Quest Overseas: Hove, E Sussex; ☎ 01273 777206; questoverseas.com; gap year projects and expeditions in South America and Southern Africa.

Raleigh International: London SE1; ☎ 020 7183 1270; raleigh.org.uk; offers young people aged 17–25 the chance to undertake demanding environmental and community projects overseas; destinations in 2009 are Costa Rica with Nicaragua, India and Malaysian Borneo; the fundraising target is £2,995 for 10 weeks.

Real Gap: Tunbridge Wells; ☎ 01892 516164; realgap.co.uk; many volunteer and other gap year/career break programmes in 49 countries.

SPW (Students Partnership Worldwide): London SW1; ☎ 020 7808 1783; spw.org; educational and environmental programmes lasting 4–8 months in Africa and Asia for 18–28-year-olds; volunteers are paired with indigenous volunteers; fee £3,600 includes airfares.

Travellers: West Sussex; ☎ 01903 502595; travellersworldwide.com; volunteers teach "conversational English (and/or other subjects) and join conservation projects worldwide.

Twin Work & Volunteer Abroad: London; ☎ 0800 804 8380; workabroad@twinuk.com; workandvolunteer.com; broad range of volunteer programmes in Latin America, Africa and Asia.

VentureCo Worldwide: Warwick; ☎ 01926 411122; ventureco-worldwide.com; gap year and career break programmes lasting 2–15 weeks in Latin America, Africa and Asia that combine language learning, community development work and an expedition.

WORKCAMPS AND OTHER PLACEMENT ORGANISATIONS

Voluntary work in developed countries often takes the form of workcamps, short projects that accept unskilled labour. As part of an established international network of voluntary organisations they are not subject to the irregularities of some privately run projects. As well as providing volunteers with the means to live cheaply for two to four weeks in a foreign country, workcamps enable volunteers to become involved in what is usually useful work for the community, to meet people from many different backgrounds and to 'increase their awareness of other lifestyles, social problems and their responsibility to society' as one volunteer has described it. Workcamps are an 88-year-old programme of conflict resolution and community development and an inexpensive and personal way to travel, live and work in an international setting.

ANDREW BOYLE, WHO HAS DONE A VARIETY OF JOBS ABROAD SUBSEQUENTLY, GOT OFF TO AN EXCELLENT START BY JOINING SEVERAL EUROPEAN WORKCAMPS:

I participated in three voluntary workcamps: two in West Germany and one in the French Alps. The former, particularly, were excellent value, both in the nature of the work (Umweltschutz or environmental protection) and in that the group of about 20 became part of the local community – meeting the locals in the kneipen or socialising with the conscientious objectors doing community service instead of military service. These camps are an excellent introduction to travelling for 16 to 20 year olds, say, sixth formers who have never been away from a family type social structure. I suspect that their value would be more limited to an experienced traveller.

Within Europe, and to a lesser extent further afield, there is a massive effort to co-ordinate workcamp programmes. This normally means that the prospective volunteer should apply in the first instance to the appropriate organisation in his or her own country, or to a centralised international headquarters. The vast majority of camps take place in the summer months, and camp details are normally published online in March/April with a flurry of placements made in the month or two following. It is necessary to pay a registration fee which has become standard across the different agencies recruiting volunteers, normally £150 for a standard project in Europe, £180 for one in a developing country to help finance future projects or to pay for specialised training. The fee covers board and lodging but not of course travel.

The largest workcamp organisation is Service Civil International with branches in 41 countries. The UK branch is International Voluntary Service (IVS-GB) in Edinburgh (☎ 0131 243 2745; info@ivsgb.org). The cost of registration on IVS workcamps outside the UK is £190 which includes £35 membership in IVS.

IVS has linked up with the four other main agencies listed below to form VINE-UK (vine-uk.org), all of whom organise International Volunteer Exchange programmes. The other organisations in the network are:

Concordia International Volunteers: Brighton; ☎ 01273 422218; concordia-iye.org.uk; programme of workcamps in 30 countries; registration fee £150.

UNA Exchange: Cardiff; ☎ 029 2022 3088; unaexchange.org; membership £12 plus £150 for overseas projects, £200+ for longer term ones.

Voluntary Action for Peace/VAP: London SE22; ☎ 0844 209 0927; vaporg.uk; workcamps held in many countries in Western and Eastern Europe, plus Mexico, the Middle East and Bangladesh; administrative fee £120–£160.

Xchange Scotland: Glasgow; xchange.scotland@yahoo.com; xchangescotland.org.

European Voluntary Service (EVS) is an initiative of the European Commission to encourage young Europeans (aged 18–30) to join short and long term projects in social care, youth work, outdoor recreation and rural development elsewhere in Eastern and Western Europe. This programme is remarkable because volunteers do not have to pay to participate; EVS provides several thousand volunteers with free travel, food, accommodation and an allowance for the duration of two to 12 months. The programme is delivered in the UK by a range of voluntary agencies such as those listed above, among others such as EIL Experiment in International Education in Malvern (☎ 0800 018 4015; evs@eiluk.org; volunteering18–30.org.uk).

American volunteers should apply to one of the two major workcamp organisations in the US:

SCI-IVS (Service Civil International-International Voluntary Service): ☎ 434 336 3545; sci-ivs.org.

Volunteers for Peace: ☎ 802 259 2759; vfp@vfp.org; vfp.org; annual membership $30; in early April VFP publishes an online *International Project Directory* with more than 2,500 programme listings in nearly 100 countries; membership costs US$30 and gives members early access to the directory; registration for most programmes costs $300.

The majority of international projects are environmental or social. They may involve the conversion/reconstruction of historic buildings and building community facilities. Some of the more interesting past projects include building adventure playgrounds for children, renovating an open-air museum in the Baltics, organising youth concerts in Armenia, constructing boats for sea-cleaning in Japan, looking after a farm-school in Slovakia during the holidays, helping peasant farmers in central France to stay on their land, plus a whole range of schemes with the disabled and elderly, conservation work and the study of social and political issues.

ARCHAEOLOGY

Taking part in archaeological excavations is another popular form of voluntary work, but volunteers are usually expected to make a contribution towards their board and lodging. Also, you may be asked to bring your own trowel, work clothes, tent, etc. Archaeology Abroad based at University College London (☎ 020 8537 0849; britarch.ac.uk/archabroad) is an excellent source of information, as they publish details of excavations needing volunteers on CD-ROM in spring and autumn; in the past year between 700 and 1,000 definite places on sites were offered to subscribers. They do stress however that applications from people with a definite interest in the subject are preferred. An annual subscription costs £22.

An online and print source of archaeology field schools is the memorably named Shovelbums (shovelbums.org) run on a shoestring by an archaeologist in Ohio. Anyone who can navigate in German can also check archaeologie-online.de.

For those who are not students of archaeology, the chances of finding a place on an overseas dig will be greatly enhanced by having some digging experience nearer to home. Details of British excavations looking for volunteers are published as online briefings by the Council for British Archaeology in York (☎ 01904 671417; britarch.ac.uk). Anthony Blake joined a dig sponsored by the University of Reims and warns that 'archaeology is hard work, and applicants must be aware of what working for eight hours in the baking heat means!' Nevertheless Anthony found the company excellent and the opportunity to improve his French welcome. See the chapter on France for information about joining one of the hundreds of summer digs.

Israel is another country particularly rich in archaeological opportunities, many of them organised through the universities. Digs provide an excellent means of seeing remote parts of the country though Israeli digs tend to be more expensive than most, typically US$35–$40 a day plus registration.

CONSERVATION

People interested in protecting the environment can often slot into conservation organisations abroad. One enterprising traveller in South Africa looked up the 'green directory' in a local library, contacted a few of the projects listed in the local area and was invited to work at a cheetah reserve near Johannesburg in exchange for accommodation and food.

For a directory of opportunities in this specialised area, consult the 2009 edition of *Green Volunteers: The World Guide to Voluntary Work in Nature Conservation* (£11.99). A number of companies and charities offer 'conservation holidays' which cost almost as much as a regular holiday. Pre-eminent among them is BTCV (British Trust for Conservation Volunteers) which runs a programme of mainly 2-week International Conservation Holidays in a dozen countries including Iceland, France, Bulgaria, USA, Cameroon and Japan. Further details are available from BTCV in Doncaster (☎ 01302 388883; information@btcv.org.uk; http://shop.btcv.org.uk). Accommodation, meals and insurance are provided; sample prices are £460 for a week of nest-building on the Black Sea to £510 for two weeks planting trees in a Cameroonian village.

The Australia-based Involvement Volunteers Association Inc. (☎ +61 3 9646 9392; volunteering.org.au) arranges individual placements worldwide open to all. Projects are concerned with conservation, animal welfare, social and community service and education. Projects last two to six weeks and can be arranged back-to-back in different countries. The programme fee is A$1,200 or AUS$1,200 (£580).

The following agencies help and staff scientific expeditions by supplying fee-paying volunteers:

Biosphere Expeditions: Norwich; ☎ 0870 446 0801; biosphere-expeditions.org; other offices in Europe, USA and Australia; wildlife conservation research expeditions to many parts of the world; volunteers with no research experience assist scientific experts on 1 or 2 week projects including jaguar and puma studies in Brazil, snow leopard projects in Central Asia and reef preservation in Honduras; fees start at £1130 for a fortnight (excluding airfares).

Coral Cay Conservation Ltd: London SE1; ☎ 020 7620 1411; coralcay.org; sends teams of paying volunteers to assist with marine conservation expeditions in the Philippines, Tobago and Cambodia; a sample six-week project for a dive trainee costs £1,850 (including credit crunch reduction).

Earthwatch Institute (Europe): Oxford; ☎ 01865 318838; earthwatch.org/europe; international non-profit organisation that recruits thousands of volunteers a year for short expeditions to assist scientific field research around the world; sample projects: to measure climate change on the edge of the Canadian Arctic (£1,350 for 11 days) and to monitor dolphin behaviour in the Bahamas (£1,660 for 11 days).

Ecovolunteer: ecovolunteer.org.uk; acts as on online travel agent matching paying volunteers with short-term wildlife conservation projects worldwide.

Operation Wallacea: Lincolnshire; ☎ 01790 763194; opwall.com; marine, rainforest or desert research projects in Sulawesi (Indonesia), Honduras, Egypt, Amazonian Peru, South Africa/Mozambique and Cuba.

DEVELOPING COUNTRIES

Commitment, no matter how fervent, is not enough to work in an aid project in the developing world. You must normally be able to offer some kind of useful training or skill unless you are prepared to fund yourself and don't mind that your effort to help will be more a token than of lasting benefit. Many organisations offer ordinary people the chance to experience life in the developing world by working alongside local people for a brief period and these are mentioned throughout the chapters on Africa, Asia and Latin America later in this book. Geoffroy Groleau from Quebec decided to spend some months in India and wanted to dedicate part of his time to volunteering in the development field. He stumbled across an Indian NGO on the internet and arranged to work for a month with Dakshinayan (see chapter on Asia).

GEOFFROY ENDED UP THINKING THAT HIS ENJOYMENT TOOK PRECEDENCE OVER HIS USEFULNESS:

Volunteers should expect to learn more from the people than they will ever be able to teach. Remember that the villagers know much more about their needs than we do, and they have learned long ago to use effectively the resources around them. On the other hand, the contacts with the outside world that the volunteers provide is a valuable way for the villagers to begin to understand the world that surrounds them. In my experience, the hardest things were to adapt to the rather slow rhythm of life and to the fact that as a volunteer you will not manage to change significantly the life of the villagers other than by putting your brick in a collective work that has been going on for many years.

The pre-eminent professional voluntary and aid organisations in the UK is VSO, London SW15 (☎ 020 8780 7500; enquiry@vso.org.uk; vso.org.uk) which recruits professional volunteers for two-year assignments in the fields of education, health, natural resources, technical trades and engineering, business and social work, among many others. VSO pays a modest local wage, various grants, national insurance, provides accommodation, health insurance and return flights. Volunteers need to be aged 20–75 – the average is now 41 – and qualified and experienced. Another long-established and respectable global agency is Inter-Cultural Youth Exchange (ICYE) (☎ 020 7681 0983; icye.co.uk) which arranges for students and others aged 18–30 to spend 6–12 months abroad with a host family and volunteering, for example in drug rehabilitation, protection of street children and ecological projects in one of 30 countries in Latin America, Africa and Asia. No specific skills are needed as this is a skills development programme. The fees are £1,200–£1,950 for the short-term programme, £3,795 for 6-month placements, and £4,495 for a full year.

NORTH AMERICAN OPPORTUNITIES

Companies and consultancies that maintain databases of opportunities (mostly unpaid) and offer personalised consultations to fee-paying clients (often young people aged 16–25) attempt to match them with a suitable work, volunteer or study placement abroad:

Taking Off: Boston; ☎ 617 424 1606; takingoff.net; taking Off provides ongoing personal assistance to those looking for international experiences that include volunteer work, internships and custom-designed situations (not paying jobs); consultation fee $1,200; ongoing consulting service $2,000.

Center for Interim Programs LLC: Princeton; ☎ 609 683 4300; interimprograms.com; consulting service with offices near Princeton and Harvard aimed primarily at pre-university and university students looking to arrange an internship or volunteer work; consulting fee from $2,100.

LEAPNow: Calistoga, CA; ☎ 888 424 5327; leapnow.org; various internships and experiential programmes in 126 countries, e.g. wildlife hospital in Greece, school in Honduras and orphanage in India; agency fee of $750 in addition to the programme costs.

Horizon Cosmopolite: Montreal, Canada; ☎ 514 935 8436; horizoncosmopolite.com; database of volunteer work, internships and Spanish immersion in 30+ countries around the world; tries to match clients with suitable placements; registration fee C$555 plus varying programme fees.

Here is a selection of major organisations, some of which offer short volunteer vacations, popular in the US, lasting no more than the length of an ordinary holiday.

A Broader View Volunteers Corp: Pennsylvania; ☎ 215 780 1845; abroaderview.org; huge range of customised opportunities lasting 1–8 weeks.

Cross-Cultural Solutions: New Rochelle, NY; ☎ 1 800 380 4777; crossculturalsolutions.org; also has office in Brighton, UK; 0845 458 2781/2; infouk@crossculturalsolutions.org; volunteers are placed in short-term volunteer projects in Ghana, Morocco, South Africa, India, China, Costa Rica, Guatemala, Peru, Brazil, Thailand, Tanzania and Russia; fee for 12 weeks is about $6,000–$6,500.

Experiential Learning International: Denver, CO; ☎ 303 321 8278; eliabroad.com; immersion, intern and volunteering programmes in South and Central America, Africa, Asia and Europe.

Explorations in Travel Inc: Guildford, VT; ☎ 802 257 0152; volunteertravel.com; international volunteers for rainforest conservation, wildlife, community and many other projects worldwide.

Geovisions: ☎ 1 877 949 9998; geovisions.org; live-in language tutors for Europe and worldwide, including Jordan, Brazil and Egypt.

Global Routes: Northampton, MA; ☎ 413 585 8895; globalroutes.org; offers 12-week voluntary internships to students over 17 who teach English and other subjects in village schools in Tanzania, Costa Rica, Peru, Ghana, India and Thailand; participation fee $6,250–$6,750.

Global Service Corps: San Francisco; ☎ 415 551 0000; globalservicecorps.org; co-operates with grass-roots organisations in Thailand, Cambodia and Tanzania and sends volunteers and interns for two or three weeks or longer.

Global Volunteers: St Paul, Minnesota; ☎ 1 800 487 1074; globalvolunteers.org; 'granddaddy of the volunteer vacation movement'.

Globe Aware: Dallas, Texas; ☎ 877 588 4562; globeaware.org; short volunteer vacations in 14 countries including Cuba, Jamaica and Laos.

Heritage Conservation Network: Boulder; ☎ 303 444 0128; heritageconservation.net; interesting independent non-profit that organises volunteer vacations in the form of building and conservation workshops to preserve endangered buildings; past projects have been in Albania, Kenya and the US.

Interexchange: New York; ☎ 1 800 597 3675; workingabroad.org; volunteer placements in Australia, Argentina, Costa Rica, India, Ghana, Namibia, Peru and South Africa.

World Endeavors: Minneapolis, MN: ☎ 612 729 3400; worldendeavors.com; volunteer, internship and study programmes lasting 2 weeks to 2 months in many countries.

GOING IT ALONE

In the course of your travels, you may come across wildlife projects, children's homes, special schools, etc. in which it will be possible to work voluntarily for a short or longer time. You may simply want to join your new Tongan, Turkish or Tanzanian friends in the fields or wherever they are working. You may get the chance to trade your assistance for a straw mat and simple meals but more likely the only rewards will be the experience and the camaraderie.

Some travellers who find themselves in the vicinity of a major disaster, such as the tsunami, think that their assistance will be welcomed. However with no practical skills, they often become a nuisance and a burden both to distressed locals and professional aid workers. If you are spending time in one place in the developing world you can try to make the acquaintance of the aid community who will be plugged into the needs of local NGOs and international agencies. While Till Bruckner was staying in the Sudan he noticed that overseas branches of Oxfam, Save the Children, etc. had huge volumes of reports to write, something that the local staff sometimes struggled to do in polished English.

Part 2
Work Your Way in Europe

UNITED KINGDOM

Many readers of this book will begin to plan their world travels in Britain, and it is in Britain that they will want to save up an initial travelling fund. The amount of savings will vary depending on the ambitiousness of the travel plans and on the individual's willingness to live rough and take risks once he or she sets out. Some people are lucky enough to have a reasonably well paid and stable job as an office temp, postman or software developer before they set out on their adventures and will be in a good position to save. Others will have to gather together as many funds as possible from doing casual work at home before pursuing the same activities abroad.

Readers in other countries will also be interested in the information contained in this chapter if they are planning a working holiday in Britain. Armies of young people, particularly Antipodeans, arrive year round and quickly plug into the network of like-minded travellers looking for work in London and beyond. Everyone knows that London is an expensive city and not a pleasant place for people with few funds. But thousands of young people from overseas overlook its defects for the excitement of spending time in one of the world's great cities.

After several years of very high rates of employment, especially in the south of England, the economic crisis has given rise to alarming increases in unemployment figures, redundancies and failed businesses. Many of the 'new Europeans' who flocked to the UK are returning to their countries, especially Poland. Of the more than half a million Poles who have arrived in the UK to work since Poland joined the EU in 2004, about half have returned home. A telling news report from March 2009 claimed that British nationals were applying in numbers for seasonal farm work that has for many years been done by Eastern European students and migrant workers.

RED TAPE

Nationals of the newly expanded European Union (referred to as the A8 for Accession 8) are entitled to enter Britain to look for work, provided they register with the Worker Registration Scheme, but there are restrictions on their right to benefits. For non-EU citizens, most of whom enter on six-month tourist visas (which can normally be renewed on re-entering the country after an absence), it is difficult to find legal work. In general the Home Office does not issue work permits to unskilled and semi-skilled workers. Until recently, employers seldom asked to see proof of status (though they would ask for your National Insurance number). However a law has been introduced to curb illegal employment by requiring employers to see documentary proof of status and not rely solely on verbal assurances. Still, the UK is not a very bureaucratic country so this practice is not universal.

At the end of 2008, the UK introduced a new five-tiered immigration system based on points. As is true throughout the world, skilled workers must have a job offer in hand before applying for a work permit. Many immigration websites explain all the permutations, such as workpermit.com. The official government site of the UK Border Agency is ukba.homeoffice.gov.uk/workingintheuk (☎ 0870 606 7766 or 0114 207 4074).

Commonwealth nationals who can produce documentary evidence that a parent or grandparent was born in the UK can gain permission to stay and work under the ancestry or patriality rules. After completing five continuous years of work they can apply for UK residency.

Working Holiday Visas

The long established working holiday scheme was radically overhauled at the end of 2008. Only four nationalities are eligible for the new Youth Mobility Scheme (in contrast to the 50

Commonwealth countries previously eligible): Australia, New Zealand, Canada and Japan. These are based on reciprocal visa provisions offered by those countries to British nationals.

To be eligible you must be between the ages of 18 and 30 inclusive with no dependants. The YMS working holiday permit entitles the holder to work in Britain at any job or jobs for up to a maximum of two years. It is essential to apply from outside the UK and you must prove that you have £1600 or equivalent in the bank. Application forms and details are available at ukba.homeoffice.gov.uk; the cost of applying for the visa is £125 (2009/2010).

Other Visas

The Training and Work Experience Scheme (TWES) allows foreign nationals to do work-based training for a professional or specialist qualification, a graduate training programme or work experience. TWES permits are issued to employers on the understanding that the individual will return overseas at the end of the agreed period. Normally, they will not be allowed to transfer to work permit employment. Applications for permits can only be made by employers based in the UK on behalf of the person they wish to employ. Trainees must be paid at the same level as resident workers, i.e. at least the minimum wage.

Non EU-students at bona fide UK educational institutions offering at least 15 hours a week of structured classes are allowed to work up to 20 hours a week during term-time and full-time in the vacations without applying for a work permit. Anyone entering the country as a visitor or tourist who intends to stay longer than a few weeks should have a water-tight story, something Woden Teachout from Vermont had not prepared:

> ***Coming into the UK I had a horribly distressing immigration experience. On the advice of my travel agent, I had bought a six-month return ticket rather than an open return and expected no problems. Everything went awry. I think it was when I wavered over how long I meant to be in the country that the immigration official became suspicious. The lady-turned-ogre forced me to produce my passport, ticket, money, address book and wrote down my entire life's history in cramped cursive on the back of my entrance card. I portrayed myself as a spoilt and privileged child, funded by Mummy and Daddy in her aimless intercontinental wanderings. When she at last grudgingly stamped me into the country, she called after me in a voice thick with derision, 'Do you think you'll ever work for a living?'***

A few weeks later Woden had five different jobs.

SPECIAL SCHEMES AND EXCHANGE ORGANISATIONS

This section describes a number of special schemes for young people from outside the European Union which allow them to work legally in Britain. One example is the Seasonal Agricultural Workers Scheme or SAWS (see section on Harvests). Students and others from EU and non-EU countries may be able to participate in work exchange programmes, many of which charge a substantial placement fee. Careers advisers in universities and colleges should be the best source of information.

A number of commercial companies and non-profit organisations are involved with providing work experience placements to international candidates; for example Interspeak in Cheshire (☎ 01829 250973; interspeak.co.uk) arranges Traineeships (stages) lasting three weeks to six months for students mainly in the fields of marketing, retail, engineering, hotel work and computing; the placement fee is £440–£500. A number of English language schools in the UK run work placement schemes (unpaid) alongside language courses such as Twin School of English in south London (☎ 020 8297 1132; workuk@twinuk.com; workuk.co.uk) which has links with hundreds of companies and hotels throughout the country.

The problem of work permits does not normally arise in the case of voluntary work, though participants will have to have a valid visa to be in Britain (where applicable). Conservation camps and other voluntary projects generally offer an enthusiastic welcome to foreign participants (see section on Volunteering at the end of this chapter). For example the UK's largest volunteering organisation, CSV (☎ 0800 374991; csv.org.uk) runs an overseas programme in which people from 12 partner countries (including Canada and the USA) are placed alongside British volunteers in projects with people who need help, such as children with special needs, adults with learning difficulties, teenagers at risk of offending and homeless people. Volunteers do not need any previous experience, special skills or minimum qualifications to join. During the projects which last from between four and 12 months, food, accommodation and £32 weekly allowance are paid together with travel expenses from the point of entry into the UK. Unfortunately the partner agencies tend to charge high placement fees; for example North Americans must apply through YR Learning Connections in Canada (yourworldtodiscover.ca) and the fee is $2,995.

Many recruitment agencies specialise in bringing EEA nationals to the UK (and to Jersey, the Isle of Man and the Republic of Ireland) to work in hotels (see 'Tourism and Catering' section below). Lots of commercial agencies on the continent sell packaged working holidays to young people. Caution should be exercised when paying over large sums to a mediating agency since some offer a very poor service as Emiliano Giovannoni from Italy explains:

> ***Every year there are hundreds of Italian, French, German and Spanish guys and girls who get to London, 'thanks' to the service of some unscrupulous agencies which operate in these countries and have the monopoly on 'advising' youngsters. These agencies charge enormous fees, promising jobs, accommodation and English lessons which they don't always deliver. I have met very many people in London who, after having paid a lot of money, had to live with rats and, after weeks, still haven't been given the chance of attending one interview for a job which they usually ended up finding themselves or thanks to the local Jobcentre. All this just because they did not have access to some genuine information.***

Working Holidays for Americans

The drastic immigration changes that were implemented in November 2008 spelled the end of the long-lived Work in Britain Program managed by BUNAC. The programme is currently closed though BUNAC is hopeful that an agreement can be reached in the future to reinstate the programme in some form or other.

US students and early-career professionals who have been offered a full-time position in the UK in their field of study or experience may apply for a work permit through the Association for International Practical Training (☎ 410 997 2200; aipt.org).

The Mountbatten Institute in New York (☎ 212 557 5380; mountbatten.org) offers a reciprocal programme to American graduates who want to become business interns in London for 12 months.

US citizens who wish to spend seven weeks from mid-June volunteering in a social service programme in Great Britain (e.g. working with inner city youth, the elderly, homeless and people with mental health problems) and then travel independently for two weeks should request an application from the Winant & Clayton Volunteers (☎ 212 378 0271; winantclaytonvolunteer.org). Free room and board are provided, and the volunteer pays all travel expenses (approximately $3,500).

Working Holidays for Commonwealth Nationals

As mentioned, Canadian students can apply for a Youth Mobility Scheme permit independently or, if they want the security of a package arrangement, they may participate in the Student Work Abroad Programme (SWAP) for C$435/$505.

Various backpacker agencies in Australia, etc. have links with London agencies and sell packages that make arrival and the initial job hunt much easier. Overseas Working Holidays (owh.com.au) part of Student Flights with various offices in Australia sells starter parks to working holiday makers bound for London and operates a scheme called Pub Work UK which brings together many British pubs, mostly in London, looking to employ Australians and New Zealanders who either have a UK passport or a Youth Mobility visa for the UK.

Tax

One clear advantage of obtaining legal working holiday status is that you are entitled to apply for a National Insurance number from the local Jobcentre Plus (☎ 0845 600 0643) which you should promptly do. Single people are entitled to a personal allowance of £6,475 per year (2009/10) after which they start paying 20% in income tax, though under the PAYE system (Pay As You Earn) you may have tax deducted straightaway, which you will have to reclaim if you earn less than your personal allowance in the tax year starting on April 6th.

Foreign nationals can claim the personal allowances if they have been in the UK for at least 183 days in any tax year. If the total is less than 183 days, they may be able to claim as a foreign national and/or resident of a country with which the UK has a double taxation agreement. HM Revenue and Customs maintains a clear and informative website (hmrc.gov.uk). If you may need to claim, keep all tax documents such as the P60 (end-of-year tax certificate). When you finish work, send both parts of the P45 which your employer has to give you to your employer's tax office. When you are ready to leave Britain and want to claim a tax rebate, complete and submit form P85, a leaving certificate which asks your intentions with respect to returning to the UK to work. Always take the precaution of making photocopies of any forms you send to the tax office for the purposes of chasing later, and be prepared to wait at least six weeks. You can make things easier for yourself by using an accountancy firm that specialises in tax rebates. They normally keep a percentage (about 18%) of whatever they get back for you. Try for example one of the London firms that advertise in the expat press like 1st Contact (1stcontact-taxrefunds.com) and Taxback (taxback.co.uk).

Foreign students are treated the same as UK students and can be exempted from tax. They should ask their employer for a P38(S) form which exempts students from paying tax on vacation earnings.

In addition to income tax, you must also pay National Insurance Contributions of 11% on taxable earnings above £95 a week (2009/10). Foreign students of English or agriculture (who can present a certificate in English from their institution proving that they are studying these subjects) can apply for an exemption.

EMPLOYMENT PROSPECTS

At the time of writing, the British economy was in disarray with unemployment escalating and many businesses failing. The foreign job seeker will now have to compete with many professionals and workers who have been made redundant, though seasonal and temporary vacancies can be found in agriculture, tourism, childcare and so on.

The National Minimum Wage from April 2009 is £5.73 per hour for workers over 22, £4.77 for workers aged 18–21. For details contact the NMW helpline 0845 6000 678 or check the government website berr.gov.uk. Unless you are very lucky in finding cheap accommodation, it will be very difficult to save on these wages especially in Southeast England where the cost of living is higher than elsewhere.

Temp Agencies

Thousands of employment agencies do business in the UK, though times are tough for them with so many businesses cutting costs. Manpower and Select Recruitment are among the biggest general agencies with dozens of branches in London alone and many more nationwide. Blue Arrow has an industrial division that signs up students and others to carry out casual cleaning, packing and warehouse work.

COLIN ROTHWELL FROM SOUTH AFRICA FOUND INDUSTRIAL AGENCY WORK A VERY SATISFACTORY WAY TO SAVE FOR HIS FUTURE TRAVELS, THOUGH HE COULDN'T STOMACH ALL HIS ASSIGNMENTS:

In England I found the easiest way to find work was through temping agencies. However, it was also the most inconvenient way as they liked you to have an address and a phone number. They were also the biggest sharks around and you got paid half the going wage as they took a very healthy cut from your hard-earned blood, sweat and tears. It did have its advantages though; you worked when and where it suited you, and some agencies sent you all over the place to do all kinds of weird jobs. For example, the worst job I did on my whole trip was at a dog meat factory. You arrived at the crack of dawn and were sent into a massive fridge where you were met with tons of semi-defrosting offal, with blood everywhere, and a stench like you wouldn't believe. So, as desperate for money as I was, I only lasted two days.

Catering agencies abound and anyone with a background as a chef will probably be in demand. (See section below Tourism & Catering.) Temping allows a great deal of flexibility, though most agencies you approach will want to be reassured that you are not about to flit off somewhere. Most will ask foreign temps for evidence of permission to work.

One recommended agency for people with working holiday visas or EU nationality is Workabout in Dorset (☎ 0871 222 4036; workabout.uk.com) which has separate departments for placing people in hospitality positions and as home helps. The Australian-linked temp agency Bligh Appointments (70 North End Road, West Kensington, London W14 9EP; ☎ 020 7603 6123; info@bligh.co.uk) always has vacancies for childcare assistants, PAs and secretaries and welcomes travellers.

Adverts

As each year goes by, fewer job ads appear in newspapers and more on recruitment websites like justjobs4students.co.uk. Gumtree.com and http://london.craigslist.co.uk/ carry hundreds of job ads for London. Several free weekly newspapers and magazines in London aimed at the expat communities, mainly of Australians, New Zealanders and South Africans, can prove to be excellent sources of casual jobs for anyone. Look for distribution boxes for *TNT* (tntmagazine.com) outside tube stations, travel agencies, etc. Recruitment agencies advertise for nurses and professionals in accountancy, banking, IT, law, etc. but unskilled and semi-skilled jobs as mother's helps, in call centres, bars and farms are also advertised.

One job that is advertised aggressively (possibly because there is such a high turnover) is as a 'charity fundraiser'. Commercial companies are regularly hired by mainstream and other charities to raise money on the streets of British cities. Companies like Flow Caritas (flowcaritas.co.uk), Dialogue Direct (dialoguedirect.co.uk) and Inspired People (inspiredpeople.org) use worthy sounding lines such as 'championing the search for a better world' in their bid to hire an army of young people to accost passers-by and try to persuade them to sign direct debit donation forms. This activity has been dubbed 'charity mugging' and hence the employees are sometimes referred to as 'chuggers'. A high percentage of those hired are foreign young people on working holiday visas, including 18-year-old David Cox from Ontario who was hired soon after arriving in London. He was invited to attend a day's training in Oxford before being dispatched to his first location, and looked forward to a chance to see different places:

> ***The last three weeks have been very interesting, but I'm starting to get into the swing of things. So far I've been posted in Brighton, Portsmouth and Newcastle areas and am leaving for Manchester tonight. I love the job but it's literally 7 days a week and can be very stressful so I'm looking forward to time off, I'm going to Norway in 2 weeks.***

Not everybody ends up loving the job by any means. Anna Ling was attracted partly by idealism to do this job in Bristol but came to consider it iniquitous since so much of the money raised goes to the 'middle-men'. In 2008 she was paid £4 an hour plus a commission per donor.

HARVESTS

The principal fruit growing areas of Britain are: the Vale of Evesham over to the Wye and Usk Valleys; most of Kent; Lincolnshire and East Anglia, especially the Fens around Wisbech; and north of the Tay Estuary (Blairgowrie, Forfar). But there is intensive agricultural activity in most parts of Britain so always check with the Jobcentre or Farmers' Union in the area(s) where you are interested in finding farm work. The annual *Summer Jobs Worldwide* lists a number of British fruitgrowers, some of whom need more than 100 pickers. Harvest dates are not standard throughout the country, since the raspberries of Inverness-shire ripen at least two or three weeks later than the raspberries on the Isle of Wight; nor are the starting dates the same from one year to the next.

Some of the biggest agricultural employers in the country belong to the Seasonal Agricultural Workers Scheme (SAWS) which is an approved means of hiring foreign nationals. At the moment the scheme is open only to Bulgarian and Romanian nationals. The quota for 2009 is 21,500 workers who are distributed among the nine participating organisations like the huge soft-fruit farm in the Norfolk Broads, R & JM Place (ifctunstead.co.uk) and specialist agencies like Fruitful Ltd in Evesham. Participating agencies and farms are linked from the SAWS site (ukba.homeoffice.gov.uk/workingintheuk/eea/saws/agents).

Agricultural Agencies

SAWS agencies that recruit on behalf of farms throughout the United Kingdom are:

HOPS Labour Solutions: c/o National Federation of Young Farmers' Clubs, YFC Centre, Stoneleigh Park, Kenilworth, Warwickshire CV8 2LG; ☎ 02476 857206; hopsgb@nfyfc.org.uk; hopsgb.org.uk.

Concordia (YSV) Ltd: 19 North Street, Portslade, East Sussex, BN41 1DH; ☎ 01273 422293; info@concordia-ysv-org.uk; concordiafarms.org; non-profit organisation.

Fruitful Ltd: Unit 3, Honeybourne Industrial Estate, Evesham, WR11 7QF; ☎ 0870 727 0050; info@fruitfuljobs.com; fruitfuljobs.com.

Sastak Ltd: 1–7, BDC, Long Lane, Craven Arms, Salop, SY7 8DZ; ☎ 01588 673636; SAWS@sastak.com; sastak.com; recruits on behalf of farms in Shropshire and Staffordshire.

CARISA FEY, AN 18-YEAR OLD GERMAN TRAVELLER, JOINED THE RANKS OF THE AGRICULTURAL WORKERS IN THE EAST OF ENGLAND AFTER ANSWERING AN ADVERT IN *TNT* MAGAZINE:

Together with a South African girl I'd met in Scotland, I went to Wisbech, the most boring place on earth. So we didn't mind working 12 hours every day with 1½ hours to and from work. We managed to save around £100 each a week. And working in the factories wasn't that bad; one just has to entertain oneself. It is very easy to get a job in the factories through the agencies that advertise. The good thing is that they handle everything like accommodation, job, bank account, but you have to be lucky to find a fair one. If you have enough money for your own job search, go to the Jobcentre in Peterborough or Wisbech or ask at the factories directly.

The press frequently reports cases of exploitation, particularly of foreign workers with little knowledge of English. A large proportion of employment in UK agriculture is in the hands of the unattractively named 'gangmasters'. If you are concerned that you may be getting involved with something dodgy, make sure that your employer is licensed under the Gangmasters (Licensing) Act 2004 whose site has a searchable database of approved agencies.

Another agricultural recruitment agency which specialises in placing working holidaymakers is called WOWO, Wapsbourne Manor Farm, Sheffield Park, Uckfield, East Sussex TN22 3QT (☎ 01825 723414; assignments@wowo.co.uk; wowo.co.uk). This agency, attached to a campsite, places candidates in grounds maintenance and food packing jobs in the area; most jobs come with caravan or other accommodation. Overtime is sometimes available, though new legislation will make that more difficult. For other leads, check adverts in *TNT* or *New Zealand News*. Caution is always required when accepting a picking job since conditions are notoriously rough and earnings can be disappointing if you are inexperienced.

The organisation WWOOF UK (World Wide Opportunities on Organic Farms) maintains a list of 350+ farm hosts throughout the UK who offer free room and board in exchange for help. Membership costs £20 (£30 for a couple) and entitles you to a copy of the their list (printed or online); details from WWOOF UK, PO Box 2154, Winslow, Buckingham MK18 3WS (wwoofers@wwoof.org.uk; wwoof.org.uk).

TOURISM AND CATERING

Despite its infamous weather and cuisine, Britain attracts millions of tourists from abroad as well as an increasing number of Britons holidaying at home because of the weak pound. It has been estimated that one in ten of the employed labour force of Britain is involved in the tourist industry.

Wages in the hotel trade are notoriously low, and exploitation is common, though the introduction of the minimum wage has alleviated the situation for the lowest paid. Hotel staff with silver service or other specialist experience can expect to earn a decent wage as can restaurant staff in London. People who are available for the whole season, say April to October, will find it much easier to land a job than those available only for the peak months of July and August. Most hotels prefer to receive a formal written application in the early part of the year, complete with photos and references; however it can never hurt to telephone (especially later in the spring) to find out what the situation is. Anyone who has acquired the Basic Food Hygiene Certificate online or in person will have an advantage when looking for catering work. As usual, many companies use online recruitment sites such as hospitalitystaff.co.uk.

Many training and exchange organisations place foreign students in hotel jobs including the following:

European Work Experience Programme Ltd: Unit 1, Red Lion Court, Alexandra Road, Hounslow, Middlesex, TW3 1JS; ☎ 020 8 572 2993; ewep.com; assist young EU nationals to find jobs in hotels, fast food restaurants, etc.; fee £271.

Exchange Training Communication International (ETCi): 248 High St, Beckenham, Kent BR3 1DZ; ☎ 020 8663 0055; etci.co.uk.

Working holidaymakers should be able to fix up work in bars, cafés, hotels, etc. without going through a mediating agency. Twenty-two year old Sarah Zimmerman from the US decided to support herself in the UK by picking up jobs, but encountered a few problems she hadn't anticipated when her first job was in a fancy hotel:

> ***You'd think it would be easier for me since I understand English, but no, the entire menu and bistro – everything was in French, I couldn't even figure out what the word for green bean was! And, I know they said that the head chef was speaking English, but I begged to differ because I have yet to understand a word he shouted at me. The others whom I worked with from Austria, Poland, Sweden and Venezuela were very nice and seemed to grasp it all better.***

Sarah set off to find a job in a non-French-speaking environment but wasn't convinced it was preferable: *'The English are self-proclaimed laid-back people, so maybe that is why it takes so long to secure something. I had a trial day at a funky/expensive bakery/restaurant that really was fun, minus the two-hour lunch rush where I was serving hot food and felt so much like a cafeteria lady from elementary school that I almost asked where my hair net was!'*

Pubs

Live-in pubs abound throughout England, especially in London and the Southeast with a sprinkling further afield. Staff work 39–45 hours a week with a couple of days off, and usually earn the minimum wage. Many people work some evenings in a pub in addition to their day job to boost their finances for future travelling. The Original London Pub Co (londonpubau.com) with its main office in Melbourne and branches in the UK, New Zealand and Canada can sort out jobs for individuals and couples before arrival for a fixed fee of $595. As usual experienced cooks and chefs are always in demand.

Waiting for an ad to appear is usually less productive than going pub to pub. An American traveller found himself nearly penniless in the popular tourist town of Pitlochry in Perthshire and made the rounds of the pubs asking for work. In each case the management were either fully staffed or were too concerned about his lack of a work permit. He claims that in the 34th and final pub, they asked him if he were free to start work that minute, and he gleefully stepped behind the bar and began work, without knowing shandy from Guinness. Americans may need to be reminded that you do not get tips in a British pub though you may be bought a drink now and then. Americans often have trouble with the different accents they will encounter as Woden Teachout found:

'I had a hard time deciphering the orders over the music; "Bakes" does not sound remotely like "Becks" to the American ear.'

Scotland

Although unemployment is traditionally higher in Scotland than England, plenty of tourist-related jobs are available.

CARISA FEY FROM GERMANY IS JUST ONE TRAVELLER FROM THE CONTINENT WHO WAS INSTANTLY SMITTEN WITH SCOTLAND:

Before all my money was gone I took the bus up to Scotland because I heard that it would be very easy to get a job in the highlands in a hotel. As the bus came through Aviemore on my way to Inverness it was love at first sight. One visit to the Jobcentre in Inverness and two days later I was back in Aviemore to work at the Freedom Inn plus extra nights at the Cairngorm Lodge (better paid but less fun). My planned stay of three months worked out to be ten and by the time I left I was speaking with a Scottish accent, could clean a room in record speed, carry four plates and still talk normally after consuming an amount of alcohol that would kill an average middle European man. I had a wonderful time.

Agents sometimes advertise in London for live-in hotel work in Scotland. Keith Flynn answered such an ad (livein-jobs.co.uk), and ended up working in an isolated place ten miles from the nearest town and with no public transport, which made it an ideal place to save money: *'I saw Dee Cooper's advert and decided to ring up. Basically you just call and say what job you do, e.g. kitchen porter, bar, waiter/waitress and she gives you a list of vacancies around Scotland at no cost to you.'*

Paul Binfield from Kent travelled further north in Scotland and was rewarded with a healthy choice of casual work in the Orkney Islands:

> ***Unemployment here is about 3% and from March to September there is an absolute abundance of summer jobs. We worked in one of the several youth hostels on the islands, have done voluntary work for the Orkney Seal Rescue and I am currently earning a very nice wage working at the historical site Skara Brae on a three-month contract. There is loads of seasonal work available in hotels and bars, cutting grass for the Council and other garden contracts, etc.***

Holiday Camps and Activity Centres

Anyone with a qualification in canoeing, yachting, climbing, etc. should be able to find summer work as an instructor. The 24 centres that belong to the British Activity Holidays Association (baha.org.uk) are a good starting point and the BAHA website has a useful link to Job Vacancies.

Plenty of jobs as general assistants exist for sports-minded young people, especially at children's multi-activity centres. Suzanne Phillips, who worked at an adventure centre in North Devon, claims that 'a person's character and personality are far more important than their qualifications'. The pay is not high but may be supplemented by an end-of-season bonus at some centres. Applicants intending to work with children will be asked to undergo a CRB check and foreign candidates will have to show police clearance forms. Normally it is the responsibility of the employer rather than the individual to apply to the Criminal Records Bureau (CRB). The standard fee charged for a CRB disclosure is £31 and an enhanced disclosure costs £36. Further details are available from crb.gov.uk or on the CRB Information Line ☎ 0870 90 90 811. One of the largest employers is PGL Travel, with a staggering 2,500 vacancies for activity instructors, group leaders, etc. for its 30 UK holiday centres. The season lasts from February to October though most vacancies are for the summer season. PGL's Recruitment Team can be contacted at: Alton Court, Penyard Lane, Ross-on-Wye, Herefordshire HR9 5GL (☎ 0870 401 4411; recruitment@pgl.co.uk; pgl.co.uk/recruitment).

Many activity holiday centres also double as English language camps for children from abroad. These also need a range of support and leadership staff in addition to EFL teachers (see list in section on Teaching below).

Here are some holiday activity centres that may require domestic as well as leadership staff:

Barracudas Summer Activity Camps: St Ives, Cambs; ☎ 01480 497533; jobs@barracudas.co.uk; 150 activity instructors, 50 arts and crafts instructors, 150 group co-ordinators, 50 lifeguards, etc. for residential and day camps throughout southern England; 6 weeks of school holidays only.

EAC Activity Camps: Edinburgh; ☎ 0131 477 7574; activitycamps.com; 100 activity staff for July/August camps in Scotland and England; accommodation is not provided.

Kingswood Learning & Leisure: kingswoodjobs.co.uk; 250 'adventure jobs' at 12 educational activity centres on the Isle of Wight, north Norfolk coast, etc.; also hire large numbers of seasonal staff for residential camps run by Camp Beaumont.

Supercamps: Abingdon, Oxon; supercamps.co.uk/join_the_team/index.asp; well-paid specialist instructor jobs and many others.

For catering, domestic and other work at family holiday centres try Butlins with centres in Bognor Regis, Minehead and Skegness, Pontins who hire for six coastal family holiday centres (careers-pontins.com), and HF Holidays based in the Lake District offering activity and special interest holidays at country house hotels (hfholidays.co.uk/recruitment). Butlins along with Warner Breaks, Haven and British Holidays all belong to the Bourne Leisure Group which is responsible for hiring 12,000 staff (bournejobs.co.uk).

Theme parks like Alton Towers and Legoland have large seasonal staff requirements, though do not offer accommodation. As well as filling the usual skivvying jobs, they require ride operators, entertainers for both children and adults, lifeguards, DJs, shop assistants, etc.

Youth Hostels

Hundreds of general assistants are employed by the Youth Hostels Association (England and Wales) from March to October each year, and they have launched a dedicated job site hokey-cokey-jobs.co.uk. to help in the running of YHA's 193 youth hostels in the UK. The job can involve cooking for large numbers, general cleaning, cash handling and some clerical work. Accommodation and food are provided along with a basic salary.

There are also a number of independent hostels and budget accommodation around the country. Three hundred of these are listed in the pocket-sized *Independent Hostel Guide* from the Backpackers Press, in Derbyshire (☎ 01629 580427; backpackerspress.com), at a cost of £4.95 (plus £1 postage). The hostel listings are searchable online. Independent hostels are a good source of temporary work, often providing a few hours a day of work in return for bed and board.

Special Events

Events such as the Henley Regatta in June, Test Matches at Headingley in Leeds, the Edinburgh Festival in August/September and a host of golf tournaments and county shows need temporary staff to work as car park attendants, ticket sellers and in catering. Sporting events like the British Open and Wimbledon employ a myriad of casual workers. Ask the local tourist information office for a list of upcoming events and contact the organisers.

Outside catering and other companies which hold the contracts for staffing special events include:

Events Staff Ltd: 25 York Road, Northampton NN1 5QA; ☎ 01604 627775; 1000+ stewards, programme sellers, car park and security staff for racing fixtures, etc.

FMC (Facilities Management Catering Ltd): Church Road, Wimbledon, London SW19 5AE; ☎ 020 8971 2465; fmccatering.co.uk; one of the largest outdoor caterers in Europe which has contracts with Wimbledon, the Oval and Chelsea Football Club.

Leapfrog International: Riding Court Farm, Datchet, Berks SL3 9JU; ☎ 01753 580880; crew@leapfrog-int.co.uk; events crew for family fun days, etc.; pay is £55 a day for first three events, £75 thereafter.

Compass Group: http://compass.peoplebank.com; bar and waiting staff for sports events.

If mass catering and cleaning seem a little tame, more interesting possibilities for entrepreneurs crop up at major events, especially at such a buzzy event as the Edinburgh Fringe Festival:

NICOLE GLUCKSTERN FROM THE US DISCOVERED POSSIBILITIES AT THE EDINBURGH FESTIVAL:

Work available breaks down into two basic categories: street vending and theatre work. Street vendors of jewelry, hairwraps, caricatures, etc. should bring their own supplies and a RAINCOAT. In theory you need a permit which has to be applied for one year in advance. In practice, as long as you don't set up on the high street, you can set up shop anywhere, until you get moved along by the (generally sympathetic) cops. Wait half an hour and set up again.

Theatre work itself is for technicians and flunkies who sell tix, make popcorn, mop floors (how much theatre experience do you need?). If you just breeze into town the week before the festival you can probably find work pasting up posters all over town; otherwise you probably have to do some advance planning. Unless you live in Bohunk Montana, you might try to find a group in your hometown who's going and offer to work as an unpaid assistant. Every group is required to bring a stage manager but a lot of them find it hard to find one at the last minute. Unlike rock festivals or Christmas markets, working the Fringe is not going to make you any fortunes but the sheer value of the experience is well worth going out of your way for.

Keith Larner recommends a variation on the classic summer job of erecting marquees for weddings and parties (see section Building and Other Seasonal Work below): *'Now I can tell you about another good avenue for casual work. I've just completed a job erecting temporary grandstands for sporting events such as golf, racing and tennis. It is very physical work, extremely heavy-going, but financially rewarding because you work 7 days per week (but only between April and October).'*

Less financially rewarding but probably a lot more fun would be to attend the Glastonbury Festival as a steward as part of a team of Oxfam volunteers. Last year Oxfam recruited 1,400 stewards who are guaranteed entry to the famous Somerset festival that takes place in the third week of June. For details go to oxfam.org.uk and search for Glastonbury. Litter picker-uppers are taken on for summer music festivals like Womad either paid or as volunteers; see eventrecycling.co.uk/workForUs.html.

CHILDCARE AND DOMESTIC

The radical restructuring of the immigration rules that took place in 2008 has had a significant impact on the au pair programme. To quote the UK Border Agency website: 'Au Pairs: This immigration category closed on 26 November 2008. Please refer to the Youth Mobility Scheme under tier 5 of the points-based system.' Whereas large numbers of au pairs used to arrive (legally) from non-EU countries like Turkey and Croatia, those nationalities are now banned. Few candidates from the Youth Mobility countries of Canada, Australia, New Zealand and Japan are interested in au pairing. European Union nationals are of course free to work as au pairs or anything else. The great majority of au pairs comes from the EU accession countries of Slovakia, Hungary, etc. Special rules apply to Bulgarian and Romanian nationals (see ukba.homeoffice.gov.uk).

Although the Home Office no longer acknowledges the au pair category, its old guidelines are deeply ingrained in the system. They stipulated that au pairs should work caring for children and doing light housework for no more than 25 hours and five days a week, plus a couple of evenings of babysitting. The recommended pocket money for au pairs is currently £55–£65 a week; this category of work has been declared exempt from minimum wage regulations.

Young women and, increasingly, men wishing to become mother's helps or nannies have a good chance of succeeding since the market in this field is booming, especially in the Home Counties. An untrained, unqualified child carer can expect to be paid at least £100 a week in addition to room and board. Mothers' helps with some experience often earn twice this amount and nannies even more.

Nannying in the UK is the option that many young women from Australia and New Zealand choose, partly because it takes care of accommodation and pays a good wage. Those with the Youth Mobility visa can make use of agencies or answer private ads.

If you decide to register with one of the approved agencies, your references will be verified and a police check will be carried out on you. Two good websites to use with links to established nanny and au pair agencies are bestbear.co.uk and nannyjob.co.uk. A couple of London agencies now specialise in supplying male live-in childcare: The Manny Service (☎ 020 8141 5224; mannyservice.co.uk) and My Big Buddy (mybigbuddyinfo@yahoo.co.uk).

If you want a live-in position but not looking after children, many agencies specialise in providing carers for the elderly and disabled, for example Cura Domi-Care at Home in Surrey (☎ 01483 420055; curadomi.co.uk) pays £350–£450 a week to residential care workers. Oxford Aunts is another venerable agency in this field (☎ 01865 791017; enquiries@oxfordaunts.co.uk).

TEACHING

Although there is a veritable epidemic of English language schools along the south coast and in places like Oxford and Cambridge, you may find it more difficult to get a job as a language tutor in Torquay than in Taipei, harder in Brighton than in Bogota. It takes more than a tidy appearance to get one of the well-paid summer jobs at one of the 500+ summer language schools operating in Britain. But with the weak pound, it is predicted that English learners from the Eurozone will arrive in increasing numbers.

The majority of language schools in Britain insist that their teachers have a formal qualification in TEFL (Teaching English as a Foreign Language) or at the very least a university degree, teacher's certificate or fluency in a foreign language. If you satisfy any or all of these requirements you should apply to a number of language schools several months prior to the summer holiday period. The average salary for certificate-qualified EFL teachers is £250–£310 per week. Many employers provide staff accommodation for which there will be a deduction from wages.

If you lack the necessary qualifications to teach, you might still consider blitzing the language schools, since many of them also run a programme of outings and entertainments for their foreign students and they may need non-teaching supervisors and sports instructors. Working at one of these language summer schools is an excellent way of making contact with Italian, French and Spanish young people who might offer advice or even hospitality once you set off on your travels.

The 400 English language schools and colleges accredited by the British Council are linked from the website of English UK (arels.org.uk). These schools employ qualified or experienced teaching staff. Schools are located throughout the UK, but are concentrated in the South-East, London, Oxford and Cambridge.

Here is a short list of major language course organisations which normally offer a large number of summer vacancies:

Anglo Continental Educational Group: Bournemouth; ☎ 01202 557414; anglo-continental.com; up to 100 EFL teachers for adult summer courses and 20 for adolescents.

Ardmore Language Schoo:l ☎ 01628 826699; jobs@theardmoregroup.com; ardmore-language-schools.com/work.html; residential multi-activity and English language camps for overseas children throughout the UK.

Concorde International Summer Schools: Canterbury; ☎ 01227 451035; concorde-int.com/recruitment; 150 teachers; £300 per week + holiday pay in return for 15 hours teaching and 6 activities per week; full board residential accommodation is available; experience and TEFL qualification required.

Discovery Summer: Kensington, London; ☎ 020 7937 1199; discoversummer.co.uk; summer courses for children/teenagers at five residential centres in England employing 40 live-in activity leaders and teachers.

EF International Language Schools: London SE1; ☎ 020 7401 8399; large number of EFL teachers for residential courses.

EJO Ltd: Hampshire; ☎ 01428 751549; ejo.co.uk/employ.asp; teachers needed at peak time (July) for about a dozen centres around England; 2–4 weeks minimum.

Embassy CES: embassyces.com; 22 summer schools need teachers and activity staff; basic pay (2009) for non-residential activity leaders is £220 per week up to age 22; accommodation can be provided for £30 per week.

Pilgrims English Language Courses: Canterbury and Oxford; ☎ 01865 258336; recruitment@pilgrims.co.uk; teachers and programme staff.

Project International: 20 Fitzroy Square, London, WIT 6EJ; ☎ 020 7916 2522; recruitment@projectinternational.uk.com; projectinternational.uk.com/employment.html; in-coming youth tour operator with ten centres from Liverpool to Dover.

Thames Valley Summer Schools: Windsor; ☎ 01753 852001; english@thamesvalley-summer.co.uk.

The shortage of certified teachers for primary and secondary schools in deprived areas is still acute, both in London and elsewhere. Many local Education Authorities, mainly in inner and outer London, are constantly in need of supply or temporary short-term teachers who are paid a daily rate ranging from £115 to £140.

APPLYING LOCALLY

British readers may decide that it is easiest to save money by working close to home. If you have had no luck through the Jobcentre, by answering online or newspaper adverts or by registering with private employment agencies, you may want to spread your net even wider. The *Yellow Pages* are an invaluable source of potential employers in anything from market gardening to market research. Personal visits are also a good idea, for example to the personnel managers of large department stores, supermarkets, national retailing chains, fast food restaurants or canneries in your area, especially as summer approaches.

Although Woden Teachout, a young travelling American woman, did not have the benefit of a work permit, she pieced together several jobs in Cambridge within a couple of weeks: *'In my terror at my shrinking funds, I accumulated five jobs: two cleaning, one nannying, one behind the bar at a red plush Turkish nightclub and one (which has stood me well) as a personal assistant to a professor.'* The latter job, which was advertised on a notice board at the Graduate Student Centre, was by far the most interesting and also lucrative. Similar notices for research assistants are posted in universities around the world, mostly in department offices and teaching buildings rather than in student unions.

Medical Experiments

There are between 50 and 100 clinical research units in the UK, many of which rely on testing their drugs on human volunteers. The demand for willing volunteers is so great that some of the larger pharmaceutical companies like GlaxoSmithKline advertise in the mainstream media. The case in 2006 of six healthy volunteers suffering catastrophic organ failure after acting as guinea pigs for a leukaemia drug has done damage to the reputation of clinical drug testing, and fewer volunteers have been coming forward. Drug testing is of course very carefully monitored and overseen by ethical committees, but the case at London's Northwick Park Hospital proved that safety cannot be guaranteed. Less dramatically many people fear that the long-term consequences of taking unlicensed drugs cannot be safely predicted.

Nevertheless many people rely on drug testing as a regular source of income, earning as much as £200 a day, or £2,000 for a complete trial. Most company literature states that expenses will be reimbursed, but payment is normally more generous than this. To obtain details about GSK's programme of experiments in Cambridge and London, see volunteers.gsk.co.uk. Other clinics to try include:

Chiltern Research Unit: Slough; ☎ 01753 512000; volunteer@chiltern.com; chiltern.com.

Parexel Clinical Pharmacology Research Unit: Northwick Park Hospital, Harrow; ☎ 0800 389 8930; drugtrial@parexel.com; drugtrial.co.uk.

Hammersmith Medicines Research: Cumberland Avenue, London NW10 7EW; ☎ 0800 783 8792; recruit@hmrlondon.com; londontrials.com.

Quintiles (GDRU Ltd): Guys Drug Research Unit, London; ☎ 0800 634 1132; ☎ 020 7910 7777; areyoutheanswer.com.

Kingshill Research Centre: Victoria Hospital, Okus Road, Swindon SN1 4HZ; ☎ 01793 437519; kingshill-research.org; specialist studies in memory and dementia.

LCG Bioscience: Bourn Hall Clinic, Bourn, Cambridgeshire; ☎ 0800 833399; lcg-bioscience.com.

Richmond Pharmacology Volunteer Recruitment: ☎ 0800 085 6464; trials4us.co.uk.

Roche: Welwyn Garden City; ☎ 0800 212 469; rocheuk.com/healthyvolunteer.

Covance Clinical Research Ltd: Leeds; ☎ 0800 591570.

Charles River Clinical Services: Tranent near Edinburgh; ☎ 01875 614545; seen advertising in 2009 for female volunteers to participate in a 23-day residential trial for £2,200 plus travel expenses.

DDS (Drug Development Solutions): Ninewells Hospital, Dundee; ☎ 0800 838249; getpaidtoparticipate.com.

ICON Development Solutions: Manchester; ☎ 0800 328 8000/ 0161 232 0391; iconvolunteer.com.

Simbec Research Ltd: Merthyr Tydfil, South Wales; ☎ 0800 691995; volunteer-research.com.

Veeda Clinical Research: Plymouth; ☎ 01752 772111; veedacr.com.

In some cases, volunteer subjects must produce a medical certificate from their own doctor attesting to their good health, and in most cases foreign volunteers must prove that they are in the country legally. Reluctantly Rob Abblett signed up for a study of hay fever tablets in his home town (Leicester) to revive his flagging fortunes between world trips: *'Lots of blood samples and lots of TV. Thankfully, my veins are too fine so I won't be making a career out of this. I'll get about £950 if I last the distance from 16th June to 11th July. This includes two nights residential and two return visits each week.'*

The majority of opportunities are in London. If you qualify as a participant for a current trial, you will be asked to attend for screening by the volunteer recruitment officer. After passing the screening (you must have taken no medications or drugs in the previous fortnight), you must undertake to abstain faithfully from nicotine, alcohol, tea, coffee, cola and chocolate for 48 hours on either side of the test. Between swallowing the experimental medications and having tests (e.g. blood tests, blood pressure, etc.), you will be given meals and entertained with television and DVDs (perhaps not *Zombie Flesheater*, *Coma* or *Love at First Bite*). If the thought of subjecting your body to unknown drugs upsets you, then psychological experiments provide an easier (if less lucrative) alternative. Psychology researchers constantly need large numbers of volunteers and often receive grants specifically to pay subjects. It is worth enquiring at any university's psychology department about this opportunity.

Men who at one time would have unthinkingly donated sperm in exchange for a small fee (normally £17–£20 once accepted, plus expenses) now have to register their details so that the children born subsequently can trace their genetic fathers. More than two-thirds of prospective donors are rejected. For the nearest clinic, see the website of the National Gamete Donation Trust (ngdt.co.uk). The London Women's Clinic on Harley Street (lwclinic.co.uk) describes itself as the 'nation's premier sperm bank'.

Building and Other Seasonal Work

The building trade is in the doldrums with the collapse of the housing market, so there is little chance of picking up casual or even skilled work for some time to come.

You may have better luck finding work building temporary rather than permanent structures. The work of erecting marquees is strenuous and pays fairly well, especially since time spent travelling to the destination is also paid, and there is usually plenty of overtime. Try, for example, Field and Lawn (Marquees) Ltd who operate throughout the UK with offices near Leeds, Edinburgh, Glasgow, London and Bristol (fieldandlawn.com). The company Danco based in Bristol has a history of hiring backpackers for marquee erecting (danco.co.uk/employment). Check the local *Yellow Pages* for other firms to contact.

Certain agricultural jobs are very seasonal in nature, such as turkey plucking in December.

ERIC MACKNESS BRAVED THE GRUELLING JOB OF WORKING ON A CHRISTMAS TREE PLANTATION IN OXFORDSHIRE FOR ONE MONTH FROM NOVEMBER 10TH:
I was recruited at the end of the summer tourist season on Sark by an Irish company which has outlets in Ireland, Scotland and Kent as well as Abingdon near Oxford where I worked. The job consists of sorting, pricing and loading Christmas trees. It's not that well paid an hour but because of the potential for working a hideous number of hours (80–90 a week with no days off) it is possible to earn a tidy sum. Accommodation is provided and the food is excellent. The work was the hardest I have ever done (and I have done some hard jobs). Working on top of a trailer loaded with frozen trees in a snowstorm is not for the faint-hearted.

Apparently many of the workers return from one year to the next, but new vacancies do crop up with the Emerald Group; applications to the Irish office in Wexford (☎ +353 53 912 2033; emeraldgroup.ie).

LONDON

Most new arrivals in the capital report that there is no shortage of work. The problem is finding affordable accommodation which allows you to save from what is seldom a startlingly good wage. Ian Mitselburg from Sydney went through the usual processes: *'The first job I got was through a hostel notice board: labouring for a shifty hotel owner, who was restoring his hotel in the Paddington/Bayswater area (where else?) for a few weeks, paid cash-in-hand. After that I worked through an agency in Earl's Court run by a couple of Kiwis who favoured Australasians.'*

The advertising pages of free magazines aimed at the ex-pat community, notably *TNT*, carry scores of ads for employment agencies specialising in everything from banquet catering to landscape gardening. You can expect to earn minimum wage as a kitchen porter (the most lowly job) and up to twice that as an assistant chef. Ask your agency about obtaining hygiene certificate training. Also check out cleaning and security work, for which there seems to be an insatiable demand in London. An active agency in the field of gardening and landscape labouring, among others, is Target Appointments near Chancery Lane (☎ 020 7242 9962; target-jobs.com).

Pubs

Anyone who has been on a pub crawl in London will know that a huge percentage of the people working behind the bar are not English, but rather Polish, Australian or one of a hundred nationalities. Although there are employment agencies specialising in bar work, they aren't usually very helpful to people looking for casual bar work. Gumtree.com is a better bet.

KRISTEN MOEN FROM NORWAY DESCRIBES HER JOB IN A LONDON PUB
I loved it: the atmosphere was great, I had so much fun and met so much nice people at work. The only thing I can complain about is that the money is not very good – or maybe the rents for flats in London are too high. If I had had a work permit, I would have gotten a job immediately, but it took me two weeks. First I went around asking in pubs and restaurants. Everybody was really helpful. They would always suggest another place I could go to or tell me to come back in a few weeks. At the same time I was also reading the job ads in the Evening Standard. 70% turned me down because of my missing work permit, but finally I got something and worked happily there for four months.

Some pub jobs come with accommodation, in which case you might expect to net £600 a month for working 45 hours a week. So many pubs duplicate as restaurants now that you can also expect to earn tips in some positions.

Couriers

Driving is a standard stop-gap job, for example of vans or as a courier. Motorcycle owners might be tempted by the money that can be earned by despatch riders. For those who don't own their own bikes, they can be leased from the firm. Despatch riders can earn up to £700 a week. But the high earnings only come when jobs come thick and fast, and if you have a good knowledge of London streets. There is also a high risk of serious injury, hence insurance premiums will be very high if you choose to declare your occupation for insurance and tax purposes.

The firm City Sprint (citysprint.co.uk) is always looking for drivers, couriers and porters, and seems sympathetic to the erratic habits of people working for relatively short periods to fund their travels (☎ 08707 384444; fleetrecruit@citysprint.co.uk). Bicycle couriers are also needed, for example by visa agencies. Top couriers cover up to 300 miles a day doing up to 40 jobs. The job carries on in all weathers (except snow which is considered too dangerous). Although cycle couriers don't earn as much as despatch riders, it appeals to some brave souls.

Accommodation

Most new arrivals in London go to one of the scores of (relatively) cheap hostels where overseas travellers congregate. Expect to pay £20–£25 for a dorm bed. Your fellow hostellers will often prove invaluable sources of inside knowledge about the job market and hostels often serve as a launch pad for money-saving careers and shared houses. If you are lucky enough to have friends with whom you can doss, offer to contribute about £5 a night towards bills. When sharing private accommodation, budget for at least £50 a week if sharing a room, £80 for a private room, and twice that for a studio flat or self-contained bed-sit. Websites can be very useful for London accommodation as well as jobs, especially gumtree.com and accommodationlondon.net.

Carisa Fey arrived in London from Stuttgart at the tender age of 18 determined to make a go of long-term working and travelling, and soon moved out of a hostel and into rented accommodation:

> ***Once in London I went – where else? – to Earls Court, and met my first fellow travellers in a hostel. I planned to be the very first one on Monday morning to grab the hostel copy of TNT and to start my hunt for a job. Well, unfortunately, we were in one of those, ehm, social hostels and until 3pm on Monday I couldn't even walk. I thought my chance was gone and that no one was going to give a job to me considering the state I was in. But just to practise I put on my suit and decided to look for a place to stay. The third letting agency I went into (I was still a spoiled brat then and believed in things like letting agencies) seemed nice, professional and not too expensive. While filling in the form, I left the space 'Occupation' empty and said that I was looking for a job. The agency's boss sat on the next desk, looked up and asked 'Do you want to work here?' So I found in one afternoon a job and a place to stay.***

Free food and accommodation in exchange for some duties is a great bonus in London. For example a number of charities recruit full-time volunteers to assist people with severe physical disabilities to live independently in the community. For example SHAD recruits volunteers, who are required to stay for a minimum of three or four months, who in turn receive a place to live and an allowance of at least £60 a week plus expenses. A shift system is worked by volunteers allowing plenty of free time to explore London. SHAD's office is in Wandsworth (☎ 020 8675 6095;

shad.org.uk). Independent Living Alternatives (Trafalgar House, Grenville Place, NW7 3SA; ☎ 020 8906 9265; ILAnet.co.uk) offers a similar arrangement for its full-time 'personal assistants'. Its website lists current vacancies offering wages of £650 per week worked. Private care agencies also employ live-in carers and pay some startlingly high wages.

DEBBIE HARRISON ARRIVED IN LONDON AFTER A FRENETIC SEASON AS A HOLIDAY REP IN GREECE, EAGER TO SAVE SOME MONEY:

After the constant dining out, excessive drinking and sunbathing, my current job as a live-in carer for an old lady in a quiet part of Surrey is quite a contrast. I went to the agency interview with no experience or qualifications but was introduced by a friend already employed by them and I was offered a job straightaway. The pay is good and the long hours mean temporary death to the social life so it's a great way to save.

The kind of clientele served by certain agencies means that they will be selective, so you will need to look respectable and have a background to match, with contactable references. A driving licence is often essential.

VOLUNTARY OPPORTUNITIES

CSV mentioned at the beginning of this chapter offers volunteer placements to anyone aged 16+ who commits him/herself to live away from home for 4–12 months supporting people who need help such as children with special needs and homeless people. Volunteers do not need any special skills, qualifications or experience. Volunteers receive £33 a week in addition to accommodation and meals (or a meal allowance of £39); freephone the Volunteers' Hotline on 0800 374991 or consult the CSV homepage csv.org.uk. Another organisation which provides board, lodging and pocket money to volunteers willing to work at centres for the homeless is the Simon Community in Camden (☎ 020 7485 6639; simoncommunity.org.uk) whose preferred minimum stay is nine months. Volunteers over 19 receive an allowance of £36 a week in addition to room and board.

Many shorter term opportunities for volunteers can be found, especially during the summer months when disability charities recruit volunteers to assist at holiday centres to give disabled people and their carers a break. Vitalise runs holiday centres in Southampton, Bodmin, Southport, Bridgford (Nottingham) and Chigwell that depend on willing volunteers (British or otherwise) from February to November. The charity pays all board, lodging and travel to the centres from within the UK; an application form can be downloaded from the site vitalise.org.uk. Break is another national charity that takes on volunteers for the holidays (☎ 01263 822161; break-charity.org).

If you are more interested in conservation work, several national bodies arrange one to three week working holidays where volunteers repair dry stone walls, clear overgrown ponds, undertake botanical surveys, archaeological digs or maintain traditional woodland. You will be housed in comfortable volunteer basecamps with about a dozen other volunteers. For a free brochure listing the 400 projects organised by the National Trust, ring 0844 800 3099 for week-long and weekend residential projects or the Central Volunteering Team on 0870 609 5383 for long-term placements (nationaltrust.org.uk/volunteering). Working holidays take place year round. Most summer projects cost £85 per week to join whereas out-of-season working holidays cost from £65. From 2009 families can participate together.

BTCV (British Trust for Conservation Volunteers) organise about 200 conservation working holidays throughout the UK from the Cornish coast to the Scottish Highlands. Accommodation, meals and insurance are provided at a cost of about £190 per week. All include relevant training, and many lead to qualifications and certificates. Visit the BTCV website http://shop.btcv.org.uk to view Natural Breaks in England and Scotland (☎ 01302 388883).

Bird-lovers can become volunteer wardens for up to four weeks with the Royal Society for the Protection of Birds (RSPB) and undertake many other volunteer roles (☎ 01767 680551; rspb.org.uk/volunteering). Accommodation is provided free but the volunteers must provide their own food. The Waterway Recovery Group (☎ 01494 783453; wrg.org.uk) runs week-long voluntary Canal Camps costing only £49 a week for accommodation and meals.

Anyone who wants to participate on an archaeological dig should consult information from the Council for British Archaeology in York; some of its fieldwork listings are freely available on their site (britarch.ac.uk/briefing/field.asp). Otherwise you can subscribe to CBA's briefings which lists archaeological digs to which volunteers can apply.

Volunteering is an excellent solution for anyone who has work permit problems. Americans, and indeed anyone, can fix up voluntary jobs independently. Janet Renard and Luke Olivieri are two particularly enterprising American travellers who arranged several voluntary positions before they left home. One of the most unusual was working for the Ffestiniog Railway Company in Porthmadog, North Wales (☎ 01766 516035; ffestiniograilway.co.uk/volunteer.htm) which operates a famous narrow gauge railway and provides hostel accommodation to volunteers.

> ***Many of the volunteers are railroad/steam engine fanatics, but accepted us even though we didn't know the first thing about it. We elected to work in the Parks & Gardens section and spent a week weeding, planting, clearing, etc. The work was hard and the evenings were busy too. We were taken to a pub one night, asked to dinner another, visited a Welsh male voice choir and went climbing in the area. Ffestiniog Railway depends completely on volunteers who come from all over, all ages, all professions. But they can always use more help, so we may just go back.***

The Centre for Alternative Technology in Wales, Machynlleth, Powys SY20 9AZ (☎ 01654 705955; cat.org.uk/volunteers) takes on short-term volunteers for a week or two between March and September; volunteers pay £10 a night for a bed and meals. Advance booking is essential.

Buddhist communities throughout Britain offer working visits whereby volunteers stay free of charge. For example the Losang Dragpa Buddhist Centre in the Pennines (Todmorden, West Yorkshire; ☎ 01706 812247 ext 201; info@losangdragpa.com) requires volunteers to pay £40 per week while assisting with various projects maintaining the Victorian castle in which it is housed.

Also in Yorkshire is the Madhyamaka Buddhist Centre, Kilnwick Percy Hall, Pocklington, Yorks. YO42 1UF (☎ 01759 304832; madhyamaka.org) where Shona Williamson enjoyed a working holiday so much she decided to make it her home for an extended period. In exchange for 35 hours of gardening, decorating, etc. per week she got free dormitory accommodation, vegetarian meals and the chance to attend evening meditations and teachings. The Manjushri Mahayana Buddhist Centre in Ulverston, Cumbria also advertises working holidays (☎ 01229 584029; workingvisit@manjushri.org).

Laura Hitchcock from New York State managed to fix up two three-month internships in the field of her career interest by agreeing to pay her own expenses if they would take her on and help her find accommodation in local homes. Her jobs were in the publicity departments of the Ironbridge Gorge Museum Trust near Telford in Shropshire, and then in a theatre-arts centre in East Anglia (The Quay Theatre at Quay Lane, Sudbury, Suffolk CO10 2AN): *'I learned when writing not to ask for "internships" but rather for "unpaid work experience"; otherwise the British will ask you what hospital you are with! The particularly good feature of my jobs was that the people were so friendly. If you were willing to help yourself they'd do all they could for you.'*

IRELAND

The astonishing rise in Ireland's fortunes hit the buffers at the end of 2008 when the banking system came close to collapsing and thousands of migrant workers from Eastern Europe began fleeing like rats from a sinking ship. The predictions for 2009 are that unemployment will top 11%. So this may not be the best time for job-seeking travellers to land on Ireland's shores.

WORKING HOLIDAY SCHEMES

US nationals who can prove Irish ancestry may be eligible for unrestricted entry to Ireland and even Irish nationality (which would confer all EU rights). Enquiries should be directed to the Irish Embassy.

Full-time North American students in tertiary education or recent graduates are eligible to apply for an 'Exchange Visitor Programme Work Permit' through BUNAC (bunac.org). For American students the permit is valid for up to four months at any time of the year and for Canadians who can make the arrangements through Travel CUTS's Student Work Abroad Programme (swap.ca) the limit is 12 months. Whereas the number of visas for Canadians with student status (no age limits) is unlimited, the number available to Canadian non-students aged up to 35 is limited so early application to SWAP is advised. The partner organisation in Ireland is the student travel and exchange agency USIT (19–21 Aston Quay, Dublin 2; ☎ 01 602 1906; usit.ie or workandtravelireland.org); their fee for overseeing the programme is US$430.

Once in Ireland, non-EU nationals intending to stay and work for longer than 90 day must register with the Garda National Immigration Bureau and pay a fee of €150. USIT can advise on this as well as advising on job opportunities. USIT does not currently administer the working holiday scheme for Australians and New Zealanders who should apply for exchange visitor permits from the Irish embassy in their own country. If you visit the USIT office on the south side of the River Liffey, you can inspect a large notice board with many Jobs Available notices.

Obviously there will be many Americans and others who are not students and therefore not eligible for this programme. Again informal arrangements with private hostels can make it possible to extend your stay in Ireland. One enterprising Californian contacted hostels via hostels.com and, after a brief exchange of emails and references and a phone conversation, was hired by a start-up hostel which gave her accommodation plus $150 a week.

THE JOB HUNT

The EURES office is at 27–33 Upper Baggot Street, Dublin 4 (☎ 00800 4080 4080; fas.ie). Jobs.ie and loadzajobs.ie are two of the country's biggest online recruitment sites, which register employers' vacancies in hotels, restaurants, bars and leisure centres, sales, etc. throughout Ireland. Chefs and experienced hotel receptionists are particularly in demand.

Note that some agencies arrange unpaid work experience placements for young people from the continent (like Job Options mentioned below) and from North America. Cultural Embrace in Austin, Texas charges astronomical fees for month-long career-specific internships and private accommodation for Americans mainly in Dublin (culturalembrace.com).

Tourism

The tourist industry is the main source of seasonal work in Ireland. Outside Dublin, the largest demand is in the southwestern counties of Cork and Kerry, especially the towns of Killarney (with well over 100 pubs) and Tralee. Contact the addresses in any guide to hotels in Ireland. Among the biggest employers are the Doyle Collection hotels group and Sinnott Hotels (humanresources@sinnotthotels.com).

When applying, you should mention any musical talent you have, since pubs and hotels may be glad to have a barman who can occasionally entertain at the piano. Directly approaching cafés, campsites and amusement arcades is usually more effective than writing. Two hundred thousand people a year visit the Aillwee Cave in County Clare; the company which manages the attraction recruits cave tour guides, plus catering and sales staff for a minimum of two months (Aillwee Cave Co. Ltd., Ballyvaughan, Co. Clare; ☎ 065 707 7036; aillweecave.ie). Hostel accommodation is provided at a cost.

Experienced assistants and instructors may be needed by riding stables and watersports centres throughout Ireland. The horse industry is still very strong in Ireland; anyone with experience of horses might have success by contacting stables, riding holiday centres or equestrian recruitment agencies. Equipeople in County Laois is a specialist agency providing work experience on Irish farms (equipeopleworkexperience.com) and also supplies horsey staff to the equine sector in Ireland and abroad (equipeoplestaff.com; ☎ +353 57 8643195; equipeople@eircom.net). Other sites to check are theequinest.com/jobs/ie and yardandgroom.com. Instructors and pony trek leaders are needed mainly for children at Errislannan Manor Connemara Pony Stud (Clifden, West Galway ☎ 0952 1134; errislannanmanor@eircom.net); the minimum stay is two months and applications must be made before March.

Innumerable musical and cultural festivals take place throughout Ireland, mostly during the summer. Big-name bands often perform at concerts near Dublin. A small fortune can be made by amateur entrepreneurs (with or without a permit) who find a niche in the market. Heather McCulloch had two friends who sold filled rolls and sandwiches at a major concert and made a clear profit of over £1,000 in just a few hours.

'The Rose of Tralee', a large regional festival held in Tralee, Co. Kerry in the third week of August, provides various kinds of employment for enterprising workers, as Tracie Sheehan reports: *'As 50,000 people attend this festival each year, guest houses, hotels, restaurants and cafés all take on extra staff. Buskers make great money, as do mime artists, jugglers and artists. Pubs do a roaring business, so singing or performing in a pub can be very profitable.'*

Dublin

According to Mig Urquhart, '*crappy jobs are very easy to get in Dublin, whereas real jobs are scarce*'. Mig has variously worked in a Dublin hostel, bed and breakfast, Irish-owned fast food company Supermacs (recruitment@supermacs.ie), canteen of a government department and for the boat taxi on the River Liffey patronised by tourists, school groups and commuters. Check the notice boards in the main travellers' hostels like the Dublin International Youth Hostel at 61 Mountjoy Street.

Try the trendy spots in Temple Bar in the city centre. Writing from Dublin a couple of years ago, the American Dan Eldridge found the city to be a land of opportunity:

> ***Restaurant and pub work is exploding in Dublin especially in Temple Bar but also north of the river on and around Grafton Street, basically anywhere you see people. My experience has been that when your would-be employer asks if you have working papers (and they all do) your best bet is to say that you're in the process of getting them together, and they'll surely get the drift.***

But not everybody is as successful as Dan. A couple of years ago a 19 year old Brazilian backpacker Manoel Netto headed for Dublin with €800 in savings and an optimistic outlook. His plan was to look for a job, save some money, make friends and go travelling afterwards. Writing his web diary on travelpunk.com, he recalls his hard landing:

> ***I heard that Dublin was a good bet, as the job opportunities were massive and the Irish people were really friendly. The Irish never disappointed me! Temple Bar has tons of bars and the huge amounts of people, trying every tap. Walking around, looking for a job in every single place, I just could not find a job. In one week all I heard was 'no' and 'what's your insurance number?' Nothing! After one week, the despair was in my face. Even though I made some friends with whom I used to go out, I knew that I wouldn't have enough money to keep that lifestyle for a long time. I felt humiliated, tired and jaded. I needed to get out of Dublin in order not to get mad.***

Buskers and street entertainers can do well in and around Dublin's Grafton Street since the Irish are a generous nation and appreciate musical talent.

Au Pairing

European Union nationals who want to learn English and some Commonwealth passport holders may wish to consider au pairing in Ireland via one of a number of agencies, for example Aupairs4Dublin makes the usual family placements in Dublin and the surrounding area. The related Aupairs4ireland agency specialises in families in the countryside in every part of Ireland, especially families who own horses where it is possible for the au pair to work with animals and children. Horse-only jobs are also an option but a work permit may be required in some instances. Contact: J. Kidd based in Downpatrick in Northern Ireland (☎ 02844 615106; aupairs4dublin@ireland.com/ aupairs4ireland@ireland.com/ horsejobs@ireland.com; aupairs4ireland.com).

The Job Options Bureau in Cork and Dublin (☎ 021 427 5369; joboptionsbureau.ie) is a founder member of the International Au Pair Association. An au pair agency called Cara International has branched out into recruiting workers from the EU for jobs in hotels and restaurants, construction, etc. (Castlebar, Co. Mayo; ☎ 0394 928 9802; carainternational.net). Other agencies worth trying are the Secret Garden in the lovely town of Kinsale (secretgardenagency.com) and for experienced nannies Hynes Agency (hynesagency.ie) which charges €85 registration fee (permitted in Ireland).The recommended pocket money for au pairs is €75–€85+ a week for 25 hours of duties, €85–€110 for 30 hours and up to €200 for a full-time six-day week. The agencies which are offshoots of language schools usually make it a requirement that au pairs sign up for English courses with them.

Fishing

Robert Abblett gave a lift to an Irish fisherman who passed on some tips on finding work in the fishing industry:

> ***He mentioned three places to try. I visited Rossaveal fish factory west of Galway and could have got a job easily extracting the roe from herrings. The work was paid piece work and the boss told me that the average experienced worker earns £50 a day, and the fastest worker double that, for a maximum of five days a week (weather permitting). Most people only last a few days as the work is dirty, smelly and boring. The season here lasts from mid-October till February only. I then visited Dingle and enquired at the fish factory. I didn't bother checking Castletownbere on the Beara peninsula which is a large whitefish port. Work on the fishing boats and factories is apparently available most of the year.***

Robert showed admirable enterprise in tracking down these opportunities. He picked out likely looking village names from the Michelin map, and dialled Directory Enquiries to phone the local post office. They were usually able to give the telephone numbers of the local fish factories.

THE NETHERLANDS

British and Irish young people continue to pour off no-frills flights and ferries, check into hostels and begin looking for the well paid jobs and liberal attitudes they've heard about. The market for unskilled non-Dutch-speaking workers is far from saturated since unemployment is the lowest in the EU at 2.7% with youth unemployment less than one third of the Eurozone average.

The job search should not be confined to Amsterdam. Scores of temporary employment agencies can be found in Rotterdam, The Hague, Haarlem, Leiden and Utrecht. Unemployment is highest in the south and north-west, so these areas should probably be avoided. Competition for work is much less outside the summer.

REGULATIONS

The Dutch have been tightening up the regulations in an attempt to clamp down on squatters, drug abusers and others perceived to be undesirable. This has been partly in response to the substantial influx of workers from the newly enlarged EU. All job-seeking EU nationals must follow the bureaucratic procedures which the majority of agencies and employers follow. For EU nationals who intend to stay for more than three months, all that is needed is an EU passport which can be taken to the local tax office (*Belastingdienst*) to apply for a Citizen Service Number (*Burger Servicenummer* or BSN). To apply for a BSN in Amsterdam go to the big black building outside the train station in Sloterdijk (Kingsfordweg 1; ☎ 0800 0543). You will have to have a BSN before being allowed to register with employment bureaux or take up a job.

Job agencies may not be willing to sign you up unless you have a Dutch bank account and banks in areas frequented by short-stay workers have become reluctant to open accounts. Look for the Fortis Bank and PostBank which allow you to open a giro account.

Non-EU Nationals

The situation for non-EU nationals is predictably more difficult. North Americans, Antipodeans and others who require no visa to travel to the Netherlands are allowed to work for less than three months, provided they report to the Aliens Police within three days of arrival and their employer has obtained a *tewerkstellingsvergunning* (work permit) for them. The first step is to acquire a sticker in your passport from the local aliens police (*Vreemdelingenpolitie*) or Town Hall, normally over-the-counter. They will expect you to provide a local address and it is best to use this same address throughout your stay.

Other non-EU nationals wishing to stay for longer than three months must obtain a provisional residence permit (*machtiging tot voorlopig verblijf* or MVV) before their arrival in the Netherlands and before their employer can apply for an employment permit from the CBA (Centraal Bestuur Arbeidsvoorziening). The MVV must be applied for through the Dutch Embassy in your country and then can be turned into a Residence Permit after arrival. In practice, the *tewerkstellingsvergunning* is unlikely to be issued for casual work.

The expatriate support organisation Access inside the City Hall in The Hague publishes various information booklets. For detailed information, contact the Dutch Immigration Service, *Immigratie en Naturalisatie Dienst* or IND (☎ 0900 1234561 or +31 20 8893045 from outside the country; ind.nl which is fully accessible in English). Canadians, Australians and New Zealanders up to the age of 30 can obtain a working holiday visa valid for up to a year.

Red Tape

The Dutch have some of the most progressive laws in the world to minimise exploitation of workers. Compulsory holiday pay of at least 8% of gross salary should also be paid on all but the most temporary casual jobs. Do not count on receiving the holiday pay immediately after finishing a job because it may have to be sent to your home bank account months later. Similarly tax rebates may be owing at the end of the tax year, and so employees should save all pay slips showing income and deductions. Health insurance contributions (*Ziekenfonds*) are compulsory.

If you feel that you are not being treated fairly by an employer or landlord, you can get free legal advice from any Jongeren Informatie Punt or JIP (Youth Information Points; jip.org) or you can make enquiries at any employment office.

A potentially useful web forum can be found at nlplanet.com which covers in English topics of interest to expats. Another worthwhile travel site is joho.org, the 'one-stop-organisation for travellers-backpackers, expats-entrepreneurs, international job-seekers, interns-language students and volunteers-development workers'. JoHo maintains shops/offices in Leiden, Amsterdam, Rotterdam, Utrecht and Groningen, with a few job vacancies on file, though the main thrust of its work is to help Dutch job-seekers to find work abroad. Its sister sites comingtothenetherlands.com and carrierebank.nl might have some useful tidbits, though mostly in Dutch. Some job information in English can be found at betaaldwerkinhetbuitenland.nl/werk/functieprofielen.

PRIVATE EMPLOYMENT AGENCIES

The majority of employers turn to private employment agencies (*uitzendbureaux* – pronounced and meaning 'out-send') for temporary workers, partly to avoid the complicated paperwork of hiring a foreigner directly. Therefore they can be a very useful source of temporary work in Holland. They proliferate in large towns, for example there are nearly 350 in Amsterdam alone.

Look up *Uitzendbureau* in the telephone directory or the *Gouden Gids* (*Yellow Pages*; goudengids.nl) and register with as many as you can in your area. Not all will accept non-Dutch-speaking applicants. You should visit or at least phone the office daily at opening time and perhaps twice a day since often the allocation of jobs is not systematic and once the phone is put down the agency forgets about you. Ian Kent thinks that Amsterdam is far more promising than the provinces for non-Dutch speakers:

> ***In Amsterdam it is very easy to get work in cafés, hostels and coffee shops. However outside Amsterdam it is somewhat tricky. It took me three months of asking round farms, greenhouses and being told by all of the uitzendbureaux that there is no work unless you speak Dutch. By chance I found work packing fruit and veg through an uitzenbureau in Rotterdam who at the time were giving work to anybody with an EU passport. The work was boring and the shifts long, 10–12 hours. I would advise anybody who does not speak good Dutch to go to Amsterdam to look for work.***

Uitzendbureaux deal only with jobs lasting less than six months. Most of the work on their books will be unskilled work. The area in the west of the Netherlands called the Randstad with the main centres of population has the most work. Many international companies are based in the Netherlands, so there are often vacancies for experienced Native English secretaries and data-inputters, usually through the uitzendbureaux. Kerian Parry spent several years when she was in her early 20s working in Sassenheim and Noordwijk-aan-Zee near Leiden.

> ***Leiden has a lot of uitzendbureaux, and in my experience about half of them will take on English speakers who don't speak Dutch. Adecco, Olympia, Dactylo, Manpower, First Start, Via Werk,***

V.A.B., and one branch of Luba definitely signed up foreign workers when I was there and all except Via Werk and Manpower offered me jobs during my stay. They are nearly always looking for people who have office experience and/or typing skills, but I didn't feel my typing was good enough. I supported myself with the following jobs: worker in flower-factories, order-picker in a clothing warehouse, cleaner of fire-damaged objects and kitchen assistant/cleaner in a hospital canteen. I hated starting at 7am, although most low-paid jobs in Holland seem to start between 7am and 8.30am. Like all employment agencies uitzendbureaux gain their income by charging the employer a percentage of the wage, which in some cases is 100% or more.

Among the largest *uitzendbureaux* are Randstad with up to 700 branches, Manpower, Creyf's and Tempo Team, all of whose websites are only in Dutch. A good online recruiter is megajobs.nl.

THE BULB INDUSTRY

Traditionally, the horticultural sector has had difficulty in finding enough seasonal labour for the processing of flower bulbs for export and related activities. Hordes of young travellers, especially from the accession countries of Eastern Europe, descend on the area between Leiden and Haarlem in the summer. Large numbers of unskilled workers are employed in fields and factories to dig, peel, sort, count and pack bulbs, especially in the early spring and through the autumn. Important export companies (*Bloembollen Groothandel*) can be found in the north around Andijk and Breezand. The Dutch *Yellow Pages*, online at goudengids.nl, can be a useful ally in the search for work. For example dozens of addresses of bulb companies are listed showing their locations on linked maps.

Finding the Work

The majority of farmers use agents or middlemen to recruit casual labour. A couple of years ago Rob Abblett travelled to Holland after the *vendange* in Switzerland, just because he'd never been before. He headed for Andijk near Enkhuizen north of Amsterdam: *'By great luck and effort I managed to find a job on foot, but later discovered that I had to go through a job agency anyway, unless I had worked there the year before. The job agencies helped me and, now that I have their telephone numbers, I can even phone them from England, say, to check on work availability.'*

Work in the Andijk factories is available mid-July to September and mid-October till February/March. He returned to Hillegom in September armed with an address given to him by a fellow traveller, and this connection made it much easier to land a job. Eighty caravans were parked behind the factory, full of Polish workers with German passports. His job was to sprinkle glitter on waxed pinecones for the Christmas market, at a rate about equivalent to the UK minimum wage (though no one received any wage slips). After a month, he couldn't face it any more and returned home.

The busy times differ among bulb employers according to their markets. For example mail-order companies (like P. Bakker mentioned below) need employees to pick and pack customers' orders from February until the end of April and again from September to December. The busy time for bulb peeling is the second half of June. Ask at the local job centre (*CWI*) or look for signs (*Bollenpellers Gevraagd*) in Hillegom, Lisse, Noordwijk, Sassenheim and Bennebroek. New arrivals will have no trouble locating the properties of the bulb barons once they arrive. In Hillegom head for Pastoorslaan or Leidsestraat where many of the factories are concentrated and in Lisse, look along Heereweg. Note that the greenhouses and flower auction houses in and around Aalsmeer also provide employment but not so seasonal.

The majority of bulb exporters consider only candidates who are around when there are vacancies and with changes in immigration patterns more of them are able to find enough workers already resident in the Netherlands. It is always worth trying the famous bulb exporter P. Bakker B.V., Postbus 600, Lisse (☎ 0252 438438; bakker-hillegom.nl) which employs up to 2,000 people at busy times doing shift work (3.30pm–11.30pm and 6.30am–2.30pm). Unauthorised days off are grounds for instant dismissal.

The long established firm Frijlink en Zoon in Noordwijkerhout (☎ 0252 343143) receives plenty of applications via word of mouth as do Baartman & Koning b.v. in Voorhout (☎ 0252 211141) and Van de Groot b.v. in Noordwijkerhout (☎ 0252 373891). Try also Van Zanten b.v. in Den Helder and Hillegom (royalvanzanten.com).

It should be noted that like all employers the bulb companies can accept applications only from European Union nationals; people from outside the EU who write are wasting their time and money. Even if you do receive a job offer in advance, you cannot be sure that the company will honour its promise. It costs them nothing to promise jobs to enquirers, to cover themselves in case of a worker shortage, as happened to Gordon Robertson from Glasgow a couple of years ago.

Traditionally seasonal workers congregate on big campsites, and will normally be willing to advise newcomers. The job hunt will be easier if you're carrying a tent. At times the need for workers is so urgent that employers have to find some way round the problem of accommodation. Renting a flat is even more problematical since foreign workers have such a bad reputation for rowdiness and irresponsibility that few landlords will risk it.

In Robert Abblett's experience, this reputation is not undeserved: '*Lots of the workers smoke dope from waking up, at work (if they can) and the rest of the day. Coming back to my house and finding my three co-habitants totally stoned is quite normal. But I can't blame them, for the work requires a positive mental attitude to withstand the boredom and if you haven't got it, then you must choose insanity, oblivion or just leave.*' Obviously if the competition is like this, it is not too surprising that his boss at De Jongs Lily Factory in Andijk made him supervisor of the night shift line (☎ 0228 591400; dejonglelies.nl).

Yet competition for jobs remains acute, though less so at the more far-flung factories. Mark Wilson recommends having some transport: *'Along with a tent, a necessity when looking for bulb work is a bicycle. While out exploring on my bike I came across an area full of factories just outside Noordwijkerhout, a village west of Lisse.'* Second-hand bicycles can be picked up fairly easily and affordably.

Pay and Conditions

The bulb industry is better regulated than it once was which means that there is less black work around. The hiring of non-EU nationals has virtually ceased and exploitation is less common than it was, though membership in the bulb workers' union (Voedingsbond FNV) is not generally available to foreigners.

Overtime paid at a premium rate is what makes it possible to save. Like most agricultural work, earnings fluctuate according to the weather; on a rainy day when the flowers don't open people are lucky to get four hours work.

Darren Slevin worked at a bulb factory in Voorhout 3km from Leiden. He did not appreciate the way the Irish workers were treated as thieves and drug-users (which they weren't) nor did he enjoy the mind-numbing work which caused pain in back, legs and feet. His boss's favourite word was *'snell, snell'* (faster, faster). But he did enjoy the international camaraderie. The most commonly heard complaint about packing is how boring it is, 'worse for your head than boxing' according to one veteran. But most workers receive enough breaks throughout the long day to make it bearable. Naturally there are good employers and bad employers and Garrett Mohan felt himself lucky to be working for one of the former: *'Our boss is quite easy-going but, like the rest of the Dutch, very big on punctuality. He has provided us with a TV and DVD and regularly records English films for us.'*

Bulb-peeling is a much more unpleasant job as Martin and Shirine recall: *'The work was hard on our hands and we soon resorted to wearing rubber gloves or plasters. The hours of work were 8am-5pm with an hour's lunch break and the choice to work until 10pm. That was a long time to spend crouched over a table, sitting on an old wobbly stool that was the wrong height for you.'*

Mark Wilson had an even more miserable experience as a bulb peeler: *'The first job I had was peeling the skin off the bulbs which was the most mind-numbingly boring job I have ever done. Later I was condemned to two weeks in the hyacinth shed which is kept away from the main factory. While working on a sorting machine in a loose T-shirt I found to my horror and my Dutch workmates' amusement that bulb dust is a very powerful irritant, so after a couple of hours of itching like a madman, I resigned on the spot, ran back to the campsite and dived into the shower to relieve my tormented skin.'*

AGRICULTURE

From mid-April to October jobs might be available picking asparagus, strawberries, gherkins, apples and pears. During the same period jobs exist in greenhouses and mushroom fields, though these jobs are popular with locals and usually can be filled with local students and other job-seekers.

Many harvests take place in fertile pockets of southern Holland for example in the Baarland in the extreme south-west and in Limburg to the east along the Belgian border. Garrett Mohan travelled to the tiny village of Kwadendamme near Goes in the Baarland (Zeeland) in early September (after local school children had returned to school) to join the apple and pear harvest which ends in early November. An agency which may be able to assist is Creyf's in Goes (☎ 0113 211223; goes@creyfs.nl).

Limburg and Brabant

The area around Roermond in the 'deep south' of Holland (about 50km southeast of Eindhoven and north of Maastricht in the province of Limburg) is populated by asparagus growers and other farmers who need people to harvest their crops of strawberries (June to mid-July), potatoes and other vegetables, especially in the spring. If possible find someone to translate ads in the local paper *De Limburger*. The agencies around here are less accustomed to dealing with non-Dutch applicants but can be all the more helpful for that. Independently Joanne Patrick and Steve Conneely found work picking potatoes and earned a tidy sum between them in two weeks in late February and early March.

Asparagus picking starts just after the middle of April and lasts through to mid-June. A tent is a great advantage here to be able to stay at campsites like the one Murray Turner stayed at in Helden north of Roermond. Despite initial hopes that earnings would be high in the peak season, he ended up earning a modest wage based on piecework rates. He moved on to the strawberry harvest where earnings from piecework were unreliable because of the weather. The asparagus harvest is similarly affected by weather; if it's hot you can work as long as you are able.

Westland

The area between Rotterdam, the Hook of Holland and Den Haag is known as the Westland. The principal villages in the area are Naaldwijk, Westerlee, De Lier and Maasdijk, but the whole region is a honeycomb of greenhouses. The tomato harvest begins in early to mid-April and this is the best time to arrive, although work is generally available all year round if you are prepared to work for at least one month. Although the work is boring and dirty with long hours – it is not unusual for workers to start work at 5am and finish at 7pm or 8pm – conditions can be reasonable with barn accommodation provided.

Try *uitzendbureaux* in Naaldwijk, 's-Gravenzande and Poeldijk for work picking cucumbers, peppers, flowers, etc. Also try the flower and vegetable auctions (*bloemenveiling/groenteveiling*) in Westerlee/de Lier and Honselersdijk which need people to load the stock for auction buyers, etc. Ian Govan's overtime pay (in cash) increased his basic earnings for a 38-hour week by about two-thirds.

TOURISM

Dutch hotels and other tourist establishments employ some foreigners, especially those with a knowledge of more than one European language. A few tour operators like Eurocamp/Holiday-break (see *Tourism* chapter) employ British young people as staff for the summer season.

In Adam Skuse's year off before university, he almost succeeded in finding hotel work but not quite:

> ***I got a list of hotels online and then systematically emailed them all asking for a job. Most had no vacancies, a couple told me to call them when I was in Amsterdam, and one actually arranged an interview with me. But even the knockbacks were pleasant. Quite a few offered to buy me a drink anyway. Alas, I never managed to find the hotel in time, ran out of funds and am now back in Blighty.***

Although you may be lucky enough to obtain a hotel job through an *uitzendbureau*, your chances will normally be better if you visit hotels and ask if any work is available, or keep your ears open in pubs and hostels.

While visiting a friend in the seaside resort of Zaandvoort south of Haarlem, Martin and Shirine tried to find work washing dishes for one of the many bars which line the beach. They knew that without speaking Dutch this was the only job they could reasonably expect to get.

A range of boating holidays for leisure and business is managed by Naupar which employs 300 crew and a catering team of 100 for its fleet of 140 traditional sailing boats such as Platbodems. Applicants must have a knowledge of German as well as English.

OTHER WORK

Labouring work may be available in some of the massive docks of Rotterdam and Ijmuiden north of Haarlem. According to Shelly Harris's partner Terry, who got work straightaway unloading fishing boats, it's just a case of turning up at the offices on the docks early (about 5.30am) and asking for work. The money is good but the work is hard, cold and irregular. It used to take Terry two hours to thaw out in front of a fire after knocking off work about 3.30pm.

Teaching

Urban Dutch people have such a high degree of competence in English after they finish their schooling that there is not much of a market for basic EFL teaching. An increasing need for advanced levels of English within both companies and universities means that institutes are always on the lookout for qualified native speakers. Language schools tend to look for people who have extensive commercial or government experience as well as a teaching qualification. For example UvA Talen in Amsterdam (☎ 020 525 46 37; jobs@uvatalen.nl) with links to the University of Amsterdam offers part-time freelance assignments to well qualified teachers and PCI (Pimentel Communications International) in Alkmaar (☎ 072 512 11 90; pcitalen.nl) looks for experience in business and technical English. Rates of pay start at around €25 per hour.

The agency Franglais Language Services in The Hague (☎ 070 361 1703; jobs@franglais.nl) claims that it is often looking for native English speakers to edit texts by e-mail written in English by non-native speakers. The pay is 5 eurocents per word.

Amsterdam

As throughout the world, hostels employ people to clean, cook, do maintenance and night porter duties. Carolyn Edwards was not dissatisfied with the wage which was paid in addition to room and board since it was equivalent to what she had been earning as a temp in London (minus the food and accommodation). More usually, people work a few hours a day for free bed and breakfast but no wage.

Saffery Ruddock enjoyed this arrangement as a *whapper* (worker) at the Flying Pig hostel near the Vondelpark; she exchanged 3½ hours of work a day cleaning, serving breakfast and doing odd jobs for a dorm bed and a 'brilliant atmosphere, busy, friendly and relaxed'. There are two other Flying Pig hostels, one downtown and one at the beach (flyingpig.nl) which were advertising jobs at the time of going to print: *'The hostels always welcome passing travellers to help us out with tasks such as cleaning, breakfast, maintenance and more.'* Most travellers work for food and accommodation, though EU passport holders and working holidaymakers do reception, bar and maintenance work. Interested people should email headoffice@flyingpig.nl.

Justine Bakker wrote to recommend her workplace in Amsterdam as a '*great place for travellers because it hires a lot of international people, especially for promotion*'. Boom Chicago on Leidseplein describes itself as a '*comedy institution*' and employs nearly 100 people as cooks, waiters, bar staff, performers and for promotion; go to boomchicago.nl and follow the links to Community and Jobs.

Busking is an ever-popular way to earn some money and the tolerance for which the Dutch are famous extends to street entertainers. The best venues are in the Vondelpark (where many Amsterdammers stroll on a Sunday) and in the city squares like Stadsplein and Leidseplein. Some pitches (like the one outside the 'smoking' coffee shop the Bulldog) are in such demand that you may have to wait your turn. Regular buskers have their favourite pitches, so be cautious about muscling in.

Schiphol Airport is a major employer. Try the employment agency Adecco at the airport (☎ 020 654 4767) or others listed at uitzendbureau.nl/schiphol. You can check out the Undutchables Recruitment Agency (the 'recruitment agency for internationals') which has offices in Amsterdam, Amstelveen, Rotterdam, The Hague, Utrecht and Eindhoven (undutchables.nl).

Proper jobs may not be outside the reach of non-Dutch speakers with relevant experience, as Paul Jones from Australia discovered:

> ***Having been working for a number of years at home in Australia and having transferable skills in IT, it made sense to find work in Europe in my field to finance my trip. Prior to leaving, I found a job by using the internet and having interviews over the phone. I still like the fact that I got my first job by having an interview on my mobile phone that was the clearest while standing on a city street that provided a nice drowning out kind of noise. Not the best conditions for an interview but it worked. The job happened to be in the Netherlands where I had never wanted to go but that was the job that I was accepted for first, so I took it as a stepping stone.***

You might try a specialist recruitment agency in the IT field like Adnexus Recruitment in Amsterdam (adnexus-recruitment.com).

Au Pairs

Since Dutch is not a language which attracts a large number of students, au pairing in the Netherlands is not well known. However a number of private agencies can place au pairs with Dutch or international families. Working conditions are favourable (e.g. pocket money of €300–€340 per month with two days off a week and insurance costs are met by the host family) but you must stay at least six months. The main agencies are reputed to offer solid back-up, guidance on contacting fellow au pairs and advice on local courses and excursions.

The international exchange organisation Travel Active (0478 551900; aupair@travelactive.nl) has an incoming programme for foreign au pairs aged 18 to 25 as well as sending Dutch young people abroad on various work exchanges. The programme is free to incoming au pairs, although some co-operating agents abroad may charge a fee. Another large agency is S- Au Pair Intermediate in 's-Hertogenbosch (☎ 073 6149483; saupair.com) with partners in many unusual countries like Botswana and Uzbekistan.

Jill Weseman from the States was very pleased with her au pair placement in a village of just 500 people 30km from Groningen:

> ***After graduation I accepted an au pairing position in Holland, mainly because there is no prior language requirement here. I really lucked out and ended up with a family who has been great to me. Though the situation sounds difficult at best – four children aged 1½, 3, 5 and 7, one day off a week and a rather remote location in the very north of Holland – I have benefited a great deal. The social life is surprisingly good for such a rural area.***

Two other agencies are located in the Hague: Au Pair Agency Mondial (☎ 070 365 1401; aupair-agency.nl) and the House-o-Orange Au Pairs (☎ 070 324 5903; house-o-orange@planet.nl; house-o-orange.nl) which also has lots of families in Belgium as well. For others see the website for the Dutch Au Pair Association, NAPO (Nederlandse Au Pair Organisatie; napoweb.nl).

BELGIUM

Belgium is a country that is often ignored. Sandwiched between France and the Netherlands, its population of 10.5 million can be broadly divided between the French-speaking people of Wallonia in the south (about 40% of the total population) and those who speak Flemish (which is almost identical to Dutch) in the north.

Belgium has no large agricultural industry comparable to those of its neighbours: it needs neither the extra fruit pickers that France does, nor the unskilled processors of Dutch bulbs. Yet the unemployment rate has been gradually falling and now stands at 7% which is only slightly higher than the UK rate.

As in neighbouring Holland, employment legislation is strictly enforced in Belgium with favourable minimum wages, compulsory bonuses, sickness and holiday pay for all legal workers. The demand for temporary workers is especially strong in Belgium because of the generous redundancy regulations which discourage employers from hiring permanent staff. Of course the many multinational companies, attracted by the headquarters of the European Union in Brussels, have a constant and fluctuating demand for bilingual office and other workers.

REGULATIONS

Although the requirement has been abolished for EU citizens to obtain residence permits when staying in other member states for more than three months, Belgium still requires foreign residents to register with the local authorities. Within four months of your arrival you should take to your local Town Hall (*Maison Communale* or *Gemeentehuis*) a valid EU passport and proof that you can fund your stay (by working, being self-employed, studying, supported by a spouse, etc.). Some local authorities will also request photos, a housing contract, birth certificate and/or European Health Insurance Card.

Non-EU citizens will have to find an employer willing to apply for a work permit (*carte professionnelle*) on their behalf from the Office National de l'Emploi. Assuming they want to stay longer than three months in paid employment, they must also be in possession before arrival in Belgium of a temporary residence permit (*Autorisation de Séjour Provisoire* or *Voorlopige Verblijfsvergunning*). Assuming all this has been done, the local council (*Commune*) will issue a *Certificat d'inscription au registre des étrangers* (C.I.R.E.) initially valid for a year.

SEASONAL WORK

Although Belgium's seaside resorts like Knokke-Heist, Blankenberge and De Panne, and other holiday centres like Bouillon in the Ardennes are hardly household names, there is a sizeable tourist industry in Belgium where seasonal work is available. The more mainstream tourist centre of Bruges is very busy in the summer. Travellers have a chance of being given free accommodation in exchange for some duties at one of the city's four or five private hostels. Venture Abroad based in Derbyshire (☎ 01332 342050; ventureabroad.co.uk) employs a few reps, including students with a background in scouting or guiding, for its programme in Belgium. Ski Ten International takes on French-speaking tennis instructors and monitors to work at summer camps (☎ 081 21 30 51; martine@ski-ten.be).

The best way of finding short-term general work, apart from contacting possible employers directly, is to visit a branch of the Belgian employment service *Agences Locales pour l'Emploi* or ALEs. A special division called T-Interim in Brussels (tbrussels.be) specialises in placing people in temporary jobs. Most jobs will require a good knowledge of at least one foreign language. People who live in the south-east of England can make use of the EURES Channel Network (eureschannel.org) which assists people looking for jobs in West Flanders and Hainaut in western Belgium, Nord-pas-de-Calais in northern France and Kent, with bilingual Euro-Advisers in Mons, Lille and Dover.

AU PAIRS

As the capital of the European Union, Belgium has a high demand for au pairs. The government stipulates that au pairs be paid €450 a month for 20 hours of work a week and €500 for au pairs plus. Non-EU au pairs are required to enrol in a language course; most study four to six hours a week. While many British and North Americans make their arrangements over the internet, the Stufam agency in Wemmel (☎ 02 460 33 95; aupair.stufam@scarlet.be; aupair-stufam.be) and Au Pair International in West Flanders (☎ 051 460 525; aupairinternational.be) make placements throughout Belgium.

Vlan is a useful classified portal with job listings in French or Dutch at vlanemploi.be. Prospective au pairs should look under the heading 'Entretien et Gens de Maison'.

TEACHING

The casual EFL teacher will probably have trouble finding work in Belgium where there is a great deal of competition from highly qualified expatriates. Yet, despite the large number of well-qualified expatriate spouses and others who take up teaching, some schools are always recruiting, among them the Thema Language School in Ixelles near Brussels (themalingua.be). Almost all foreign teachers who begin to work for an institute do so on a freelance basis and will have to deal with their own tax and social security. The starting pay at most schools falls between €10 and €27 an hour.

Berlitz have several schools in Belgium which employ a number of native English speakers with a university degree after they have done the compulsory Berlitz training and a trial teaching period of three months; contact Berlitz Language Services, Avenue Louise 306–310, 1050 Brussels; (teaching@berlitz.be or joke.vandaele@berlitz.be). They pay employees €9.89 for a 40-minute lesson, and €15 to freelancers.

Other organisations in Brussels to try if you have a TEFL background include Kiddy & Junior Classes asbl (☎ 02 218 3920; kiddyclasses.net), May International Training Consultants (☎ 02 536 0670; mayintl.com), Call International (☎ 02 644 9595; callinter.com), CLL (Centre de Langues) based in Louvain-la-Neuve which employs about 100 teachers to work on a freelance basis, and Phone Languages (☎ 02 647 4020; phonelanguages.com). The latter employs people with American or British accents to teach over the phone and pays about €10 an hour.

Prolinguis runs language courses for children, teenagers and adults in remote countryside near Arlon in the province of Belgium called Luxembourg (6717 Thiaumont; ☎ 063 22 04 62; prolinguis.be). EFL-trained teachers are hired by Prolinguis on 12-month or 2-month contracts and are paid €80–€96 a day plus board and lodging on campus.

CONTACTS

The Federation Infor Jeunes Wallonie-Bruxelles is a non-profit making organisation which co-ordinates youth information offices in French-speaking Belgium (inforjeunes.be). These can give advice on work as well as leisure, youth rights, accommodation, etc. The website of the Brussels branch has links to useful job info at inforjeunes-bxl.be/offresdejob.htm. Advising on temporary and holiday jobs is among Infor Jeunes' services.

Belgium's long-standing English language weekly publication *The Bulletin* carries job adverts such as live-in positions and language tuition (xpats.com/jobs); the magazine is published on Thursdays and can be bought from newsstands for €2.70. *Newcomer* is a bi-annual publication published in March and September (available from newstands for €3); this guide is aimed at new arrivals in Belgium and carries useful sections called 'Getting to Grips with the Red Tape' and 'Job-Seekers' Guide'.

VOLUNTARY OPPORTUNITIES

The Flemish association of young environmentalists called Natuur 2000 in Antwerp (☎ 03 231 26 04; natuur2000@telenet.be; natuur2000.be) is a Flemish conservation organisation that hosts short summer workcamps and study projects throughout Belgium open to all nationalities. The fee of €60 for five days covers accommodation, food, insurance and local transport. Other possibilities exist in their bat reserve-cum-nature education centre situated in an old WWI fortress near Antwerp (May till September).

Young people interested in participating in residential archaeological digs in Namur lasting one to three weeks in the summer should contact Archeolo-j in Rixensart (☎ 81 611073; archeolo-J@skynet.be; skene.be). Residential archaeological digs accept paying volunteers, some for teenagers, some for adults. The fee is €299 for 8 days, €549 for 15 days and €670 for 22 days (2009).

LUXEMBOURG

If Belgium is sometimes neglected, Luxembourg is completely by-passed. Yet it is an independent country with an unemployment rate of less than 5% (among the lowest in the EU) and a number of useful facilities for foreigners. The national employment service (Administration de l'Emploi or ADEM) at 10 rue Bender, L-1229 Luxembourg (☎ 352 2478 53 00; adem.public.lu) operates a Student Employment Service (info.jeu@adem.public.lu) for students and young people looking for summer jobs in warehouses, restaurants, etc. To find out about possibilities, you must visit this office in person. Or it might be just as fruitful, keeping your eyes and ears open in hostels. While cycling through the countryside, Mary Hall was struck by the number of travellers working on campsites and in restaurants in Luxembourg City.

With a total population of 486,000 and an area of just 999 square miles, job opportunities are understandably limited. However, they do exist especially in the tourist industry for anyone who has mastered a European language in addition to English. Check an online directory of hotels such as hotels.lu for leads or the specialist job site horesto.com/jobs/luxembourg.html where the Hotel Eden Au Lac near Echternach was advertising a number of positions at the time of going to print.

The main language is Luxembourgish (variously called Luxembourgeois and Letzeburgesch) but both German and French are spoken and understood by virtually everyone. Casual workers will normally need a reasonable knowledge of at least one of these. Temporary office work abounds for linguists since many multinational companies are based in Luxembourg. Addresses of potential employers can be obtained from the membership list of the British Chamber of Commerce in Luxembourg (bcc.lu).

Helpful Organisations

The Centre Information Jeunes (CIJ), 26 Place de la Gare, Geleria Kons, 1616 Luxembourg (☎ +352 26 29 32 00; cij.lu) runs a holiday job service between January and August for students from the EU. Wages in Luxembourg are very high; for example as of 2009, the minimum for those over 18 is €1,122 per month and the hourly minimum is €10.

Since 2003 Luxembourg has not recognised the special legal status of au pairs so that they are treated like all foreign workers which means they must have a written contract of employment and pay social security contributions. There is plenty of demand from families, so the best way is to browse through online au pair matching services such as findaupair.com. Check ads also on 352.lu/babysitting-au-pair.html.

FRANCE

Although you may occasionally encounter the legendary hostility of the French towards the English, more often you will be treated with warmth and helpfulness especially in the countryside. So many English-speaking people reside in France that expatriate grapevines are an invaluable source of job information. Unemployment is among the highest of the old EU countries, just a shade under the EU average of 8% at the beginning of 2009, and the rate among young people is much higher. It would be a mistake to expect to walk into a job just because you have a GCSE in French and enjoy eating *pains au chocolat.*

Although the French tourist industry offers many seasonal jobs, there are even more in agriculture: approximately 100,000 foreign workers are employed on the grape harvest alone. Workers come from all over, but mainly from Eastern Europe and the Balkans, North Africa and Southern Europe. You may find yourself working in the fields next to a student from Québec, an Armenian migrant worker or a young Dane or Scot who is touring Europe as a nomadic worker. It is possible to support yourself throughout the year in France by combining work in the various fruit harvests with either conventional jobs such as tutoring in English, or more unusual occupations from busking to gathering snails.

One important feature of working in France is that you should be paid at least the *SMIC* (*salaire minimum interprofessionel de croissance*) or national minimum wage. There are slightly different rates for seasonal agricultural work and full-time employees; at present the basic SMIC is €8.71 per hour or €1,321 per month (gross) based on a working week of 35 hours, the statutory maximum in France. These are adjusted annually to take account of inflation.

REGULATIONS

Tax inspectors and immigration officers carry out spot checks in tourist resorts, and employers in even the most out-of-the-way places have refused to hire anyone who lacks the right documents. Wine-makers in Bordeaux have been told that if they are caught employing non-EU nationals without papers, they will not be allowed to bring in their harvest the following year.

EU Nationals

Since 2003, EU citizens have been free of the obligation to obtain residence permits to live and work in other EU countries. Once you take up paid employment in France, your employer must complete all the necessary formalities for registering you with social security (*sécu*) at the local

URSSAF office where you will be issued with a registration card and start to have contributions deducted from your wages. After working a summer season at Disneyland Paris (described later), Keith Leishman offered what he considers a crucial piece of advice, which is to take a certified copy of your birth certificate translated into French. It must include your father's full name and your mother's maiden name. Keith arrived without this abstruse document and as a result had trouble registering for social security and furthermore in getting paid.

Legal employers will deduct about 20% for social security payments, even before you have a number. These can be counted towards National Insurance in Britain, if you subsequently need to claim benefit. You may also lose a further 5% in tax.

Non-EU Formalities

Australians and New Zealanders under 30 are eligible for one-year working holiday visas for France. Non-EU nationals must obtain work documents before they leave their home country in order to work legally and this is fiendishly difficult since it depends on finding an employer who can argue that no French or EU national could do the job.

A more manageable approach is to turn yourself into a student. Foreign students with a *carte de séjour* and who are enrolled in an institution that registers its students with the national health insurance system (*sécu*) have the right to work during their studies. The maximum number of hours worked in a year is 964 which equates to approximately 15–20 hours a week in term-time and full-time in the vacations. In order to obtain a student visa, you will have to have good French language skills, two years of higher education (which may be waived if attending art college) and proof of financial support in the form of a notarised statement from a bank or benefactor that you can access enough per month to live on. Students based in Paris should apply at the Centre des étudiants étrangers, 13 rue Miollis in the 15th arrondissement; otherwise apply at the local Sous-préfecture.

Special Schemes for North Americans

A Paris organisation, Centre d'Echanges Internationaux (CEI), administers a Work in France programme for higher education students over 18 or occasionally new graduates from outside Europe. Participants are given temporary work permits (*autorisation provisoire de travail*) to work in France for up to six months starting any time. Candidates in training programmes may stay for up to one year. All candidates must be conversant in French. The basic placement fee for independent job-seekers is €360. CEI can also arrange jobs and internships for a fee of €825 to €980. Details are available from CEI Paris (☎ 01 43 29 60 20/40 51 11 81; wif@cei4vents.com; cei4vents.com).

BUNAC in the US (bunac.org) administers a Work in France programme for full-time university students aged 18–35 who must prove that they can function in French (this will be tested in writing) and who can take with them €1,500. Participants may work only up to three months in the period between May and September. They will be assisted on arrival by BUNAC's partner organisation in Paris, Aquarius (aquariusabroad.org).

The Cultural Services of the French Embassy in Washington, DC (☎ 202 944 6011) collates information of use to Americans who wish to study or intern in France and oversees an internship programme for French-speaking Americans (www.frenchculture.org) that helps them with the formalities and provides support information. It also manages the long-established English Teaching Assistants programme (assistant.washington-amba@diplomatie.gouv.fr) which runs from October 1st for seven to nine months. Up to 1,500 undergraduates and graduates under 30 who have a good working knowledge of French can be placed. The gross monthly stipend is €950.

Americans who are interested in arranging an internship in France may contact AIPT (see Introduction) or the French-American Chamber of Commerce in New York which oversees an International Career Development Program (☎ 212 867 0123; icdp@faccnyc.org). The programme is for graduates aged 18–35 with relevant professional experience. The Chamber can assist suitable candidates arrange a six-month visa that can be renewed twice.

The French American Center in Montpellier (☎ 04 67 92 30 66; frenchamericancenter.com) arranges au pair placements for Americans aged 18–25 with families in the Languedoc region plus internships in local businesses lasting up to three months. It also runs a local English language teaching programme for adults and young people. Application can be made on-line; the fee is $125–$160. Details are available from the French-American Center of Montpellier (jeanettefranklin@gmail.com).

A one-year visa is available to Canadians aged 18–35 with a working knowledge of French (swap.ca). In addition to paying the registration fee of $230, SWAP participants must have access to support funds of C$3,000. Special exchange visas are available for students who are residents of Québec through the Association Québec-France (9 Place Royale, Québec G1K 4G2; prog@quebecfrance.qc.ca). They can issue special work permits to cover the grape harvest or a summer job in youth hostels, holiday camps, etc.

THE JOB HUNT

Internet browsers might start with several useful websites: paris-anglo.com in English has articles and links on working in France plus job classified ads; http://france.angloinfo.com has reams of practical information specific to 16 regions, while the French-language youth information site phosphore.com incorporates a job search function with quite a lot of hard information and contact details. The online community noticeboard kijiji.fr has a large number of employment classifieds. As usual the *Pages Jaunes* are available online (pagesjaunes.fr) which can prove a great help when drawing up a list of relevant places to ask for work.

Once you get into the countryside, the French can be remarkably generous not only in offering lifts but in helping their passengers to find work. If you are offered seasonal work ahead of the start date and plan to leave the area in the meantime, stay in constant touch with the employer; not only can start dates vary but farmers and hotel managers don't always keep their promises.

ANPE

The former Agence National pour l'Emploi or ANPE is now known as Pôle emploi (pole-emploi.fr). The national employment service of France has dozens of offices in Paris and hundreds throughout the country. The website lists all the branches by region or postcode (anpe.fr), providing addresses, telephone and fax numbers. For example the ANPE in Narbonne (ANPE, BP 802, 29 rue Mazzini, 11108 Narbonne Cedex) has seasonal hotel vacancies from May to September, and others can provide details of when agricultural work is available. Although EU nationals should have equal access to the employment facilities in other member states, this is not always the case in France unless the job-seeker speaks good French and has a stable local address. If possible foreign job-seekers should work with a EURES Adviser.

Seasonal employment offices are set up in key regions to deal with seasonal demands like the *vendanges* for the grape harvest and in ski resorts.

CIJ

There are 27 regional *Centres d'Information Jeunesse* (CIJ) and 1,300 smaller youth information points in France which may be of use to the working traveller. Helping people to find jobs is only one of their activities: they can also advise on cheap accommodation, the legal rights of temporary workers, etc. The main Paris branch is CIDJ (Centre d'Information et de Documentation Jeunesse) whose foyer notice board is a useful starting place for the job-seeker in Paris. It also sells books and leaflets (mainly €2.50) on such subjects as au pairing and the regulations that affect foreign students in France. Check the site cidj-librairie.com for a complete list, which includes *Etrangers en France: Vos Droits* (2003) for €22. CIDJ may be visited at 101 Quai Branly, 75740 Paris Cedex 15 (☎ 01 44 49 12 00; cidj.com).

In order to find out about actual vacancies you must visit the CIDJ offices in person, preferably first thing in the morning. Employers notify centres of their temporary vacancies; some offices just display the details on notice boards, while others operate a more formal system in co-operation with the local ANPE (e.g., CIDJ in Paris registers about 10,000 summer jobs).

Private Employment Agencies

Agences de travail temporaire (temporary work bureaux) or *agences d'intérim* may be of some use. Among the largest are Manpower (manpower.fr) and Adecco (adecco.fr); others can be found in the *Yellow Pages* under the heading *Travail Intérimaire* or from the Franco-British Chamber of Commerce in Paris (☎ 01 53 30 81 30; francobritishchambers.com/recruitment.asp). Almost all will require good French, and many specialise in a field such as industrial, medical or office work. Although vacancies for unskilled jobs are few and far between, some travellers have made good use of agencies.

ON HIS YEAR ABROAD DURING HIS DEGREE COURSE, MATTHEW BINNS WENT TO A JOB AGENCY IN PARIS WITHOUT HIGH HOPES OF SUCCESS:

I foolishly said I was prepared to do anything. The bloke in the agency looked astonished and gave me, I think, the most unpopular job on his books – plongeur in a factory canteen in the suburbs. George Orwell's account in Down and Out in Paris and London about his time as a plongeur should be required reading for all would-be dishwashers in Paris. I did three weeks in this job until the regular plongeur came back, poor sod. The worst bit is arriving at work with a hangover and putting on yesterday's wet clothes. But the pay was excellent.

TOURISM

The best areas to look for work in the tourist industry of France are the Alps for the winter season, December-April, and the Côte d'Azur for the summer season, June-September, though jobs exist throughout the country. The least stressful course is to fix up work ahead of time with a UK campsite or barge holiday company in summer or ski company in winter. For example the giant First Choice Holidays (firstchoice4jobs.co.uk) hires people, not necessarily with qualifications, to work in hotels in the Alps and Normandy. Esprit Alpine Sun hires resort managers, chalet hosts and childcare staff for their summer programme in the Alps (☎ 01252 618318; recruitment@esprit-holidays.co.uk).

Eurolingua offers hotel work experience in the south of France lasting three to six months. The work is paid and comes with free staff accommodation and meals in the hotel. The programme is preceded by an appropriate language course at the nearest Eurolingua school, for instance in Montpellier, Nice and Toulon. These programmes are suitable for both EU and non-EU students meeting French immigration requirements; details at eurolingua.com/Work_Experience(France).htm. The programme fee is €995 for 2–3 months, and €1,290 for 4–6 months (30% extra for non-EU students).

If you set off without anything pre-arranged, one of the easiest places to find work is at fast food establishments like Pizza Hut France or Quick Restaurants (quick-restaurants.com); the latter employ nearly 5,000 people in France (recrute@quick.fr). Americana is still quite trendy in France and English-speaking staff fit well with the image. The hardest place to find work, except at the lowest level (e.g. dishwasher) is with reputable French-owned hotels and restaurants, where high standards are maintained. Your best chances will be in small family-run hotels where the hours and conditions vary according to the temperament of the *patron.*

Hotels and Restaurants

Remember that the vast majority of restaurants are staffed by waiters rather than waitresses. Newspapers in holiday towns may carry adverts, e.g. *Nice Matin* (http://emploi.nicematin.com). But most people succeed by turning up at a resort and asking door to door and, in the opinion of veteran British traveller Jason Davies, 'door-to-door' should be just that:

> ***Before I was down to my last few coins I had been choosy about which establishments to ask at. 'That doesn't look very nice' or 'that's too posh' or 'that's probably closed' were all thoughts which ensured that I walked past at least three in five. But in Nice I discovered that the only way to do it is to pick a main street (like the pedestrianised area in Nice with its high density of restaurants) and ask at EVERY SINGLE place. I visited 30–40 one morning and I would say that at least 20 of those needed more employees. But only one was satisfied with my standard of French, and I got the job of commis waiter.***

Speaking French to a reasonable standard greatly improves chances of finding a job, though fluency is by no means a requirement. Kimberly Ladone from the American east coast spent a summer working as a receptionist/chambermaid, also in Nice:

> ***I found the job in April, at the first hotel I approached, and promised to return at the start of the season in June. While there, I met many English-speaking working travellers employed in various hotels. No one seemed bothered by work permit regulations as most jobs paid cash in hand. My advice to anyone seeking a job on the French Riviera would be to go as early in the season as possible and ask at hotels featured in English guidebooks such as Let's Go: France, since these tend to need English-speaking staff. My boss hired me primarily because I could handle the summer influx of clueless tourists who need help with everything from making a phone call to reading a train schedule.***

It must be said that not everyone finds work easily, as Alison Cooper found: *'Last summer I tried to find work along the French Riviera, but was unsuccessful. I met many people at campsites who were in the same position as myself. From my experience most employers wanted people who could speak fluent French, and German as well. Otherwise you have to be very very lucky.'*

The best time to look for work on the Côte d'Azur is the end of February when campsites well known to working travellers, such as Les Prairies de la Mer and Camping de la Plage at Port Grimaud near St Tropez host representatives from camping holiday companies trying to get organised in time for Easter. If you are on the spot you can often wangle free accommodation in exchange for three or four hours of work a day. If you can't be there then, try the middle of May at the beginning of the peak season. When Peter Goldman couldn't find work on boats as he had hoped (because of rainy September weather) he tuned in to Riviera Radio and heard about a local job stripping wallpaper from luxury apartments in Monte Carlo.

Campsites

An estimated 7,000 campsites in France employ an army of seasonal staff even though some of them are small family-run operations which need one or two assistants. You can make direct contact with individual campsites listed in any guide to French campsites (e.g. Michelin's *Camping France*), or you can simply show up. Jobs are not glamorous, like cleaning the loos, manning the bar or snack bar, doing some maintenance, etc. Even if there are no actual jobs, you may be given the use of a tent in exchange for minimal duties, outside the peak season.

A number of British-based travel companies offer holidaymakers a complete package providing pre-assembled tents and a campsite courier to look after any problems that arise. Since this kind of holiday appeals to families, people with a childcare background or who can organise children's activities are especially in demand. In addition to the Europe-wide companies like Eurocamp and Vacansoleil (addresses in *Tourism* chapter), the following all take on campsite reps/couriers and other seasonal staff:

Carisma Holidays: Hertfordshire; ☎ 01923 287344; personnel@carisma.co.uk; carisma holidayjobs.co.uk; 2009 wage range £125–£175 per week.
In2Camping: Blackpool; ☎ 01253 593333; in2camping.com.
Matthews Holidays: Surrey; 01483 284044; matthewsfrance.co.uk/MH/jobs.html.
Venue Holidays: Kent; ☎ 01233 629950; jobs@venueholidays.co.uk; website carries job information.

The best time to start looking for summer season jobs from England is between November and February. In most cases candidates are expected to have at least A-level standard French, though some companies claim that a knowledge of French is merely 'preferred'. It is amazing how far a good dictionary and a knack for making polite noises in French can get you. Many impose a minimum age of 21.

The massive camping holiday industry generates winter work as well. Brad Europe Ltd has depots in Nantes and Beaucaire near Avignon that clean and repair tents and bedding on behalf of many of the major companies. Staff (who need not speak French though it is an advantage) are needed for the laundry and distribution for four to six months in winter and summer. Gite accommodation is provided free of charge in addition to the UK minimum wage. A driving licence is essential for the delivery drivers but not for the laundry operatives. Brad Europe's UK office is in Wigan (☎ 01942 829747; info@bradeurope.com; bradeurope.com/vacancies.html).

Short bursts of work are available in the spring (about three weeks in May) and autumn (three weeks in September) to teams of people who put up and take down the tents at campsites, known as *montage* and *démontage*. For example the Dutch company Vacansoleil takes on English-speaking people to work in small international teams between September 8th and October 24th to break down and store tents for the following season (camping-jobs@vacansoleil.com).

Holiday Centres

Outdoor activity centres are another major employer of summer staff, both general domestic staff and sports instructors. Try the companies mentioned in the chapter on Tourism such as PGL and Acorn Adventure (acorn-jobs.co.uk). Manor Adventure based in Shropshire (☎ 01584 861333;

manoradventurejobs.com) hires holiday co-ordinators and sports instructors for its adventure centre Le Chateau du Broutel along the coast from Boulogne.

Keen cyclists could try to get a job with a cycling holiday company active in France such as Belle France in Kent (☎ 01580 214010; enquiries@bellefrance.co.uk), Bent's Bicycle & Walking Tours in Shropshire (☎ 01568 780800; info@bentstours.com), and Susi Madron's Cycling for Softies in Manchester (☎ 0161 248 8282; cycling-for-softies.co.uk) whose staff are over 25. Headwater Holidays in Cheshire (☎ 01606 720033; headwater.com) looks to hire French-speaking reps (minimum age 21) and British Canoe Union qualified canoe instructors.

For work in a more unusual activity holiday, contact a hot air balloon company such as Bombard Balloon Adventures in Beaune (jobs2009@bombardsociety.org; bombardsociety.org/jobs) or France Montgolfieres based in Montrichard (☎ 02 54 32 20 48; jane@franceballoons.com). Ground crew are hired for the summer season May to October and must have physical fitness and strength, a cheerful personality, clean-cut appearance and year-old clean driving licence and driving experience. Whereas Bombard has a large American clientele, Montgolfieres requires its staff to speak French. The minimum French wage is paid.

Ski Resorts

France is the best of all countries in Europe for British and Irish people to find jobs in ski resorts, mainly because it is the number one country for British skiers, 200,000 of whom go there every year. Most of the resorts are high enough to create reliable snow conditions throughout the season. The main problem is the shortage of worker accommodation; unless you find a live-in job you will have to pay nearly holiday prices or find a friend willing to rent out his or her sofa. Since many top French resorts are purpose-built, a high proportion of the holiday accommodation is in self-catering flats or designed for chalet parties. This means that not only is there a shortage of rental accommodation, but there are fewer jobs as waiters, bar and chamber staff for those who arrive in the resorts to look for work. There is an increasing number of English and Irish style pubs which are good places to find out about work.

If you are employed by a British tour operator, be aware that you will not be paid according to French employment law. The French authorities have estimated that 10,000 staff are employed to work for ski chalet companies and all of them are being paid much less than the SMIC, typically between £65 and £80 plus living expenses and lift pass. If trying to fix up a job from Britain, there are one or two agencies that arrange for young people with at least A level French to work in ski resorts. Jobs in the Alps (jobs-in-the-alps.co.uk) recruit EU nationals only as waiting staff, porters, kitchen porters and housekeepers in mountain resorts. Employers pay a net salary of approximately £500 in addition to free room and board. NBV Leisure in Hove (☎ 0870 220 2148; nbvleisure.com/recruitment.html) recruits staff for a huge range of seasonal jobs in French resorts operated by the French tour operator Eurogroup (eurogroup-vacances.com) which owns hotels, restaurants and chalets in ski and beach resorts in France (and the rest of Europe). Applicants must hold an EU passport and a UK National Insurance number.

Excellent ski recruitment websites include natives.co.uk, seasonworkers.com and freeradicals.co.uk, all of which match job-seekers with alpine and other vacancies. Qualified/experienced nannies are especially sought after. Specialist nanny agencies supply nannies to holidaying British families such as Jack Frosts in the Portes du Soleil (☎ 06 13 79 07 17; jackfrosts.net/jobs.htm).

Up to 30 British tour companies are present in Méribel alone, so this is one of the best resorts in which to conduct a job hunt. It may even be worth calling into the tourist office to ask about seasonal employment, though it is more promising to ask for work in person at hotels, bars, etc.

Looking for work out-of-season in October and November has the added advantage that well-placed youth hostels like the one in Séez les Arcs are empty and relatively cheap.

Resorts like Méribel are flooded with British workers just before the season and eventually by British guests, many of them school groups. The functioning language of many establishments is English. British chalet operator have also established a strong presence in Courchevel; at least one UK tour operator has its French office in the picturesque village of Le Praz, one of the five villages that comprise the resort of Courchevel. If you are not already familiar with the resorts, try to do some research beforehand, something Susan Beney regretted not doing: *'We took pot luck with the resort and on reflection would have done a bit more homework on resorts we might have preferred. La Tania was very limited; La Plagne would have been one hundred percent better.'*

Most jobs with British companies pay low wages but allow workers to ski or snowboard between 10am and 4pm. UK operators that recruit staff for Méribel and France generally include the following:

Esprit Holidays/Ski Total: Hampshire; ☎ 01252 618318; recruitment@esprit-holidays.co.uk or recruitment@skitotal.com; skijob.co.uk.

Family Ski Company: Malvern; ☎ 01684 540333; jobs@familyski.co.uk; offer many jobs in the French Alps.

Inghams: ☎ 020 8780 8803; inghams.co.uk/general_pages/jobosea.html.

Le Ski: Huddersfield; ☎ 01484 548996; recruitment@leski.com; leski.com/alpinejobs; jobs in Courchevel, La Tania and Val d'Isère.

Meriski: Cirencester; ☎ 01285 648518; hr@meriski.co.uk; meriski.co.uk; chalet cooks and nannies in greatest demand.

Scott Dunn: London SW17; 020 8682 5087; scottdunn.com/winter-season-ski-jobs.html; summer season jobs also.

Ski Beat: Chichester; ☎ 01243 832510; jobs@skibeat.co.uk; jobs in La Plagne, Tignes, Val d'Isère, La Tania and several others.

Ski Olympic: Doncaster; ☎ 01302 328820; skiolympic.co.uk/recruitment.

Supertravel Ski: London SE1; ☎ 020 7962 1369; skijobs@lotusgroup.co.uk; supertravel.co.uk/jobs.asp; takes on winter staff for France, primarily chalet chefs, chalet hosts with excellent cooking skills, chalet assistants with customer service skills, chalet managers fluent in French, and handymen/drivers; all applicants must hold an EU passport and have a National Insurance number.

Nannying is a very promising area of employment in ski resorts. Matt Tomlinson, who spent a year near Paris as an au pair, spent the winter season in Courchevel:

> ***I'm not sure if I just lucked out getting work or whether it is a question of having done most jobs, being presentable and enthusiastic. There certainly doesn't seem to be any shortage of employment opportunities in Courchevel and Le Praz during the busy periods. My first job was as a private nanny: easy work, good pay plus extra for babysitting. I moved on to doing Children's Club with one operator and then Snow Club with Ski Esprit. Not everyone was NNEB qualified though all had substantial childcare experience and most were hired in England. I would recommend anyone thinking of doing a nanny job in the Alps to think seriously before taking it on. The days were very long and tiring, especially when you have to keep track of 18 sets of ski gear.***

Success is far from guaranteed in any ski resort job hunt and competition for work is increasing. Val d'Isère attracts as many as 500 ski bums every November/December, many of whom hang around bars or the employment office for days in the vain hope that work will come their way. If looking for work in Val, listen to Radio Val d'Isère or pay the small registration fee to access jobvaldisere.com.

Yachts

Kevin Gorringe headed for the south of France in June several years ago with the intention of finding work on a private yacht. His destination was the British favourite of Antibes, where he began frequenting likely meeting places like La Gaffe English pub and the Irish bar as well as the agencies like Adrian Fisher and Blue Water. A number of crewing agencies are housed in the same building, La Galerie du Port, 8 Blvd d'Aguillon, 06600 Antibes; a list can be found on the useful directory site http://riviera.angloinfo.com.

Kevin recommends staying at one of the cheap campsites at Biot on the other side of Antibes, which is easily reached by public transport. Alternatively there are several crew hostels like Stella's Crew House (☎ 04 93 13 64 30) that could be goldmines of information. He and his girlfriend went round the quays asking for work but soon tired of begging for scrubbing jobs and decided to move on. They concluded that to find work in Antibes you have to be 'persistent, focused and able to get into the click'. Bill Garfield is one traveller who stuck at it. After a week of failure, Bill began asking at every single boat including the ones already swarming with workers and also all the boats big and small in the 'graveyard' (refitting area). Two weeks after leaving Solihull this tactic paid off and he was hired for a nine-week period to help refit a yacht in preparation for the summer charter season.

Look tidy and neat, be polite and when you get a job work hard. The first job is the hardest to get, but once you get in with this integrated community, captains will help you find other jobs after the refitting is finished. Of course many continue through the summer as deckhands on charter yachts and are paid €100+ a week plus tips (which sometimes match the wage). The charter season ends in late September when many yachts begin organising their crew for the trip to the West Indies.

A British tour company which hires instructors, reps and entertainers for its four sailing holiday centres in Southwest France is Rockley Watersports based in Poole (☎ 01202 677272; rockley-watersports.com/wiw).

Barges

The holiday barges that ply the rivers and canals of France hire cooks, hostesses, deckhands and captains. The best time to apply to the companies is in the new year. All prefer to employ only people who feel comfortable functioning in French even if the majority of their clientele is American or British.

European Waterways with an office in Middlesex (☎ 01784 482439; GoBarging.com) employs seasonal staff for its hotel barges in Europe. The season lasts from April to October and vacancies exist for barge pilots, chefs, deck hands, tour guides and housekeepers for the luxury barge fleet. All applicants must have an EU passport (or the right to work in the UK), a current driving licence, and some knowledge of French culture and language. Wages start at £780 per month. All positions include on-board accommodation, meals and uniform. Croisières Touristiques Françaises based in Venarey-les-Laumes on the Burgundy Canal (☎ 03 80 96 17 10; ctf.boat@club-internet.fr) operates five luxury hotel barges employing chefs, guides, stewardesses, deckhands and pilots. Inexperienced crew members are paid from £900 per month and gratuities are divided among the crew.

GRAPE-PICKING

Every year the lure of the *vendange* attracts many hopefuls, whether for financial gain or the romance of participating in an ancient ritual. Past participants agree about the negative aspects of the job: the eight or nine hours a day of back-breaking work, often for seven days a week, and the weather, which is too cold and damp in the early autumn mornings and too hot at mid-day. Waterproofs are essential because you will be expected to continue picking in the pouring rain and mud. The accommodation may consist of a space in a barn for a sleeping bag, and the sanitation arrangements of a cold water tap. But despite all this, every year the grape-growing regions of France are flooded with job-seekers.

Part of the attraction is the wage. Although it is not usually much higher than *le SMIC* of €8.71 (porters sometimes earn more, especially when the vineyards are located on steep hills), there is little opportunity to spend your earnings on an isolated farm and most people save several hundred pounds during a typical fortnight-long harvest. Anna Ling joined the vendange in Epernay in September 2008, and after working ten straight days for eight hours a day, earned a lump sum in cash of €800.

If you work for the same *patron* for seven consecutive days, you should be paid an overtime rate. Be prepared for at least 15% to be deducted for social security.

The major threat to jobs at present comes from mechanisation. A great many farmers are clubbing together to invest in the great noisy juggernauts harvesting day and night, which have almost completely replaced human beings in some areas like Cognac and south of Bordeaux. However, many chateaux are sticking with traditional hand-picking.

Work and Conditions

Working and living conditions can vary greatly from farm to farm. Obviously it is easier for the owner of a small vineyard with a handful of workers to provide decent accommodation than for the owner of a chateau who may have over 100 workers to consider. Farmers almost always provide some sort of accommodation, but this can vary from a rough and ready dormitory to a comfortable room in his own house. Food is normally provided, but again this can vary from the barely adequate to the sublime: one picker can write that 'the food was better than that in a 5-star hotel, so we bought flowers for the cook at the end of the harvest', while another may complain of instant mashed potatoes or of having to depend on whatever he or she can manage to buy and prepare. When both food and accommodation are provided there is normally a deduction of one or two hours' pay from each day's wage.

Free wine is a frequent feature of the job, for example Dustie Hickey was allowed a seemingly endless supply of wine which '*lifted up the workers' spirits but often left me falling into the bushes*'. (When she was offered the same perk during the olive harvest later in the autumn, she wisely sold her daily two litres of wine.)

Hours also vary. Whereas one traveller found the structuring of the working day ridiculous, with a 1½ hour lunch break and no other breaks between 7.45am and 6pm, others have found themselves finishing the day's picking at lunchtime, especially in the far south near the Spanish border, where the sun is unbearably hot in the afternoon.

The work itself will consist of either picking or portering. Picking involves bending to cut the grapes with secateurs from a vine that may be only three and a half feet tall, and filling a pannier that you drag along behind you. Gloves are useful if you don't want your hands stained by grape juice (white grapes are the worst) and rubber boots are the footwear of choice. The panniers full of grapes are emptied into an *hotte*, a large basket weighing up to 100lb which the porters carry to a trailer. The first few days as a *cueilleur/cueilleuse* or *coupeur* (picker) are the worst, as you adjust to the stooping posture and begin to use muscles you never knew you had. The job of porter is sought after, since it does not require the constant bending and is less boring because you move around the vineyard.

The further south you go the more likely you are to find yourself competing with migrant workers from the new Europe, Spain, Portugal and North Africa. Large and famous chateaux (like Lafite) often use a contracted team of pickers who return every season and who can stand the fast and furious pace. These immigrant workers tend to return to the same large vineyards year after year, where they work in highly efficient teams which are normally preferred to individual travellers.

How to Find Work

Provided you are prepared to disregard their advice if it is discouraging, the local ANPE in a wine-growing region is worth visiting in case they are able and willing to tell you which farmers need workers. As mentioned they are not usually helpful unless you speak good French. But if you can navigate a computer in French, you can conduct a DIY job hunt and print out relevant numbers to phone (after buying a local phone card). One traveller who was informed 'C'est complet' by the ANPE in Saumur, the tourist office, a *maison de vin* and a private employment agency, decided to persevere and, after a ten-mile walk east along the Loire, found a job.

When Michael Jordan was looking for grape-picking work in Alsace, he noticed that every *mairie* had a poster up advising job-seekers to present themselves to the ANPE in Colmar. Alsace Vendanges is a seasonal service of the ANPEs in Colmar, Guebwiller, Molsheim and Sélestat which operates a recruitment telephone number 'Allo Vendanges' on 03 89 20 16 65. The jobs that tend to go unfilled are for people with their own accommodation (tent, caravan) and their own transport. Because of its more northerly location, Alsace can be very cold during the harvest, which puts some potential competition off.

Below are listed some major wine-producing regions, with rough guidelines as to the starting dates of the harvest. It should be stressed that these dates can vary by days or even weeks from year to year. After a very hot summer, the harvest can start a full month early. Even vineyards a few miles apart may start picking up to a week apart.

Alsace – October 15th
Pôle emploi offices in Colmar, Strasbourg and many others.
Beaujolais – September 10th
Pôle emploi in Villefranche-sur-Saone
Bordeaux – September 25th
Pôle emploi in Bordeaux and Pauillac
Burgundy – October 6th
Pôle emploi Macon and Dijon
Champagne – October 1st
Pôle emploi in Reims and Epernay
Languedoc-Roussillon – September 15th
Pôle emploi in Perpignan, Carcassonne, Nimes, Bagnols sur Cèze, Beziers, etc.
Loire – October 6th
Pôle emploi in Tours and Angers

For those who do not want to beard the ANPE/Pôle lion, there is an easier way. A Dutch agency called Appellation Controllée (☎ +31 50 549 2434; info@apcon.nl; apcon.nl) mediates between grape-growers (in Beaujolais north of Lyon, Burgundy, Chablis and Champagne) and up to 500 Europeans looking for jobs in the *vendange*. Work lasts between one and three weeks in September. In exchange for working eight hours a day, seven days a week you will earn €57 a day plus get full board and lodging. The ApCon agency fee is €99 and they have a good message board.

After signing up with ApCon, Danielle Thomas from the Netherlands was set up with a grape-picking job in Beaune starting September 21st. In 11 days, she earned about €650 gross, €550 after deductions were made for tax and food costs. At her farm in Meloisey, accommodation was provided for grape-pickers who had worked with the farming family before, but first-timers were asked to bring their own tents and sleep in the garden. Danielle had no trouble identifying the good and bad aspects of her experience:

> ***The work was very hard, though very enjoyable because of the team. Back pain was experienced often and at the end I had a lot of cuts in my hand, 22 to be exact. I would not advise sleeping in a tent, since at that time of year, I woke up cold every day and not in the right mental mood for the day's work. Breakfast was limited, though both lunch and dinner were very large and impressive, five course meals, including soup and bread, salad and vegetables, meat or fish, a variety of cheeses and finally a dessert. With each lunch and dinner, local wine or their own wine was also provided. Dinners were very social and fun.***
>
> ***This was my first Vendange and I must say, even though the work was hard, it was a very pleasant experience. The family was very welcoming and the food was exceptional! I met a lot of really nice people and I hope to go back next year. I'd advise anyone thinking of doing Vendange in the future, that it would certainly be a good idea – as long as you have an open mind and are ready for hard work.***

Her practical tips to future grape pickers include the following: bring waterproof clothing and Wellingtons, as the weather may change at any moment. Also, bring rubber washing-up gloves (not cloth gloves), since in the mornings the grapes are wet and your hands get very wet. Hand cream is also a good idea. And most importantly do not expect the French to be able to speak English, so bring a phrase book.

The demand for pickers in all regions is highly unpredictable. Whereas there is usually a glut of pickers looking for work at the beginning of the harvest (early to mid-September), there is sometimes a shortage later on in the month. Harvests differ dramatically from year to year; a late spring frost can wreak havoc. The element of uncertainty makes it very difficult to fix a starting date from afar.

Experienced grape-pickers recommend visiting or phoning farms well before the harvest starts and asking the farmer to keep a job open. According to Jon Loop the key to success is serial phoning: *'The best time to phone is July. Then phone in August to ask when to phone for starting dates. Then phone in September to say you are coming, to ask when it starts. You may also have to phone a week before the start to confirm.'*

OTHER HARVESTS

Although the *vendange* may produce the highest concentration of seasonal work, there are numerous opportunities for participating in other harvests and with potentially less competition for the available work. While increasing mechanisation threatens the future of grape-picking by hand, there are not yet any machines which can cope with apples, plums, peaches and olives.

One longstanding source of seasonal work is maize castration or maize topping (*l'écimage*) which consists of picking off the flowers of the male maize plants. Demand for temporary workers has fallen sharply over the years partly because of the introduction of a sterile maize plant. Try the ANPE in Riom in the Auvergne, though its information is discouraging: the working period lasts only three to seven days, no accommodation is provided and the starting date is not known until the very last minute, which make it impractical for people from outside the region to look for work with maize farmers.

France is an overwhelmingly rural country. The *départements* of Hérault, Drôme and Gers are among the most prolific fruit and vegetable producers, especially of plums, cherries, strawberries and apples. Crops ripen first in the south of the country, and first at lower altitudes, so it is difficult to generalise about starting dates. For example the strawberry harvest on the coastal plain around Beziers normally takes place between mid-May and late June, whereas 60km inland in the Haut Languedoc near Sauclieres, it starts in mid-July. Cherries and strawberries are the first harvests, normally taking place between May and July. Blueberries are picked throughout July and August. Peaches are picked from June after the trees have been pruned, while pears are picked throughout the summer but especially (like apples) from mid-September to mid-October. Apples are grown throughout France including in Normandy.

THE BELGIAN TRAVELLER VINCENT CROMBEZ WROTE FROM THE VILLAGE OF MONETIER-ALLEMONT (BETWEEN GAP AND SISTERON) TO RECOMMEND THIS AREA OF THE HAUTES-ALPES SOUTH OF GRENOBLE:

Apple picking starts about the 1st of September and lasts until the end of October. I was paid the SMIC and worked 9 or 10 hours a day every day except Sunday. It's no problem to save £400+ a month if you don't go to the only pub in this wonderful village every day. Now I'm back here for the apple thinning. I'm working 9 hours a day, but it's easy, always sunny and I will save £800 for the two months.

After landing a job in the vendange with her first phone call to a proprietor in Champagne, Anna Ling's luck ran out when trying to follow up with an apple picking job. She and her boyfriend followed up every imaginable lead but were led on a wild and unproductive goose chase. Apple growers all seemed to want relevant experience, certainly for the months of pruning following the harvest.

Harvest work is paid either hourly (normally the SMIC) or by piece rates. If you are floundering with piece work, you may be transferred to a different job where you can earn an hourly wage. It is normally up to workers to provide their own food and accommodation, and so a tent and camping equipment are essential. If a farmer does provide board and lodging he will normally deduct the equivalent of two hours' wages from your daily pay packet. If you are planning to leave as soon as the harvest is over, bear in mind that agricultural wages are often not paid until seven to ten days after the harvest finishes (to ensure workers do not leave prematurely). Furthermore the wages may have to be cashed at a local bank, so be prepared to hang around.

The Loire Valley

Strawberries, apples, pears and many other crops can be found along the River Loire: the towns of Segré, Angers and Saumur are especially recommended. For example the strawberry harvest around Varennes-sur-Loire lasts six to eight weeks from early/mid April.

Two unusual crops are grown round Saumur, both of which are picked from the beginning of July, mushrooms and blueberries or bilberries. While working on a farm in Kent, Andrew Pattinson-Hughes found out that the farm secretary owned a blueberry farm in Brain-sur-Allonnes, a few kilometres north of Saumur:

After hounding her to write us a letter of recommendation, she gave in. I borrowed money from my dad for the coach fare to Tours, then caught a train to Saumur and an over-priced taxi to the farm, Anjou Myrtilles (myrtille is French for blueberry). The farmer spoke fluent English and agreed to hire us. We stayed on a campsite in Brain-sur Allonnes about a 40 minute walk away, as the farm is in the middle of the sticks.

It is possible to print out an application form from the site anjoumyrtilles.fr and submit it to Emploi Saisonnier, Sarl Myrtilles Anjou, Le Bourg, 49390 La Breille les Pins (☎ 02 41 52 83 81). It may be possible to continue picking until the end of August and then move on to the apple harvest in the nearby village of Parcay les Pins where it will be easy to save most of your earnings.

Apple picking takes place around Tours throughout September and October; try the villages of Brèches and further west, Les Rosiers sur Loire.

Organic Farms

The national organisation Sésame (Services des Echanges et des Stages Agricoles dans le Monde) fixes up *stages* or work experience placements for agricultural trainees of all nationalities on French organic farms (Paris; ☎ 01 40 54 07 08; sesame@agriplanete.com; agriplanete.com). Their brochure and website are in English as well as French.

The organic movement is powerful in France, and now WWOOF France (2 place Diderot, 94300 Vincennes; wwoof.fr which is also in English) maintains an up-to-date list of hundreds of organic farmers looking for volunteers. The membership fee is €15 for one, €20 for two for an electronic list, €10 extra for printed booklets. In his gap year, Jack Standbridge was looking for 'an experience', which he found first on the grape harvest and later by WWOOFing in France:

I went to a WWOOF place where there was no electricity, no running water, no heating or a house or anything, because I thought it would be interesting. The work has been difficult in places, like when I had to build a dry-stone wall for pretty much a month solid with stones that weighed quite a good deal more than myself.

TEACHING

So many expatriates live in Paris and throughout France that being a native speaker of English does not cut much ice with prospective employers of English teachers. Without a TEFL qualification, BA or commercial flair (preferably all three) it is very difficult to get a teaching contract. Of course if you can make yourself look ultra-presentable and have an impressive CV, you should ring to make appointments and then tramp round all the possible institutes and training centres to leave your CV. (As is usual in Europe, there is virtually no hope of success in July and August.)

In Paris many companies advertise in the *métro*, or you can look up addresses in the *Yellow Pages* under *Enseignements Privé de Langues* or *Ecoles de Langues*. A great many of these cater for the business market, so anything relevant in your background should be emphasised. Most schools pay between €15 and €25 (gross) per lesson. As is increasingly common, schools are reluctant to take on contract teachers for whom they would be obliged to pay taxes and social security, and so there is a bustling market in freelance teachers who work for themselves and are prepared to teach just a few hours a week for one employer.

In Paris it is often a case of offsetting the high cost of living by doing some tutoring which sometimes shades into au pairing. Language exchanges for room and board are commonplace and are usually arranged through advertisements (in the places described below in the section on

Paris) or by word of mouth. This is one way for Americans and other non-Europeans to circumvent red tape difficulties, as Beth Mayer from New York found in Paris:

> ***I tried to get a job at a school teaching, but they asked for working papers which I didn't have. I checked with several schools who told me that working papers and a university degree were more important than TEFL qualifications. So I placed an ad to teach English and offer editing services (I was an editor in New York City before moving here) and received many responses. I charged a decent fee but after I had spent time going and coming, I earned only half that. It would be better to have the lessons at your apartment if centrally located. I not only 'taught' English but offered English conversation to French people who wanted practice. I met a lot of nice people this way and earned money to boot.***

The usual methods of scouring on-line message boards, advertising in local newspapers, sticking up photocopied ads in libraries and stores such as Monoprix supermarkets could work.

University language students who would like to spend a year as an English language *assistant* in a French school should contact the Language Assistants Team of the British Council (☎ 020 7389 4596; assistants@britishcouncil.org). They send hundreds of undergraduates studying French at British universities and recent graduates aged 20–30 to spend an academic year in primary or secondary schools throughout France. *Assistants* give conversation classes for 12 hours a week and are paid €940 (gross) a month. As mentioned earlier, Americans can also become *assistants* in France through the French Embassy in Washington.

Emily Sloane from the US was posted as an *assistant* to a small town in Lorraine (where the quiche comes from), unknown to any English-language guidebook that she could find:

> ***I taught English to about 170 students in three different primary schools, two 45-minute sessions per class per week, for a total of 12 hours of work each week. In general, the teaching and lesson planning were thoroughly enjoyable, although I wasn't given much guidance and received no feedback throughout the year, so I'm sure the fact that I was already comfortable and experienced with teaching and working with children made a big difference in my enjoyment. The kids, although adoring and very enthusiastic, were a lot rowdier than I had expected, and I was obliged to spend a lot more time on behaviour management than I'd anticipated. The kids were never mean, just excitable and chatty, especially so because my class offered a break from their usual blackboard-and-worksheet style routine. The fact that I was the only assistant in my town meant that my French improved noticeably, especially my slang and listening comprehension, although it made for some lonely weekends, because I was forced to get by in French all the time.***

Outside the bigger cities, your chance of picking up freelance work is quite strong, something Emily Sloane discovered:

> ***Through word-of-mouth and no active self-promotion, numerous townspeople contacted me about private English tutoring. By the middle of the school year I had five private students, whom I taught once a week each for €10, with sometimes a meal on top of that. It was nice to be able to work through more complicated material with older students and really nice to have an inside look into various French households. Plus, the tutoring sessions kept me busy. I also earned some extra cash by doing freelance writing work for the mother of one of my students, which helped to supplement my fairly meagre salary and allowed me to take long and stress-free vacations during the numerous school breaks.***

CHILDCARE

Au pairing has always been a favoured way for young women to learn French and for young men too. The pocket money for au pairs in France is linked to the *SMIC* and is currently €67.50 per

30-hour week plus a city transport pass, though some families pay more. Au pairs plus should earn €100 for a 35-hour week and nannies far more. Dozens of agencies both in Britain (see list in *Childcare* chapter) and in France arrange placements. Most agencies make enrolling in a French course a necessary condition.

Quite a few foreigners are too hasty in arranging what seems at the outset a cushy number and only gradually realise how little they enjoy the company of children and how isolated they are if their family lives in the suburbs (as most do). Unless you actively like small children, it might be better to look for a free room in exchange for minimal babysitting (e.g. 12 hours a week). Matt Tomlinson went into his au pair job with his eyes open:

> ***I'd heard too many horror stories from overworked and underpaid au pair friends to be careless, so chose quite carefully from the people who replied to my notice on the upstairs notice board of the British Church (just off the rue de Faubourg St Honoré). My employers were really laid back, in their mid-20s so more like living with an older brother and sister. The little boy was just over two whilst the little girl was three months old, and they were both completely adorable. On the whole it was great fun. Baking chocolate brownies, playing football and finger-painting may not be everybody's idea of a good time but there are certainly worse ways to earn a living (and learn French at the same time).***

Applying directly through a French agency is commonplace. The most established agencies are members of UFAAP, the Union Francaise des Agences Au Pair, an umbrella group set up ten years ago, currently with its headquarters in the Oliver Twist Association agency below (ufaap.org). All the agencies charge a registration fee, normally around €240 which should guarantee a quality service. UFAAP agencies warn applicants against free online matching services which can lead to big problems and some swindles.

Here are some agencies to contact:

Alliance Francaise: Marseille; ☎ 04 96 10 24 60; info@alliancefrmarseille.org.

Association Familles & Jeunesse: Nice; ☎ 04 93 82 28 22; info@afj-aupair.org; afj-aupair.org; places more than 300 au pair girls and boys, mainly in the South of France plus the French Riviera and Corsica.

Butterfly et Papillon: Annecy; ☎ 04 50 67 01 33; aupair.france@wanadoo.fr; butterfly-papillon.com; member of IAPA.

Europair Services: Paris; ☎ 01 43 29 80 01; europairservices@wanadoo.fr; europair services.com; member of IAPA.

France Au Pair – Eurojobs: Saint Palais sur Mer; ☎ 05 46 23 99 88; contact@eurojob.fr; eurojob.fr.

Institut Euro'Provence: Marseille; ☎ 08 75 82 55 62 or 0 91 33 90 60; myriam@europrovence.org; europrovence.org; largest au pair agency in southern France.

Inter-Séjours: Paris; ☎ 01 47 63 06 81; bureau.intersejours@wanadoo.fr; http://asso.intersejours.free.fr; registration fee of €240.

Oliver Twist Work & Study: Pessac; ☎ 05 57 26 93 26; oliver.twist@orange.fr; oliver-twist.fr.

By law, families are supposed to make social security payments to the local URSSAF office on the au pair's behalf, though not all do and you might want to enquire about this when applying. Au pairs in or near Paris should receive the *carte orange* (monthly travel pass) which is worth about €55 to cover the central zones.

The online matching service frenchaupairs.com is free to au pairs. North Americans can fix up au pair placements directly with a French agency, bearing in mind that the placement fees must be paid upfront and that in some cases little information about the family is available in advance.

BUSINESS AND INDUSTRY

You will normally need impeccable French in order to work in a French office which eliminates the sort of temping jobs you may have had back home. Specialist agencies like the Sheila Burgess Agency in Paris place bilingual secretaries in office positions (☎ 01 44 63 02 57; sheilaburgessint.fr).

Fee-paying training programmes can provide an opening to employment and boost the quality of a participant's CV. Andy Green participated in a scheme run by Interspeak (interspeak.co.uk) and spent two months in an office in Limoges. As is usual with placements in France, Andy's *stage* was on an unpaid basis, yet he still considered the £1,000 investment worthwhile for the experience.

A cheaper way to find a base in France from which to improve your knowledge of the language is to participate in a Work Exchange Program such as the one offered by the Centre International d'Antibes, a French language school on the Côte d'Azur. Volunteers with the right to work in Europe do administrative or domestic work in exchange for free accommodation and/or French tuition. Details of the scheme are available from CIA, 38 Boulevard d'Aguillon, 06600 Antibes (☎ 04 92 90 71 70; info@cia-france.com; learn-french.fr/work_exchange_program.htm).

A number of British-run building firms (not all of them licensed) are active in areas like the Dordogne where many English people build homes. You are more likely to come across building work informally as the American Peter Goldman did:

> ***I was hitching south from Paris when a kind woman stopped near Tours. She was heading to her farmhouse near Bordeaux where a Dutchman was putting a new roof on the house. I explained that I had some experience in construction and I was hired on the spot. I worked for ten days, received good wages plus tons of food, beer and wine and a bed. The Dutchman was happy with my work and took me to Biddary near Bayonne to help him renovate another house. There I earned a small wage on top of all living expenses, learned a lot about European building methods, rural France and met some great people.***

It can be profitable to let your fingers do the walking when you are in France: the telephone directory (pagesjaunes.fr) can be an invaluable ally when you are looking for new addresses to contact. Here are a few headings to look under: *Publicité direct* and *Distributeurs en publicité* for jobs handing out leaflets (a job which phosphore.com describes accurately as 'un job harassant mais facile à trouver'), *Démenagement* for house removals, *Entreprises de nettoyage* for domestic work cleaning houses and *Surveillance* for security work. Leaflet distribution pays either according to the number you offload or by the day. Another job readily available to French speakers is *animateur de supermarché*, i.e. product promotion in supermarkets.

VOLUNTEERING

France has as wide a range of opportunities for voluntary work as any European country, and anyone who is prepared to exchange work for subsidised board and lodging should consider joining a voluntary project. Projects normally last two or three weeks during the summer and cost between €8 and €18 a day. Many foreign young people join one of these to learn basic French and make French contacts as well as to have fun.

Archaeology

A great many archaeological digs and building restoration projects are carried out each year. Every May the Ministry of Culture (Direction de l'Architecture et du Patrimoine, Sous-Direction de l'Archéologie) publishes a national list of summer excavations throughout France requiring up to 5,000 volunteers which can be consulted on its website (culture.gouv.fr/fouilles) from March/April. Most *départements* have *Services Archéologiques* which organise digs. Without relevant experience you will probably be given only menial jobs but many like to share in the satisfaction of seeing progress made.

Anthony Blake describes the dig he joined which the History Department of the University of Le Mans runs: *'Archaeology is hard work. Applicants must be aware of what working 8.30am–noon and 2–6.30pm in baking heat means! That said, I thoroughly enjoyed the working holiday: excellent company (75% French so fine opportunity to practise French), weekends free after noon on Saturday, good lunches in SNCF canteen, evening meals more haphazard as prepared by fellow diggers. Accommodation simple but adequate.'*

Conservation

France takes the preservation of its heritage (*patrimoine*) very seriously and there are numerous groups both local and national engaged in restoring churches, windmills, forts and other historic monuments. Many are set up to accept foreign volunteers, though they tend to charge more than archaeological digs:

APARE/GEC: Association pour la Participation et l'Action Régionale, L'Isle sur la Sorgue; ☎ 04 90 85 51 15; apare-gec.org; an umbrella organisation that runs volunteer workcamps at historic sites in Provence (plus a few in North Africa); cost of €97 for 1 week, €133 for 2 weeks, €169 for 3 weeks.

Chantier Histoire et Architecture Médiévale (CHAM): Paris 75014; ☎ 01 43 35 15 51; cham@cham.asso.fr; cham.asso.fr; volunteer projects to protect historic buildings, not just in mainland France but in farflung places including Réunion Island (a *département* of France in the Indian Ocean near Mauritius); see the CHAM website (which is in English) for details; camps cost €10 a day plus €30 registration fee.

REMPART: Paris; ☎ 01 42 71 96 55; rempart.com; similar to the National Trust in Britain, in charge of endangered monuments throughout France; most projects charge €5–8 per day plus €38 for membership plus insurance.

La Sabranenque: Centre International, rue de la Tour de l'Oume, 30290 Saint Victor la Coste; sabranenque.com; $630–$710 per fortnight; US applicants should contact Jacqueline Simon, 124 Bondcroft Drive, Buffalo, NY 14226; ☎ 716 836 8698.

UNAREC (Etudes et Chantiers): Délégué International, Clermont-Ferrand; 04 73 31 98 04; unarec.org; hundreds of international volunteers for short-term conservation projects and longer-term professional training, accepted via partner agencies.

Try to be patient if the project you choose turns out to have its drawbacks, since these organisations depend on voluntary leaders as well as participants. Judy Greene volunteered to work with a conservation organisation and felt herself to be 'personally victimised by the lack of organisation and leadership' or more specifically by one unpleasantly racist individual on her project. Tolerance may be called for, especially if your fellow volunteers lack it.

PARIS

Like all major cities in the developed world, Paris presents thousands of ways to earn your keep, while being difficult to afford from day to day. Unless you are very lucky, you will have to arrive with some money with which to support yourself while you look around. When house-hunting, check notice boards (see below) and local papers or (if you can afford it) use an agency which will cost you at least a month's rent but will help to ensure that you get your deposit of two months' rent back.

The Grapevine

Expatriate grapevines flourish all over Paris and are very helpful for finding work and accommodation. Most people find their jobs as well as accommodation through one of the city's many notice boards (*panneaux*). The one in the foyer of the CIDJ at 101 Quai Branly (*métro* Bir-Hakeim) is good for occasional studenty-type jobs such as extras in movies, but sometimes there are adverts for full-time jobs or *soutien scolaire en Anglais* (English tutor). It is worth arriving early to check for new notices (the hours for most CIDJ services are Monday–Friday 9.30am–6pm and Saturday 9.30am–1pm). They also have a telephone information service on 08 25 09 06 30.

The other mecca for job and flat-hunters is the American Church at 65 Quai d'Orsay (☎ 01 40 62 05 00; *métro* Invalides). Official notices are posted on various notice boards inside and out; the cork board in the basement is a free board where anybody can stick up a notice. Obviously it is necessary to consult the notices in person; they are not available by phoning the church or on the internet. Also pick up the free monthly magazine for English speakers in Paris, *Paris Voice* with a classified section of job offers.

The American Cathedral in Paris at 23 avenue George V (americancathedral.org; *métro* Alma Marceau or George V) has a notice board featuring employment opportunities and housing listings. The Cathedral also offers volunteering opportunities, for example it operates a soup kitchen every Friday lunch.

Arguably the most eccentric bookshop in Europe is Shakespeare and Company at 37 rue de la Bûcherie in the fifth *arrondissement* (on the south side of the Seine). It has a notice board and is also useful as a place to chat to other expats about work and accommodation. The shop operates as a writers' guest house. If you are prepared to write a short account of yourself and pitch in with doing chores for a couple of hours a day, you can stay free for a limited period, assuming there is space. The elderly American expat owner George Whitman has passed on the shop to his young daughter Sylvia who carries on the tradition and still hosts open house events for aspiring *literati*. English-speaking volunteers are still accepted to clean, run errands and work behind the till.

HANNAH ADCOCK DESCRIBES HERSELF AS A 'RATHER SOLEMN' EIGHTEEN YEAR OLD WHEN SHE READ AN EARLIER EDITION OF THIS BOOK AND SET OFF FOR PARIS:

Soon after, I found myself living at this hippy Parisian bookstore with a view of Notre Dame, a treat of inedible pancakes to look forward to and orders to clean the floor using newspaper and cold water. Kids staying at Shakespeare's do most of the jobs for free. You'll only get a paid job if (a) the owner really likes you, (b) you went to a university like Cambridge or Harvard and (c) you're really cute. The room overlooking Notre Dame is lovely but when I was there it smelt foul and a highly evolved species of bed bug lurked, as big as rats (ok – exaggeration). Shakespeare's is brilliant, but working there has its 'interesting' aspects!

Most expat places like Shakespeare & Co, the WH Smith Bookshop on the rue de Rivoli and dozens of others distribute the free bilingual English magazine *France-USA Contacts* or *FUSAC*

(fusac.org) which comes out the first Tuesday of each month. *FUSAC* comprises mainly classified adverts including some for English teachers which are best followed up on the day the paper appears. The cost of an ad for example under the heading 'Work Wanted in France' starts at €36. Other possible sources of job and accommodation leads are the weekly free ads paper *J'Annonce* and the online resource http://paris.kijiji.fr.

Disneyland

The enormous complex of Disneyland Paris, 30km east of Paris at Marne-la-Vallée, employs about 12,000 people in high season, both on long-term and seasonal contracts. Seasonal positions from March or May to September are open to EU nationals or others with permission to work in the EU. The minimum period covers the high season from the end of June to the end of August.

'Cast members' (Disneyspeak for employees) must all have a conversational level of French and preferably a third European language. The only positions for which you might get away with weak French are in the parades (where the emphasis is on dancing ability) or in the more menial positions as sweepers, etc. Working conditions are reasonably good, with two consecutive days off a week, reimbursed travel (most recently €76 each way from the UK) and accommodation provided in shared flats a bus-ride away from the park.

The majority of jobs are in food and beverage, housekeeping, merchandising and custodial departments, though one of the best jobs is as a character like Micky Mouse. The French standard working week is 35 hours long for which staff are paid a salary which is roughly equivalent to SMIC depending on the job; social security deductions will be at least €170 and staff accommodation costs €250 per month. Further details are available from Service du Recrutement-Casting, Disneyland Paris, BP 110, 77777 Marne-la-Vallée Cedex 04 (http://disneylandparis-casting.com). Casting tours are conducted around Europe in February for the start of the season in March.

For all jobs the well-scrubbed look is required (though the no-facial-hair rule has been dropped), and of course they are looking for the usual friendly, cheerful and outgoing personalities. Whether you will be impressed by the fringe benefits is a matter of individual taste; they consist of discounts on merchandise and in the hotels and some free entrances to the theme park itself.

KEITH LEISHMAN FROM DUNDEE WAS A CAST MEMBER A FEW SUMMERS AGO BEFORE TAKING A LAW DEGREE (WITH FRENCH):

Getting the job was initially quite frustrating. I first sent a letter to the company around November. After another couple of letters and e-mails without reply I was just about giving up hope. Finally around March I received notification of an interview in Edinburgh and was offered the job. After that you are pretty much left to your own devices and simply expected to turn up at Disney the day before your contract begins. (This was rather a shock to me after working for Eurocamp the year before who provided transport to France and some preparatory material beforehand.)

I was employed on the ticketing side of operations. I had to wear a Prince Charming costume and supervise the entrance of guests to the Park, stamping their hands for readmission. This meant standing for the whole shift in what were often scorching conditions. This was very beneficial for my French as people would ask a whole range of weird and wonderful questions.

The staff apartments were comfortable enough and equipped with kitchens, though I did not cook much due to the cheapness and accessibility of Disney canteens. I could eat well for a few euros a day. Another of the main advantages of working at Disneyland is the mixture of nationalities. The sheer number of young people from all over the world means there are always lots of parties and barbecues in the residences. On days off I usually went into Paris which is only 40 minutes away on the train. I stayed for two months of the peak summer season and found it quite hard to keep up the Disney smile when I was hot and tired. The job is demanding because you are creating an illusion. All the same I would urge anybody with an interest in people and a desire to improve their French to try the experience. I intend to return at Christmas or Easter.

Survival

Talented musicians should consider joining the army of buskers on the Left Bank on a Friday or Saturday night and graduating to the highly competitive métro. Transit authorities issue licences (free of charge) which allow you to perform in prescribed locations. Playing on the trains themselves is not allowed, though many ignore the regulations. Anna Ling from Cambridge developed a short and dazzling fire poi show (spinning two flaming balls on a flexible chain) which she performed outside restaurants in August 2008, wherever she could find enough space, while her accomplice circulated with a hat.

It has been mentioned elsewhere in this book that English churches are often helpful sources of contacts. Jonathan Poulton found himself very short of money in Menton (near Monte Carlo) after discovering that the starting date of his job in a patisserie had been postponed. He wandered into the English church which happened to be next door, explained his situation to the vicar and within five minutes had secured a job as a gardener for one of the congregation. Religious foundations also run many emergency shelters and free hostels throughout France, mostly for men only.

If you would like to survive in rural France, communal living is a possibility. Roberta Wedge enjoyed several months at the 'bleakly beautiful' Le Cun de Larzac Peace Centre (Route de Saint-Martin, 12100 Millau; larzac.org/cun) and says that they need work-for-keep volunteers in the summer to look after visitors, tend the gardens, preserve the fruit, etc.

Several Gandhian Communities of the Ark accept volunteers, including La Borie Noble (34650 Roqueredonde) and La Flayssière (34650 Joncels). Robert Abblett enjoyed his stay on a community a few years ago:

> ***From the WWOOF list, I found the address of Domaine de Courmettes. This was my favourite WWOOF for it was situated on an 800-metre plateau above the Côte d'Azur. I spent a wonderful 3½ weeks here one August in a most peaceful place camping and swinging in my hammock, contemplating life and exploring the top of the mountain nearby. On my days off I would go swimming in some of the most beautiful rivers and swimming holes with the other volunteers. I would work four days washing up followed by three days off. My French really helped me enjoy the experience.***

If you are more into private enterprise, you may wish to follow Tessa Shaw's example. She learned that there were many edible snails to be found along the canal and riverbanks in the *département* of Vaucluse which she could sell in the market. The snails move about only on still, dank nights: so Tessa would be found between the hours of 2am and 7am scouring the waterside with the help of a torch. She would then keep them in a sack or bin for four or five days until they exuded all the poison in their systems, and then sell them in the market of Carpentras. There is a closed season for snail collecting between April 1st and June 30th.

While you're waiting for something to turn up, it is possible to sleep in parks, railway stations or on beaches, though this is unlikely to be trouble-free. If you are sleeping overnight in a station, you may be asked to show a valid ticket; otherwise the patrolling police will not be over-gentle when evicting you.

GERMANY

Ever since the reunification of Germany two decades ago, foreign workers have been flocking to Germany especially from the former Yugoslavia, Poland and the other EU accession countries. German hotels have been turning in great numbers to eastern and central Europe for their staff, leaving fewer vacancies for British and other students. The global recession has bitten hard into the German economy, and the rate of unemployment has risen to 8.5% at the time of writing, with forecasts that it will climb further. Yet, work experience placements for students of German are still numerous, albeit unpaid. Perseverance by anyone who has a reasonable command of German may yet be rewarded with a decently paid job at some level in Germany.

REGULATIONS

EU nationals are free to travel to Germany to look for work, but are still subject to the labyrinthine German bureaucracy. The first step is to register your address with the local authority of the district you are living in (*Einwohnermeldeamt*) or at your local registry office (*Meldestelle*), as German citizens must also do. For this you will need proof that you are living locally, e.g. a copy of your contract with your landlord. You should do this within 14 days of arriving in Germany. Only after doing this is it possible to apply for a residence permit (*Niederlassungserlaubnis*) from the residence office (*Landeseinwohneramt*) or from the aliens' authority (*Ausländerbehörde*) probably located in the *Rathaus* (town hall) or the *Kreisverwaltungsreferat* (local authority's offices). You have to go to your local authority in person with a completed residence permit application form, a valid passport and a recent passport photograph.There is still a high level of people working black (*Schwarzarbeiter*) and employers who hire large numbers of workers under-the-table are subject to raids and huge fines of €5,000–€30,000 if caught. For many jobs (e.g. childcare, food service, etc.) you must also acquire a *Gesundheitszeugnis* (health certificate) from the local *Gesundheitsamt* (health department). Again, restaurants will be heavily fined if they are caught employing anyone without it.

Australians and New Zealanders under 30 are eligible for one-year working holiday visas for Germany. Other citizens of Australia and New Zealand plus Canada, the US, Israel and Japan are permitted to apply for a work permit after arrival in Germany provided they have found an employer willing to support their application. Other nationalities will have to apply to a German consulate in their home country.

Non-Europeans wishing to stay in Germany for an extended period require an *Aufenthaltserlaubnis* or residence permit. For this, applicants will require a notarised certificate of good conduct, evidence of health insurance as well as a *Gesundheitszeugnis* (as above), proof of accommodation and means of support. The permit must specify that employment is permitted before the bearer has any chance of going on to obtain an *Arbeitslaubnis* (work permit) from the *Arbeitsamt* (Employment Office, described below).

Anyone who earns less than €400 a month (like an au pair) does not need to obtain a tax card. Above that level, you will start to pay contributions on a graduated scale up to the maximum deduction of 9.75% on a monthly income of €800 or above. If you earn less than €7,664 in a tax year, you can apply for a tax rebate.

SPECIAL SCHEMES

Internships for American students and graduates up to the age of 30 who can function in German are available in business, finance, technical and other fields through CDS International Inc. in New York (☎ 212 497 3502; cdsintl.org). If appropriate, the first month can be spent at an intensive language course, after which participants undertake a paid or unpaid internship which they have secured previously with the help of CDS's partner agency InWEnt (Internationale Weiterbildung und Entwicklung gGmbH) in Bonn (inwent.org). The summer programme is open only to enrolled students (whose placement must be less than six months) whereas graduates are permitted to stay up to 12 months, extendable to 18. The average monthly compensation will cover living expenses. The CDS programme fee is $575.

InterExchange in New York (workingabroad.org) runs Au Pair in Germany whereby young Americans aged 18–24 spend 6 or 10 months living in a Germany family (see below). SWAP in Canada (swap.ca) dispenses 12-month work permits to Canadians aged 18–35 who need not be students. A knowledge of German is helpful but not a requirement. The programme fee is C$400 plus participants must have access to C$2,750.

The IJAB (International Youth Exchange) in Bonn has a EuroDesk at Godesberger Allee 142–148 which administers European student exchanges (☎ 0228 95 06 250; eurodesk.de). The website prabo.de, available in English, describes itself as 'the free internship database on the internet for companies and students and everybody who is offering or searching for internships' in Germany and elsewhere.

The Working Holidays in Germany scheme places language and gap year students from the UK and the old EU countries in the field of rural tourism. Participants are given weekly pocket money of €51 and full board and lodging with families on farms or in country hotels. In return they look after children and/or horses and farm animals or take up serving and kitchen duties. The preferred stay is three to six months though a six-week commitment is also allowed; details available from Terre des Langues e.V. in Regensburg (☎ 0941 565602; terre-des-langues@t-online.de; workingholidays.de). A fee of €180 is payable after the placement is agreed, at least 4 weeks before the start date.

WORK EXPERIENCE

Internships are commonplace in German companies. Work placements can be organised in a wide range of sectors including tourism, trade, telecommunications, marketing and banking depending on timing and availability. Most internships are organised in conjunction with an intensive language course. Normally an upper intermediate level of language ability is required for work experience to be successful. Most are unpaid or are rewarded only with a subsistence wage. Board and lodging will generally be provided only in the tourism sector.

The federal employment service (see next section) can assist with arranging internships for post-graduate students and recent graduates who wish to gain international work experience in a German company. The preferred faculties are engineering, economics, business administration and tourism management. The duration of the internships should be at least three months and not longer than one year. The students should have a good knowledge of the German language. Applications should be sent to ZAV's Project-Team Incoming (☎ 0228 713 1570; incoming@arbeitsagentur.de).

DID-Deutsch Institute (Hauptstrasse 26, 63811 Stockstadt am Main; ☎ 6027 41770; did.de) is a major language course provider which can arrange two to six month internships following their language courses in Berlin, Frankfurt, Munich and Wiesbaden; the processing fee for an unskilled work placement is €350 while a qualified internship placement will cost €450 in addition to the preceding language course (e.g. €1,460 for 8 weeks). Similarly GLS (Global Language Services; german-courses.com) combines a minimum 4-week language course with an unpaid internship in a Berlin-based company of 6, 8 or 12+ weeks. Host companies want their trainees to speak German to at least an intermediate (B-1) level.

Astur GmbH (☎ 661 92802 0; info@astur-gmbh.de; astur-gmbh.de) organises linguistic stays in about 50 cities and towns around Germany with unpaid work experience placements lasting four to 12 weeks. Applicants must be students from the old Europe aged 18–25 with an excellent standard of German to work in a German company, normally in industry, sales, marketing, administration, accountancy, tourism, law, translation or computers. Astur also arrange hotel experience placements for which candidates need an intermediate level of German after a compulsory pre-placement language course. The Astur fee (2009) includes homestay accommodation starting at €1,280 for four weeks, €2,290 for ten weeks.

GERMAN NATIONAL EMPLOYMENT SERVICE

The whole of Germany is covered by the network of employment offices run by the state *Bundesagentur für Arbeit* (arbeitsagentur.de). There are nearly 200 principal *Arbeitsamter* (job centres) and a further 650+ branch offices. These are all connected by a number of co-ordinating offices that handle both applications and vacancies that cannot be filled locally. If you speak German and aren't in a hurry, it's probably worth registering.

The Zentrale Auslands- und Fachvermittlung (International Placement Services), ZAV, part of the German Federal Employment Agency, has an international department (Auslandsvermittlung) for dealing with applications from German-speaking students abroad. Details and application forms are available from ZAV (Villemombler Strasse 76, 53123 Bonn; ☎ 0228 713 1330; fax 0228 713 270 1525; ZAV-Bonn.Ferienbeschaeftigung@arbeitsagentur.de). All applications from abroad are handled by this office. Although people of any nationality can apply through the ZAV, only citizens of old EU countries (who have German language skills) are entitled to expect the same treatment as a German.

This special department of the ZAV finds summer jobs for students of any nationality (Team 327 – Ferienbeschäftigung), because this is felt to be mutually beneficial to employers and employees alike. Students who wish to participate in this scheme should contact ZAV before the beginning of March. Students must be at least 18 years old, have a good command of German and be available to work for at least two months. ZAV places students in all kinds of jobs, but mainly in hotels and restaurants, in industry, cleaning and agriculture. The ZAV assigns jobs centrally, according to employers' demands and the level of the candidate's spoken German. For example those with fluent German may be found service jobs while those without will be given jobs such as chambermaiding and dishwashing. If you decline the first job offered by the ZAV, there is no guarantee of being offered another.

OTHER SOURCES OF WORK

Anyone with office experience and a knowledge of German should look for branches of private employment agencies such as Adecco and Manpower in the big cities; these will be listed in the *Gelbe Seiten* (*Yellow Pages*) under *Personalberatung* or *Stellenvermittlungsburo*.

Most of the main dailies like *Frankfurter Allgemeine Zeitung* carry their job supplements on Saturdays which go on sale on Friday evening. *BZ* in Berlin has a good selection of vacancies for unskilled people or check online at thelocal.de/jobs and toytowngermany.com/jobs, both in English.

If you are looking for labouring or other casual work after arriving in Germany, seek out the local Irish bar or British pub. There are dozens of these from the Oscar Wilde in Berlin to Mulligans in Oldenburg. Many tend to be staffed by British and Irish people and are often meeting places for expat workers.

TOURISM AND CATERING

The German tourist industry depends heavily on immigrants and students during the busy summer months. Despite the huge number of immigrants from Eastern Europe and the Balkans who are often willing to work for exploitative wages, other nationalities do find jobs in hotels and restaurants.

If you are conducting a door-to-door search of hotels and restaurants in the cities, you will be at an enormous advantage if you speak decent German. For example every time Danny Jacobson turned around in Freiburg (after a fruitless search for harvesting work in the countryside), he met young people from around the world working at campsites and in bars. You may be lucky and find a manager who speaks English and who needs someone behind the scenes to wash dishes, etc. Robin Gray lived to regret accepting a job in a kitchen without really understanding what he was meant to do:

> ***The manageress told me she was looking for a salad chef and I said I was a chef. The waitresses were coming in with the orders, but I didn't know there were about seven different salads. I was just putting a couple of slices of lettuce, tomatoes, bit of cucumber, etc. on all the plates and they were going off their heads because there wasn't enough watercress or no tomatoes with that certain salad. I started at 10am and got the sack at 2pm, but I got paid for it so I wasn't too bothered.***

You can try to fix up a summer job ahead of time by sending off speculative applications. This worked for Dean Fisher who went to wash dishes in Berchtesgaden on the Austrian border: *'I spent 2½ months working in a very orderly and efficient kitchen on the top of a mountain in the Kehlsteinhaus (Eagle's Nest) with the most amazing view I've ever seen. I actually enjoyed the work even though it was hard going. I met loads of good people and learned a lot of German.'*

Munich is estimated to have more than 2,000 pubs and restaurants and Berlin is similarly well endowed with eateries (try the American style places on Kurfürstendamm). The Munich beer gardens, especially the massive open-air Chinese Tower Biergarten, pay glass collectors and washers-up (most of whom have lined their jobs up at the beginning of the season) €70–€80 a day tax free at the height of the season, when people work 14-hour days. Look for adverts in the local press, especially *Abendzeitung* in Munich. Key words to look for on notices and in adverts are *Notkoch und Küchelhilfe gesucht* (relief and kitchen assistant required), *Spüler* (dishwasher), *Kellner*, *Bedienigung* (waiters/waitresses), *Schenkekellner* (pub type barman); *büffetier* (barman in a restaurant), *Büffetkräfte* (fast food server), or simply *Services*.

Be prepared for hard work. In hotels, it is not unusual to work 10 or 12 hours a day and to have only a day or two off a month. Those whose only experience of hotels and catering has been in Britain are usually taken aback by German discipline. Waitresses are normally expected to keep all customers' payments until the end of a shift, when the total is calculated and handed over as a lump sum. Those who lose track while being shouted at in German will not last long.

The punitive hygiene laws do not help matters. Once you realise that restaurants and hotels are frequently visited by the health department you will appreciate why it is that the head cook orders you to scrub the floors and clean the fat filters regularly. Paul Winter worked several seasons on the lakes near Munich:

> ***I found that it is best to apply around April/May in person if possible. What they usually do is to tell you to come back at the beginning of June and work for a couple of days to see how you get on. As long as you are not a complete idiot they should keep you on until September. Even as late as July I knew of places looking for extra staff but as a rule most places are full by the end of May. I worked for the summer as a barman/waiter earning a good net wage. With the tips I got I generally managed to double this.***

Both Ammersee and Starnbergersee can be reached by S-Bahn from Munich. These two lakes are ringed by towns and villages which all have hotels and restaurants, popular mainly with German tourists. Be warned that competition for work from German students and migrant workers will make it difficult.

Other recommended areas to try for a summer job are the Bavarian Alps (along the border with Austria), the shores of Lake Constance (especially in and around Friedrichshafen which is a Ryanair destination), the Bohmer Wald (along the Czech border), the Black Forest (in south-west Germany), and the seaside resorts along the Baltic and North Seas. One employer on the Baltic coast hires a number of general assistants, food and beverage staff, child carers and sports instructors at a coastal campsite/golf and holiday park. The hours are long and you must be able to speak German but the wages are good. Students only should apply in the spring to Riechey Freizeitanlagan GmbH, 23769 Wulfen/Fehmarn (☎ 04371 86280; wulfenerhals.de/ENGLISCH/jobs.shtml).

Movie World employs between 400 and 500 staff for food concessions (restaurants, bakeries, ice cream stalls, fast food, etc). Applicants should be able to converse in German as well as English, and preferably Dutch too since the park is not far south of the Dutch border. Accommodation is not provided (teammoviepark.de).

Anyone with some experience working in hotels or restaurants might check the website eurotoques.org (click on *Chefkoche* and then on *Jobborse*) where top chefs offer unpaid work experience placements.

Winter Resorts

Germany is a good place to pick up jobs in ski resorts although few British tour companies operate there compared to France and Austria. The two main skiing areas are Garmisch-Partenkirchen (which also has hotels and services for the American Army) on the Austrian border 50 miles southeast of Munich, and the spa resort of Oberstdorf in the mountains south of Kempten. Seasonal vacancies are mostly in the kitchen or housekeeping departments.

As always, timing is crucial. One highly qualified job-seeker (with experience in hotels and restaurants, a knowledge of German, French and English, and a good skier) went on the old 'hotel-trot' in Garmisch Partenkirchen and was repeatedly told that they wouldn't be hiring until the beginning of the season (circa December 15th). Up-to-date job listings, including entry level jobs, can be found on http://jobs.meinestadt.de/garmisch-partenkirchen.

Work on Military Bases

Cutbacks in military spending have necessitated the withdrawal of resources and personnel from British and American military bases in Germany. Yet there are still jobs around for Americans and Britons on the relevant bases. Heidelberg is the HQ for the US Army in Europe, home to about 16,000 serving soldiers and their families, which creates many ancillary jobs.

Military bases throughout Germany have Civilian Personnel Advisory Centers (CPACs) that are responsible for recruiting auxiliary staff to work in bars, shops, etc., on base and as ski instructors. For further information see http://cpolrhp.belvoir.army.mil/eur/cpac/heidelberg/index.htm. The best bet for US citizens to obtain entry level jobs in the hotel and recruitment department for a period of 13 months is at Edelweiss Lodge and Resort in Garmisch-Partenkirchen and Chiemsee. Details are available from the Human Resources Department Unit 24501, APO AE 09006; fax +49 8821 9440; ELRinterview@aol.com; edelweisslodgeandresort.com/employment.html. They interview exclusively in the United States three or four times a year, and candidates must go through rigorous interviews and background checks before being selected. Edelweiss never hires Americans who are already in Europe. Americans do not require work permits to work on US bases.

Jobs on British Forces Germany (BFG) bases along the Rhine such as Münster/Osnabruck and Paderborn are now very scarce though British nationals are occasionally still hired at the Berlin base for waitressing, bar work, cleaning and administration. See lecsupport.bfgnet.de for links to the Rhine Area Labour Support Unit and other specific vacancies for civilian labour.

Special Events

Oktoberfest starts each year on the second last Saturday of September and lasts a fortnight. They begin to erect the 14 giant tents for the festival about three months ahead so you can begin your enquiries any time in the summer. Some of the hiring is done directly by the breweries, so it is worth contacting the Hofbräuhaus and Löwenbräu for work, as well as pubs, restaurants and hotels. Nicole Gluckstern from California wrote to confirm that Oktoberfest is always looking for people to sell pretzels, wash glasses, take photos, etc. but she advises job-seekers to set their dignity temporarily aside since the atmosphere will be zoo-like. There is also work after the festival finishes as Brad Allemand from Australia discovered: *'On the Monday after Oktoberfest finished I went around to all of the Beer Halls which were being taken down asking for some work. The first one I went to was Spatenbräu and the boss obliged. Even though my German was almost non-existent, I managed to understand what was needed of me. Many other foreigners were also on the site – English, Australian, Yugoslav, etc.'* Brad enjoyed the work, which lasted about six weeks. He worked 7am–5pm five days a week.

Many other international trade fairs and special events may need large numbers of people to set up stands and deal with maintenance, catering, etc. Some of the major ones include the Frankfurt Trade Fair in March and the Hannover Trade Fair in April. Hamburg hosts a big festival ('DOM') three times a year, for a month before Christmas, over Easter and in August. Casual labour is needed to dismantle the place at the end of the events, so look for 'Help Wanted' signs on the stalls. Many high-profile trade fairs are held at the huge Frankfurt Exhibition Hall (*Messe*), such as the Frankfurt Book Fair in mid-October. Applications for work at one of the numerous fairs held in Frankfurt can be addressed to Messe Frankfurt GmbH, Ludwig-Erhard-Anlage 1, 60327 Frankfurt; messefrankfurt.com. Only people with a stable base in Frankfurt and a good command of languages (for example for running messages) can be considered.

TEACHING

If you enquire at an *Arbeitsamt* about teaching, translation or secretarial work in the major cities, you will probably be told (truthfully) that there is a surplus of people offering those services. However you may find that they are more helpful in smaller cities.

Graduates with a background in economics or business who can speak German have a better chance of finding tutoring work in a German city than arts graduates, since most of the demand comes from companies. Private language schools have multiplied in the eastern *Länder*, many with an American bias. Try for example ICC Sprachschule in Leipzig and Chemnitz (☎ 0341 550 36 73; info@icc-sprachinstitut.de; icc-sprachinstitut.de) which employs about 35 teachers; and Lingua Franca in Berlin (☎ 030 863 98 080; lingua-franca.de) which makes use of 50 freelancers at any one time. A wage of €13–€16 per lesson is typical.

A TEFL Certificate has less clout than relevant experience, as Kevin Boyd found when he arrived in Munich in September, clutching his brand new Cambridge Certificate: *'I was persuaded by a teaching friend to go to Munich with him to try to get highly paid jobs together. As he spoke some German and had about a year's teaching experience, he got a job straightaway. Every school I went to in Munich just didn't want to know as I couldn't speak German and only had four weeks teaching experience.'*

If you do intend to look for a teaching job take evidence of any qualifications and some good references (*zeugnisse*) which are essential in Germany. You can always try to arrange private English lessons to augment your income, though you are unlikely to be able to make a living this way. Many secondary schools in Germany (including the former East) employ native English-speaking *assistenten*. Applications are encouraged from students who have at least AS level, Higher Grade or equivalent in German. UK applicants should contact the Language Assistants Team at the British Council (10 Spring Gardens, London SW1A 2BN; ☎ 020 7389 4596; assistants@britishcouncil.org; britishcouncil.org/languageassistants). Altogether they place about 400 assistants who work 12 hours a week for one academic year and are paid about €800 a month (net).

Language teaching organisations whose addresses are included in the introductory chapter *Teaching English* have a sizeable presence in Germany: Berlitz Deutschland (http://careers.berlitz.com) with 61 institutes, Bénédict with 25 branches, inlingua (inlingua.de) with 70 branches and Linguarama which specialises in language training for business. Linguarama Spracheninstitut Deutschland (Sendlinger-Tor-Platz 7, 80336 Munich; ☎ 089 200 009 3 0; munich@linguarama.com) employs between 25 and 70 teachers at its eight centres in Germany. Wall Street Institute (wallstreet-institute.de) has 24 schools and hires 100 teachers who have a TEFL background. Current vacancies are recorded on their website.

Many commercial institutes employ teachers on a freelance basis, often resident expatriates willing to work just a few hours a week. The best source of language school addresses is once again the *Yellow Pages* which can be consulted online (gelbeseiten.de). Another way of accessing potential employers is via the local English Language Teachers Association, a branch of which can be found in most major cities. The Munich Association (MELTA) is especially vigorous and devotes one page of its website to potential jobseekers (melta.de/jobs.htm). Look for English-language magazines aimed at expats and you should come across some relevant adverts. For example the English-language magazine *Munich Found* (munichfound.com) carries occasional TEFL vacancies.

CHILDCARE

Au pairs must have some knowledge of German and experience of childcare and those from outside the European Union must be aged 18–24. Among the longest established agencies is the non-profit Roman Catholic agency IN VIA with 40 branches throughout Germany (0761 200206; au-pair.invia@caritas.de; aupair-invia.de). Its Protestant counterpart is affiliated to the YWCA: Verein für Internationale Jugendarbeit headquartered in Frankfurt (☎ 069 469 39 700; au-pair-vij.org). VIJ has 14 offices in Germany and places both male and female au pairs for a preferred minimum stay of one year though six-month stays are also common.

Scores of private agents operate all over Germany, many of them members of the Aupair-Society e.V. (au-pair-society.org) which carries contact details for its 45 members (some of which specialise in sending German au pairs abroad). Commercial au pair agencies do not charge a placement fee to incoming au pairs.

Au-Pair Vermittlung AMS: c/o Anna-Maria Schlegel, Freiburg; ☎ 0761 70 76 917; info@aupair-ams.de; aupair-ams.de; information in English on website.

Abroad Connection: Landsberg; ☎ 08191 941378; abroadconnection.de.

MultiKultur AuPair Service: Köln; ☎ 0221 921 30 40; multikultur.info; places international au pairs throughout Germany.

The minimum monthly pocket money for an au pair in Germany is fixed by the government at €260. Some families offer to pay for a monthly travel pass, a contribution of up to €100 per semester to your language course and even your fare home if you have stayed for the promised period of nine months, typically up to €150. In return they will expect hard work which usually involves more housework than au pairs normally do, as Maree Lakey found during her year as an au pair in Frankfurt:

> ***I found that Germans do indeed seem to be obsessed with cleanliness, something which made my duties as an au pair often very hard. I also found that from first impressions Germans seem to be unfriendly and arrogant, however once you get to know them and are a guest in their home, they can be the most wonderful and generous people. The Germans I met were sincerely impressed by my willingness to learn their language and at the same time genuinely curious about life in Australia, my home country.***

It is possible for non-EU citizens to become au pairs through one of the above organisations provided they are not older than 24. Interexchange in New York simplifies placement for eligible young Americans willing to pay the $495 programme fee. Upon arrival, Americans will need to apply for a temporary residence permit that allows them to live and work in Germany as an au pair for up to 12 months

FARM WORK

Farms in Germany tend to be small and highly mechanised: most farm work is done by the owner and his family, with perhaps the help of some locals at busy times. Only on rare occasions are harvesting vacancies registered with the local *Arbeitsamt*.

Grape production is the only branch of agriculture that employs casual workers in any great number. The harvest, which takes place mostly in the west of the country, is usually later than the one in France, taking place throughout the month of October. While hitching through the Rhine Valley a few years ago, Danny Jacobson asked repeatedly about grape-picking and every response included a reference to Polish migrant workers who appear to have a monopoly on the harvest work.

As usual your chances are better if you can visit the vineyards a month or two before the harvest to fix up work. Ask any German tourist office for a free leaflet about wine festivals which is bound to include sketch maps of all the grape-growing regions of Germany. The main concentration of vineyards is along the Rivers Saar, Ruwer, Mosel and Nahe, centred on places familiar from wine labels like Bernkastel, Bingen, Piesport and Kasel. There are ten other areas, principally the Rheingau (around Rüdesheim and Eltville), Rheinpfalz (around Deidesheim, Wachenheim and Bad Dürkheim) and Rheinhessen (around Oppenheim and Nierstein).

Apart from grapes, the most important area for fruit picking is the Altland, which lies between Stade and Hamburg to the south of the River Elbe and includes the towns of Steinkirchen, Jork and Horneburg. The main crops are cherries, which are picked in July and August, and apples in September and October. Apples and other fruit are grown in an area between Heidelberg and Darmstadt called the Bergstrasse, and also in the very south of the country, around Friederichshafen and Ravensburg near Lake Constance. The Bodensee area has been recommended for apple picking: small villages such as Oberdorf, Eriskirch and Leimau sometimes employ migrant workers.

An account of the strawberry harvest near Wilhelmshaven in northern Germany from a Polish contributor Kristof Szymczak goes some way to explaining why so few travellers work on German fruit harvests: *'I was strawberry-picking in June/July, and I don't recommend this kind of work to anybody who isn't desperately short of money. Strawberry picking for me is really hard work, almost all day under the sun or rain. Of course it's piece work. The pickers are only from Vietnam and Turkey (already resident in Germany) and of course Poles like me. After travel and living costs, there wasn't much left.'*

Those who wish to volunteer to work on organic farms should contact the German branch of WWOOF or World Wide Opportunities on Organic Farms, (info@wwoof.de; wwoof.de). Membership costs €20, whereupon the farm list containing about 150 addresses in Germany will be sent to you in less than a month.

VOLUNTEERING

Most of the international organisations mentioned in the introductory chapter *Volunteering* operate schemes of one sort or another in Germany. Justin Robinson joined a workcamp to restore an old fortress used by the Nazis as a concentration camp. The green movement in Germany is very strong and many organisations concentrate their efforts on arranging projects to protect the environment or preserve old buildings. For example Internationale Jugendgemeinschaftsdienste (IJGD) organise summer 'eco-camps' and assist with city fringe recreational activities. This organisation was highly praised by a former volunteer who wrote: *'The camp was excellent value both in the nature of the work and in that the group became part of the local community. These camps are an excellent introduction to travelling for 16 to 26 year olds.'*

As usual workcamps organisations in Germany normally recruit through national partners:

IJGD: Kasernenstr. 48, 53111 Bonn; ☎ 0228 22 800 0; workcamps@ijgd.de; ijgd.de; scores of camps in Germany; British applications accepted by Concordia and UNA Exchange.

Internationale Begegnung in Gemeinschaftsdiensten (IBG): Stuttgart; ☎ 0711 649 11 28; ibg-workcamps.org; many projects in both eastern and western Germany; applications in UK as above plus via VFP (vfp.org) in the US.

Mountain Forest Project (Bergwald Projekt e.V.): Würzburg; ☎ 0931 452 6261; bergwaldprojekt.de; one-week education and conservation projects in the alpine forests of southern Germany; basic knowledge of German is useful since the foresters conduct the camps in German; hut accommodation, food and insurance are provided free though participants must pay an annual membership fee of SFr60/€40.

NIG: Rostock ☎ 0381 492 2914; campline.de/nig/fger.

Vereinigung Junger Freiwilliger (VJF): Berlin; ☎ 030 428 506 03; vjf.de; camps take place in the former East Germany; camp details in English on website; registration fee €60.

There are some longer term possibilities as well. Internationaler Bund (Internationaler-Bund.de) takes on young people for a period of six or twelve months in various social institutions such as hospitals, kindergartens, homes for the elderly or disabled people. In some German states, young people aged 16–27, including foreign nationals, may work on ecological projects for a year starting at the end of the summer (foej.de).

Local opportunities to volunteer can be sought out by anyone staying in a city. For example, Sitske de Groote wanted to spend time with her boyfriend in Berlin. With a background in biological sciences and a liking for working out of doors, she approached the Botanical Gardens to ask about volunteer work. At first they said no because they were worried that her German was not good enough to understand instructions and that she did not have a German tax card. But when she pursued it with the director, he said that she did not need a tax card because the work would be unpaid and that they would take her on, and she ended up really enjoying the experience.

GREECE

While many backpackers have been moving further afield to Turkey, Thailand and Tahiti, thousands gather on the islands and mainland of good old Greece every summer. They laze on the beaches, indulge in calamares and Kalamata olives, and try to work out how to afford to stay longer. Jobs in cafés, bars and hostels pop up throughout the busy season and are usually given to attractive young women.

Agricultural work in the orange and olive fields that was once readily available to travellers now goes almost exclusively to the many job-seeking Albanians, Serbs, Romanians, Bulgarians, Georgians, Egyptians, etc. Outside Athens the hiring of itinerant workers to pick fruit, build houses, unload lorries, etc., often on a day-to-day basis, tends to take place in the main café or square of the town or village, where all the locals congregate to find out what's going on and possibly offer a day's work to willing new arrivals.

The work that remains for Western Europeans in addition to resort work is in English language schools, as holiday reps and in private households looking after children where English is prized.

REGULATIONS

A European Union directive implemented recently states that EU nationals who intend to stay for more than three months should apply for a registration certificate (*veveosi eggrafis*) at the local aliens bureau, which is valid indefinitely. This is free of charge and should be issued on-the-spot after the applicant produces the necessary documents, i.e. an EU passport and proof of employment, self-employment or (if not working) medical insurance and proof of funds.

EU nationals in employment should try to make sure that their employer registers them with the Greek national health and social insurance scheme, IKA (ika.gr). Contributions will be up to 16% of earnings. After 60 days of paying contributions, you must go with your employer to apply for an IKA book; thereafter you are entitled to free medical treatment and reduced cost prescriptions. IKA offices can provides a list of participating doctors who treat IKA patients free of charge.

Note that since January 2009 Romanian and Bulgarian citizens have been able to live and work in Greece without a permit, further reducing the supply of casual jobs for travellers.

Non-EU Nationals

The situation is confused. According to the *Athens News*, a special seasonal work permit was introduced for which employers can petition to employ non-EU workers. However official sources do not confirm this. The reality is that the majority of people working with non-European passports are doing so informally and without permits. Many employers are not only willing to employ non-EU workers but eager because they do not want to pay contributions and taxes for legitimate workers.

The immigration police conduct occasional raids on bars or clubs hiring people under the table, but usually the rumour of a raid provides some advance warning. If the draft EU law comes into force in 2010 as proposed, illegal workers could be jailed for up to 18 months before being deported. For more high profile and longer-term jobs like English teaching, it seems that most employers will hire outside the EU only if they are desperate. Non-EU citizens working in Athens should regularise their status at the Aliens Bureau at Antigonis Street 99, Kolonos, Athens (☎ 210 510 2833).

A Schengen visa entitles non-EU nationals to enter Greece and stay for up to 90 days. For longer stays, it is necessary to pop over a border and re-enter to be given a further 90 days. Be careful not to stay longer than the three months or you risk a hefty fine when leaving. Richard Ferguson from New Zealand was fined an eye-watering €600 (September 2008) when he left Greece after working at a bar in Faliraki.

> ***I found out from the Greek yellin' at me: 'Pay 600 Euros in cash or 4 years no Europe it will be!' I had overstayed 22 days and paid the fine. Stupid when I could have gone on a boat to Turkey and back in one day with a fresh stamp in my passport. But being hungover for two months, the brain didn't think this through so well!***

TOURISM

Recession, the falling pound and the political disruptions of 2008 have prompted some to predict drastic falls in the number of tourists visiting Greece, especially from Britain and Germany. But the response of the big package holiday operators in marketing good-value packages may mean the decline is not so serious, and many young Europeans will still be needed to work in bars, clubs and restaurants. Women have the advantage, although young men are hired as touts to persuade groups of young women into clubs. A good time to look is just before the Orthodox Easter (usually in April) when the locals are beginning to gear up for the season. In a few cases there is work outside the May to September period especially if you are willing to work on a commission-only basis.

You are more likely to find work in places that are isolated from the local culture, in American/European style bars and clubs in the cities and resorts. Well-known party resorts like Faliraki in Rhodes, Gouvia in Corfu and Malia and Hersonissos on the north coast of Crete employ many young European and English-speaking staff. As long-time expat writer and entrepreneur Louis Tracy concludes, '*The work scene for students is the same as always – people need to prepare well, speak some Greek, arrive early and have lots of chutzpah and determination*'. For detailed information about the resort of Malia, look at *Greece Monkey* (malia.co.uk/service/working) a site maintained by a long-time expat.

Patient web-surfing will lead to the websites of individual bars and restaurants that have a 'Jobs' icon, for example the Tex-Mex restaurant Escoba with branches in a suburb of Athens and on Naxos (escoba.gr). While hunting on the net for a suitable summer vacancy, Annelies van der Plas made use of wereldwijzer.nl, the largest online travel community in her native Holland. After spending days of online searching and placing adverts, she finally received a reply from a Dutch man who asked her if she would like to work behind the bar at the Camel Bar on Kos (camel.gr/jobs.php). She was asked to send a picture to the Greek boss (which, alas, is typical) and was soon offered a job but no contract (again typical):

> ***It was a kind of gamble to go alone as a blonde girl of 19, and my parents were a little bit worried, but they did not object to it, especially because many Dutch people worked on Kos. The boss had an apartment ready for me, for €200 per month or €100 if I shared. The apartment itself was nothing special but the beautiful view of the harbour from the balcony made it worth the money.***
>
> ***When I was working at the Camel bar I saw that it was not hard to find another job on the island. Mostly jobs behind the bar were already taken so the jobs consisted of getting people in. I noticed that the salary was most of the time the same, about €30 a night. I luckily received my money every week, although I did not get my salary for my last week which means I worked a whole week for nothing. There was nothing I could do; the police were very corrupt.***
>
> ***A good feature of the job was the free drinking and the contact with the people. I met a lot of people and every evening seemed like a night out. The tips were much better on the terrace and I could talk more to the people.***
>
> ***In two months I have seen that most Greek people see the tourists as idiots. Most bosses think only of money, and they don't care if the customer is not happy with their drink because they will never see them again. My last piece of advice: if you are a (blonde) girl, be careful of the Greek men.***

Undoubtedly the motives of some employers in hiring women are less than honourable. If you get bad vibes, move on. On her gap year, Emma Hoare lasted precisely 20 days in a job as receptionist in a hotel on Mykonos before realising that (a) she was being totally ripped off and (b) her boss was a '*big fat disgusting immoral bully*', whom another disgruntled ex-employee described as '*feral*'.

Even people who love Greece and have enjoyed working there offer warnings about Greek employers. Crete resident Louis Tracy was disillusioned with his working conditions:

> ***I do not envy those coming to find seasonal work. My own experiences in a hotel last year were an eye opener; I was given a waiter's job because my wife knows someone who deals with the hotel manager. I speak French and have had long-ago experience in hotel, restaurant and bar work. The introductory talk with the manager did not cover hours or wages, and I assumed these would be relayed to me in due course; we are, after all, in Greece. After some 12-hour days I understood that I would be expected to work these hours and be paid for only 8, split into two shifts, early and late. If the rest of the team and I could not finish within that time, it was our problem. I saw three people summarily told to go home because there were fewer tourists than expected, including my co-waiter. I was told that I would be kept because I speak French. And now I was to run the restaurant on my own, with equally inadequate staff numbers in the kitchen. Of course I walked out. They paid me €60 for 140 hours.***

According to the website livingincrete.net/employment.html (which also carries some job vacancies), adverts for seasonal work in hotels, cafés, tavernas and shops can be found in the Greek language newspapers, *Haniotika Nea* and *Patris* in February/March. The site also recommends the notice board at the secondhand shop, To Pazari, on Daskalogianni St. in Chania, which sometimes has ads in English for job vacancies, or you can advertise your services here.

Corfu, Ios, Kos, Rhodes and Naxos seem to offer the most job openings in tourism, though Paros, Santorini and Mykonos and, to a lesser extent, Aegina, Spetsai, Skiathos and the Ionian island of Zakynthos have all been recommended. One place to look for job feedback is the gumtree.com forum on 'Seasonal Work in Greece'. A 2009 posting makes the situation sound hopeful:

Last summer me and my friend from New Zealand went over to Santorini and worked in a bar. We got over at the start of June which was the start of the season but if you're looking at going to Ios (where all the Australians and Kiwis go) you would have to go in May to get the good jobs and good accommodation. We worked every second night over June as it wasn't too busy. Come mid-July till the end of September, you work every day of the week, often till closing time at 4am. We were only doing bar work but saved about €6000 between us so that was good! We had the best time ever in Santo and are going back to do it again!

It should be noted that it is more usual even for careful savers to end up with no more than €1000 after a long busy season. Flamboyant personalities might want to investigate the Remarc Agency in Athens which supplies entertainers, animators and sports services to hotels and resorts in the region (☎ 210 985 8553; sunseafun.com); the promised wage starts at €400 per month plus room and board. An alternative in this field is NewTime Entertainment in Athens (☎ +30 211 7152675; newtime-entertainment.com).

Working in very heavily touristed areas can leave you feeling jaded. Although Richard Ferguson had a great season in Faliraki, he was relieved when he finally had a ticket out of 'ChavLand'. He had had enough of his PR job outside Q Nightclub with the nightly patter, 'hullo luff, yoo awright? where yoo goin' tanite? come ta Q Club. I'll give ya sum free shots I will 'n awl.' Q Club Nightclub on Club Street is the one favoured by other foreign workers in Faliraki who go along at the end of their shifts.

To find out about occasional openings for people to deliver cars for car rental firms or to act as transfer couriers, ask around at those local travel agencies which act as the headquarters for overseas reps. Some enterprising long-stay foreigners have moonlighted as freelance guides. For example you could hire a jeep and offer to take small groups on an off-the-beaten-track tour of a region you know well, taking in the cheapest tavernas and most remote beaches.

Seasonal jobs can be arranged from the UK as well for example at beach resorts run by Mark Warner (☎ 0871 703 3955; markwarner-recruitment.co.uk). They employ a range of seasonal staff from nannies to aerobics instructors for a weekly wage starting at £50 on top of free travel, accommodation, meals, use of facilities, medical insurance and so on. Similarly Neilson (neilson.co.uk/Jobs.aspx) takes on a similar range of summer staff.

Good possibilities exist with Olympic Holidays (☎ 0870 499 6739 or 6742; olympicholidays.com) who are always on the lookout for outgoing EU nationals to work a season as resort reps (candidates must have at least 12 months' customer service experience) or guiding reps. Tax-free wages are £350–£600 per month plus flights and accommodation. Brighton-based Pavilion Tours (☎ 0870 241 0425; paviliontours.com) needs qualified windsurfing, kayaking and sailing instructors willing to help with evening entertainment.

TOUR OPERATORS SEEM TO BE MORE INTERESTED IN FINDING THE RIGHT ATTITUDE RATHER THAN EXPERIENCE WHEN RECRUITING REPS, AS DEBBIE HARRISON DISCOVERED:

Despite the fact that I had no qualifications or relevant experience, had never been to Greece and had never even been on a package holiday, I was offered a job on the island of Kos immediately at the end of my interview. Perhaps this had something to do with the fact that it was mid-March, less than a month before training began and they obviously still had positions to fill. However tour operators do hire reps as late as May or June to help out with the extra workload of high season. Six or seven months is a long time to stay in one place.

A recruitment agency based in Thessaloniki and registered with the Ministry of Labour aims to find staff from all over Europe to fill positions in holiday resorts in Greece and Cyprus. The In-Globe Agency recruits up to 2,000 Europeans aged 18–55 for tourist hotels on the islands through its 'Work & Travel in Greece' programme and its internship programme for trainees. In most cases jobs last from four to 18 months. Basic monthly salaries start at €400 in addition to free accommodation, meals, social insurance and the possibility of paid flights. For details contact Maria Tsilempi Kaltsidou (☎ 2310 588200; maria@inglobe.com.gr). Internships open to students only last four months (June to September) and pay €400 a month; contact the internship co-ordinator Stella Kampa (info@inglobe.com.gr).

Hostels

The competition for business among hostels and cheap pensions is so intense that many hostel owners employ travellers to entice/bully new arrivals into staying at their hostel. In exchange for meeting the relevant boat, train or bus, 'runners' (otherwise known as couriers, touts or hawkers) receive a bed, a small amount of cash-in-hand and a small commission for every 'catch'.

Many enjoy the hostel atmosphere and the camaraderie among hostel workers, and regard the job as a useful stop-gap while travel plans are formulated, often based on the advice of fellow travellers. Anyone who sticks at it for any length of time may find themselves 'promoted' to reception; in this business a fortnight might qualify you for the honour of being a long-term employee.

A great many hostels offer the same wage and perks to people who will spend a few hours a day cleaning. This work is easy-come, easy-go, and is seldom secure even when you want it to be.

Selling and Enterprise

Creative entrepreneurs often find a ready market in the tourist ghettoes of the Greek islands. In the past people have sold sunglasses at a big mark-up, made jewellery and cut hair to supplement their travel fund.

Anyone who can paint or draw quick portraits may be in for a bonanza in the main resorts. There may be work painting signs and notice boards (primarily at the beginning of the season) or decorating the walls and doors of tourist places themselves. This can be quite well paid if you are good at it and get a good reputation. One reader reported that after noticing so many misspelled signs on Zakynthos (her favourite advertised 'daft Cider'), she was sure that someone with both artistic and orthographic talents could persuade Greek bar owners to pay for a sign.

Boating

Yachting holiday companies are a possible source of jobs, which can be fixed up either ahead of time or on the spot. Sailing holiday operator Sunsail (☎ 0844 463 6512; sunsail.co.uk/hr) uses an online recruitment process to hire a large number of sailors, watersports instructors and qualified nannies, etc. for their Sunsail Club Vounaki and their flotilla holidays in Greece. Sailing Holidays Ltd in London (☎ 020 8459 8787; sailingholidays.com) look to hire flotilla skippers and hostesses, boat builders and marine engineers for their upmarket holiday programme in the Greek and Dalmatian islands. The specialist tour operator Setsail Holidays in Suffolk (☎ 01787 310445; boats@setsail.co.uk) recruits a similar range of staff for the May–September season in the eastern Med, promising pocket money of £120–£160 per week.

For casual work it is worth doggedly enquiring around yacht marinas on any island from Corfu (Gouvia) to Crete (Agios Nikolaos).

AGRICULTURE

Working in the English-speaking environment of tourism is not for everyone and certainly does not conform to Ben Nakoneczny's philosophy of travel:

> ***If you are to work abroad it is preferable to be employed in a capacity which allows an insight into the people of the country you are visiting. To serve English tourists bottled beer in a western-style bar is merely to experience the company of those travellers who cling to what they know, unprepared to risk the unfamiliarity of an alien culture. I believe that the best way of breaking cultural boundaries is to work outside the tourist areas, probably in agriculture.***

Unfortunately these days you might end up deserting an English-speaking environment only to find yourself in an Albanian, Bulgarian or Romanian one. Most of the feedback received over the past couple of editions of this book has read more like an epitaph than a how-to guide.

For example Siôn from Wales revisited the Peloponnese on a sentimental journey, recalling his experiences as a fruitpicker and casual worker when he was a contributor to this book in its infancy: '*The citrus pickers I watched in the Sparta region seemed to be Romanians and Greeks. I didn't notice any of the sort of seasonal workers in Kalamata, Mystras and Sparta that I knew in the early eighties in Greece. I remembered my time on the mainland when I and others had been offered seasonal work by drivers merely by walking along roads.*'

Inevitably, travellers will continue to meet farmers in cafés and be asked to lend a hand here and there in the harvesting of oranges, olives, grapes and other crops. But the employment of young international travellers does not take place on the massive scale it once did. The orange harvest between Corinth and Argos and south to Tolo runs from late November or early December to late February, with the crop at its peak between mid-December and mid-January.

Crete, the largest of the Greek islands, was once able to provide a huge amount of work to travellers, from the bananas in Arvi on the south coast (the most northerly commercial banana plantations in the world) to the potato harvest around Ayios Georgios in the Lassithi Plain in August, but mainly involving the grape and olive crops and the massive greenhouses around Ierapetra.

The olive harvest begins in late November though mechanisation has replaced much of the hand-picking.

Although much of northern Greece is rugged and forbidding, parts of Central Macedonia are very fertile. The area west of Thessaloniki, encompassing the market towns of Veria in the prefecture of Imathia, and Yiannitsa in Pella province, comprises a rich agricultural plain, producing asparagus, peaches, pears and tobacco. The asparagus harvest takes place in the spring while the peach harvest gets started in mid-July and peaks after August 1st. As elsewhere this area once attracted armies of migrant workers, both Greek and Western European. Now the work has been taken over by Albanians and Bulgarians (whose borders are not far away).

OTHER WORK

It is sometimes worth checking the classified ads on the website of the English language daily *Athens News* (athensnews.gr), which is updated every Thursday. Adverts range from the distinctly dodgy ('Smart-looking girls required for co-operation in luxury bar') to the legitimate ('English girl wanted for babysitting'). Most are for au pair, nanny or English-tutoring jobs in private households.

You could also try placing your own advertisement in the Situations Wanted. The minimum rate for advertising is €11 for 15 words.

Also check out the American-biased ads-in-greece.com which lists a few job vacancies, though as is so often the case 'Jobs Offered' are outnumbered by 'Services Offered' (Employment Wanted) postings. The Athens Chamber of Commerce and Industry (7 Academias Str, 106 71 Athens; acci.gr) may be able to advise skilled candidates on jobs with Greek companies.

Childcare

The Nine Muses Agency accepts applications from young Europeans and American women for au pair positions and can also place candidates after arrival in Athens. Hotel positions are also sometimes available. Contact the Athens agency on ☎ 210 931 6588; ninemuses@ninemuses.gr; ninemuses.gr. The owner Kalliope Raekou prides herself on her after-placement service, meeting regularly with au pairs at coffee afternoons. There is no fee to au pairs. Among her satisfied au pairs is Riitta Koivula from Finland who, from an unsatisfactory situation on Kos, moved with Popy Raekou's help to a much better one in Athens:

> ***I started my work as an au pair on Kos when I was 19. At first I was so excited about my new family and the new place since I had never been to Greece before and I loved the sun and the beach. I lived in a small village called Pili where almost no one spoke English. But soon I got tired of the village because winter came, tourists left and it wasn't so warm to spend time on the beach any more. I also got tired of the family. The three little girls didn't speak English and they were very lively. The working hours were also terrible: 8 to 12 in the morning and then 4 to 10 in the evening every day except Sundays. I was very homesick on Kos and decided I wanted things to change. So I went to Athens in November and was soon given a new family. I fell in love with Athens and its people right away. My new family was the best and we are still very close.***

The advantage of waiting until you get to Greece to look for a live-in job is that you can meet your prospective family first. It is far better for both parties if you can chat over a cup of coffee and bargain in a leisurely fashion for wages, time off, duties, etc. Most families looking for nannies live in the well-off suburbs of Athens like Kifissia, Politia, Pangrati and Kolonaki as well as in Thessaloniki, Patras and the islands.

Teaching English

Thousands of private language schools called *frontisteria* are scattered throughout Greece, creating a huge demand for native English speaker teachers. This is one job for which there will be no competition from Albanians, though it should be noted that Australians, South Africans and North Americans of Greek ancestry are often given teaching jobs in preference to people with non-Greek surnames.

Standards at *frontisteria* vary from indifferent to excellent, but the run-of-the-mill variety is usually a reasonable place to work for nine months. By no means all of the foreign teachers hired by *frontisteria* hold a TEFL qualification, though all but the most dodgy or desperate schools will expect to see a university degree (which is a government requirement for a teacher's licence) and EU nationality.

The majority of jobs are in towns and cities in mainland Greece. Athens has such a large expatriate community that most of the large central schools are able to hire well-qualified staff locally. But this is not the case in Edessa, Larisa, Preveza or any of numerous smaller towns of which the tourist to Greece is unlikely to have heard.

The minimum hourly wage is currently €8.81 gross (2008). Anyone with some training or experience should be able to ask for a slightly higher rate. Earnings can be increased substantially by compulsory bonuses at Christmas and Easter and holiday pay at the end of the contract. The average number of hours assigned to teachers has been shrinking to 18 per week, which means reduced earnings.

Chains of schools are always worth approaching with your CV. Try for example ISON Foreign Language Centres, part of the Strategakis Group with head office in Thessaloniki (☎ 2310 264276; centralschool@strategakis.gr) which employs 25 British and Irish teachers for 100 foreign language centres all over northern Greece. Several teacher recruitment agencies actively seek teachers to work for one academic year. Interviews are carried out in Greece or the UK during the summer for contracts starting in September. These agencies are looking for people with at least a BA and normally a TEFL certificate (depending on the client *frontisterion*'s requirements). The following undertake to match EU teachers with *frontisteria* and do not charge teachers a fee:

Anglo-Hellenic Teacher Recruitment: PO Box 263, 201 00 Corinth; tel/fax 27410 53511; jobs@anglo-hellenic.com; anglo-hellenic.com; scores of posts in wide choice of locations for university graduates from the UK, preferably with a CELTA or Trinity TESOL; interviews conducted in London, Corinth or Athens during the summer; via Lingua TEFL certificate training courses also offered monthly (info@teflcorinth.com).

Cambridge Teachers Recruitment: 17 Metron St, New Philadelphia, 143 42 Athens; tel/fax 210 258 5155; macleod_smith_andrew@hotmail.com; one of the largest agencies, placing up to 60 teachers per year in vetted schools; applicants must have a degree and a TEFL Certificate, a friendly personality and conscientious attitude.

Hyphen: Vas. Olgas 24b (4th floor), 54641 Thessaloniki; ☎ 2310 888125; hr@hyphen.gr; hyphen.gr; among its services to language publishers and schools, it tries to fill vacancies on behalf of its client schools (teaching vacancies listed on website).

Linguistic Lab: PO Box 12, 20400 Xylokastro, Corinth; tel/fax 27430 22135; info@linguisticlab.com; linguisticlab.com; variable vacancies for those with a BA and TESOL certificate; training courses run by Global TESOL are offered monthly.

After travelling and working in Greece for a couple of years, Jane McNally wrote from a school in Macedonia with some advice:

> ***Most English speakers find work in private English schools. It can be difficult to find work by just knocking on school doors. Most school owners recruit their staff through agents two or three months in advance of the new term. All my colleagues and myself have had discipline problems in the classroom. Be prepared for employers that range from nutty to demented!***

Private lessons, at least in the provinces, are possible to find. The going rate is about €25–€30 an hour for tutoring candidates to pass the B2 (Independent User) and C2 (Proficient User), the new EU standards

Volunteering

Elix-Conservation Volunteers Greece in Athens (210 382 5506; elix.org.gr) is a non-profit organisation promoting intercultural exchanges and nature and heritage conservation. Projects include work in protected landscapes, conservation of traditional buildings and work on archaeological sites. Applications can be sent directly or through a partner organisation in your country (e.g. UNA Exchange and Concordia in the UK).

Organisations involved in the protection of sea turtles actively use volunteer helpers. Archelon is the Sea Turtle Protection Society of Greece (tel/fax 210 523 1342; volunteers@archelon.gr;

archelon.gr) which carries out research and conservation on the loggerhead turtle on Zakynthos, Crete and the Peloponnese. A free campsite is provided for those who stay at least a month; volunteers will need at least €15 a day for food plus pay a registration fee of €150 or €250 (the lower fee is for those who arrive before mid-June or after August 21). Melanie Leather was interviewed about her experiences for the *Independent*:

> ***I spent a month on the island of Zakynthos in Greece working for Archelon. The base camp was very basic: two cold showers, chemical toilets, a simple kitchen and eating area and everyone's tents. We were assigned duties such as beach patrol, which involved explaining about the turtles to the tourists. We did a lot of public awareness work. I presented slide shows at local hotels and manned the information booth. I also gave brief talks on turtle spotting boats, which involved some background reading. There were more mundane duties such as cooking for 40 people. After that, I spent three nights on the beautiful island of Marathonissi. We were the only ones living there. Apart from beach patrol, we conducted morning and night surveys. At 6am we searched for turtle tracks on the beach, recording all the data and mapping the nests. It was a steep learning curve. It never got boring. I'd recommend it to everyone. The Greeks aren't big on conservation, so you really feel you are doing something worthwhile.***

Another turtle conservation organisation is MEDASSET (Mediterranean Association to Save the Sea Turtles; ☎ 210 361 3572; medasset@medasset.org; medasset.org/volunteer1.htm) which offers volunteers free accommodation in central Athens in exchange for working for a minimum of three weeks in the Medasset office providing administrative back-up for a sea turtle rescue project in Zakynthos and elsewhere in the eastern Mediterranean.

Bears are even more threatened than marine turtles. Arcturos accepts short-term volunteers at its environmental centre in the Prefecture of Florina in northern Greece, which serves as a bear protection centre (tel/fax 23860 41500; mstyliadou@arcturos.gr; arcturos.gr).

Another interesting possibility for people willing to work for at least three months from April or July is at the holistic holiday centre on the island of Skyros in the northern Aegean. A number of 'work scholars' help with cleaning, bar work and domestic and maintenance duties at the Atsitsa Bay centre in exchange for weekly pocket money of £50 plus the opportunity to join one of the 250 courses on offer, from yoga to windsurfing. Details are available from Skyros's UK office (9 Eastcliff Road, Shanklin, Isle of Wight PO37 6AA; ☎ 01983 865566; office@skyros.com).

CYPRUS

The Cypriot economy like its Greek counterpart relies heavily on tourism (nearly three million tourists visited the island last year) as well as agriculture. In late 2008, the rate of unemployment was 3.7%, among the lowest in the European Union. The accession of Cyprus to the EU in 2004 has dispensed with the bureaucracy of work permits since it elected not to implement a transitional period before labour could move freely in and out of the country. (The Turkish Republic of Northern Cyprus is dealt with separately at the end of this chapter.)

A visitor to Greek Cyprus will be struck by the similarities with Greece (language, cuisine, architecture, landscapes and culture) but then surprised by the relative prominence of English and the widespread British influence left over from when Cyprus was a British colony until 1960. Also the cost of living is higher.

REGULATIONS

According to the website of the Ministry of Foreign Affairs, the formalities for EU nationals are as follows:

> ***Nationals of any Member State who move to Cyprus in order to pursue activity as employed persons are granted a residence permit. The residence permit is valid for not less than five years from the date of issue and it is effective throughout the territory of the Republic. It is automatically renewable upon request. Application forms for the issue of a residence permit are available at the Civil Registry and Migration Department of the Ministry of Interior and at the District Aliens and Immigration Branches of the Police. The application form must be submitted within three months of entry in the Republic to the above mentioned Department or Police Branches. For the issue of a residence permit for employment, the following documents are required: a valid passport or identity card, a confirmation from the employer or a certificate of employment stamped by the Labour Department of the Ministry of Labour and Social Insurance, in which the duration and type of the work provided by the employee is stated; and two recent passport-sized photographs. Completion of the formalities for obtaining a residence permit do not prevent the immediate employment of the applicant.***

Australians are lucky that there is a reciprocal working holiday scheme whereby people aged 18–25 can apply in Australia for a one-year working holiday visa for Cyprus.

Anyone with qualifications and experience, particularly in IT, should look at the job vacancies listed by the recruitment agency Global Recruitment Solutions with offices in Limassol and Nicosia (grsrecruitment.com) or consult recruitment sites like jobs.com.cy.

THE TOURIST INDUSTRY

Most big tour operators consider placement in Cyprus as a perk to be offered to staff who have worked well for the company elsewhere, especially if they have worked in Greece and picked up some of the language. Cyprus has the advantage of offering work during the winter as well as the summer, though it has special short seasonal attractions when it is especially busy, such as for the spring flowers.

To track down companies to which you can apply, check any Winter Sun travel brochure or check recruitment websites like jobincyprus.com and cyprusjobs.com (the latter with undated job adverts). Hotel chains such as Louis Hotels (louishotels.com) and Amathus Hotels (amathus-hotels.com) are worth investigating. As in Greece, women are at an advantage when looking for work in cafés, bars and restaurants, but they should exercise caution according to Karen Holman:

> ***In my two years there I heard stories about Cypriot employers expecting more of their barmaids than just bar work. I worked in two pubs and I would say that both bosses employed me with an ulterior motive. I was lucky – both of them were shy. By the time they realised I wasn't going to be their girlfriend, they had found me to be a good worker and were used to me being around. Many employers will sack the girls, or threaten to report them for stealing.***

Tom Parker had little success with a job search along the seafront in Limassol in April:

> ***We headed for the tourist area and were soon told that we would stand a better chance if we bought a drink for the manager before asking about jobs. The only concrete result was that we got very drunk. No job opportunities (they told us we were too early). The next day we concentrated on the small cafés in the back streets of the old town. Here my two companions (both girls) were offered jobs in separate cafés.***

TURKISH REPUBLIC OF NORTHERN CYPRUS

As is well known, Cyprus is a divided island. The southern part is the Republic of Cyprus, a member of the British Commonwealth and European Union. The north, occupied by Turkey since the intervention of 1974, is called the Turkish Republic of Northern Cyprus (Kibris). It is not recognised by any country except Turkey. However there is a sizeable expat community that has acquired many properties along the north coast of the island. Although hampered by the lack of direct flights (incoming tourists must travel via Turkey), the tourist industry is flourishing. Because it is off the beaten track, the pool of potential seasonal or casual labour is smaller than it is elsewhere on the Mediterranean.

The red tape for foreign workers is relatively straightforward. Before working in the TRNC, you will first have to overcome your qualms about working in a place whose regime was responsible for the forcible eviction of so many Greek Cypriots and destruction of property and artefacts following the invasion of 1974. On the other hand, the increased interest in reunification and the recent easing of border restrictions looks set to continue with the symbolic re-opening of Ledra Street in central Nicosia in 2008.

Turkish Cyprus is a very small place (population 265,000) and job vacancies become known as soon as they exist. For every one advertised in the English language weekly *Cyprus Today*, there are dozens heard of on the grapevine. The notice board outside the Post Office in the main town of Kyrenia (Girne) is a good source of information on jobs, accommodation, etc. The British Residents' Society can be found in 'the hut' behind the post office on Saturday mornings and also meet on Friday mornings (11am–1pm) at the Pegasus Restaurant. Opportunities exist in restaurants and holiday apartments, especially those owned or managed by expats. The wages are low by British standards, but food and accommodation may be provided. The highest concentration of restaurants and bars is along the picturesque harbour of Kyrenia, with a further concentration in Lapta, Karaman and Alsancak to the west.

Tour Companies

Northern Cyprus is not a cheap package holiday destination and tends to attract a more discerning clientele, who are interested in visiting the sites as well as enjoying the marvellous scenery and climate. It is a popular destination for Germans, so some knowledge of German would be an advantage.

Some times ago, Pat Kennard landed a job with Kibris Travel Services (kibristravel.com), the ground handling agent for a number of UK tour operators. She enjoyed a fantastic season as a holiday rep even though, as she admits, it is a very demanding job having to do early morning and late night airport runs, sort out clients' problems with their accommodation and conduct tours of the island. Nowadays they prefer people who can speak Turkish as well as English.

Red Tape

As in Turkey it will be necessary to leave Cyprus every three months to renew your tourist visa; this entails a two-hour catamaran trip to mainland Turkey at a cost of about €55 return. Do not overstay your three-month stay because you will be fined for every extra day. Work permits can be applied for on your behalf only by a local employer, though technically you should be out of the country. Further information can be found on the websites cyprus44.com or aboutnorthcyprus.com.

ITALY

Italy is a remarkably welcoming country. Once Italians accept you, they will go out of their way to find you a place in their communities, without any emphasis on the barriers of nationality. Once you get a toehold, you will find that a friendly network of contacts and possible employers will quickly develop. Without contacts, if only a sympathetic landlady at your pension, it is virtually impossible to find work.

In Italy you find the best-dressed and most sophisticated people in the world. Image counts for a great deal in Italy, and it has to be said that good-looking smartly dressed people have far more chance of success than their dowdy counterparts. With a gradually rising unemployment rate (6.7% autumn 2008), it is going to take time to find a job no matter what your dress sense. The situation for casual job-seekers has been made more difficult by the arrival of more than half a million Romanians since Romania joined the EU, although they cannot work without a work permit, which has led to resentment and animosity on both sides.

REGULATIONS

Since 2007 the bureaucracy for EU nationals in Italy has been simplified. EU nationals intending to stay in Italy longer than 90 days are required to apply for a *carta di soggiorno* or *certificato di residenza* (residence certificate). To obtain this, you must take some proof of income (employment contract, financial backing from home) to the *anagrafe* office of the local town hall.

Non-EU citizens must still apply for a permit to stay (*permesso di soggiorno*) within eight days of arrival in Italy. It is now possible to apply at a post office rather than from the *Questura* (police department) as formerly. Detailed information can be found at portaleimmigrazione.it including templates of the forms in English needed to apply for the *permessi*.

Australian and New Zealand citizens aged 18–30 are eligible for a 12-month working holiday visa in Italy. The best chances for other non-EU citizens (*extracomunitari*) of getting their papers in order are to be a dual national, to obtain a student visa which permits 20 hours of work a week (living in or out) or to arrange a firm offer of a job while they are still in their home country. Note that American citizens may be able to avoid work permit hassles by working for the US military. The large base in Vicenza sometimes hires catering and other staff; contact the Vicenza Civilian Personnel Advisory Center's Job Information Centre on 0444 71. If you want to open a bank account, you need to take proof that you are resident and proof of income (tax return or contract). Tax is a further headache for long-stay workers. As soon as you sort out the work documents, you should obtain a tax number (*codice fiscale*) from the Uffici delle Entrate. The rate of income tax (*Ritenuta d'Acconto*) is usually about 20% in addition to social security deductions of up to 10%.

Remember that medical expenses can be very high if you're not covered by the Italian Medical Health Scheme (ASL or *Azienda Sanitaria Locale*). Once you locate the local office, you must apply for an EU Health Insurance Card for Italy (*Tessera Sanitaria*).

FINDING WORK

If you can't speak a word of Italian, you will be at a distinct disadvantage. Provided you can afford it and are sufficiently interested, you should consider studying a little Italian before you set off on your travels or enrolling in one of the many short Italian language courses offered in most

Italian cities. Italian is one of the easiest languages to learn, especially if you already have some knowledge of a Latin-based language.

Although you should not neglect scouring the newspapers and online recruitment sites for job adverts, you may be disappointed. Sometimes requests by *stranieri* (foreigners) for work outnumber the situations vacant.The first free-ads papers in Europe were published in Italy in 1977. *Secondamano* is published in ten regional editions and online (Italian only) covering the industrialised north of the country. The British Embassy in Italy site lists English-language publications both internet and print, such as the fortnightly *Easy Milano* and *Wanted in Rome* (wantedinrome.com) which has job vacancies for teachers, au pairs, etc. You can also search recruitment websites like jobrapido.it.

Contacts

Contacts are even more important in Italy than in other countries. Many of the people we have heard from who have worked in Italy (apart from TEFL teachers, au pairs, etc.) have got their work through friends. They may not necessarily have had the friends or contacts when they arrived, but they formed friendships while they were there as visitors.

Staff at the local CTS branch may be helpful. CTS (Centro Turistico Studentesco e Giovanile) is the main student travel agency which does far more than arrange flights and travel, e.g. its website cts.it has links to language courses (*corsi di lingua*) and conservation volunteering as well as to its offices (*sedi*) throughout Italy.

In Rome try the notice boards in the following locations: the English language Lion Bookshop and Café at Via dei Greci 36, the Church of England on nearby Via del Babuino and CTS at Via Solferino 6A (☎ 06 462 0431).

Language school notice boards are always worth checking; at the Centro di Lingua & Cultura Italiana per Stranieri where Dustie Hickie took cheap Italian lessons in Milan, there was a good notice board with adverts for au pairs, dog-walkers, etc. Dustie got a cleaning job this way.

Even with contacts you are not guaranteed to find work, as Edward Peters found one summer: *'After travelling through Eastern Europe and Austria, we had hoped to find something in Italy; but three sets of contacts were unable to find us anything – perhaps because it was August (national holidays) or perhaps because we were too busy enjoying ourselves in Milan, Rome and Ischia.'*

TOURISM

Italy's tourist industry employs between 6% and 7% of the Italian workforce and has limited openings for unskilled non-Italians. Anyone who has had the pleasure of dining out in Italy or even buying 200 grams of cheese or salami at a delicatessen will know that Italian standards of service are very professional and indeed people (usually men) consider waiting on tables as a career. Any openings for casual bar staff that come along are likely to be in (for example) Irish themed pubs or American-style bistros.

Although less well known than the seaside resorts of other Mediterranean countries, there may be seaside possibilities for foreign job-seekers, especially in the resorts near Venice. Lake Garda resorts like Desenzano, Malcesine, Sirmione and Riva del Garda are recommended as are the seaside resorts near Venice like Lido di Jesolo, Bibione, Lignano, Caorle and Chioggiaa, all of which are more popular with German and Austrian tourists than Britons, so a knowledge of German would be a good selling point. Apart from the job of *donna ai piani* (chambermaid), a knowledge of Italian will be necessary in most cases.

The Blu Hotels chain has hotels and holiday villages in Lake Garda, Sardinia, Umbria, Abruzzo, Tuscany, Rome, Palinuro and Calabria (as well as Austria); its website bluhotels.it has a Jobs icon. Michael Cullen worked in three hotels around Como and Bellagio and found 'a nice friendly and warm atmosphere, despite the heat and long hours'. Even in flourishing resorts like Rimini, there seem to be nearly enough locals and Italian students to fill the jobs in hotels, bars and on the beach, although one company has been advertising heavily in the English-speaking media. The Life Club in Rimini (lifemedias.com/job.php) hires lots of young people to work in the club scene over the summer and starts its recruitment in October (info@lifediscos.com).

If you don't get a job in a hotel, you might get work servicing holiday flats or gardening. If you plan far enough in advance (and speak some Italian) you might get a job as a campsite courier with one of the major British camping holiday organisers such as Canvas Holidays or with a tour operator like Headwater Holidays (see the chapter on Tourism). The smaller Venue Holidays (☎ 01233 629950; jobs@venueholidays.co.uk) employs summer season reps at campsites on the Venetian Riviera, Lake Garda and in Tuscany. Catherine Dawes enjoyed her campsite job near Albenga on the Italian Riviera – '*a fairly uninspiring part of Italy*' – even more than she did her previous summer's work on a French campsite. She reports that the Italians seemed to be more relaxed than the French, especially under high season pressure, and would always go out of their way to help her when she was trying to translate tourists' problems to the mechanic or the doctor.

The British company Brad Europe Ltd (bradeurope.com/vacancies.html) provides a linen hire service to over 300 campsites in Europe, and has opened a new laundry in Vicenza. Staff are paid the UK minimum wage and provided with free accommodation.

Many mountain resorts with busy ski seasons (see section below) also need workers from outside the area for the summer. One UK tour operator that takes on domestic staff and summer reps to work in the Dolomites is Collett's Mountain Holidays (☎ 01763 289660; colletts.co.uk/work).

You can also try Italian-run campsites which have a large staff to man the on-site restaurants, bars and shops. The two main campsites in Rome including the Flaminio Village may take on English help before the season begins (i.e. March). Boat mechanics and other staff can approach holiday barge companies; for example the British company Connoisseur Holidays Afloat (☎ 0870 160 5648; connoisseurboating.co.uk) keeps six boats at Casier and Porto Levante south of Venice in the Po delta.

Holiday Animators and Entertainers

Various agencies recruit musicians, singers, DJs and entertainers for holiday villages and summer resorts around Italy. Italian companies would be unlikely to hire anyone unless they spoke more than just English. Here are a handful of companies that hire substantial numbers:

Planet srl, Animazione Turistica: Rimini; ☎ 0541 787597; planetvillager.com; this company recruits hundreds of staff not only in Italy but on recruiting trips to Belgium, Switzerland and the Czech Republic.

Darwin srl, Turismo e Spettacolo: Florence; tel/fax 055 292114; darwinstaff@yahoo.it; darwinstaff.com; large numbers of staff needed, e.g. 150 mini club animators to arrange children's holiday programme plus hostesses, DJs, musicians, etc.

RossodiSero: Foggia; ☎ 0881 709951; rossodiseranimazione.it; recruitment reps in Rome, Bari and Naples; 3 or 4 day training courses for €95 or €130.

Associazione Nazionale Animatori: Rome; tel/fax 06 678 16 47; associazionenazionaleanimatori@hotmail.com; ilportaledegliartisti.it/ana.htm.

Hostels

As throughout the world, backpackers' haunts often employ travellers for short periods. One that has been recommended is the Fawlty Towers hostel at Via Magenta 39 (☎ 06 445 0374; fawltytowers.org) near the Termini Station in Rome, where many native English speakers find work in reception, maintenance and cleaning.

Raised in New York and largely cut off from her family's Italian roots, one traveller decided at age 30 to spend some time in Italy.

BY MAKING USE OF HOSTELS.COM STEPHANIE FUCCIO HAD LITTLE DIFFICULTY PRE-ARRANGING A HOSTEL JOB:

Never in a million years did I think that watching MTV would be part of my daily life in Rome, Italy. But it was. I was working at a really cute, small hostel in Rome, seven days a week. The shifts would alternate from evening to morning every day: one day doing the morning shift when the hostel was cleaned and the next day the evening shift. As well as getting to stay there for free, they paid me and my co-worker 20 euros per day in cash which was really nice. Rome was so cheap (from a San Francisco point of view) and with great weather, it was easy to save. I came to Italy with $700 cash and a plane ticket, I left with about $600 and a plane ticket to England and Ireland. I was there about five weeks total.

Winter Resorts

On-the-spot opportunities are possible if not plentiful in the winter resorts of the Alps, Dolomites and Apennines. Many of the jobs are part-time and not very well paid, but provide time for skiing and in many cases a free pass to the ski-lifts for the season. Sauze d'Oulx and Courmayeur are the best resorts for job hunting.

Cathy Salt describes her success in Sauze d'Oulx:

> ***Upon arrival at Sauze d'Oulx on 14th November, we found we were much too early for on-the-spot jobs. The place was practically dead. Only a few bars were open. Fortunately an English guy working in a bar informed us that the carpenter was looking for help. My partner Jon was able to get four weeks work with him, sanding down and varnishing, also enabling him to be on the spot for other work that would come up. The same day I found a babysitting job for a shop owner's son, but I wouldn't start until 5th December. We were both fortunate in finding this since we came up on a Thursday and have since found out that the weekend is a much better time to look because the ski shops and restaurants are open.***

Such stories are counterbalanced by the inevitable failures: Susanna Macmillan gave up her job hunt in the Italian Alps after two weeks when she had to admit that her non-existent Italian and just passable French were not getting her anywhere. Perhaps she was looking in the wrong resorts like Cortina d'Ampezzo, which is sophisticated and expensive and has a high percentage of year-round workers.

Crystal Holidays, part of the TUI Travel Group (☎ 020 8541 2223; jobsinwinter.co.uk) hire resort reps and chalet staff for work in the Italian Alps as well as staff for summer holidays. Interski based in Nottinghamshire specialise in ski holidays in the Aosta Valley and recruit lots of winter staff (☎ 01623 456333; interski.co.uk/employment.htm). The Ski Department of PGL Travel Ltd offer some jobs as ski reps, leaders and ski/snowboard instructors (to BASI-qualified skiers), especially for short periods during half-term and Easter holidays. Mark Warner (markwarner-recruitment.co.uk) also hires winter staff for Courmayeur.

Not nearly as many chalet jobs can be found in Italy as in France, due to the very strict regulations that govern chalets in Italy. You are more likely to find a job in a small family-run bar or hotel than in one of the big concerns. The large hotels usually recruit their staff in southern Italy and then move them en masse from the sea to the mountains in the autumn.

AU PAIRS

Many European au pair and nanny agencies deal with Italy, so you should have no trouble arranging a family placement. The London-based agency Totalnannies.com (☎ 020 8542 3067) specialises in Italy and has up to 100 vacancies in Italy at any given moment.

ANGIE COPLEY WAS DELIGHTED WITH THE SITUATION TO WHICH HER BRITISH AGENCY SENT HER:

After finding the address of agencies in your book, I wrote to one and before I knew it they had found me a family in Sardinia. I couldn't believe it was so easy. All I had to do was pay for a flight out there and that was that. When I arrived, the family met me and took me to their house. Some house. It wasn't just a house but a castle where the Italian royal family used to spend their holidays. What was even better was that the family had turned it into a hotel, the best possible place for meeting people. I ended up having the best summer of my life in Sardinia. Once I picked up the language I went out, met lots of people, had beach parties. My work involved not much more than playing with their two-year old boy all day and speaking English to him. Basically it was one big holiday.

Summer-only positions are readily available. Most Italian families in the class that can afford live-in childcare go to holiday homes by the sea or in the mountains during the summer and at other holiday times which did not prove as idyllic as it sounds for Jacqueline Edwards:

> ***My first job as an au pair in Italy was with a family who were staying in the middle of nowhere with their extended family. It was a total nightmare for me. I could just about say hello in Italian and couldn't understand a word of what was going on. After three weeks I was fed up, homesick and ready to jump on the next plane to England. But a few days later we moved back to town (Modena) and from then on things improved dramatically.***

The average wage for au pairs is in the range €70–€100+ per week, mothers' helps €500–€800 monthly and trained nannies €1000+. Wages are slightly higher in the north of Italy than central and southern parts of the country because the cost of living is higher. The demand for nannies and mothers' helps able to work 40+ hours is especially strong since a high percentage of families in Italy have two working parents.

Most of the Italian agencies speak English and welcome applications from British au pairs. Some agencies charge a registration fee or other fees for ancillary services, so always enquire. Try any of the following:

ARCE (Attivita Relazioni Culturali con l'Estero): Genoa; ☎ 010 583020; arceaupair.it; long established agency makes placements throughout the country.

Celtic Childcare: Via Sant Antonio Da Padova 14, 10121 Turin; ☎ 011 533606; celticchildcare.com; IAPA member.

Euroma: Rome; ☎ 06 806 92 130; euroma.info; member of IAPA.

Intermediate srl: Via Bramante 13, 00153 Rome; ☎ 06 57 300683; intermediateonline.com; intermediate has its own language school in the Aventino district of Rome; registration fee for au pairs €280; member of IAPA.

Roma Au Pair: Via Pietro Mascagni 138, 00199 Rome; ☎ 06 863 21519; romaaupair.com; no placement fee for au pairs.

TEACHING

Hundreds of language schools around Italy employ native English speakers. Unfortunately for the ordinary traveller, the vast majority of the jobs require a degree, TEFL qualifications and knowledge of Italian. Xuela Edwards arrived with a friend who was a qualified English teacher at the right time (September) and reported that the language schools were flooded with teachers and just being able to speak English was not enough.

Doing a TEFL course will improve your chances, as always. After '*stressing and sweating*' his way through a CELTA course in Edinburgh one summer, Fergus Cooney posted a message on Dave's ESL Café (see intro chapter *Teaching English*) 'Teacher with degree + CELTA seeks job in Italy/Spain' and soon his inbox began to fill (and not only with job offers from Korea). He chose a school in Calabria (and it is unlikely that the Calabria Tourist Promotion Board will be giving him a job in the near future):

> ***To cut it short (forgive the pun), I was sacked after two months for what might well be the most unreasonable reason ever in the field of TEFL, for falling ill with appendicitis. My appendix burst and I nearly died. The small private school in the village far from anywhere wanted me back at work two days after the operation. I could barely walk and couldn't talk for a week. I certainly couldn't shout loudly which was necessary in the south of Italy in a class full of screaming 12 year olds. After a week, the bosses told me that I was no longer needed and that I had to be out of their flat by Monday. I found a job in a nice school run by two English guys in the city 50km away although I had problems there too trying to obtain a contract. I now know that getting a contract is of the utmost importance and next time I will not plunge into a job before researching the school, town, amenities, etc. To inexperienced teachers: don't go to Reggio Calabria. It has to be Europe's most boring and ugly city. There is nowhere to eat during the day except Mc-bloody-Donald's; there is nowhere in the city centre to sit down, no cinema, no pubs, no live music and a general lack of culture. OK the local food and, especially the oranges in winter, are fantastic. But I would definitely NOT go back to Calabria.***

Similarly Natalia de Cuba could not persuade any of the language schools in the northern town of Rovereto where she was based to hire her without qualifications. So she decided to enrol in the Cambridge (CELTA) Certificate course run by International House in Rome (ihromamz.it). She found the month-long course strenuous but not terribly difficult, and worth the fee (which now stands at €1,750). Often employers notify IH of job vacancies, and Natalia had no problem finding a job back in Rovereto.

Fortunately the online version of the Italian *Yellow Pages* is reasonably user-friendly. Go to paginegialle.it and search under *Scuole di Lingue* in the cities and towns in which you're hoping to work. Make sure you use the Italian version of the name, e.g. Napoli, Torino, Venezia, etc. (although you can also search in English). The ones listed first have email and web addresses. International language school groups like Benedict Schools, Linguarama, Berlitz and inlingua are major providers of English language teaching in Italy. Wall Street Institutes now have about 90 centres in Italy and actively recruit native speakers (wallstreet.it has a link to 'lavora-con-noi').

Several Italian-based chains of language schools account for a large number of teaching jobs, though most operate as independent franchises so must be applied to individually. Chains include the British Schools Group (britishschool.com) with more than 60 member schools and an on-line teacher application procedure. Other chains include British Institutes with 175+ associated schools (britishinstitutes.it) and Oxford Schools based in Venice (☎ 041 570 2355; oxforditalia.it) with 13 schools in northeastern Italy.

Another possibility is to set up as a freelance tutor, though a knowledge of Italian is even more of an asset here than it is for jobs in schools. You can post notices in supermarkets, tobacconists, primary and secondary schools and advertise in a free paper. As long as you have access to some premises, you can try to arrange both individual and group lessons, and undercut the language institutes significantly. One enterprising traveller presented himself to a classroom teacher who asked her class of 12 and 13 years olds if they would like to learn English from a native. They all said yes and paid a small sum to attend his after-school class.

As in other European countries, summer camps for unaccompanied young people usually offer English as well as a range of sports. The organisation called ACLE (Associazione Culturale Linguistica Educational) runs summer camps throughout Italy, though its HQ is in San Remo, Liguria (☎ 0184 506070; acle.org). They advertise heavily for more than 200 young people 19 or over with a genuine interest in children to teach English and organise activities including drama for four to eight weeks. The promised wage is €220–€260 per week plus board, lodging, insurance and travel between camps within Italy. However summer staff must enrol in a compulsory four-day introductory TEFL course for which a deduction of €150 will be made from earned wages.

A less well known organisation also based in San Remo might be worth comparing: Lingue Senza Frontiere (☎ 0184 508650; linguesenzafrontiere.org). They promise to pay their tutors €450 net plus board and lodging every two weeks in their English immersion summer camps. A smaller outfit to try is the English Camp Company (info@theenglishcampcompany.com).

AGRICULTURE

In most Italian harvests, there is no tradition of hiring large numbers of foreign young people. With the arrival of so many migrant workers from Romania, the Balkans and elsewhere joining the traditional Moroccan workers, the situation has become even less promising. Seasonal jobs in the grape and olive harvests are reserved and carefully regulated among locals and other Italian unemployed. However if you have local friends and contacts or if you speak some Italian it is worth trying to participate in one of the autumn harvests which by most accounts are thoroughly enjoyable. Wages are also good.

There may be seasonal agricultural work in the strawberry harvests of Emilia Romagna. Cherries are grown around Vignola (just west of Bologna) and are also picked in June. The Valtellina area, near the Swiss border, is another area with a multitude of orchards. Olives are almost never picked by foreigners. Andrea Militello investigated possibilities for olive pickers in Tuscany (around San Miniato) but the wages were so low he didn't pursue the idea.

The contact for World Wide Opportunities on Organic Farms (WWOOF) in Italy is Bridget Mathews in Castagneto Carducci in Livorno (info@wwoof.it; wwoof.it). WWOOF volunteers in Italy must join the national association at a cost of €25 for insurance purposes and in return will be sent the list of more than 50 organic farmers in Italy looking for volunteers.

Val di Non Apple Harvest

The main exception to the shortage of harvest jobs for foreign travellers is the apple harvest in the Val Venosta and Val di Non around the town of Cles in the valley of the River Adige north of Trento.

ANDREA MILITELLO (FROM ANOTHER PART OF ITALY) HAS PARTICIPATED IN HARVESTS FROM SPAIN TO TASMANIA, BUT HIS FAVOURITE IS THE APPLE HARVEST IN REVO NEAR CLES WHERE HE HAS PICKED FRUIT FOR MANY YEARS:

This year I had a great time with the other pickers. The harvest starts about the 20th-25th September and lasts until 25th October, but it's better to arrive at least ten days early. In the beginning it's best to go to Cles. This harvest unites people from everywhere, South America, Spanish, black people... so there's a meeting of many cultures.

Women normally sort the apples, which the men have picked (for a slightly higher wage). To get the crop picked as quickly as possible, the farmers expect workers to pick ten hours a day with no days off. The standard arrangement is for a proportion of the hourly wage to be deducted for lunch and accommodation.

Of course not everyone is successful at finding a job. Kristof Szymczak from Poland described the area as a tower of babel and couldn't find an orchard owner willing to hire him. But if you do manage to break in, it sounds one of the most enjoyable harvests in this book, at least as described by the American Natalia de Cuba:

> *Apple picking is great on the ground. The ladders require much more concentration (beware of drinking too much wine!) and are considered a man's job. Lunch with the family was included – pasta, salad, wine and a shot of grappa. It was delicious and friendly, as all the pickers – many of them family members – ate together and gossiped and joked. There is always plenty of opportunity to chat while working, especially if you are assigned the job of sorting the fruit. The Italian pickers really do sing opera in the orchards.*

Grape-picking

Several people have reported success in finding a place on the grape harvest (*vendemmia*). Italy was called Oenotria by the ancient Greeks meaning 'the land of wine' and it remains the biggest producer of wine in the world. Today there are no regions of Italy which are without vineyards. Once you are in a fruit-growing area, a good place to look for work is the warehouse run by the local cooperative where all the local farmers sell their produce to the public. There may even be a list of farmers who are looking for pickers. Try visiting the Societá Agricultura Vallagarina in Rovereto in the region of Trentino, a major agricultural area. In the German-speaking South Tirol, strawberries are picked in June in the Val Martello and Val Isarco.

The style of grape-picking is reputed to be easier than in France since the plants are trained upwards onto wire frames, rather than allowed to droop to the ground, so that pickers reach up with a clipper and catch the bunch of grapes in a funnel-type object, which is less strenuous than having to bend double for hours at a stretch. Accommodation can be a problem since it is not normally provided by farmers.

VOLUNTARY OPPORTUNITIES

Many Italian organisations arrange summer work projects which are as disparate as selling recyclable materials to finance development projects in the developing world to restoring old convents or preventing forest fires. Here is a selection of voluntary organisations that run working holidays. In some cases, it will be necessary to apply through a partner organisation in your home country:

Abruzzo, Lazio and Molise National Park: Centro Operativo Servizio Educazione, Via Roma, 67030 Villetta Barrea; ☎ 0864 89102; centroservizi.villetta@parcoabruzzo.it; parcoabruzzo.it; volunteers carry out research and protection of flora and fauna in remote locations, e.g. in Pescasseroli and Villetta Barrea; volunteers must cover their insurance and registration fees: €80 for 7 days, €140 for 14 days.

AGAPE: Centro Ecumenico, Prali (Torino); ☎ 0121 807514; agapecentroecumenico.org; volunteers help run this ecumenical conference centre in the Alps, about 80 miles from Turin; stays usually last 3–5 weeks in summer but can be shorter at other times of the year.

Emmaus Italia: Boves; tel/fax 0171 387834; emmauscuneo.it; workcamps to collect, sort and sell second hand equipment to raise funds for social and community projects worldwide.

International Building Companions (Soci Costruttori): Ferrara; ☎ 0532 243279; iboitalia.org; renovation projects in deprived communities.

LIPU (Lega Italiana Protezione Uccelli): Parma; ☎ 0 521 273043; lipu.it; long-established environmental and bird conservation association which publishes a catalogue of summer projects at its bird reserves (*gasi*) throughout Italy.

Lunaria: Rome; ☎ 06 884 1880; workcamps@lunaria.org, lunaria.org; international workcamps accept about 400 incoming volunteers.

Mani Tese: Milan; ☎ 02 407 5165; manitese.it; international campaigning organisation raises funds for projects in developing countries and hosts study camps for which a basic knowledge of Italian is needed.

Pithekos: Milan; ☎ 02 3091 2320; asspithekos@tiscali.it; pithekos.it; eco-volunteer organisation.

La Sabranenque: Centre International, rue de la Tour de l'Oume, 30290 Saint Victor la Coste, France; ☎ 04 66 50 05 05; sabranenque.com; French-based organisation uses voluntary labour to restore village and monuments in Altamura (inland from Bari in Southern Italy); the cost of participation is £180 for three weeks in July/August.

WWF Italia: Servizio Campi, Via Po 25/C, 00198 Rome; ☎ 06 844971; wwf.it; click on *Campi di Volontariato*.

A few environmental conservation camps are organised in cooperation with regional organisations like naturasicilia.it. Volunteers can also join archaeological camps. The national organisation Gruppi Archeologici d'Italia in Rome is the umbrella group for regional archaeological units that co-ordinate two-week digs (☎ 06 3937 6711; segreteriagruppiarcheologici.org; gruppiarcheologici.org). Paying volunteers may join these digs (e.g. €365). The Archeoclub d'Italia in Rome (☎ 06 4420 2250; archeoclubitalia.org) has website links to local branches around Italy that arrange archaeological digs, some of which accept paying volunteers.

MALTA

Since Malta joined the European Union in 2004, EU nationals have been entitled to work in Malta. Despite its small size and population and resulting fear of having its labour market swamped, Malta welcomes all EU nationals to enter freely and look for work. Australians and New Zealanders under the age of 25 (exceptionally 30) may apply for a working holiday visa to Malta valid for one year.

Although small in area (30km by 15km), Malta has much of interest for the traveller. Its economy is in good shape with a relatively healthy rate of unemployment of just less than 4% in 2008. The procedure for non-Europeans obtaining an employment licence is to obtain a signed form (Employment Engagement Form) from their prospective employer and submit it to the Maltese Employment & Training Corporation: etc.gov.mt.

TOURIST INDUSTRY

Tourism plays such a large part in the island's economy that it may be possible to get a job on the spot. Try cafés, bars, hotels and shops in Sliema, Bugibba and beach resorts in the south. Wages are far from high.

The Employment & Training Corporation (ETC) maintains an up-to-date online vacancy database. Vacancies range from skilled tradesmen to part-time waitresses. Many of these job openings overlap with the ones registered by EURES. Spring and summer see far more listings than winter.

TEACHING

Malta has undergone an English language teaching boom over the past decade and a number of private language schools cater to groups of language learners from around the Mediterranean, especially for holiday summer courses. English-speaking monitors and tour leaders may be needed by companies like Cultural English Tours in Iklin, central Malta (cost@cetleisure.com). The promised wage is €4–€5 an hour.

The interests of mainstream English language institutes are represented by FELTOM, the Federation of English Language Teaching Organisations Malta in Sliema (☎ +356 2744 5422) whose website feltom.com has good links to its 15 members schools including schools that recruit EU teachers like Inlingua in Sliema (inlinguamalta.com) and the Global Village in St. Paul's Bay (gvmalta.com).

The student and youth travel organisation NSTS in Valletta (☎ 2558 8000; nsts.org) markets English courses in conjunction with sports holidays for young tourists to Malta. NSTS runs weekly vacation courses from June to August, and it might be worth approaching them for a job, particularly if you are a water sports enthusiast. NSTS was keen to hire Robert Mizzi from Canada, especially when they learned he was half-Maltese:

> ***I was offered a job quite casually when NSTS found out I was volunteering conversational English in the main youth hostel in Valletta. Perhaps one reason they wanted to hire me was they knew the visa would not be a problem. However I was surprised by how relaxed the offer was. It was just mentioned in passing rather than at an actual interview. I guess it is the Maltese way; once you are one of them, then everything is gravy.***

SCANDINAVIA

The Scandinavian countries of Denmark, Sweden, Finland, Norway and Iceland exercise their own fascination, though working travellers must be prepared for the notoriously high cost of living and of travel in this region, especially Norway. Iceland's disastrous economy means that it is cheaper to visit than it once was, though the employment situation is dire.

Denmark, Sweden and Finland are full members of the European Union, whereas Norway and Iceland have decided to stay outside the Union. However they are part of the European Economic Area (EEA) which permits the free movement of goods, services and people from the EU. European citizens are entitled to enter any Scandinavian country for up to three months to look for work. When they find a job and get a 'Confirmation of Employment' from their employer, they can then apply to the police for a residence permit which, in the case of open-ended (i.e. permanent) jobs, will be for five years; otherwise it will be for the duration of the job. At least in principle, the only prohibition in the two non-EU countries is that foreign workers are not entitled to claim social security.

The accession of the ten new member countries into the European Union in 2004 has had a major impact on the job markets of Scandinavia. A large number of students and migrant workers from Poland and other countries have been attracted to the high wages and low unemployment that contrast so strongly with their home countries. For example the hourly rate in Norway for an unskilled job like cleaning, house renovations or in farm work is 115 Norwegian kroner, seven or eight times more than would be paid in Poland, though of course the relative costs of living must be taken into account.

Australian and New Zealand citizens aged 18–30 may obtain a working holiday visa valid for one year for Denmark, Sweden, Norway and Finland. In all the programmes, participants must undertake not to work for the whole 12-month validity of the visa and be able to show sufficient back-up funds, e.g. 18,000 Danish kroner for Australians going to Denmark.

No such reciprocal schemes exist for Americans, though Canadians can enter Denmark and Sweden on working holiday visas now. In order to work legally, people not eligible for working holiday visas have to obtain work permits before leaving home, which is well-nigh impossible. The American-Scandinavian Foundation in New York (☎ 212 879 9779; amscan.org) places about 30 American trainees aged 21–30 each summer in the fields of engineering, chemistry, computer science and business in Scandinavia, primarily Finland and Sweden. (It also has an English teaching programme in Finland – see below.) The ASF can also help 'self-placed trainees', i.e. those who have fixed up their own job or traineeship in a Scandinavian country, to obtain a work permit (amscan.org/self-placed.html).

A knowledge of a Scandinavian language is not essential in landing a job since English is so widely used throughout Scandinavia. One contributor humorously points to the few areas where English will not cut any ice (literally): 'among migratory Lapp shepherds, among polar Eskimo hunters in North Greenland and among Russian coal miners in Spitzbergen'.

One of the features that unifies these countries is that the cost of living and of travel is very high. One possibility for keeping costs down is to join WWOOF and work four hours a day in return for bed and board at organic farms (national contact details below). Susan and Eric Beney, a couple from Australia with two grown-up daughters, did this when they found themselves 'pretty broke' driving their camper van from Norway to France where they had been hired as chalet hosts for the winter season.

Busking, begging and street-selling are illegal in many places, however prosecutions are rare. As long as you are not causing a nuisance or blocking traffic you should be left alone by the authorities but will attract the attention of many passers-by for whom busking is a novelty. Scandinavians have the reputation of being both rich and generous.

AU PAIRING

The demand for English-speaking au pairs is not vast but remains steady, especially in Denmark, where a certain number of young women over 18 are placed with families for 10–12 months. Au Pairs International in Copenhagen (☎ +45 32 841002; aupairsinternational.dk) makes placements in Denmark, Norway and Sweden as well as worldwide. Some agencies take account of religious affiliation, and in Scandinavia there is a much higher proportion of requests for Protestant than Catholic au pairs (and almost none for atheists). Weekly wages vary a lot but many are around €100. Another possibility is the Scandinavian Au-Pair Center (scandinavian@aupair.se; aupair.se) whose website provides contact names, phone numbers and email addresses for its representatives in Helsingborg (Sweden), Oslo (Norway) and Roskilde (Denmark) among others.

DENMARK

Denmark has the highest average wage of any EU country and the second highest spending power. Most wages are at least 90–95 Danish kroner per hour. It also has a very low rate of unemployment (2.3% in 2009) though the rate is higher among people aged 16–24 in Copenhagen. Denmark is an undeniably rich country and there are many opportunities for casual work. Employers are obliged to pay legal workers an extra 12.5% holiday pay (*feriepenge*).

Work exists on farms and in factories, offices and hotels: the main problem is persuading an employer to take you on in preference to a Danish speaker. May Grant from Glasgow corroborated that the attitude in the job centres seemed to be 'Denmark for the Danes' and to find work it was necessary to explore other avenues.

Although initial impressions are that non-Danish speakers have little chance of finding work, some find that the reality is not so bad, provided you speak English. Partly because benefits are so generous in Denmark, many unemployed people are reluctant to move to find work, to take on unpleasant jobs or work at unsocial hours, which leaves some opportunities for the energetic foreigner.

Regulations

The rules on how to obtain a work or residence permit can be found on the Immigration Service's website at: nyidanmark.dk and in the Ministry of Employment manual on residence and work, which can be found at: bm.dk. EU nationals who intend to stay longer than three months should apply for a residence certificate from the regional state administration where you are based. Take the approved form (downloadable from nyidanmark.dk), two photos, passport and, if possible, a contract of employment or, alternatively, proof of means of support. The contract should show that you are employed for a minimum of ten hours a week and that your monthly wages before tax are at least kr4,583 if you are under 25 or kr5,527 if over. If your application is straightforward, you should be sent the permit within a week.

Non-EU nationals will find it much more difficult, though certain categories may be eligible (such as au pairs). As usual, work and residence permits must be applied for at a Danish consular representative in the applicant's home country. The office and service centre of the Immigration Service is at Ryesgade 53, 2100 Copenhagen Ø.

The minute you find employment, even if it is going to be very temporary, apply for a tax card in the municipality where you are working (or where your employer has his head office). You can find contact addresses at skat.dk (☎ 7222 1818). You will need a CPR (Civil Registration) number from the Folkeregisteret in order to apply. Give your tax card to your employer the day you get it. Without one, you will be taxed at a punitive 52% on all earnings. The tax card entitles you to a personal allowance of kr38,500 per year (and then a tax rate of 30%-35%). If you do end up overpaying, you won't have a chance of getting a rebate until six months after the calendar year in which you worked.

Because of the acute shortage of workers especially in seasonal harvests, the authorities have taken the unprecedented step of bestowing significant tax breaks on foreign workers. They are entitled to a tax deduction of kr650 per day (assuming accommodation is not provided by the employer) to cover expenses in their home country. In other words the exemption is calculated according to how much it would cost you in your home country per month so you may need to show documents to prove your home situation. In some locales, the worker will be given a *frikort* (tax card) which shows the exemption; in others the tax will be deducted at source and will have to be reclaimed after leaving Denmark. Tax can also be set against travel expenses as well; the 2009 rate is kr0.92 per kilometre travelled from home, including the ferry.

If successful, seasonal workers should end up paying only 8% plus 5% of earnings which is compulsory for all workers in this sector. The EURES website (seasonalwork.dk) explains the scheme in detail.

Copenhagen

Copenhagen, the commercial and industrial centre of the country, is by far the best place to look for work. It is also the centre of the tourist industry, so in summer it is worth looking for jobs door to door in hotels, restaurants and the Tivoli Amusement Park. The highest concentration of restaurants is located from Vesterbros Torv to Amalienborg Slot and from Torvet to Christiansborg Slot. Many of the large hotels have personnel offices at the rear of the hotel which should be visited frequently until a vacancy comes up. Also try the Old English Pub, the Scottish Pub and Rosie McGee's bar/nightclub (job@rosiemcgee.dk) at Vesterbrogade 2A.

Some job-seekers may have no trouble finding hotel work, as in the case of the Dutch traveller Mirjam Koppelaars:

> ***My Norwegian friend Elise and I rather liked Copenhagen but realised that money was going quick again and decided to try to find some work. After filling in an application form and having a very brief interview at the Sheraton, we both got offered jobs as chambermaids starting the next day.***

Jobcenters (*Arbejsformidling*) in Copenhagen should be able to assist EU nationals with a sought-after skill and a knowledge of Danish. They can do nothing for people who send their CVs. The casual work centre (*Løsarbejderformidling*) is at Tøndergade 14, Vesterbro (☎ 33 55 10 09), next door to the *Studenterformidlingen* (Student Job Centre) though a knowledge of Danish is a prerequisite.

Private employment agencies (*vikarbureauer*) will also expect clients to speak Danish. It may still be worth registering with a few of those listed in the *Yellow Pages* such as the multinational Adecco, which is the largest in Denmark.

Among the largest employers of casual staff in Denmark are newspaper distribution companies. More than 100,000 Danes subscribe to a daily or weekly newspaper and an army of 3,000 workers is needed to deliver them. This job is not done by school children as in Britain and North America because most of the deliveries are done at night. Typically, papers must be collected from a local depot at midnight and delivered by 7am. The job is much easier if you have invested in a second-hand bicycle or a wagon.

Bear in mind that the reason for the chronic shortage of workers is that the work is no doddle. Mr Stonemann describes what is involved:

> ***Few buildings in Denmark have private mail boxes at the entrance, so deliverers must go up to the fourth or fifth floor to put the paper through the right slots. Hence this is physically demanding work, especially in winter. Payment is according to quantity of work done. New workers take only one or two routes, whereas some veteran workers can do six or seven by themselves. After the first week of practice, a new worker can usually earn kr500 per night (before taxes). So in less than two nights he has financed his bicycle, especially if he chooses to work on Sundays and holidays. In winter the payment is 10% more. Payment is made every 14 days by bank transfer, so the worker needs to open a bank account before beginning a contract.***

To get a job as an *omdeler* or 'paper boy/girl', contact A/S Bladkompagniet's office in Rødovre (☎ 70 20 72 25; bladkompagniet@bladkompagniet.dk) or in Copenhagen (☎ 35 27 73 20). Otherwise check the *Yellow Pages* under the heading 'Aviser Distriktsblade' for other companies. Another big hiring company is the morning paper *Morgenavisen Jyllands-Posten.* They employ 4,000 people on weekdays and 5,000 on Sundays to deliver all their papers before 6.30am (8am on weekends). Ring 80 81 80 82 or email avisbud@jp.dk or cni@daoas.dk for details.

Agriculture

Farming plays an important part in the Danish economy and farm work is arguably the easiest door by which to enter the working life of Denmark. The main crops are strawberries (picked in June and July), cherries (picked in July and August), apples (picked in September and October), maize (month of August) and Christmas trees (October-December). The Danish fruit industry is flourishing and worker shortages are a problem, something that is being energetically addressed by EURES whose website (seasonalwork.dk as mentioned earlier) provides a wealth of information about harvest work and an online application. EURES estimates that in 2009 2,000 foreigners will be offered jobs in seasonal harvests and invites applicants to subscribe online.

The hours of strawberry picking are normally early in the morning until noon or 1pm leaving the afternoons free for cycling, swimming and socialising. Most employers expect you to bring your own tent and cooking equipment, and in most cases will make a daily charge from kr25 to cover the cost of electricity, water and rubbish collection. The island of Fyn has often been recommended for fruit-picking work, especially the area around Faaborg. But Samsø is where most pickers head in June. The website samsobaer.dk is a central resource for four Samsø strawberry farms which are included in the list that follow. All the farmers stress that they can accept only people with an EU passport and an EHIC (European Health Insurance Card).

Birkholm Frugt & Baer ApS: Hornelandeveg 2D, 5600 Faaborg; ☎ 62 60 22 62; fax 62 60 22 63; birkholm@strawberrypicking.dk; strawberrypicking.dk; season lasts from early June to nearly the end of July and applications are processed between 1st April and 15th May; piecework rates are calculated over the whole season, varying from kr5.25 per kilo if you pick less than 500kg during the season up to kr6.50 if you pick a superhuman 2,000kg or more, with an average falling between these two; minimum period of work is two weeks. Picking starts at 5am; campsite available for pickers at a cost of kr20 a day; minimum age 18.

Guldborgland Frugtplantage: Vigsnæsvej 36, Guldborg L., 4862 Guldborg; ☎ +45 54 77 05 14; mobile +45 22176301; guldborgland-frugt@post.tele.dk; contact Gillian and Lars Hansen; accommodation charge kr50 per day.

Holmgaard: Sildeballe 35, 8305 Samsø; ☎ 86 59 14 03; holmgaard@brdr-madsen.dk; 70–100 pickers needed by Inge and Aage Madsen.

Maries Minde: Permelille 26, 8305 Samsø; ☎ 86 59 08 72; mahlers@tdcspace.dk; mahlers.dk; 100 pickers needed; daily charge of kr25 for use of campsite facilities.

Morten Alexandersen: Storegade 34, Pillemark, 8305 Samsø; 86 59 22 64; morten@samsobaer.com; 80–100 pickers employed from early June for 6–8 weeks.

Starting dates and picking hours are unpredictable so do not count on making a quick fortune. Whereas you will get 40 or 50 hours of work one week (and can expect to pick between 5kg and 20kg of strawberries an hour), you might only get ten hours the next. Be sure to take wet weather gear since picking carries on through the rain. And even in July the 5am starts can be chilly. Other crops like apples, pears and cherries are paid either by the hour (which because of the high minimum wage is usually very worthwhile) or by piece work.

The long-established WWOOF Denmark (VHH) distributes a list of their approximately 30 members, most of whom speak English. In return for three or four hours of work per day, you get free food and lodging. Always phone, email or write before arriving. The paper list can be obtained only after sending €10/£5/US$10/kr50 to Inga Nielsen, Asenvej 35, 9881 Bindslev (98 93 86 07; info@wwoof.dk; wwoof.dk) or you can access it online by sending the same amount to VHH, Horsevadvej 200, 9830 Tårs. May Grant and her boyfriend Ian visited two VHH places, one very relaxed where they only had to weed the garden, the other more strenuous. Rob Abblett had a very positive experience working briefly for a friendly farmer who took him to Copenhagen to visit the Botanical Gardens and other sites.

If communal living appeals, you may want to visit the Svanholm Community which consists of about 120 people including lots of children. Numbers are swelled in the summer when a few extra volunteers arrive to help with the harvest of the organic produce. This possibility is open to all nationalities. Guests can stay for a month and work 30 hours a week for food and lodging but no pocket money. If interested, write to the Visitors Group, Svanholm Gods, 4050 Skibby (svanholm.dk).

As usual it is best to find out as much as you can about what you're letting yourself in for.

DAVID ANDERSON MADE PRIVATE ARRANGEMENTS TO WORK ON AN ORGANIC FARM ON MORS IN THE NORTH OF JUTLAND. HE REGRETTED HIS HASTE IN DECIDING TO TAKE THE JOB:

I arrived at the doorstep with the equivalent of £10. The owner was a strict vegetarian (all home-grown) and expected me to be the same. And there was no hot water. I was the only staff to pick the fruit and vegetables plus I had to help him build a greenhouse in the shape of a pyramid since he was convinced pyramids have some special power. When I received my pay for the first three weeks, I left and headed straight for the McDonald's in Esbjerg.

Volunteering

If you are already in Denmark, Mellemfolkeligt Samvirke in Copenhagen (globalcontact@ms.dk; ms.dk) organise about a dozen summer workcamps in Denmark which last two or three weeks. The main objective of these camps, which carry out projects such as building playgrounds, conservation work, etc., is to bring participants into contact with the social problems found in every society. MS also co-ordinate three month-long summer workcamps in Greenland (minimum age 20). The anticipated fee for Greenland is approximately €2,000 including airfares. Past tasks in Greenland include the renovation of a Viking village.

Survival

Contributors have suggested various ways to survive, including bottle-collecting from bins early in the morning or from annual festivals like the Roskilde Festival. The pickings are rich along certain Copenhagen streets especially on Sunday morning when only a few supermarkets are open to accept returns; try for example the Aldi on Rantzausgade.

Denmark is one of the most prolific sources of sperm for infertile couples in the world. Cryos is a franchised network of sperm banks with four centres in Aarhus, Copenhagen, Aalborg and Odense, as well as New York and India (cryosinternational.com). The company recruits both anonymous and non-anonymous donors from all races and ethnicities. No minimum commitment period is necessary but they ask donors to deliver at least ten ejaculates. Be warned that nine out of ten men's sperm is rejected. Payment is usually about kr280 (€38) but varies according to quality and volume.

Buskers head for the pedestrian streets of Central Copenhagen like Købmagergade and Strøget where, on a busy summer's day, it is not unusual for a talented musician, juggler or acrobat to earn 200kr in an hour. Buskers must not use amplifiers and must not perform in groups of more than three. Hours are restricted in some places, though Radhuspladsen and Kogens Nytorv by Krinsen are open to buskers between 7am and 10pm. Whereas most musicians need not apply for a licence, street performers like magicians and jugglers do.

FINLAND

Finland offers far fewer short-term paid training opportunities to foreign students and recent graduates than formerly. The International Trainee Exchange programme in Finland is administered by CIMO, the Centre for International Mobility, though application must be made through a partner organisation in the student/graduate's own country. British students and graduates who want an on-the-job training placement lasting between one and 18 months in the fields of agriculture or in technical subjects should apply to IAESTE for technical placements.

Short-term training takes place between May and September, while long-term training is available year round. Applications for summer positions must be in to CIMO by the middle of February. To qualify for the trainee exchange, you must have studied for at least one year, preferably with a year's experience as well, in a related subject. Despite the designation 'trainee', wages are on a par with local Finnish wages for the same work. Among CIMO's programmes is a language teaching programme for a month, a term or preferably an academic year, open to native speakers who are university students or recent graduates in arts or education. CIMO has opened an Information Center on the 5th floor, Hakaniemenranta 6, in Helsinki (☎ +358 206 90 501; cimoinfo@cimo.fi; studyinfinland.fi, which is in English). The office is open Tuesday to Thursday afternoons only.

Applicants in the US should contact the American-Scandinavian Foundation mentioned above. If an individual does succeed in fixing up a traineeship, work and residence permits are granted for the specific training period offered by a named Finnish employer. Immigration queries can probably be answered by looking at the English language website of the Finnish Immigration Service, PO Box 18, 00581 Helsinki or in person at Lautatarhankatu 10 in Helsinki (☎ 071 873 0431; migri.fi).

Teaching

One of the programmes that has been offered by the American-Scandinavian Foundation (58 Park Avenue, New York, NY 10016; ☎ 212 879 9779; training@amscan.org; amscan.org/tefl.html) is an English teaching programme in Finland. American students and recent graduates over 21 teach in a variety of companies and educational establishments from kindergartens to colleges, for an academic year. However at the time of writing, no paid teaching placements were anticipated for September 2009, possibly another victim of the world economic crisis.

Anyone with experience of the business world might persuade Richard Lewis Communications with offices in Helsinki, Turku, Tampere and Oulu (info.finland@rcglobal.com; crossculture.com) to hire them to teach English to corporate clients. RLC has its headquarters near Southampton in the UK (☎ 01962 771111).

For a quite different clientele wanting to learn English, a Russian language school (☎ +7 812 303 86 96; nordicschool.ru/eng) hires native speakers of any nationality to teach conversational English to Russian teenagers at short summer and winter language camps in northern Finland. In addition to board and lodging, a payment of €300–€400 is paid per camp.

Casual Work

Finland's rate of unemployment is 7% which is considerably higher than that of its neighbouring Nordic countries, so job opportunities are never going to be abundant. However certain areas of employment do experience occasional labour shortages, such as the flower nurseries around Helsinki, language tutoring and in hotels, especially in resorts like Hämeenlinna and Lahti. Jobs with UK tour operators are rare but possible: Esprit Santa's Lapland have positions for tour reps, chalet hosts and child care staff for their Finnish Lapland programme which operates for the month of December (Esprit Holidays; ☎ 01252 618318; recruitment@esprit-holidays.co.uk; workaseason.com). Hotels in the Lapland ski resort of Sirkka-Levi sometimes look for hospitality trainees for the winter season. The Lapland Hotel group (laplandhotels.com) has nine hotel-restaurants. The hourly wage for shift work is €7–€10 with deductions of between €150 and €500 per month for rent and €4.13 per day for meals.

Some time ago, Natasha Fox fixed up her own work with private families:

> ***I found work as a nanny in Finland simply by placing advertisement cards in a few playgroups. The best area to place them if you are in Helsinki, is Westend Espoo, the most affluent area of the capital. My job paid £110 a week for working Monday to Friday 8am-4pm.***
>
> ***If you have Finnish friends, ask them to translate newspaper advertisements for you. Helsingin Sanomat, Finland's daily newspaper, has several vacancies for domestic positions each day. It's certainly worth ringing up and asking if they would like an English speaker for the children's benefit. (Since so many Finnish parents want their children to learn English, this often works.) If you advertise yourself, try to write in Finnish; it shows you aren't an arrogant foreigner. You probably won't have to speak a word of it in the job.***
>
> ***Here is the advert I put up:***
> ***Haluaisitko vaihtaa vapaale', lasten hoidon lomassa? Iloinen, vastuullinen Englandtilais-tytto antaa sinulle mahdollisuuden! Olen vapaa useimpina päivinä/iltoina.***
>
> ***This translates as, 'How would you like a break from the kids? Responsible cheerful English girl will give you the chance! I am free most days and evenings.'***

On a more frivolous note, busking might be one way of stretching your travel fund, especially outside Helsinki. According to a correspondent in Finland, buskers (especially Russian accordionists) are a familiar sight; average hourly earnings are €8–€15. As in Denmark, collecting empty bottles, both alcoholic and non-alcoholic, can be profitable.

Volunteering

The co-ordinating workcamp organisation in Helsinki is called KVT, the Finnish branch of Service Civil International (kvtfinland.org). They organise about 15 summer camps each year undertaking lots of interesting projects. The workcamp joining fee is €85 in addition to the €17 KVT membrship fee.

The Finnish Youth Cooperation organisation, Allianssi (☎ +358 20 755 2614; kv@alli.fi), co-operates with the members of the Alliance of European Voluntary Service Organisations placing volunteers sent by their counterparts in other countries in workcamps in Finland (though the majority of their work involves sending Finnish young people abroad).

ICELAND

With a tiny population of not much more than 300,000, any job losses translate into large percentage falls. Iceland's rate of unemployment increased nearly fivefold over 2008, as the banks collapsed and the country's economy crumbled. This situation does not make Iceland a good bet for the job-seeker for the next year or so.

Demand for labour is traditionally within the fish, farming, tourism and construction industries and often during the summer season only. The international demand for fish will persist, though it is not known how many vacancies will be open to those who do not speak Icelandic. Some lucky individuals may find unskilled jobs in agriculture and hotels.

There are eight regional Employment Offices in Iceland and the EURES Advisers can be conulsted at the main office at Borgartún 7, 105 Reykjavik (☎ +354 554 7600; eures@vmst.is; eures.is/english). The Icelandic EURES website includes a job application form in English. Efforts are also concentrated on recruiting workers from other Scandinavian countries primarily through the Nordjobb scheme which arranges summer jobs for Nordic citizens aged 18–28 in other Nordic countries for at least four weeks (nordjobb.net).

The private employment agency Ninukot (PO Box 12015, 132-Reykjavik or Skeggjastadir 861, Hvolsvöllur, ☎ +354 561 2700; ninukot@ninukot.is; ninukot.is) originally specialised in agricultural and horticultural jobs throughout Iceland but has branched out to offer jobs in babysitting, fisheries, gardening, horse training and tourism as well. Their welcoming website is in English and holds out the prospect of an easy-to-arrange working holiday in Iceland for EEA nationals.

Qualifying Europeans may stay up to six months before they need a residence permit. The number of such permits applied for increased hugely after Poland and other new accession countries were admitted to the Union, but the influx has diminished. Processing of permit applications takes about two months and proof of payment of the kr4,000 fee must accompany the application. Information in English is available from the Icelandic Directorate of Immigration (Utlendingastofnun ☎ 510 5400; utl.is). If you are planning to take advantage of the freedom of all EEA nationals to go to Iceland to look for work, take plenty of money to cover the notoriously high cost of living. If touring, accommodation costs can be very high unless you are hardy enough to camp (and it is often cold). An alternative is *svefnpokaplass* which means 'sleeping bag accommodation' whereby you pay £10–£15 for a mattress in a school, farm, etc. Another way of solving the problem is to arrange to live with a family in exchange for minimal duties (housekeeping, English conversation, etc.).

Au Pairing

The Ninukot Employment Agency has vacancies for live-in childcarers who are paid about 10,000 kronur a week pocket money plus room and board. After completing six months, the family pays for one way airfare to Iceland and return fare after 12 months.

The Fishing Industry

The fishing industry is fairly labour intensive, directly employing 8% of the working population (down from 14% a decade or so ago) and many more indirectly. Fish products account for nearly half of the country's exports. It is a seasonal industry and the busiest season coincides with the long dark winter. The demarcation of jobs seems to be strictly adhered to according to sex: men go to sea or do the heavy lifting and loading in the factories and women do the processing. Work on fishing trawlers was available to some travellers a generation ago but not any more.

Fish processing in Iceland was once upon a time one of those classic travellers' jobs where you could earn a lot in a relatively short time in an interesting part of the world. But the work is much less popular and not as well paid as it once was. Yet there is enough demand from employers in the fish processing industry and from foreign job-seekers to justify the involvement of the Ninukot Agency mentioned above. Provided you are prepared to stay for at least five months from January in an Icelandic town or village, the agency will try to find a job in a fish factory. The minimum pay promised is 153,000 kronur a month gross with the possibility of earning overtime wages. The employer always provides reasonably priced accommodation.

The factories are always located by the seaport. Work is pressurised because the fish must be processed quickly to maintain freshness. Shifts of 12 or 14 hours with few breaks are the rule. The peak season is February and April/May and again in September/October.

Tasks to be done in a fish-processing plant include sorting, cleaning, filleting, weighing, deworming and packaging. The worst job is in the *Klevi* or freezer where the temperature is around –43°C (–45°F). The work of packing and shifting boxes of fish would not be too bad were it not for the intense cold. Without proper gear including fur-lined boots and gloves, a balaclava and layers of sheepskin, this work is unendurable. In the rest of the factory the temperature is 10°C–16°C (50°F–62°F).

It takes weeks of practice before you can fillet and pack fish expertly. Standards are usually very high and if the supervisor finds more than two bones or worms, the whole case will be returned to you to be checked again. Since pay is normally according to performance, your earnings will increase as your technique improves, but the wages will not be wonderful in view of the high cost of living. Debbie Mathieson described her work at a small factory in Hnfisdal as '*not really difficult, but mind-blowingly boring*'.Conventional social life is almost non-existent in the fishing villages of northern Iceland, though many are so prosperous that they offer facilities that would be unheard of in a village of similar size elsewhere. The five dark months of winter, when villages are cut off from their neighbours, can be depressing. Vicki Matchett signed a six-month contract with a factory in the village of Vopnafjörd in north-east Iceland and describes the life: *'Fishing villages usually have about 800 inhabitants with almost no social life, no pubs, not even any wildlife, and the weather between December and May made sightseeing risky. For the sake of saving £1,000 I'm not sure it's worth vegetating for six months. I must admit I spent most of my spare time reading travel journals to remind myself that civilisation still existed.'*

Other

Agriculture is a major enterprise in Iceland. Hay-making is an important summer job; much of the grass is cut by scythe as tractors cannot work the steep slopes, particularly in the narrow valleys where many of the farms are located. However this work is mainly done by school children.

Ninukot specialises in finding agricultural and horticultural jobs throughout Iceland. Many jobs are in picking and packing plants or greenhouses in the south and west of the country, but can also be with riding stables, on holiday farms between May and September or planting trees. The pay starts at €1,015 a month with a deduction of €12 a day for board and lodging, and terms for flight reimbursement are the same as for au pairs mentioned earlier.

It is also possible to fix up this kind of summer job independently or through EURES, especially if you know more than one European language. Janet Bridgeport was staying as a tourist at a guesthouse in Hvolsvöllur which happened to be next door to a horse trekking centre: *'Because I'd worked with horses and wasn't in any rush to get home, I knocked on the door of the trekking centre and asked if they needed any casual help for the summer. I was really amazed when they said they'd take me on (for board and lodging only). A lot of the riding guests spoke English so I suppose that weighed in my favour.'*

The Icelandic Environment Agency in partnership with BTCV (British Trust for Conservation Volunteers) runs a summer programme of projects (not for the faint-hearted!) at eight locations throughout Iceland lasting from between one and 16 days, which are open to everyone. Transport from Reykjavik is usually provided, as is the food and accommodation in huts or (weather permitting) tents. Recent projects have been mainly involved with building paths and steps in national parks such as Jökulsárgljúfur National Park. You can fix up a conservation holiday in Iceland through btcv.org or call BTCV Customer Services 01302 388883. The cost for a fortnight is £390 excluding flights.

A voluntary organisation called Worldwide Friends (WF; veraldarvinir in Icelandic) offers an interesting range of two-week projects (workcamps) which international volunteers can join. Many are concerned with the environment but in others volunteers help prepare for and work during summer festivals in several towns including Heimaey on one of the remote Vestmannaeyjar Islands. WF can be contacted at Einarsnes 56, 101 Reykjavík (☎ +354 55 25 214; wf@wf.is; wf.is). The participation fee is €90, €120 or €150 depending on the project and the duration.

NORWAY

Norway has been more resistant than most countries to embracing Europe and sometimes this attitude is apparent when foreigners look for jobs in Norway. Robert Abblett is not convinced that equality of opportunities is being taken seriously enough in employment offices in Norway:

> ***Before I flew out to Norway, I thought I would test the water a bit by phoning the Oslo Jobcentre and a private employment agency. I think I was a bit naïve, really. When I phoned Oslo I was passed on to three different people each of whom flatly refused to give me any information because I could not speak Norwegian. The same happened when I phoned Manpower in Bergen. In perfect English we argued over the point that this was a racist barrier against foreign workers from Europe from claiming their legal right to work in Norway.***

The EURES department of the Norwegian Labour & Welfare Administration (nav.no) may be more willing to assist job-seekers in person; contact the EuresAdviser, Postboks 354, 8601 Mo i Rana. The NAV Servicecenter operates a telephone information line (toll free within Norway) providing information on vacancies throughout the country; ring +47 800 33 166.

No matter how long the duration of your employment, you will need to apply for a tax card from the local tax office (*Likningskontor*) before starting work; otherwise half of your wages will be withheld for tax. EU nationals intending to stay longer than three months must apply for a residence permit; see udi.no for general immigration information. The fee is NOK1,100.

To make contact with private temp agencies, look up *Vikartjenester* in the *Yellow Pages* (gulesider.no) or look for the usual suspects like Manpower, Adecco and Kelly Services. Also check ads in the main daily paper *Aftenposten* or try placing one yourself. (As in Denmark, the delivery departments of the main newspapers employ lots of people; check the website for *Aftenposten*'s delivery or 'Avisbud' department, http://avisbud.aftenposten.no which gives the phone numbers to which you should apply for different parts of Oslo and beyond.)

As throughout Scandinavia, wages are high, though the high cost of living makes it difficult to save. Travellers have commented on how friendly and generous Norwegian people are. Because buskers are a relative novelty, earnings can be remarkably high. Mary Hall plucked up the courage to do some busking in Bergen on her newly acquired penny whistle. Although she knew only two songs, she made £15 in 15 minutes, mostly due to the fact that her audience was drunk.

Oslo also has a Use It office (Ungdomsinformasjonen) which is a young person's travel information service which might be able to advise on longer term accommodation and job options. Use It is located at Møllergata 3, 0179 Oslo (☎ 24 14 98 20; use-it@unginfo.no) and is open year round from 11am to 5pm with longer opening hours during the summer. Their free online and print guide to Norway called 'Streetwise' is updated every year (http://use-it.unginfo.oslo.no/sider) and appears in English with lots of concrete tips for making the most of your stay in Oslo.

A cleaning agency with offices in Oslo, Stavanger, Bergen, Trondheim and Akershus called City Maid recruits cleaners; see their website which is partially in English (☎ 40 00 63 30; citymaid.no).

Tourism

A reasonable number of English-speaking tourists visit Norway each summer, so there are bound to be openings for English-speaking staff. You can also try winter resorts like Geilo, Hemsedal, Lillehammer, Nordseter, Susjoen, Gausdal and Voss. For either season, you can try to get something fixed up ahead of time by emailing or writing to hotels listed on websites such as hotelsinnorway.com. There is a greater density of hotels in the south of Norway including beach resorts along the south coast around Kristiansand, and inland from the fjords north of Bergen (Geilo, Gol, Vaga, Lillehammer, and in the Hardanger region generally). Remember that even in the height of summer, the mountainous areas can be very chilly.

Wages and deductions for board and lodging for the hotel industry are revised annually. The starting net monthly wage of an unskilled hotel worker is about NOK12,000, NOK21,000 gross less tax and deductions for board and lodging, etc. The ski holiday market is much smaller in Norway than in the Alps and not many British tour operators hire staff for holidays in Norway. Lillehammer is probably the best bet. Travellers have shown resourcefulness in extending their time in ski resorts (primarily to ski), by doing odd jobs like snow clearing and car-cleaning, waitressing, DJing (since the British are thought to know their way around the music scene), au pairing and English teaching.

Norwegian Working Guest Programme

Atlantis Youth Exchange in Oslo (☎ 22 47 71 70; atlantis@atlantis.no; atlantis.no) runs the 'Working Guest Programme' which allows people aged between 18 and 30 of any nationality to spend two to six months in rural Norway (Americans and other non-Europeans may stay for no more than three months). The only requirement is that they speak English. In addition to the farming programme open to all volunteers, placements in family-run tourist accommodation are available to European nationals.

Farm guests receive full board and lodging plus pocket money of at least NOK890 a week (nearly £100) for a maximum of 35 hours of work. The idea is that you participate in the daily life, both work and leisure, of the family: haymaking, weeding, milking, animal-tending, berry-picking, painting, house-cleaning, babysitting, etc. A wardrobe of old rugged clothes and wellington boots is recommended.

Application should be made through partner organisations where available; all are listed on the Atlantis website. British participants can apply through Twin Work & Volunteer Abroad in London SE13 (☎ 0800 80 483 80; workandvolunteer.com) whereas North Americans will have to apply directly. After receiving the official application form you must send off a reference, two smiling photos, a medical certificate confirming that you are in good health and a substantial registration fee which varies according to country of origin and mediating agency (and which therefore does not appear on the Atlantis website). Twin's set of charges ranges from £550 for two months to £850 for six months.

ROBERT OLSEN ENJOYED HIS STAY SO MUCH THAT HE WENT BACK TO THE SAME FAMILY ANOTHER SUMMER:

The work consisted of picking fruit and weeds (the fruit tasted better). The working day started at 8am and continued till 4pm, when we stopped for the main meal of the day. After that we were free to swim in the sea, borrow a bike to go into town or whatever. I was made to feel very much at home in somebody else's home. The farmer and his daughter were members of a folk dance music band, which was great to listen to. Now and then they entrusted me to look after the house while they went off to play at festivals. Such holidays as these are perhaps the most economical and most memorable possible.

Outdoor Work

One of the best areas to head for is the strawberry growing area around Lier, accessible by bus from Drammen. Wages are notoriously bad in this area, and as a result the majority of harvesters are foreign. Kristin Moen and her Italian friend Maurizio were given jobs at the first farm phoned, but earned a pittance. The strawberry season here reaches its peak in early July.

The steep hillsides on either side of the many fjords support abundant wild blueberries. It is possible to freelance as a berry picker and then sell the fruit to the local produce and jam co-operatives. In Lapland it is not permitted to pick certain berries in certain seasons, since only native Lapps have the right, so make local enquiries first. Autumn brings wild mushrooms – Norway has about 2,500 varieties. In some of the larger towns, there are weekend mushroom controls where you can have what you have picked checked.

The major industry in the far north of Norway is fishing. Not enough locals are prepared to work in the fish processing plants, as Rob Abblett had confirmed when he rang a fish factory in Vardø:

> ***I spoke to a manager who had picked up an American accent somewhere and he told me almost everyone at the factory was Finnish because the local people don't want to do the work. Speaking Norwegian was not a pre-requisite here (hurray) but he did say that he would only consider long-term applicants, minimum one year, as it takes up to six months to train someone in the finer arts of fish processing, which sounded a little incredible to me.***

Apparently lots of money can be made by engineers in Norway, or others experienced in the oil or fisheries industries.

Au Pairs

The situation is promising for au pairs of all nationalities (provided they speak some English), though the red tape is still considerable for non-Europeans and the majority of au pairs are from the EU. Atlantis runs a programme for 200 incoming au pairs who must be aged 18–30 and willing to stay at least six months but preferably 8–12 months. The programme has become so popular that applications are accepted only through partner agencies, and at the moment there is none in the UK. Interested Britons should seek advice from Atlantis since it may be possible to apply through an agency in another country such as YES Au Pair in the Netherlands (yesaupair.com).

Information about the programme is readily available on their website atlantis.no. Atlantis charges a sizeable registration fee, a quarter of which is non-refundable if the placement doesn't go ahead. Au pairs from an EEA country can obtain the residence permit after arrival; others must go through a complicated procedure in their home country. The pocket money in Norway is NOK4,000 per month which sounds generous until you realise that wages plus the value of room and board will be taxed at 25%–35% depending on the region. Atlantis can advise on possibilities for minimising tax by obtaining a *frikort*, which entitles you to a personal allowance of NOK4,000 (2008).

SWEDEN

EU/EEA nationals may enter Sweden to look for work as in any other member state. Until 2007, non-Europeans could obtain permits to do seasonal work but that scheme has been suspended, due to the availability of legal migrant labour from the EU accession countries. All information on the regulations and fees are set out in the admirably clear English-language website of the Swedish Migration Board: Migrationsverket (migrationsverket.se/english.jsp). Immigration queries should be addressed to one of the immigration offices in Swedish cities or by phone to 0771 19 44 00 (upplysningen@migrationsverket.se; migrationsverket). It is possible to apply for work and au pair permits electronically.

The addresses of employment offices (*Länsarbetsnämndeni*) around Sweden can be found on the website of the Swedish Employment Service (arbetsformedlingen.se). Once you find work, you must register at the local taxation office (*Skattemyndigheten*) within three days and get a *personnummer*.

Casual Work

State handouts are so generous in Sweden that many natives are unwilling to undertake jobs like dishwashing and fruit picking for a few kroner an hour. Even without the benefit of having the right stamp in your passport, there are possibilities, as the American Woden Teachout discovered:

> *In southern Sweden I did the cleaning lady's tour of Swedish mansions. I found the first job through a couple who picked me up hitch-hiking and who contacted a friend of theirs. There are a great number of large country houses in Skane, and all the families I worked for were the acme of respectability, so a neat appearance is probably very important. So I had several weeks of sweeping out from behind stoves, washing windows, and generally helping with the spring clean. Housework has never been my great speciality, but the living was easy since the relics of Swedish gentry are both rich and hospitable. I had my own room, four-course meals under the evening sun and they took me merrily along to celebrate midsummer, or on outings to the beach or theatre.*

A rather more elevated casual job has been found by well-educated foreigners as proof-readers and polishers. So many documents in Sweden are translated into English that it is worthwhile phoning publishing companies for freelance work which should pay £20+ an hour.

New Zealander, Richard Ferguson, arrived in Stockholm just after the new year in 2009 with a one-year working holiday visa (Australians are also eligible for this visa). His plan was to find work in a bar, café or restaurant as he had in Portugal and Greece the year before. Not surprisingly, he found January was not the ideal month to job-hunt, especially given the worldwide economic slump. Despite his nationality, he trawled all the Irish pubs to submit his CV, and soon was given a job at Galways in the city centre at Kungsgatan 24 (galwaysirishpub.se):

> *Anyone who speaks English has about a 95% chance of getting a job there. The reason I (and no one else) is stoked with the job is that it's run by Turkish families. Most importantly you do get paid, no question. I get 96 kroner an hour and maybe 10–15 kroner an hour tip-wise. Also I get paid extra after 8pm and more still after midnight. In the winter it's hard to work 40 hours there but it's enough to pay rent and basic costs. From what I hear it's easier to get a job in the summer. Apparently in Gamla Stan (the old town and main tourist area), the bars and restaurants are more relaxed about visas and language, often employing anyone to serve drinks and clear tables. I imagine they don't get paid much but again, if you need to start somewhere... It's very difficult (some say impossible) to find accommodation, but somehow I found an apartment in three days; thelocal.se is a good site to search for apartments. Just email every single ad and you will get something.*

A friend of Richard's, also a New Zealander, who has been living on and off in Stockholm for several years, works in construction which can be tough in the cold dark months of winter and requires some experience. For this he is rewarded 120 kroner an hour. The government has a scheme by which employers are subsidised a considerable percentage of a worker's salary, provided the employee enrolls in a free Swedish language course. However these are so intensive that it would be impossible to combine a course with a full-time job.

It may be worth trying to find work in hotels, usually in the kitchen. Your best bets are hotels in remote areas where if you are touring before the season begins you may find jobs going. Alternatively try popular tourist areas in summer like the Sunshine Coast of western Sweden including the seaside resorts between Malmö and Göteborg, especially Helsingborg, Varberg and Falkenberg. Other popular holiday centres with a large number of hotels include Orebro, Västeras, Are, Ostersund, Jönköping and Linköping. The chances of fixing up a hotel job in advance are remote. After writing to dozens of Scandinavian hotels, Dennis Bricault's conclusion was 'Forget Sweden!'

For outdoor work, try the southern counties, especially Skane, where a wide variety of crop is grown, especially strawberries. Peas, cucumbers, spinach and many other vegetables are grown under contract to canneries and if you can't find work in the fields, you might find it in the processing plants. In the eastern part of Skane there is specialised fruit growing: apples, pears, plums, cherries, strawberries and raspberries.

Au Pairs

Au pairs are subject to the same regulations as all other foreign employees so non-EU nationals must obtain a work permit before leaving their home country. As mentioned it is possible to apply online or by post, provided you have the necessary documents including a job offer from a family (showing hours and pay) and a certificate of intended studies in Swedish. The Swedish Migration Board stipulates that au pairs must work no more than 25 hours a week, must be serious about studying Swedish and must earn at least SEK3,500 a month before tax.

An agency that sends many Swedish au pairs abroad will try to place British and other girls as au pairs in Sweden: Au-Pair World Agency Sweden in Uddevalla (☎ 522 140 00; aupairsweden.com).

Teaching

Casual work teaching English is rarely available in Sweden. For many years the EFL market has been in a slow but inexorable decline, as standards of English among school leavers have improved. The Folkuniversity of Sweden has a long-established scheme (since 1955) by which British and other native English speakers may be placed for one academic year in a network of adult education centres throughout the country, but they no longer have a policy of actively recruiting applicants from abroad. They take on new staff who are already resident in Sweden and even then, the work is part-time, at least initially (Box 2116, S-22002 Lund; ☎ 46 19 77 00; fax 46 19 77 80; peter.baston@folkuniversitetet.se; folkuniversitetet.se).

Voluntary Opportunities

WWOOF is represented in Sweden (wwoof.se). In order to obtain the list of 50 WWOOF farms you must pay the membership fee of €15 online. Susan and Eric Beney enjoyed rural Sweden a few summers ago:

> ***When we were looking for work in Sweden the number we rang no longer took Wwoofers but they put us on to someone who did. Lotte and Matthias had a smallholding with a lovely old farmhouse not far from Orebro. Their greenhouse had collapsed after a huge snowfall so our job was to dismantle it so they could erect a new one. They were very friendly, fed us very well and sent us on our way with fresh meat and vegetables. During our time off we would explore the local area – beautiful forest walks were close by.***

Stiftelsen Stjärnsund (Bruksallén 16, 77071 Stjärnsund; ☎ 225 80001; info@frid.nu; frid.nu) is located amongst the forests, lakes and hills of central Sweden. Founded in 1984, the community aims to encourage personal, social and spiritual development in an ecologically sustainable environment. It operates an international 'Participating Guest' programme lasting one week to three months starting throughout the year, but is at its busiest between May and September when most of the community's courses are offered. Carpenters, builders, trained gardeners and cooks are especially welcome. First-time working guests pay SEK500 for their first week of work (four hours a day for five days) and, if the arrangement suits both sides, it can be continued with a negotiable contribution according to hours worked and length of stay. Enquiries should be made well in advance of a proposed summer visit.

Another possibility for lovers of the outdoors is the Falsterbo Bird Observatory on the south-western tip of Sweden, where they need people who are familiar with bird ringing to work during the autumn migration (August–November). Volunteers who stay for several weeks are given an allowance of SEK150 a day, free accommodation and travel expenses within Sweden; details from the FOB, Fyren, SE-23940 Falsterbo (☎ +46 40 470688; skof.se/fbo).

Survival

Collecting discarded bottles and cans can be a fairly profitable way to earn some money anywhere in the country. The carnivals and music festivals that take place in July and August are recommended as prime targets for bottle-collecting. British and American souvenirs are trendy, so you can make up to 500% profit by selling such things at local weekend markets. Medals, caps, books, etc. are worth stocking up on at home for possible sale in Sweden.

SPAIN

Spain's economy is in almost as big a mess as Britain's, and the building industry in particular has been paralysed by the recession. The climbing rate of unemployment hit a massive 15% and it is predicted that one in five of the workforce will be jobless before long. Yet, the demand for foreign labour, particularly in English language teaching and tourism, has not completely evaporated, and Spain's tourist industry continues to absorb foreign young people in temporary and part-time jobs.

REGULATIONS

All EU citizens planning to live in Spain for more than three months are obliged to register in person at the Foreigners' Office (*Oficina de Extranjeros*) in the province of residence or at a designated police station. You will be issued with a Residence Certificate stating your name, address, nationality, identity number and date of registration. The number on your resident card is your NIE (*Número de Identidad de Extranjeros*), an identification number necessary for filing taxes, opening a bank account, and for almost any other form. Once you start work, your employer should apply for a social security number on your behalf; if you are self-employed, this is your responsibility.

Many long-stay foreigners engage a specialist lawyer called a *Gestoria Administrava* to assist negotiating the bureaucracy. The websites of the British Embassy in Spain (http://ukinspain.fco.gov.uk) and Spain Expat (spainexpat.com) are full of useful information about living and working in Spain.

The immigration situation for people from outside Europe is very difficult. Most employers refuse to tackle the lengthy procedures involved in obtaining work permits which involve submitting an official job offer form, original official company fiscal identity document, certification that the job on offer has already been advertised in the official Provincial Unemployment Office, and so on. Once your home country's Spanish Consulate has processed your work visa, you have to fetch it in person.

One way for North Americans to get round the draconian immigration laws is to join an organised cultural exchange. For example InterExchange in New York (workingabroad.org) and AIDE (aideabroad.org) arrange Teach in Spain programmes whereby fee-paying young Americans (mainly women) live with a family in exchange for speaking English and providing 15 hours of tutoring a week. The Californian company Adelante LLC (☎ 562 799 9133; adelantespain.com) places interns who are learning Spanish in Barcelona, Madrid, Seville, Jerez de Frontera and Marbella.

Americans, Canadians, Australians, etc. sometimes find paid work as monitors in children's camps, tutors at language schools and in private households, touts for bars and discos, etc. When their 90-day Schengen visa is about to expire, they are obliged to leave the Schengen area (most of Europe) for 90 days before returning.

Strict rules make it almost impossible for people from outside Western Europe to pick up casual work legally. With high rates of unemployment, resentment is strong against the huge number of immigrant workers who have arrived since 2005 from Ecuador and Bolivia and this has resulted in a clampdown on the issuing of all visas, including tourist visas.Online recruitment agencies might be of some use to those looking for permanent jobs, such as the Malaga-based jobfinderspain.com which deals with vacancies along the south coast and Gibraltar. A commercial agency called Exit Experience in Marbella charges a programme fee of €420 in return for which it arranges paid work experience jobs in the retail or customer service sector (restaurants, kitchens, etc.) in Marbella and Puerto Banús (☎ 952 779223; exitgate2.com). The agency arranges interviews before arrival and helps with the red tape of settling in. Participants must be EU passport-holders and under 26; university students up to the age of 35 are accepted.

TEEMING TOURISM

Spain hosts a staggering 57 million visitors a year, including 15.7 million Britons. Despite strong competition from Turkey and the unfavourable exchange rate of the euro against sterling, Spain's resorts and cities continue to draw hordes of tourists. The proverbial British tourist to the Spanish Costas is not looking for undiscovered villages but wants to have the familiar comforts of home along with the Mediterranean sunshine.

You almost always have to be on hand to secure a job, so people should take a cheap flight to the area that interests them in April and ask door to door. The going rate for a bar job is €6 per hour without accommodation. It is always worth checking the English language press for the sits vac columns which sometimes carry adverts for cleaners, live-in babysitters, chefs, bar staff, etc. Look for the giveaway weekly *Ibiza Sun* (theibizasun.com), the *Lanzarote Gazette* (gazettelive.com), the *Costa Blanca News* and *SUR in English* (surinenglish.com) which has an employment section and is used by foreign and local residents throughout southern Spain including Gibraltar. It is published free on Fridays.

Spainexpat.com mentioned above carries an annotated list of job sites at spainexpat.com/spain/information/jobs_in_spain. Among these are Loquo.com, which describes itself as the premiere classifieds site in Spain, and uses a format like that of Craigslist. Also try recruitspain.com. If you can arrange to visit the Spanish coast in March before most of the budget travellers arrive, you should have a good chance of fixing up a job for the season. The resorts then go dead until late May when the season gets properly underway and there may be jobs available. If you are heading for the Canary Islands, the high season for British package tourists is November to March.

Competition for jobs is predictably keen in the popular cities and so without EU nationality chances are very poor, as New Zealander Richard Ferguson found in 2008:

> ***I went to Barcelona to work but it is very very hard to get work without the right papers. Saying that you can get jobs in hostels or handing out flyers, doing walking tours of the city, but these didn't go my way so I went to Palma de Mallorca to try there. Palma is THE place to try to get a job***

on a superyacht but everyone knows this so nowadays there are heaps and heaps of Kiwis, Aussies, Saffas and Brits trying their luck. All have their STCW (see chapter 'Working a Passage' – Ed). But few have any experience which is really what the yachts are after. It seems the most demand was for stewardesses (boys need not apply), engineers and chefs. If you do land a job you can get well paid.

Anyway I was never going for one of these jobs but found a job in a pub. Palma is also very hard to get jobs without papers, but luckily I was taken on. But it was not great, the boss was a dragon and apparently thinks New Zealand is in Europe as she thought I was legal. She began to cut my hours down drastically, and earning €6 an hour in Palma on only 20 hours you can't survive. So after a month I decided to leave, without my tips – she promised to send them to me which I figured should be €200–€300, but she is only sending €115.

Year-round resorts like Tenerife, Gran Canaria, Lanzarote and Ibiza afford a range of casual work as bar staff, DJs, beach party ticket sellers, timeshare salesmen, etc. If you are in Ibiza, a good meeting place is the Queen Victoria Pub in Santa Eulalia (ibizaqueenvic.com) which posts jobs and accommodation on its notice board. Anyone can drop by and consult these though it is polite to buy a drink as well. If you are on the other side of the island around San Antonio ask around at the Ship Inn in West End (known as Bar Street) or the Do Drop Inn in Es Cana popular with seasonal workers and reps, with a jobs and accommodation message board.

CAROLINE SCOTT, WHO HAS WRITTEN A DISSERTATION ON YOUTH CULTURE IN IBIZA, DESCRIBES THE EMPLOYMENT SCENE SHE FOUND A COUPLE OF SUMMERS AGO:

Bar work was the highest paid, then waitressing, postering and worst touting which is what I did, where wages were enough to get by. Accommodation becomes harder to find in July, so it's recommended to go May/June when the better jobs are also available. This year I went back for a second season working for a different club, which I obtained by sending my CV to British clubs in January. (I got the addresses from Mixmag, a club magazine.)

The big clubs like Privilege and Amnesia are on the road between San Antonio and Ibiza. A good site for up-to-date information on clubs is ibiza-spotlight.com. Thousands of Britons try to find work on Ibiza each year so it is important to offer a relevant skill. If you haven't got one it is probably best to get your face known round the neighbouring pre-club bars before approaching the clubs for a job.

Jobs with British tour companies such as Canvas and Eurocamp (see *Tourism* chapter) can be fixed up months in advance from home. Siblu Holidays (siblu.com/contact_us/recruitment) and TJM Travel (jobs@tjm.co.uk) need reps and children's staff to work at mobile home, tent parks and adventure centres from early May to the end of September. Agencies in the major Spanish cities may be able to assist, for example the Easy Way Association (☎ 91 548 86 79; easywayspain.com/ingles/employment.htm) in Madrid charges a fee starting at €370 for placing Spanish-speaking or hospitality-trained people in restaurant jobs for a minimum of two months. Agencies of a different kind supply teams of entertainers and animateurs to Spanish resorts. AnimaJobs (http://animajobs.com) is a recruitment portal that posts current vacancies.

Odd Jobs and Touting

There is a job which is peculiar to the Spanish resorts and which allows a great many working travellers to earn their keep for the season. The job is known variously as 'PRing', 'propping', 'blagging' or touting, that is to entice/bully tourists to patronise a certain bar or club.

MANY READERS HAVE FOUND 'PROPPING' A GOOD WAY TO SPEND THE SEASON, AMONG THEM IAN GOVAN FROM GLASGOW IN LLORET DE MAR ON THE COSTA BRAVA:

There are literally hundreds of British props and a fair number of other nationalities too. I worked as a prop for over a dozen bars in three months and by the end I was earning up to £280 a month with free beer to boot. Be warned that saving is virtually impossible, but you will have one hell of a social life, and will soon enjoy the job and the challenges which arise as you try to match the experienced props and develop your own routine. The highest compliment is when the old hands start using your lines. It's pure unadulterated showbiz.

The job can involve dressing up to promote a themed event, putting up posters or sticking leaflets under windscreen wipers, as well as simply leafleting and chatting up passers-by. Some pay a nightly wage, while others pay a commission, e.g. €2 for every 'capture' plus a bonus after every 20. Sometimes new people are taken on on a drinks-only basis for one or two sessions and, after they have proved their effectiveness in drawing in customers, begin to earn a wage. When you first arrive, try to get a toe-hold by working at one of the less sought-after places. The authorities normally turn a blind eye to this activity provided props carry out their work discreetly. The hours of work are usually midnight onwards, as late as 7am.

Timeshare touting is another of those jobs that some find objectionable but others recommend. The industry is much better regulated than it was a decade or two ago, and there are fewer shady practices. Respectable companies like Thomas Cook and the Marriot Hotel Group are involved and do not employ the hard-sell which gave timeshare such a bad name. Many companies provide a one-week sales training course beforehand. Check timesharestaff.com for leads on who is hiring. One company seen advertising in 2009 was the Cyprus-based Lion Resorts (lionresorts.com) who were looking to hire sales reps and admin staff for their sales operation in Playa del Ingles, Gran Canaria (☎ +357 2620 2620; grancanariaservices.com).

Off-Premises/Outside Public Contacts (OPCs) or Vacation Promotion Reps (VPRs) have the job of persuading holidaymakers to visit the holiday development, where they are handed over to a sales rep. Those who succeed have to be aggressive and prepared to face a lot of rejection. Instead of buttonholing people on beaches (which in some cases is against the law), a more common practice for timeshare reps is to visit package holidaymakers in their rooms and invite them to a welcome meeting. The commission paid is 8%–10% which, on an investment of thousands of pounds, means that high earnings for the reps are possible.

The English and Irish pubs that advertise in the English language press are usually good places in which to make contact with like-minded job-seekers, for example Kitty O'Shea's, the Shamrock and the Haddock Scottish bar in Barcelona; and Finbar's, Finnegans (finnegansmadrid.com has a Jobs icon) and the Irish Rover in Madrid.

TEACHING ENGLISH

Major companies in every sector from transport to fashion employ English teachers to improve their staff's English skills; language schools continue to attend to the massive demand from students and young adults just out of university keen to improve their CVs, and from parents who continue to send their young children and teenagers to English classes, so they can pass school exams and eventually cope with a job market that often demands fluency in English. Thousands of foreigners find work as English teachers in language institutes from the Basque north (where there is a surprisingly high concentration) to the Canary Islands. The entries for language schools run to more than 500 in the online *Yellow Pages* for Madrid.

Job Hunting on-the-Spot

Most teaching jobs in Spain are found on the spot and, with increasing competition, it is necessary to exert yourself to land a decent job. Many job-seekers use the usual method of pounding the pavements of likely neighbourhoods. The best time to look is at the beginning of September, after the summer holidays are ended and before most terms begin on October 1st. Spanish students sign up for English classes during September and into early October. Consequently the academies do not know how many classes they will offer nor how many teachers they will need until quite late. It can become a war of nerves; anyone who is willing and can afford to stay on has an increasingly good chance of becoming established. Barry O'Leary wrote from Seville in 2008, having been a teacher there for three years. In his first year he worked for a disorganised and crafty academy where there was no mention of a contract, classes started at 8am and were staggered throughout the day until 10pm, and it was difficult to predict how much you would earn from month to month because of all the unpaid festivals in Spain.

Luckily in his second year, after mingling with the other ex-pat teachers, he was able to land himself a job with a more professional establishment. He now works fixed hours from 4pm until 10pm, Monday to Thursday leaving the mornings free, and there are excellent on-going training sessions on Friday mornings:

> ***The students, who are often passionate and keen to learn English, range in age from six to sixty so there is never a dull moment. Classes have a maximum of twelve, all material is provided and there is scope to move away from the syllabus now and then. A lot of extra work is necessary in February and June when the exams take place but it's worth the agony. Life in Seville is fun and varied, with an abundance of festivals including the religious Semana Santa and the livelier Feria. The city is a great place to live and a base for exploring Andalucía. Evenings can be spent in the many bars enjoying tapas, watching flamenco or Sevillanas (a local dance) or just mingling with the locals. Seville is generally safe and with the year-round blue skies it's a great place to brush up on your Spanish and experience a different way of life.***

After finishing her degree at Sussex University, Sophia Brown decided to spend a year in Barcelona if possible. She acquired a Cambridge CELTA qualification from the Lewis School of Languages in Barcelona (lewis-school.com) and was lucky enough to be given teaching hours by the Lewis School. Conditions were not ideal but she was grateful that she didn't have to knock on doors looking for work.

The great cities of Madrid and Barcelona act as magnets to thousands of hopeful teachers, some of whom struggle to get as many hours as they want and any job security because the supply of willing teachers is so endless. For this reason other towns may answer your requirements better. There are language academies all along the north coast and a door-to-door job hunt in September might pay off. This is the time when tourists are departing so accommodation may be available at a reasonable rent on a nine-month lease.

Berlitz is a long established big player in Spain but pays notoriously low wages starting at €12 an hour. The Madrid branch at Gran Via 80 (☎ 91 541 6104) undertakes recruitment for schools in Madrid and Seville (teach@berlitz.es) and the Barcelona branch for Valencia, Palma de Mallorca, Seville and Barcelona. Applicants must have a degree but not necessarily teaching experience or qualifications.

Other sources of job vacancy information include the Madrid daily *El Pais* (http://empleo.elpais.com) which usually carries a few relevant classifieds. Also try *Segundamano,* the free ads paper published in most big Spanish cities. Good information about teaching in Madrid, with a long list of potential employers, is available on madridinsider.com.

One way to make contact with the local community is to attend (or organise) an *intercambio* in which Spanish speakers and English speakers exchange conversation in both languages. Some are listed in the English-language free-ads magazine *Catalunya Classified* (catalunya-classified.com), which is linked to the magazine *Barcelona Metropolitan* (barcelona-metropolitan.com).

In Advance

Anyone with an ELT component on his or her CV might try to fix up work ahead of time. Addresses of language centres that have been known to hire native speaker teachers can be found in the online *Yellow Pages* and in the 2009 edition of my *Teaching English Abroad* (Crimson Publishing, £14.99). One option which makes the job hunt easier is to do a TEFL training course in Spain, of which there is a considerable choice. Specialist websites can be invaluable sources of information and potential employers, such as madridteacher.com.

Summer-only positions are available at language camps for children. The Educational Consortium of Spain (TECS) in El Puerto de Santa María, Cádiz (☎ 956 853000; tecs.es/employment) hires native English speakers for summer work or for longer-term work in the academy.

For voluntary work as an English assistant on summer language/sports camps, try Relaciones Culturales, the youth exchange organisation at Calle Ferraz 82, 28008 Madrid (☎ 091 541 71 03; spain@clubrci.es), which also places native speakers with Spanish families who want to practise their English in exchange for providing room and board.

It is also possible to arrange an informal exchange of English conversation for a free week in Spain. At least two companies, Vaughan Town and Pueblo Ingles, offer programmes whereby holiday resorts in Spain are 'stocked' with native English speakers and Spanish clients who want to improve their English. In the case of the former, seventeen English native-speaking volunteers participate alongside about the same number of Spanish adults in an intensive six-day 'talk-a-thon' on a one-to-one basis. In exchange for making English conversation, participants receive free room and board, and transport from Madrid. The Pueblo Ingles programme lasts eight days and the average age of participants from all over the world is 40. More information is available from:

Vaughan Systems: Madrid; ☎ 91 748 5950 ext 126; anglos@vaughantown.com; vaughantown.com.

Pueblo Ingles: Madrid; ☎ 91 391 3400; anglos@puebloingles.com; puebloingles.com.

CATHARINE CARFOOT WENT ON WHAT AMOUNTS TO A CLASSIC WORKING HOLIDAY AT THE VAUGHAN VILLAGE A COUPLE OF SUMMERS AGO:
Back in June I took part in an English Language immersion programme in Spain. They want native English speakers (any flavour, although in practice North Americans predominate) to go and talk a lot of English to Spaniards. The Spaniards are generally professional manager-types paid to be there by their companies to improve their English. All people have to do is get themselves to Madrid in time for the pick-up. At the end of the week, you will be delivered back to Madrid, unless you have extraordinary stamina and can manage two (or more) continuous weeks in the programme. It isn't a way to make money, but of course people can and do make friends and contacts both with the other 'Anglos' and with the Spaniards. It's also a week off worrying about food, drink and where to sleep.

Vaughan is initiating a new project from 2009 in various locations in the Castile-León region, in which volunteers work as teaching assistants with young children for two or three months (vaughantown.com/EnglishNew/programavolunteers.asp; same contacts as above).

Conditions of Work

Salaries for English teachers are not high in Spain. The standard net salary is €850–€900+ per month for a full-time load of about 25 hours a week. Compulsory social security (*seguridad social*) payments are between 4% and 7%. One of the worst problems in the classroom is the difficulty in motivating students. Many are children or teenagers whose parents enrol them in classes in order to improve their performance in school exams. David Bourne echoes this complaint after completing a nine-month contract in Gijón: *'I have found it very hard work trying to inject life into a class of bored ten year olds, particularly when the course books provided are equally uninteresting. The children themselves would much rather be outside playing football. So you spend most of the lesson trying (unsuccessfully in my case) to keep them quiet.'*

Private Tutoring

As usual, private tutoring pays much better than contract teaching because there is no middle man. Freelance rates in distant suburbs of big cities should be higher to take account of travelling time. It is difficult to start up without contacts and a good knowledge of Spanish; and when you do get started it is difficult to earn a stable income due to the frequency with which pupils cancel. Getting private lessons is a marketing exercise and you will have to explore all the avenues that seem appropriate to your circumstances. Obviously you can advertise on relevant websites as well as on notice boards at universities, corner shops and wherever else you think there is a market. Send neat notices to local state schools asking them to pin it up broadcasting your willingness to ensure the children's linguistic future.

AU PAIRS

Au pair links between Spanish agencies and those in the rest of Europe are strong because the Spanish language is gaining popularity as a modern foreign language. The pocket money for au pairs in the big cities at present is from €55, though €75 a week is possible, plus €25 per month for transport if the family lives outside the city centre. As mentioned in the section above on teaching, people can also arrange to stay with Spanish families without having to do much domestic or childcare duties. If you deal directly with a Spanish agency, you may have to pay a placement fee.

B.E.S.T.: Pozuelo de Alarcón, Madrid; bestprograms.org; au pair placements for Americans and Europeans; fee $1,050 for three months; B.E.S.T. also organises internship and work-study programmes for varying fees.

Easy Way Association: Madrid; ☎ 91 548 8679; easywayspain.com; also makes hotel and restaurant placements.

GIC Educational Consultants: Javea (Alicante); ☎ 096 646 0410; ecsl@telefonica.net; gic-idiomas.com/aupair.htm; au pair placements and live-in language tutors (registration fee €250).

Globus Idiomas: C/ Gómez Cortina 5, 2°B, 30005 Murcia; ☎ 0968 295661; globus@ono.com; globusidiomas.com; member of IAPA; registration fee €100.

Instituto Hemingway de Español: Bilbao; ☎ 094 416 7901; institutohemingway.com; accepts most nationalities; also places interns in local companies, as volunteers and English teachers.

International Au-Pair & Language Abroad Group: Marbella; ☎ 0952 90 15 76; languageabroad.info; member of IAPA; €175 fee for placements of up to 3 months; €320 for up to 1 year.

Relaciones Culturales: Madrid; ☎ 091 541 71 03; spain@clubrci.es.

Anyone with a childcare qualification or reasonable experience should approach tour operators that offer creche facilities or a dedicated babysitting and childcare agency like the British-run company Cosytoes in Majorca; tel/fax 01623 420866 in Nottinghamshire, UK (cosytoes-mallorca.com).

AGRICULTURE

Reports of people finding harvesting work in Spain are far less common than in France and Greece, but they do filter through every so often. Traditionally there is an excess of immigrant labour from Africa and landless Spanish workers especially from Andalucia to pick the massive amounts of oranges, olives, grapes, and latterly avocadoes and winter strawberries. In fact Spain and Senegal recently signed an agreement under which 2,700 Senegalese will receive work permits, including some specifically for the strawberry harvest. In places where migrant pickers congregate like Almeria, the Caritas charity often sets up a temporary food stall or even arranges basic accommodation.

In 2008 Anna Ling looked into almond-picking but concluded it was almost impossible to find an opening or to make it worthwhile since the pay was terrible – €4 an hour.

Brendan Barker hitched to an organic farm near Granada (whose address he had noticed on a card displayed in a health food shop in Brixton!) and worked happily there on a work-for-keep arrangement for six months, while picking olives at a neighbouring farm in his free time. The strawberry harvest lasts from Easter to June around Huelva on the southwest coast of Spain. Dozens of strawberry farms are located around the village of Moguer (from which half of Columbus's sailors came), plus Cartaya and Lepe. The usual struggle to find work pertains; newcomers must go to the hiring café at 6am each morning until a farmer picks them up. Then there is the usual struggle to earn decent money.

Tomatoes and many other crops are grown on Tenerife. The Canaries are normally valued by working travellers only for their potential in the tourist industry, but there is a thriving agricultural life outside the resorts. Just a bus ride away from Los Cristianos, the farms around Granadilla, Buzanada, San Isidro and San Lorenzo may take on extra help between September and June. Jon

Loop is one contributor who succeeded in linking up with an organic farmer in southern Spain where he soon got down to some serious work weeding, building a pig enclosure, searching for water when the mountain stream dried up, etc. with no days off. But the surroundings were stunning, and the desolate beauty and harshness of the semi-desert made his stay very enjoyable. He even managed to enjoy goat-herding, that most challenging of rural activities:

> ***This could be quite difficult since their range was 10km by 5km, and they could get through dense undergrowth while I had to follow dried-up rivers and footpaths. Also they had a habit of disappearing, even though they wore bells. The family were quite friendly, the food was exquisite, the accommodation adequate but the temperatures were unbearable. Walking out of the house at 5pm for the evening stint was like walking into a Swedish sauna without the steam. After three weeks I decided to call it a day, and headed up north in search of rain.***

Sunseed Trust, an arid land recovery trust, has a remote research centre in southeast Spain (near the village of Sorbas in Almería) where new ways are explored of reclaiming deserts. The centre is run by both full-time volunteers (minimum five weeks) and working visitors who stay two to five weeks and spend half the day working. Weekly charges for part-time volunteers are £65–£118 according to season and for full-time volunteers £40–£78. Typical work for volunteers might involve germination procedures, forestry trials, hydroponic growing, organic gardening, designing and building solar ovens and stills, and building and maintenance. Living conditions are basic and the cooking is vegetarian. Occasionally workers with a relevant qualification in appropriate technology, etc. are needed who are paid a small stipend. The centre can be contacted by phone (☎ 0950 525770) or email (sunseedspain@arrakis.es; sunseed.org.uk).

VOLUNTEERING

The Atlantic Whale Foundation is working to protect whales and dolphins in the Canary Islands. Volunteers join the project for four or more weeks and contribute £150 per week. A new database of conservation volunteering opportunities is available on their website whalenation.org.

Jacqueline Edwards wanted a live-in position but her status as the single mother of a two-year-old boy made her quest more complicated. She used her initiative and contacted vegetarian/vegan societies around Europe, asking them to put her details in their newsletter. Several of the replies she received were from Spain including from a natural therapies retreat centre in Zamora.

Squats and Communities

Not long after arriving in Granada, 19-year-old Anna Ling bumped into an English girl who was involved in squatting. She and a number of other people of various nationalities were setting up a new one, and Anna was invited to join. The building had been abandoned for at least ten years and was absolutely vile, with no water supply. With very little money, Anna took up 'skipping', i.e. rescuing edible food from skips near supermarkets. Anna earned her keep by helping prepare meals, paint her room, etc. Almost all squatters are musicians and try to earn some money by busking. She stayed for about a month and in that time developed a quickfire 10-minute *fire poi* show which she performed outside restaurants. One of her record bad days earned her €5 an hour but mostly it was quite a bit more. Seville proved a more lucrative destination than Granada. It has more of a shopping culture and here she earned €10–€11 per hour.

Anna also spent time at the famous community, Beneficio, in the foothills of the Sierra Nevada, two hours from Granada. Beneficio is a 30-year-old commune in a beautiful location, where the resident hippies and musicians welcome visitors willing to work for their keep, for instance by collecting wood, preparing meals, etc.

GIBRALTAR

Gibraltar is an anomaly, an accident of history. It is a tiny British dependent territory on the Spanish coast, less than six miles square and with a population of just 28,000. Gibraltar is still separated from Spain by a wire fence and border guards. It has the same currency, the same institutions, the same language (though with a unique accent) as the UK. Although Gibraltarians do not necessarily want to be a British colony, they have little choice. Under the 1713 Treaty of Utrecht Gibraltar must revert to Spain if Britain ever gives up sovereignty, a claim Spain would be unlikely to give up.

Spain has been harder hit by the depression than almost any other country of Europe but this has barely spilled over into Gibraltar. In fact because of the weak pound and strong euro, exchange-rate tourism has become common among Spaniards crossing the border for bargains. Unlike in Spain where the building industry is in crisis, it continues to flourish in Gib, where the rate of unemployment remains low at just 2%. Jobs continue to crop up in the many bars and clubs in the busy summer tourist season.

But new arrivals are finding it much tougher than it used to be. EU nationals of the original member states plus Cyprus and Malta are free to take up any offer of employment made to them in Gibraltar. Non-EU nationals must obtain a work permit from the Ministry of Employment and Vocational Training, Unit 76–77, Harbours Walk (☎ 200 40408/fax 200 73981) after the employer has applied for one. To have an application for a work permit approved, the prospective employer must prove that no Gibraltarian or EU national is available to fill the vacancy, undertake to repatriate the worker if necessary and show that suitable accommodation has been found.

Tourism continues to flourish, partly because Gibraltar's tax-free status makes it a popular shopping destination. Candidates with experience in a field like admin, marketing, IT, engineering, online gaming and so on should look at online recruitment websites for Gibraltar (and Spain) such as www.ambientjobs.com and wemploy.com.

Out of the scores of drinking holes, Andrew Giles recommends Charlie's Steakhouse and Tavern on Admiral's Walk, which has in the past been a good source of job information. Charlie's is favoured by the owners and crews of boats moored in Marina Bay.

Even Adam Cook, who complained of the shortage of work in 'that litter-strewn blob of all that's undesirably British', managed to find a little yacht-varnishing work, and then was taken on to help redecorate a restaurant, before his big break came and he was taken on as paid crew back to England.

ACCOMMODATION

There are neither campsites nor youth hostels on the Rock and free camping is completely prohibited on the beaches. A property boom in the wake of the expanding gambling businesses means that rental property is almost non-existent. The cheapest accommodation we have heard of is at a very basic hostel run by the charity TOC H (Line Wall Road; ☎ 73431). Most non-resident workers choose to commute from La Linea, the port town in Spain just across the border, where accommodation is much cheaper.

Sheppards Marina is where most of the yacht work is carried out, whereas Marina Bay with more than 200 berths is where the long distance yachts are moored. A good source of information on jobs and lodgings in the marinas is the newsagents next door to Bianca's Bistro in Marina Bay and to a lesser extent the Star Bar on Parliament Lane or Aragon Bar on Bell Lane in central Gibraltar. A notice board worth using is located in Sheppards Marina chandlery shop at the Old Marina.

Opportunities for fixing up a crewing position on a yacht exist, though normally on a shared-expenses basis; see the chapter *Working a Passage.*

PORTUGAL

Although Portugal's economy seems to be weathering the recession reasonably well so far, unemployment is predicted to rise to 8.8% in 2010 which means that the job market is definitely shrinking. Furthermore, Portugal has been inundated with a great deal of cheap Brazilian labour over the past few years and it is hard for backpackers to compete. Even without this factor, wages are low. The minimum wage in Portugal is €450 per month (2009), the lowest among the original EU member states (compared to around €1,000+ in Britain and €1,356 in the Netherlands). Chances of finding work are best with tour operators or in hotels, restaurants and clubs along the Algarve coast.

There is a long and vigorous tradition of British people settling in Portugal, and the links between the two countries are strong. Large numbers of expatriates live around Lisbon and on the Algarve, many of whom are retired. English-speaking travellers might expect to find odd jobs in this community, but the friendly relations between foreigners and locals mean that the former are quite happy to employ the latter for many such jobs.

Ask expatriates for help and advice. Probably the best idea is to scan the advertisements in the English language press or place an ad yourself. For example check the classified ads in the weekly *Algarve Resident* published every Friday for €1.50 (www.algarveresident.com, though the classified ads cannot be read online).

REGULATIONS

Portugal has always had comparatively liberal immigration policies, possibly because it has never been rich enough to attract a lot of foreign job-seekers. EU citizens are supposed to apply for a residence permit (by the end of the fourth month after arrival) if they intend to stay for more than three months. The usual documents will be needed: proof of accommodation and means of support plus adequate health insurance or proof of paying social security contributions. Wage earners must prove that they are being paid at least the Portuguese minimum monthly wage. The registration certificate should be obtained from the nearest immigration office or SEF (*Serviço de Estrangeiros e Fronteiras*), although in the future it will be available from the local town council (*Câmara Municipal*).

The Consular Section of the British Embassy in Portugal (☎ 021 392 4000; http://ukinportugal.fco.gov.uk/resources/en/pdf/pdf1/Taking_up_residence_Portugal) distributes information on taking up residence in Portugal (updated 2009).

Non-EU nationals must provide the usual battery of documents before they can be granted a residence visa, including a residence visa obtained from the Portuguese Consulate in their home country, a document showing that the Ministry of Labour (*Ministerio do Trabhalho*) has approved the job and a medical certificate in Portuguese. The final stage is to take a letter of good conduct provided by the applicant's own embassy to the police for the work and residence permit. All of this takes an age, as Rachel Beebe, an American, discovered in 2008 when she worked in Portugal as an English teacher:

> ***I was not able to obtain a work visa of any kind. I found that this is very difficult for Americans living and working in Portugal. I had to work using recibos verdes ('green receipts') which are intended for use by self-employed workers. This situation prevented me from securing a contract with my school; a contract would have allowed me a more permanent position as well as vacation***

time and other benefits. To get a work visa, you need a work contract in hand. While my school offered me a letter of intent to employ me, you are required to have a legal contract when applying for the visa, which can then take a year or more to process. In the meantime, you are only allowed to stay in the country on a 'temporary stay visa', which will allow you to stay up to nine months from the time of your arrival in Portugal. Needless to say, this period of time will expire before you are able to obtain a work visa. After the nine months, you would be expected to leave the Schengen area, which includes most Western European countries (with the notable exception of the UK). Ostensibly, this would prevent most would-be American teachers from being able to teach long-term in Portugal. You could always try to secure a contract 12 months in advance of your planned arrival date, but I have never heard of a school hiring more than five or six months before the start date. In my case, I managed to get my hands on a book of green receipts and taught for a few months using those. However, many government offices will give you conflicting information, and I was only able to get the receipts with the help and direction of a friend who was able to tell me exactly where to go and what to say to whom.

More information about green receipts and related topics can be found at http://lisbon.angloinfo.com/countries/portugal/employ.asp.

Portugal has more than its fair share of foreigners working without the right papers as a New Zealand traveller discovered when he was hired (with his rudimentary knowledge of Brazilian Portuguese) to wait on tables in a Lisbon restaurant:

The first restaurant I was in was actually raided by the immigration officials because of people working without visas, but this was before I arrived. The thing that kind of surprised me was the amount of immigrants – Indians, Bangladeshis, Chinese, Angolans, etc and so many Brazilians, who have a hate-hate relationship with the Portuguese. I think that restaurants need the immigrants as the Portuguese don't like doing service so I think many employers will be willing to look the other way.

TOURISM

Tour operators with beach resorts in Portugal include Mark Warner (☎ 08717 033955; www.markwarner-recruitment.co.uk) which employs lots of live-in seasonal staff. Thousands of Britons and other Europeans take their holidays on the Algarve creating many job opportunities in bars and restaurants in resorts like Lagos and Albufeira.

ACCORDING TO MANY TRAVELLERS LIKE EMMA-LOUISE PARKES, THE ALBUFEIRA AREA IS THE PLACE TO HEAD:

I arrived at Faro Airport in June, and went straight to the Montechoro area of Albufeira. A job hunter here will be like a kid in a sweet shop. By 12.15pm I was in the resort, by 12.30pm I had found somewhere to stay and had been offered at least four jobs by the evening, one of which I started at 6pm. All the English workers were really friendly individuals and were a goldmine of information. Jobs-wise, I was offered bar work, touting, waitressing, cleaning, packing ice cubes into bags, karaoke singing, nannying for an English bar owner, timeshare tout, nightclub dancer... I'm sure there were more. Touts can earn £16 a night with all the drink they can stomach while waitresses can expect a little less for working 10am–1pm and 6pm–10pm. Attractive females (like myself!) will be head-hunted by lively bars, whereas British men are seen by the locals as trouble and are usually kept behind bars (serving bars that is) and in cellars.

Emma-Louise recommends visiting the many bars and diners along Av. Sá Carneiro in Albufeira, known as the Strip.

Attractive females have a definite advantage in partying resorts like Albufeira. Typically the March 2009 issue of the *Jobs Abroad Bulletin* (www.jobsabroadbulletin.co.uk/tourism_jobs_index.shtml) carried an advert from a bar owner who was looking for five female bartenders to work for the summer season; cocktail-making experience was not required but an emailed photo was. Finding somewhere to stay can be more difficult than finding employment. Not surprisingly, accommodation is quite expensive during the high season. Ask around so you can avoid the dodgy landlords. It would be cheaper to stay at Campismo Albufeira which may offer discounts to long-stayers.

Lisbon will be a harder nut to crack, although Richard Ferguson managed it last year, helped by his knowledge of the language. He suggests trying the bars and restaurants at the docks (*docas*), especially the Irish bars, all of which are full of tourists in the summer. The other key area of the city is the Bairro Alto, jammed with revellers and clubbers till the wee small hours.

> ***I've been working in Lisbon for two months now. Through a friend in New Zealand, I met a local who got me my first job in a pizzeria. We simply asked the owner when we were eating there and I was told to start the next day. I was working six days from 11.30am to 4pm then an evening shift 7pm till late for €750 a month plus tips of about €80. All the workers were immigrants and these wages were below par as the minimum should be about €1000 per month. After 5 weeks I was offered a job by a rival pizzeria where I'm now working evenings only for €650 a month plus about €40 a week in tips. Finally I have some decent free time. It's an awesome environment – like a family – living with colleagues in an apartment owned by the owner for next to nothing. I'm loving it.***

Buskers congregate around the busy tourist avenues and squares of the Bairro Alto, especially around Praça de Camões near the famous Café a Brasileira.

TEACHING

The market for English tuition is fairly buoyant, especially in the teaching of young children and especially in northern Portugal. Apart from in the main cities of Lisbon and Oporto, both of which have British Council offices, jobs crop up in historic provincial centres such as Coimbra (where there is also a British Council) and Braga and in small seaside towns like Aveiro and Póvoa do Varzim. The Cambridge Certificate (CELTA) is widely requested by schools, but a number (especially those advertising vacancies in June, July and August) seem willing to consider candidates with a BA plus a promising CV and photo.

One of the most well-established groups of schools is the Cambridge School group (☎ 021 312 46 00; www.cambridge.pt) which every year imports about 100 British teachers for its eight schools. Other chains of language schools to try are the Bristol School Group (☎ 0229 48 88 03; www.bristolschool.pt) with four schools in the Oporto area, two in the Azores and three inland; Royal School of Languages with its main school in Aveiro (☎ 0234 42 91 56; www.royalschooloflanguages.pt) and the Oxford School in Lisbon and Cacém which hires 40 teachers (☎ 021 354 6586; www.oxford-school.pt). The consensus seems to be that wages are low, but have been improving at a favourable rate in view of the cost of living. On the positive side, working conditions are generally relaxed. The normal salary range is €800–€1,000 net per month. Some schools pay lower salaries but subsidise or pay for flights and accommodation. Teachers being paid on an hourly basis should expect to earn between €11 and €17 an hour.

BUSINESS

If you know some Portuguese, you might find an opening in an office; without knowing the language, chances are remote. For agencies specialising in temporary work, look up the *Yellow Pages* or *Paginas Amarelas* (www.pai.pt) under the heading *Trabalho Temporário*. The *Blue Pages* (http://portugalbluepages.com) are a searchable directory in English of services and businesses in the Algarve. For temporary office or manual vacancies, try Manpower in Lisbon (☎ 021 313 40 00; lisboa@manpower.pt) and also in Oporto (☎ 0222 00 24 26). See also www.manpower.pt. Two of the other main agencies are SELGEC (www.selgec.net) and Adecco (www.adecco.pt).

The British-Portuguese Chamber of Commerce (*Camara de Comércio Luso-Britanica*) is in Lisbon (☎ 021 394 20 20; servicos@bpcc.pt; www.bpcc.pt). CVs of members may be sent by e-mail to info@bpcc.pt though the Chamber cannot respond unless they have already been notified of a relevant opportunity. They attempt to match qualified job-seekers with their members who might be looking for staff.

AGRICULTURE

Although it is the fifth largest wine producer in the world, we have never heard of any traveller picking grapes. The farms are generally so small that hiring help from beyond the local community is simply not done. On the other hand, a large strawberry farm in São Teotónio (www.wellpict-portugal.com) on the Atlantic coast south of Lisbon hires pickers for the harvest season which is between January and June, with the peak season from March until the end of May. Jobs include picking and general farm work as well as supervisors.

Your best chance of success is to follow up leads passed on by the army of Portuguese migrant workers.

As of 2009, Portugal now has a national WWOOF association (www.wwoofportugal.org); membership costs €15 and allows you to access the list of about 70 member organic farms, including romantic sounding olive groves and cork tree woodlands.

SWITZERLAND

Switzerland is not a member of the European Union. However a bilateral agreement with the European Union has removed the main obstacles to free movement of persons. The immigration system is now more in line with the rest of Europe so that EU job-seekers can enter Switzerland for up to three months (extendable) to look for work. If they succeed they must show a contract of employment to the authorities and are then eligible for a short-term residence permit (valid for up to one year and renewable) or a long-term permit (up to five years) depending on the contract.

With a low rate of unemployment (3.4% at the end of 2008, down from the previous year) and a high proportion of foreign workers (more than a quarter of the workforce), it is easy to understand why the Swiss want to tread carefully when it comes to integrating with Europe. The high cost of living while you are job-hunting and the (deserved) Swiss reputation for hard work discourage many travellers from going to Switzerland to look for work. But many people who have spent time working in Switzerland and have come to know the Swiss have nothing but compliments. According to Tony Mason who picked grapes four seasons running and worked as a builder: *'The Swiss are a genuinely friendly and hospitable people and we are often invited to local homes for meals and on outings to the mountains. I can't say enough good things about the Swiss.'*

REGULATIONS

No permit is needed for EU nationals who stay for less than three months. If they want to stay beyond that, e.g. to continue job-hunting or to do a seasonal job, they must apply for an L permit (short-term residence permit). The L-EC/EFTA permit (*Kurzaufenhalter/Autorisation de Courte Durée*) is issued for periods of work lasting less than 12 months and can be renewed once for a further year. EU nationals simply need to take their passport and contract of employment to the local cantonal office. L-permits are no longer tied to a particular job or canton.

If the contract of employment is going to extend beyond two years, it is possible to apply for a B-permit, valid for between one and five years. Note that until 2011, Switzerland will continue to impose quotas on the number of permits granted for foreigners who want to stay longer than four months. However slowly, the Swiss are opening to the outside world. In a popular vote held in February 2009, nearly 60% of the Swiss people voted in favour of the continuation of the agreement on the free movement of persons. Detailed information about the regulations is published by the Federal Office of Migration (bfm.admin.ch). Detailed information in English is sometimes available from the cantonal authorities, for example downloadable brochures about living and working in Zurich are available at welcome.zh.ch. The canton of Zurich also allows foreigners to apply for a work permit online via their eWorkPermits gateway, which shortens the application time. The searchable forum englishforum.ch can also be helpful on technical matters.

All of these changes are of course bad news for non-EU citizens who will now find it harder to gain access to Switzerland's labour market unless they apply in special categories like spouse or au pair or the trainee permit. If a non-European does find an employer willing to sponsor their application, the applicant will have to collect the documents from the Swiss Embassy in his or her home country.

All legal workers are eligible for the high wages (minimum of SFr3,300/€2,150 a month) and the excellent legal tribunal for foreign workers which arbitrates in disputes over working conditions, pay and dismissals. Accident insurance is compulsory for all foreign workers and often the employer pays this. However health insurance, also compulsory, is the responsibility of the individual. Trainee exchanges between Switzerland and a number of non-EU countries including the US and Canada are available to candidates aged 18–35 with at least two years of vocational training. Permits for temporary trainee placements (*stagiaires*) can be obtained from the Swiss Federal Office for Migration in Bern (☎ 031 322 42 02; swiss.emigration@bfm.admin.ch; swissemigration.ch). Normally the Swiss embassy administers the programme abroad, but in some cases a co-operating partner organisation such as AIPT in the US handles the formalities. Guidance may be given to applicants on how to find an employer, though the programme is for individuals who can find a suitable position in their field independently.

CASUAL WORK

Particularly in the building trade and for agricultural work, the local supply of labour is so clearly inadequate that people without a residence permit do find jobs.

DANNY JACOBSON FROM WISCONSIN SPENT SEVERAL SUCCESSFUL SEASONS PIECING TOGETHER ODD JOBS IN THE TOWN OF BULLE:

I still feel Switzerland is a working traveller's best friend in Europe. If you're willing to get dirty, there's tons of work around. If you can speak French or German, head into the more rural parts or the less touristy towns. I've based myself in Bulle, an over-sized village in the Préalpes. The word on the street is that in the off-the-beaten-track parts of Switzerland, the authorities look the other way because the hotels and restaurants are usually desperate for workers. The hotel owner has offered me a full-time position cleaning the staircases and washing dishes five days a week for a generous wage paid cash in hand plus food. If I choose to stay here for a bit, I shouldn't need to work again for a long time when I hit the road again.

He clearly preferred this boss to a previous one, a '*drunken madman with 800 ways to mop a floor, of which a new one would be demonstrated each day because I was too inept to realise I was using yesterday's*'.

In winter you may be able to find occasional work chopping firewood or mending roofs and be paid a handsome SFr100+ per day. A special opportunity for odd jobbers – assuming global warming doesn't kill it off – is afforded by the Swiss law that prohibits snow on roofs from reaching more than two metres depth.

Although Switzerland doesn't go so far as to demand that buskers get a work permit, Leda Meredith was surprised to find that the city of Bern (a 'goldmine for buskers') publishes a leaflet about when and where busking is permitted. In fact it hosts an annual buskers' festival in August, which feeds and houses eligible musicians and entertainers for three days (buskersbern.ch). Assaf de Hazan from Israel found Switzerland a Shangri-La for buskers: *'If you have a guitar (and can play it) here in Geneva, you are a king. If you have a bit of impudence and are willing to go around cafés and bars (not too fancy) and ask to play three songs, you are more than a king. I was getting more than £50 for a day's playing around the train station part of the lake. You just go and ask and they always say yes. After playing just three songs, you go around with an ash-tray and get money, and lots of it.'*

TOURISM

It has been said that the Swiss invented tourism. Certainly their hotels and tourism courses are still the training ground and model for hoteliers worldwide. For the hotels and catering industry, a rapid short-term injection of labour is an economic necessity both for the summer and winter season – June/July to September and December to April.

Swiss hotels are very efficient and tend to be impersonal, since you will be one in an endless stream of seasonal workers from many countries. The very intense attitude to work among the Swiss means that hours are long (often longer than stipulated in the contract): a typical working week would consist of at least five nine-hour days working split shifts.

On the other hand, the majority are *korrekt*, i.e. scrupulous about keeping track of your overtime and pay you handsomely at the end of your contract. Alison May summarised her summer at the Novotel-Zürich-Airporthotel: *'On balance, the wages were good but we really had to earn them'*. Remember that from the gross (*brutto*) monthly wage of SFr3,000–3,300, up to half will be lost in deductions for board and lodging, tax and insurance (with slight cantonal variations).

The Job Hunt

Provided you have a reasonable CV and a knowledge of languages (preferably German), a speculative job hunt in advance is worthwhile. One hotel group worth trying (provided you are a European national) is Mövenpick on moevenpick-hotels.com (with a link to current vacancies) while the Park Hotel Waldhaus, 7018 Flims-Waldhaus (☎ 081 928 48 07; waldhaus-flims.ch) always seems to be recruiting staff with EU nationality.

The Swiss Hotel Association's online recruitment site http://jobs.htr.ch may be useful. For example in February 2009 there were 460 vacancies being advertised, most for German speakers with professional experience.

Becoming part of a hot-air balloon crew is physically demanding work but would be an unusual way to spend January and February in the Swiss Alps around Chateau d'Oex; details from Bombard Balloon Adventures in Beaune, France (jobs.bombardsociety.org).

Quite a few British travel companies and camping holiday operators are active in Switzerland such as Canvas and Eurocamp. Venture Abroad (Derby; ☎ 01332 342050; joanne.keighley@rayburntours.co.uk; ventureabroad.co.uk) are often looking for 'practical, resourceful and calm' people to work as resort reps. The work consists of meeting and guiding youth groups around Gstaad, Grindelwald, Interlaken, Adelboden and Kandersteg. The Jobs in the Alps Agency (jobs-in-the-alps.co.uk) places waiters, waitresses, chamber staff, kitchen porters and hall and night porters in Swiss hotels, cafés and restaurants in Swiss resorts, 150 in winter, 50 in summer. The agency is now allied with the online seasonal recruitment specialist Free Radicals.

Most ski tour operators mount big operations in Switzerland, such as Crystal Holidays and Ski Total (see intro chapter). The main disadvantage of being hired by a UK company is that the wages will be on a British scale rather than on the much more lucrative Swiss one. A Swiss company that advertises for resort staff and ski instructors is Viamonde in Anzère (fax 27 398 4883; viamonde.com); for the 2009 season they were paying their domestic hotel staff SFr383 per week net in addition to board and lodging.

The Swiss organisation Village Camps advertises widely its desire to recruit staff over 21 in their multi-activity language summer camp for children in Leysin. They also hire up to 100 ski counsellors and other staff for the winter season. Jobs are available for EFL teachers, sports and activity instructors, nurses and general domestic staff. For jobs with Village Camps, room and board are provided as well as accident and liability insurance and a weekly allowance from €175. Recruitment starts just after the new year; an application pack is available from Village Camps, Recruitment Office, 14 rue de la Morache, 1260 Nyon (☎ +41 22 990 9405; personnel@villagecamps.ch; villagecamps.com/personnel). Applications from North Americans and Antipodeans are welcome.

Another camp operator looking for seasonal summer or winter staff is Les Elfes (CP 174, 1936 Verbier; ☎ 027 775 35 90; info@leselfes.com; leselfes.com). Winter contracts for ski/snowboard instructors and activity staff are from 1st December to 30th April. They also hire kitchen and domestic staff for their various camps.

On-the-Spot

Although many people fix up jobs ahead with a tour operator or via an online seasonal recruitment site, others go out armed with a couple of references and try to fix up their jobs in person by job-hunting in the lesser known resorts such as Les Portes de Soleil at Champery or Les Crosets as well as the major resorts of Leysin, Verbier, Thyon and Crans Montana. This valley is a major road and rail route and is ideal for concentrated job hunting. Another area which has been recommended is the Jura between La Chaux-de-Fonds and Delémont.

Surprisingly, tourist offices may be of use. Naturally their lists of local accommodation are a useful starting point, but tourist information staff may also keep a register of job-seekers to which you can add your details, possibly for a small fee. Like most people, Andrew Winwood found the job hunt tough going:

> ***All in all I asked in over 200 places for ski-season work, but eventually could have counted 10–12 possibilities. As far as I can see, it's a simple case of ask, ask, ask and ask again until you get work. It was costing me so much to live in Switzerland that I couldn't let up until I definitely had a way of getting the money back.***

The most promising time to introduce yourself to potential employers is near the end of the previous season, so late April/early May for the summer season and September for the winter. November is a bad time to arrive since most of the hotels are closed, the owners away on holiday and most have already promised winter season jobs to people they know from previous seasons or ones who approached them earlier.

Danny Jacobson's tip is to bypass the large ski stations in favour of the less tourist-filled smaller stations and the surrounding villages. Joseph Tame's surprising tip is to go up as high as possible in the mountains. After being told by virtually every hotel in Grindelwald in mid-September that they had already hired their winter season staff, he despaired and decided to waste his last SFr40 on a trip up the rack railway. At the top he approached the only hotel and couldn't believe it when they asked him when he could start. Although he had never worked in a hotel before, they were willing to take him on as a trainee waiter, give him full bed and board plus the standard Swiss wage. At first he found the job a little boring since there were few guests apart from Japanese groups on whirlwind European tours. But things changed at Christmas:

> ***Christmas and New Year was an absolute nightmare. Three shifts a day for everyone with very little sleep and no time off. When a promised pay rise didn't materialise, I decided I had had enough and handed in my notice. But by January 5th, business had slumped and we had at least two hours off daily to ski. When my overdue pay rise came through I withdrew my notice. If you can stick the Christmas rush, things do get better. Switzerland was definitely the best thing that ever happened to me.***

So good that Joseph returned for three subsequent seasons and says that he is very glad that he stumbled across this 169-year-old hotel in a blizzard. The proprietors sometimes have trouble filling vacancies and so he recommends sending a CV with photo to Hotel Bellevue des Alpes, Scheidegg Hotels AG, 3801 Kleine Scheidegg (welcome@scheidegg-hotels.ch; ☎ 033 855 12 12).

A recommended meeting place is Balmer's Herberge in Interlaken (Hauptstrasse 23, 3800 Interlaken; ☎ 033 822 19 61; mail@balmers.ch). They take on English-speaking staff for a minimum of six months and only after interviewing them in person. The owner is pleased to pass on information about other job openings in the area, as the hostel is often contacted by local hotels asking for workers.

Casual work opportunities crop up in some alternative establishments in Bern and the other big cities, such as the socialist, hippy/punk type restaurant/cafés around town that the police don't bother much due to their tricky politics. One reader found weekend bar work at the Reithalle in Bern, a socialist collective arts centre housed in the former city stables, where he had some fairly wild and woolly times. For serving drinks over the pounding electro-beats and cleaning up as dawn broke, he was paid SFr15 an hour cash-in-hand.

AGRICULTURE

Official Schemes

Young people who are more interested in rural experiences than in money may wish to do a stint on a Swiss farm. The Landdienst Zentralstelle (Archstr. 2, Postfach 2050, 8401 Winterthur; ☎ 52 264 00 30; admin@landdienst.ch) runs a programme called Horizon Ferme (Power deim Bauer in German) by which farm placements are made for a minimum of three weeks for young people from the old EU countries who know some German or French. Last year about 3,000 young people (including Swiss) were placed through the Landdienst. Workers are called 'volunteers' and can work for up to two months without a permit. They must pay a registration fee of SFr56.

In addition to the good farm food and comfortable bed, you will be paid SFr16–20 per day worked (a rate that has remained the same for many years). Necessary qualifications for participating in this scheme are that you be between 18 and 25 and that you have a basic grounding in French or German. On these small Swiss farms, English is rarely spoken and many farmers speak a dialect which some find incomprehensible.

Most places in German-speaking Switzerland are available from the beginning of March to the end of October and in the French part from March to June and mid-August to the end of October, though there are a few places in the winter too. Despite Switzerland's reputation as an advanced nation, thousands of small family farms practise traditional farming methods, especially in the German-speaking cantons. Part of the reason for this is that not many mechanical threshers or harvesters can function on near vertical slopes (neither can every human harvester for that matter).

The hours are long (up to 48), the work is hard and much depends on the volunteer's relationship with the family. Most people who have worked on a Swiss farm report that they are treated like one of the family, which means both that they are up by 6am or 7am and working till 9pm alongside the farmer and that they are invited to accompany the family on any excursions, such as the weekly visit to the market to sell the farm-produced cheeses. The arrangement is similar in many ways to the au pair arrangement; in fact young women who get placed on a Swiss farm may be asked to do more chores inside the house than out. Life on an isolated farm can be lonely with few chances to improve your spoken German or French if you are alone in the house with a baby or in the fields with the goats.

Ruth McCarthy gives an idea of the range of tasks to do on the farm, and a taste of village life, which sounds like something out of *Heidi*:

> ***The work on my farm in the Jura included cleaning out cow stalls, hay making, grass cutting, poultry feeding, manure spreading, vegetable and fruit-picking, wood cutting, earth moving, corn threshing and also housework, cooking and looking after the children. The food was very wholesome and all produced on the farm: cheeses, fresh milk, home-made jam, fresh fruit, etc. The church bells struck throughout the day and peeled at 6am and 9pm to open and close each day. As well as church bells the sound of cow bells was also present so that it was quite noisy at times. There was little night life unless you went to a gasthof bar in the village. Anyway it's probably better to get a good night's sleep.***

WWOOF Switzerland (wwoof@gmx.ch; http://zapfig.com/wwoof) keeps a constantly updated list of farmers around the country, currently 45. To obtain the list you must join WWOOF at a cost of SFr20/€15/$21 in cash. Volunteers must apply with a photocopy of their passport and an accompanying letter stating why they want to become unpaid volunteers.

JOSEPH TAME MADE USE OF THE WWOOF WEBSITE TO FIX UP A PLACE ON A FARM IN THE SPRING:
I can honestly say that it has been an absolutely fantastic experience. The hours could be thought fairly long by some (perhaps 35 per week) considering there is no money involved, but I absolutely love the chance to work outside in this land that reminds me so much of the final setting in 'The Hobbit.' From our farm your eyes take you down the hillside, over the meadows covered in flowers, down to the vast Lake Luzern below and over to the huge snow-capped mountain Pilatus. It really is paradise here. The family have been so kind, and as I put my heart into learning all that I can about the farm they are only too happy to treat me with generosity. I really feel a part of the family.

Grape-picking

Like every country in Europe south of Scotland, Switzerland produces wine. The main area is in the Vaud north of Lake Geneva, but also in Valais around Sion and Sierre, where the harvest begins in late September though sometimes a few days in October. Every year scores of hopeful *vendangeurs* begin pouring into the region. Robert Abblett calculated that if he had arrived in time to catch the beginning of the harvest, he could have saved £350 from 11 days of work.

Almost everyone who over the years has written about the Swiss harvest writes in glowing terms. A Canadian Kyle MacDonald travelling with his girlfriend at the beginning of September were delighted to see a small notice pinned up in the hostel in Lyon just a few hours after arriving in Europe. They made haste to the destination, St. Saphorin, on the shore of Lake Geneva and were soon put to work at a chateau in Chexbres. Kyle recorded his experiences on his blog (http://kylemacd.blogspot.com/2005_07_01_archive.html):

> ***The next day we were aboard the appropriately named 'Le Train des Vignes' zipping along high above the shores of Lake Geneva. The thousands of acres of vineyards we passed through were going to fill thousands of bottles with Swiss wine. A cheerful Madame greeted our arrival at the train station in St. Saphorin and drove us up the road, stopping at a massive four-storey Chateau overlooking sparkling Lake Geneva and the vineyards below. In the distance were the glacier-covered peaks of the Alps. If a handful of experts had ever sat down to agree where the best place on earth to harvest grapes was located, this had to be it.***
>
> ***Dominique's job was to cut bunches of grapes from each vine. Using a small set of garden clippers, she filled plastic containers left along each row and were picked up by 'un porteur' like me. My job was to carry 'small' containers of grapes to a 'large' container waiting on the closest roadway. Each 'small' container weighed about 35 pounds each and we carried three containers at a time on our backs using a metal rack. The incredibly steep terrain made work difficult. Hauling grapes down steep staircases was tricky, but the real test came when grapes had to be hauled up staircases. We were called 'les porteurs' but I think of myself as a wine and chocolate-fuelled Swiss grape sherpa.***

In addition to free room and generous board, *vendangeurs* usually earn SFr75 (£45) per day, and in some cases even more.

Vineyards are found along the north shores of Lake Geneva on either side of Lausanne. One district is known as La Côte, between Coppet and Morges west of Lausanne, and the other is the Lavaux, a remarkably beautiful region of vineyards, rising up the hillside along the 25km between Pully on the outskirts of Lausanne and the tourist city of Montreux. The vineyards, enclosed within low stone walls, slope so steeply that all the work must be done by hand, and the job of portering is recommended only for the very fit.

One suggestion is to visit the tourist office outside the railway station in Biel on the Lake of Biel (Bielersee) and obtain the leaflet about wine in the region, which gives the names, addresses and phone numbers of nearly 50 vineyard owners (*weinbauern*). August and early September can be a good time to ask, since you might be taken on early to help with netting the grapes, to minimise bird damage. Try also the northern shores of the two adjoining lakes Murtensee and Lac de Neuchâtel.

TUTORS AND AU PAIRS

Private tutoring is a possibility for those who lack a permit, as an American world traveller discovered when he was living with his Swiss girlfriend (now wife) in Bern:

> ***A Swiss friend advised me to apply at one of the English schools but I didn't think it would work without a permit. So I just made my own flyer and put it up around town and the next thing I knew I had a bunch of people calling me up to help with proof-reading seminar papers/assignments and to give private lessons. I figured I'd go for quantity and low-ball the market, charging only SFr20 per hour. But I found a few adverts for people looking for teachers and with those, I went with their offered price which was sometimes twice as much.***

Note that a qualified EFL teacher can charge SFr80 an hour in the cities, so a rate of SFr40 might strike some as a bargain.

For those interested in a domestic position with a Swiss family there are rules laid down by each Swiss canton which principally apply to non-EU nationals since Europeans can work in Switzerland in any capacity. The regulations were relaxed in 2008, and au pairs/nannies from any country of the world are now able to work in Switzerland, provided they come through one of the handful of authorised agencies (contact details below). Non-EU candidates must be under 26, can stay as an au pair for one year only and are required to spend at least three hours a week studying the language. Families usually pay the language school fees (worth perhaps SFr100 a month) or at least make a substantial contribution. The agencies are at pains to remind potential au pairs that Swiss German is very different from the German learned in school, which often causes disappointment and difficulties.

Au pairs in Switzerland work for a maximum of 30 hours per week, plus babysitting once or twice a week. The monthly salary varies among cantons but the normal minimum is SFr700–800. Rates may be slightly higher for older girls and are generally higher in Geneva than Zürich. In addition, the au pair gets a four or five week paid holiday plus SFr18–20 for days off (to cover food). Au pairs are liable to pay tax and contributions which can mean a deduction of up to a fifth of their wages unless the family is willing to pay or subsidise these costs.

Pro Filia is a long-established Catholic au pair agency with branches throughout the country: the St. Gallen office makes placements in German-speaking families and the Lausanne office in French-speaking households (tel/fax 01 361 5331; profilia.ch). The agency registration fee is SFr40 plus a fee of SFr290 is to be paid on taking up the placement.

Independent au pair placement agencies include Perfect Way in Brugg (☎ +41 56 281 39 12; info@perfectway.ch) which vets all families and distributes a list of other au pairs and their contact details. The agency Au Pair Link (part of Wind Connections) in Erlenbach near Zurich (☎ 01 915 4104; aupairlink.ch) accepts au pairs mainly from Australia and Canada where it has in-country interviewers.

The Haut-Lac International Centre (1669 Les Sciernes; ☎ 026 928 4200; jobs@haut-lac.com; myswisscamp.com) is a language and sport camp for adolescents that employs teacher-monitors and domestic staff for seasonal language camps held year round. The American School in Switzerland (TASIS) also employs TEFL tutors and children's counsellors for their Summer Language Programs, 6926 Montagnola-Lugano (☎ 091 960 5151; wwwsummer.tasis.com, with an Employment icon). Hiring takes place between January and March. Net salaries are $2,100 for counsellors and $3,200 for teachers; American staff may be eligible for a SFr1,300 contribution to their transatlantic airfares and Europeans up to SFr500.

VOLUNTEERING

Several of the international workcamp organisations operate in Switzerland mainly to carry out conservation work. For example Gruppo Volontari dalla Svizzera Italiana (GVSI) in Arbedo (☎ +41 9 1857 4520; fmari@vtx.ch; gvsi.org/en) organises one-week summer workcamps for individual volunteers, to help mountain communities in Fusio, Maggia and Borgogne (Ticino region). Volunteers pay a weekly charge to cover modest living expenses.

The Mountain Forest Project (Bergwald Projekt e.V.) publishes its literature and website in English and is welcoming to foreign volunteers who know some German. It provides hut accommodation, food and accident insurance for the one-week education and conservation projects:

> ***People from overseas travelling in Europe will surely enjoy a week's workcamp with MFP in Switzerland, Germany or Austria. You will learn a lot about alpine forests and nature in general. We do not, however, consider it reasonable to fly to Europe just for one week to work with us. We all know that airplanes pollute the air and endanger our atmosphere, climate and forests. For these reasons we offer our workcamps only to people who are in Europe anyway.***

For details contact MFP in Trin (☎ 081 650 40 40) or register online (bergwaldprojekt.ch). The camps are free to join.

AUSTRIA

With thriving winter and summer tourist industries, Austria offers much seasonal employment. Its rate of unemployment is among the lowest in Europe at 4.3% (2008) and with net labour shortages, at least a quarter of people employed in tourism are not Austrian citizens. A good knowledge of German will be necessary for most jobs, apart from those with UK tour operators. The government website help.gv.at gives information about immigration and social security procedures for those working in Austria.

Once you are in Austria, you should visit the state-run employment office AMS (*Arbeitsmarktservice*) though it would be virtually essential to speak German before they could assist. The AMS runs offices at the national, provincial and regional levels. The AMS web pages (ams.or.at) and searching in the so-called e-JobRoom might be of assistance to German speakers. The site also provides links to EURES Advisers, for example to the Vienna office specialising in youth employment at Neubaugasse 43 (☎ 01 87871 30200). For seasonal workers in tourism, the AMS organises special job fairs. Most *Saisonstellen im Hotel und Gastgewerbe* (seasonal hotel jobs) for the winter season are notified in November for the start of the season at the end of November. Job centres that specialise in seasonal work are called *BerufsInfoZentren* or BIZ. The cross-border

EURES-BIZ office in Innsbruck can be especially helpful, as it registers many hotel and catering vacancies in the South Tyrol (Schöpfstrasse 5, 6010 Innsbruck; ☎ 512 5903 202; otto.hosp@ams.at). Anyone under 25 might find it worthwhile asking for advice at InfoEck, the Youth Information Centres in Innsbruck, Imst and Wörgl (infoeck.at).

Nationals of non-European countries must find an employer willing to apply for a work permit on their behalf. The Austrian government has quotas for temporary labour. Employers may apply to employ a non-EU national for six months and then can renew this once. For example English for Kids (see below) asks that non-EU applicants submit their certificates, references and photos so that the application can be submitted to the Austrian authorities by mid-March and processed by mid-April for a summer job. The residence permit can be processed after arrival for a cost of €70.

THE JOB HUNT

Tourism

There is no shortage of hotels to which you can apply either for the summer or the winter season, especially in the west of Austria. Get a list from the local tourist office or on the net. The largest concentration is in the Tyrol, though there are also many in the Vorarlberg region. Wages in hotels and restaurants are lower than they are in Switzerland, but reasonable.

Adventure activity organisers in Kirchberg and elsewhere may require guides for white-water rafting, mountain biking or hiking. For example Fankhauser Rafting confirmed for this book in 2009 that it needs guides for whitewater rafting, mountain biking and hiking as well as support staff (office@tirolrafting.com).

Austrian ski resorts have traditionally been popular with British skiers which creates a demand for English-speaking staff. The main winter resorts to try are St Anton, Kitzbühel, Mayrhofen, St. Johann-im-Pongau, St. Johann in Tyrol, Lech and Söll. The ski season in the Innsbruck region is fairly reliable since the Stubai Glacier normally ensures snow from early December until the end of April. As usual, it will be necessary to enquire everywhere for jobs in hotels, shops, as an au pair, in specialist areas like the 'skiverleih' (ski hire), as a technician or just working on the drag-lifts. It is probably best to target one or two villages where there are a lot of guesthouses and hotels. The Tourist Information office and the bus drivers who convey skiers from hotels to slopes are both good sources of information. You could try to fix up a job with a British tour operator beforehand, ideally in September, for example with Esprit, Equity Travel, Inghams and Travelbound (see introductory chapter *Tourism* for addresses). For example Equity Travel (☎ 01273 648273; equity.co.uk/employment) recruits chefs, housekeeping and waiting staff, handymen, night porters, plongeurs and bar staff (EU nationality essential) for its sizeable operation in the Austrian Alps. Supertravel Ski (☎ 020 7962 1369; supertravel.co.uk/jobs.asp) takes on winter staff for Austria, primarily chalet chefs, chalet hosts with excellent cooking skills, chalet assistants with customer service skills, chalet managers fluent in German, and handymen/drivers. All applicants must hold an EU passport and have a NI number.

First Choice Holidays (☎ 020 8541 2223; sla.recruitment@tuiski.com; jobsinwinter.co.uk/firstchoice) hire hundreds of people for the winter season. Also go to firstchoice4jobs.co.uk to apply for summer employment; in some cases qualifications are not required because staff are given in-house training, but you must be available to stay for the whole season from May to September.

English Teaching

As in Germany, the market for EFL in Austrian cities is primarily for business English, particularly in-company. Most private language institutes such as SPIDI in Vienna (spidi.at) depend on freelance part-time teachers drawn from the sizeable resident international community. The hourly rate at reputable institutes starts at €25, which is none-too-generous when the high cost of living in Vienna is taken into account.

Berlitz is well represented with four separate premises in Vienna alone, including the one at Graben 13 (☎ 01 512 82 86; berlitz.at). In fact all centres recruit new English trainers of British, Irish, American or Australian nationality. Candidates must have permission to work in the EU and be at least 23; a business and university background would be advantageous.

Summer language and sport camps provide more scope for EFL teachers and others. Village Camps based in Switzerland (villagecamps.ch) run a summer activity camp at Piesendorf near Zell-am-See. Some experience of teaching children and a knowledge of a second European language are the basic requirements.

Two Vienna-based organisations active in this field are the similarly named English for Children (☎ 01 958 1972; englishforchildren.com) and English for Kids (☎ 01 667 45 79; e4kids.co.at) both of which are looking for young monitors and English teachers with experience of working with children and preferably some TEFL background. English for Kids promises a salary from €1,188 per month gross, plus full board and accommodation. Try also the English Camp Company (theenglishcampcompany.com) for summer jobs teaching English and supervising activities.

Au Pairs

Austria, together with Switzerland, was one of the first countries to host au pairs. Recently, however, the number of agencies active in the field has declined with the long-established Catholic agency ceasing to be active in this field.

Au pairs from EU countries will have no trouble sorting out the paperwork in Austria whereas non-EU candidates must obtain a work and residence permit (*Aufenthaltstitel*). According to new regulations that came in from January 2009, all au pairs must receive €450 per month for working 20 hours per week. Placement agencies include: Au Pair Austria, Vermittlungs-agentur in Vienna (☎ 01 405 405 0) and Asten (07224 68359; aupairaustria.com) which charges a registration fee of €25. Another to try is Friends Au Pair Vermittlung (aupairvermittlung.at).

It should be possible to find babysitting work if you are based in a resort. Ask for permission in the big hotels to put up a notice. The going rate according to InfoEck is €7 an hour.

Outdoor Work

WWOOF Austria is in Stainz (☎ 03463 32096; wwoof.welcome@utanet.at; wwoof.welcome.at.tf). Membership costs €20/$28 per year which entitles you to the list of around 130 Austrian organic farmers looking for work-for-keep volunteer helpers.

The fact that the Austrian government grants 7,000 short-term labour permits specifically for harvest helpers indicates that demand for seasonal workers is strong. The farmers prefer workers who know some German since few of them speak any English. Normally you will be expected to stay for the whole season though people who are free to work for the first four weeks before the school holidays begin are in demand. Try the large co-operatively run farms rather than the small ones that usually rely on family members.

CENTRAL EUROPE AND RUSSIA

With the accession of Bulgaria and Romania to the European Union in 2007, the divide between Eastern and Western Europe has been further eroded. Together with Hungary, Poland, the Czech Republic, Slovakia, Slovenia, Lithuania, Latvia and Estonia, the former Soviet bloc countries are looking to the west and to the future, where the English language dominates. The demand for native speakers to teach English continues to be enormous in the cities and most farflung corners of this vast region. The vast majority of working opportunities in the region is in the field of English language teaching.

Thousands of foreigners continue to fall under the spell of Prague, Budapest and Kraków. Even those who find themselves in the less prepossessing industrial cities normally come away beguiled by Central European charm. The English language teaching industry in those cities has grown up, and is now much more likely to hire teachers with proven experience or an appropriate qualification.

TEACHING ENGLISH

In the early days, foreigners were welcomed into the state education system but nowadays most foreigners teach in the private sector which offers less financial and job security but better pay. Fewer vacancies in Central and Eastern Europe are being advertised in the educational press and on the internet, even in Poland, but it is still worth checking the *Guardian* online or the main EFL job sites.

The major chains have multiple franchise schools in the region, chief among them International House, EF English First and Language Link (see chapter Teaching English). Certification is often required and one attractive option is to train on-the-spot. For example ITC Prague (part of the ubiquitous TEFL International group) offers a four-week certificate course followed up with career support which is especially strong in Eastern European vacancies (tel/fax 224 817530; itc-training.com). Language Link in London (☎ 020 7225 1065; languagelink.co.uk) is mainly active in Russia, Central Asia and Slovakia. Contracts for new teachers pay $800–$1200 per month.

Other placement organisations are less commercial. Sharing One Language (SOL) in Devon (☎ 01271 327319; sol.org.uk) is a non-profit-making organisation which annually recruits teachers with a degree (ideally in Education or Languages) plus at least an introductory TEFL/TESOL certificate to teach in schools in the state sector in many Eastern and Central European countries, especially Hungary, Slovakia and Romania. All posts include local salary and free independent housing.

Once you have a work base, the supply of private teaching is usually plentiful. The pay for private lessons can be excellent compared to wages offered by schools. A small notice placed on a prominent university notice board or in a daily newspaper would have a good chance of producing results. Sometimes notices are posted in less likely places like shop windows and lamp posts.

Czech and Slovak Republics

There seems to be an equal demand for English in both the Czech and Slovak Republics, though the majority of TEFL teachers gravitate to the former. In Prague, the glut of well-qualified teachers is so bad that salaries are actually lower than in smaller cities like Brno, even though the cost of living is higher.

TEACHING IN THE CZECH REPUBLIC

The centralised contact for recruitment of teachers for state primary and secondary schools is the Academic Information Agency (AIA) in Prague (☎ 02 2422 9698; aia@dzs.cz). AIA is part of the Ministry of Education and acts as a go-between, circulating CVs and applications (due by the end of April) among state primary and secondary schools that have requested a teacher. Schools (mostly in small Czech towns) then contact applicants directly to discuss contractual details. They place university graduates, preferably with TEFL training or experience, in schools from September 1st to June 30th. The net salary per month is in the range 11,000–20,000 crowns often with free or subsidised accommodation.

Most people wait until they arrive in Prague before trying to find teaching work, which is what Linda Harrison did: *'The best time to apply is before June (I arrived in September which was too late) but if you persevere there are jobs around. A lot of teaching work here seems to be in companies. Schools employ you to go into offices, etc. to teach English (though not usually business English)'*. Most private language schools in the major cities can count on receiving plenty of CVs on spec from which to fill any vacancies that arise. Anyone who is well qualified or experienced should eventually find employment. The *Yellow Pages* (*Zlaté Stranky*) are an excellent source of addresses and can be consulted in English (http://en.zlatestranky.cz). The market in Brno is booming, with more than 80 language schools listed as operating in the country's second largest city (many will be one-person outfits), catering to a population of just 380,000.

Among the schools with the largest demand for teachers are:

Akcent International House: Prague 4; ☎ 02 6126 1638; akcent.cz; degree plus CELTA or equivalent is minimum requirement.

Brno English Centre: Brno; ☎ 541 212262; brnoenglishcentre.cz; 14 teachers of any nationality needed for one academic year.

Caledonian School: Prague 5; ☎ 02 5731 3650; jobs@caledonianschool.com; employ 300+ teachers for schools in Prague, and throughout the Czech and Slovak Republics; teachers must have a BA plus Trinity or Cambridge Certificate or equivalent; approximate salary of 20,000 crowns per month for qualified teachers plus free accommodation provided.

St. James Education Center: Prague 2; ☎ 02 2251 7869; stjames.cz; recruitment info on website.

Compared to the starting monthly wage in state schools of 11,000 crowns, private sector wages are normally about 20,000–22,000 crowns (gross). But this does not include accommodation which will account for between a quarter and a third of a teaching salary. Hourly fees start at 180 crowns net, though a more usual fee is 200–250 crowns less 20%–30% for tax and deductions. Since accession, EU nationals no longer have to apply for a visa or work permit. However, those who stay for more than 30 days are required to register with the Alien and Border police by filling in an application form and presenting a copy of their contract. Other foreigners who want to stay more than 90 days must apply for a long-stay Czech visa before arrival in the country. This requires gathering a raft of documents including a work permit issued by the employer, proof of accommodation, etc. all presented in the original or a notarised copy.

TEACHING IN SLOVAKIA

As the poor cousin in the former Czechoslovakia, the republic of the Slovaks has been somewhat neglected not only by tourists but by teachers as well. As one language school director put it: *'Many teachers are heading for Prague, which is why Slovakia stands aside of the main flow of the teachers. That's a pity as Prague is crowded with British and Americans while there's a lack of the teachers here in Slovakia.'*

The density of private language schools in the capital Bratislava and in the other main cities like Banska Bystrika makes an on-the-ground job hunt promising.

A UK agency that actively recruits teachers for Slovakia is London-based Language Link which is affiliated with the largest semi-private language school in Slovakia, the Akadémia Vzdelávania (tel/fax 02 5441 0040; aveducation.sk). It offers approximately 30 posts in adult education centres and schools throughout Slovakia.

HUNGARY

English is compulsory for all Hungarian students who wish to apply for college or university entrance, and university students in both the arts and sciences must take courses in English, creating a huge market for English teachers. But because of the high calibre of Hungary's home-grown teachers, native speakers do not have the cachet they have in other central European countries.

Yet native speakers continue to find teaching opportunities in Hungary, especially in the business market. The invasion of foreigners in Budapest was never as overwhelming as it was (and is) in Prague, but still Budapest has a glut of teachers. The opportunities that do exist now are mostly in the provinces.

Teachers are poorly paid in Hungary, apart from in the top-notch private schools. The hourly rate at commercial centres is normally in the range 1,200–1,800 forints (from £3.50). Freelance teachers can ask for about 1,700 forints per lesson. In the US, the Central European Teaching Program (CETP, 3800 NE, 72nd Avenue, Portland, OR 97213; ☎ 503 287 4977; cetp.info) places 50 university graduates who are native speakers of English in Hungary. The placement fee in 2008/9 is US$2,500 which includes a week-long orientation in Budapest. A furnished apartment with utilities is provided free and a monthly salary ($500–$550) is paid in local currency.

Another option is the SELTI Teach Abroad programme (Sheppard English Language Teacher Institute) in Budapest. This company (selti-hungary.com) recruits native speakers with a qualification and some higher education to teach English for a variety of language schools throughout Budapest. Candidates must acquire some TEFL training, for example an online TEFL course; the fee (currently $199) is reimbursed after the first month of teaching. The package provides accommodation, meals, group activities and a stipend in exchange for 20 contact hours per week for 6–12 months.

Since Hungary's accession in 2004, EU nationals no longer require a residence permit and immigration procedures have been much simplified. However before the 93rd day of their stay, they should report their presence to their nearest regional Office of Immigration and Nationality. The office will issue a registration certificate, which permits indefinite stays. EU nationals working full-time in Hungary are subject to the same social security and pension obligations as Hungarians. Employees must make payments into the National Health Insurance Fund and into a pension fund.

Non-EU citizens must arrange work permits and residence permits before leaving their country of residence. A foreign employee cannot be legally paid until she or he has a work permit (which costs $120). Those nationals who require a work permit must find a Hungarian employer who is entitled to apply for a work permit from the relevant Regional Employment Office. General information in English is available on the website of the Hungarian Ministry of Foreign Affairs (kulugyminiszterium.hu).

POLAND

Prospects for English teachers in Poland, western Poland in particular, remain reasonable, even if the seemingly insatiable demand for English teachers that has characterised the last 15 years is now a thing of the past. Poles are still incredibly keen to learn English but, with the explosion of cheap flights to and from Poland and the opening of borders, millions of Poles simply get on a plane and come to Britain or Ireland, mainly to work but sometimes to sign up for English language courses. This means that certain types of English class taught by native English speakers are increasingly popular, i.e. 'realistic' conversation classes that teach Poles how to rent a flat, order a drink, and fill in forms.

Even the major cities of Warsaw, Wroclaw, Kraków, Poznan and Gdansk are worthwhile destinations, though the job hunt is of course easier in the many lesser known towns and cities of Poland. As in the Czech and Slovak Republics numerous possibilities exist in both state and private schools. The monthly salary range is 1200–1600 zloties. Generally speaking, private language schools in Poland offer reasonable working conditions, with fewer reports of profit-mongers and sharks than in other countries experiencing a TEFL boom.

Private language teaching organisations run short-term holiday courses in summer and sometimes winter which require native speakers. The English School of Communication Skills whose Personnel Department is located in the charmless city of Tarnów (tel/fax 14 690 87 49; personnel@escs.pl; escs.pl) hires 100 EFL teachers for five language schools in southern Poland and summer language camps at the Polish seaside. Pay is 25–30 zloties an hour, 2,200 zloties a month. ESCS offers its own three-week TEFL training course in September at a cost of $450.

American Alicia Wszelaki was full of praise for ESCS after spending a year immersing herself in Polish culture in the southern town of Myslenice. Similarly Will Gardner greatly enjoyed his summer job with ESCS which he had fixed up from England in the spring:

> ***I spent one month working for ESCS at their summer camp on Poland's Baltic Coast. The camps were well organised and great fun. As an experienced teacher who has worked in several different countries for a range of schools, I would just like to say what a pleasure it was to work with such a well organised group of people and for a school that completely lived up to its promises. The school supplied a wide range of resources to assist teachers, although a lot of emphasis was placed on originality. The focus was always on communication and fun. The camp facilities were perfect for the situation. Food and accommodation were supplied and the weather was beautiful. Although the students were attending lessons daily, a holiday atmosphere prevailed over all activities.***

International House (ih.com.pl) maintains a contingent of language schools in Poland employing many certificate-qualified EFL teachers, including at affiliated schools in Katowice, Kraków, Opole, Wroclaw, Bielsko-Biala and Bydgoszcz.

On the Spot

Semesters begin on October 1st and February 15th, and the best time to arrive is about a month beforehand. After arrival, try to establish some contacts, possibly by visiting the English department at the university. Although some school directors state a preference for British or American accents, many are neutral. After obtaining some addresses, would-be teachers should dutifully 'do the rounds' of the *Dyrektors*. Some of the bigger schools include:

Angloschool: 7 schools in Warsaw (tel/fax 022 663 8833; angloschool.com.pl).

EF (English First): ul. Pelczynskiego 30, 01–471 Warsaw (☎ 48 22 666 00 55/ 666 05 67; tomasz.urban@ef.com; englishfirst.pl). 15 EF schools in Poland employ about 20 native speaker teachers.

ELS-Bell School Of English: Al. Niepodleglosci 792/2, 81–805 Sopot (recruitment@elsbell.com). 90 teachers for centres in Gdansk, Gdynia, Bydgoszcz, Sopot, Szczecin and Warsaw. Other Bell affiliates include Program Bell in Poznan (program-bell.edu.pl/english/work_for_us.htm).

International Language Centers (ILC): Kraków (☎ 12 429 67 88; info@ibes.pl, ibes.pl). Native speakers needed. No qualifications necessary, though experience of teaching with the Callan Method useful.

Lektor Szkola Jezykow Obcych: Wroclaw (tel/fax 071 343 2599; rmyszkowski@lektor.com.pl). 50 British, American, Canadian or Australian teachers with certificate in TEFL.

York School of Language: Kraków (☎ 012 415 1818; york.edu.pl). 40 qualified teachers.

Poland's requirements for EU teachers are broadly in line with the rest of Europe. They no longer need to apply for a work permit however teachers wishing to stay for more than three months should obtain a residence card from the regional governor of their chosen city/town. Applicants will need to justify their stay in Poland and confirm that they have sources of income (e.g. a statement from a bank account). Employers should assist with the documentation and the necessary translation of official documents into Polish.

RUSSIA AND THE INDEPENDENT STATES

The employment situation – like the rouble – has stabilised and there are ample English teaching opportunities for those wishing to experience the real Russia. Many qualified teachers work for the major foreign-owned language chains like Benedict, Language Link and EF English First (see below). The situation in the Central Asian Republics is somewhat different because demand for English there is largely funded by international oil investment and so highly qualified teacher trainers are needed.

Barry Robinson spent a number of years in Moscow working the EFL circuit:

> ***When living in Moscow patience is priceless. Expect to queue, wait longer, and endure a certain amount of discomfort when travelling around the city from lesson to lesson. Yet Moscow is an expansive, vibrant, culturally rewarding city in which to live. The people at first appear a tad abrupt, but this is usually just to cope with the breakneck pace of life in Russia's capital. When you make friends – and you will as Russians are quite sociable and always interested in native English speakers – you'll find them warm and generous people, who will let you into their hearts and homes if they genuinely like you.***
>
> ***Be warned: Moscow is a very expensive city. Increasing prosperity and the influx of foreigners have driven up rents so, if you don't want to rent a roach-infested shed, you'll have to spend hundreds of dollars on some living space. Often teaching contracts will include a flat, but these tend to be rather manky and often shared with another teacher. Freelance opportunities are abundant, and extremely lucrative. However you'll have to wade through the quagmire that is Russia's ever-muddled, ever-changing visa and entry requirements.***

Finding a Job

Anyone with contacts anywhere in the region or who is prepared to go in order to make contacts should be able to find a teaching niche on an individual basis. Many educational institutes outside Moscow and the other major urban centres can't afford to attract Western teachers through the usual recruitment channels, so any willing native English speakers who show up in the flesh have a very good chance of finding some hours of work.

A thriving English language press has established itself in Moscow and St. Petersburg. Check adverts in the *Moscow Times* and the weekly *St. Petersburg Times*.

Among the major language teaching organisations, the following employ substantial numbers of native speaking teachers with a TEFL qualification:

Benedict School: St. Petersburg; ☎ 812 315 3596; benedict@peterlink.ru; employ about 20 teachers who earn $800–$1,500 a month.

BKC – International House: Moscow; ☎ 495 737 5225; recruit@bkc.ru; bkcih-moscow.com; around 200 contract and hourly-paid teachers in Moscow, plus 50 more in the Moscow region.

EF English First: ☎ 495 937 3887; englishfirst.com/trt/english-language-teaching-in-russia.html; 40 teachers for 30 schools in Moscow, St. Petersburg, Vladivostok, etc.

Language Link Russia: Moscow; ☎ 495 250 6900; jobs.languagelink.ru; 200 teachers throughout Russia (Moscow, St. Petersburg, Volgograd, Siberia, Urals, etc.); freshly certified EFL teachers can be placed in Russian schools; unqualified people can join Teacher Internship Training Programme.

ROBERT JENSKY, DIRECTOR OF LANGUAGE LINK RUSSIA, IS CONVINCED THAT HIGH STANDARDS ARE ESSENTIAL:

I have personally seen many unqualified teachers fail because they did not fully realise the difference between speaking English and teaching English. Although Russians can vary in temperament and personality, they share a respect for education. Their only concern is that they get their full money's worth from each and every lesson. Russian students are demanding and place high expectations on their teachers, and so do the companies which employ them (including those that hire EFL teachers illegally). Given these circumstances, it is strongly recommended that any teacher coming to Russia has with him or her a good grammar book, a dictionary and a concise guide to TEFL methodology.

Russians have taken to the internet with unbounded enthusiasm and opportunities may be discovered by doing some concerted surfing. A few schemes offer volunteers the chance to teach English at any level from university to businesses to summer camps. For example the youth exchange company CCUSA with offices in the UK and California runs a Summer Camp Russia Programme whereby teacher/counsellors are placed in youth camps in Russia lasting four or eight weeks between mid-June and mid-August. Camps are widely scattered from Lake Baikal in Siberia to the shores of the Black Sea. Australian Paul Jones gradually came to enjoy the programme:

> ***I worked as a counsellor in a summer camp near the city of Perm. When I first arrived, my heart sank because it looked like a gulag (for which the area around Perm is famous). But you soon forget the physical conditions, mostly anyway. If I didn't like the food at the start, I definitely learnt to like it by the end and now reminisce about the worst of it. My job, as with American summer***

camps for kids, was to help lead a group of up to 30 children for their 3-week stay at the camp. Because I did not speak the language, I was placed with two other leaders so my services weren't really necessary. However, this region of Russia doesn't exactly get many international visitors so the role I played at camp sometimes felt more like being rockstar! The types of activities the kids did ranged from football, basketball and swimming (the colour of the pool was scary) to singing, dancing and crafts. But while I tried as best I could to lead my group of kids in their daily activities, every single kid in the camp wants a piece of you because you're the foreigner! So a lot of the job is to just be there and share a different culture with the kids (and their parents sometimes), other Russian counsellors and the Camp Director. In return, they also shared their culture. I've actually stayed in contact with a number of the local counsellors. The ones that don't speak English very well make up for it with sign language and friendliness. I found that a few words in Russian go a long way to bridging the culture gap. And if possible take some souvenirs for the kids. Even a pack of cards with the British flag on them provides 52 little gifts.

Participants must be aged 18–35 and have experience working with children. The substantial programme fee includes visa, insurance and orientation and room and board (ccusa.com).

A new development catering to the oligarch classes is a rise in the number of jobs for English speakers to tutor and look after young children in kindergartens or as nannies. Agencies as well as individual families post adverts in newspapers and on websites like expat.ru.

Since 1982 the Serendipity Russian-English Program has been sending Americans to work for a year at the American Home in Vladimir Russia, a city 200km east of Moscow. Not only do they teach English but also deliver lectures on American culture. The programme is administered from Illinois by Dr Ron Pope (☎ 309 454 2364; serendipity-russia.com/engculture.htm teaching%20opportunity).

Regulations

For people participating in established international exchanges, the red tape is usually straightforward. Russia is a place where the regulations change as often as the government ministries responsible. In the commercial sector, work permits are problematic, because few Russian companies are willing to embark on the time-consuming and expensive process.

The difficulty lies in finding an organisation which is registered with the authorities and has permission to invite foreigners to Russia for the express purpose of working for them. Many language schools would prefer to avoid this route as it means they have to pay both income and social welfare taxes on their foreign employees. Obviously, the easiest way for language schools to avoid these costly taxes is not to employ teachers legally. In the past, this was done by employing English teachers who had arrived in Russia on twelve-month multiple entry business visas. Certain underhanded employers even went so far as to tell their newly hired teachers that possessing a business visa allowed them to work legally in Russia, which it does not. In order to crack down on this abuse, the authorities now stipulate that foreigners who enter the country on multiple entry business can remain in Russia for only three months during any six-month period. This has cut down on the number of foreigners working without proper authorisation, apart from those working for very short periods.

Baltic States

As traditionally the most westernised part of the old Russian Empire, the Baltic countries of Lithuania, Latvia and Estonia were all admitted to the European Union in 2004. This has significantly eased the bureaucracy for EU passport holders, while other citizens will need to apply for a work permit which can take six months. For this reason and due to extra costs, most schools strongly prefer to employ EU citizens. A number of budget airlines as well as national carriers operate to the region (e.g. Ryanair to Kaunas and Riga) and ticket prices can be remarkably low. The English language teaching industry continues to experience growth partly as a result of all the new business and tourism links.

The most promising time to make contact with schools is just before the summer holidays in June. There are more opportunities for teachers in Kaunas, the second city of Lithuania, and the surrounding areas than in the capital.

Even voluntary opportunities are few and far between. One of the few volunteer and gap year agencies that deals with Latvia is Changing Worlds (changingworlds.co.uk). Karen Rich decided in her 30s to get some TEFL training and do something completely different from her career as airline cabin crew. The country that took her fancy was Latvia, so she made contact with Changing Worlds, paid the programme fee and ended up enjoying herself enough to extend her three-month stay to a full year, ending in June 2008:

> ***It's truly been a life-changing year for me. I changed careers, I moved to the small town of Tukums where I'm the only English person and I've travelled to many new and exciting countries including Russia, Lithuania and Estonia. I hadn't expected to have so many students and classes. I had to call a halt at around 50 students and working weeks of 40 hours. I felt so proud that students who had been shy and reserved at the beginning of the year were relaxed and able to chat to me quite openly at the end. However loneliness was a problem. All my colleagues in the school were Latvian and had their own families, so it was difficult to mix with the local people as the culture was different and it's not acceptable for a single woman to sit in a café and drink coffee. I noticed that the people didn't laugh much.***

Ukraine

The vast republic of the Ukraine's EFL market is still in its infancy, although demand is increasing as citizens realise that they may be able to double their earning power by learning English and open up opportunities for their children by sending them to private tutors. This increase in demand has not been met by an influx of native English teachers, partly because the government lacks a centralised recruitment policy for foreign teachers and partly because wages can be very low and conditions primitive. Computers and televisions may be in short supply outside the major cities, whilst books can be out-of-date and old-school. Students are trying to make the transition from Soviet-style language learning techniques to the more flexible communicative methods favoured these days.

CENTRAL EUROPE

Romania

English was barely taught before the downfall of Ceaucescu in 1989 and the collapse of communism. Demand for English has been intense ever since though there are still relatively few private language institutes, even now that Romania is in the European Union. The association of quality language services (QUEST Romania; quest.ro) based at the Prosper-ASE Language Centre in Bucharest has less than a dozen members.

Despite the demand for native English speakers, however, the government doesn't always make it easy for foreign teachers to work in Romania. The American organisation Central European

Teaching Program (cetp.info) used to supply teachers to schools, particularly in the Hungarian-speaking areas of Transylvania, but decided to pull out last year. They found that the government would reassign their teachers to locations like Bucharest, regardless of promises made to CETP.

Wages will be equivalent to those earned by Romanian teachers, from US$250 a month. Teachers would be advised to take as many teaching materials as possible, e.g. magazine articles, postcards, language games, photos and pictures. Information about the teacher's hometown always goes down well.

Bulgaria

Since Bulgaria joined the EU in 2007 it has attracted EU tourists in large numbers, whilst property speculators and foreign business have not been far behind. There is a substantial demand for English teachers, although the market has moved on from the excitable years following the 1989 transition to a market economy. Those without a degree or teaching qualifications are much less likely to secure a position than they once were. Almost all schools ask for at least a degree and teaching certificate.

Opportunities in the private sector are still very scarce. A Bulgarian agency of long standing appoints 60–80 native speakers to teach in specialist English language secondary schools for one academic year for which the deadline is the end of May. Details are available from Teachers for Central and Eastern Europe (21 V 5 Rakovski Blvd, Dimitrovgrad 6400; tel/fax +359 391 24787/27174; tfcee@usa.net; tfcee.8m.com). University students, preferably with a TEFL background, are accepted from the US, UK, Canada and Australia. The weekly teaching load is 19 40-minute classes per four-day week. The salary in Bulgarian leva is equivalent to $200. Benefits include free furnished accommodation, 60 days of paid holiday, paid sick leave and work permit. A summer programme is also available at Black Sea resorts for which the application deadline is June 15th.

Slovenia

As in Croatia, there are a good many private schools and many opportunities can be created by energetic native speakers both as freelance teachers for institutes or as private tutors. The British Council in Ljubljana has a list of private language schools throughout the country (britishcouncil.org/slovenia-exams-cambridge-how-to-prepare-language-schools.htm, shows postal addresses only). The Council remains closely in touch with language schools and may be prepared to refer qualified candidates to possible employers. The average hourly wage starts at about €8–€10 net. Two private language schools which hire native speaker teachers are Berlitz in Ljubljana; (☎ +386 1–433 13 25; berlitz.ljubljana@berlitz.si) and Nista Language School in Koper (☎ +386 562 50400; nista@siol.net).

Albania

A decade ago Albania was a rather desperate and lawless place, but its economy has been growing and the country is more stable. Private schools have opened, though are staffed almost exclusively by Albanian teachers. Wages are low while the cost of living is rising. The largest provider of English to Albanians is the organisation LSIA (Language Schools in Albania), a foundation founded in 1994 by a group of Albanian university teachers and students. They currently enrol around 3,500 students in 14 locations across Albania and Macedonia, with plans to expand into Kosovo and Montenegro. Out of 120 English teachers a handful are native speakers. The salary is €300 per four weeks (no taxes and social security paid). Accommodation is free and the association organises work permits. Albania might be a good bet for newly qualified teachers, as the LSIA website explains (lsiaal.com/teachforus.php): *'There are relatively few native-speaker teachers in Albania, and we offer rapid career development not normally available to new or recently qualified teachers.'*

Butrint National Park in the far south of Albania has impressive archaeological remains and extensive wetlands. The Albanian National Trust (butrinti.com) accepts international volunteers for conservation and archaeological projects, teaching English, etc.; details by email from visitbutrint@albmail.com.

VOLUNTARY OPPORTUNITIES

Service Projects

The main workcamp organisations in Britain (IVS, Concordia, and UNA Exchange) and in the US (SCI-USA and VFP) can provide up-to-date details of projects and camps in all the countries of the region. Often discussion sessions and excursions are a major part of the three or four week workcamps.

The registration fee will be £150 minimum. The national workcamp partners handle the travel and insurance arrangements once you arrive in their country. The language in which camps are conducted is usually English. Projects vary from excavating the ancient capital of Bulgaria to organising sport for gypsy children in Slovenia. Applications for workcamps should be sent through the partner organisation in the applicant's own country (see introductory chapter on Volunteering). If you are particularly interested in one country it is worth checking the websites of their main voluntary organisations at regular intervals.

While Russia continues to experience socio-economic and organisational problems, anyone interested in volunteering there would be advised to keep abreast of developments through a local workcamp organisation. For example the annual *Workcamp Directory* from VFP in the US (online from March at vfp.org) provides advice on visas for Russia and recommends that North Americans contact the specialist Russian-American Consulting Agency (russianconsulting.com). The Russian Youth Hostels Association (ryh.ru) also offers visa support. Note that the processing is much cheaper if you apply well in advance, for example $156 (if you have an invitation from a Russian organisation) with two weeks warning, but $475 for a same-day service.

Environmental Volunteering

A number of non-profit organisations are involved in protecting the ecology of Lake Baikal in Siberia. One of the best known is the Great Baikal Trail (GBT), whose main aim is to protect the unique environment of Lake Baikal by creating a network of environmentally friendly trails and by developing eco-tourism. The GBT conducts summer camp projects in national parks and reserves where volunteers have a chance to spend two weeks on the shores of the lake in pristine Siberian taiga (greatbaikaltrail.ru/programs/summer_camps_en.html). The Earth Island Institute in San Francisco (☎ 415 788 3666 ext 109; baikal@earthisland.org) is the main partner organisation. Volunteers pay a contribution of 10,900 roubles (approximately $300 or €235).

Volunteers/interns are needed to stay for at least two months to work with at-risk youths on an outdoor education programme in the mountains of Kyrgyzstan; details from the Minneapolis-based Alpine Fund (alpinefund.org). Organisations in the countries of the region organise workcamps independently, such as HUJ in Armenia with an office in the capital Yerevan (☎ +374 10 522788; huj.am). It accepts 150 foreign volunteers to do ecological and renovation work, take care of sick and disabled children, and so on. Also in Armenia, AIEP (aiep@arminco.com; aiep.am) sponsors camps to restore and maintain mediaeval buildings in Armenia and runs an internship programme for students and recent graduates.

A new WWOOF branch has opened in the Czech Republic (wwoof.cz@seznam.cz; wwoof.ecn.cz) which charges €15 (cash) for its list of 44 hosts. The newest of all is WWOOF Bulgaria (wwoofbulgaria.org) whose short list of potential hosts is freely available after registering online. They also participate in the EVS scheme for fully funded European volunteers willing to stay for a year.

Lindsay Whitlock and her family paused in their round-the-world adventure to spend some time on a WWOOF farm in Hungary, which turned out to be one of the highlights of their year-long travels. The family arranged to stay on a goat farm in a remote area about 25km from Kaposvár where they picked fruit and helped in the kitchen and where 10 year old Tom helped look after the herd of goats, meanwhile all staying in an idyllic old farmhouse.

Volunteers who are willing to pay €740–€890 for 11 days spent assisting researchers to monitor dolphin behaviour and habitats along the coast of Croatia should contact the Adriatic Dolphin Project (☎ 51 604666; blue-world.org). Students with a background in biology or geography may be accepted as interns. The Eco-Centre Caput on the Croatian island of Cres (tel/fax +385 51 840 525; supovi.hr) welcomes conservation volunteers to assist in the conservation of the Eurasian griffon vulture, repairing dry stone walls, saving small ponds, picking olives and helping local shepherds. Volunteers pay €164 for one week in summer or €298 for 2 weeks; winter fees are much less, €108/€135. Long stays of up to six months can also be arranged.

CCUSA (mentioned earlier in this chapter) runs a summer camp in Croatia, where English-speaking counsellors are needed from early June till the end of August; details and application form can be found at campcalifornia.com.

The Laboratory of Geoarchaeology of the Kazakh Institute on Nomads recruits international volunteers for archaeological fieldwork. Details are available from the Department of Geoarchaeology in Almaty, Kazakhstan (☎ 07 3272 914386; ispkz@nursat.kz; lgakz.org). The three camps last 15–30 days between May and October and cost €250 per week.

The Center for the Study of Eurasian Nomads carries out fieldwork in Southern Russia and Mongolia which paying volunteers over 20 may join. A contribution of $1,350/$1,550 is requested to join the three-week excavation in summer 2010; see csen.org for details.

Social Projects

Kitezh Children's Community for orphans in Kaluga 300km south of Moscow has close links with the Ecologia Trust in Scotland (☎ tel/fax 01309 690995; ecologia.org.uk). The Trust recruits volunteers, particularly Russian language students, to spend at least two months at Kitezh and provides extensive preparatory information, including profiles of the individual residents. The joining fee is £845 for two months, £100 for each additional month, including visa support but not airfares to Moscow. Knowledge of Russian or TEFL is preferred.

MANY VOLUNTEERS HAVE FOUND KITEZH A FRIENDLY, WELCOMING AND RELAXING PLACE TO SPEND SOME TIME, AMONG THEM SARAH MOY:
Kitezh life is so different from the rest of the world that it took a while to know where you could go, how to get involved in work/play with the children, etc. I felt very much a part of the community and enjoyed sharing my talents (but would have liked to have taught more English). Apart from the obvious benefits of improving Russian and learning more about Russian culture and people, I gained much from the slower pace of life. I was very impressed by the idea of people who have made a career out of genuinely caring and giving. I learnt more about a rural way of life and appreciated being reminded how many luxuries we have here. Altogether it was a fantastic experience.

British-Romanian Connections, PO Box 86, Birkenhead, Merseyside CH41 8FU (tel/fax 0151 512 3355; b-r-c-uk@ntlworld.com) operates summer language schools in Romania for local pupils and orphanages in Piatra-Neamt. The project is suitable for sixth formers and undergraduates, native speakers or highly proficient speakers of English as a second language.

Voluntary organisations working with displaced persons inside the former Yugoslavia sometimes take on foreign volunteers. One of the most important is Balkan Sunflowers which works for social reconstruction in the Balkans and is always looking for volunteers; its main office is in Prishtina, Kosovo (☎ +381 38 246299; balkansunflowers.org). Projects take on volunteers over 21 in Kosovo, Macedonia and Albania for a minimum of six months. Volunteers must contribute at least €200.

Bridges for Education (tel/fax 716 592 4090; bridges4edu.org) recruits and trains volunteer teachers to spend July on an international peace camp in Belarus (as well as Turkey and China). Volunteers are given basic ESL training before departure. Participants pay their airfare and programme administration fee of about $1,000.

OTHER OPPORTUNITIES

Many people based in the cities of Eastern Europe over the past decade have taken advantage of the new entrepreneurial spirit by engaging in conventional employment. Companies and recruitment agencies advertise in the English language papers and on the internet for computer programmers, administrators, etc.

The westernising democracies of Eastern Europe are all targeting tourism as a means of aiding their economies and are encouraging foreign tour operators to develop resorts, etc. that in time may have large staff requirements. Ski tour operators like Balkan Holidays (London W1; balkanholidays.co.uk/careers.htm) recruit children's reps and entertainers outside the countries, but mostly try to hire locals.

Young people in east European capitals are so eager to embrace western culture that American-style restaurants and Irish pubs are plentiful, and some hire English speakers. Such jobs will be heard about by word-of-mouth or possibly advertised in the English-language press. For example the classified section of the weekly *Prague Post* can be read online at praguepost.com. An advert of up to 300 characters can be placed free of charge. If you are looking for some casual work, ask discreetly in hostels, around the universities or among expatriates teaching English. Your services as anything from a DJ to a freelance business consultant may be in demand.

Marta Eleniak started as a volunteer in Warsaw teaching English in a primary school and within a year listed her various paid activities as assistant to the Vice-President of a consulting firm, translator and teacher at a real estate agency, UK representative of a Polish musician and exporter of paragliders. She concludes that 'England seems so sleepy in comparison'. Obviously there are many niches which keen foreigners willing to stay for a while can fill.

Part 3
Work Your Way Worldwide

AUSTRALIA

In some ways this chapter is superfluous. Australia has developed a magnificent industry to cater specifically for backpackers and working holidaymakers. Most hostels both in the cities and the countryside are well informed about local jobs available to travellers; some act as informal employment agencies. Bus companies have routes that shuttle between fruit-picking regions for the benefit of working travellers. Outback properties offer training in the skills necessary to work on a station and then double as a placement agency. Recruitment agencies and employers with seasonal requirements target the backpacking community by advertising in the places they frequent. Free newspapers, magazines and websites specifically address an audience of backpackers, carrying employment advertisements. Employers even co-operate with regional tourist offices to find seasonal staff, as in the South Australian fruit-growing region of the Riverina. So there is no shortage of information and assistance available for the newly arrived working holidaymaker.

The number of working holiday visas granted has been rising steadily from 33,000 in 1995 to more than 150,000 in 2008, demonstrating the strength of the Australian economy. In fact the number of UK applicants increased by 20% in 2008 compared to 2007. Recently, the rules were relaxed to encourage more working holidaymakers to do jobs in country areas. Even if the rate of unemployment rises sharply in the wake of global recession, as is predicted, vacancies for backpackers will still be numerous. The vast majority of unemployed Australians do not want to pick fruit, collect for charity, work on a sheep station, or do any of the other kinds of work visitors to Australia do. This is the conclusion to which a longstanding contributor to *Work Your Way Around the World*, Armin Birrer, came when he worked as recruiting officer at a vineyard in northern Victoria:

> ***Local unemployment was high at that time, and yet I had severe problems getting pickers. Most of the unemployed didn't want to pick grapes because it is too hard for them. Plus lots of them don't think it's worthwhile to go off the dole for three to four weeks and then wait to go back on again. I came to the conclusion in Mildura that I can always find some work even if unemployment rises to 20%, if I go to where the work is. People who can work hard and don't make trouble are always in demand.***

This is not too difficult in a country where unskilled workers can expect to be paid $17 an hour, sometimes cash-in-hand, and people with keyboard skills (for example) earn at least $20 an hour (note that dollar rates quoted throughout this chapter are in Australian dollars). Provided you arrive with the right visa, some references (most Australian employers are sticklers for references and will check them) and some decent clothes, you should find a way to earn a crust.

But do not expect the job hunt to be a doddle. Partly because of the overwhelming numbers of young foreigners on working holiday visas, it is an employer's rather than a job-seeker's market and the job hunt can be a struggle in some sectors. Travelling job-seekers often find themselves at the bottom of the heap in the job market, especially in places like Bondi Beach and Cairns which have been swamped by noisy, sometimes anti-social backpackers. Until three years ago, the working holiday visa limited holders to jobs of less than three months. However it is now permitted to work for an employer for up to six months, which means that there is less turnover in backpacker jobs than there once was.

Roger Blake who spent two separate spells as a working holidaymaker in Australia is someone who is willing to turn his hand to anything and has successfully 'blagged' (talked) his way into all manner of jobs around the world. Yet he found Australia an uphill struggle, certainly compared to New Zealand. Although he managed to survive on his occasional earnings (having arrived with next to nothing), he warns to expect a 'rough ride': *'I have met SO many travellers who are leaving Australia after just 3 months or less of their WHV, thoroughly disgusted with the attitude of employers towards backpackers and the associated struggles of finding an (often lousy) job in the first place. .... But it is not all doom and gloom and I've had fun between troublesome times.'*

The kinds of job you are likely to get in the rural areas are of a very different nature from city jobs. To discover Australia's more exotic features, you will have to penetrate into the countryside. While some experienced travellers declare that the big cities are the only places you can work on a steady basis at reasonably good wages, others advise heading out of Sydney as soon as you've seen the harbour. Chris Miksovsky from Connecticut found computer work in both Sydney and Melbourne offices with ease. However after a few months he realised that the reason he had left home was to get away from spending his days in an office, so he headed north to look for station work. Work in the country or the outback often comes with accommodation whereas city rents can eat into your wages, as can the social life.

WORKING HOLIDAY VISAS

Australia has reciprocal working holiday arrangements with Britain, Ireland, Canada, the USA, Netherlands, Germany, Japan, Korea, SAR of Hong Kong, Taiwan, Sweden, Denmark, Finland, Norway, Cyprus, Malta, France, Belgium, Italy, Estonia and soon Indonesia.

The Working Holiday visa is for people intending to use any money they earn in Australia to supplement their holiday funds. Working full-time for more than six months for the same employer is not permitted, though you are allowed to engage in up to four months of studies/training. Applicants must be between the ages of 18 and 30 and without children. The Working Holiday visa is valid initially for 12 months after entry, which must be within 12 months of issue. You can leave and re-enter Australia during that 12 months but this does not alter the maximum duration of the visa. You can apply for a 12-month extension provided you can prove that you have spent at least three months working in regional Australia, for example fruit-picking, pearling, sheep-shearing or fishing.

Most people apply for a Working Holiday Maker (WHM) visa online, though you can also submit a paper application to any Australian representative outside Australia. When you apply online for an e-WHM visa there is no need to provide proof of funds nor do you send in your passport. Applying online via the Australian Department of Immigration website immi.gov.au is normally straightforward and hassle-free and should result in an emailed confirmation inside the promised 48 hours which is sufficient to get you into the country. Your passport isn't physically inspected until you arrive in Australia when you must take it along to an office of the Department of Immigration and Citizenship to obtain the visa label, avoiding, if possible, the busy downtown Sydney or Melbourne offices where the queues can be long. In either case the fee for the WH visa is $195 (currently £90).

Visas 2 (☎ 020 8123 7454; visas2-australia.co.uk), the Visa Bureau (visabureau.com) and Visa First in Dublin (visafirst.com) all offer a visa service and typically add £30–£35. All visa information can be checked at immi.gov.au or by ringing the Australian Immigration and Citizenship Information line 09065 508 900 (charged at £1 per minute).

A top tip when filling out the application form is to answer the question: What type of employment do you intend to seek in Australia? with the reply 'fruit harvest/seasonal work'. This is primarily what the government wants WHMs to do while in Australia and therefore they are more likely to approve a visa application on this basis. Once you have the visa you are free to seek any job and do any kind of work (within the terms of the visa).

The second step is to get as much money in the bank as possible. Each application is assessed on its own merits, but the most important requirement is a healthy bank balance. You must have enough money for your return fare, although it is not essential to have a return ticket at the time of entry. You must show evidence of having saved a minimum of A$5,000/£2,250. Anyone intending to work in health care or a childcare centre must undergo medical tests by an approved doctor.

If you overstay your visa and they notice on the way out, you will be automatically barred from returning to Australia for a minimum of three years. People found working without the necessary visa will be placed on the Movement Alert List (whose acronym means 'bad' in French) which may count against them in future visa applications.

The Work and Holiday Visa programme for Americans was introduced in late 2007 which for the first time allows students and graduates aged 18–30 from the US to spend up to a year working in Australia. Tourism Australia hopes that there will be around 30,000 visa holders annually by the fourth year (though in 2008 there were only 4,200 applications for the visa).

Alternative Visas

Those not eligible for a working holiday visa may want to investigate the range of alternative options. People with a skill in short supply, anything from carpentry to dental hygiene, architecture to IT, may be eligible for the Temporary Business Visa (457) which requires sponsorship from an Australian employer. Special allowance is made for those willing to work in regional Australia. It is even possible to be sponsored by an employment agency like Geoffrey Nathan (geoffreynathan.com or gnjobs.com.au). In that case you must already be in Australia on a valid visa, be looking for work in an area of skills shortage, have a degree and/or five years relevant experience in your profession, and be available to work for at least three months and up to four years. A separate range of Business Visas is available to senior managers and investors with significant assets. All of these visa programmes are described on the Department of Immigration site (immi.gov.au) and further helpful information can be found on the websites of specialist immigration law firms such as Parish Patience in Sydney (parishpatience.com.au) which specialise in assisting clients with visa applications.

Obtaining a resident's visa (for permanent migration) is, predictably, much more difficult, though not impossible if you have a skill in short supply (like nursing or teaching and are prepared to work in a rural area) and/or a close relative in Australia. Form 1126i is the initial migration form, available online at immi.gov.au. Since 1970 Consyl Publishing in Bexhill-on-Sea (consylpublishing.co.uk) has been publishing a monthly newspaper *Australian Outlook* about emigrating to Australia.

Pre-departure Schemes

A number of competing travel and youth exchange agencies can assist those who want some back-up on a working holiday. They offer various packages which may be of special interest to first-time travellers. Some are all-inclusive especially the gap year placement organisations; others simply give back-up on arrival. Given how relatively straightforward it is to orient yourself and find work, you should weigh up the pros and cons carefully before paying a substantial fee. Typically, the fee will include airport pick-up, hostel accommodation for the first few nights and a post-arrival orientation which advises on how to obtain a tax-file card, suggestions of employers and so on. Some even guarantee a job. Various perks may be thrown in like a telephone calling card and free maps.

BUNAC: London EC1; ☎ 020 7251 3472; downunder@bunac.org.uk; offers a Work Australia package.

CCUSA: London (ccusa.com); offers a 12-month WorkExperience Downunder programme; US applicants should contact CCUSA in Sausalito.

Intern Options: London; ☎ 020 7353 7699; internoptions.com; mainly paid internships in the tourism and events sector, in horticulture or in summer jobs in Sydney; arrangement fee starts at £650; also offer graduates with an appropriate background glamorous-sounding internships in for example video editing and marketing.

International Exchange Programs (IEP): Level 3, 362 Latrobe St, Melbourne 3000; ☎ 03 9329 3866; or Level 18, 233 Castlereagh St, Sydney 2000 ☎ 02 9299 0444; national enquiries ☎ 1300 300912; iep.org.au; BUNAC's partner organisation.

VisitOz: Springbrook Farm, 8921 Burnett Highway, Goomeri 4601 Queensland; ☎ 07 4168 6185; visitoz.org; provides a year-round programme for young people with a working holiday visa who wish to live and work in outback and rural Australia for one year; the first nine days consist of a meet and greet programme, paperwork and jet lag recovery at the beach, followed by five days on the farm having an introduction to Australian agricultural techniques; participants go to their first job on the ninth day in Australia; jobs are guaranteed for the duration of the visa as the participant travels around Australia, with holiday breaks in between; there are 1800 employers Australia-wide offering jobs in agriculture, with horses, in hospitality, childcare and distance education teaching; the programme price is $1,990 and can be booked in the UK; ☎ 07966 528 644; will@visitoz.org.

AIFS Australia Pty Ltd: Sydney; ☎ 02 8235 7000; sydney@aifsaustralia.com; workinaustralia.net; arrival programme for working holiday makers, co-operating with partners abroad e.g. Globetrotters in Canada; ☎ 416 565 4420; laura@globetrotterseducation.ca.

Changing Worlds: ☎ 01883 340960; david@changingworlds.co.uk; changingworlds.co.uk; paid hotel placements in Surfers Paradise, Queensland; placements last 3 or 6 months starting September, March and July; fee £2,400–£2,600 for hotel and farm work, £3,975 for zoos, all including return flights from UK; farm and zoo work provides food and accommodation.

Involvement Volunteers Association Inc: Port Melbourne; ☎ 03 9646 9392; ivworldwide@volunteering.org.au; volunteers are placed within a network of voluntary projects around Australia (and worldwide) for up to a year. Package costs $1200.

Backpacker Agencies

Any travel agency that specialises in the backpacker market will almost certainly promote their ability to assist clients on working holidays, since such a high proportion of that market wants to work. There are a maze of alliances between travel and recruitment agencies, hostel groups and working holiday providers though most of them seem to be offering similar services. Try to shop around if you have the stamina.

Travellers Contact Point (travellers.com.au) sells working starter packs for Sydney for $260 including airport pick-up, two nights' hostel accommodation, access to Job Search service, 12-month mail-holding service, etc. In Sydney the TCP office is at Level 7, Dymocks Building, 428 George St, Sydney 2000 (☎ 1300 855569).

Downunder Jobs at 167 Franklin Street in Melbourne helps people with a working holiday visa to set up work as well as providing a range of other back-up services for a fee of A$330. Ring 1800 154664 or go to downunderjobs.com which is part of the Bakpak Group of hostels. Backpacker agencies tend to outsource their recruitment service to specialist agencies such as Travellers at Work in Sydney (☎ 02 9221 4810; taw.com.au). For example the company OzIntro, with offices in Plymouth in the UK and Coogee in Sydney, sells a membership in the Travellers at

Work Australian Job Search Club for £20 (ozintro.com). The Work Travel Company (234 Sussex St, Sydney 2000; workandtravelcompany.com) maintains job listings for working travellers. Jobs are mainly in hospitality, labour/factory/warehouse, call centre and white collar.

Workstay Australia (workstay.com.au) is a source of working holiday and general travel information for backpackers travelling in Western Australia with links to the job site work2excite.com. Workstay runs the Country Pub Barmaid's Programme, by which mainly young women are placed in jobs for 5–12 weeks. Also in Western Australia, the Job Shop has offices in Perth and Kununurra (thejobshop.com.au) and specialises in finding employment for backpackers. Another Perth-based agency for working backpackers is Go Workabout (info@goworkabout.com) which charges $699 for their 'Complete Working Holiday Starter Pack' that includes the working holiday visa and a job arranged before you arrive.

The agency freespirit (freespirit.com.au) offers a service to support foreign travellers relocating temporarily to Australia.

Unofficial Work

Those who don't qualify for a working visa should not despair, though escalating concern at all levels of Australian society and government about illegal immigration means that new measures to prevent visa-less workers are making it harder. Tax file numbers are compulsory (see below) and immigration raids are not uncommon. Discretion is therefore essential. Employers who at one time did not ask to see the stamp in your passport are more likely to do so these days to avoid paying huge fines if caught.

Jane Harris thinks it should be stressed that anyone working without a visa alongside others in a similar position should be very careful, and suspicious of anyone nosing around. She describes what happened at the campsite she was staying on in Stanthorpe, Queensland:

> ***I got back to our campsite to discover that Immigration had raided farms throughout the area. Apparently, a local man had been running an illegal bus service to all the local farms from the three campsites in town. Someone from Immigration started checking the visas of everyone on the bus, and found seven people with tourist visas. They were told to leave the country within two weeks. That evening, four car loads of Immigration officials turned up at the campsite. They had lists of local farm employees and were matching these with people's passports, so it seems best to work under a false name (especially as the local pubs will cash salary cheques without seeing any ID). Meanwhile we stayed inside our campervan and hid all signs we'd been working (e.g. gloves, boots, pay slips). It seems that they do not have to see you physically working but can act on circumstantial evidence.***

Tax

All people in employment in Australia must either provide their employer with a 9-digit tax file number or be taxed at a punitive 46.5% for non-residents. Therefore it is greatly to your advantage to obtain one. We have heard of several cases of people being deported for inventing tax file numbers (but giving their real names).

Foreigners must apply at a tax office, for example in downtown Sydney, where queues are long (national telephone number 132861; ato.gov.au). Processing normally takes between four and six weeks. You must submit a passport with appropriate visa plus one of a number of documents such as an original or certified copy of your birth certificate, Australian driving licence, bank statement at an Australian address, etc.

The ultimate tax liability for non-residents of Australia is 29% of all earnings whereas residents are taxed at 15%. Non-residents are not eligible for the tax-free threshold of $6,000 nor for concessional rebates (for example residents who work in a 'remote zone' and those who work in seasonal harvests pay only 13% tax). Working holidaymakers are automatically categorised Non-Resident which means you must expect to lose nearly a third of your earnings. If you are lucky enough to have obtained a Resident's Visa on the basis of your education and skills, you can legitimately claim the tax status of a resident. In this case, you should obtain a Group Certificate (statement of earnings and tax deducted, equivalent to a P45) after you leave each job, arranging to have it posted on to you if necessary. If you have earned less than your tax-free threshold of $6,000 during the tax year (starting July 1st), you could be eligible for a refund. All earners are supposed to submit a tax return by October 31st.

Anyone who can show that they will be resident in a certain place for more than three months is eligible for a Medicare card which allows you refunds on doctors' fees and prescriptions.

THE JOB HUNT

Employment National

Although everybody finds some kind of job in the end, it isn't always easy. You are likely to encounter a surprising degree of competition from others on working holidays, many of whom are chasing the same kinds of job. For example a company which operates tours of Sydney Harbour received 50 replies to an advertisement for waiting staff and a receptionist, 42 of which were from Poms. The glut of travelling workers is especially bad in Sydney, Perth and in Queensland resorts before and after Christmas. In addition to asking potential employers directly (which is the method used by at least a third of successful job-seekers in Australia), the main ways of finding work are via the internet, newspaper advertisements, notice boards (especially at backpackers' hostels) and private employment agencies.

Anyone intending to work in Australia should have an up-to-date and properly thought out CV. With few exceptions (like fruit picking) prospective employers will ask to see your resumé before they'll so much as entertain your application and often they'll ask for references from an Australian too. A further frustration is the rampant bureaucracy and government insistence on paper qualifications which means that employees must have specific certificates to work in certain industries, for example the RSA (Responsible Service of Alcohol) and/or RCG (Responsible Conduct of Gambling) for jobs in hospitality and the Occupational Health and Safety (OHS) green or blue card for the building and construction industry. Most training courses last one day and cost $90–$130. A certificate issued in one state is often not recognised in another; one never knows whether an employer will strictly enforce the regulations or be willing to flout them (and risk a fine).

The door-to-door job hunt will require huge reserves of stamina and patience, as Roger Blake discovered:

> ***Another frustrating aspect of the job hunt downunder is the oh-so-frequent scenario where I have walked into a bar, restaurant or wherever (CV in hand) to express an interest in the job seen advertised in their window. The response has varied from: 'Sorry, the job has been taken, we just haven't taken the sign down' (yet two weeks later the sign is still up in their window) to 'Sorry, we're looking for a female' to 'We want a local, sorry, mate'. Obviously they're not allowed to put that on their advertisements.***

Private Employment Agencies

As in Britain, private employment agencies are very widespread and are a good potential source of jobs for travellers, especially those with hospitality experience or office skills, computer, data processing or financial experience. In addition to the specialist backpacker agencies mentioned earlier, a surprising number of mainstream temp agencies positively encourage English speakers on working holidays, often by circulating their details to hostel managers. Competition will be most acute at those agencies that court the backpacking market so some people purposely avoid those. The offered wages are good too: from $16 an hour for clerical work, $20 for secretarial and $22 for computer work.

Major agencies include Drake, Bligh and Adecco. Most agencies do not occupy the equivalent of high street premises, and you will often find yourself in some obscure office block. You should make an appointment to register and allow up to an hour for each one to have your skills assessed and your references checked. George Street in Sydney has dozens of agencies including the long established Bligh Appointments (Level 7, Dymocks Building, 428 George St, Sydney 2000; ☎ 02 9235 3699; bligh.com.au) who welcome working holidaymakers, and Goldstein and Martens Recruitment Consultants (Level 4, 285 George St; ☎ 02 9262 3088; goldsteinmartens.com.au) which is reputed to pay $2–$3 above the average hourly wage.

In Melbourne head for the Franklin Street area of downtown where you will find (among others) Staff Gap Solutions at 18 Anthony St (staffgapsolutions.com.au) which deals with the usual range of urban jobs for travellers: data entry clerks for people who can type, call centre workers, furniture removers, market research interviewers, general labourers and so on. Periodic shortages of temporary secretaries crop up, so if you've got decent skills, you're practically guaranteed work. Drake (drakeintl.com) has been recommended by several readers; the company has offices in all the major cities. Try also Manpower (manpower.com.au) with 34 branches in Australia. Because these major recruitment agencies have offices all over the world, it can be useful having a letter of reference or introduction if you have worked for your local branch.

Some agencies specialise in certain kinds of work for example work on stations and farms, in tourist resorts or as nannies and au pairs (see relevant sections). Troys Hospitality Staff (☎ 02 9290 2955; troys.com.au) and Alseasons (☎ 02 9324 4666; alseasonsagency.com) both in downtown Sydney have been recommended for placing casual catering staff in Sydney. Pinnacle Hospitality and Travel People recruitment agency have offices in Melbourne, Sydney, Perth, Cairns and Brisbane (pinnaclepeople.com.au). They will all be able to advise on where to do the appropriate training, such as a one-day course in Bar Skills or Food and Beverage delivery or the RSA and RCG mentioned earlier.

Hostels and Notice Boards

Youth hostels and backpackers' lodges everywhere are a goldmine of information for people working their way around the world. And nowhere are they better than in Australia. A growing number of hostel managers, especially in the major fruit and vegetable growing areas of Queensland, run their own informal job-finding service and try to put backpackers in touch with local employers. The disadvantage of being hard to contact when based in a big city hostel has largely been overcome by the mobile phone.

You may find employment in the hostels themselves of course. Stephen Psallidas describes the proliferation of work, especially on the 'Route' between Sydney and Cairns:

> ***I've met loads of people working in backpackers' hostels. Typically you work two hours a day in exchange for your bed and a meal. Work may be cleaning, driving the minibus, reception, etc. and***

is always on an informal basis so there are no worries about visas, etc. I will be jumping on the bandwagon myself soon. I'll be completely shattered from picking tomatoes so I'm going to 'work' in a hostel in Mission Beach, where the owners invited me to work when I stayed there earlier. I'm going to rest up in a beautiful place before continuing my travels, and not spend any of my hard-earned dollars.

Australia has 140 YHA hostels, many of which distribute details about employment available within their region. A free booklet listing all hostels and state offices is widely available (yha.com.au). One of the most successful groups of non-YHA backpackers' hostels is VIP Backpackers Resorts of Australia which is especially strong in New South Wales and Queensland (vipbackpackers.com). A booklet listing their Australian hostels is distributed far and wide or can be obtained from overseas by purchasing their VIP card for A$43 (£20 in the UK) which gives various discounts and benefits. Hostel beds start at $25 a night in a dorm.

The disadvantage of using hostels as your main source of jobs is that they are full of your main competition for available work. Andrew Owen was discouraged to find that every backpackers' hostel seemed to be populated almost entirely with Brits on working holidays. Also be a little suspicious of claims such as 'Plenty of farm work available for guests' since this may just be a marketing ploy on the part of the hostel (see section on Queensland).

Most Sydney hostels are well clued up on the local job scene, especially in the main backpackers' areas like King's Cross, Glebe and Coogee. In King's Cross, the Pink House at 6–8 Barncleuth Square (☎ 02 9358 1689) has good work contacts and promised to be able to get jobs for guests who stay for four weeks 'in telephone sales, IT, hospitality, labouring, gardening, clerical, etc'.

ROGER BLAKE COULD NOT AFFORD TO BE TEMPTED BY THE SOCIAL LIFE OF SYDNEY AND GOT STRAIGHT DOWN TO FINDING A JOB:

Having enjoyed the East Coast to the full, I arrived in Sydney at make or break point with $70 to my name, leaving me with no choice but to sort myself out and quickly. I found a reasonable and certainly affordable place to stay in King's Cross on day one. I found a job on day two, once again through scouring the backpacker noticeboards and making a hundred and one phone calls. A desperate backpacker is willing to turn his or her hand to anything for a dollar (no choice but). I spent six hours a day, seven days a week parading the city streets in a sandwich board handing out flyers promoting of all things, tapestry, knitting and needlecraft. This went on for about three weeks and I was one of the few who stuck it out from start to finish. I only made it through this mind-numbing, leg-cramping job because of the comedy moments and observations of life on Sydney's streets. A couple of times I saw buskers being casually thrown a $50 note and on several occasions beggars being given $10–$20 as if they were 20 cent coins. The owners took us out for a nice meal and all drinks paid for at the end of the sale. I did quite well out of it actually and didn't mind being paid to parade the city streets looking like a fool… all too easy and good fun. I did two brilliant tours of the outback paid for by my antics in Sydney.

The Cronulla Beach YHA (☎ 02 9527 7772; cronullabeachyha.com/backpacker-jobs.html) actively assists backpackers to find local jobs as waiting staff, labourers, nannies, etc. and invites them to submit an online employment request form. In the beach suburb of Coogee (pronounced Coodjee) try the Wizard of Oz at 172 Coogee Bay Road (02 9315 7876) and Sydney Beachside next door. Both are regularly contacted for casual workers. People looking for day labour regularly come in early (7.30am). Apparently it helps if you are built like a barn, especially if they are looking for someone to move grand pianos. It is also worth sticking close to reception in the evenings when employers ring with their requirements for the next day. When working like this, insist on being paid daily.

When I was researching this 14th edition of *Work Your Way*, I visited Glebe Village Backpackers in Sydney (☎ 02 9660 8878; glebevillage.com) in July 2008. While chatting to the Canadian backpacker manning the desk about job opportunities in Sydney, the hostel phone rang. As if on cue, the phone call was from an employer in North Sydney looking for a casual employee to start work the following day and my obliging informant invited me to watch her informal job agency in action. I followed her into the courtyard of the backpackers' hostel where the first person we bumped into eagerly jotted down the phone number of the employer and within five minutes had fixed up a job doing manual work for a very good hourly wage of $23.

In fruit-picking areas, certain hostels and campsites are populated almost exclusively by workers; see the relevant sections below.

The Internet

Many of the sites listed above in the section on Backpacker Agencies will provide an excellent starting point. Searching the web for employment leads is especially productive in Australia. Dozens of routes exist for finding out about job vacancies. The government's http://jobsearch.gov.au is a superb resource listing up-to-date vacancies throughout the country in an easily searchable format with contact details, normally to a local employment agency. The site seasonalwork.com.au tries to link employers and workers on the 'Great Australian Harvest Trail' (though not all jobs listed are agricultural).

Also have a look at jobaroo.com, a well-maintained work site for backpackers with pages on outback and harvest jobs; and jobmap.com.au (☎ 02 9475 7116) whose tagline is 'Number 1 Job Site for Working Holiday Travellers', with most listed job vacancies in Sydney. Travellersxpress (travellersxpress.com) owns Jobmap.com and is one of Australia's largest specialist work/travel companies with stores in Cairns, Manly, downtown Sydney, Bondi and St Kilda (Melbourne) with more stores planned for central Melbourne and Brisbane. Their recruitment division specialises in finding work for white collar working holiday travellers.

Plenty of other sites cater for more corporate job-seekers, such as seek.com.au or http://mycareer.com.au.

RURAL AUSTRALIA AND THE OUTBACK

Most of Australia's area is sparsely populated, scorched land which is known loosely as the outback. Beyond the rich farming and grazing land surrounding the largest cities, there are immense properties supporting thousands of animals and acres of crops. Many of these stations (farms) are so remote that flying is the only practical means of access. Sandra Gray describes the drawbacks of spending time on a station:

> ***Be warned! Station life can be severely boring after a while. I managed to land myself on one in the Northern Territory with very little else to do but watch the grass grow. If you have to save a lot of money quickly station work is the way to do it since there's nothing to spend it on. But make sure the place is within reasonable distance of a town or at least a roadhouse, so you have somewhere to go to let off steam occasionally.***

Your chances of getting a job as a station assistant (a jackaroo or jillaroo) will be improved if you have had experience with sheep, riding or any farming or mechanical experience. Several farmers are in the business of giving you that experience before helping you to find outback work, like the one mentioned above in the VisitOz Scheme. Shaun Armstrong thoroughly enjoyed a similar four-day Jackaroo/Jillaroo course in Queensland:

> ***I braved the jackaroo course with three other travellers (all Dutch). Horse riding, cattle mustering, ute driving, trail biking (the 'ings' were numerous) and other tasks occupied our days: wonderful hospitality ended each evening. Memorable days. Station placement was arranged afterwards as was transport if needed. I was sorry to leave really. I'd say the course did prepare me for most experiences encountered in the job. For example I was able to muster cattle on horseback with four experienced riders having spent only 15 hours in the saddle. It wasn't easy, but I did it.***

Such an outback training course is offered by the Leconfield Jackaroo and Jillaroo School in Kootingal NSW 2352 not far from Tamworth/Armidale (tel/fax 02 6769 4230; leconfieldjackaroo.com/info.html). On completion of the group course lasting 11 days and costing $950 (or $1050 through agents), successful participants will be guided in the direction of paying jobs.

Shearing is out of the question for the uninitiated. Although the post of roustabout (the job of fetching, carrying, sweeping and trimming stained bits from the fleeces) is open to the inexperienced, jobs are generally more scarce on sheep stations than they once were because of the decline in the wool industry. Check adverts in agricultural journals like The Land, part of Queensland Country Life (http://qcl.farmonline.com.au/classifieds.aspx).

Chris Miksovsky was not impressed with the assistance he received from two outback placement services in Alice Springs so resorted to cold-calling stations after looking them up in the phone book for northern Western Australia, the magical land where Baz Luhrmann's film *Australia* is set. After making more than 40 calls (and spending as many dollars on phone cards) he found a cattle station willing (or desperate enough) to take him on. He advises against exaggerating your experience: if you say you can ride a horse, the station manager will probably put you on 'Satan the Psycho-mare' your first day.

CHRIS DESCRIBES STATION LIFE AS HE EXPERIENCED IT:

The days were long (breakfast sometimes at 3am), never-ending (I worked 32 days straight once), often painful and sometimes gruesome. But then again, where else can you gallop across the outback chasing (or being chased by) a Brahman bull and sleep out under the stars listening to other jackaroos spinning yarns around a campfire, all while getting paid? Three months on the station earned me about $3000 net. It was the best thing I've done since I started travelling.

Australia's first specialist harvesting recruitment agency is flourishing: Grunt Labour Services has offices in Darwin, Katherine, Kununurra, Broome, Cairns, Bundaberg, Mareeba, Brisbane, Sydney and Melbourne (gruntlabour.com).

Some city-based employment agencies deal with jobs in country and outback areas, primarily farming, station, hotel/motel and roadhouse work. In Western Australia try the Rural Enterprises Employment Agency in a suburb of Perth (☎ 08 9398 8016; ruralenterprises.com.au). Experienced farmworkers and tractor drivers are paid $18–$25 an hour for 10–12 hour days, seven days a week at seeding time (April to June) and harvest time (October to December). Housekeeping, nannying and cooking positions are available for two or three months at a time throughout the year. The standard wage is $500+ a week after board, most of which can be saved. For work in outback roadhouses and hotels, previous experience is essential to earn $400–$500 a week after lodging. The three-month commitment enables travellers to experience the regional country towns, and save $4,000–$5,000 during their stay.

While travelling back from Ayers Rock, chef Sara Runnalls popped into an employment office in the Northern Territory town of Katherine to ask about local jobs. That day she was driven 80km to a property at Scott Creek:

> ***Here I found 15 hungry workers and a disgustingly dirty, dusty, insect haven for a kitchen. I had few fresh ingredients, ample beef, plenty of salt and tomato ketchup. My mission was to feed them five times a day with a variety of beef dishes and homemade cakes. I came up with some typically English cuisine and no complaints. I saw plenty of wildlife and enjoyed my two weeks on the cattle station. They asked me to stay the whole season but I'm here to travel.***

Anyone with experience of the horse industry should contact the agency IEP-UK in the UK (☎ 0845 347 9105; ws@iepuk.com), whose Australian partners are TEP trading as Stablemate Staff Agency, PO Box 1206, Windsor, NSW 2756 (☎ 02 4587 9770; info@tepeople.com.au) and IRE (International Rural Exchange) in rural WA (☎ 08 9064 7411; ire.org.au).

Stablemate deal exclusively with placing equestrian and thoroughbred staff but are sometimes able to assist people with limited experience with horses if they want to work in an ancillary position or as a nanny, general farm assistant or even in unskilled harvest work sometimes. People over 18 with a year's practical experience should enquire of the UK office about the International Exchange Programme in Australia. An Adelaide-based firm, Bibber International, oversees exchanges specifically for the wine industry (☎ 08 8227 1955; bibber.com.au).

Although you may not be forced to eat witchetty grubs for tea, there are some obvious disadvantages to life in the outback, viz. the isolation, the heat and to some extent the dangers. Even if you have had experience of living in the rural areas of Europe, it may be hard to adjust to life in the outback. Lots of towns have nothing more than a post office and small shop combined, a hotel (pub) and petrol pump. The sun's heat must not be underestimated. It is important to cover your head with a cowboy hat or a towel and to carry a large water bottle with you. Droughts are increasingly common; in fact the Australia-wide drought in 2008/9 is thought to be the longest and worst on record, which led to the terrible bush fires in Victoria in the summer of 2009. Be prepared to cope with severe water restrictions.

Finally there is the ever-present hazard of spiders and snakes which Tricia Clancy describes: '*The hay barn attracted mice and the mice attracted snakes, so whenever we entered the barn we had to make a loud rumpus to frighten them away. Huntsmen spiders proliferated. These great tarantula-like creatures were not poisonous, however it was still frightening when they emerged from behind the picture frames in the evenings.*' Once you get into the habit of checking inside your boots and behind logs for snakes, and under the loo seat for redback spiders, the dangers are minimised. The outback is often a rough male-dominated world, and not suited to fragile personalities.

Conservation Volunteers

Several organisations give visitors a chance to experience the Australian countryside or bush. The main not-for-profit conservation organisation in Australia is called, predictably enough, Conservation Volunteers Australia (CVA) and it places volunteers from overseas in its 'Conservation Experience' projects, though the charges are quite steep. Sample projects include tree planting, erosion and salinity control, seed collection from indigenous plants, building and maintaining bushwalking tracks, etc. Overseas volunteers are welcome to become involved by booking a four-week or six-week package which includes food and accommodation and all project-related transport at a cost of A$1,037 and $1,500 respectively (which works out at less than $37 a day for accommodation, food and transport). Further details are available from the National Head Office in Ballarat (☎ 03 5330 2600; conservationvolunteers.com.au).

DANIELE ARENA FROM ITALY STUMBLED ACROSS AN INDEPENDENT PROJECT ON THE COAST OF QUEENSLAND THAT APPEALED TO HIM:

One of the most amazing experiences I had in Oz was the time I was volunteering at the Turtle Rookery in Mon Repos Beach. We could pitch our tent for free, and gave a small contribution of $5 a day for food. The work was to patrol the beach waiting for nesting turtles and, when they come in, to tag and measure them and the nest. This goes on between November and March. I was fortunate enough to get this by chance but normally there's quite a few people who want to do it, so you should probably contact the Queensland Parks and Wildlife Service for info.

For further information, contact the Mon Repos Conservation Park on ☎ 07 4159 1652.

The World Wide Opportunities on Organic Farms organisation is very active in Australia and has a huge supply of unpaid work opportunities. WWOOF headquarters are near Buchan in Victoria (☎ 03 5155 0218; wwoof.com.au) though their publicity is widely distributed through backpacker haunts. The Australian WWOOF Book that they publish contains about 1,500 addresses throughout Australia of organic farmers and hosts looking for short or long term voluntary help or to promote cultural exchange. The list is sold with accident insurance at a cost of A$60 within Australia, A$70 for a couple ($65 and $75 including overseas postage).

A free internet-based exchange of work-for-keep volunteers can be found at helpx.net where nearly 600 Australian hosts are listed.

Before becoming a volunteer with CVA, Susan Gray joined WWOOF Australia and worked on several farms on a work-for-keep basis. *'They are all growing food organically and usually in beautiful countryside. Most are very keen to show you around and show off their home region to you. The work was as hard as you wanted it to be, but about four hours of work were expected. I usually did more as I enjoyed it, and I learned a lot from those experiences.'*

Interesting research projects take place throughout Australia and some may be willing to include unpaid staff looking for work experience. For example a rainforest research station in northern Queensland operated by the Australian Tropical Research Foundation (PMB 5, Cape Tribulation, Qld 4873; ☎ 07 4098 0063; austrop.org.au) welcomes 50 volunteers a year who normally stay two or three weeks, though extensions are possible. Volunteers assist in research and station activities such as radio-tracking bats, counting figs, stomping grass for forest regeneration, constructing buildings, digging holes, and running the Bat House visitor centre. Volunteers are asked to pay US$20 a day to cover food and accommodation.

Wildcare is a Tasmanian NGO (wildcaretas.org.au) which anyone can join for just $25 and then request a volunteer placement, from monitoring orange-bellied parrots to becoming a temporary caretaker on a remote southern island.

The Australian Institute of Marine Science (AIMS) at Cape Ferguson near Townsville (☎ 07 4753 4260; aims.gov.au) maintains an Employment Register for people who have expressed an interest in short-term casual work up to three months or temporary employment up to a year. Opportunities are mainly open to graduates and undergraduates looking for work experience in marine research.

Fruit Picking

In the rich agricultural land between the coastal ribbon of urban development and the outback, a multitude of crops is grown: grapes around Adelaide and in the Hunter Valley of New South Wales, tropical fruit on the Queensland coast and north of Perth, apples in the southwest part of Western Australia and in Tasmania, etc. Although fruit farms may be more fertile than the outback, the same considerations as to isolation, heat and dangers from the fauna hold true. The standard hours for a fruit picker working in the heat are approximately 6am-6pm with two or three hours off in the middle of the day.

During certain harvests, the farmers are desperate for labour and put out appeals over the radio, on the notice boards of backpackers' hostels and via harvest employment agencies. On one Queensland farm where Mary Anne Mackle from Northern Ireland worked, the farmer had to bring in a team of prisoners to finish off the cucumber harvest since there was such a shortage of pickers. If you find yourself falling behind your fellow-workers during the first few days of the harvest, you should console yourself that some may be professionals who have been following harvests round the country for years.

Recent visa changes that allow working holiday makers to work for up to six months (increased from three) for one employer mean that farmers now want to hire backpackers who are willing to work for longer periods. They are not usually interested in considering people who are available for just a couple of weeks.

But if you are prepared to stay for a spell on a farm, opportunities abound. A short surf of the internet will soon take you to a huge amount of harvesting information. The National Harvest Labour Information Service based in Mildura, Victoria (☎ 1800 062 332; nhlis@madec.edu.au; jobsearch.gov.au/harvesttrail) is funded by the federal government and therefore free to users. Alternative sources of vacancies are harvesthotlineaustralia.com.au and goharvest.com.

Harvest seasons are often diverse: crops ripen first in Queensland and finish in Tasmania as you move further away from the equator. Even the two major grape harvests take place consecutively rather than simultaneously. For easy reference, we have included tables showing crops, regions and times of harvest (omitting grapes, which appear on a separate chart) for the most important fruit-growing states of New South Wales, Victoria, South Australia, Western Australia and Queensland.

Quite often farmers will offer a shack or caravan for little or no money. Not all fruit farmers can supply accommodation, however, so serious job-seekers carry a tent. On the other hand backpackers' hostels are never far away and in the main picking districts organise minibus transport between hostels and farms. Campervans are of course very versatile and comfortable but expensive to run and expensive to buy.

MARY ANNE MACKLE PARTICIPATED IN A NUMBER OF HARVESTS DURING HER WORKING HOLIDAY AND OFFERS THESE TIPS TO UNSUSPECTING FRUIT PICKERS:

1. *Although a car is not essential, it is often necessary in looking for work, and then getting to town to shop.*
2. *Be prepared for extremes of temperature. Although it may be in the 80s during the day, the nights are often very cold.*
3. *Don't expect any nightlife. A typical evening for us involved showering, washing dishes, making dinner, reading, writing and chatting with fellow fruit pickers.*

4. *Forget about vanity. You will stink at all times even after a shower. Your socks will never be the same again and your skin won't like the sunblock and build-up of dirt either.*
5. *Forget about modesty. Don't expect to have the use of toilet facilities out in the fields.*
6. *On an optimistic note, you will be a fitter person and, if things go well, a wealthier one too. You can then go off and take a dive course on the Great Barrier Reef, snorkel in Coral Bay, canoe down Katherine Gorge, get drunk in Darwin, hike in national parks, swim in waterfalls, until your money runs out and you start all over again.*

Mary Anne's conclusion is that harvesting is certainly preferable to packing videos in a warehouse in Sydney or selling hotdogs for $15 an hour.

The Grape Harvest

Australian wines have made a startling impact on the rest of the world as the volume, quality and consumption increase each year. Regardless of their quality, the important fact for itinerant workers is that there is a large quantity of grapes to be picked. The main centres for grape-picking are the Mildura region of Victoria, the Riverland of South Australia (between Renmark and Waikerie) and the Hunter Valley of New South Wales (around Pokolbin and Muswellbrook), though grapes are grown in every state including Tasmania. Detailed tables are set out below. The harvests usually get under way some time in February and last through March or into April. If you work solidly for six weeks, it is possible to earn more than $2,000.

Picking for a winery is easiest; it doesn't matter too much if the grapes are squashed or there are a few leaves left in (a blockie would have a fit if he read that). Picking for drying means the grapes shouldn't be squashed and picking for market (i.e. table grapes) demands extreme care and is usually paid as wages or at a higher rate per box.

The fairest way to pick is by weight. The only time you are likely to get a break in the afternoon is when it is too hot to leave the grapes out in the sun, though ads noticed in 2009 (for sultana pickers in Irymple near Mildura) included a promise of 'smokos', i.e. breaks.

Certainly the demand for pickers is intense in many regions. After deciding that the Sydney employment scene was unremittingly grim, Henry Pearce phoned some employment agencies in mid-February and decided that Griffith in New South Wales was the best bet. When he arrived, he was delighted to see that the job board was full of grape-picking jobs. He was hustled into the harvest office, allocated to a farmer and driven to a farm in the region, where he began work the next morning. The International Hostel at 112 Binya Street in Griffith (☎ 02 6964 4236; info@griffithinternational.com.au) helps with finding work.

Across the River Murray the situation is the same around Mildura in Victoria, the grape capital of the area. Armin Birrer reported from the town of Cardross that 300 picking jobs were advertised in the local papers and on roadside signs. This is the area to which agencies in Melbourne are most likely to send you if you arrive in January/February. The Western Australian wine industry is flourishing. Some vacancies for vineyard work between October and January in Margaret River and Busselton are filled through the Margaret River agency Down to Earth (☎ 08 9758 7074) or Bacchus Contracting in Busselton (☎ 08 9753 1338). The starting wage is $16 an hour.

GRAPE HARVESTS	
SOUTH AUSTRALIA	**DATES OF HARVEST**
Clare-Watervale	February-April
Barossa Valley	February-April
Adelaide and Southern Vales	February-March
Coonawarra	February-April
Langhorne Creek	February-April
Riverland (Waikerie, Berri, Loxton, Renmark)	February-April
NEW SOUTH WALES	
Orchard Hills	late Jan-mid March
Camden	early February-mid March
Wedderburn	mid February-mid March
Nolong	late February-April
Orange	March-April
Mudgee	late February-April
Hunter Valley (Pokolbin, Bulga, Denman, Broke, Muswellbrook)	early February-March
Murrumbidgee Irrigation area (Griffith, Leeton)	mid February-March
Dareton	Jan-April
Curlwaa	Mar-April
Buronga	February-June
Mid-Murray (Koraleigh, Goodnight)	late February-April
Corowa	February-March
VICTORIA	
Goulburn Valley	February-March
Swan Hill	February-March
Lilydale	February-March
Mildura/Robinvale	February-March
Great Western-Avoca	February-March
Drumborg	February-March
Glenrowan-Milawa	February-March
Rutherglen	February-March
WESTERN AUSTRALIA	
Swan Valley (near Perth)	February-April
Margaret River	February-April
Mount Barker	February-April

The Apple Harvest

Although apple-picking is notoriously slow going for the beginner, you can usually pick up enough speed within a few days to make it rewarding. Seasonal pickers are needed in Western Australia throughout the year but especially between November and May, with the peak of the apple harvest falling in the summer. In harvests where the conditions seem at the outset to be unattractive, it is not hard to get work especially when it is the time of year (normally February to May) when students return to college and the weather is getting colder.

Many travellers flock to the Western Australian harvest that takes place around Donnybrook, Manjimup and Pemberton. Brook Lodge Backpacker Accommodation on 3 Bridge St, Donnybrook (☎ 08 9731 1520; brooklodge.com.au) maintains a register of job vacancies in the area. It can take between a couple of hours and seven to ten days to find work locally, depending on the time of year. The season starts in November with thinning out the immature apples and plums and progresses to stone fruit picking December to March, though apple picking carries on until July. Other crops are grown in the vicinity such as tomatoes (picked January to March) and pears (February to April). During the picking season, a contract rate is the norm, ranging from $600 to $800 for a six-day week. Otherwise a straight hourly wage is paid of $17.60. Transport to work is arranged by Brook Lodge.

Climatic conditions will determine what else you take in addition to a long novel to keep you amused until work materialises. High summer temperatures mean that you will need to take water, sunblock and a brimmed hat into the orchards. Later on warm clothes will come in handy as Armin Birrer discovered one chilly autumn: *'The only problem with the south of WA is that the wet season starts in May which lasts till August. And as the season progresses it gets colder and colder and more and more miserable.'*

Mary Anne Mackle spent six weeks picking in Manjimup and found that being paid by the bin was a great motivator to work long hard hours. She and her companion started on a meagre three bins a day but by the end they were filling 16 a day, which shows what a difference some practice can make. By the time she finished, her clothes were in shreds and her body not far behind, but she had saved several thousand dollars.

Tasmania is not known as the 'Apple Island' for its shape alone. The apple harvest takes place between March and early May, though other fruit harvests start at the beginning of November with strawberries and apple thinning, followed by cherries and blueberries in late December. Grape picking is available in March/April. The work is available in the Huon region around Cygnet and Geeveston not far south of Hobart. Like many before him, Robert Abblett recommends Huon Valley Backpackers, on Sandhill Road in Cradoc (☎ 03 6295 1551; huonvalley@tassie.net.au): *'As the main accommodation in the area, the hostel finds work for guests and provides transport too. I spent two months working hard for several different orchards, as the crop was intermittent. With previous experience, I saved £1,000. I was put with 20 other strange people for the whole season. The owners (bless 'em) thought I would have a calming influence on them because of my age. No chance.'* Working travellers are charged $175 per week and transport/shopping costs are an extra $25 per week.

Other Harvests

From asparagus to zucchini there is an abundance of crops to be picked from one end of Australia to the other, and the energetic itinerant picker can do very nicely. Australia has such an enormous agricultural economy that there will always be jobs. Gordon Mitchell from Aberdeen is just one Briton who has worked out a profitable route:

> ***I've been picking fruit in Australia for a few years. I make the best money between November and April/May, starting at Young NSW picking cherries. When they finish I do the smaller cherry harvest in Orange NSW, then on to Shepparton Victoria in early January for the pear picking. When the sultanas start in Mildura in early February I do them, though most people stay in Shepparton to finish the pears and apples. This takes me to early or mid-March when the apples start in Orange and finish in late April or early May. Sometimes it's very hectic but that's when the picking is good.***

Queensland

As you travel north the produce, like the weather, gets more tropical so that citrus, pineapples, bananas and mangoes grow in profusion in the north, while stone fruits, apples and potatoes grow in the Darling Downs, 220km inland from Brisbane. In the tropics there are not always definite harvest seasons since crops grow year round.

Work in the Queensland harvests is strongly monopolised by the hostels. Farmers for the most part rely on hostel managers to supply them with a workforce, making it hard to fix up a job directly with a farmer and accommodation on farms is rare. Shuttle transport between hostel and farms is often laid on. Job-seekers are not always in a strong position to ensure they get paid a decent wage and pay a fair price for transport and accommodation.

About 400km north of Brisbane, the agricultural and rum-producing centre of Bundaberg absorbs a great many travelling workers. All the hostels in town advertise help with employment including Federal Backpackers (☎ 07 4153 3711; federalbackpackers@hotmail.com) and City Centre Backpackers (07 4151 3501) both on Bourbong St. The hostel at 64 Barolin St (☎ 07 4151 6097) calls itself the Bundy Workers and Divers Hostel, though it attracts more workers than divers. Bundaberg is such a magnet for working travellers that it is often bursting at the seams. Bridgid Seymour-East was not impressed with the scene: *'There are too many hostels and too few jobs to go around. Hostels take about 100 people each so lots of desperate people all together. Most people get only one or two days of work a week, just enough to pay for their hostel bed and food. You cannot choose your jobs and if you quit or get fired they might not give you a job for another week.'*

The town of Bowen, centre of a fruit and vegetable-growing region (especially tomatoes) 600km south of Cairns, is another well known destination for aspiring pickers. Julian Graham spent part of his working holiday in Australia as manager of Barnacles Backpackers in Bowen, which sounds an excellent place to find out about work:

> ***Part of my duties consisted of finding work for travellers at the many local farms. All sorts of picking and packing are available and Bowen is a superb place to recover considerable funds. My girlfriend and I arrived broke and left with enough money to fly to Tasmania for the Sydney–Hobart race and finance a month's travelling in Tas. Anyone arriving in Bowen should do themselves a favour and go straight to Barnacles where they will find you work (May–December) and make you more welcome than anywhere else in the town by a large margin.***

One working hostel in Bowen is Reefers at the Beach (☎ 07 4786 4199; reefers.com.au/work.htm). In fact all the hostels in Bowen cater for working travellers. As always, count on paying $140 a week for a dorm bed, or $150 a week in a double.

The farmers usually provide a minibus once the picking really gets going, which costs a couple of dollars from Bowen. Otherwise a bicycle would be handy. If you're job-hunting farm-to-farm, go out on the Bootooloo or Collinsville Roads or to the Delta or Euri Creek areas. Apparently the tail end of the harvest in November can be a good time to show up, when lots of seasonal workers are beginning to drift south. If the farmers are desperate enough, they pay premium rates, sometimes even double.

Further north, Cardwell, Innisfail and Tully offer work in banana and sometimes sugar plantations. Farmers around Tully (the wettest place in Australia) organise transport between town and the properties. If you pay for two weeks' accommodation upfront plus a $150 deposit at the purpose-built working hostel Banana Barracks at 50 Butler St (☎ 07 4068 0455; bananabarracks.com/work.html), they will do their best to find you work. Henry Pearce describes his gruelling job as a banana cutter in October:

> ***The bananas all grew together on a single stem which could weigh up to 60kg. The farmer cut into the trunk to weaken it and, once I had pulled the fruit down onto my shoulder, he cut the stem and I staggered off to place them on a 'nearby' trailer. The work was physically shattering and the presence of large frogs and rats inside the bunch (thankfully no snakes) jumping out at the last minute didn't do anything to increase my enjoyment. We were paid by the hour and worked an eight hour day, five days a week which was standard for the area.***

Working with Queensland fruits seems to be an activity fraught with danger. If you decide to pick pineapples, you have to wear long-sleeved shirts and jeans (despite the sizzling heat between January and April) as protection from the prickles and spines. Caroline Perry advises anyone who packs rock melons to wear gloves; otherwise the abrasive skin rips your hands to shreds.

Southern Queensland is also a good destination. Head for Stanthorpe almost on the NSW border in November for peach and pear picking, and January/February for tomato picking.

New South Wales

The southern part of the state around Wagga Wagga is known as the Riverina. Seasonal work opportunities can be found in Batlow, Jugiong, Leeton and Young as well as Darlington Point, Gundagai, Hay and so on.

The asparagus harvest at Jugiong on the Hume Highway northwest of Canberra attracts many seasonal pickers, as does the cherry harvest around Young half an hour north of Jugiong, which starts as the asparagus finishes. The packing season is a long one from about late September to at least mid-November. The work is notoriously back-breaking but can be lucrative. Whereas some have been disappointed with working conditions and earnings in the cherry harvest near Young between mid-November and Christmas, others recommend it. The unpredictable weather and piecework pay rates can make things difficult.

Of all the many picking jobs that Henry Pearce found, the best money was earned working on onions around Griffith, where he and his girlfriend saved an impressive $5,000 in ten weeks between early January and March. You have to be lucky to find work in this harvest particularly if you don't have your own transport. Ask at all the onion-packing sheds in Griffith.

Victoria

The tragic bush fires of February 2009 did not destroy any fruit farms, but only burnt the edges of some vineyards, so the demand for harvest help in 2009 was as great in Victoria as ever. The summer fruit harvests in northern Victoria annually attract many participants on working holidays. The best time to arrive is mid to late January and work should continue until the end of March. The National Harvest Labour Information Service mentioned above now carries out most of the recruitment in Northern Victoria. CVGT Employment and Training are the government's contracted provider of recruitment services with offices in Cobram and Shepparton, and a harvest hotline ☎ 1300 724788.

Mooroopna is just outside Shepparton and is a good place to look for work. Ask in the pub about tomato-picking possibilities in February and March. You might want to buy a second-hand bicycle from the shop on the main street of Shepparton to get around the area. R J Cornish & Co in Cobram are major employers too (☎ 03 5872 2055; picking@rjcornish.com; rjcornish.com) though in 2009 they had far more applicants than vacancies. Plunkett Orchards in Ardmona in the Goulburn Valley (☎ 03 5829 0015; plunkettorchards.com.au) and McNab & Son also in Ardmona (☎ 03 5829 0016; fruitpicking.com.au) are also worth a try. Pickers coming to the area can stay at the Cobram Willows Caravan Park on the Murray Valley Highway (☎ 03 5872 1074) where they will meet lots of people earning $60–$100 a day between December and March. The hourly rate for fruit grading (for instance at Plunkett Orchards) is in the range $16–$20.

In the northwestern corner of the state, Mildura (mentioned above as a centre for grape-growing) is a major agricultural district and Cardross across the river is also a promising destination. Work is available virtually year-round (May is the slowest month) due to the sunny climate and epic irrigation schemes. Contact the MADEC Harvest Jobs Australia office in Mildura (☎ 03 5022 1797; MADEC.edu.au). A high proportion of the travellers staying in Mildura's hostels take advantage of the job-finding and transport-providing services of places like Working Hostels Mildura (27 Chaffey Avenue; ☎ 0447 WORKER/967537; workinghostels.com.au) where the majority of guests are working or looking for work. Although harvesting work is often not hard to get, some find it hard to make any money. The pear crates may look quite small at the outset but will soon seem unfillable with mysterious false bottoms. Many eager first-timers do not realise how hard the work will be physically, and give up before their bodies acclimatise. But you should have faith that your speed will increase fairly rapidly.

South Australia

The Riverland region of South Australia (not to be confused with the Riverina in NSW) consists of Renmark, Loxton and Waikerie but is centred on Berri where most of the backpacker accommodation and job agencies like Select and Rivskills and the harvest Labour Office are located. In recent years work has been available all year round due to the expansion of the wine and citrus industries, though the ongoing drought in the Murray Basin has resulted in fewer jobs while the number of job-seekers coming to the area has increased. Berri Backpackers (☎ 08 8582 3144; berribackpackers.com.au) gets positive reviews from long-stay residents. Daniele Arena called this hostel 'the most wonderful probably in the whole world' since he greatly enjoyed their regular barbecues for $5.

According to an earlier report from Bridgid Seymour-East who also loved this hostel, landing some work is a bit of a free-for-all:

> ***Whoever answers the phone first gets a job first, which can seem a bit daunting at first (survival of the fittest). We started on citrus picking for a big company Yandilla Park. Whilst the contract rate is high, you don't get that many hours in the long run because you can't pick citrus until the fruit is dry on the tree. Often you can't start picking until 11am or 12 noon, which can be very frustrating. But it gives you enough money to survive until the vine work begins. At the end of June I got a job cutting canes which involves taking a cutting from the grape vines, trimming it to size and bundling it in bunches of 100. Whilst extremely boring, I never made less than $120 a day after tax and on good days $200, so I was getting pay cheques of $800–$900 a week.***

The biggest employers in the Berri area are:

Angas Park: ☎ 08 8561 0800; angaspark.com.au; apricots and peaches are picked December to April; men only; 7 days a week, 10 hours a day; extra money paid at weekends; no days off (or you're fired).

Simarloo: ☎ 08 8583 8269; apricots and plums picked in Lyrup December to March; contract work (i.e. per bin).

AgriExchange (formerly Yandilla Park): Renmark; ☎ 08 8586 1200; agriexchange.com.au/empop.html; peak period April–November.

In addition to these big companies, there are at least 1,000 small family blocks which need helpers. Other accommodation for pickers is available on campsites.

Nearer Adelaide, a major employer of travellers and casual fruit pickers is Torrens Valley Orchards (Forreston Rd, Gumeracha; ☎ 08 8389 1405; tvo@hotkey.net.au), located just south of the Barossa Valley wine region and only a cheap bus ride from the state capital less than an hour away. Cherry picking and packing takes place in December/January for up to 25 backpackers at a time, while others are needed year round to plant trees, do pruning, maintenance and office work. Accommodation is available on-site for about eight workers.

It seems almost a contradiction in terms but Nomads on Murray describes itself as a 'funky working hostel'. It is located west of Berri on the Sturt Highway (☎ 1800 665166).

Western Australia

There are over 100 vegetable and banana plantations around the cities of Geraldton and Carnarvon north of Perth, many of which are very short of pickers in the winter when they are busy supplying the markets of Perth. The tomato harvest lasts from early August until mid-November, with the month of September being the easiest time to find work. The banana harvest starts in October, but there is casual work available anytime between April and November. One way of meeting farmers is to go to the warehouses or packing depots where growers come to drop off their produce.

Agricultural development around Kununurra in the extreme north of the state is extensive, and every traveller passing through seems to stop to consider the possibility of working in the banana, melon, citrus or vegetable harvests. Travellers are regularly hired during the first part of 'The Dry' (the dry season lasts from May to July) and beyond. If you can't fix up work through the Youth Hostel or the Backpackers Resort hostel, contact Ord River Bananas and Oasis Bananas. For the melon harvest between May and October contact Bluey's Outback Farm (☎ 08 9168 2177; blueysoutbackfarm.com.au); the hourly pay for pickers is $16.49.

AUSTRALIAN HARVESTS

CROP	NEW SOUTH WALES	DATES OF HARVEST
Strawberries	Glenorie and Campbelltown	Sep-Dec
Cherries	Orange	Nov–Jan
	Young	Oct–Dec
Peaches and Nectarines	Glenorie	Oct–Jan
	Campbelltown	Nov–Jan
	Orange	Feb–Mar
	Bathurst	Jan–Mar
	Leeton & Griffith, Forbes	Feb–Apr
	Young	Feb–Mar
Plums	Glenorie	Nov–Jan
	Orange	Jan–Mar
	Young	Jan–Mar
Apricots	Leeton & Griffith	Dec–Jan
	Kurrajong	Nov
Apples and Pears	Oakland, Glenorie and Bilpin	Jan–Apr
	Armidale	Feb–May
	Orange	Feb–May
	Bathurst	Mar–May
	Forbes	Feb–Apr

CROP	NEW SOUTH WALES	DATES OF HARVEST
	Batlow	Feb–May
	Griffith & Leeton	Jan–Apr
	Young	Mar–Apr
Oranges (Valencia)	Outer Sydney	Sep–Feb
	Riverina, Mid-Murray	Sep–Mar
	Narromine	Sep–Feb
	Leeton	Dec–Jan
Lemons	Outer Sydney, Riverina, Mid-Murray, Coomealla	Jul–Oct
Grapefruits	Mid-Murray	Nov–Apr
	Curlwaa	Jun–Feb
Asparagus	Dubbo, Bathurst, Cowra, Jugiong	Sep–Dec
Wheat	Narrabri, Walgett	Nov–Dec
Cotton	Warren & Nevertire, Wee Waa	Nov–Mar
Onions	Griffith	Nov–Mar
Corn de-tasselling	Narromine	Jan
CROP	**SOUTH AUSTRALIA**	**DATES OF HARVEST**
Apricots	Riverland (Waikerie, Barmera, Berri, Loxton, Renmark)	Dec–Jan
Peaches	Riverland	Jan–Feb
Pumpkins and	Riverland	May–Jul
Oranges	Riverland	Jun–Apr
CROP	**VICTORIA**	**DATES OF HARVEST**
Pears and Peaches	Shepparton, Ardmona, Mooroopna	Jan–Mar
	Kyabram	
	Invergordon, Cobram	
Tomatoes	Shepparton/Mooroopna, Tatura	Jan–Apr
	Kyabram	
	Echuca, Tongala	
	Rochester	
	Swan Hill	
	Elmore	
Tobacco	Ovens and Kiewa Valley	Feb–Apr
Potatoes	Warragul, Neerim	Feb–May
Cherries	Silvan, Lilydale, Warburton, Lilydale	Nov–Dec
Berries	Silvan, Wandin, Monbulk, Macclesfield, Hoddles Creek, Daylesford	Nov–Feb
Apples and Pears	Myrtleford	Mar–May
	Goulburn Valley	Jan–Apr
	Mornington Peninsula	Mar–May
Flowers and Bulbs	Emerald	Jan–Dec
CROP	**WESTERN AUSTRALIA**	**DATES OF HARVEST**
Apples and Pears	Donnybrook, Manjimup, Balingup, Pemberton	Mar–Jun
Oranges	Bindoon, Lower Chittering	Aug–Sept

(continued)

CROP	WESTERN AUSTRALIA	DATES OF HARVEST
Oranges	Harvey	Jun–Jul
Lemons and	Bindoon, Lower Chittering	Nov–Feb
Grapefruit	Harvey	
Apricots, Peaches and Plums	Kalamunda, Walliston, Pickering, Brook	Dec–Mar
Tomatoes, vegetables	Carnarvon, Geraldton	Aug–Nov
Bananas	Carnarvon	Oct
Melons, Bananas, etc.	Kununurra/Lake Argyle	May–Oct

CROP	QUEENSLAND	DATES OF HARVEST
Bananas	Tully	October
Tomatoes	Bowen	Aug–Nov
Peaches and Plums	Stanthorpe	Dec–Mar
Watermelons	Bundaberg	Nov–Dec
Potatoes	Lockyer Valley	Oct–Dec
Onions	Lockyer Valley	Sep–Oct
Pineapples	Nambour, Maryborough,	Jan–Apr
	Bundaberg, Yeppoon	
Apples	Stanthorpe	Feb–Mar
Citrus	Gayndah, Mundubbera	May–Sep
Strawberries	Redlands	Jul–Nov
Mangoes	Bowen	Nov–Dec
	Mareeba	Dec–Jan
Cucumbers, etc.	Ayr	May–Nov
Courgettes	Mackay	Aug–Sep

INDUSTRY

Construction and Labouring

Darwin has always been a mecca for drifters, deportees and drop-outs looking for labouring work, though there are fewer job adverts in the Territory's papers than there once were. As the rains recede in May, the human deluge begins and competition for jobs is intense. It is better to be around at the end of the Wet (April) to fix something up beforehand.

Tradesmen of all descriptions usually find it easy to get work in Australia, especially if they bring their papers and tools. Plumbers, electricians and carpenters have been having a field day, especially in Sydney. A pair of steel-capped boots would also be a useful accessory.

TOURISM AND CATERING

This category of employment might include anything from cooking on tourist boats in the Whitsunday Islands in Queensland, to acting as a temporary warden in a Tasmanian youth hostel. You might find yourself serving beer at a roadhouse along the nearly uninhabited road through the Australian north-west or serving at a Sizzler diner (which claims to have invented 'casual dining in Australia'). Whatever the job, expect to present yourself as a serious candidate. According to Ken Smith who noticed plenty of 'Help Wanted' signs posted in restaurant and shop windows in Melbourne, '*even a job washing dishes usually requires several months relevant experience*'.

Casual catering wages both in the cities and in remote areas are higher than the equivalent British wage. The award rate for casual waiting staff in New South Wales starts at $17.50 an hour, with weekend loadings on Saturdays (25%), Sundays (50%) and holidays. Although tipping was not traditionally practised in Australia, it is gradually becoming more common and waiting staff in trendy city establishments can expect to augment their basic wage to some extent.

Standards tend to be fairly high especially in popular tourist haunts. A common practice among restaurant bosses in popular places from Bondi Beach to the Sunshine Coast is to give a job-seeker an hour's trial or a trial shift and decide at the end whether or not to employ them. Stephen Psallidas was taken aback when he approached a hospitality employment agency in Cairns: *'I was in Cairns in April and thought I'd have little trouble getting work. But though I had a visa and experience, I had no references, having worked as a waiter in Greece, where they wouldn't know a reference if one walked up and said "Hi, I'm a reference", so I was doomed from the start. The agency told me that if I'd had references they could have given me work immediately. Curses.'*

Queensland

Because of Queensland's attractions for all visitors to Australia, the competition for jobs comes mostly from travellers, who are more interested in having a good time than in earning a high wage. The pay is generally so low in seasonal jobs in the Queensland tourist industry that the work does not appeal to many Australians, since they can earn nearly as much on the dole. When employers need to fill a vacancy, they tend to hire whomever is handy that day, rather than sift through applications. For example if you phone from Sydney to enquire about possibilities, the advice will normally be to come and see.

If you want a live-in position, you should try the coastal resorts such as Surfers Paradise and Noosa Heads and islands all along the Queensland coast where the season lasts from March, after the cyclones, until Christmas. If Cairns is choc-a-bloc with job-seekers try the huge resort of Palm Cove just north of the city. Many of the small islands along the Barrier Reef are completely given over to tourist complexes. You might make initial enquiries at employment offices on the mainland for example in Proserpine, Cannonvale, Mackay or Townsville, though normally you will have to visit an island in person (and therefore pay for the ferry).

Among the many possibilities are the Kingfisher Bay Resort and Eurong Beach Resort on Fraser Island (☎ 07 4120 3381; kingfisherbay.com); a manager wrote to stay that they have a high demand for food and beverage staff and that vacancies are listed on their website. Also try the Heron Island Tourist Resort.

Voyages Hotels and Resorts dominates the upscale resort market of Australia, operating resorts on Heron Island, Lizard Island, Bedarra, Brampton and Dunk Islands plus Silky Oaks Lodge in the Daintree Rainforest of North Queensland, Wrotham Park Station in the Far North Gulf region and others. They employ large numbers of seasonal staff, mainly with relevant experience in hospitality, but also international travellers at busy periods usually for a minimum of three months. Their employment website (voyages.com.au/corporate/careers) includes detailed fact sheets on living and working in each of their resorts including number of employees, perks and accommodation (most resorts charge from $50 a week for staff accommodation plus $80+ for meals) and contact details for job-seekers in each resort, e.g. careers@heron.voyages.com.au. You could also try in advance Rydges Hotels and Resorts such as the Capricorn Resort and the Oasis Resort on the Sunshine Coast (rydges.com/about/jobs.asp).

Tourist development along the Queensland coast has been rampant, especially with an eye to the Japanese market. Anyone who has travelled in Japan or who has a smattering of Japanese might have the edge over the competition (unless the competition happens to be a Japanese working holidaymaker of whom there are many in Cairns and elsewhere). James Blackman, who hadn't studied any Oriental languages, describes how he got his job at a resort in the Whitsunday Islands:

> ***Giving up on Airlie Beach I went to Hamilton Island to search for work. I went to practically every establishment and was turned away. However I persevered and the second last place gave me a job as a kitchen hand in a restaurant which was on the beach front. Lots of different people staffed the resort and most were quite friendly, always asking, 'How're ya going?'***

Roger Blake was lucky in Airlie Beach when the initial fortnight of work as a handyman, gardener, labourer and jack-of-all-trades at some swanky apartments was extended to six:

> ***I saved a tidy sum and figured I had enough to do the East Coast. I loved Airlie Beach and not without good reasons. Besides the obvious – the climate, crystal clear and turquoise Whitsunday waters and stunning ocean views – being a familiar face in this one-street town also had perks. I made good friends with many locals and was treated as one. For example I qualified for $2 beers at a popular bar which otherwise charges absurd resort prices.***

The Gold Coast has a number of theme parks with opportunities for casual work during holiday periods, mainly in food and beverage and retail service. It will be difficult to save any money since wages are not high and you will have to pay for transport between a hostel in town. Check for adverts in the *Gold Coast Bulletin* or in the Brisbane *Courier Mail* on Saturdays. Alternatively contact Warner Bros Theme Parks which recruits centrally for Movie World, Sea World, Wet 'n' Wild Water World and Australian Outback Spectacular The contact address for the Human Resources Department is Warner Village Theme Parks, Pacific Motorway, Oxenford, Queensland 4210 (hr@wvtp.com.au; myfuncareers.com.au). Many short-term vacancies occur in the holiday periods and are ideal for backpackers, i.e. Easter, a four-week period in September during school holidays and four to six weeks during the Christmas holidays.

Another big employer is Dreamworld in Coomera which welcomes applications by post or in person only.

Diving and Watersports

One of the larger employers is the dive industry. Although not many visitors would have the qualifications which got Ian Mudge a job as Dive Master on *Nimrod III* operating out of Cookstown (i.e. qualified mechanical engineer, diver and student of Japanese), his assessment of opportunities for mere mortals is heartening:

> ***Anyone wishing to try their luck as a hostess could do no worse than to approach all the dive operators with live-aboard boats such as Mike Ball Water Sports in Townsville, Down Under Dive, etc. 'Hosties' make beds, clean cabins and generally tidy up. Culinary skills and an ability to speak Japanese would be definite pluses. A non-diver would almost certainly be able to fix up some free dive lessons and thus obtain their basic Open Water Diver qualification while being paid to do so. Normally females only are considered for hostie jobs.***

The sailing season in Sydney lasts from October to April with the peak in December. There is no point in looking for work in the Antipodean winter. To take one example Northside Sailing School at Spit Bridge in the Sydney suburb of Mosman (☎ 02 9969 3972; northsidesailing.com.au/employment.htm) offers casual instructing work during school holidays to travellers who have experience in teaching dinghy sailing especially to kids. There is often a shortage of staff in early September though opportunities would not be full-time.

Flying Fish (see *Tourism* chapter) run a structured Work Experience programme in Australia. After yacht and dive training, graduates can be helped to find work in the industry. Many trainees who have completed Professional Dive Training with the Pro Dive Academy in Sydney (prodive.com.au) go on to work on Pro Dive's Work-Away scheme whereby they build up experience in one of Pro Dive's resorts in Australia and the South Pacific.

Ski Resorts

Another holiday area to consider is the Australian Alps where ski resorts are expanding and gaining in popularity. Jindabyne (NSW) on the edge of Kosciuszko National Park and Thredbo are the ski job capitals, though Mount Buller, Falls Creek, Baw Baw and Hotham in the state of Victoria are relatively developed ski centres too. The best time to look is a couple of weeks before the season opens which in Jindabyne is usually around the 11th of June. The employment offices in Wangaratta and Cooma can advise, though most successful job-seekers use the walk-in-and-ask method. In 'Jindy' try the Brumby Bar, Aspen Chalet Hotel, Kookaburra Lodge or any of the dozens of other hotels and pubs.

Denise Crofts went straight from a waitressing job in Sydney to the large Arlberg Hotel in Mount Buller, where she had a terrific season, with excellent snow conditions. The hotel accepts applications for vacancies posted online (arlberg.com.au/jobs.html). Staff accommodation and full board are provided at a cost of about $195 a week. Henry Pearce's experiences looking for work were not very positive, despite heavy radio advertising:

> ***When we hitched to Cooma on June 2nd, we enquired about the progress of the applications we had sent in April. We were told that there had been 4,000 applications and two vacancies for bar staff to date. We carried on up to Thredbo and half-heartedly asked around a few chalets and hotels and it seemed most of them had already fixed up their basic requirements. We were told of several definite posts available once the snow fell. In Jindabyne we were hired to work at the 'highest restaurant in Australia' (at the top of the ski lift). But accommodation was uniformly expensive in Jindabyne as was the cost of lift passes and ski hire.***

Anyone qualified as a ski instructor should attend the hiring clinics held in the big resorts before the season gets underway. Kosciuszko Thredbo Pty Ltd at the Alpine Ski Village, Thredbo (☎ 02 6459 4100; recruitment@thredbo.com.au) hire the full range of ski resort staff in three categories: on-the-mountain, hotel and instruction. Their website thredbo.com.au provides detailed information about recruitment procedures; applications must be in by the beginning of April. The names of short-listed candidates are listed on the website shortly afterwards; interviews take place in Sydney, Brisbane and Thredbo in early May.

Cities

Melbourne is arguably better for work than Sydney, partly because it is much less packed with working travellers and also the cost of living is slightly lower. Temp agencies are the first port of call for most job-seekers. Apart from restaurants and cafés, pubs and clubs, temporary catering jobs crop up in cricket grounds, theatres, yacht clubs and (in Sydney) on harbour cruises. Function work is usually easy to come by via specialist agencies provided you can claim to have silver service experience.

Looking for work in a Sydney suburb apart from the ones inundated by backpackers might prove more successful. For example Danny Jacobson, a pizza chef from Chicago, had better luck in Newtown than he did in Bondi. He also was hired as a walking advertisement for a designer clothing sale:

> ***I just approached a guy on Oxford Street holding a huge sign on a wooden stick. This backpacker told me his boss doesn't fuss about work permits and he pays $10 an hour cash. The work consists of just standing for up to ten hours a day on a specific street corner or sometimes walking a beat. It's not bad because you get to people-watch and meet all the street freaks. They also hire the more attractive people to work in store selling clothes or checking bags. Check around the Town Hall in the city or in Paddington. The best way to tap into these jobs is to talk to the people with the signs who will send you straight up to the boss.***

The best opportunities for bar and waiting staff in Perth are in the city centre, Fremantle and Northbridge, the area around William and James Streets. Rhona Stannage and her husband Stuart Blackwell arrived in Perth in November, and having had chalet experience in the French Alps and restaurant experience in Cyprus en route, were in a strong position to find hospitality work:

> ***Since there were lots of adverts in the newspapers for bar/restaurant staff we didn't go door-knocking, but we did meet a Canadian guy who had been in Perth one week and who had immediately found work in Northbridge just by asking around in the restaurants, bars and night-clubs. We both got jobs fairly quickly – me within a week and Stuart a couple of weeks later. (I put my relative success down to the usual sexism in the hospitality trade since we have virtually the same experience.) I'm working in an Irish pub called Rosie O'Grady's (they prefer Irish accents but stretched a point when it came to my Scottish one). I would also recommend the 'traditional British pub' the Moon and Sixpence on Murray St in the City, since they seem to have only Poms and no Aussies working there.***

Rhona was also offered a job at the Burswood Entertainment Complex which is one of Western Australia's largest employers. Employees enjoy a range of benefits including free meals. Vacancies are registered at burswoodjobs.com.au.

Catering agencies like Pinnacle (pinnaclepeople.com.au) and Hoban (hoban.com.au) in Melbourne supply short-term staff to casinos, corporate events, etc. The preference for females is strong in places like Kalgoorlie where waitresses are sometimes known by the offensive name 'skimpies' (scantily clad bar maids). Partly because Darwin has such a small population (121,000), tourist bars and restaurants rely heavily on transients for their staff. As well as being easier to find work than in Sydney or Melbourne, the cost of accommodation is substantially less. To take one example, Skycity Darwin, the casino-hotel complex, advertises 'Jobs for Travellers' on its website skycitydarwin.com.au.

Bridgid Seymour-East thinks that new arrivals should be warned of the dangers which Sydney poses to the traveller: '*You may plan to stay a week or two and set off to travel or find work. However one or two months later, after a lot of fun, you find yourself still there and your funds severely depleted. Sydney traps you because you do have so much fun. Jimmy and I met in a youth hostel in Glebe and love blossomed.*'

HOLIDAY LANGUAGE COURSES

Travellers with a TEFL certificate can take advantage of the seasonal demand for English tuition created by 'study tours', popular among Japanese, Indonesian and other Asian students during their autumn and winter holidays. Demand for these holiday English courses has been increasing as middle class prosperity has escalated in Pacific Rim countries and the Australian immigration authorities have relaxed the restrictions on visas.

When Barry O'Leary arrived in Sydney with a working holiday visa, he had very little money left so needed a job fast. He had emailed a number of language institutes in Sydney in advance and fixed up an interview the day after he arrived. In addition to walking round all the schools he could find, he used Australian search engines like seek.com.au, jobsearch.gov.au and mycareer.com.au. Soon he found a job with Maewill English College in Brookvale, an outer suburb of Sydney (mec.edu.au):

> ***This was my first full-time job and I was thrown in at the deep end. Initially I was doing maternity cover and working 15 hours a week, but this later increased to 45 including preparation time. The wages were fantastic, I wasn't paying any tax because I set myself up as a contractor and I was paid A$30 an hour (the going rate then) and $300 every two weeks for the evening business course I taught. I managed to save about A$8,000 in three months which paid for a brilliant trip up the east coast of Australia. There was always a laugh in the staff room and a lot of banter between England and Australia. I really enjoyed the mixed classes because there was such a range of opinions and at times more challenging because each nationality would have different weaknesses.***

SPECIAL EVENTS

Special events like test matches and race meetings can be seen as possible sources of employment. If you happen to be in Melbourne in late October or early November for the Melbourne Cup (held on the first Tuesday of November which is a public holiday in Victoria) or for the Grand Prix, your chances of finding casual work escalate remarkably. An army of sweepers and cleaners is recruited to go through the whole course clearing the huge piles of debris left by 15,000 race-goers. Hotels, restaurants and bars become frantically busy in the period leading up to the Cup, and private catering firms are also often desperate for staff.

At a swanky backpackers in the hip suburb of St Kilda, an opportunity came up for Roger Blake to do some work. A company setting up exhibition stands at the MEC (Melbourne Exhibition Centre) was short-staffed so came looking for casual workers. He worked for them on and off throughout his stay in Melbourne which meant that he could move on to New Zealand with a few hundred dollars saved up.

A couple of years ago Daniele Arena had the chance to work at the Phillip Island Racing Circuit just south of Melbourne. They are especially keen to employ casuals before the Australian Motorcycle Grand Prix in October and the Superbikes in March. Odd jobs like scrubbing floors, hosing the pit lanes and even painting tyre walls paid well and you get lots of hours.

All the major cities have important horse races. Rowena Caverly was hired for the Darwin Cup Races 'mainly to check that none of the Lady Members had passed out in the loos'.

Travelling fairs are very popular and have frequent vacancies. Richard Davies joined the Melbourne Show in September and was paid $100 a day tax-free to work 12–14 hours. It travels from Adelaide to Melbourne, Sydney and on up the Gold Coast staying a week or ten days. Ask at the local tourist office. Geertje Korf was at first thrilled to land a job with a travelling fair but it wasn't all as exciting as she had hoped:

> ***The work itself was good enough, helping to build up the stalls and working on the Laughing Clowns game. But the family I got to work for were not extremely sociable company. As a result, when we left a place and headed for the next I would spend time (about a week) until the next show day wandering lonely around incredibly hot and dusty little country towns where there was absolutely nothing to do while the showmen sat in a little circle drinking beer and not even talking to me. Also, the public toilets on the showgrounds were not usually open until showday, never cleaned since the last showday and usually provided some company (at last!) such as frogs, flies and redback spiders. I got paid $200 a week plus the use of a little caravan and evening meals which was not bad. Apparently a Dutch guy had spent six months with them the year before and had a great time, so I suppose it all depends on your personality.***

THE INTERIOR

Uluru or Ayers Rock is a place of pilgrimage for more than a third of a million visitors a year. The nearest facilities are in the Ayers Rock Resort village about 20km north of the Rock. Ayers Rock Resort (formerly known as Yulara) is the fourth largest settlement in the Northern Territory and a good place to look for a job. Although the resort has a waiting list of job-seekers, many people have moved on before they reach the top of the list. The resort employs about 1,000 people in catering and cleaning and many other departments. Staff accommodation is available. Like the Queensland resorts mentioned earlier, this one is also operated by Voyages; applications should be made to the Human Resources Department, Ayers Rock Resort, NT 0872 (08 8957 7380; human.resources@ayers.voyages.com.au). Be prepared to pay up to $140 a week for staff accommodation.

Alice Springs is a very popular tourist destination because of Ayers Rock. One traveller who stayed at one of the many backpackers' lodges reported that 8 out of the 12 women staying there were working as waitresses or bar staff. Occasional vacancies occur for hostesses to work on upmarket special interest tours. Personality and presentation are more important than qualifications and experience for jobs as hostesses and cooks.

Coober Pedy (opal capital of Australia in the South Australian outback), Alice Springs, Kununurra and Broome are other places worth trying for tourist work in the Dry (May to October). Broome hosts a big festival in early September just prior to the monsoon (when travel becomes hazardous and uncomfortable) which is a good time to try.

THE AUSTRALIAN PUB

The tradition in male-dominated pubs of heavy drinking and barmaid-taunting continues, so you should be prepared for this sometimes irritating (though almost always good-natured) treatment. You may get especially tired of hearing sporting comparisons between Australia and Britain.

Standards of service in pubs and restaurants are high and many hotel managers will be looking for some experience or training. Only those desperate for staff will be willing to train. Even if you have had experience of working in a British pub, it may take you some time to master the technique of pouring Australian lager properly. There is a bewildering array of beer glasses ranging from the 115ml small beer of Tasmania to the 575ml pint of New South Wales with middies, schooners, pots and butchers falling in between. Names and measures vary from state to state.

Working at a road station can be a lonely business. A typical station consists of a shop, a petrol pump and a bar, and they occur every couple of hundred miles along the seemingly endless straight highways through the Australian desert. The more remote the place (and these are often the ones that are unbearably hot) the more likely there will be a vacancy. If you see a job going in Marble Bar, for example, remind yourself that it is arguably the world's hottest inhabited town with summer temperatures occasionally nudging 50°C (122°F).

CHILDCARE

The demand for live-in and live-out childcare is enormous in Australia and a few agencies in Britain cater to the demand, such as Childcare International (London NW7; childint.co.uk). But it is easy to conduct the job hunt on arrival. Applicants are often interviewed a day or two after registering with an agency and start work immediately. Nanny and au pair agencies are very interested in hearing from young women and men with working holiday visas. Geertje Korf's experience in Tasmania illustrates the ease with which childcare work can be found: *'I decided to go to Tasmania for a cycling holiday. At the second place I stopped I got offered a job as a nanny to four children, just by mentioning I had been nannying in Sydney. The place had beautiful surroundings, restaurants, etc. so I decided to accept. It was a good job and I left quite a bit richer.'*

A typical weekly wage in addition to room and board would be $250–$300 with some families paying up to $450 to live-in child carers who promise to stay for 12 months. A number of au pair agencies place European and Asian women with working holiday visas in live-in positions, normally for a minimum of three months. Not all placements require childcare experience. Try any of the following:

Australian Nanny & Au Pair Connection: Kooyong, Vic; tel/fax 03 9824 8857; australian-nannies.info.

Dial-an-Angel: ☎ 1300 721111; administration@dialanangel.com; dial-an-angel.com.au; long established agency with franchised branches throughout Australia; qualified nannies can earn up to $1000 a week.

Family Match Au Pairs & Nannies: ☎ 02 4363 2500; familymatch.com.au; agency places many working holidaymakers; 25–35 hours per week for pocket money of $180–$250 plus all live-in expenses.

People for People: Brookvale, NSW; ☎ 02 9971 1393; peopleforpeople.com.au; welcome working holidaymakers for three-month summer positions.

Most agencies will expect to interview applicants and check their references before placement. As in America, a driving licence is a valuable asset. As well as long-term posts, holiday positions for the summer (December–February) and for the ski season (July–September) are available. Matt Tomlinson worked as a nanny in a ski resort on the strength of the year he'd spent as an au pair in Paris: '*Being a male nanny in Australia was an interesting experience. I got used to being asked if I was a child molester. On the upside, I was also offered a number of live-in jobs in Melbourne. And in case you're wondering, yes, I did get a lot of ribbing from the guys when I told them what job I was doing.*'

Anyone considering a childcare position may be interested in Rowena Caverly's experiences: *'I looked after a 15-month-old boy at a permaculture farm set in a rainforest. The job taught me new skills daily, such as how to persuade a baby that the Huntsman Spider on the wall really does not want to play. My task in summer was to teach him to toddle heavily to scare off snakes. Otherwise a nasty situation might have developed (and my money would not necessarily be on the baby as the victim).'*

FISHING AND BOATING

It is sometimes possible to get work on prawn fishing vessels out of Broome, Darwin, Cairns, Townsville, Bowen or even Karumba on the Gulf of Carpentaria. Stephen Psallidas noticed lots of trawler and yachting jobs in the *Cairns Post* (especially on Wednesday and Saturday) and on noticeboards in town. You can either try to get work with one of the big companies like Raptis (raptis.com.au) in Queensland, South Australia, etc. or on smaller privately-owned boats.

There has also been a recent geographical shift from Darwin to Cairns. The prawn fleets usually spend six or more weeks at sea catching banana prawns, and then go out in August/September for tiger prawns, with the season finishing by Christmas. Trawlers depart from the Francis Bay mooring basin in Darwin, invariably referred to as the Duck Pond, in mid-April and return at the beginning of June. The skippers complain that they can't get enough labour. A manager at one of the biggest companies Austral Fisheries (☎ 08 9202 2444 in Perth or 07 4035 1843 in Cairns;

newfish.com.au) wrote in 2009, '*Working on our boats can be and usually is hard physical work with long hours that can be financially and personally rewarding. We are more than happy to give someone a start if they are prepared to commit themselves to the task. Going to sea can be a trip to self enlightenment or a trip from hell, it's all up to the individual.*'

Any traveller who goes down to the docks at the beginning of the season has a chance of being taken on for a short trip, even without experience, though wages will be a fraction of those earned by the old hands, as Sam Martell learned:

> ***After chatting to some Aussies in Darwin, the allure of $15,000 over six weeks was too tempting. So I trooped down to the harbour with a few beers to bribe my way and chatted to some fishermen and got shown around a couple of boats. Unfortunately I found that because I was 'green' I would not be paid what everyone else was. Rather than $2,500 a week it would be $300 – definitely not worth it as it works out at about $4 an hour. Only those who are gluttons for punishment or with experience should try the prawn trawlers. There are other fishing boats around though.***

The main jobs assigned to male deckhands are net-mending and prawn-sorting. Work is especially demanding during the banana prawn season of April/May, since banana prawns travel in huge schools which are caught in one fell swoop, requiring immediate attention. Much of the fishing for tiger prawns takes place at night. Women are taken on as cooks. They should make it quite clear before leaving harbour whether or not they wish to be counted among the recreational facilities of the boat, since numerous stories are told of the unfair pressures placed on women crew members at sea. The most that some women have had to complain about is that they were expected not only to cook but to help sort out sea snakes and jellyfish from the catch. Men are not immune to problems, of course: if the skipper takes a dislike to any of his crew, he can simply leave them stranded on an island or beach.

The backpacker press carries an alarming ad placed by Maritime Safety Queensland which mentions 'pirates' operating out of the Whitsundays.

> ***Pirates cruise the Whitsundays ripping off travellers. They hang around pubs and clubs offering cheap cruises if you work as part of the crew. Once you are on board, you are trapped. Their yachts are usually unsafe, unregistered and extremely unfriendly. Only sail with an authorised operator. You'll have a much better time. Look for the Whitsunday Charter Boat Industry Association sign and ask the right questions.***

Pearling is an industry that takes place in relatively remote places and makes extensive use of itinerant labour, provided they are willing and strong. 'Pearling' gets its own heading on the working traveller job site: jobaroo.com/job-pearling.html. The capital is Broome where you can simply ask at the companies farming oysters. The harvest season lasts from April/May to September, though there are jobs year round. Work on the boats can be live-aboard or not, but in either case means very early mornings and hard physical work, which will be rewarded with $120–$145 a day with all expenses paid. Pearling companies operate out of Exmouth and Broome on the coast of WA north to the Coburg Peninsula near Darwin.

CONCLUSION

Ian Fleming sums up what many working travellers have observed about Australians:

> ***The opinion that we formed regarding Australian employers is that they are hard but fair. They demand a good day's work for a fair day's pay, and if you do not measure up to their expectations they will have no hesitation in telling you so. I also found the Aussies to be much more friendly and helpful than anticipated and very easy to socialise with (in spite of the fact that I was nicknamed 'P.B.' for Pommy Bastard).***

There is a marvellous range of jobs even if you are unlikely to repeat Sandra Grey's coup of being paid $50 for three hours 'work' testing a sunscreen on her lily-white back, or Jane Thomas's bizarre jobs, one in a sex change clinic, the other in a morgue typing up the labels for dismembered parts of bodies.

Even after several setbacks with bosses and jobs, Louise Fitzgerald concludes: *'To anybody not sure about going, I'd say, go, you'd be stupid not to. Australia is a wonderful country and the Australians are great people, even if the males do have a tendency to be chauvinists. If you prove to them you're as good as they are, they tend to like you for it!'*

NEW ZEALAND

New Zealand is a charmingly rural country where just over four million human beings are substantially outnumbered by sheep. While the main cities become more sophisticated by the year, they remain friendly and manageable in scale. Travellers have found hitch-hiking easy, the backpackers hostels congenial, camping idyllic (when it's dry) and the natives very hospitable. The minimum wage is NZ$12.50 (as of April 2009), equivalent at the time of writing to about £4.50. Furthermore the NZ cost of living is low and therefore you should aim to spend your earnings before leaving the shores of New Zealand.

With a low unemployment rate of 4.6%, even in these recessionary times, a demand for both skilled and unskilled workers continues. Supplementing your travel fund with temporary jobs, cash-in-hand work, odd jobs or work-for-keep arrangements is usually good fun. Camping on beaches, fields and in woodlands is generally permitted. Even more than elsewhere in the world, backpackers' accommodation in New Zealand is a good place to hear about local opportunities for casual work, particularly the ubiquitous fruit-picking.

REGULATIONS

New Zealand deserves its national reputation for friendliness to visitors. Tourists from the UK need no visa to stay for up to six months, while Americans, Canadians and Europeans can stay for three visa-free months. Tourists entering the country may be asked to show an onward ticket and about NZ$1,000 per month of their proposed stay. In practice, respectable-looking travellers are most unlikely to be quizzed at entry.

The UK Working Holiday Scheme was considered so successful in addressing severe labour shortages in seasonal work that the maximum duration was extended recently from one year to two years, and the quota removed. The scheme allows any eligible Briton aged 18–30 to obtain a working holiday visa, allowing her or him to do temporary or full-time jobs in New Zealand. Applicants must have the equivalent of NZ$350 for each month they intend to stay, so if you are applying for the 12-month visa you must show £1,500 and also have enough to cover a return airfare. Participants are permitted to work for up to 12 months of the two-year visa validity, either consecutively or cumulatively. Anyone who has worked for at least three months in horticulture or viticulture can apply to extend their working holiday permit by three months. Information can be obtained from the New Zealand Immigration Service at New Zealand House, Haymarket, London (fax 020 7973 0370) in person, by phone on 09069 100100 (charged at £1 per minute) or via the internet at immigration.govt.nz, an admirably comprehensive and up-to-date site.

Applications for all working holiday schemes can be done online so that you can apply from anywhere in the world. The fee (currently NZ$120/£45) will be payable by credit card at the time of application. Other working holiday schemes (maximum duration one year) are open to Irish, American, Canadian, Dutch, Japanese and many other nationalities, mostly on a reciprocal basis.

A possible alternative to the working holiday visa for those who have contacts in New Zealand or special skills in short supply or with a firm offer of employment before leaving the UK is to apply for a temporary work visa (for a non-refundable fee of £70/NZ$200). Your sponsoring employer in New Zealand may have to prove to the NZIS (NZ Immigration Service) that it is necessary to hire a foreigner rather than an unemployed New Zealander. The work visa does not in itself entitle you to work, but does make it easier to obtain a work permit after arrival. If you are granted a work visa before departure it will allow you to stay for up to three years. (In general the term 'visa' is used for permission applied for from outside New Zealand, while 'permit' is for applications lodged within New Zealand.)

If you think that permanent migration is a possibility, you must first submit an Expression of Interest to the New Zealand Immigration Service. Consyl Publishing (☎ 01424 223111; consylpublishing.co.uk) specialises in publishing information for potential migrants.

Special Schemes

BUNAC in London (☎ 020 7251 3472; downunder@bunac.org.uk) has a Work New Zealand programme that provides a 'Work Exchange Visa' (unique to BUNAC) or ordinary working holiday visa, job assistance from BUNAC's partner organisation IEP and other benefits for a programme fee of £429. You can also buy a package directly from IEP (worknewzealand.org.nz).

Work Adventures Downunder programme from CCUSA in London (ccusa.com) operates to New Zealand as well as Australia. Fees start at £370 to include initial accommodation and a post-arrival orientation at the partner office in Auckland. IST Plus (☎ 020 8939 9057; info@istplus.com) offers UK residents eligible for the working holiday visa the Work and Travel New Zealand programme. One of the gap year placement companies to operate in New Zealand is Changing Worlds (☎ 01883 340960; changingworlds.co.uk) which offers 3- or 6-month job placements in hotels in Paihia or Queenstown, or the chance to volunteer on farms or on small boats in the Bay of Islands. The programme fee including flights is £3,145.

Globetrotters Education Consulting in Ontario (globetrotterseducation.ca) arranges unpaid internships lasting 6–16 weeks for a fee of C$1,200–C$1,500. Similarly Intern Options in London (☎ 020 7353 7699; internoptions.com) arranges mainly paid placements in the farming and tourism sectors; their arrangement fee is £895 for six months or £950 for a year.

New Zealand Job Search (stayatbase.com/work) is a specialist job search centre for travellers attached to BASE Auckland ACB backpacker hostel (Level 3, 229 Queen St; ☎ 0800 462 396; info@nzjs.co.nz). Work starter packs starting from NZ$355 include a 12-month registration with NZ Job Search, job placement service and various perks (one-way airport transfer, orientation session, SIM card, etc.).

An excellent resource is Seasonal Jobs NZ (seasonaljobs.co.nz), which provides splendidly full details on current job vacancies. Also check vacancies on seasonalwork.co.nz. The sites gapyearnewzealand.co.uk/jobs/gap-year-jobs.php and backpackerboard.co.nz/work_jobs/job_listings.php are active with recruitment agency listings and some dated vacancies. A couple of sites specialise in agricultural jobs (see Fruit Picking below).

Tax

In the majority of cases employers will be more concerned to see a tax number from the Inland Revenue Department (IRD) than a work visa. Without a tax number you will be taxed at the punitive rate of 46%. According to the IRD (ird.govt.nz) applications must be posted or faxed, and accompanied by a photocopy of the ID page of your current passport plus you must provide a NZ address to which the tax number can be sent.

People who have worked for part of the year may be eligible for a tax rebate. About a month before you are due to leave the country, phone the IRD free phone number (☎ 0800 227774) and ask for the refund form. Any money due to you – as much as 20% of earnings – will be paid into a nominated bank account or credited to your credit card account. In Roger Blake's case the processing took three months but eventually a rebate of NZ$130 was posted to his home address in the UK which he thought worth the bother. Normally you must have stayed in the country for at least six months to be eligible. Make sure you tell the tax office when you are leaving the country permanently to prevent them sending you an IR3 (self-assessment) form and trying to tax you on your subsequent earnings in your home country.

CASUAL WORK

Because New Zealand has a limited industrial base, most temporary work is in agriculture and tourism. As in Australia, backpackers' hostels and campsites are the best sources of information on harvesting jobs and other casual work. Farmers often make contact with hostels and backpackers' lodges looking for seasonal workers as Ian Fleming observed: *'During our travels around the North and South Islands, the opportunity to work presented itself on several occasions. While staying in the Kerikeri Youth Hostel, we discovered that the local farmers would regularly come into the hostel to seek employees for the day or longer. My advice to any person looking for farm work would be to get up early as the farmers are often in the hostel by 8.30am.'*

Alternatively local farmers co-operate with hostel wardens who collate information about job vacancies or they may circulate notices around youth hostels, for example, 'Orchard Work Available January to March; apply Tauranga Hostel' so always check the hostel board. At the same time, be on your guard as Roger Blake warns:

> ***After a couple of weeks in Auckland with a little work here and there I was barely breaking even as the cost of living is quite high. Acting on an ad I had seen on the YHA notice board, I phoned a hostel in Hastings which had placed an ad for 30 apple pickers 'Needed Immediately' which they confirmed. So the following day I jumped on a bus to Hastings. Although a few of the travellers there were working, the others were hanging on for another day as work was assured, 'maybe tomorrow'. After a week I had learned for myself that the season was late. A warning that hostels can and do use these tactics to fill their beds.***

A website maintained by the Budget Backpackers Hostels group includes job information (bbh.co.nz/travellers/billboard_home.asp). At the time of writing (2009) there were 46 vacancies for hostel jobs listed plus 13 other vacancies. Hostels often employ travellers for short periods, either part-time in exchange for free accommodation or full-time for a wage as well. After the engine of Roger Blake's campervan blew up, he scoured the hostel notice boards of Wellington and fixed himself up with a cleaning job on a work-for-accommodation basis. Many travellers are dotted around New Zealand cleaning in hostels for three hours each morning six days a week in return for a free dorm bed. The job is usually not difficult.

Louise Hawkes spent more than a year doing a variety of transient jobs which kept her afloat:

> ***The majority of work I did was in the hospitality industry, as a waitress, barmaid or barista. I even managed a backpackers' for six months in beautiful Kaikoura, which was a lovely change from waiting on tables. Other little jobs picked up along the way included working on a vineyard planting and guarding vines, driving a tractor on a farm, thinning kiwis on a kiwi fruit farm and working in a barley field pulling out wild oats.***

Matt Tomlinson recommends buying a vehicle to travel and job hunt in New Zealand. He bought one at a Sunday morning car market-cum-auction in the Auckland suburb of Manukau City. Also try the Ellerslie Car Fair in South Auckland or autotrader.co.nz where you might be lucky enough to find a decent vehicle for $1,200. Backpackers' car markets take place in Auckland at 20 East Street in the city centre and in Christchurch (near the corner of Colombo and Battersea Streets); details on http://backpackerscarmarket.co.nz. Look for a vehicle with a couple of months of WOF remaining (equivalent to MOT).

Greenpeace frequently recruits fund-raisers (greenpeace.org/new-zealand/jobs/overseas-applicants). The job involves standing around in a busy shopping area and trying to persuade people to sign up for a monthly direct debit donation to Greenpeace.

If planning to be in or near Dunedin for a period of time, you could see if Zenith Technology is conducting any clinical trials in which you might be able to pick up $200 for a weekend's volunteering: Zenith Technology, 156 Frederick St, Dunedin (☎ 03 477 9669; zenithtechnology.co.nz).

Rural and Conservation Volunteering

World Wide Opportunities on Organic Farms (WWOOF) NZ is active and popular, with 830 farms and smallholdings on its fix-it-yourself list which welcome volunteers in exchange for food and accommodation. The list can be obtained from PO Box 1172, Nelson (☎ 03 544 9890; support@wwoof.co.nz; wwoof.co.nz) for a fee of NZ$40 or $45 (to an overseas address). WWOOF hosts often have leads for paid work in market gardens, nurseries and other farms.

Farm Helpers in New Zealand lists nearly 200 farmers around New Zealand where working travellers can arrange a farmstay lasting from three days to several months. FHiNZ in Palmerston North (fhinz.co.nz) charges NZ$25 for their membership booklet and list of farms which is updated monthly. No experience is necessary and between four and six hours of work a day are requested. Another possibility is the free internet-based exchange of work-for-keep volunteers which can be found at helpx.net where an impressive 724 hosts in New Zealand are listed. Originally set up by a British backpacker in New Zealand, the scheme is flourishing and expanding.

Adrienne Robinson and her partner and young son joined FHiNZ and arranged two enjoyable farmstays. Because they were looking for farms at the height of the summer and at Christmas, they found that many of the listed farms were already booked up for that period. They found that the general picking, weeding and mulching work they were asked to do was fairly easy to manage alongside three year old Jordan.

LEONA BALDWIN THOUGHT SHE WOULD TRY SOMETHING COMPLETELY ALIEN TO HER, A WWOOF STAY ON A NEW ZEALAND FARM:

Growing up in Toronto, the closest I'd ever come to experiencing life on a farm was driving past deserted cornfields on my way into the city with billboards boasting 'Prime Site for Housing Development'. The appeal of one day 'getting back to nature' lingered.

After touring New Zealand we began to long for a taste of real life in Kiwiland. Becoming a WWOOF volunteer presented the ideal scenario, satisfying our need to take a break from the ordinary, and our bank balance's need to take a break from all the spending. Luckily, our first choice in horse trekking farms had a vacancy for two Wwoofers, and after a brief informal telephone interview, we were invited to come and stay at a farm just outside the ski resort of Ohakune.

The self-sufficiency of life on this farm was quite amazing. Seeing firsthand how easy and economical it is to live without the aid of supermarkets and pre-packaging builds an inarguable case for sustainable living. But admittedly, after weeks without even a glimpse of the golden arches and its chemically enhanced flavor additives, I was craving a Mc Anything. I guess old habits die hard. For someone who was not entirely sure what the term 'organic' even meant prior to my stay, being a part of the daily regime on an organic farm truly was a breath of fresh air. I learned more about gardening than I ever thought possible, I developed muscles in places no amount of circuit training or yoga has ever come close to and I formed friendships with people from around the world.

The New Zealand Department of Conservation (DOC) carries out habitat and wildlife management projects throughout New Zealand and publishes a detailed Calendar of Volunteer Opportunities; see their website doc.govt.nz for links to regional projects such as counting bats, cleaning up remote beaches and maintaining historic buildings. Most require a good level of fitness and a contribution to expenses, though not always. The DOC also needs volunteer hut wardens at a variety of locations. Details are available from any office of the Department of Conservation.

Conservation Volunteers New Zealand with an office in Auckland (☎ 09 376 7030; conservationvolunteers.co.nz) is a not-for profit organisation operating on both islands, that was set up by Conservation Volunteers Australia in 2006. It operates its own team-based projects which accept overseas volunteers to monitor wildlife, plant trees, maintain tracks and so on. Overseas volunteers can book a four-week or six-week package through CVA's office in Victoria, through agents abroad (see website) or on arrival in Auckland.

The New Zealand Trust for Conservation Volunteers was set up a decade ago to match both local and international volunteers with conservation projects of all kinds to counteract the loss of native bush and wildlife. Whereas DOC projects take place only on DOC lands, NZTCV registers projects run by many local and national organisations as well as DOC projects. Details are available on their website conservationvolunteers.org.nz (tel/fax 09 889 3711). NZTCV has created a central database on which individuals can register in order to be put in touch with organisations running conservation projects.

PAUL BAGSHAW FROM KENT AND HIS GIRLFRIEND SPENT A THOROUGHLY ENJOYABLE WEEK ON AN UNINHABITED ISLAND IN MARLBOROUGH SOUND MONITORING KIWIS, THE FLIGHTLESS BIRD WHOSE NUMBERS HAVE BEEN SERIOUSLY DEPLETED. AN ONGOING PROGRAMME REMOVES THEM FROM THE MAINLAND TO SMALL ISLANDS WHERE THERE ARE NO PREDATORS:

The object of the exercise was to estimate the number of kiwis on Long Island north of Picton. As the kiwi is nocturnal, we had to work in the small hours. As it's dark, it's impossible to count them so we had to spread out and walk up a long slope listening for their high-pitched whistling call. During the day they hide in burrows and foliage so it is very rare to see one. One night, when we heard one rustling around our camp, my girlfriend went outside with a torch and actually managed to see it. She was so excited that she couldn't speak and resorted to wild gesticulations to describe its big feet and long beak. The island has no water source except rainwater which collects in tanks, all very basic. We lived in tents and prepared our own meals from supplies brought over from the mainland. Our one luxury was a portaloo.

FRUIT PICKING

The climate of New Zealand lends itself to fruit and vegetable growing of many kinds including not only the apples and kiwifruit well known from every British supermarket but carrots, citrus fruit and other produce. Just turning up in towns and asking around is usually a safe bet for work while the season is on. Expect to earn between $350 and $450 a week. Below are some general guidelines as to what areas to head for in the appropriate seasons. Motueka/Nelson, Tauranga/Katikati, Hawke's Bay and Kerikeri are the favourites among travellers.

Most farmers are able to provide some kind of shack or cottage accommodation (known as a 'bach' in the North Island, a 'crib' in the South), though the spring and summer weather is suitable for camping provided you have a good waterproof tent. Farmers often provide fresh fruit and vegetables, milk and sometimes lamb, or organise end-of-harvest barbecues with free drinks. As Roger Blake concluded after picking pears in Motueka, 'Very nice people Kiwis!' If the farmer doesn't have accommodation, you can stay in backpackers' hostels or holiday parks/campsites. Long stays in the off-season usually cost $100–$130 per week.

Several New Zealand-based companies specialise in matching seasonal workers with agricultural employers – try pickapicker.co.nz and picknz.co.nz (☎ 0800 742569). Both started in Hawke's Bay but cover the whole country.

FRUIT AND VEGETABLE HARVESTS

PLACE	CROP	SEASON
Nelson/Blenheim/Motueka	apples (also pears and peaches)	Feb/Mar/Apr
Motueka	apple thinning	mid-Nov/Dec
Blenheim	cherries	late Dec/Jan
Motueka	apple thinning	Feb/Mar/Apr
Wairau Valley (Marlborough area)	cherries, grapes	Dec
Nelson/Tapawera	raspberries	Dec
Kerikeri (Bay of Islands)	peaches, apricots	Dec/Jan
	citrus packing	Oct/Nov
	kiwifruit	late Apr
Northland (peninsula north of Auckland)	kiwifruit	May
	strawberries	mid-Oct
Paiumhhue (just south of Auckland)	kiwifruit	May
Poverty Bay (Gisborne)	kiwifruit	May
Poverty Bay Flats	grapes	from Feb
Tauranga/Te Puke (Bay of Plenty)	citrus	Oct/Nov
	kiwifruit	May-Jul
Clive/Napier (Hawke's Bay)	apples, pears and grapes	late Feb/Apr
	pruning work	Jun

PLACE	CROP	SEASON
Hastings	tomatoes	
	apples	late Feb/Apr
Ohakune	carrots	June
Martinborough (north of Wellington in the Wairarapa area)	grapes	Mar
Central Otago (Alexandra and Roxburgh)	plums, apricots	Jan/Feb
	apples and pears	Mar/Apr
Christchurch area	peaches	Mar
	apples, berries and mixed fruit	Jan-May
	potatoes	Jan–Mar
Invercargill	tulips	early Dec

Bay of Plenty

The Bay of Plenty is where the majority of New Zealand's kiwifruit is grown. The tiny community of Te Puke swells in number from 6,000 to 10,000 for the harvest which traditionally starts on May 1st (though it is best to arrive a week or two early to line up a job). Picking lasts four or five weeks and the packing season extends to August. Workaholics can work an evening shift packing after a day in the orchards. An hourly wage is paid for this boring work (5pm–11pm).

Hawke's Bay

The shortage of people to bring in the autumn harvests of apples and pears in the Hawke's Bay area can be acute. The area can absorb 15,000 workers, a seven-fold increase on the numbers needed outside the harvest times. Any working holidaymaker who shows up in early to mid-February at the apple orchards around Napier will almost certainly be taken on.

Even workers who are paid on a piece-work basis have to earn minimum wage, i.e. $500 for a 40-hour week plus holiday pay of 6% of gross earnings.

This is one area in which it is wise to keep an eye out for immigration officials. Craig Ashworth arrived in late February and found that there was lots of no-questions-asked apple picking work around. He found it tough at first but was eventually earning above the minimum. There is also pruning work in the area in June.

A former RTW working traveller Paul Foulkes now runs Travellers Labour Services Ltd in Hastings (☎ 021 1292607; utbnb2004@hotmail.com), a work-broking company that aims to place backpackers in outdoor and indoor jobs in the seasonal fruit industry of New Zealand, mainly in apples, onions, pumpkins, carrots, peaches, apricots, grapes and kiwifruit.

Apollo Pac Ltd in Hastings and Whakatu (apollo.gen.nz) operates a large apple packhouse and storehouse in Hawke's Bay (☎ 06 873 0404) employing several hundred graders and packers in the season between mid-February and July.

A harvest of boysenberries takes place in Hastings on Hawke's Bay between early December and mid-January. The fruit cannot be picked in the heat of the day so working holidaymakers are invited to swim and fish in the Ngaruroro River during the day.

Travelling east, the largest carrot-producing region in the southern hemisphere is around Ohakune. Work is available for up to nine months of the year here. While waiting for the ski season to begin, Matt Tomlinson rang some farmers out of the *Yellow Pages* and was soon hired to pack carrots. High staff turnover means that hiring goes on continuously. The work is boring and hard and pays not much more than minimum wage.

Northland

The tropical far north of the country, which specialises in citrus growing, is another favourite destination. In addition to growers in the region, several major packing sheds employ a large number of casual workers in November/December. Contract pruning can be more lucrative than picking. Kiwifruit pickers normally work in gangs of ten and are paid piecework, while kiwifruit packers and citrus pickers are paid by the hour. The six weeks between early April and mid-May is a busy kiwifruit season. Any of the hostels in Kaitaia and Kerikeri will be able to advise. Especially recommended is the Aranga Backpackers in Kerikeri (☎ 09 407 9326; aranga.co.nz). It provides transport to the kiwifruit and mandarin orchards for a small fee and has tent sites which are available at discounted weekly rates in the off season; the weekly charge for a dorm bed is $110. Similarly Pukenui Holiday Park in Kaitaia (☎ 09 409 8803) recruits and runs the mandarin gangs on behalf of Kerifresh, the company that manages the four largest mandarin orchards in the area. Mandarin thinning starts in early January and lasts four to six weeks.

Nelson/Motueka/Blenheim

The Nelson/Motueka area is a great area for travellers for its jobs as well as its beaches. The supply of seasonal work is so great that there is a specialist government agency in Motueka called Seasonal Solutions Nelson (236 High St; ☎ 03 907 0234; ann.riley003@msd.govt.nz).

Many foreign travellers are hired for the apple harvest, and also at the apple packing and processing works in Stoke, just outside Nelson. One of the main employers of seasonal workers, whose numbers peak at 6,500 doing three shifts in the New Zealand autumn, is Enza Foods on Nayland Road in Stoke (enzafoods.co.nz/careers). The season lasts from late February till September. The hourly wage range for 2009 was $13.25–$16.75 with bonuses paid for cleaning, night shifts and for completing the season.

Many of the backpack operators in Nelson have created a useful website backpacknelson.co.nz/seasonalwork.php which has useful links. Farmers generally provide accommodation other than just a campsite; some charge will be made though often the deduction is negligible.

In Blenheim, make enquiries at the Grapevine hostel (29 Park Terrace; queries@thegrapevine.co.nz) about local picking, packing and pruning work in local vineyards. Rob Abblett spent several months earning money in the South Island. Apple thinning between mid-November and Christmas was fairly lucrative though he fared less well with contract cherry picking around Blenheim for six weeks from late November or early December:

> ***The season starts with select picking (on November 20th) on which nobody made any wages worth bothering about. Things picked up after the first two or three weeks but unfortunately many backpackers were paid by the kilo throughout the season, even on select picking. I was aghast to earn about £40 in the first week, £60 in the second. Way too fickle a fruit. Yeah, in an excellent year with good pollination, ideal weather and a good orchard, it might be possible to earn $800 a week (the figure used by the orchard owners to motivate the thoroughly disillusioned backpackers). But in a bad or average year, I would stick with apple thinning.***

Many employers can be found by trawling the internet as well as asking locally. For example the wine giant Pernod Ricard at http://jobs.pernod-ricard-nz.com needs about 700 people to prune and wrap vines in their Marlborough and North Canterbury vineyards from mid-May to August and to carry out hand-harvesting in March/April. Sai Viticulture Ltd in the Blehheim area also hires vineyard workers in large numbers (☎ 021 516 533; http://saiviticulture.com/_wsn/page4.html).

Roger Blake stayed on in 'Mot' (Motueka) until the season ended in June:

> ***It has been three months since I arrived in this small town which is a haven for working travellers (plenty of hippies in these parts). Surrounded by the marvellous Mount Arthur, Motueka is the gateway to the world famous Abel Tasman National Park which has fantastic walking trails. I came to Mot to work with a friend and have been flat out ever since. The first job was a three-week stint picking pears which was good as it goes (fruit picking is really fun, not!) then went to an orchard to pick apples. But I hated every minute of it and quit on my first day and was ready to up and leave the town, thoroughly disillusioned with this fruit picking lark. As if by fate I got a job in a packing shed (apples and pears) and have been packing ever since. The job is work as work is meant to be – monotonous and semi-hard labour. But for some reason I have enjoyed spending 8–14 hours a day for six days per week running back and forth between conveyor belts, sorting, standing tirelessly at a grader throwing out bad apples and (my preference) stacking the boxes after they are packed. And that for a pittance of a wage. Worked with a great crowd of people though which made work more of a social thing.***

Although Roger calls his wage a pittance, he managed to save $2,000 in three months, while living in a tent pitched at the holiday park on Fearon Street (☎ 03 528 7189; motuekatop10.co.nz) which gives seasonal workers a special affordable weekly rate.

Southland

Cherries are picked in Otago over the winter with the peak period from December 10th to January 20th. Bennie & Son Orchards in Alexandra (☎ 03 448 8497) accepts up to 200 pickers who camp on the farm, some of whom stay on for the apple harvest from mid-March to late April. It is also worth travelling to the far south of the South Island in late December for the tulip bulb harvest during the month of January at Van Eeden Tulips, 370 West Plains Road, R.D.4, Invercargill; ☎ 03 215 7836.

Massive investment in cherry production around Cromwell (not far from Alexandra) has created additional seasonal jobs for the area. For instance Orchard Fresh in Cromwell in Otago (☎ 03 445 1402; orchardfresh.co.nz/employment.php) employ up to 250 picking and packing staff from mid-December to the end of January. Picking is usually more popular than sorting but at this farm sorters are paid piece rates, which provides an incentive to sort faster. For seasonal work in this area, consult Seasonal Solutions in Alexandra (☎ 0800 545567; jobscentral.co.nz), the job centre for seasonal work in central Otago.

TOURISM

Openings in New Zealand's flourishing tourist industry continue to proliferate. Waiters and waitresses are usually paid only a little above the minimum wage. On the plus side, restaurant kitchens tend to be more relaxed places than they are in Europe. Based on his experience of looking for catering work on Auckland waterfront, Colm Murphy from Ireland recommends cold calling at all the bars and restaurants in the smart Viaduct Harbour, Princes Wharf, Parnell, Ponsonby and Jervois Road areas. Remember that there is only a very recent tradition of tipping in New

Zealand, though it is possible to make a little extra. Colm Murphy made up to $100 a week in tips, especially when foreign tourists came to dine: *'Admittedly waiting on Kiwis is soul destroying. On numerous occasions I had big tables of 10–12 Kiwis and they never tipped me. They will thank you profusely for the service but they will not tip. To a certain type of Kiwi (especially those from south of the Bombay Hills, i.e. south of Auckland) tipping is an alien concept.'*

Well south of the Bombay Hills, the capital Wellington is not the first city you think of in the context of New Zealand tourism. But the base used by Peter Jackson in the making of the *Lord of the Rings* trilogy has brought fame and fortune to the city. It has a remarkably high ratio of cafés to citizen and a booming job market. Catharine Carfoot showed up there one November with a working holiday visa (though she wasn't always asked to show it) and easily found work first and accommodation second:

> ***I worked weekends driving for Wellington Cable Cars which has its ups and downs (cable car joke). And I was doing various things during the week, mostly temping through Select Appointments, and life modelling at the Inverlochy Art School and Vincents Art workshop ($80 cash for five hours). Bizarrely, I ended up practising my French conversation skills more than I had done for years, both at the Cable Car and with people met on the street asking for directions. It seems very odd that even the bigger hotels here don't always have a francophone on duty.***

Note that the cable car and many tourist operations become very busy in February which marks the cruise ship season. The tourist industry in New Zealand adopts many adventurous and sporting guises. You might get taken on by a camping tour operator as a cook; perhaps you could find a job on a yacht or in a ski resort (see below).

Queenstown and the South Island

The lakeside resort of Queenstown is particularly brimming with opportunities. It is a town whose economy is booming due to backpacker tourism and whose population is largely young and transient. It is one of the few places in which restaurants and bars (especially those that have been caught out in the past) may ask to see your working holiday visa.

Writing from Queenstown, 28 year old Roger Blake describes how he had set about the job hunt a few months earlier:

> ***I arrived in Queenstown late one night with only NZ$90 in my pocket (and to my name). I immediately set about studying the internet café/backpackers notice boards and phoned for every job going, no matter what. Early the following morning I got a call asking me if I could start work right away. (A mobile phone really is the most valuable asset to gaining work.) Since then I have been a builder's mate, a landscape gardener, deliveries off-sider, done house and furniture removals, dug holes for scientists, dug trenches, planted trees, been a refuse collector and much more besides. Generally only working Mon to Fri, my average week was around 45 hours (optional weekend work is available but I chose to enjoy them otherwise). Quite an achievement to save money in Queenstown with so much temptation and so many establishments willing to take your money. After 4 months here (and having had a damn good time in the process) I have saved a little over $3000.***

Roger claims not to have met anyone who had a problem obtaining work in Queenstown whatever their nationality or visa status. As always in travellers' meccas, finding affordable accommodation is the main challenge. Roger shared a house with seven like-minded working travellers.

One of the perks of being a worker in Queenstown and therefore an honorary resident (instead of a 'loopy', the local term for tourist), is that often workers can get discounts on local activities like rafting or 'zorbing' (rolling down a hill in a plastic ball). If you want to leave the scene behind, try ringing resort hotels in Milford Sound, Fox Glacier, Franz Josef and Mount Cook to ask about job vacancies.

Ski Resorts

The ski season lasts roughly from July to October. Of the dozen commercial ski fields in the country, the main ones on the South Island are Coronet Peak and the Remarkables (serviced by Queenstown), Mount Hutt and Treble Cone (with access from Wanaka). On the North Island, Mount Ruapehu is the main ski area, at least when its volcanic activity is dormant. The ski field at Turoa is serviced by the resort of Ohakune and the ski area of Whakapapa by the settlement called National Park.

Catering and related jobs are widely available in these resort towns. In addition to a wage, you may be given a lift pass and subsidised food and drink. Matt Tomlinson enjoyed his two jobs in Ohakune as a barman in the ski resort bar and a waiter in a restaurant, though he came to the conclusion that New Zealand bosses like to get their money's worth. When there weren't many customers, he was put to work building shelves, chopping wood and cleaning drains. He found the jobs by checking notice boards (by the library in Ohakune and in the supermarket), reading the local newspapers and asking around. Altogether the Ruapehu/Ohakune area absorbs about 700 seasonal workers so there is plenty of scope. One of the main employers in the area is Ruapehu Alpine Lifts Ltd (Private Bag, Mount Ruapehu; ☎ 07 892 3738; mtruapehu.com/winter/employment) which accepts applications until mid-April and interviews candidates over the first weekend of May. You will also have to keep your ears open if you are to find affordable accommodation.

The biggest company on the South Island is NZSki Ltd whose employment pages can be found at www3.nzski.com/employment/welcome.jsp, including an online application form. If you have a specific skill, e.g. ski or snowboard instructor, ski patroller, ski hire technician, snowcat/plough driver, then it is worth applying to the resort in advance. Opportunities also exist for carpenters and painters in the months before the season begins; ask around in the pubs. Most resorts are linked from http://skicentral.com/newzealand.html.

A BASI level III certificate or equivalent (see introductory chapter *Tourism: Winter Resorts*) is essential to get full-time instructing work. Part-timers or rookie instructors usually get a lift pass plus instructor training sessions and loggable hours of practice. Snowboard instructors are in demand.

Fishing

Fishing is a profitable business for New Zealand and fishermen (seldom fisherwomen) can be found in most coastal towns. Nelson is one of the important centres for fishing and fish processing, and one of the largest operations is called Sealord where you might get a job on the boats (seven weeks on, seven weeks off) or in fish processing, especially during the mussel season starting in early January (sealord.co.nz/jobs). Overtime is usually available. Compare sea and land vacancies at the other major fishing company Talley's (☎ 03 528 2800; amaltal.co.nz/employment.htm). They are constantly hiring workers to unload their boats which is a very tough job. Provided you have a tax number and a NZ bank account, you should get hired if you show up at the Gatehouse in Port Motueka or at the Amaltal Building on Akersten St in Port Nelson.

Of course recreational fishing creates work, as the American Chris Miksovsky describes:

Queenstown was such a nice place that I decided to stay for a while. I happened upon a job with a chartered fishing boat business. We'd take small groups of angler-wanna-be's out in a motorboat and try to help them catch some rainbow trout or lake salmon. I got to go on several outings but mostly I sat at a small desk by our dock in the town harbour giving information to people about the trips and getting a commission on the trips I booked. The money was excellent some days ($150 was my record) and nil others, all paid cash-in-hand. It was probably the most relaxing and scenic job I've ever had, right on the water, surrounded by mountains, watching the tourists of the world go by. The only downside was that I often had to listen to die-hard fishermen go on and on about all the fish they'd caught around the world. The Americans were the worst: 'Now y'all see that there Barracuuuuda?' (pointing to photo) 'I caught that big ol' boy in Faayjaay. Tuk me fowr hours to brang that there sucker in.'

BUSINESS AND INDUSTRY

Experienced secretaries are in constant demand in Auckland and Wellington by the big agencies like Adecco (adecco.co.nz) with 19 branches. Temping secretaries in the main cities earn $18–$22 an hour, data entry pays $15–$18 while clerks start at the minimum wage and telemarketers earn $16+. Holiday pay of 8% is also accrued.

EMILIANO GIOVANNONI SPENT SEVERAL SUCCESSFUL MONTHS IN TELESALES IN WELLINGTON:

There are lots of opportunities for travellers in Wellington to get a little job. The big thing seems to be telesales and telemarketing. There are loads of agencies recruiting people for that sort of job and no particular skills are required but to be able to 'blag' it. The money is reasonably good for New Zealand and it is easy clean work.

A specialist agency in Wellington, Auckland and Christchurch is Select Teleresources whose vacancies can be searched on seek.co.nz. Among the agencies in Auckland to try for a range of jobs is Kelly Services (☎ 09 303 3122; kellyservices.co.nz).

Without secretarial skills, try market research and labouring agencies, which sometimes require only an IRD number. Labouring agencies can be a good bet such as Allied Workforce which is the largest casual labour supplier in New Zealand (labourhire.co.nz).

TEACHING AND AU PAIRING

Shortages of early childhood, primary and secondary teachers of maths, sciences, technology and special education are acute, especially in Auckland. The NZ government has been providing incentives such as $2,000 or $4,000 international relocation grants in order to attract teachers from overseas, many from Britain, to hard-to-fill posts; details on teachnz.govt.nz.

Au Pair Link in Auckland invites applications from young people from abroad who want to spend up to a year working for a family (☎ 0800 287247; aupairlink.co.nz). Au pairs are paid on average $150 a week and $1000+ if they stay for a full 12 months.

ANTARCTICA

As well as the highly trained scientists and others needed to run an Antarctic research station such as McMurdo Station, a certain number of dogsbodies are needed. The Raytheon Polar Services Company is subcontracted by the US government's National Science Foundation to hire between 800 and 1,000 Americans to run the station, a third of whom are women. Of these, a certain number are general assistants (GAs) who, among many tasks, do quite a lot of snow shovelling. Openings also exist for chefs, electricians, computer programmers, typists, construction workers and so on. Contracts are for four, six or twelve months.

Colorado-based Raytheon Polar Services Company (rpsc.raytheon.com) begin considering applications in April though may not choose their summer season personnel (to work October to mid-February) until the last moment. They host job fairs as part of the selection process. Even though the work schedule is nine hours a day, six days a week, the unskilled jobs are massively oversubscribed, so perseverance will be needed, plus excellent health (physical, mental and dental) and a willingness to travel at short notice. Interested people might want to take a look at coolantarctica.com/Community/find_a_job_in_antarctica.htm which has a jobs forum.

Britain's five research stations and two research vessels in Antarctica are overseen by the British Antarctic Survey in Cambridge (☎ 01223 221508; antarctica.ac.uk/Employment). Most vacancies are for tradespeople like plumbers and electricians plus IT engineers at the BAS stations of Rothera and Halley. All support staff hired by BAS must be suitably qualified or experienced and willing to sign a fixed term or open-ended contract, usually for up to 18 months. They also offer short-term vacation and casual labour contracts, which range for a period of weeks up to a maximum of one year, usually to committed students.

UNITED STATES OF AMERICA

The great American Dream has beckoned countless people who have left their homelands in eager pursuit of the economic miracle. America's image that has been so battered by George W. Bush's foreign policy has been polished up again with the election of Barack Obama. It is early days, but it is likely that the new President will be less wedded to Homeland Security and more sympathetic to reaching out. So the rules and barriers that escalated around exchange programmes under Bush may gradually recede.

However the US authorities continue to make a concerted effort to protect their borders, partly in the interests of post 9/11 'homeland security' but also because the economy is struggling since the credit crunch. The rate of unemployment has increased by nearly 3% over the past year and stands at 7.6% in 2009.

Despite the wide open spaces and warm hospitality so often associated with America, their official policies are discouraging for the traveller who plans to pick up some casual work along the way. The choice of the word 'alien' in official use to describe foreigners may not be intentionally symbolic, however it does convey the suspicion with which non-Americans are treated by the authorities. It is very difficult to get permission to work. But as we have found in so many other countries, there are some special provisions and exceptions to the rule.

The most important exception is the special work visa, the J-1, available through work and travel programmes like the ones run by BUNAC, the British Universities North America Club in London (☎ 020 7251 3472; bunac.org.uk). Various programmes, including the summer camp agencies, are described in detail since they arrange for large numbers of people to work legitimately in the USA.

Other possibilities include joining the one-year Au Pair in America Programme (see section on Childcare below) or joining one of the work exchange or internship programmes, which require you to find your own position in your field of study. According to the US State Department Office of Exchanges there are 3,917 approved programmes, listed at http://eca.state.gov/jexchanges/index.cfm and searchable by category such as summer work, au pair and camp counsellor.

The other side of the coin is the possibility of working without permission, which carries a number of risks and penalties to be carefully considered beforehand. As described below, the laws are always changing in order to tighten up on security in general and black work in particular. The missing link between you and a whole world of employment prospects is a social security number to which you will not be legally entitled unless you have a recognised work visa.

VISAS

Under the Visa-Waiver Program, citizens of the UK and 34 other countries who have a machine-readable passport do not need to apply for a tourist visa in advance for stays of less than 90 days. However as of 2009, they have to obtain prior authorisation via ESTA, the Electronic System for Travel Authorization, which can be easily done on-line free of charge. Individuals entering visa-free or with a visitor visa for business or tourism are prohibited from engaging in paid or unpaid employment in the US. Those planning trips of more than 90 days, including those who wish to work or study, must obtain a visa in advance from the Embassy. This now requires a pre-arranged face-to-face interview and a $131 visa fee (even if the visa is denied) as well as completing a long and detailed form.

British travellers and tourists arriving in the US on the visa waiver programme face increasingly rigorous restrictions. Upon arrival you will have a digital photograph and an inkless fingerprint taken. Check the Embassy website (usembassy.org.uk) or dial the premium line 09042 450100 (£1.20 per minute) for visa information and application forms or request an outline of non-immigrant visas from the Visa Branch of the US Embassy (5 Upper Grosvenor St, London W1A 2JB).

The non-immigrant visa of most interest to the readers of this book is the J-1 which is available to participants of government-authorised programmes, known as Exchange Visitor Programmes (EVP). The J-1 visa is a valuable and coveted addition to any passport since it entitles the holder to take legal paid employment. You cannot apply for the J-1 without the right form and you cannot get form DS2019 without going through a recognised Exchange Visitor Programme (like BUNAC and Camp America) which have approved sponsors in the US. Many are available only to registered students.

Other Visas (Non-J-1)

Apart from the J-1 visa available to people on approved EVPs, there are three possible visa categories to consider, all of which must be applied for by the employer on the applicant's behalf and will take at least three months. The H category covers non-immigrant work visas in special circumstances. The H2-B is for temporary or seasonal vacancies that employers have trouble filling with US citizens. For example, the chronic shortage of workers on the ski fields of Colorado means that many employers can obtain the necessary Labor Certification confirming that there are no qualified American workers available to do the jobs. A petition must be submitted by the employer to the United States Citizenship and Immigration Services (USCIS) which is a bureau of the Department of Homeland Security and which has taken over many functions of the old INS (Immigration and Naturalization Service). The maximum duration of the H2-B visa is one year. The quota is currently 33,000, controversially halved in 2008, leaving many American employers unable to fill their vacancies. Holders of the H2-B must work only for the employer that has petitioned for their visa. The seasonal work visa for agriculture is the H-2A (see foreignlaborcert.doleta.gov/h-2a.cfm).

The non-immigrant Q-1 visa is the 'Cultural Exchange Visa', affectionately dubbed the 'Disney' visa, since it was introduced partly in response to their lobbying. If you find a job in which it can be argued that you will be providing practical training or sharing the history, culture and traditions of your country with interested members of the American public, you might be eligible to work legally for up to 15 months. This is potentially possible in amusement parks, restaurants, museums, summer schools, etc. As usual this visa must be applied for by the prospective employer in the US and approved in advance by USCIS.

It is exceedingly difficult (not to mention expensive) to get an immigrant visa or 'green card' (actually it's off-white) which allows foreigners to live and work in the US as 'resident aliens'. Nearly all the permanent resident visas which are issued each year are given to close relations of American citizens or world experts in their field. Money and love are not the only reasons to marry, though this course of action is too drastic for most.

Arrival

If you have a visa/visa waiver, a return ticket and look tidy and confident, chances are you will whiz through immigration. But American immigration is so notoriously tough and unpleasant that it is worth describing some of the techniques used by readers to avoid possible catastrophe. The length of time given seems to be completely discretionary and you can't count on being stamped in for as long as you request. Note that you can cross land borders with a Visa Waiver as long as the crossing takes place within 90 days of your return ticket from North America to Europe.

Whichever method you choose, be prepared for a gruelling inquisition when you first arrive. Whatever you do, don't confess that you hope to find work. Dress neatly but remember to look like a tourist, not an aspiring professional. If you are taken away to be interviewed, expect to have your luggage minutely examined. Be prepared to explain anything in your luggage which an average sightseeing tourist would be unlikely to have, such as smart clothes (for possible interviews). Better still, don't pack anything which could be incriminating such as letters of reference, letters from an American referring to jobs or interviews, or even a copy of this book. Having written proof that you have a full-time job to return to, property ties or a guaranteed place in higher education in the UK are also an asset. It can be helpful to provide them with a travel itinerary, a list of places and people you want to see in your capacity of tourist.

Although having a return or onward ticket is no guarantee that you will not be hassled, it helps your case. Many travellers recommend entering the US on a short-term return ticket which can be extended after arrival, for instance with Kuwait Airways or Virgin Atlantic. If you do choose this option, make sure before you buy a ticket that the date can be changed without an excessive penalty. If you don't have much money or an onward ticket, it is a good idea to have the names of Americans willing to put you up or a letter from a friend, undertaking to support you for a month or so. Laurence Koe had asked his grandmother to type up a list of all their family connections on the continent which he showed to the suspicious immigration officer at Hawaii Airport, accompanying it with a touching story of how it had been his boyhood dream to encircle the globe.

WORK AND TRAVEL PROGRAMMES

A welter of exchange organisations help candidates from round the world to obtain a J-1 visa. Participants on an Exchange Visitor Programme can work on a J-1 visa in any job for up to four months between 21st May and 30th October or for the winter season between 21st November and 30th April (see section on Ski Resorts below). After the work period finishes, they are permitted a further 30 days for pure travel in the US. BUNAC (16 Bowling Green Lane, London EC1R 0QH; ☎ 020 7251 3472; bunac.org.uk) administers three summer programmes in the US: one is the 'Work America Programme' which allows full-time university students to do any summer job they are able to find; the second is 'Summer Camp USA' which is open to anyone over 18 interested in working on a summer camp as a counsellor; the third is 'KAMP' (Kitchen and Maintenance Programme) which is open to students who want to work at a summer camp in a catering and maintenance capacity. (The camp programmes are described below under the heading 'Summer Camps'.) All participants must join the BUNAC Club (£5), travel between June and the beginning of October either independently or on a BUNAC flight (for £450), pay the varying programme fees and purchase compulsory insurance (£138).

If you are considering a summer job in America, it is worth contacting BUNAC headquarters or your local club branch (in most universities) as early as possible and wading through the details of their programmes and procedures. There is no easy way of circumventing the red tape and accompanying uncertainty though BUNAC are very experienced at guiding applicants as gently as possible through the processes. With tightening US security it is essential that you keep abreast of changes, for example the SEVIS tracking programme means that if you intend to leave the country temporarily (e.g. to visit Canada), you have to register your intention at least two weeks in advance by sending your DS2019 form to your sponsoring organisation.

BUNAC's Work America programme (bunac.org/uk/workamerica) offers several thousand places to students who may take virtually any job anywhere in the US over the summer. In addition to the registration fee of £249 for first-time applicants, you must submit a letter from your principal, registrar or tutor on college headed paper showing that you are a full-time degree-level student. You are also required to take at least $400 in support funds. If you are going over with a commission sales job or plan to job hunt on arrival, you must take at least $800. The J-1 visa application fee is £101 and the SEVIS fee is a further £25. To assist applicants in finding work, BUNAC publishes job listings online; many employers have taken on BUNAC participants in the past. Accommodation may be provided by the employer, particularly if a British student takes a job in the hospitality industry. Jobs can be pre-arranged through BUNAC's resources or they can be found on-the-spot.

In addition to BUNAC, the principal work and travel programmes (as distinct from career-oriented internship programmes described in the next section) are broadly comparable. These programmes provide full-time or deferred place students aged 19 to 30 with the opportunity to live and work in the US for a maximum of four months.

IST Plus Ltd: Richmond (☎ 020 8939 9057; info@istplus.com; istplus.com) is the agency appointed to operate programmes on behalf of CIEE (Council on International Educational

Exchange; ☎ 207 553 4002), including Work and Travel in the USA and Internship USA (described later); participants, who must be students in full-time education, are free to find their own summer jobs before departure and are required to show minimum back-up funds; the fee starts at £415 excluding travel.

Real Gap Company: Tunbridge Wells; ☎ 01892 516164; realgap.co.uk; offers the USA Summer Casual Work for Students Programme; programme fee of £499 includes a job offer.

CCUSA: London W1; ☎ 020 7637 0779; ccusa.com; has a sizeable Work Experience programme, in addition to its summer camp programme (described below); CCUSA participants can work on a J-1 visa in any job for up to four months in the summer; candidates choose whether to find their own job before or after arrival or to have CCUSA find a job for them; respective fees are £298 and £476; most recruitment takes place before April 1st; the company has a network of interviewers around the UK and organises various open houses and recruitment fairs.

Outbreak Adventure Recruitment: ☎ 07971 051097; outbreak-adventure.co.uk/recruitment; supplies seasonal staff for both summer and winter resorts in North America. The agency assists with transport, accommodation and the legal paperwork.

Global Choices: London SE16; ☎ 020 7394 7319; info@globalchoices.co.uk; work and Travel summer programme for students among others; jobs can be found independently or basic, entry level summer jobs are guaranteed, mainly in housekeeping, as restaurant support staff, and in amusement parks; fee £385–£450 for self-arranged programmes and £520–£590 for assisted placements.

Twin Training and Travel Ltd: Lewisham; ☎ 020 8297 3251; workandvolunteer.com; work and Travel USA summer programme; fee £750.

Note that a number of other student travel organisations place students from around the world in similar work and travel programmes. For example Sayit is an Irish student travel agency with an office in Cork which operates a J-1 programme (sayit.ie). Student Placement Australia near Sydney does likewise for Australians and also offers a 12-month working programme for the USA (studentplacement.org.au). APEX USA Ltd (PO Box 8, Clinton, Oklahoma 73601; apexusa.org) is just one of many approved exchange agencies with partner organisations around the world that conduct interviews on its behalf.

Internships

Internship is the American term for traineeship, providing a chance to get some work experience in your career interest as part of your academic course. These are typically available to undergraduates, recent graduates and young professionals, and are almost always unpaid. Several organisations in the UK are authorised to help candidates find work placements in the USA and obtain a J-1 visa valid for up to 18 months. IST Plus, Realgap, Twin UK and Global Choices in the UK (contact details above) help full-time students and recent graduates to arrange course-related placements in the US lasting from 3 to 18 months. The placement can take place at any time during your studies, during the summer, as a sandwich year or up to 12 months after graduating. Although you are responsible for finding your own course-related position, the programme organisers supply practical advice on applying for work and a searchable database of internships/work placements. Those who qualify get a J-1 visa. Programme fees differ but may start at £400 for students who can fix up their own training position but rise to more than £2,000 for non-students who want a placement arranged for them. Realgap charges interns £799 for six months, £1,299 for up to 12 months and £1,559 for 18 months, which includes arranging an internship for example in the hotels industry. Wages are paid on a par with US co-workers.

The UK/US Career Development Programme is administered by the Association for International Practical Training (AIPT) in Maryland (aipt.org). This programme is for people aged 18–35 with relevant qualifications and/or at least one year of work experience in their career field. A separate section of the programme is for full-time students in Hospitality and Tourism or Equine Studies. InterExchange (interexchange.org) and the Alliance Abroad Group (allianceabroad.com) are both accredited to grant J-1 and H2-B visas to European candidates.

SUMMER CAMPS

Summer camps are uniquely American in atmosphere, even if the idea has spread to Europe. An estimated 8 million American children are sent to 10,000 summer camps each year for a week or more to participate in outdoor activities and sports, arts and crafts and generally have a wholesome experience. The type of camp varies from plush sports camps for the very rich to more or less charitable camps for disabled or underprivileged children. British young people are especially in demand as soccer coaches on summer camps.

It is estimated that summer camps employ nearly a third of a million people. Thousands of 'counsellors' are needed each summer to be in charge of a cabinful of youngsters and to instruct or supervise some activity, from the ordinary (swimming and boating) to the esoteric (puppet-making and ham radio). Several summer camp organisations are authorised to issue J-1 visas, primarily Camp America and BUNAC, but some smaller ones are also mentioned below.

After camp finishes, counsellors have up to six weeks' free time and normally return on organised flights between late August and the end of September. Camp counselling regularly wins enthusiastic fans and is worth considering if you enjoy children (even the rambunctious American variety who might threaten to sue you if you shout at them) and don't mind hard work. Some camps are staffed almost entirely by young people from overseas, which can be useful if you are looking for a post-camp travelling companion. If the idea of working at a remote lakeside or mountain location appeals to you but the 24-hour-a-day responsibility for keeping children entertained and well-behaved does not, you might be interested in a behind-the-scenes job in the kitchen or maintenance. Camp directors often find it difficult to attract Americans to do these jobs, partly because the wages are low, and both BUNAC and Camp America can arrange this for British and European students.

Bear in mind that your enjoyment of a summer camp job will be largely determined by the style of the camp, the standard of facilities and its proximity to interesting places to visit on your days off. One way of making an informed choice is to attend one of the recruitment fairs held in the new year by Camp America where you can meet camp directors. This might have helped Amy Jones, a student at Nottingham University, to avert her disastrous experience:

> ***On arrival we were launched into a 75-hour week, looking after the children and the 37 horses. This increased to 85 when the only American counsellor quit after just two weeks. Apart from the exhaustion, this might have been tolerable. But the couple who ran the camp were intimidating. They seemed worried we might run away (which we did often think about). One of the new rules they imposed was that we were not allowed to speak to each other unless it concerned camp organisation. There was no privacy and no freedom. The atmosphere was filled with tension.***

Amy's conclusion was that, seen from one point of view, the recruitment agencies supply cheap labour who are not at liberty to leave because they then forfeit their free flight.

Camps have to impose rules and in many cases these are quite strict, such as no alcohol (apparently Irish and Australian counsellors, true to their reputations, are the most likely to be fined for drinking at camp.)

BUNAC

With its Summer Camp USA programme, BUNAC is one of the two biggest counsellor placement organisations in the field, sending several thousand people over 19 (or 18 if expert in something in demand) as counsellors at children's camps. The registration fee of £144 includes camp placement, return flight and land transport to camp and pocket money of $985–$1,215 (depending on age) for the whole nine-week period. The fact that you do not have to raise the money for the flight is a great attraction for many; the camp which decides to hire you advances the amount from your wages to BUNAC who in turn put it towards your flight. Interviews, which are compulsory, are held in university towns throughout Britain between November and May.

Summer camps provide more scope for employment than looking after the kids. BUNAC's Kitchen and Maintenance Programme, otherwise known as KAMP USA, is open only to degree-level students (including final year students) who are given ancillary jobs in the kitchen, laundry or maintenance department, for which they will be advanced their airfare and in some cases paid more than the counsellors, i.e. a guaranteed minimum of $1,350 for the eight or nine-week period of work. Initial registration costs £144.

Camp America

Camp America (London SW7; ☎ 020 7581 7373; campamerica.co.uk) is another major recruitment organisation in Britain, which arranges for up to 9,000 people aged 18 or over, from around the world, to work on children's summer camps in the USA. The work is for nine weeks between June and August where you could be teaching activities such as tennis, swimming and arts and crafts. Camp America provides a free return flight from London to New York and guidance on applying for a J-1 visa. The camp provides free board and lodging plus pocket money.

At the end of your contract, you will be given a lump sum of pocket money which will range from $575 to $1,200 depending on your age (as of 1st June), experience, qualifications and whether you've been a camp counsellor in the US before. Upfront charges include the registration fee of £469 which excludes the US visa fee of £108 and the compulsory police check (£36).

AFTER THE FIRST YEAR OF HER SOFTWARE ENGINEERING COURSE AT BIRMINGHAM UNIVERSITY, VICTORIA JOSSEL SPENT A WONDERFUL SUMMER IN THE US WITH CAMP AMERICA WHICH SHE FELT REALLY ENHANCED HER CV:

On June 9th, I apprehensively boarded my flight to Blue Star camp in North Carolina. Not only did I have the privilege of bonding with the children in my cabin from whom you receive constant love, caring and attention, but I also met new people from all over the world and received amazing references for my future career. I learned how to organise, motivate and lead people as well as negotiate positive outcomes to conflicts. From a normal 19 year old girl, I became a responsible, motivated, adaptable and independent person with 14 children who were my responsibility. I had never been camping and had never wanted to go camping. Yet it was the most amazing experience: I learned to start a fire on my own, cook food for all 14 girls and organise it so the kids all got EXACTLY the same amount of Hershey's chocolate.

One way to secure a placement early and avoid last-minute uncertainty is to attend one of Camp America's recruitment fairs in various British cities between January and March, which is what Colin Rothwell did: *'At the recruitment fair, you could actually meet the camp directors from all over the States and find out more about particular camps. If you are lucky, like me and a thousand others, you can sign a contract on the spot. Then you leave all the "dirty work" to Camp America and wait until they call you to the airport in June sometime.'*

Camp America's other summer programme is Campower, for students who would like to work in the kitchen/maintenance areas at camp and earn a little more ($1,000–$1,300 for the summer).

Other Summer Camp Organisations

Camp Counselors USA (CCUSA) works with 850 camps in 48 states and since 1986 has placed more than 200,000 young people over 18 from over 60 countries. CCUSA's programme includes return flight to the US, one night's accommodation in New York City, visas and insurance, full board and lodging during placement as well as the chance to earn more than on the other programmes. CCUSA tries to place counsellors at camps which suit their skills and personality. Enquiries should be made as early as possible to the relevant CCUSA office (see ccusa.com).

The pocket money for first year participants aged 18 is $800 for the nine-week programme rising to $1,210 for those over 21 in addition to international flights, one way domestic flight and living expenses. CCUSA is reputed to offer a good service, as reported by Joseph Tame: *'CCUSA were very good to me. They visited us during the summer and were very efficient when it came to my flight home. All I did was call their freefone number with the date I wanted to return; there and then they said yes. The overall impression I got was that CCUSA offered a good and friendly service.'*

Several au pair agencies co-operate with Interexchange in New York by placing candidates over the age of 19 on the Camp USA programme: contact Worldnet UK (☎ 0845 458 1551; worldnetuk.com). Other possibilities include:

International Camp Counselor Program: New York; run by YMCA International in New York; ☎ 212 727 8800; internationalymca.org; special needs counsellors and life-guards especially needed; in UK, camp support roles can be applied for through West London YMCA, London W5 5RE; international@londonymca.org.

Camp Leaders in America (CLIA): Liverpool; 0845 430 1219; campleaders.com; partner of Cultural Homestay Program; programme fee £399.

International Counselor Exchange Program: New York, NY 10024; ☎ 212 787 7706; icep-usa.org; no British representative.

Note that some of the smaller less publicised programmes may charge lower fees than the big companies.

CASUAL WORK

A law stipulates that all employers must physically examine documents of prospective employees within three working days, proving that they are either a US citizen or an authorised alien (see Documents below). All US employers are obliged to complete an I-9 form which verifies the employee's right to work. Employers who are discovered by the immigration authorities to be hiring illegal aliens are subject to huge fines. Yet it is estimated that there are up to 200,000 British workers living and working illegally in California alone.

The law is considered to be unenforceable in seasonal industries such as fruit growing and resort tourism where it is still not uncommon for more than half of all employees to be illegal. Farmers and restaurateurs have claimed that they can barely stay in business without hiring casual workers without permits. Yet those who are caught working illegally run the risk of being deported, prohibited from travelling to the US for five years and in some cases for good. If your place of work is raided and you are caught, you will be detained while your case is being 'processed', which can take up to three weeks. If you are 'in-status' (which means your tourist visa has not expired) you are given the option of departing voluntarily. If not, you will be automatically deported.

The law seems to be more strictly enforced in areas like California, Texas and Florida which are traditional strongholds for illegal workers from Mexico and the rest of Latin America.

Documents

Every American can reel off his social security number by heart. J-1 visa holders are entitled to apply for one. Social security offices are required to check the J-1 visa with the USCIS database which has caused delays, which in turn can mean delays in being paid by your employer. Other routes to obtaining a social security number apart from having an approved visa include getting one for the purposes of banking but this will be stamped 'Not Valid for Employment'.

False social security cards circulate in their thousands (so much easier to produce with today's digital technology), though the Department of Homeland Security has been cracking down harder on fraudulent ID papers and mounting large-scale raids on workplaces thought to hire large numbers of undocumented aliens. A recent approach has been to bring charges against people with forged documents for committing 'identity theft' rather than simply immigration violations.

Hostels

Round-the-world backpackers are sometimes shocked by the contrast between your average city hostel in the US and in Australia/New Zealand, as gap year student David Hardie (RIP) reported in 2008:

> ***In LA the hostel was a dive. This seems to be the case with most hostels in the US. One of the people staying at our LA hostel was a black dwarf named Jacky whose job it was to impersonate Chucky, the evil doll from those films. Another hostel resident wanted us to join him to go and trash his ex-girlfriend's car. There isn't really a backpacking scene in the USA. Unlike Australia everyone in US hostels seems to be older and in between jobs, usually low lives.***

Therefore it might be wise to choose your accommodation with more care than elsewhere. There are of course travellers' hostels which will trade food and a bed for some work. Occasionally notices of casual jobs appear on the bulletin boards of youth hostels and backpackers' haunts. The Green Tortoise Hostel at 494 Broadway in San Francisco sometimes has strange odd jobs for pleasant and persistent travellers. One way to search for openings is to go to craigslist.org for the city where you want to work and search for 'hostel' in the Jobs pages. A sample search for San Francisco revealed opportunities at the USA Hostel on Post Street (usahostels.com) including a job as a 'graveyard receptionist' to cover the night shift.

Carolyn Edwards had a discouraging time looking for work in Hawaii, but came across plenty of travellers spending four hours a day cleaning in hostels in exchange for bed and board. Richard Davies was given free accommodation and paid $10 an hour to clean toilets at his Los Angeles hostel which allowed him time to look for other work. Employment in your hostel is always worth asking about since some operate an informal work-for-keep system. Ask at privately owned travellers' lodges in the Grand Canyon area. Mark Horobin patronised a different sort of hostel when he found himself skint in California:

Males who line up in the early afternoon outside the San Diego Rescue Mission have a good chance of being given a bed and meals for three days. If you need a longer stay you may consider signing up as a helper as I did, but to do this you'll have to explain your reason (claiming to be an ex-alcoholic goes over well) and attend a compulsory daily Bible study session. If you are accepted you work about four hours a day. Later I stayed at the Prince of Peace Monastery in Oceanside.

Drive-aways

The term 'drive-away' applies to the practice of delivering private cars within North America. Prosperous Americans and Canadians and also companies are prepared to pay several hundred dollars to delivery firms who agree to arrange delivery of private vehicles to a different city, usually because the car-owner wants his or her car available at their holiday destination but doesn't want to drive it personally. The companies find drivers, arrange insurance and arbitrate in the event of mishaps. You get free use of a car (subject to mileage and time restrictions) and pay for all gas after the first tankful and tolls on the interstates. Usually a deadline and mileage limit are fixed (e.g. 400 miles or 650km a day), though these are often flexible and checks lax. A good time to be travelling east to west or north to south (e.g. Chicago to Phoenix) is September/October when a lot of older people head to a warmer climate. On the other hand, when there is a shortage of vehicles (e.g. leaving New York in the summer), you will be lucky to get a car on any terms.

The only requirements are that you be over 23, have a clean driving licence, plus an International Driving Permit, and able to pay a deposit in cash or travellers cheques (generally $350–$400) which will be refunded on successful delivery. You may also have to produce references and/or an official motor vehicle driving record from your home country.

Check *the Yellow Pages* under 'Auto Transporters' for a local provider, though the company with national coverage is Auto Driveaway (1 800 346 2277; autodriveaway.com) which has dozens of franchised operators across the US, from Salt Lake City to Syracuse, Saint Louis to Seattle. Go to autodriveawaydc.com/carlist.html for a current list of available cars. Try also Custom Auto Delivery (driveaway.com) though they tend to use staff drivers rather than occasional ones. From Toronto, an established company is Toronto Drive-Away Service (☎ 1 800 561 2658; torontodriveaway.com) whose website contains driver recruitment information; the minimum age is 25. An alternative is to ask at a travel information centre for car rental agencies which arrange delivery of rental cars to the places where there is a seasonal demand, for example to Florida or to ski resorts in the winter.

The greater your flexibility of destination, the quicker you'll be out of town. Bridgid Seymour-East and Jimmy Henderson enjoyed a wonderful 'potluck' trip around the USA, picking up a car in Los Angeles and driving to a town in Minnesota. If you are travelling with one or more people, you can save money by splitting the cost of the gas. The company allows you to take co-drivers and/or passengers provided they register for insurance purposes. The type of vehicle you are assigned and its gas consumption can make a significant difference to the overall cost. Few agencies store cars themselves so you will need to find your own way to the car's home. When you are introduced to the vehicle, check through a list of existing damage with the owner (or agent) and fill in a 'Condition Report'. Be very thorough, since otherwise you may be held liable for existing damage or faults. If you do have mechanical problems on the road, you pay for any repairs costing less than a specified sum (perhaps $75), which you reclaim from the recipient of the vehicle. For more expensive work you should call the owner (collect) and discuss how he or she will arrange payment for the repairs. Many travellers have concluded that drive-aways are an excellent wheeze, among them Mig Urquhart:

One day somebody in Fort Lauderdale was talking about fishing in Alaska and about a week later three of us had a driveaway to Seattle. It was the most outstanding car to do the journey in – a Mitsubishi Montero, one of those big jeep-type 4X4s. Only two of us could drive. We did 4,700 miles in nine days which included a birthday party for me in Tampa, lunch in New Orleans, the Grand Canyon, Las Vegas, a weekend with a friend in San Francisco and finally the glorious drive from SF to Seattle. The trip cost each of us $200 including food, gas, the motel in Vegas and a really nice meal in SF.

THE JOB HUNT

Working holidaymakers from Britain and countries worldwide can capitalise on current employee shortages during the summer season by participating in one of the approved Work and Travel programmes mentioned earlier. A headline in the *Daily Telegraph* in November 2008 revealed the extent of the problem for employers in just one area: 'US ski resorts face severe staff shortages', and the same is true of summer resorts too.

The majority of seasonal jobs will pay the minimum wage of $6.55, rising to $7.25 July 2009, though some states have legislated a higher wage, e.g. California and Massachusetts ($8), New York ($7.15), etc. and five southern states have no minimum wage. Trainee workers aged under 20 may be paid the youth minimum of $4.25 for the first 90 days of their employment. People in jobs that rely on tips earn a pittance since the minimum hourly wage for tipped employees in the US is an appalling $2.13. These can be checked on the Department of Labor's website (dol.gov/esa/minwage/america.htm).

Prospects for job-hunters in the cities are not so rosy. Dan Jacobson returned to his home town of Chicago after several years of roaming the globe but was not welcomed back with open arms by local employers:

With all the experiences I've had getting work all over the place, when I'm finally legal I can't find a job. It's a laugh really... I've applied around town like crazy and nothing's come up so far. Temp agencies don't call back and won't let you come in to interview any more. I've hit I don't know how many cafés and restos, all to no avail, plus plenty of shops and various other stuff (like a dog daycare centre) but nobody's hiring me. I guess all the anecdotes about a bad economy are for real. I'm heading back to the mountains of Switzerland.

But if you're prepared to travel and to work for a whole summer season, you will have better luck. Time can productively be spent searching the internet. Dozens of sites may prove useful, though resortjobs.com, coolworks.com and jobmonkey.com are especially recommended for seasonal jobs in the tourist industry. If you wait until you arrive in the States to look for a job, bear in mind that it is more difficult to lead a hand-to-mouth existence in North America than elsewhere. Word of mouth and personal contact are particularly important in the States. Travellers are frequently offered some casual work while chatting to local residents. Many of these jobs have been in building, landscape gardening, furniture removal, or similar. Other jobs are less conventional. Paul Donut didn't have to look too hard for work in the capital of Louisiana, but the opportunities that presented themselves were distinctly unappealing:

When I arrived in Baton Rouge I looked up a friend of a friend who, I was told, might be able to help me find work. She did. She found me a job escorting customers from a bar at the gates of Louisiana State University to their cars, as many of them had been mugged on this short but perilous journey. After considering this job for about 30 seconds, I declined it, since the murder rate in Baton Rouge is among the highest in the country. The only other job opportunity to arise was helping out on an alligator farm which I wasn't sure would be any safer than protecting people from mugging.

TOURISM AND CATERING

Labour demands in summer resorts and national parks sometimes reach crisis proportions especially along the eastern seaboard. Because tipping is so generous, employers in many states are allowed to pay next to nothing, provided tips bring the take-home pay up to at least the state minimum. This means that you can earn the derisory wage of $10 for an evening shift. An average weekly take in tips for a full-time waiter/waitress might be $120 with possibilities of earning twice that. Bar staff can earn as much as $200 a night (but note that bar staff have to be the legal drinking age of 21). Apparently a British accent helps, except in the case of Briton Jane Thomas who was accused of putting it on to attract a higher tip! Even if you don't get a job serving drinks or a 'waitperson', busboys (table clearers) are usually given a proportion of tips by the waiter whom they are helping, typically 10%.

The recruitment needs of national and state parks can often be found on the internet, for example Glacier National Park in Montana near the Canadian border on gpihr.com and Denali Park in Alaska (summerdenalijobs.com); the latter hires 900 people each summer (early May to mid-September). Facilities in the famous national parks of Utah (Bryce Canyon and Zion Canyon) are run by Xanterra Recreational Services (xanterra.com or coolworks.com/utahparks). Xanterra also recruit for the even more famous Yellowstone National Park in Wyoming which offers 2,500 seasonal jobs (yellowstonejobs.com) Grand Canyon North Rim is now operated by Forever Resorts which also makes use of coolworks.com. The DNC Parks and Resorts concessionaire at Yosemite National Park in California can be contacted by ringing 209 372 1236 or checking the Employment section on yosemitepark.com about its 800 open summer vacancies.

California is a magnet for Brits, though many find the cost of living higher than elsewhere in the States. Plenty of foreigners find work in Los Angeles, in the restaurants, bistros and cafés of Santa Monica, San Francisco and so on. Paying your way in Manhattan with a fast food or equivalent job will be a challenge. Jane Thomas solved this problem by getting on a house-sitting circuit via contacts. Through a friend, she met various people who were only too glad to have a nice reliable English girl live in their houses while they were away on holiday, to discourage burglars, water the plants, etc. One of the places she stayed in was a luxury apartment overlooking Central Park. The incongruity of passing the commissionaire every morning arrayed in the orange polyester uniform of Burger Heaven struck her as highly amusing.

Seaside Resorts

Popular resorts are often a sure bet, especially if you arrive in mid-August (when American students begin to leave jobs), or in April/May (before they arrive). Part-way through her second year of a social anthropology degree at Manchester Uni, Julia Wilson realised that she did not want to fritter her summer away as she had the previous year, so a round-robin email from BUNAC caught her eye. As she reported in 2009, she soon enrolled on the Work America programme and was emailing her CV to some employers listed in the BUNAC Directory. She received three job offers, and was shocked that two of them imposed a ceiling on tips earned, so that waiting staff could earn only up to $8 an hour. Instead she accepted a job at the West Chop Club in Martha's Vineyard, all Republican Senators, heiresses and spoilt kids. At first she was bowled over by the beauty of the place, so clean and well-groomed near pristine beaches. But the lack of spare time working 40–50 hour weeks, and the apartheid between guests and staff soon began to grate. When after a month her manager told her that she was sacking her because it was evident her heart was not in the job, Julia couldn't disagree and was given a scant 48 hours to vacate her room.

But she liked Martha's Vineyard enough to want to stay on the island, and scoured the local paper for accommodation and jobs. She soon found a room in the home of some colourful locals, bought a bicycle for $50 and juggled three part-time jobs that left her more free time and brought in more money than the pre-arranged job. She concluded that being fired was the best thing that happened to her. If she had stayed around for the $300 end-of-season bonus, she would have had to work up until Sept 16th and flown home on the 17th. Her jobs consisted of life-modelling for the local art society which paid $50 for two hours, working as a hostess in a restaurant (attached to a health spa which staff were allowed to use) and working in a boutique where she had plenty of time between customers to read books and use her laptop, while earning a generous $12 an hour.

According to Andrew Boyle, there seemed to be more BUNACers in the Maryland resort of Ocean City than natives, and in fact he noticed considerable tension and a 'clash of ideologies' between the party-loving young workers and the older year-round residents. In fact a lot of young foreigners go to resorts like this simply to party and anyone who is willing to work really hard stands out and is usually treated better. Other popular resorts to try are Wildwood (New Jersey), Virginia Beach (Virginia), Myrtle Beach (South Carolina) and Atlantic Beach (North Carolina).

Boats

For a yachting job, Florida is the best place to look. Innumerable pleasure craft and also fishing boats depart from the Florida Keys (at the southern tip of the state) bound for the Caribbean, especially between Christmas and Easter. You might also try for work on a cruise ship (see section on the Caribbean). There is usually plenty of bar and kitchen work in the Keys, the second largest gay centre in North America. Florida resorts are swamped by tens of thousands of students during their spring breaks, so accommodation is almost impossible to find in March and early April.

Fort Lauderdale creates plenty of casual work on yachts year round which regularly pays $11–$13 an hour. A good place to hear about day work on yachts, as well as opportunities in landscaping and restaurants, is Floyd's Hostel and Crew House in the southeast section of town, which accepts only international travellers. Floyd Creamer, the owner/manager (who contributed to an earlier edition of this book), invites people to ring 954 462 0631 or email floydshostel@gmail.com to find out about bed availability and arrange a free pick-up from bus or train station.

Ski Resorts

There truly is an abundance of winter work in ski resorts, especially in Colorado, between November and the 'Mud Season' in May. Aspen, Vail and Steamboat Springs Colorado have all been recommended. Much of it can be investigated online, e.g. through jobmonkey.com/ski.

If you are prepared to travel in person, the best time to arrive is October/November when the big resorts hold job fairs. Jobs are available as lift operators, restaurant workers, ticket clerks, basket check (like left luggage for skiers), etc. As ever, the main problem in big resorts (especially Vail) is a lack of employee accommodation. Unless you arrive in August/September, you will have to be very lucky to find a room of any kind. Check adverts in the local papers for example in *Steamboat Pilot* and *Today* whose employment classifieds are posted online (steamboatpilot.com). Hundreds of 'help wanted' ads appear in the winter months and even more in the summer. Also check the resorts' websites which have links from the employment website coolworks.com/ski-resort-jobs.

You should also be aware that immigration raids are frequent, which make employers reluctant to hire people without papers even when desperate for staff. The Steamboat Springs site steamboat.com posts some vacancies or email hr@steamboat.com. If in the resort visit the Human

Resources office of the largest local employer, the Steamboat Ski and Resort Corporation (☎ 970 871 5132). Job Fairs are held around the first weekend of November where employers can meet job-seekers. Neil Hibberd worked a season as a ski lift operator for the Steamboat Corporation on a J-1 visa fixed up through an internship programme in London (now IST Plus described at the beginning of the chapter).

Condominiums or 'condos' are sometimes a good bet for casual employment. If you're just looking for occasional work, chopping wood in late autumn is a simple way of making a quick profit and contracts for clearing snow from roofs are sometimes available. Hotels aren't a big feature of American resorts (though two of the principal ones at Steamboat, the Sheraton and the Ptarmigan Inn, hire large numbers of non-local workers). Resort companies like Mountain Resorts and the Steamboat Ski and Resort Corporation hire room cleaners, maintenance men, drivers, etc. It is common for one company to own all the facilities and control all employment in one resort, and in some cases provide accommodation to all staff.

In another of Colorado's famous resorts, try Vail Resorts which has a dedicated freephone jobs line 1-888-Ski-Job-1 and an employment website http://skijob1.snow.com with detailed information for foreign applicants. Aspen is one of the wealthiest resorts and supports a large transient working population. The Aspen Skiing Company is heavily involved with the hiring of foreign workers through CCUSA. Due to popularity of the programme they encourage interested candidates to start the application procedures as early as May for the following ski season. The company is permitted to submit visa applications in July; the website aspensnowmass.com/companyinfo/employment/visa.cfm contains a wealth of detailed information about the recruitment procedures for non-US citizens. One of the major employers in Aspen for the summer as well as the winter season is the Gant Condominium Resort (610 West End St, Aspen, CO 81611; ☎ 970 925 5000; gantaspen.com/ski-resort-employment.php).

If you decide to show up in Aspen, visit the Cooper Street Pier bar and listen for foreign accents. Unfortunately wages tend to be low in this setting and saving very difficult after you have paid for room and board, ski pass and equipment rental. It is worth hanging on to the end of the season when many employers pay sizeable bonuses or distribute a share of the season's tips. Another major Colorado resort is Winter Park Resort (☎ 1 970 726 1536; skiwinterpark.com/employment).

Californian ski resorts that also hire in large numbers include Sugar Bowl in Norden (sugarbowl.com/employment) and Mammoth Mountain Resort (☎ 760 934 0654; http://jobs.mammothmountain.com). Many other ski resorts around the country hire seasonal staff in November/December.

Theme Parks

Although British people are acquainted with fun fairs and theme parks, they will be amazed at the grand scale on which many American amusement parks and carnivals operate, sometimes employing up to 3,000 summer assistants to work on the rides and games, food service, parking lot and maintenance, warehouse, wardrobe and security. One chain of parks is Six Flags Theme Parks which have huge operations in a number of states which together hire 2,500 international staff. Some of the biggest employers of this kind co-operate with the work and travel programme organisers described earlier. Representatives from Six Flags sometimes liaise with the major summer work agencies and recruit summer staff abroad. One of the biggest amusement parks is Cedar Point in Sandusky, Ohio (cedarpoint.com) which hires international students via CIEE and CCUSA. The opportunities afforded to young people looking for summer work by just one of these enormous commercial complexes are enormous and dwarf Butlins and Alton Towers entirely.

On a smaller scale, travelling carnivals and fun fairs may need a few assistants to set up, operate and dismantle game stands and rides. Since the keynote of American business is to encourage competition and provide incentives, many of these carnival operators let you take home a cut of the profits on your particular stall, which can be stressful.

The Disney International Programs at the Walt Disney World Resort near Orlando in Florida are made up of two programmes: the 'Disney International College Program' (5–12 months for students and recent graduates) and the one-year 'Cultural Representative Program'. Participants in both programmes work in front line roles at Disney's theme parks and resorts. For information about the College Program contact ☎ 407 934 7470 (wdw.int.recruiting@disney.com; disneyinternationalprograms.com) Specifically for the Cultural Representative Program, people from the UK and about a dozen other countries are hired to represent the culture, heritage and customs of their countries in themed pavilions and other areas of the resort. In the UK, the annual recruiting presentations normally take place in March and October; for details contact Yummy Jobs (The Georgian Village, Unit 5, 100 Wood Street, London, E17 3HX; fax 020 7691 7820; enquiries@yummyjobs.com). Any job which involves tips is usually more lucrative than others; pay rates start at $7.21 per hour, and wages can be swelled by more than $100 in a five-hour shift. The gated staff apartments have lots of facilities and a buzzing social life.

Kevin Eastwood from Huddersfield participated as a Cultural Representative in 2008–9 and focused on the perks of the job:

> ***The programme has been a fantastic opportunity for me and one I will remember forever. I worked in food and beverage at the UK Pavilion in Epcot... Disney understands how sometimes it can be difficult being so far away from family and friends for so long, and have provided many resources, from computer labs to free internet access in our apartments, to housing events... I now have friends from places such as Canada, Norway, China, Mexico, Italy, Japan, America and France. I also enjoyed all of the Cast-exclusive opportunities available to us such as admission to Disney theme parks and discounts on resort accommodation and dining.***

After checking out the feedback on the unofficial website for International Program alumni (wdwip.com), most of it very enthusiastic, Catherine Howard from Cork, Ireland decided to apply to work in Florida. Unfortunately there is no separate Irish pavilion, but she sent an application off to Yummy Jobs anyway for their J-1 Cultural Resort Program and, after she had paid their processing charges of about $2,000, they found her a Front Desk position at the Walt Disney World Swan and Dolphin Hotel next to Epcot but not owned by Disney. Interestingly, the literature from the sponsoring organisation in the US made the training and visa scheme sound far more rigorous a process than it actually was and in the end her interview at the US embassy in Dublin lasted all of 60 seconds.

DESPITE SOMETIMES BAULKING AT AMERICAN BUSINESS CULTURE, CATHERINE HOWARD HAD A WONDERFUL 18 MONTHS:

I loved my job. Everyone was really nice and helpful, and I did actually enjoy chatting with guests. You are in Disney World after all, so for the most part, guests are usually happy to be there. Sometimes it was difficult to stomach the touchy-feely parts of corporate America. At pre-shift meetings, we would talk about 'core values' and making our guests feel special, and no pre-shift was complete without each of us reciting an example from our own lives where we were made to feel special as well. The Americans did this willingly without irony or self-consciousness, but it wrecked my head. The way I saw it, our time would be better spent fixing the actual problems the hotel had, instead of feeling special, but this attitude got me into trouble with the manager, so my advice would be to smile and suck it up instead!

(This was the same manager, mind you, that introduced a directive whereby, if a guest asked us how we were today, we had to reply with a word of three syllables or more, e.g. 'Good' was not allowed, but 'wonderful' or 'fantastic' was okay. My favourite was 'homicidal'.)

I loved my time in Florida and going there is one of the best decisions I ever made. But my first three months or so were one of the lowest points in my entire life, because I made one crucial mistake: I never learned to drive. I couldn't quite fathom what people meant when they said that in Orlando you couldn't walk anywhere. Not only was I a freak – the only person over the age of 16 in the entire state of Florida who couldn't drive a car – but when it came to finding an apartment, my options were severely limited. Four months in, I learned to drive, bought a car and moved into a much nicer apartment with one of my new best friends.

During my eighteen months in Orlando, I got to:

- *See a Space Shuttle launch from Cape Canaveral – one of my Top 3 Dreams.*
- *Spot celebrities. The best one was seeing Steven Tyler in the queue for Pirates of the Caribbean!*
- *Attend a Hallowe'en screening of the Rocky Horror Show, in costume.*
- *Watch fireworks every night on my way home from work (and the Seaworld fireworks from my patio every night in the summer).*
- *Go to Mickey's Very Merry Christmas Party at the Magic Kingdom – twice.*
- *Drink and eat my way around Epcot's Food and Wine Festival.*
- *Go to Washington DC, Miami, Mardi Gras in New Orleans, New York at Christmastime, etc.*
- *Wake up to sunshine almost every single morning.*

OTHER POPULAR JOBS

Selling

By reputation, anyway, American salesmen are a hardbitten lot. Some travellers have found that their foreign charm makes selling surprisingly effortless. ('Are you really English? I just love that accent.') Americans are not as suspicious of salesmen as other nationalities and you may be pleasantly surprised by the tolerance with which you are received on the doorstep and, even more, by the high earnings which are possible. The BUNAC Job Directory contains details of a number of commission selling jobs but you must have at least $800 on arrival to tide you over the low periods.

Advertisements for sales positions proliferate. You may find telesales less off-putting than door-to-door salesmanship, but it will also be less lucrative. On the other hand, some working holidaymakers and gap year students do not shy away from the hard edge of selling and tackle commission-only jobs. The Southwestern Company with its headquarters in Nashville markets educational books and software door-to-door throughout the US and has a recruitment office in Edinburgh (☎ 0131 445 7408) which targets gap year and university students. Its website (southwestern.com) contains glowing reports from past students whose earnings have been impressive. They claim that the average seller saves $8,000 over a summer. Their statistics possibly exclude all the students who give up in disgust after a few weeks of failure.

Soccer Coaching

Soccer continues to gain popularity in North America, including among girls, and demand is strong for young British coaches to work on summer coaching schemes. A number of companies recruit qualified coaches to work all over the States including Hawaii. Some (like Sonesoccer) employ staff only on long-term contracts, but others offer shorter contracts:

Goal-Line Soccer Inc: PO Box 1642, Corvallis, OR 97339; ☎ 541 753 5833; info@goal-line.com; goal-line.com; minimum age 21; mostly in Oregon and Washington; recruits through BUNAC for July and early August only.

Major League Soccer Camps: Connecticut. UK recruitment, Leeds; ☎ 0113 276 8826; chir.andrew@mlscamps.com; mlscamps.com/employment; the largest and best known company. Package costing £575 includes kit, training, flights from UK, rental car plus gas and insurance expenses, emergency health care insurance and a wage of at least $150 per week; MLSC assists with processing of H-2B visas.

Soccer Academy Inc: Manassas, Virginia; soccer-academy.com; European-based coaches should apply to Mark Jennings, 38 Shawfield Road, Hadfield, Glossop, Derbyshire SK13 2BJ; ☎ 07814 390740; mmarkjenco@aol.com.

UK Elite Soccer: Cedar Knolls, NJ; 973 631 9802; jobs@UKElite.com; offers soccer camps, coaching and programmes in 16 states, mainly on the east coast; seasonal coaches needed March–November and 70 summer coaches July–August; summer coaches earn salary of $1,400 plus $4,000 in expenses.

BUNAC knows about these companies, since they normally process the necessary J-1 visa. It is more important to be good at working with kids than to be a great football player, though of course it is easier to command the respect of the kids if you can show them good skills and a few tricks. Most companies prefer to hire candidates with a National Coaching Licence, e.g. FA level 1 coaching which can be acquired after doing a course lasting 24–40 hours (see 1st4 sportqualifications.com). You are likely also to need an enhanced CRB check and emergency first aid certificate.

Manual Work

Cash-in-hand work can be found, especially as a loader with removal firms, as security guards and in construction (especially for those with skills). The best time (for men) to look for removal work is just before the end of the month when many leases expire and more people tend to move house. Dan Eldridge worked at a hostel in San Francisco for a year and so knows the working scene well: *'An interesting option is to open up the phone book to "Movers" and personally visit them, especially any with Irish names. They all employ foreigners paying a decent hourly wage cash-in-hand. I sent many people to the moving companies and most quit after a couple of weeks, but were happy to have the cash.'*

Since houses throughout the States are wood-framed, carpenters can do well, even those without much experience. It is common practice to pay employees as contract labour, which leaves them with the responsibility of paying taxes, social security, etc.; this is a definite advantage if your papers are not in order. Even if you can't find work building new houses, you can offer your painting or maintenance skills to any householder, preferably one whose house is looking the worse for wear.

A more definite but offbeat suggestion has been proffered by Mark Kinder who wrote from rural Maryland:

> ***After spending the summer on the Camp America programme, a friend and I decided to do a parachute jump. Once you have made about ten jumps, the instructors expect you to learn how to pack parachutes, which takes about five hours to learn. Once you have learnt how to pack you get paid $5 per chute cash and with a bit of practice can pack three or four chutes an hour which is good***

> ***money. I would say that 90% of parachute centres in the US pay people cash for packing the chutes but you generally have to be a skydiver to do the job. It is definitely a fun way of earning money. Skydivers are very friendly people and are thrilled to meet foreigners, so they will often offer a place to stay. If not, you can always camp at the parachute centre.***

A list of the 275 parachute centres in the US can be obtained from the national association USPA, 1440 Duke St, Alexandria, VA 22314 or via the Drop Zone Directory section of their website uspa.org.

Medical

Nurse shortages are chronic in the US and qualified nurses might like to investigate possibilities through a specialist UK agency. For people with a more casual interest in medicine, there is the possibility of testing new drugs as well as donating blood. While filling in the time until her flight out of Seattle, Mig Urquhart sold plasma at the Plasma Center. She was turned down on her first visit since there was too much protein in her urine (she reckoned it was because she had been living on peanut butter sandwiches).

When Lindsay Watt arrived in the US, he intended to sustain himself with conventional kinds of employment. But almost immediately he discovered that the longish-stay male travellers staying at his hostel in New York were all earning money solely through medical studies. Invariably, a social security number is needed though it can bear the stamp 'Not Valid for Work'. Most studies pay at least $100 a day and provide all food, accommodation and entertainment. On the three studies in which Lindsay participated, he earned $300 in five days in New York, $475 for four days in Philadelphia and $3,000 for a month in West Palm Beach (Florida). Together these funded a tour of South America. The best he ever heard of was a three-day study in Baltimore which paid $800 which no doubt involved some unpleasant procedures. There are Drug Research Centers in many American cities especially Massachusetts, New York, New Jersey, Pennsylvania, Maryland and Florida. Women are seldom accepted unless they are sterile.

Two excellent sources of information on drug testing centres are the websites centerwatch.com, a listing service for clinical trials, and biotrax.com, an online directory of clinics and research centres. Try also clinicaltrials.gov which lists thousands of clinical studies sponsored by the National Institutes of Health, other federal agencies and the pharmaceutical industry; they indicate which ones are recruiting but mainly they are looking for people who are actually suffering from the relevant disorder or disease. Healthy volunteers are needed only for Phase 1 trials.

Alaskan Fishing

Fishing off the coast of Alaska and fish-processing are classic money-spinning summer jobs in the US, still advertised in west coast newspapers, though the possible earnings are often exaggerated since the Alaskan salmon industry has been in decline for some time. It has been known for deckhands to weather full three-month seasons on mediocre boats and go home with no more than $3,000 for their effort, though $10,000+ is more typical.

Therefore think carefully before buying a one-way ticket to Alaska where the cost of living is very high and the competition for work intense, particularly from American students. Be sure your expectations are realistic. There is no guarantee of finding a job on a productive boat and, even if you do get work, it's unlikely that you'll make any more than minimum wage considering the long hours. What is certain is that you will work harder, longer and faster than you ever have or ever will; you will be cold, beyond exhausted, made to feel stupid, and at times, miserable. Yet the determined can still succeed.

Do not rely on the promises of websites that offer to arrange jobs in the fishing industry for a fee. With profits and the safety of all onboard at stake, boat captains cannot afford to rely on email or long distance phone calls to size up potential crew. The only reliable way to land a deckhand job in Alaska is to show up before the season begins and beat the docks. You will have to obtain a commercial fishing licence which costs about $130, plus rubber boots and raingear for at least the same amount again. Novices can be found frequenting the docks at Kodiak, Ketchikan, Homer and Petersburg in Alaska as well as Astoria and Newport in Oregon. Due to the proximity to the mainland US, work is generally harder to find in the ports of the Southwest. Venturing further north to Kodiak Island or the Bristol Bay fisheries, which boast large fleets and are less accessible, holds more promise. In Kodiak, check the ever-popular job board at Harborside Coffee, perpetually plastered with post-it notes like 'Deckhand needed immediately, no experience necessary'. A good place to stay to hear about openings is the St. Francis Bunkhouse two blocks from the harbour.

The first halibut are caught over a 24-hour period in early May and this opens the fishing season. It is easier to pin down job openings between then and early June when salmon crews are doing pre-season gear work. Often a skipper will take inexperienced newcomers on a trial basis. If you are willing to do prep work without pay, e.g. mending nets, scrubbing hulls, chances are you will have the job when the season opens around the 1st of June. By putting in some hard time for hanging participle free, a skipper can better discern if you have the necessary tenacity, as Jason Motlagh puts it, '*to grind through sleepless two-day benders, jellyfish facials, raw hands and screaming muscles*'.

This is a way of life for the boat owners, not a summer job. Try to convey that you will take your work seriously, but are easygoing enough to live with under cramped conditions for months at a time. Do not forget that taking orders and insults on the chin is a rite of passage; take it personally and you'll soon find yourself back on the dock.

Rejection is an inevitable part of the deckhand job search; never take no for an answer. Many skippers will turn you down several times before taking you on. If you can pass this initial test of your resolve, the prevailing logic is that it may reflect your work ethic, which will be tested like never before.

If you start your job search late, be wary of boats with crew vacancies deep into the season. Some skippers are notorious for being abusive, reckless, withholding pay, or simply bad at catching fish. Ask around the docks to get the straight story on which boats are reputable and which ones to avoid. Deckhands like to talk and you'll generally get a consensus. Boats talk too. If a vessel looks like it hasn't seen a fresh coat of paint since the Cold War, move on. Safety should be a top priority. Between 1991 and 1998, 239 boats sank and 97 people died fishing Alaskan waters. Each year a lot of fingers and a few lives are lost usually because of irresponsible captains cutting corners.

Most of the newcomers that flock to Alaskan ports each summer looking for deckhand jobs have no idea what they are letting themselves in for. Fishing is dangerous work in which adrenaline and fatigue are in constant conflict. A salmon boat crew typically numbers four or five men; each must pull his weight under monotonous, often brutal conditions that push the limits of physical and mental endurance. Amazingly, it is not impossible for women to find work as deckhands, though they will be spared none of the harshness of life at sea. Needless to say, privacy is in short supply, while crude language and pornography are not.

To remain in business fishermen must offset lower prices with higher volume, which translates to even longer hours. Unable to cope, many naïve hopefuls quit their jobs within the first few days which is how Jason Motlagh managed to get a job on board a 'highliner'.

AFTER FINISHING A DEGREE IN FOREIGN AFFAIRS, AMERICAN JASON MOTLAGH CAUGHT THE FISHING BUG. ON RETURNING FROM KODIAK TWO AUTUMNS AGO, HE WROTE ABOUT THE 'GRUELLING, TEDIOUS WORK ABOARD A COMMERCIAL FISHING VESSEL WITH REWARDS FEW OTHER JOBS COULD HOPE TO OFFER':

Like countless others before me, I decided to head north to be a 'greenhorn' for a crack at fortune and adventure as an Alaskan fisherman. Three months later, I returned to the lower 48 a lean-mean-fishing machine with a respectable pay cheque, a wealth of stories, and the self-knowledge that while I could brave 20+ hour work days on the water, 9 to 5 at a desk would never again be as easy.

Less than ten hours after landing in Kodiak on a puddle jumper from Anchorage, with nothing more than a backpack and blind faith, I walked onto one of the top five boats in the entire fleet. A skipper who had come into port to refuel that morning got word on the dock that I was looking for deckhand work and told me he 'might be short a man, check back in two hours'. Apparently, after three rough weeks on the fish, one of his deckhands wanted off the boat. When I returned I was instructed to get some new rain gear and a fisherman's license, as we'd be leaving in less than an hour. This was all the more remarkable as it was already weeks into the summer salmon season. The first guy I'd spoken with told me he had beaten the docks for eight days without success. But I didn't take his word for it, and neither should you. Make it happen.

If you can cook well, this is also the time to show your expertise in the galley. After a long day in foul weather, a tasty meal might be all a crew has to look forward to. Cooking duties invariably fall on greenhorns. Bad cooks are hated, skilled ones will be cut some slack. During my first weeks, when I could do no right on deck, some extra effort preparing meals kept me in my skipper's good graces.

If you are fortunate enough to find a job on the right boat, fishing can still be safe and lucrative. Thanks to a little bit of initiative and a lot of dumb luck, I walked away with just under $10,000 for ten weeks' work on a boat that netted well over one million pounds of salmon for the season. But you must not forget that the good jobs are likely to be filled by return crew, who know just how rare they are.

But if you go in search of an experience that will sharpen life's edge, you will not be disappointed. Think of your pay cheque in terms of learning a real trade, earning the respect of hardened men, of gazing out over calm seas as humpback whales breach under a midnight sun. A moment's rest, a fresh cut of fish, the feel of solid land under your feet after two weeks on the water, will never be as sweet. And when the season finally comes to a close, you'll walk away with the unmistakable swagger of an Alaskan fisherman.

CHILDCARE AND DOMESTIC WORK

The US State Department administers the au pair placement programme which allows thousands of young people from around the world with childcare experience to work for American families for exactly one year on a J-1 visa. They apply through agencies in their country which are partnered with one of the 12 sponsoring organisations in the US, who all follow the federal guidelines, so there is not much difference between them.

The basic requirements are that you be between 18 and 26, speak English, show at least 200 hours of recent childcare experience, have a full clean driving licence and provide a criminal record check. The childcare experience can consist of regular babysitting, helping at a local crèche or school, etc. Anyone wanting to care for a child under two must have 200 hours of experience looking after children under two and must expect the programme interviewers to test their claims carefully. The majority of candidates are young women though men with relevant experience (e.g. sole care of children under five) may be placed. (It is still not unusual to have just a handful of blokes out of hundreds of au pairs.)

The job entails working a maximum of 45 hours a week (including babysitting) with at least one and a half days off per week plus one complete weekend off a month. Successful applicants receive free return flights from one of many cities, a four-day orientation in New York and support from a community counsellor. The time lag between applying and flying is usually at least two months. The counsellor's role is to advise on any problems and organise meetings with other au pairs in your area. Applicants are required to pay a good faith deposit of $300–$400 which is returned to them at the end of 12 months but which is forfeit if the terms of the programme are broken.

The fixed amount of pocket money for au pairs is $176.85 a week which is a reasonable wage on top of room, board and perks. On arrival participants must join a four-day orientation which covers child safety and development. Legislation has made first aid a compulsory component. An additional $500 is paid by the host family to cover the cost of educational courses (three hours a week during term-time) which must be attended as a condition of the visa. Au pairs are at liberty to travel for a month after their contract is over but no visa extension is available beyond that.

A separate programme exists for qualified child carers/nannies, called by Au Pair in America the 'Au Pair Extraordinaire' programme or 'Premiere Au Pairs', 'Au Pair Elite', etc. by other companies. Candidates with the appropriate NNEB, BTEC, Diploma in Nursing or NVQ3 qualification or who are over 20 with two years verifiable childcare experience are eligible to earn $250 a week. Another 12-month programme is called Educare for students who want to have shorter working hours (up to 30 per week) and more time for formal studies. In this programme the pocket money is $132.64, the family's contribution to non-degree studies is up to $1,000 and the upfront fee $805 plus airfare.

At any one time 12,000 American families are hosting a foreign au pair and the vast majority of placements are reasonably successful. This is not to say that problems do not occur, because it is not at all unusual for au pairs to chafe against rules, curfews and unreasonable expectations in housework, etc. When speaking to your family on the telephone during the application period, ask as many day-to-day questions as possible, and try to establish exactly what will be expected of you, how many nights babysitting at weekends, restrictions on social life, use of the car, how private are the living arrangements, etc. The counsellors and advisers provided by the sending organisations should be able to sort out problems and in some cases can find alternative families.

Consider carefully the pros and cons of the city you will be going to. Emma Purcell was not altogether happy to be sent to Memphis, Tennessee which she describes as the 'most backward and redneck city in the USA':

> ***I was a very naïve 18 year old applying to be an au pair for a deferred year before university. I have been very lucky with my host family who have made me feel one of the family. I have travelled the USA and Mexico frequently staying in suites and being treated as royalty since my host dad is president of Holiday Inn. On the bad side, I have lost numerous friends who have not had such good luck. One was working 60 hours a week (for no extra pay) with the brattiest children, so she left. Another girl from Australia lasted six months with her neurotic family who yelled at her for not cleaning the toaster daily and for folding the socks wrong. Finally she plucked up the courage to talk to her host parents and their immediate response was to throw her out. A very strong personality is required to be an au pair for a year in the States.***

Au Pair in America is the largest organisation, making in excess of 4,000 au pair and nanny placements throughout the country. Brochures and application forms can be ordered online (aupairinamerica.co.uk) or by phone in the UK on ☎ 020 7581 7322. The programme operates under the auspices of the American Institute for Foreign Study or AIFS (37 Queens Gate, London SW7 5HR) though some of the selection has been devolved to independent au pair agencies such as Childcare International Ltd, Trafalgar House, Grenville Place, London NW7 3SA (☎ 0870 774 7475; 020 8906 3116; childint.co.uk). Au Pair in America also has representatives in 45 countries and agent/interviewers throughout the UK.

Other active au pair Exchange Visitor Programmes in the US are listed on the State Department website (http://eca.state.gov/jexchanges/index.cfm). All are smaller than Au Pair in America but may be able to offer a more personal service and more choice in the destination and family you work for. A selection of these includes:

Agent Au Pair: San Francisco; ☎ 415 552 6500; UK partner: IAPO, 37 Great Russell St, London WC1B 3PP; ☎ 020 7580 3106; agentaupair.co.uk; $300 deposit plus $200 placement fee.

Au Pair Care Inc: San Francisco; ☎ 415 434 8788; aupaircare.com; partner agency in UK is the Au Pair Shop in Radlett, Herts; ☎ 01923 289737; the-aupair-shop.com.

Cultural Care: ☎ 020 7101 2933; aupair.de@culturalcare.com; culturalcare.co.uk.

EurAupair: Laguna Beach, CA; ☎ 949 494 5500 ext 201; euraupair.com; UK partner is EurAupair UK, 17 Wheatfield Drive, Shifnal, Shropshire TF11 8HL; ☎ 01952 460733; maureen_asseuk@yahoo.co.uk.

goAUPAIR: Murray, UT 84107; ☎ 801 255 7722; 2baupair@goaupair.com; goaupair.com.

Au Pair USA: New York; 1-800-AU PAIRS or ☎ 212 926 0446; aupairusa.org; administered by Interexchange (interexchange.org).

Au Pair Foundation, Inc: Novato, CA; ☎ 1 866 428 7247; aupairfoundation.org; UK partner: Quick Au Pair Agency, Norwich; ☎ 01603 503434; quickaupair.co.uk.

It should be possible to fix up a job working with a family after arrival in the States, though the penalties for working illegally described earlier in this chapter apply equally. There are some job notices for au pairs and nannies on hostel notice boards (especially in San Francisco) and in big city dailies.

Gerhard Flaig found a congenial employer by the simple expedient of pestering a contact he had (organist in the church next to his hostel in Los Angeles who had kindly let him play the organ) until he finally introduced him to the church secretary who did have an idea:

> ***The secretary arranged a meeting with an old man who wanted someone to organise his files and house, to do some transcriptions and other odd jobs. He gave me my own room and free food plus paid me an hourly wage. I was overjoyed and left the hostel at once. After I'd done the transcribing, he wanted me to paint his rooms. His landlady was so satisfied with the job I did that she asked me to paint her house and then a friend of his asked me as well. I got one job after the other and was very busy working as a painter. I had a wonderful time in Hollywood and earned quite a lot of money to travel on. And I still keep in touch with the man.***

AGRICULTURE

Students of agriculture can find exchange schemes which allow them to receive further training in the US (see information for instance on the International Agricultural Exchange Association in the introductory chapter on *The Countryside*). Also described in that chapter is the International Exchange Programme which allows equine and horticultural trainees to be placed in the US by the international agency IEP-UK (iepuk.com).

Like everything else in America, many farms (often agribusinesses rather than farms) tend to be on a massive scale, especially in California and the Midwest. This means that the phenomenon of cycling along a country road, finding the farmer in his field and being asked to start work in an adjoining field is virtually unknown in the US. Furthermore it could be dangerous, since anyone wandering up a farmer's driveway would be suspected of being a trespasser and liable to be threatened with a vicious dog or a gun.

In many important agricultural areas, much of the fruit and vegetable harvesting has been traditionally done by gangs of illegal Mexicans or legal Chicanos (naturalised Americans of Spanish descent) for notoriously low wages. It is very common for an agent to contract a whole gang, so that there may be no room for individuals and pairs of travellers.

A gentler form of agriculture is practised on organic farms that flourish in many corners of the USA. One centralised place to make contact with them is via the website organicvolunteers.com where members can contact organic farmers throughout the country who are looking for volunteers; membership costs $20. Alternatively WWOOF USA has established a national organisation (☎ 831 425 3276; wwoofusa.org); individual membership costs $20 which gives you access to the 700 member farms. WWOOF Hawaii is a separate organisation run by the Canadian branch of WWOOF; membership of $20 entitles you to receive the booklet listing 150 host farms, most of which are on the Big Island (see wwoofhawaii.org). Unfortunately working for keep on a farm counts as employment for the purposes of Immigration so as usual it is important not to mention the word 'work' or 'employment' in any immigration context, but rather cultural exchange.

Work on dude ranches might be more congenial than heavy farm work and anyone with horse experience might find work as a wrangler. Michael Cooley moved from California to the Rockies with one thing in mind, apart from skiing and riding, and that was 'room and board' since both are so expensive in seasonal resort towns:

> ***I decided to look for work on a guest ranch (dude ranch) in April which is the right time. I picked up the Yellow Pages and started calling from A. Many wanted a season's commitment (mid-May to September) which was fine with me. One owner of a small ranch needed someone immediately, so I went for an interview the next day. Being from another country himself, he was nervous about hiring me, but he decided that I was OK for mucking out stalls, etc. I worked hard, he was pleased and I soon became the person who would answer the phone and talk to people looking for work themselves – how satisfying! I didn't make much money but I didn't spend anything either. The starting wage on most ranches is $400–$800 with the promise of a bonus for those who stay the whole season. It's hard work and long hours – you are there for the beauty of the area and fresh air, not for the $$ (I say this a lot to myself).***

In the world of conventional agriculture, there is scope for finding work. In every state in the Union (except perhaps Nevada, Montana and Alaska) there is some fruit or vegetable being picked throughout the summer months. Both in large-scale harvests and on small family farms there is a chance that no one will be concerned about your legal status. This is what Jan Christensen from Denmark found when he looked for summer farm work in Minnesota a few years ago:

> ***The farmers seemed to have a very relaxed attitude towards permits. The best places to look are along route 210 just off Interstate 94 at Fergus Falls which is a rich farm area with good employment prospects from April/May till mid-October. But it's best to have some experience in tractor driving and combine harvester work. If you try to bluff, you will find yourself on the road PDQ. I found that my farmer expected me to know just about everything about farming and had no time to train me.***

Fruit pickers congregate in the counties of Yakima, Chelan, Douglas and Okanogan in Washington State. Another example of a large-scale harvest is the peach harvest in Western Colorado around

Palisade. Several hundred pickers are suddenly needed between 20th July and 4th September and especially during the second fortnight in August. One large hiring peach farm is Rancho Durazno in Palisade, Colorado (ranchodurazno.com/rd/FarmLabor.htm). Although many positions are filled in advance there are opportunities for travellers willing to work hard. The owner, Thomas Cameron, encourages applications from international travellers but not the kind who casually make plans only to abandon them and let him down.

Cherries are also grown here and must be picked in June. Similarly the three-week cherry harvest around Traverse City Michigan in late June/early July employs large numbers of non-locals. The employment site michaglabor.org has links to growers throughout Michigan.

California and Florida are the leading states for agricultural production, especially citrus, plums, avocados, apricots and grapes. Most of these are grown along the Central Valley particularly the San Joaquin Valley around Fresno. The work is notoriously poorly paid. Some have fared better in the Salinas Valley on the California coast, which is a huge vegetable growing area, again predominantly Spanish-speaking.

VOLUNTEERING

The main workcamp organisations in the US such as VFP (vfp.org) listed in the chapter *Volunteering* have incoming programmes. Prospective volunteers must register through a workcamp organisation in their own country. In the past, volunteers have been placed on environmental projects in San Francisco's Golden Gate National Park and the Hawaii Volcanoes National Park, assisted with urban renovation and preservation of historic landmarks in New York and New Jersey, and worked with disabled children and adults on their summer holidays.

Voluntary opportunities in the US range from the intensely urban to the decidedly rural. In the former category, you can build houses in deprived areas throughout the US with Habitat for Humanity (habitat.org). Each summer Winant-Clayton Volunteers place 12 participants in community projects in the USA, mainly in New York, working with inner city youth, the elderly, homeless people and people with mental health problems. Volunteers with a British passport are taken on to work for eight weeks from mid or late June followed by two or three weeks of travel. For application info contact WCV based in East London (☎ 020 8983 3834; winantclayton.org.uk) in advance of the application deadline of 31st January. If you want a less structured spell of volunteering in New York City, go along to the University Soup Kitchen at the Church of the Nativity at 44 Second Avenue, on Saturdays from 11.45am–3.30pm (streetproject.org). Volunteers receive a free lunch.

Working outside the big cities is an attractive prospect. For example the US Forest Service organises workcamps to maintain trails, campsites and wildlife throughout the country; volunteers should apply to the individual parks; state-by-state opportunities are posted on the internet at volunteer.gov/gov. The Heritage Resource Management department of the US Forest Service operates a volunteer programme called 'Passport in Time' to conduct archaeological surveys, record oral histories, etc.; details from the Clearinghouse in Rio Rancho (New Mexico) on ☎ 800 281 9176; volunteer@passportintime.com; passportintime.com.

The American Hiking Society collates volunteer opportunities from around the United States to build, maintain and restore foot trails in America's backcountry. No prior trail work experience is necessary, but volunteers should be able to hike at least five miles a day, supply their own backpacking equipment (including tent), pay a $275 registration fee ($245 for AHS members) and arrange transport to and from the work site. Food is provided on some projects. For a schedule of projects, go to AmericanHiking.org or ring the Volunteer Vacations department of the AHS on 301 565 6714 or 800 972 8608.

The ever-growing Student Conservation Association Inc. (☎ 603 543 1700; thesca.org) places anyone 18 or older in conservation and environmental internships in national parks and forests nationwide. If accepted, interns are placed with a land-management agency (National Park Service, US Forest Service) anywhere in the U.S. for three to six months. Positions range widely, from wildlife management to native plant restoration to wilderness ranger-ing to trail work to fisheries. During the internship, participants work alongside agency employees, basically doing the same work as they do, and gain insight into normally impenetrable organisations. Travel expenses within the US, housing, training and a weekly stipend are provided.

At a loose end after university, Emily Sloane decided to spend some time in the great outdoors:

> ***I did a six-month internship in the glacier-covered North Cascades National Park in Washington state. I was a member of the native plant propagation team and spent my season taking care of nursery plants, gathering seeds and swinging pick-mattocks to loosen up restoration sites so that we could re-vegetate them. I had ample time to explore the mountains, picking up some mountaineering equipment and skills, and as an intern was given occasional special privileges, like a spot on an elite botanical expedition for a nearby university and a ride over the mountains in my boss's friend's ultralight glider. My supervisors were lovably insane, leading us in Pilates sessions at the beginning of every workday, screaming out classic rock songs as we planted in the November snow and (per my request) donning wigs for an entire workday as a birthday gift to me. One of my best summers EVER.***

It is also worth trying the Appalachian Trail Conservancy based in Harpers Ferry, West Virginia 25425 0807 (☎ 304 535 6331; crews@appalachiantrail.org; appalachiantrail.org) which organises work parties to maintain the Appalachian Trail lasting one to six weeks. Volunteers receive food, accommodation and insurance. Emily Sloane worked for the Appalachian Mountain Club (outdoors.org) for two summers as a backcountry campsite caretaker, during which one of her more glamorous duties was mixing sixty gallons' worth of human faeces with a pitchfork (while wearing long rubber gloves, of course) to keep the composting outhouse operational. The AMC hires plenty of Europeans to work at its base lodge at Pinkham Notch at the foot of Mt. Washington, New England's tallest peak (notorious for its horrendous weather). The work there might not itself be terribly exciting – kitchen or housekeeping duties, most likely – but it provides access to a very beautiful area and a community of rugged outdoorsy folks. It might be possible for a foreigner to score a backcountry job although, as these positions are much more competitive, it would be prudent to plan ahead (apply by December for the following summer). The busiest season at the AMC's facilities runs from late May to late August.

In her year out between school and university, Elisabeth Weiskittel from New York State fixed up a short internship at the Ocean Mammal Institute (oceanmammalinst.com) on the island of Maui in Hawaii. Every January, the woman in charge of the Institute takes some of her students and a few interns (often people taking a year off) to Hawaii for 2–3 weeks for a fee of $2,400:

> ***The purpose of the Institute was to study humpbacked whales and the effects of nearby boats on their behaviour. Our data was intended to support a pending law restricting the use of speedboats and other craft in these small bays where the whales and calves were swimming. One group watched and recorded the whales' behaviour in the morning and had the afternoon off, and the other group watched in the afternoon and had the morning off. I had no problem adjusting to life in Hawaii. Most people were there to get a tan and go to bars, but even if that's not your scene it's still lots of fun in Hawaii. During our last week there was a large conference on environmental issues, which all the interns were invited to attend. Some of the speakers were well-known, and one or two spoke to our group, such as the founder of Greenpeace.***

CONCLUSION

This chapter has only scratched the surface, but has been written in the hope that it will spark a few new ideas for your trans-American trip. As one of our less intrepid correspondents recalls: *'When we first arrived in the States we went immediately to visit the parents of a friend. I'd never met them before but they made us welcome. A good thing too, because America seemed so strange to me and expensive and complicated, that I just wanted to get on the first plane back.'*

There is no denying that it is preferable to qualify for an Exchange Visitor Programme like BUNAC, Au Pair in America or equivalents. One of the advantages is that these approved agencies choose a comprehensive insurance policy for you. If you go on your own, make sure you have purchased enough insurance cover since medical care is astronomically expensive in the US.

You must balance caution with a spirit of adventure, accepting and even revelling in the bizarre. When Julia Wilson from Oxford found lodgings in ultra-posh Martha's Vineyard, she was alarmed at first that they had guns and would regularly go out hunting for skunk, not quite what she expected of a place so beloved of old Boston money. You may end up in some unlikely situations, but some of them may also lead to a few days of work helping a trucker with his deliveries, joining an impromptu pop group to perform at private parties, gardening on a Californian commune, building solar houses, and so on. If you aren't lucky enough to have the appropriate visa, you should grasp every opportunity to take advantage of offers of genuine hospitality.

You should be able to get some kind of job which will introduce you to the striking cultural differences between Europe and America and which will provide you with some capital with which to explore this amazing country.

CANADA

Wide open spaces, a high standard of living and none of the excesses of south of the border, Canada is a very attractive prospect for the working traveller. Students and some other categories are eligible for visa schemes which make it possible to get round the 'Canada-only' immigration policies. Canadians are hospitable and eager for visitors to like their country.

RED TAPE

British citizens require only a valid passport to enter Canada. Normally on arrival they will be given permission to stay as tourists for six months; incoming tourists may be requested to show that they have sufficient funds, adequate medical insurance and a return ticket or, failing that, some Canadian contacts. Although Canadian Immigration is reputed to be less savage than its American counterpart, many young travellers without much money have been given a rough ride and are categorically prohibited from working including working-for-keep.

The Canadian government administers three similar working holiday programmes for Britons (and other nationalities), primarily for full-time students or recent graduates but for a limited number of non-students too. BUNAC (the British Universities North America Club) has the exclusive right to dispense 12-month Open Employment Authorisation working holiday visas to students and non-students under 31.

Participants of programmes via BUNAC do not require a definite job offer but must show sufficient funds. It is also possible for full-time students with a letter of acceptance at a UK university and a concrete job offer from a Canadian employer to apply for the Student General Working Holiday Programme directly to the Canadian High Commission. Participants are permitted to work only for the named employer for the duration of their visa, so it is much less flexible.

The Canadian government offers a quota of temporary authorisations each year to students and non-students from eligible countries The Canadian High Commission in London administers the programme for students of British, Irish, Swedish and Finnish nationality. Other nationalities (like Australian and New Zealand) should consult the Canadian Consulate locally or check whpcanada.org.au. The quotas have been lifted in some countries like Australia and are fairly generous in the others (e.g. 4,000 for New Zealand).

The website of the Canadian High Commission in London canada.org.uk carries the relevant information; the visa info number is 020 7258 6699. Processing of work authorisations can take six weeks and the fee is £85.

Certain special categories of work are eligible for authorisation, such as nannies who are in great demand but must be qualified (see *Childcare* section below). There is also a category of work permits for voluntary work which takes about a month to process if you have found a placement through a recognised charitable or religious organisation.

Americans are not allowed to enter Canada in order to look for work. Like all foreign nationals, they must fix up a job (before arrival) which has been approved by the employer's local Human Resources and Skills Development Canada or HRSDC (the name for employment offices). BUNAC in the US (bunac.org/usa/workcanada) runs a working holiday programme for college students aged up to 30 to work in Canada for up to six months.

Australians should check their eligibility online via the Canadian Consulate General in Sydney (☎ 02 9364 3082; whpcanada.sydney@international.gc.ca; whpcanada.org.au). The working holiday visa is an open Employment Authorization valid for a year, available to young people (not necessarily students) aged 18–30 with no criminal record. People with an employment authorization are entitled to apply for the essential Social Insurance Number (SIN). This should be done at an HRSDC office in one of the big cities, listed in the government pages of telephone directories. Health insurance regulations differ from province to province for foreign workers, but you will generally have to rely on private cover for at least the first three months.

Special Schemes

As mentioned, BUNAC in London (☎ 020 7251 3362; bunac.org/uk/workcanada) is the main route for British working holiday makers going to Canada. The BUNAC programme fee is £200, and insurance costs from £115 for three months. A new requirement is for applicants to submit a police background check that adds at least £35 to the cost. Participants can choose to travel on a BUNAC group flight (costing approximately £500 return to Toronto) or independently which could be cheaper. Anyone intending to work in childcare, teaching or healthcare must undergo a medical examination with a designated doctor which will cost an estimated £135 and add up to five weeks to the application process. Places are allocated on a first come, first served basis so early application is advantageous (from December).

BUNAC distributes to Work Canada participants a free *Canada Handbook* which includes contact details for companies that have employed foreign students in the past. The majority of jobs are in hotels and tourist attractions in the Rockies, a beautiful part of the world in which to spend a summer. For summer season jobs, British university students have an edge over their North

American counterparts since they don't have to return to their studies until mid to late September rather than the beginning of September.

All participants of approved student schemes benefit from orientations and back-up from the Canadian Federation of Students' SWAP offices in Toronto and Vancouver which have job boards, internet access and staff advisors. They even organise pub outings and excursions for participants, as well as advising on nitty-gritty issues like social insurance cards, which can be processed in six working days. Students on work exchanges should receive the same tax exemption as Canadian students, though filing for a tax rebate is complicated and it might be a good idea to enlist the help of a tax refund specialist like taxback.com.

CASUAL WORK

The lack of an Employment Authorization or Social Insurance Number (the SIN is comparable to the American social security number) is a perpetual thorn in the sides of itinerant workers. Without them, you will have to steer clear of official bodies such as employment offices, tax offices, etc. and many employers will be unwilling to consider you or, more importantly, pay you.

If you decide to work without proper authorisation, you should be aware that you are breaking a law which is taken seriously in Canada with a very real danger of deportation. If you are working in a job known to hire large numbers of foreigners (e.g. tree-planting and fruit-picking in British Columbia), there is a chance that the area will be raided by immigration control. Raymond Oliver could hardly believe their efficiency: at 10am he gave his British Columbia employer a made-up SIN, at noon a phone call came to say it was fake and at 11am the next day an immigration officer arrived to tell him he had to leave the country within a fortnight. If you cannot fund your own departure, you will either be given a 'departure order' which gives you 30 days to leave the country, an exclusion order which means you are barred from returning to Canada for a specified period or, worst of all, a deportation order which permanently bars a return. If you are caught and want legal advice, contact the nearest legal aid lawyer whose services are free.

Anyone on shaky legal ground should keep a very low profile. It is rumoured that it is not difficult for people without permits to find winter work in ski resorts in the Rockies but not on the slopes. Brigitte Albrech worked as a tree planter in Prince George B.C. using a SIN number given to her by her employer. But because she was German, it was hard to blend in and the authorities somehow heard of her (after she had been working for three months) and sent her a request in writing to leave within six weeks or face a court hearing.

Statutory minimum wages vary by province, mostly in the range $8–$9.50, the latter being the rate for Ontario (2009) and $10.25 from 2010. Most working holidaymakers (like most Canadian students) earn the minimum wage, with an average weekly wage of $320 and average accommodation costs of $400+ a month in a shared house.

THE JOB HUNT

The job hunt in Canada has always been tough, and recent events in the economy haven't made it any easier. It takes BUNACers an average of seven to ten days to find a job in Canada, which can be a dispiriting time. Even Canadian students find it hard to get summer jobs and there will be competition for most kinds of seasonal work. It will be necessary to look presentable, eager to please, positive and cheerful, even if the responses are negative or the employers rude. On the other hand, some find the job hunt relatively easy, as Australian Rebecca Wootten did not long ago, after spending seven months in Canada on a working holiday visa:

> ***I worked in Vancouver and had a great time working for a float plane company called West Coast Air. It isn't too hard to get a job. I joined an employment service straight after we were issued with our social insurance numbers, and handed out resumés. Lots of cafés are willing to hire Aussies and other foreigners. Also a great spot would have been the resort of Whistler, where you can work summer or winter.***

Toronto and other major cities have fleets of rickshaws which employ runners. The most lucrative areas are around the base of the CN Tower, the Skydome and Harbourfront in downtown Toronto. The best times are during Caribana, the annual Caribbean festival at the end of July, and over the Labour Day weekend at the beginning of September. If interested, ask the vendors for the name and number of their boss. Matthew Shiel from the University of Swansea did it for the summer and at one point was saving an astonishing C$1,000 a week. Companies to try for a summer season job include Rickshaw Runners of Toronto (rickshawservices.com) and Kabuki Kabs in Victoria (kabukikabs.com). Runners must rent the rickshaw from the company and work as independent contractors.

As ever, youth hostel notice boards are recommended for information on jobs. According to one informant, staff at the Edmonton Youth Hostel can advise on local work opportunities. Only students with working holiday permits will be allowed to work in hostels.

To illustrate the stringency of immigration regulations, even work-for-keep arrangements are difficult to find, as described by the Jericho Beach Youth Hostel in Vancouver: *'Unfortunately, due to Canadian employment regulations, we are unable to have foreign nationals participate in our work exchange programme at the hostel (two hours work in exchange for a free overnight). We do have an employment board at the hostel where we post notices from local companies and individuals offering employment. In addition, the front desk staff are a valuable resource for finding employment in the city.'*

In addition to Vancouver, the best cities to look for work are Toronto, Calgary and Edmonton. Jobs for sales staff are advertised wherever you go in Canada. One of the easiest ways to get a job is to apply to branches of European companies like the Body Shop and Gap. Tanufa Kotecha joined BUNAC's Work Canada programme and quickly learned that Canadian selling techniques are just as aggressive as American ones: *'I landed a job within a week in Toronto working in a French Canadian clothing store. In my store as soon as a customer walked in, they had to be greeted by a "sales associate" within 15 seconds! The North American way of selling is pushy and upfront, but it does get results. One must have confidence to sell.'* Almost all shop jobs of this kind pay the minimum wage.

TOURISM

The Rocky Mountain resorts of Banff, Jasper, Lake Louise, Sunshine Mountain and Whistler are among the best places to try, both summer and winter. Banff and Whistler seem to absorb the largest number of foreign workers as catering and chamber staff, ski staff, etc. Both are expensive towns in which to job-hunt though in summer some people have been known to camp free well out of town.

The huge Fairmont Banff Springs Hotel alone employs 900 people, as do its sister hotels in the Fairmont group of luxury hotels like Chateau Lake Louise, Jasper Park Lodge and Chateau Whistler. The Fairmont Group's website describes its recruitment needs and links to current vacancies (fairmontcareers.com). Also try Lake Louise Inn (lakelouiseinn.com/employment.htm), Inns of Banff Park, Banff International Hotel and Athabasca Hotel in Jasper. One of the main employers in Jasper is Mountain Park Lodges (hire@mpljasper.com). The standard wage at these hotels is the provincial minimum ($8.40 in Alberta, $8 in BC). During the height of the season there may be very little time off. Employers are permitted to deduct $2.60 a day for staff accommodation plus $2 a meal.

One traveller to Western Canada reported:

> ***While on holiday in Banff, I met a lot of Australians and Britons staying at the youth hostel. All of them were just on holiday visas, and all of them had found work in the height of the tourist season. I was offered hotel work. There is a lot of work to be had in Canada and men in particular would have no trouble supporting themselves. Canadians are very warm towards foreigners and employers are generally prepared to risk hiring casuals 'black' if they can't get through the red tape. Wages are very good for this type of work.***

As always, special events like the Calgary Stampede every June, result in a stampede of temporary workers. Anyone working front-of-house in the hospitality industry should be liable to earn a lot of tips in a short time. The classified ads, online or print, of local newspapers like the *Vancouver Courier* (http://classified.van.net) are usually promising. Also check kijiji.ca for the town in which you want to work (kijiji is the North American equivalent of gumtree) and of course craigslist.ca. Tourist industry jobs in the cities will be hard to find out-of-season, since most openings are part-time and filled by local students.

SKI RESORTS

Ski resorts throughout Canada create a great number of seasonal employment vacancies which can't be filled by Canadian students since they're all studying. As is the case throughout the world, affordable accommodation is in very short supply in the main ski resorts. Most of the accommodation in ski towns is full by October, well in advance of the start of the season. The hosting of the Winter Olympics in Vancouver and Whistler will make it impossible to find a place to stay in February 2010.

Banff is always in desperate need of cheap labour; there are literally thousands of young travellers, mainly Canadian students, Australians, Kiwis and Brits in town. No one seems to struggle to find employment, and as a result many employers are very flexible with hours. Many offer staff accommodation at a heavily subsidised rate which is incredibly useful since rents in Banff are a killer. It's not unheard of for five people to share a two bedroom flat to save money.

For Banff, consider Sunshine Village Resort which employs about 400 seasonal staff, with limited basic accommodation provided depending on the position. Their website skibanff.com has lots of useful information for prospective staff including dates of their annual hiring clinic held at Banff International Hostel in mid-October. You can contact the Human Resources department for more information by email at jobs@skibanff.com or on a toll-free number within North America 1 877-WORK-SKI (☎ 877 967 5754) or ☎ 403 762 6546 from abroad.

Other useful contacts for seasonal job-hunting summer and winter in the Alberta Rockies are the Job Resource Centres in Banff and Canmore, a resort nearer Calgary. A spring hiring fair takes place in the Cascade Plaza in Banff in late May (see jobresourcecentre.com).

Moving west to the Pacific, the Whistler Chamber of Commerce posts employment information at whistlerchamber.com/er-finding-a-job.html. Intrawest is the company that runs the ski operations at Whistler (as well as many other North American ski resorts). The Employment link on the site whistlerblackcomb.com gives details of the annual recruiting fair (usually first few days of November) and allows you to apply online for jobs in retail, guest services, food and beverage, etc.; alternatively you can ring the jobline on 604 938 7367. A large number of workers leave after the Christmas rush so it is possible to get a job once the season begins even if you haven't lined anything up at the main autumn hiring season.

James Gillespie spent the winter and summer of his gap year working in Whistler. After taking the beautiful train ride from Vancouver, it soon became clear that getting a place to stay would be a major problem. But soon he had a job as a ticket validator which came with a free ski pass and subsidised accommodation: *'It was an excellent job and, although sometimes mundane, it was often livened up by violent and abusive skiers trying to get on the lift for free. Going there was the best thing I've ever done and I hope to be living there permanently eventually. I came home with a diary full of experiences, a face full of smiles, a bag full of dirty washing and pockets full of... well nothing actually. I was in debt, but it was worth it.'*

Applications for work in Ontario resorts like Blue Mountain near Collingwood (fax 705 444 1751; bluemountain.ca/employment.htm) are normally considered in November, whereas the deadline is somewhat earlier for work in western resorts since the season starts earlier. Blue Mountain is another Intrawest resort and the centralised recruitment site sums up the aims of the working traveller: wework2play.com. Blue Mountain employs up to 700 staff for the season which is running on full steam from Christmas to the March break. If considering ski resorts in Québec like Mount Tremblant, a knowledge of French is necessary.

Other popular holiday areas in summer are the Muskoka District of Ontario centred on the town of Huntsville, and the shores of the Great Lakes, particularly Lake Huron. Most of the holiday job recruitment in Ontario is done through Canadian universities, though someone willing to stay until mid or late September will be preferred. Among the biggest resorts are Deerhurst (☎ 705 789 7113 ext 4236; deerhurstresort.com), Clevelands House and Delawana Inn (delawana.com/employment.html) with a summer staff of 170.

TREE-PLANTING

The archetype of the working Canadian is the lumberjack. Nowadays there are fewer jobs for tree-choppers than tree-planters. In areas which have been logged or burnt, forestry officials are encouraging massive reforestation and every March planting contractors begin to recruit crews for the season which begins in April. The payment is piecework usually between 9 and 11 cents per tree in Ontario, more in the West where conditions are tougher and even more on steep or uncleared terrain. Novices can usually earn $40–$100 a day after a few weeks' practice. In some cases 'rookies' are earning more than $100 though you usually have to have done a few seasons before you're earning $150–$200 a day. A deduction is made for camp expenses, e.g. $25 a day in Ontario. You will need a waterproof tent and work clothes including boots and waterproofs. Many firms do not lend out the equipment, so the cost of shovels and bags (which will run to between $200 and $600) are deducted from your wages. The internet is a goldmine of insiders' information with extensive listings of companies updated every January; see tree-planter.com.

Prince George is an important centre for tree-planting. While travelling in Mexico on annual leave from her job in Germany, Brigitte Albrech met up with a van full of French Canadians who were heading for Prince George to plant trees, and decided to follow them rather than return to her job. Among the many companies based in Prince George, try Folklore Contracting (folklorecontracting.ca).

Dates are uncertain due to weather. There is a spring and a summer season with two to four weeks in between. Some BC contractors start as early as late March and finish in August, though others don't begin until early May. Around Fort Frances and Thunder Bay in Ontario, the season is shorter, late April until the first week of July. An average season consists of 50 days of work.

Although Brigitte Albrech agrees that the work is hard and the hours long, she greatly enjoyed the team spirit and solved a few problems she didn't know she had. Chris Harrington paints a fairly negative picture (while concluding that he had a great time):

> ***Tree-planting itself consists of a ten-hour day starting about 6am, though overtime is available to masochists. This is awful work, make no mistake. The job is monotonous and weather conditions can be appalling (snow in June!). Coupled with the bugs, this can lead you to question your sanity. One of the worst aspects is 'down time' which occurs regularly between contracts, where you will find yourself hanging around expensive motels with no idea when and if you will be working again. How much you earn depends on how well you can motivate yourself.***

FRUIT PICKING

British Columbia

The fruit-growing industry of Western Canada takes place in decidedly more congenial surroundings. The beautiful Okanagan Valley of British Columbia is tucked away between two mountain ranges in the interior of British Columbia and supports 26,000 acres of orchards. The Valley stretches north from the American border at Osoyoos for over 200km to Armstrong. Cherries, peaches, plums, pears, apricots, grapes and apples are all grown in the Valley, with a concentration of soft fruits in the south and hard fruits (apples, pears) in the north. All of these must be picked by hand.

Anyone interested in summer seasonal employment should register with the Agricultural Labour Pool which runs a centralised province-wide placement service from its office in Abbotsford near Vancouver (☎ 604 823 6222; info@agri-labourpool.com; agri-labourpool.com). Six WorkZone employment offices are located in Penticton, Summerland, Keremeos, Oliver, Osoyoos and Princeton; see workzonebc.com which can help seasonal job seekers with job boards, use of telephone and an agricultural information pack. Lots of fruit pickers stay at the Loose Bay campsite in Oliver, which is cheap and basic. Detailed fruit-picking information about Oliver can be found at http://oliverbc.ca/oliver-bc-farm-labour-and-pickers.

The harvests in Kelowna, a town approximately in the centre of the Valley take place at the times given in the chart below.

FRUIT HARVESTS IN BRITISH COLUMBIA

SPECIES OF FRUIT	APPROXIMATE STARTING DATE	APPROXIMATE DURATION
cherries	June 25	through July
apricots	mid-July	approx. 3 weeks
Vee peaches	August 5	2 or 3 weeks
Elberta peaches	August 28	2 or 3 weeks
Red Haven peaches	July 20	6 weeks
Prune plums	mid-August	till mid-September
Bartlett pears	August 12	till Sep/early Oct
Anjou pears	late September	October
Macintosh apples	early September	3–4 weeks

SPECIES OF FRUIT	APPROXIMATE STARTING DATE	APPROXIMATE DURATION
Spartan apples	late September	3–4 weeks
Newton apples	late October/November	3–4 weeks
Winesap apples	late October	3–4 weeks
Golden Delicious apples	September	3–4 weeks
Red Delicious apples	September	3–4 weeks
Rome Beauty apples	September	3–4 weeks
Fuji apples	September	3 weeks
grapes	September 8	6 weeks

Picking jobs are assigned by the WorkZone office on a first come first served basis (all things being equal) and so it is important to arrive early in the day. Sometimes 100 hopeful job-seekers have gathered at the door by 7am. When the office is less busy, job-seekers are required to register, giving their name, social insurance number and contact address. Some attempt is made to screen applicants to avoid sending out a picker who has caused trouble elsewhere. You can also make contact with the farmers directly. For example the Okanagan and Kootenay Cherry Growers' Association (bccherry.com) posts the contact details of its more than 50 member farms.

Professional migrant pickers (many of whom are from Quebec) begin with the cherries in the south of the valley and move up the valley to pick only the peak cherries. Then they come south again to work the apricots in the same way and so on. Note that even when fruit-pickers are paid piecework, they must earn at least the BC minimum wage of $8 an hour. Of course once your speed improves, it is to your advantage to be paid piecework. Inexperienced pickers usually start by earning not much more than $50 a day whereas the pros touch $200. Most people's wages are paid directly into a bank account, which is a further difficulty for casual workers without proper papers.

Apples are the Okanagan's most famous export product. There is continuous picking of one variety or another from mid-August to the end of October. Apple-picking can be slow and poorly paid. A basket is worn at the front of the body and this becomes very heavy as it fills up. Experience is not so important for the apple harvest. Especially towards the end of the harvest when all the students have returned to university (approximately mid-September) and the weather is getting colder, the farmers begin to take almost anyone.

Raspberry, blueberry and cranberry picking and pruning take place nearer Vancouver in Richmond, Chilliwack, Abbotsford, Aldergrove and Langley between June and August, though this work is notoriously badly paid. Bulb work is offered over the winter by Van Noort Bulbs in Langley (vannoortbulb.com). Tales of mass exploitation of migrant farm labourers emerge from this area at intervals. Most growers do not provide accommodation and campsite charges are considerable relative to wages. There are pickers' huts but these are mainly occupied by Asian immigrants. A further problem is the controversy over pesticides that may harm skin. A trawl of the internet will result in directories of fruit farms such as the one at http://bcstrawberries.com/FarmList.php. To take just one example, Driediger Farms in Langley (☎ 604 888 1685) employ an average of 150 pickers in the season to harvest blueberries, strawberries and raspberries.

Ontario, Quebec and Eastern Canada

The micro-climate in the fertile Niagara region bordering Lake Ontario is excellent for growing peaches, pears, plums, grapes (mostly for wine) and cherries. But local unemployment is high and it will be difficult to get a decent job, even though there is no shortage of fruit needing to be picked. To meet farmers, it is a good idea to go to the Saturday farmers' market at Sylvia Place in Niagara Falls, around the corner from the employment office on Main Street.

The Maritimes

High unemployment in some Maritime areas has driven many locals west in search of employment. However if you are travelling in the eastern provinces in August/September, you might try to find paid work picking or 'raking' blueberries in the Nova Scotia towns of Parrsboro, Minudie, Amherst or Pugwash and elsewhere. Earlier in the summer (i.e. mid-June to mid-July), strawberry picking is available. In the autumn you can also look for work picking apples. Head for the Bay of Fundy coast of Nova Scotia around Annapolis Royal, Bridgetown and Middleton. If you're lucky, fruit picking wages will be paid cash-in-hand.

Casual fruit pickers are sent to various farms on the outskirts of Montreal by registering with the Agrijob Agency (☎ 514 273 1503; agrijob.info) who organise buses from several suburban metro stations to the farms. One picker found it all fairly joyless.

OTHER FARM WORK

If you are interested in working your way from farm to farm and want to meet Canadians, you might consider volunteering for WWOOF-Canada (World Wide Opportunities on Organic Farms). You can access all the 800+ host farms at the WWOOF Canada website wwoof.ca after becoming a member. Membership costs C$45 or $55 per couple (cash or via paypal; a printed version costs $10 extra). All volunteers must have valid tourist visas. Canada permits volunteer work in exchange for accommodation and meals, provided it is not the main object of the trip.

CHILDCARE AND SUMMER CAMPS

Live-in nannies and mothers' helps are in great demand in Canadian cities. However domestic employment in Canada is governed by a number of carefully formulated and strictly enforced regulations. Details of the 'Live-in Caregiver Program' may be obtained from the Canadian Immigration Department's website cic.gc.ca/english/work/caregiver/index.asp. Qualifying nannies must either have six months of full-time training in a related field (teaching, nursing, childcare) or 12 months experience in full-time paid employment as a nanny or mother's help within the previous three years, at least half of which must have been continuously for the same employer. The other main requirements are that the nanny must have a job confirmation letter from an employer in Canada, have completed secondary school and speak English or French.

If you are eligible and have found an employer (possibly through an agency), you can apply for an Employment Authorization for Canada valid for one year and renewable once. There is a handling fee of C$150 (£85). The procedure for getting an Authorization usually takes between one and four months and will include a very strict medical examination by an appointed private doctor who will charge at least £130. The Authorization will be valid for one employer, though it can be changed within Canada as long as your subsequent job is as a live-in child-carer. At the end of two years as a care-giver, it is possible to apply to become a permanent resident.

Working as a nanny or mother's help in Canada has more status attached to it than au pairing in Europe, and the conditions of work reflect this. The federal and provincial governments set out guidelines for hours, time off, holidays, minimum salary and deductions. For example nannies can expect to earn no less than the provincial minimum wage and in many cases they earn $10 an hour. From a monthly salary of (roughly) $1,500, you might lose a fifth in taxes and up to the permitted maximum for room and board which is $420 a month, depending on province. That means that net wages are $1,000+ per month based on a 44-hour week, a sum that has remained static for many years.

A search of the internet will take you to many Canadian agencies offering the Caregiver programme, though some are more experienced in bringing in nannies from countries like Peru, Mexico, the Philippines, Hong Kong, Ukraine and Slovakia rather than the UK. In all cases, nannies must satisfy the government's Live-in Caregiver requirements. Here is a small selection of agencies:

ABC Nannies Agency: Vancouver; ☎ 604 581 1018; abcnannies.ca; placements across Canada.

Care Solutions Inc: Vancouver, Toronto and USA; 1 877 925 8474; absolutecarenanny.com.

Elite Care/Au Pair Canada: Toronto; ☎ 416 590 7429; info@nannies-canada.com; elitenanniescanada.com; also place caregivers for the elderly; member of IAPA.

Nannies on Call: Vancouver, Calgary and Whistler; nanniesoncall.com; lots of short-term work, all of it live-out.

Nanny Finders Directory Agency: Richmond, BC; ☎ 604 272 1622; nannyfindersbc.com.

OptiMum Children & Nannies Inc.: Vancouver; ☎ 604 671 4965; info@opti-mum.com; opti-mum.com; nannies looking for work in and around Vancouver can add their details to a searchable internet database free of charge.

Scotia Personnel Ltd: 6045 Cherry St, Halifax, NS; B3H 2K4; ☎ 902 422 1455; scotia-personnel-ltd.com.

Selective Personnel International: 12 Irwin Avenue, Suite 300, Toronto, Ontario M4Y 1K9; ☎ 416 962 5153; selectivepersonnel.ca. Placement agency that recruits and markets caregivers, nannies, nurses and housekeepers from all over the world.

Canadian children flock to summer camps in the great outdoors in huge numbers. Young people are needed to work as camp counsellors, swimming instructors, canoeing and wilderness guides and so on. Potentially useful online resources include ontariocamps.ca and camppage.com/canada.htm. CCUSA (ccusa.com) places British and other foreign counsellors on 800 camps in Canada, and cooperates with Nyquest Training and Placement based in Toronto (☎ 416 932 1370; go-nyquest.com). The CCUSA programme fee for Britons is £299 for early applicants; £399 for later ones.

VOLUNTEERING

Some interesting practical community projects are organised by Frontiers Foundation in low-income communities in Canada, including native communities in isolated northern areas. Volunteers of many nationalities, who must be at least 18 and energetic, work as tutors (e.g. of maths, science, English, music, drama), teaching assistants or recreation workers, along with assisting in First Nations offices. Most projects take place on wilderness camps for Native children or in schools in the three northern territories (Yukon, Northwest Territory and Nunavut). Placements last ten months from September. Some volunteers, preferably with relevant experience, are taken on for at least three months over the summer to help build and renovate housing. All expenses are paid within Canada including domestic travel and medical insurance, plus pocket money of $50 a week.

ACCORDING TO EMILY SLOANE, WATCHING THE RIVERS BREAK UP IN THE SPRING WAS ONE OF THE MOST SPECTACULAR THINGS SHE HAS EVER SEEN, AND HER TIME WITH FF TURNED OUT TO BE ONE OF THE BEST EXPERIENCES OF HER LIFE:

From February to June I worked as an education volunteer in a Gwich'in village in the Northwest Territories through Frontiers Foundation. The school I worked in desperately needed help and positive energy. I became the teaching assistant in the grade 4–6 classroom, and I think that my presence allowed the overly-stressed teacher to relax a bit. I eventually got to help design and implement parts of the reading and social studies curricula, too. And of course, being in the Arctic had its perks. I was able to attend a caribou hunting field trip in the Yukon in March, during which I got up in the middle of the night to use the outhouse in 60 below temperatures. I'd go cross-country skiing after school every day, sometimes with several husky puppies at my heels, and as the days grew longer, my skis were sometimes postponed until 10 or 11 at night. All in all, a thoroughly satisfying experience.

Frontiers Foundation-Operation Beaver has its head office in Toronto however the British Columbia office co-ordinates projects in the north (☎ 604 585 6646; frontwest@shaw.ca; frontiersfoundation.ca). The organisation can assist with obtaining a work visa for international volunteers, a process which takes between two and five months.

Another contributor stumbled (or rather strode) across a different way to experience the Canadian bush. Obbe Verwer from Amsterdam spent part of the summer hiking in British Columbia:

> ***After enjoying my visits to a couple of farms listed by WWOOF, I went on by myself to Vancouver Island. I set off to hike through the rainforest along the Clayoquot Valley Witness Trail. When I came to the trailhead, I met the trail boss who was working with a group of volunteers to build boardwalks at both ends of the trails. This was to enable more people to walk part of the trail which is important because this valley has to be saved from clearcut logging. I decided to join them. Actually you are supposed to go through the organising committee to become a volunteer worker but I just pitched my tent and joined on the spot.***
>
> ***All the wood to build the boardwalk had to be carried into the trail, steps, stringers, nails and tools. We worked till 4pm, but it was not strict at all. Sometimes it was pretty hard, but it was fun. The forest impressed me more and more. The big trees, the berries, the mushrooms and the silence in the mist. It was just amazing. It was very satisfying to be helping to save this forest.***

The Western Canada Wilderness Committee can be visited at 341 Water St or 227 Abbott St in Vancouver (☎ 604 683 8220; volunteer@wildernesscommittee.org) and can also arrange internships for international candidates. Volunteers should bear in mind that while working in rainforests one is bound to get wet. It also has offices in Victoria and Winnipeg.

A searchable database of volunteering opportunities in British Columbia and Alberta can be found at govolunteer.ca. This is especially good for special events like the 2010 Winter Olympics or the Celtic Festival in Vancouver every March which needs volunteer participants.

Clinical research is often carried out in university towns by university medical departments and teaching hospitals. The website centerwatch.com gives easy-to-use links to major research centres in Canada such as the Clinical Research Centre at the McGill University Health Centre (☎ 514 934 1934; muhc.crc@mcgill.ca).

LATIN AMERICA

As a travel destination, South and Central America has been gaining popularity among Britons and Europeans faster than almost any other regional destination. Many gap year students as well as older travellers are setting their sights on a trip to Argentina or the Amazon or the Andes possibly in between a stint of teaching or volunteering.

Most Latin American nations do not need unskilled workers from abroad to perform the menial tasks associated with agriculture and industry. For every such job, there are several dozen natives willing to work for a pittance, and gringos (white westerners) will not be considered for such work. However, people who can speak competent Spanish may find opportunities in the cities, especially bilingual secretaries. Because Britain has few colonial ties with Central and South America, there is a general cultural and economic orientation towards Uncle Sam which means that Americans tend to occupy many jobs rather than Britons. Apart from volunteering opportunities, the main sphere of employment in which foreign travellers have any prospect of gaining acceptance is the teaching of the English language.

In Lima, Quito, Cusco or Buenos Aires, visit the South American Explorers clubhouses (saexplorers.org) which keep a list of local opportunities including at language institutes. SAE offices are staffed by expats who will be happy to share information and valuable databases of volunteer opportunities with members. SAE membership costs US$60 per year, $90 for a couple (SAE, 126 Indian Creek Road, Ithaca, NY 14850, USA; ☎ 607 277 0488; saexplorers.org/zen).

TEACHING

Spanning 75 degrees of latitude, the mammoth continent of South America together with the Caribbean islands and the eight countries of Central America, offer a surprising range of teaching opportunities. All but Brazil have a majority of Spanish speakers and, as in Spain itself, there is a great demand for English teaching, from dusty towns on the Yucatan Peninsula of Mexico to Punta Arenas at the southern extremity of the continent, south of the Falkland Islands.

The countries of most interest to the travelling teacher are Mexico, Bolivia, Colombia, Ecuador, Peru, Venezuela, Chile, Argentina and Brazil. Despite high levels of economic and often political uncertainty, demand for English language tuition continues to increase in the various kinds of institution engaged in promoting English, from elite cultural centres supported by the British and American governments to technical centres, from prestigious bilingual secondary schools to agencies which supply private tutors to businessmen. Experience is not always essential to land a teaching job on-the-spot.

It is advisable to take a professional approach, by having at your disposal a smartly turned out CV, qualifications and references, though not all schools will ask to see them. Obviously, you'll need a local contact number, so get yourself a mobile phone and then distribute your CV as widely as possible. When you drop your CV in, the school may ask you to take a written English test on the spot which is sometimes quite elaborate with a composition section. If you pass the test, you may get invited to a group interview in which you will be asked to perform various tasks in small teams or pairs. If you are successful at this stage, you may then be asked to do a one- or two-week training course (usually unpaid). Only once this has been completed will you be offered work. Some of the smaller companies will offer some hours if you pass their test and give a satisfactory demonstration lesson so try to bring some teaching materials with you.

You can also arrange jobs before arrival. Sheona Mckay managed to set up her own project as a volunteer teacher in Peru between March and June through a personal contact:

> ***Especially for people wanting to teach English, I think it is easy enough to find out the names of some schools in an area you are interested in working in. Then you can e-mail the school directly and hopefully come to an agreement with them.***

A surefire way to get a teaching job is to do a TEFL training course in your destination country, such as the TEFL Academy in Santiago (tefl-academy.com), EBC TEFL in Buenos Aires (ebc-tefl-course.com), Maximo Nivel in Cusco and San José (maximonivel.com), TESOL Training Costa Rica (tesoltrainingcostarica.org) and Teachers Latin America in Mexico City (innovative-english.com). Most courses last four weeks and cost between $1,200 and $2,000. More detailed information about teaching and training in Latin America can be found in the 2009 edition of my book *Teaching English Abroad* (£14.99 from Crimson Publishing or bookshops, or in libraries; $24.95 in the US).

THE JOB HUNT

In a land where baseball is a passion and US television enormously popular, American (and also Canadian) job-seekers have a distinct advantage. The whole continent is culturally and economically oriented towards the States and there is often a preference for the American accent and for American teaching materials and course books. On the other hand, many Britons have found themselves highly valued from Colombian universities to language agencies in Santiago. Business English is booming throughout the region and anyone with a business background will have an edge over the competition.

If you are looking for casual teaching work after arrival, check adverts in the English language press such as the *Buenos Aires Herald* or the Caracas *Daily Journal*. English language bookshops are another possible source of teaching leads. Ask in expatriate bars and restaurants, check out any building claiming to be an English School, however dubious-looking, and in larger cities try deciphering the telephone directory for schools or agencies which might be able to use your services.

The crucial factor in becoming accepted as an English teacher at a locally run language school may not be your qualifications or your accent as much as your appearance. You must look as professionally turned out as teachers are expected to look.

Travellers working their way around the world are more likely to find a few hours of teaching here and there earning $3–$6 an hour, and have to patch together hours from various sources in order to make a living. If you have a good education, are carrying all your references and diplomas and are prepared to stay for an academic year, it may be possible to fix up a relatively lucrative contract.

Even when you land a paying job, be prepared for possible problems extracting your wages. Till Bruckner didn't manage to guard against the problem and offers this advice based on hard experience:

> ***It's easy to find teaching work in these countries (Bolivia, Peru, Ecuador) but hard to get your pay if you're working for a cowboy outfit. Insist on weekly payment and make clear to the boss straight from the first day that it's against your culture to work if you're owed money. Make clear that you'll happily walk out the second you don't get paid. In Bolivia, I was stuck in a catch-22 where I had to go on working because if I stopped I'd definitely not get a penny of the money owed me (and boy was I broke). But if I continued, I might never get paid. The episode ended when the boss of***

the language school crammed a cool $60,000 into his briefcase and ran off to Argentina. I had a great time anyway.

For a more conventional pre-arranged teaching post, consider the British Council's Language Assistants Scheme (☎ 020 7389 4596; assistants@britishcouncil.org; britishcouncil.org/languageassistants-latin-america.htm). Applicants aged 18–30 with at least A Level Spanish and a degree, or undergraduates currently studying Spanish are placed for an academic year in Argentina, Chile, Colombia, Ecuador, Mexico, Paraguay and Venezuela. Application forms are available from October and interviews take place in January/February.

Some US-based organisations arrange for paying volunteers to teach in South and Central America including AIDE (☎ 512 457 8062; aidebroad.org) with volunteer teaching programmes in Argentina, Costa Rica, Ecuador and Peru, plus a handful of paid teaching positions in Chile (minimum age 21, programme fee $800 for four months, $1,000 for eight months). World Endeavors in Minneapolis (☎ 866 802 9678 toll free in North America; worldendeavors.com) sends paying volunteers to Costa Rica, Guatemala, Ecuador and several other countries.

Red Tape

Of course requirements vary from country to country but it is standard for work visas to be available only to teachers on long-term contracts after a vast array of documents has been gathered including notarised copies of teaching qualifications, police clearance, etc. This means that a high percentage of teachers work on tourist visas throughout Latin America. These must be kept up-to-date by applying for an extension from the immigration department or by crossing into and back from a neighbouring country. Occasionally extensions are available from the appropriate office, for example the 90-day visa given on entering Chile can in some cases be extended for a fee, though most long-stay Britons simply cross the border to Mendoza in Argentina every three months, for up to ten years. Shane Donavon, world traveller and editor of the admirable e-magazine *Jobs Abroad Bulletin* reported that in order to spend some months in Cusco, Peru, he had to renew his visa stamp twice by crossing the border into Bolivia. Even though he had lost his Peruvian immigration card and the Bolivian officials sent him back, a well placed $5 bill fixed the problem with minimal inconvenience.

Mexico

Companies of all descriptions provide language classes for their employees during all the waking hours of the week but especially in the early morning and at weekends. Roberta Wedge even managed to persuade a 'sleek head honcho in the state ferry service' that he needed private tuition during the siesta and that busy executives and other interested employees of a local company needed English lessons at the same time of day.

Demand is not confined to the big cities but exists in the remotest towns, at least one of which must remain nameless in order to preserve Roberta Wedge's dreams:

After doing a 'taster' ESL course in Vancouver, I set out for Nicaragua with a bus ticket to San Diego and $500 – no guide book, no travelling companion, no Spanish. On the way I fell in love with a town in Mexico (not for worlds would I reveal its name – I want to keep it in a pristine time warp so I can hope to return) and decided to stay. I found a job by looking up all the language schools in the phonebook and walking around the city to find them. The problem was that many small businesses were not on the phone. So I kept my eye out for English school signs. I had semi-memorised

> ***a little speech in Spanish, 'I am a Canadian teacher of English. I love your town very much and want to work here. This is my CV.' Within two days I had a job at a one-man school.***

Mexico City is a thousand times more polluted, yet offers the best prospects for language teachers who have every chance of being invited to attend a disconcertingly informal interview.

AMERICAN BRADWELL JACKSON DIDN'T HAVE TO LOOK FAR FOR HIS FIRST TEACHING JOB IN MEXICO:

After reading Work Your Way Around the World, I made the decision to ... wander the earth freely. I wondered if it was really possible to get a job teaching English so easily. Well I found out that it is. I was sitting at a metro stop in Mexico City, trying to figure out what school to go to for my first planned job enquiry. After I decided that the particular school I had in mind was too far away, I looked up and saw an English school right across the street. Providence, I thought. I was right. I sauntered on upstairs, cheerfully asked if they needed an English teacher, and about an hour and a half later, I was told when to start my training. It really was that easy.

The starting wage at the large chains will be 60+ pesos per hour though opportunities exist to make 14,800 pesos (gross) a month at universities like the Universidad del Mar in Oaxaca.

The red tape situation in Mexico is bound to cause headaches. Visitors are not allowed to work or engage in any remunerative activity during a temporary visit. Established schools are not normally willing to contract people with only a tourist visa, unlike private institutes who often employ teachers on tourist visas and expect them to renew it every 90 or 180 days by crossing the border. Among the required documents for a work permit are a CV in Spanish, notarised TEFL and university certificates which have been certified by a Mexican consulate and, if you are already in Mexico, a valid tourist visa. Volunteers with letters from a sponsoring organisation in Mexico and the UK may apply for a one-year FM3 work visa from the Mexican consulate for a fee of 2,593 pesos.

A volunteer placement organisation in the UK specialises in Mexico, placing people in teaching jobs as well as environmental and social projects. The £2,800 cost of a three-month placement with Outreach International (☎ 01458 274957; outreachinternational.co.uk) includes insurance and Spanish language course. Sarah Elengorn from Middlesex wanted to learn Spanish and so was attracted to a six-month project with Outreach International, working with street children in Puerto Vallarta, Mexico. She was the only female and the only non-Mexican on her placement at a shelter for street boys, so her Spanish (albeit street Spanish) improved very quickly. Sarah did some work on the streets but mainly worked at the shelter, organising, teaching (including safe sex) and playing with the children. She has stayed on in Puerto Vallarta working for various NGOs and charities.

Bolivia

Even the poorest of Latin American nations offers possibilities to EFL teachers, provided you are prepared to accept a low wage. In contrast to the standard hourly wage of $10–$20 in Europeanised cities like Rio de Janeiro and Santiago, the wages paid by language schools in La Paz start at 14 bolivianos ($2). Because of the low salaries, many schools find it hard to attract teachers to Bolivia. However many travellers prefer the country to others in South America for cultural reasons, for its colourful social mix.

If you have a good standard of education, are carrying all your references and diplomas plus a CV translated into Spanish and are prepared to stay for an academic year, it is possible to fix up a teaching contract after arrival. Terms begin in early February and late September, so try to arrive a few weeks in advance of these dates. Look up the handful of language schools and *colegios* (private schools) in the *Yellow Pages* (guia-amarilla.com), deliver your application dossiers by hand to the directors and tell everyone what you are trying to do.

JONATHAN ALDERMAN WAS HAPPY TO PUT UP WITH LOW PAY IN EXCHANGE FOR THE EXCELLENT QUALITY OF LIFE HE FOUND IN BOLIVIA, WHICH HE SAYS 'CAN FEEL LIKE AN IDYLLIC PARADISE SOMETIMES BECAUSE OF THE CLIMATE'. HE DID THINGS THAT WOULD BE UNIMAGINABLE AT HOME IN BRITAIN SUCH AS SWIMMING IN A POOL IN ORURO WHOSE WATERS WERE HEATED UNDERGROUND BY A VOLCANO, AND ATTENDING ONE OF THE MANY CARNIVALS IN FEBRUARY AND THROWING WATER BALLOONS AT THE LOCALS.

I came back to Cochabamba after exploring South America and took a job in the institute, El Britanico Boliviano de Cultura (BBC, Calle España 171, Cochabamba; 422 0936). The lessons were mostly in the evening, but I was lucky to get some one-to-one classes through the school to teach during the day as well. This school was professionally run and the director paid me on the last day of the month without any hassle. In this school I also taught mostly adults rather than kids. One thing that makes this school stand out from the many others in Cochabamba is the strong emphasis on British rather than American English (as the name would suggest). BBC often finds it quite hard recruiting teachers, simply because it is difficult to attract teachers to Bolivia due to the low salaries.

I would highly recommend staying and working in Bolivia – and if you are staying in Bolivia, it just has to be Cochabamba, because of the perfect spring-like climate. Teaching Bolivian students can be fun, though the kids can be boisterous (I especially found teenage boys to be a pain in the arse). When teaching adults, it was nice to be able to establish friendships with the students.

Last year Jonathan went back to Cochabamba to concentrate on teaching private classes and doing some translation work, while still teaching part-time in the Britanico. He concludes: *'If someone wants to earn a decent wage teaching English in Bolivia, one has to turn to private classes.'* When he first arrived, he advertised in the local newspaper for private classes charging 30–35 Bolivianos an hour. The best place to advertise private English lessons is the Sunday edition of the newspaper *El Diario*.

Most teachers arrive on a tourist visa ($100 for Americans) and should in theory apply for a work visa. Yet most simply continue to work on a tourist visa.

The biggest language school in the country is the bi-national Centro Boliviano Americano (cba.com.bo) which has a couple of locations in La Paz and schools in other cities like Sucre and Santa Cruz.

Brazil

The appetite for English has always been massive in Brazil though the country does well at producing its own highly qualified English language teachers. But there is always room for native speakers, as reported by a well-travelled TEFLer, Barry O'Leary. Barry arrived in Salvador (northern Brazil) just before *Carnaval*, which marks the break between terms every February.

BARRY O'LEARY BOUGHT A MAP, BORROWED A TELEPHONE DIRECTORY FROM HIS HOSTEL AND WALKED ROUND ALL THE 25 LANGUAGE ACADEMIES WITH HIS CV. HIS LUCK WASN'T AS QUICK AS IT HAD BEEN IN ECUADOR (DESCRIBED LATER) BECAUSE MOST ACADEMIES COULDN'T TELL HOW MANY STUDENTS THEY WOULD HAVE UNTIL AFTER CARNAVAL. BUT BARRY EVENTUALLY SUCCEEDED:

I taught in three Institutes, PEC (pec.com.br), Okey Dokey and AEC Idiomas. The business academy sent me to various offices which were all fully equipped and well organised. Generally working conditions were excellent and so was the pay; i received about $8 an hour which was a good rate for Brazil. The pupils were a mixed bag, yet they all had a great sense of humour and participated in the lessons, though some students were there only because their boss wanted them to be and had little interest.

I worked at another academy one afternoon a week. The approach here was to teach English through music, followed by group conversation lessons. Each week the director would translate two or three songs for the students to sing along in English. The students enjoyed this immensely, and I thought it was a very original way to learn. Most students seemed to be more interested in asking me questions about England and my life rather than pay attention to the lessons, but it was a good way for them to improve their fluency. I found Brazilian students very happy go-lucky people, they were always smiling and interested in learning English.

I was lucky enough to live in the old quarter of Salvador called Pelourino which was the hub of the nightlife, but also the hub of any trouble. I lived in a house with 15 people including Brazilians, Nigerians, French and Irish, for which I paid $20 a month and had a brilliant three months.

If you want to study Portuguese, you can apply for a student visa which would make it easier to stay on. For example, many foreigners register at the Pontificia Universidade Católica in Rio de Janeiro. This is an excellent place to link up with students and advertise classes if you want to offer private lessons (which pay much better than working for an institute). Richard Ferguson from New Zealand studied Portuguese with a tutor in Belo Horizonte, but decided not to try to teach. However he did meet an American who gave private English lessons in Sao Paulo for a few months charging a steep 50 reais an hour (£15). He bemoaned the fact that the sprawling city was hard to get around and he also insisted that students should be asked to pay in advance because Brazilians are notorious for no shows, being late or last minute cancellations.

Rates of pay for qualified and experienced teachers in institutes vary from R$13 an hour for classroom teaching to R$30 working for language agencies that will send you to companies like IBM.

Argentina

Argentina was crushed in 2000–2002 by an economic crisis that drastically devalued its currency, making it incredibly cheap for foreigners. But the country is making a steady recovery and has a real buzz about it at the moment. Although language schools, many of which specialise in the business market, have not made a full recovery, there is cause for some optimism with an economic growth rate predicted. Demand for English is back on the agenda, with several companies accepting untrained foreigners from North America and Europe as interns who are given free board and lodging with a family, free Spanish tuition, a small stipend and plenty of opportunities to travel and see the country.

For example Road2Argentina in Buenos Aires (☎ 011 6379 9391; road2argentina.com) offers cultural exchange and language immersion programmes in which international interns of any nationality undertake various placements in and around the capital, including some as ESL teachers (for which no knowledge of Spanish is required). Participants are aged 18–30, stay with families for between one and six months and take up various extracurricular activities such as tango lessons, cookery and photography. Programme fees start at $975 for one month including accommodation. Road2Argentina also offer a four-week TEFL training course from $1,975 including accommodation.

The hourly teaching wage is normally between 20 and 24 Argentine pesos which is now equivalent to about $5.40–$6.50. The *Buenos Aires Herald* carries job adverts for English teachers, as might the useful notice board in El Ateneo, the English language bookshop at 340 Calle Florida (the main shopping street). Another good contact point is the Instituto de Lengua Espanola para Extranjeros or ILEE where many foreign residents take Spanish classes.

Luke McElderry from Texas and his girlfriend Jenny Jacobi spent hours researching potential teaching employers in Buenos Aires on the internet. After completing a training course, he sent a mass e-mail with CV attached to at least 40 addresses and waited for responses to trickle in, and ended up hearing from about a quarter. He describes his job hunt:

> ***The first interviews were varied, some in English, one in Spanish, but all fairly casual. Most take 30 minutes and they seem to care more about your availability than your experience. I was asked a couple of times if I had any visa/permit and said no, and the employers didn't seem to care at all. I have heard the biggest institutes are the ones that care, and ironically pay the least!***

Before long, they were working for an institute (Speak Spanish which also teaches English; speakspanish.com.ar) which sent them out to teach 1½-hour classes in businesses. The wages were enough to take advantage of BA's sophisticated social life, though prices were steadily rising while they were there. All went smoothly apart from finding accommodation, which was a real hassle.

Chile

More than most other South American economies, Chile's is flourishing although the unemployment rate has been climbing and is expected to reach 8% by 2010. The market for English language teaching is very healthy, with at least 30 major language schools in the capital Santiago alone. Short-term casual teaching is not well paid: non-contractual work starts at 4,000–5,000 pesos per hour but rises with experience. If you arrive in February at the beginning of the school year with a recognised TEFL certificate and preferably some teaching experience, it will be easy to find teaching work. Whereas some schools expect their teachers to cross the border to renew a tourist visa every three months, others provide a contract which is a prerequisite for a work visa (except for Australians and New Zealanders who are eligible for one-year working holiday visas).

Early in 2008, Doug Burgess went job hunting in Santiago, armed with a CELTA and a few months of teaching experience:

> ***When I finished university I realised I wanted to learn another language and decided that Spanish was the one as I love Latin culture. I decided the best way to do this was to teach abroad so I decided to do the CELTA at home in Cambridge and work in some institutes over the summer in order to save***

> ***money and get some experience so that I wouldn't arrive in Chile as a green teacher. I chose Chile as it's probably the most developed country in South America, with a healthy currency and favourable exchange rate with other countries in South America.***
>
> ***When I arrived in Chile I worked an exchange system for the first three months in a school called Woodward in Providencia (woodward.cl). I taught two classes of English and in exchange received two classes of Spanish every day for three months, which was great because I didn't speak any Spanish when I arrived and this saved me a lot of money.***

Doug went on to be offered teaching work by some of the well-known institutes like Burfords and EF, and in the end signed a one-year contract with the prestigious Instituto Chileno Britanico. Another school which operates a language exchange programme of interest to newcomers is the Chileno Swiss Institute (info@chilenosuizo.cl).

TeachingChile in Santiago is an agency supplying native speaker teachers to various schools for a minimum of six months; it has contact numbers in the US (☎ 720 221 3831) and the UK (☎ 020 8150 6981); see teachingchile.com.

The following schools in Santiago, most located in the upper middle class area of Providencia, are among the best known language schools in the capital. Typically these schools offer a newcomer with a TEFL certificate the chance to teach a trial lesson and, if successful, a probationary three months.

American Business English Language Services: ☎ 02 946 2629; dday@netexpress.cl; more than 50 qualified native speakers.
Berlitz: with five branches (berlitz.cl).
Burford English Center: ☎ 02 235 1056; burford.cl; agency that sends teachers to off-site locations.
EF English First: chile@ef.com; up to 40 teachers for two branches. Full-time monthly salary is 500,000 pesos.
Fischer English Institute: ☎ 02 235 9812/235 6667; fischerinstitute.cl; teaches very structured lessons both on and off-site.
Polyglot-Mitford Ltd: Santiago; ☎ 02 233 3250; polyglot-mitford.cl; 40–50 teachers hired a year.

On arrival in Chile, you will automatically be given a tourist visa valid for 90 days, which is in the form of a small slip of paper which you must hang on to, since you will need it if you want to renew the visa by crossing the border or if you apply for a *visacion de residencia.*

To find private clients, it may help to advertise. The best results are obtained by putting a small ad in *El Mercurio,* the leading quality daily or checking ads on Craigslist (http://santiago.en.craigslist.org) or in the free ads paper *El Rastro.*

Ecuador

Compared to its neighbours, Peru and Colombia, Ecuador represents an oasis of political stability with its currency not only pegged to the dollar but it actually is the US dollar. The demand for English thrives more than ever, particularly American English in the capital Quito and in the picturesque city and cultural centre of Cuenca in the southern Sierra. The majority of teaching is of university students and the business community whose classes are normally scheduled early in the morning (starting at 7am) to avoid the equatorial heat of the day and again in the late afternoon and evening. Many schools are owned and run by expatriates since there are few legal restrictions on foreigners running businesses.

Teaching wages have climbed back so that a respectable hourly wage is now $6, with some schools still offering $4 or $5. Quito is not as large and daunting a city as some other South American capitals, though certain areas are dangerous. It should be easy to meet longer term expats who can help with advice on teaching.

WHEN BARRY O'LEARY ARRIVED IN QUITO, HE VISITED A TOURIST AGENCY WHICH HAD THE ADDRESSES OF ALL THE POSSIBLE ACADEMIES AND INSTITUTES. HE STARTED HIS FIRST TEFL JOB HUNT ARMED ONLY WITH A BASIC TEFL CERTIFICATE AND SPEAKING VERY LITTLE SPANISH. AS LUCK WOULD HAVE IT HE FOUND TWO JOBS IN 24 HOURS JUST BY WALKING ROUND THE CITY WITH COPIES OF HIS CV:

I can still remember the buzz I felt when José, my first employer, said 'Yeah we're looking for someone to start next week.' I couldn't quite believe it. With this institute there wasn't really a formal interview or application process. With another school I had a basic interview to make sure I could speak and wasn't a monster, they didn't even ask for my TEFL certificate. In Ecuador everyone I knew was working without a work visa. I remember being worried about telling them I was only staying for three months but they were just happy to have a native speaker teaching their students.

Here is a brief list of language schools in Ecuador:

Centro de Estudios Interamericanos (CEDEI): Cuenca; ☎ 07 283 9003; cedei.org.
EF English First: Quito; ☎ 02 224 8651; steve.tomkins@ef.com.
Inlingua: Quito; ☎ 02 245 8763; inlinguaquito@inlingua.com.
Key Language Services: Quito; ☎ 02 222 0956; kls@andinanet.net.

If you want to get away from commercial language schools in the cities, many agencies in Ecuador place volunteer teachers. The Children of Ecuador programme based in the coastal town of Bahía de Caráquez is part of the Genesis of Ecuador Foundation, a non-profit organisation created to raise the level of education of Ecuadorian children. Volunteers receive a week of supervised in-class training, and are expected to teach 6 hours from 7.30am, Monday–Thursday, helped by the class instructor. The cost of a minimum four-week homestay is $1,290, a third of which is donated to the programme. Spanish classes and other extras are provided (bahiacity.com/volunteer).

Technically you shouldn't work on a tourist visa but there is little control. Britons and Americans can stay 90 days as tourists, though this can be extended by leaving the country. A tourist visa cannot be changed into another kind of visa without leaving the country. Many teachers work on a study or cultural exchange visa valid for one year.

Peru

Lima has a sprinkling of language institutes, especially in the port area of Miraflores, many of which hire and pay a salary to native speakers. The other main cities offer some opportunities too like Arequipa, Trujillo, Nazca and Piura. The town of Cusco is a favourite among travellers, many of whom settle down for an extended stay, possibly by swapping English lessons for Spanish or for a room with a local family. Check the display adverts in the 'Seccion Empleos' of the Sunday edition of the main daily *El Comercio*. Among the most prestigious are the Instituto Cultural Peruano Norteamericano (icpna.edu.pe), the Instituto Cultural Peruano Britanico (britanico.edu.pe) and the Instituto de Idiomas de la Universidad Catolica (idiomas.pucp.edu.pe), but many other less well known schools offer pay at the lower end of the spectrum, i.e. US$3–$6.

James Gratton arrived in Lima looking forward to what had sounded like a dream job. He had contacted some institutes ahead and was contacted enthusiastically by one (on the strength of a certificate earned from a one-week intensive TEFL training course in London and nine months of living and teaching in Venezuela the year before). Despite the job not living up to expectations (many of his employer's promises were not honoured), he concluded that the experience could be used as a stepping stone to better opportunities. When he put a cheap advertisement (written in English) in *El Comercio* he immediately signed up two private clients.

Venezuela

The prospect of the leftist president Hugo Chavez remaining in power for the foreseeable future may continue to make life difficult for the business community, which is in love with learning American English with a view to doing business with *El Norte*. Despite this, language schools with names like Iowa Institute (iowainstitute.com) and big international chains like Wall Street (wsi.com.ve) and inlingua (caracas@inlingua.com) still recruit native speaker teachers from time to time.

Nick Branch from St. Albans investigated most of the schools and agencies in Venezuela several years ago and worked outside Caracas where the pay was substantially less than in the capital: *'Merida is very beautiful and a considerably more pleasant place to be than Caracas. The atmosphere and organisation of the institute where I worked were very good. But alas. As with all the English teaching institutes in Merida, the pay is very low. Merida is three times cheaper to live in than Caracas, but the salaries are 5–6 times lower.'*

Check adverts in Caracas' main English language organ, the *Daily Journal*. Most give only a phone number. Surprisingly, opportunities for English teachers also exist on the popular resort island of Margarita. Two exchange programmes worth investigating are run by Centro Venezolano Americano del Caracas (cva.org.ve) which places a large number of North American graduates as teacher-interns, and VENUSA College in Merida (venusacollege.org) whereby up to 40 interns stay with families and teach English for 3–12 months.

Most people work on a tourist visa which is valid for 90 days non-extendable. It is possible to apply for a multiple entry visa (about $30) if you can provide proof of employment, sufficient funds and a return ticket.

Central America

If you keep your ears open as you travel through Central America, you may come across opportunities to teach English, especially if you are prepared to do so as a volunteer. Salaries on offer may be pitiful but if you find a congenial spot on the 'gringo trail' (for example the lovely old colonial town of Antigua in Guatemala), you may decide to prolong your stay by helping the people you will inevitably meet who want to learn English.

As the wealthiest country in Central America, Costa Rica is sometimes referred to as the Switzerland of the region and there are plenty of private language academies in the capital San José. The school year runs from March 1st to December 1st. Temporary six-month renewable working visas are sometimes issued to teachers working for established employers like International House in San José (institutobritanico.co.cr). After deciding that she needed a complete change from Hounslow and an office job, Jane Roberts signed up for a CELTA course at International House in London and had to decide where she wanted to job-hunt:

> ***I wanted to work in a hot Latin country. IH had said don't expect to get a job straightaway in your dream destination, but I have proved this wrong. I got the address of Instituto Britanico (from your book!), emailed them my CV and a covering letter, within two weeks was offered a job and a couple of weeks later I was here in Costa Rica. My students are very motivated, lovely to work with, keen to learn, really want to speak a lot. I have the greatest admiration for them as they often come after a hard day at work to a 3-hour lesson and put a lot into it. I have to ensure that it is as interesting as possible for them. At first I didn't have much spare time, however I have now visited mountains, volcanoes and the beach when I had a long weekend. My advice is to smile, relax, be nice to people. I have not found any problems with Latin machismo, no hassles with men. They love my accent but have not been pushy or offensive. Costa Rican people are so friendly and helpful. It's a very chilled country.***

VOLUNTEERING

Short-term voluntary work projects are scattered over this vast continent, though the two easiest countries in which to find organised projects are Ecuador and Costa Rica. Many of the opportunities that become widely known are concerned with conservation (treated separately below) and charge a substantial fee. But an approach to almost any environmental, health or childcare non-governmental organisation might be greeted warmly, especially if the enquiry is made in Spanish. The better funded of these projects might even be able to offer accommodation and expenses.

The internet has made it much easier to unearth opportunities for volunteering, whether from one of the mainstream databases like idealist.org, traveltree.co.uk or wwv.org.uk. One specialist website is volunteersouthamerica.net, conscientiously maintained by its founder Steve McElhinney. He set out to list free and low-cost volunteer opportunities in South and Central America for the benefit of backpackers and independent travellers looking for a real volunteer experience abroad, without paying any middle-man or agency fees.

A specialist advisory service based in Brighton will tailor-make a list of voluntary projects in Latin America to which clients can apply directly; see volunteerlatinamerica.com (price £20.50). The excellent online guide to Ecuador EcuadorExplorer.com has listings and links to teaching and voluntary projects as well as what to do. Another good source of opportunities is on volunteeringecuador.org whose listed projects charge $15–16 a day to cover living expenses, plus a registration fee of $190. In some cases a centralised placement service makes choosing a project much easier, though you will have to pay for the service as in the case of Volunteer Bolivia (volunteerbolivia.org) located in Cochabamba. They encourage their clients to sign up for a month of Spanish tuition while staying with a local family before becoming a volunteer; a combined language course, homestay and volunteer placement programme costs $1,670 for one month, $2,450 for 12 weeks. Bolivia Volunteers (freewebs.com/boliviavolunteers) charges somewhat less, from $1,080 for four weeks to $1,800 for eight weeks.

ProWorld Service Corps with headquarters in the US (☎ 877 429 6753; myproworld.org/internships.htm) offers a range of internships in fields from business to journalism, lasting 2–26 weeks with aid agencies in Peru, Belize, Mexico and Brazil. Fees start at $1,895 which includes project work with local NGOs, language training, room and board, and cultural activities. ProWorld has a UK office in Sheffield (☎ 0870 750 7202).

Spanish language course providers and cultural exchange organisations can often arrange interesting volunteer or internship programmes. Among the largest are the following:

Adelante LLC: Seal Beach, CA; ☎ 562 799 9133; adelanteabroad.com; internships, volunteer placements, teaching abroad and semester/summer study opportunities from 1–12 months in Costa Rica (San José), Mexico (Oaxaca), Chile (Vina del Mar/Valparaiso) and Uruguay (Montevideo); prices start from $1,995 for 1 month in Chile, Uruguay and Mexico to include language classes, various housing options and work assignment placement.

Amerispan Unlimited: Philadelphia; ☎ 800 879 6640; info@amerispan.com; specialist Spanish-language travel organisation with expertise in arranging language courses, voluntary placements and internships throughout South and Central America.

Amigos de las Americas: Houston; ☎ 800 231 7796; amigoslink.org; summer training programme for 700+ high school and college student volunteers mostly in community health projects throughout Central and South America; participation fee is $4,040 including travel from the US; all volunteers must have studied Spanish at school or university and undergone training.

Cactus Volunteers Abroad: Brighton, UK; ☎ 01273 725200; volunteers-abroad.com/language_volunteering.php; spanish language courses followed by voluntary placements in range of countries; examples include working at a hatchery for Leatherback turtles on Guatemala's Pacific Coast, animal breeding projects in El Puma Ecological Park in Argentina and teaching English in a school in Cusco, Peru.

Caledonia Languages Abroad: Edinburgh; ☎ 0131 621 7721; caledonialanguages.co.uk; educational consultancy which books individuals of any nationality onto volunteer projects following on from language courses (minimum three weeks) in Costa Rica, Argentina, Bolivia, Chile, Ecuador and Peru; arrangement fee of £250 plus VAT in addition to cost of language course and accommodation.

EIL: Malvern, UK; ☎ 0800 018 4015; overseasvolunteering.org.uk. Provides language and volunteering programmes with Experiment in International Living partners in Argentina, Brazil, Chile, Ecuador and Guatemala; sample price for Chile programme is £1,886 for 12 weeks.

Individual language schools often have links with local projects and can arrange for students of Spanish to attach themselves to projects that interest them. Typically Carisa Fey started her big trip round South America with a short language course in Quito which led to some voluntary work afterwards teaching knitting to street kids. For example Mundo Verde Spanish School in Cusco, Peru (☎ +51 84 221287; mundoverdespanish.com) has links with a development project in the rainforest and with many other voluntary projects to which students can be assigned for no fee.

As you travel throughout the region you are bound to come across various charitable and voluntary organisations running orphanages, environmental projects and so on, some of which may be able to make temporary use of a willing volunteer. The Quaker-run peace and service centre in Mexico City, Casa de los Amigos, has information on a variety of volunteering opportunities throughout Mexico City and Mexico. The Casa also has its own volunteer programme for those who speak Spanish and are able to commit for at least six months to a year, working for peace and social justice. The Casa is at Ignacio Mariscal 132, 06030 Mexico, D.F., Mexico (☎ +52 55 5705 0521; amigos@casadelosamigos.org) and provides simple accommodation starting from 100 pesos (US$7) per night. All are welcome to stay at the Casa; most of the guests are involved in volunteer work and other peace and social justice activities.

Many worthwhile social projects rely on volunteers. One of the most famous and long-established is Casa Guatemala, an orphanage and attached backpackers' hostel which relies on travellers to carry out maintenance, cooking, building, organic gardening, teaching the children

English, etc. They can use as many as 100 volunteers a year, preferably for a minimum of six months (casa-guatemala.org). The director warns that volunteers should expect a certain amount of hardship. Long-stay volunteers must pay a refundable fee of $300.

Almost any Spanish language school in Guatemala can help arrange a volunteer position. To find links to many of these language schools, visit xelapages.com/schools.htm. The cultural institute Casa Xelaju in Quetzaltenango (☎ 502 7761 5954; casaxelaju.com) runs Spanish courses and refers clients to internships and voluntary work in Guatemala. The fee for volunteers is $80–$200 plus $60 a week for homestay accommodation. The city of Quetzaltenango offers many opportunities to do volunteer work in the community.

The children's charity TASK Brasil (Trust for Abandoned Street Kids) has an office in London (☎ 020 7735 5545; taskbrasil.org.uk) or in the US ring 215 732 5985. They are looking for volunteers over 21 to work with street children in Rio.

Conservation

An increasing number of organisations, both indigenous and foreign-sponsored, is involved in environmental projects throughout the continent. The highest concentration of projects is probably in Costa Rica where the National Parks and Communities Authority runs a voluntary programme Asociacion de Voluntarios para el Servicio en las Areas Protegidas (ASVO). To be eligible you must be willing to work for at least 30 days, be able to speak at least minimal Spanish and provide a copy of your passport and a photo. The work may consist of trail maintenance and construction, greeting and informing visitors, beach cleaning, research or generally assisting rangers. There is also a possibility of joining a sea turtle conservation project. Details are available from the San José office (☎ 506 258 4430/223 4260; info@asvocr.org or lmatarrita@asvocr.org; asvocr.org). Food and accommodation cost $17 a day in addition to a $30 registration fee. One volunteer warned that security at the national parks is lax, allowing the odd confidence trickster to pose as a volunteer and rob money and valuables from the volunteers' dorms.

A cultural exchange organisation in Argentina, Grupo de Intercambio Cultural Argentino, invites paying volunteers and interns from abroad (normally with a working knowledge of Spanish) to work in projects in Buenos Aires and Patagonia. Assignments last a week or more and many involve community outreach. Accommodation is provided and starts from $1,000 a month. Details are available from GIC in Buenos Aires (☎ 011 5353 9497; gicarg.org). Two other volunteer agencies in Argentina are Insight Argentina (volunteers@helpargentina.org) and Buenos Aires Volunteer (bavolunteer.org.ar).

BUNAC has volunteering programmes in Costa Rica and Peru under the auspices of partner organisations which provide back-up during the two or three month placement. Any British resident 18 or over who can speak intermediate level Spanish (minimum GCSE) may apply. The Volunteer Peru programme fee for 2009 is £1,199 for two months, £1,449 for three months, and Volunteer Costa Rica is £100 less.

Trawling the internet for other eco-projects in Central and South America will turn up lots of lively possibilities. For example in a remote corner of Surinam you can monitor nesting sea turtles with STINASU, the Foundation for Nature Conservation in Surinam (stinasu.volunteerwork@gmail.com; stinasu.com/program_eng.html). They accept volunteers from February to September and expect a minimum contribution of $100. The Eco-Escuela de Español in the Petén region of Guatemala arranges for language students to assist local conservation and development projects for two hours a day (☎ 502 5940 1235; EcoEscuelaEspanol@gmail.com, ecoescuelaespanol.org). People with a TEFL qualification may be able to find paid work.

A project in Brazil charges volunteers about $550 a month to donate their time to carry out general duties; iracambi is a farm and research centre in the state of Minas Gerais (☎ 032 3721 1436; iracambi.com). A new volunteer programme run by the Picaflor Research Centre in Peru (picaflor_rc@yahoo.com) accepts volunteers for any period of time to work on habitat restoration and the establishment of an environmental education centre in the Tambopata area, close to Lago Sandoval.

One way of spending time in the famous Galapagos islands is to become an International Volunteer with the Charles Darwin Foundation. Volunteers must be at least second year undergraduates and preferably able to stay for a minimum of six months. The skills required vary according to project. International volunteers have to cover all their expenses including airfares to and from the islands, food and accommodation. More information is available at darwinfoundation.org/es/get-involved/volunteer/international or by post from the Volunteer Program Manager, Charles Darwin Research Station, Puerto Ayora, Isla Santa Cruz, Islas Galapagos, Ecuador (vol@fcdarwin.org.ec).

For animal lovers the Inti Wara Yassi wildlife reserve in Bolivia accepts volunteers to help care for injured animals (intiwarayassi.org). The relatively new Flor de la Amazonía Animal Rescue Centre in Ecuador accepts volunteers through the administrative office in the UK (youvolunteer.org) which also sends volunteers to teach and care for children as part of the Arajuno Road Project in Amazonian Ecuador. Both schemes start at an affordable $500 for four weeks.

Organic farming has a healthy sprinkling of proponents in Latin America and WWOOF has branches in Argentina, Belize, Brazil, Chile, Costa Rica, Ecuador and Mexico.

THE IDEA OF VISITING ORGANIC FARMS APPEALED TO ROB ABBLETT:
I stayed on a WWOOF farm in Paraguay for two weeks, living and working with a Swiss German family on a large isolated plot of land, learning about their many trials and tribulations as they struggled (in vain) to adapt from Swiss efficiency to third world conditions. Afterwards I became the first WWOOFer a German woman host in Uruguay had ever had. She worked as a teacher in Montevideo and had integrated well into the country. She provided great food and wine for working on her large garden, picking strawberries, weeding and painting. But I didn't stay long: I'd been robbed in Paraguay, got scared in Buenos Aires and decided that eight years of working around the world has been fantastic and worthwhile but now I need to do something different.

OTHER OPPORTUNITIES

Apart from teaching, the only paid work available in Latin America tends to be for bilingual professionals. Engineers, business managers, highly specialised technicians have all found work in the private sector especially in international companies that operate in the mining, oil, hotel, banking and telecommunications sectors. Interesting volunteer opportunities are also available, as Sara Ellis-Owen discovered when she decided she needed to get out of London, and the law firm that employed her was sympathetic to her desire to take a break. Not only did they give her three months of unpaid leave but they contributed financially to her placement by the Edinburgh-based charity Challenges Worldwide (challengesworldwide.com) with a legal NGO that advocated for the rights of all children in Belize. She was delighted to have plenty of free time to explore Belize which is an 'unspoilt, happy, relaxed place' and she loved every minute of it.

The Iko Poran Association in Rio de Janeiro (☎ 021 3852 2916; ikoporan.org) assigns several hundred volunteers in their 20s to various development projects in Rio, Salvador and Amazonia for 3–24 weeks. The programme fee is R$1,500 ($630) which covers volunteer lodging for the first month and a donation of R$400.

ELEP (Experiential Learning Ecuadorian Programs) in Quito, Ecuador (☎ 02 254 3231; elep.org) arranges unpaid internships and volunteer placements in many fields in Ecuador such as media, tourism, computing, marine biology, event management, engineering, finance, medicine and law. Locations include the highlands, coastal regions and Galapagos Islands. Participants must do a four-week course in intermediate/advanced Spanish (at a cost of about $1,500) before being assigned to an eight-week internship.

Bilingual secretaries who can produce letters in proper English are in demand from commerce and law firms. Americans should find out if there is a local American Chamber of Commerce (as there is in Caracas) and Britons may do likewise. For example the British-Chilean Chamber of Commerce will supply the names of British companies in Chile. The US-Mexico Chamber of Commerce (usmcoc.org/usa/bvecino.html) sponsors a summer internship programme whereby bilingual American and Mexican students from certain universities are placed in companies in each other's countries.

A new opportunity for paid work in Costa Rica might appeal to some. Like Gibraltar, Costa Rica has become the location of choice for many online sports bookies. English-speaking staff (preferably American) take bets on sporting events over the telephone and do basic clerical work. Wages are on a par with office work in the US, i.e. the minimum wage, and reports indicate that companies are not too strict about work permits. Among the estimated 300 companies active in the business, a couple of the biggest are Skybook and Bodog. Knowledge of sports is preferred but not essential.

Translators, particularly of scientific, medical and technical papers, tend to be well paid by universities and large industrial concerns. Both types of vacancy are advertised in English language newspapers, which may themselves need proofreaders and editors or know of companies that do. In many large cities there is a sizeable English-speaking expatriate community, predominantly involved in international commerce. The bars and restaurants that they frequent are good job-hunting grounds: not only might you hear about opportunities for temporary work in business, but you could obtain work serving in the establishment itself.

Tourism

Only highly able candidates who have extensive Latin American travel experience and a knowledge of Spanish are hired as overland expedition guides and drivers with UK operators like Tucan Travel (tucantravel.com) and Journey Latin America also in London (journeylatinamerica.co.uk). In most cases, the company pays for food and accommodation plus a daily rate of $20–$25. If you get to know an area well, you may be able to act as a freelance guide though, not surprisingly, this will probably incur the locals' resentment, as Mónica Boza found when she lived in Cusco, Peru:

> ***If you have a good knowledge of the trails and want to become an outdoor guide, contact the tour agencies on arrival. But Peruvian guides are very jealous of foreign ones. I have known cases where they called the Migration Service and deportation followed. The adventure tour agencies are mainly along Plateros St or on the Main Square.***

Local opportunities may crop up in one of the many places where tourism is booming. Many expat-style bars and clubs employ foreigners. For example Venezuela's Margarita Island in the Caribbean has dozens of places catering to package holidaymakers. Few corners of the world have escaped the fashion for Irish pubs; in Cusco, try Paddy Flaherty on Santa Catalina St. Mexico is another country in which travellers have been approached to work not as waiters or bar staff, but as hosts, entertainers and touts. For a realistic assessment of job prospects in the resort of Cancun, check out cancunassist.com.

Anyone who can fix engines, especially on camper vans, should find no trouble earning a living in any touristy area of Mexico. You might be able to find day work on boats in harbours before the yachts set sail or perhaps an opportunity to boat-sit as Anne Wakeford did in Puerto Vallarta. She recommends asking boat owners to radio your request for work to their fellow yachtsmen in the morning. She also noticed that there might be work further south helping boats to navigate the locks of the Panama Canal.

At the other end of the continent, reports from the Falkland Islands indicate that they have been experiencing a mini-boom. Many of the tiny population have been drawn away from the countryside and into Stanley where a range of bars, shops and restaurants has opened. The island government is worried about rural depopulation and abandoned farms, so hard working people with agricultural experience might well be able to find work on the land. The few hotels there very occasionally recruit staff from abroad; the Sea Lion Lodge (sealionisland.com) tends to employ Chilean staff and a British chef.

THE CARIBBEAN

The Caribbean is far too expensive to explore unless you do more than sip rum punch by the beach. A host of Britons, Australians, South Africans, etc. are exchanging their labour, mostly on yachts, in order to see this exotic part of the world.

JOBS AFLOAT

Perhaps the easiest jobs to find are those working on the countless sailboats, charter yachts and cruise ships which ply the Caribbean each winter and spring. From November until May the Caribbean becomes a hive of marine activity. Since it marks the start of the main tourist season, Christmas is a particularly good time to look for work. The main requirement for being hired is an outgoing personality and perseverance in the search more than qualifications or experience. Hours are long and wages are minimal on a charter boat, but most do it for the fun. Board and lodging are always free and in certain jobs tips can be high. It would not be unusual to work for a wage of less than $100 a month and then earn ten times as much in tips.

Cruise Ships

For general information about cruise ship work see *Working a Passage*. Contracts are normally for six to nine months and the hours of work are long, often 14 hours a day, seven days a week living aboard the passenger ship with all onboard facilities provided by the ship owner. Most cruise ships active in the Caribbean contract their staff from Florida-based personnel agencies (known as concessionaires), some of which liaise with UK and European agencies. Workers aboard passenger ships require a C-1/D seafarer's visa issued by the United States Embassy which is only granted after a face-to-face interview.

Charter Yachts

The charter season in the Caribbean is November to May when an experienced deckhand can earn US$400 a week cash-in-hand plus tips. But there will be many weeks when the boat will not be chartered and the wage will fall away while you may have to hang around a boring marina. It is important to stress that a deckhand job is not compatible with a great vacation. It's a tough job with long working hours during which you must never stop smiling. When the guests are snorkelling on the reef, the deckhand will be helping the skipper repair the toilet. While the guests are hiking up a volcano, the deckhand is polishing the winches.

The lack of a work permit can be a definite hindrance in the search for work with a charter company. Immigration authorities are consistently tough throughout the Caribbean. When you leave any boat as a crew you sign off the crew list in immigration where they want to see a ticket not only out of the country but one that connects with a flight to your home country. They also want to see an address where you intend to stay and may ask to see sufficient funds.

Yacht charter companies are unwilling to publicise vacancies, both because they have enough speculative enquiries on the spot and also they are forbidden by their respective island governments from hiring anyone without proper working papers. However once you are on the spot, it is easier to hear of possibilities, and there are brokers and agents who match up crew with boats. These crew placement agencies may be able to help people on-the-spot, particularly in late October, who complete an application form and pay the registration fee (usually $20):

Jane's Yacht Services: English Harbour, Antigua; ☎ 268 460 2711; antyacht@candw.ag; yachtservices.ag; offers a crew placement service.
Nicholson & Sons Antigua: Stanley's Tavern, English Harbour, Antigua; ☎ 268 460 1530; nicholson-charters.com.

If you don't get anywhere with the agencies or charter comanies, it will be a case of implementing all the tactics outlined in the *Working a Passage* chapter to commend yourself to skippers, by asking at docks, putting up notices, following up leads, frequenting bars and so on. One way of breaking into the world of Caribbean yachties is to help with the drudgery of maintaining boats when at anchor. Try to find out when and where boat shows and races are being held as people are always in a rush to get their boats looking first class.

JOBS ON LAND

People occasionally find work in nightclubs and hotels on the islands. The Cayman Islands are meant to be one of the best places to look for this sort of work, with over 1,500 Americans alone working there. Construction work may also be available on Grand Cayman; ask around at bars. Without a 'Gainful Occupation Licence' or work permit (difficult to obtain with hundreds of locals after the same jobs) you should not take for granted that you will be treated fairly. Plenty of horror stories circulate concerning maltreatment by employers, such as failure to pay wages and to honour agreements to provide a homeward flight. Keep your beach-scepticism handy, and don't hesitate to cut your losses and run, if you sense you're on to a bad deal.

The Dominican Republic has built up a flourishing package tour industry and jobs can be found by people with hospitality experience or a knowledge of several languages. There are 14 hotels in the resort of Playa Dorada and two more in Costa Dorado where you can ask for work which will pay only $50–$100 a month. Beware of promises of earning a fortune since these jobs will involve selling on commission.

There are some opportunities for voluntary service including in the Dominican Republic. For instance the Canadian charity the Smiles Foundation (smilesfoundation.org) accepts volunteers over 21 with some Spanish to join their projects in health care, education and social development. The Bermuda Institute of Ocean Sciences (St George's GE01, Bermuda; ☎ 441 297 1880 ext 206; bios.edu) accepts volunteer science interns to help scientists conduct research for three to six months. Applicants (who are normally upper level undergraduates or recent graduates in relevant subjects) should make personal contact with the faculty member(s) for whom they wish to work (see website). Note that immigration restrictions mean that the Station cannot hire foreigners to carry out work other than research.

Greenforce (London SW6; ☎ 020 7384 3343; greenforce.org) recruits fee-paying volunteers to help with a biodiversity marine project in the Bahamas. Projects involve studying endangered species and habitats. No previous experience is necessary as dive training is provided. The cost is £2,500 for ten weeks plus flight; shorter stays are also offered.

Volunteers collaborate with marine biologists at the Bimini Biological Field Station in the Bahamas studying the behaviour of lemon sharks and other captive animals for at least a month. They also take on routine maintenance and catering chores. Volunteers contribute $695 per month to cover meals and housing. For further information contact bbfssharklab@gmail.com (miami.edu/sharklab).

With the beleaguered economy of Cuba, few opportunities will present themselves, though the Cuba Solidarity Campaign (London N4; ☎ 020 8800 0155; finance@cuba-solidarity.org.uk) still runs its work/study 'brigade' twice a year in which volunteers undertake agricultural and construction work for 15 days in July and December/January. No specific skills or qualifications are required but applicants must be able to demonstrate a commitment to solidarity work. The cost of the brigade in 2009 is approximately £975 which covers the full cost of flights, visas, transfers, accommodation and food.

St. Eustatius National Parks Foundation in the Netherlands Antilles has a volunteer programme to maintain park trails and a botanical garden, plus participate in a marine turtle monitoring programme organised by the STENAPA Foundation, Gallows Bay, St. Eustatius (tel/fax +599 318 2884; statiapark.org). Volunteers from overseas available for one to six months should apply though the British-based workingabroad.com. The cost for two months is £990.

AFRICA

Nearly a decade into the new millennium, Africa struggles with continuing challenges involving ethnic violence, disputed elections, famine and HIV. Mounting death tolls in Zimbabwe, chaos in Congo and Somalia, terrorist attacks in Egypt, criminal gangs in Johannesburg and unrest in many places persuade many travellers that it is too difficult and dangerous a destination. Madagascar suffered a coup in early 2009 which badly affected some projects and scared western volunteers away but it is amazing how resilient development agencies can be; many are functioning again. Vast swathes of the continent are of course safe and marvellous, with an astonishing diversity of scenery and culture. According to the Year Out Group, South Africa and Kenya are the most popular destinations for gap year placements, with Ghana and Tanzania also appearing in the top ten.

It is impossible to generalise about countries as different from each other as Morocco, Uganda and South Africa; however, the level of paid employment opportunities is negligible throughout the continent and certainly does not warrant a country-by-country treatment here. The principal means of experiencing Africa other than as a gawking tourist is as a volunteer.

All travellers will have to come to their own conclusions about personal safety. Every so often a tragedy occurs in which someone is mauled by lions or a safari jeep overturns in a ravine. Statistically, the level of violent crime in the urban areas of South Africa poses a more realistic threat, though victims tend to be the well-heeled types who stay in smart hotels. A tragedy of more far-reaching proportions is the spread of HIV/AIDS on the African continent. In 2008 an estimated 22 million people were living with HIV/AIDS in Sub-Saharan Africa and 1.5 million died. In much of Africa the teaching of safe sex has become far more important than the teaching of English. Many agencies are working tirelessly to spread the message and volunteers may well find themselves involved in raising awareness of the dangers of spreading the virus.

The concept of a true working holiday is well developed in Africa. Eco-tourism – where non-mass tourists pay for a holiday that may enhance not harm the local culture or environment – can take the form of participating in conservation projects or learning bush lore.

TEACHING

Because English is or has been the medium of instruction in state schools in many ex-colonies of Britain including Ghana, Nigeria, Kenya, Zambia, Zimbabwe and Malawi, the majority of English teachers in these countries is local and the need for native speakers is much less than in Asia or Latin America. Still there is some demand for volunteers in secondary schools, especially in Ghana, Kenya and Tanzania.

The majority of foreigners teaching in Africa are not 'teacher-travellers' but on one or two year volunteer contracts fixed up in their home country, while a number of others are placed by recognised gap year organisations in the UK. Missionary societies have played a dominant role in Africa's modern history, and some religious organisations continue to be active in the field of education and teacher recruitment, like Christians Abroad and the evangelical AIM International (☎ 0115 983 8120; aimint.org/eu).

Anyone who has fixed up a contract should try to gather as much up-to-date information as possible before departure, preferably by talking to people who have just been there. Otherwise local customs can come as a shock. A certain amount of deprivation is almost inevitable; for example teachers, especially volunteers, can seldom afford to shop in the pricey expatriate stores and so will have to be content with the local diet, typically a staple cereal such as millet usually made into a kind of stodgy porridge, plus some cooked greens, tinned fish or meat and fruit.

One gap year agency sent Sarah Johnson from Cardiff to Tanzania to teach English and geography at a rural secondary school:

> ***The expectations which Zanzibari children have from school are worlds away from those of British school children. They expect to spend most of their lessons copying from the blackboard, so will at first be completely nonplussed if asked to think things through by themselves or to use their imagination. I found that the ongoing dilemma for me of teaching in Zanzibar was whether to teach at a low level which the majority of the class would be able to understand, or teach the syllabus to the top one or two students so that they would be able to attempt exam questions, but leaving the rest of the class behind. Teaching was a very interesting and eye-opening experience. I believe that both the Zanzibari teachers and I benefited from a cultural exchange of ideas and ways of life.***

The British Council (britishcouncil.org) places a large number of qualified EFL teachers worldwide, and the Peace Corps in the US (☎ 1 800 424 8580; peacecorps.gov) recruits hundreds of volunteer teachers every year. Also the major gap placement agencies such as Lattitude, Project Trust and Africa & Asia Venture are active on the African continent and charge (see chapter *Volunteering: Gap Year and Career Break Placements*).

A selection of other charities that recruit volunteer teachers includes:

Mondochallenge: Newbury; ☎ 01635 45556; mondochallenge.org; sends volunteers (average age 27) to help with teaching and business development programmes in Tanzania, Kenya, Gambia and Senegal (though the latter involves teaching French); normal stay is 3 months and start dates are flexible; fee of £1,400 for 3 months. Board and lodging in local family homes costs an extra £15 (approximately) per week.

Sudan Volunteer Programme: London NW3; tel/fax 020 7485 8619; svp-uk.com; needs volunteers to teach conversational English to university students and adults in Sudan for 6 months (preferred) from September or January; undergraduates and graduates with experience of travelling abroad (preferably in the Middle East) are accepted; TEFL certificate and knowledge of Arabic are not required; volunteers pay for their airfare (about £500) plus UK travel expenses for selection and briefing; local host institutions cover living expenses in Sudan; most are in the Khartoum area.

Village Education Project (Kilimanjaro): Sevenoaks, Kent; ☎ 01732 459799; project@kiliproject.org; kiliproject.org; volunteer and gap year programmes to help teach EFL and other subjects in village primary schools in Tanzania for an academic year (8–9 months); fee is £3,250.

Egypt

Respectable and dubious language teaching centres flourish side by side in the streets of Cairo and to a lesser extent Alexandria. Teaching jobs are not hard to come by, especially if you have a Cambridge or Trinity Certificate. Many parents enrol their children to do intensive language courses in the summer, so this is a good time to look for an opening (assuming you can tolerate the heat).

The British Council in Agouza, Cairo (britishcouncil.org/egypt.htm) is one place to check for work. The Director of ELT may send or give you a form to fill in (teacherapplications@britishcouncil.org.eg) and then invite you for an interview and demonstration lesson. Normally they hire people with qualifications and two years' teaching experience but may be less fussy for summer courses. During exam time there is also a need for paid invigilators. The US-based Amideast English Teaching Program hires teachers in Cairo (23 Mossadak St, Dokki) and in Alexandria (3 Pharana, Azarita; alexandria@amideast.org).

An American traveller about to start law school posted the following on the thorntree forum in 2008:

> ***Back in December I posted a message asking people if they thought it was possible to get short term jobs abroad or if it was a good idea to possibly make tutoring flyers to put up around town. Both were ideas to supplement the money I already had saved and to have some new adventures/meet locals while traveling. I got a ton of negative responses telling me those ideas wouldn't work, etc. etc. Just wanted to post back on here six months later that it IS possible and my friend and I just did it. We got teaching jobs in Egypt that paid fairly well, without having work permits, without having TEFL, and the classes were for business professionals and thus were short terms (five weeks). Also, we put up tutoring flyers all over Cairo and made a decent amount of money doing private tutoring.***

One way of advertising your availability to teach might be to place an advert in the expatriate *Egypt Today* or on the job board of the monthly *Maadi Messenger* (maadimessenger.info) published by the Maadi Women's Guild and distributed through expat haunts like English-speaking churches.

The American University, centrally located at the eastern end of Tahrir Square in Cairo, is a good place to find work contacts.

If you are looking for good causes to which you can volunteer your time, ask at All Saints Anglican Cathedral (dioceseofegypt.org/english) behind the Marriott Hotel in Zamalek. Zamalek, along with Heliopolis and Maadi, are the best areas to look for private clients.

Ghana

As one of the most stable countries in Africa, Ghana supports a large number of organised schemes for volunteer teachers, since it has a long tradition of welcoming foreign students to participate in its educational and commercial life. Quite a number of exchange organisations like BUNAC, gap year programmes and charities operate to Ghana, many in co-operation with the Student and Youth Travel Organization in Accra (sytoghana.net). Fees differ for the Volunteering and Internship programmes among international agents, but the local charge for lodging and meals is fixed at $200 per month. The Accra-based organisation Volunteer in Africa (volunteeringinafrica.org) mentioned later in this chapter arranges positions (among others) as English and maths teachers in primary and junior secondary schools in Ghana for fee-paying volunteers.

Ikando is a volunteer and intern recruitment agency based in Accra which deals with education positions lasting up to eight weeks, as well as many others (☎ +233 21 222726; ikando.org). Volunteers stay in the Ikando house in the centre of Accra and cover their living expenses (£87 per week after their initial fortnight at £481).

Kenya

Kenya has had a chronic shortage of secondary school teachers for some time, mostly in Western Province. It may still be possible to fix up a teaching assistant's job by asking in the villages, preferably before terms begin in September, January and April. Be prepared to produce your CV, diplomas and official-looking references. Basic accommodation and a monthly salary (local rates) may be provided, though not all schools can afford to pay it, especially non-government self-help *Harambee* schools. According to the Kenyan High Commission in London (kenyahighcommission.net/employment.html), all non-Kenyan citizens who wish to work must be in possession of an Entry/Work permit issued by the Principal Immigration Officer in Nairobi before they can take up paid or unpaid work.

VAE Teachers Kenya sends British school-leavers and university graduates on six-month teaching placements from January to poor rural schools in and around Gilgil in the central highlands of Kenya. The cost of about £3,350 is all-inclusive of flights and living expenses. Details are available from Simon Harris who divides his time between Herefordshire and Gilgil (☎ 01568 750329; vaekenya.co.uk).

AVIF UK, administered from North Yorkshire (☎ 0777 171 2012; volunteer@avif.org.uk) sends volunteers to teach English at children's summer schools in Kenya which will cost the volunteer only the price of the airfare plus subsistence costs of £25 per week. At the end of each programme, AVIF organises an optional group safari from a base camp in Oropile, Masai Mara or a climb of Kilimanjaro with an experienced guide.

French West Africa

Even in ex-colonies of France, English is a sought-after commodity. World traveller Bradwell Jackson recently discovered paid on-the-spot teaching opportunities in Mali, Mauritania and Senegal.

Mauritania is becoming a more popular overland route from Morocco to Senegal now that the tensions of the Western Sahara seem to have cooled. Bradwell found a teaching job by a '*happy accident of fate*'. On striking up a conversation with a westerner walking on the other side of the street, he asked her about English language schools, and was promptly taken to the front door of The English Language Centre.

> ***I was lucky enough to speak with the owner right away. I was talking to her while she was busy doing some other things, so it was not a formal interview. I did not have to fill out an application, though she asked me to write a letter explaining why I wanted to work in Mauritania. She seemed very interested, and asked me to come back in a couple of days to do a mock class in front of her teachers. I was hired based on this.***

Getting a work permit was refreshingly simple. The school simply took his passport to the employment office and paid for a one-year work permit. The students were a joy to work with, because they were hungry to learn.

Networks like Couch Surfing (couchsurfing.com) have hosts registered all over Africa, who might be interested in exchanging hospitality for English lessons. Bradwell Jackson stayed with a couch surfing host in Bamako, Mali, for two months. Mali is one of West Africa's poorest countries, however his host was a wealthy man who treated him generously in exchange for two hours of English lessons a day.

TOURISM

Once again travellers' hostels are one of the few providers of casual work in the developing nations of the African continent. It is something that many independent trans-Africa travellers do for the odd week, from Dahab on the Red Sea to the backpackers' haunts of Johannesburg, and is a very nice way to have a break without having to pay for it. While cycling through Africa, Mary Hall stopped at a backpackers' hostel in Malawi where she was even offered a permanent job, but the road called.

Tourism is well established both on the Mediterranean coast of Africa and in the countries of East and Southern Africa where game parks are the major attraction. (Opportunities in South Africa are discussed separately below.) It is possible to find work in hotels and bars in resort areas; try the so-called trendy establishments rather than humble locally staffed ones. When you're in places like Dahab on the Sinai peninsula, keep an eye out for notices in bars and travel agencies for staff. Wages will be low and so will living expenses.

Anyone with a diver's certificate might be able to find work at Red Sea resorts like Sharm el Sheikh and Hurghada. If you aren't sufficiently qualified but want to gain the appropriate certificates, the Red Sea might be a good place to train. Emperor Scuba Schools (emperordivers.com/ess_career_packages.php) have four schools on the Red Sea and run a career development programme for divers who want to gain instructor status and then find a job. Another company to try is Sinai Divers (sinaidivers.com/english.htm) with dive centres in Dahab, Marsa Alam and Sharm el Sheikh.

At local dive centres, you can sometimes get free lessons in exchange for filling air tanks for a sub-aqua club. It is possible to be taken on by an Egyptian operator (especially in the high season November to January); however the norm is to be paid no wage and just earn a percentage of the take.

Long-term possibilities may be available with overland companies like the Imaginative Traveller and Kumuka mentioned in the section *Overland Tours* in the chapter *Working a Passage*. For courier work, applicants are required to have first-hand knowledge of travel in Africa or must be willing to train for three months with no guarantee of work. Requirements vary but normally expedition leaders must be at least 23–25 and be diesel mechanics with a truck or bus licence. Some African specialists are listed here; others can be found on internet sites like go-overland.com.

Absolute Africa: London W4; ☎ 020 8742 0226; absoluteafrica.com.
Acacia Africa: London W2; ☎ 020 7706 4700; acacia-africa.com/work_for_us.html.
African Trails: Kent; ☎ 01580 761171; africantrails.co.uk.
Economic Expeditions: ☎ 020 7262 0177; economicexpeditions.com; Africa specialist.
Oasis Overland: Somerset; ☎ 01963 363400; oasisoverland.co.uk/work.html.

Anyone with skills as a mechanic might be able to find work with an overland company, especially if based along one of the major routes.

OPPORTUNITIES IN SOUTH AFRICA

Frightening levels of urban crime have prompted an enormous brain drain in South Africa. Hundreds of thousands of South Africans have emigrated over the past decade and more than two-thirds of skilled and educated South Africans have said that they have considered or are considering emigration, mainly to escape the crime but also the AIDS epidemic and an unemployment rate that exceeds 23% (including people no longer looking for work). Affirmative action policies mean that it is very difficult for foreigners to land jobs (legally) which could be done by locals.

Classified adverts in a range of South African papers can be accessed online via ioljobs.co.za. Temporary employment agencies such as Kelly with 50 branches (kelly.co.za) might be willing to register likely candidates whom they are persuaded plan to settle in South Africa. Prospects are generally rosier outside the popular destination of Cape Town.

Red Tape

The government is (understandably) not keen to hand out work permits to Europeans and other nationalities when so many South African nationals are unemployed. Tony Forrester found the situation very discouraging: '*With affirmative action, it's a nightmare being a white male and looking for a job.*' The Department of Home Affairs (home-affairs.gov.za/temp_residence.asp) takes the usual line of immigration authorities that '*the main consideration in dealing with work permits is whether a South African citizen/permanent resident cannot perform the employment task to be undertaken*'.

Because of the huge influx of illegal aliens from neighbouring states like Zimbabwe, Mozambique and Angola, the authorities have tightened up on casual workers and the fines for employers caught employing them are fierce.

Skilled and qualified people can apply to South African embassies for a Work Seeker's Permit (BI-159) provided they have a confirmed offer of a full-time job which the three-month permit will allow them to assess face-to-face. After a job is officially accepted, the foreigner can obtain a work permit from the nearest office of the Department of Home Affairs. Good information is available online at southafrica.info/travel/documents/workpermits.htm or consult the Consular Section of the South African High Commission in London (southafricahouse.com).

Most people who do casual work have only a three-month tourist visa, which must be renewed before it expires. A 90-day extension can be obtained from the Department of Home Affairs in Johannesburg or Cape Town for a fee. If you try to do this more than once, the authorities will become suspicious.

One solution to the problem is to consider BUNAC's Work South Africa programme, run in partnership with the South African Student Travel Services (11 Bree St, Cape Town 8000; ☎ 021 418 3794; sasts.org.za). The 12-month work permit is available to full-time university students under 30 of any nationality or those who have graduated in the past six months. The programme fee is from £500 plus flights, special work permit (currently £100) and insurance. Participants are allowed to take any job they can find. BUNAC warns that finding a job can be tough, though easier in the high season between October and March.

WorkTravelSA (WTSA, Somerset West, South Africa; ☎ 21 851 9494; worktravelsa.org or gapwork.co.za) arranges diverse work, volunteer, internship, gap year and study programmes in both humanitarian and conservation areas. Opportunities in townships and game reserves are all directly managed by WTSA. Most volunteer placements last 4–12 weeks and cost from £710 to £1,730, whereas internships in guest houses and game lodges last from 12 weeks up, for a fee starting at £680.

Willing Workers in South Africa (WWISA) is a community service volunteer organisation based in The Crags, near Plettenberg Bay. Whatever their age and skills, volunteers work on projects alongside local villagers according to their interests, options and available dates, in the areas for example of schooling and education, youth development, business development, health care and environmental research. Programmes are geared to the social and economic enhancement of the local rural community of Kurland Village. Prices should be checked on the website wwisa.co.za, though as a rough guide participants pay from £800 per month (2009).

Another volunteer placement company is AVIVA who are based in Cape Town (☎ 021 557 4312; aviva-sa.com). Their wide range of placements includes working with orphans (fee from £1,030/$1,520 for six weeks), contributing to wildlife conservation in the Kruger area (£900/$1,320 for a fortnight), rehabilitating endangered African penguins (£800/$1,170 for six weeks) and helping to introduce computer literacy and sports skills to rural schools (£1,310/$1,940 for four weeks). Several other conservation opportunities in South Africa are provided at the end of this chapter under the heading 'Conservation and Wildlife'.

Tourism

Cape Town is the tourist capital of South Africa including for backpackers, though jobs are harder to find here than elsewhere. The Backpack Hostel and Africa Travel Centre (☎ 021 423 4530; backpackers.co.za) has been recommended for its notice board but many others will be able to advise. Roger Blake expected to stay in South Africa for three months but ended up spending seven:

> ***There are more than 100 hostels in South Africa, many of which 'employ' backpackers on a casual basis. Within two weeks of arrival I was at a hostel in George on a work-for-keep basis. Through contacts made here I also sold T-shirts at the beach for a small profit and I did a few days at a pizza place for tips only. Then I was offered a job at a hostel in Oudtshoorn (Backpackers Oasis). They gave me free accommodation and 150 rand a week to run the bar and help prepare the ostrich braai (BBQ) that they have every evening. Also I did breakfasts for fellow travellers which was like being self-employed as I bought all the ingredients and kept all the profit. It was a small but worthwhile fortune after six weeks here.***

Everyone who has looked for a tourist job in Cape Town recommends Seapoint, a beach suburb lined with cafés, ice cream kiosks, snack bars and other places which have high staff turnovers, though wages are low. Ice cream is also sold from cycle carts; find out whom to contact for work by asking the sellers. Also try using the door-to-door approach in the flashy Victoria and Alfred

Waterfront development, Camps Bay and the beaches along the Garden Route. Note that openings along the Garden Route are seasonal, i.e. the peak periods fall at Christmas and Easter. The summer season starts around the 10th of December and so the best time to look for restaurant/ bar work is the last week of November.

Bear in mind that these high-profile tourist meccas have been the target of immigration raids. Smart places downtown sometimes hire temporary staff e.g. on posh Loop Street. Casual workers might prefer more discreet places. Suburban restaurants such as the Spur Steak Ranches (a leading South African franchise), Mike's Kitchen Family Restaurants (mikeskitchen.co.za) and St. Elmo's are often hiring, though the first two are liable to pay only commission. Suburbs to concentrate on are Observatory, Rondebosch, Wynberg and Plumstead.

Although Johannesburg is often maligned as a big, bad city, it is the earning capital of South Africa with better job possibilities than many other places. Unfortunately some of the inner city areas where backpackers used to congregate and find jobs (Yeoville, Brixton) have succumbed to the crime and grime for which the city is known. Now the areas to head for restaurant and pub work are the northern suburbs of Sandton, Rosebank and Dunkeld West. Try for example the Ritz in Dunkeld West (1A North Road, ritz@iafrica.com; backpackers-ritz.co.za).

Sandton is an area where within a 5km radius there are more than 60 restaurants and bars, five huge clubs, the new Montecasino complex and backpackers' lodges. Travellers can often get jobs waiting tables, working on the bar, etc. The backpackers' travel website backinafrica.com includes a Jobs Offered and Jobs Wanted forum (more of the latter than former). Resorts along the east coast between Cape Town and Port Elizabeth and even as far as the Ciskei provide employment opportunities, as does the Natal coast especially Durban and Margate. Particularly recommended on the east coast are George, Knysna, Jeffreys Bay, Plettenberg Bay and of course Port Elizabeth. As in the cities, December/January is the high season.

Tekweni Backpackers and Travel Info Centre in the Morningside area of Durban (169 Ninth St; ☎ 031 303 1199; info@tekwenibackpackers.co.za) sometimes employs foreigners for free rent and a small wage (which soon gets swallowed up at the numerous night spots on Florida Road on the hostel's doorstep).

Work may be available in the boatyards of Cape Town and other places, especially doing the dogsbody jobs of sanding and painting. Activity peaks before the early January departure of yachts on the Heineken Cape to Bahia Yacht Race.

Farm Work

The towns of Stellenbosch and Paarl to the east and north of Cape Town respectively are the centres of South Africa's wine industry. Around Stellenbosch picking begins in late January/early February and lasts four or five weeks. Further inland (e.g. around Worcester) it starts a few weeks later, and continues well into March. If you find a farmer willing to put you up and give you work, the problem of work permits is unlikely to arise. The Antipodean farm volunteer exchange website helpx.net records 14 properties in South Africa including a property with camels and bush pigs, and game reserves that need skilled riders.

BUSINESS AND INDUSTRY

If you are interested in joining a business in Africa (especially if you have a technical or managerial skill) start by surfing the internet. For example the site africaguide.com/work.htm carries links to recruitment companies and a few actual job vacancies, though there are far more 'Work Wanted' listings. You can also contact the Commercial Section of the embassy of the country which interests you for general information about job prospects. If you are on the spot, the expatriate community may be willing to offer advice or practical assistance.

Other work opportunities in Africa include translating business documents from and into French, German or English, depending on the particular country's position and trade. You could put an ad in the paper or visit firms.

VOLUNTEERING

Africa is still partially reliant on aid agencies and voluntary assistance. The majority of volunteers in Africa are trained teachers, medical staff, agricultural and technical specialists who have committed themselves to work with the support of their churches back home or through mainstream aid organisations like VSO (vso.org.uk) and Skillshare International (Leicester, skillshare.org) for at least two years. Vacancies in Africa with various charities and commercial agencies are posted on the internet, for example on responsibletravel.com on which Volunteer Travel options are searchable by country, etc.

Thirty-year-old Australian Paul Jones gave up a full-time position in the IT industry in order to go freelance and work and travel in Europe and beyond. While working in England, he came across VolunteerAfrica (volunteerafrica.org):

> ***It was almost an accident that I found an organisation called VolunteerAfrica. I wish I'd known about these kinds of groups years ago because I would have done it then. The idea evolved from a pure holiday in Africa to some volunteer work mixed in with travel. I found out that VolunteerAfrica support a local NGO in the Singida region of Tanzania. At first I was surprised that I had to pay so much to participate in a 4-week programme but learnt very quickly that it was my donation of money that was most important and my presence on the ground in Tanzania was secondary. Once I understood how it worked and that even charity organisations are businesses, even if not to make a profit, I set my sights on going and knew that while the outlay of money might seem a lot for me, it would mean a lot more to those I would be helping.***
>
> ***VolunteerAfrica interview all applicants to make sure participants are normal people. I say that because you don't have to have any particular skills, but be willing to try something new, be flexible and get along with other people. I had every vaccination possible, got a medical test and police check which all added to the costs, but again you get over it. All transport was taken care of and language lessons were organised while in Tanzania. I'm still amazed at my experience in Tanzania. I can sit for hours at my computer and stare at my photos, remembering the village I worked in, my trek up Mt Kilimanjaro and the safari. There are such stark contrasts between different parts of Tanzania that I would recommend a similar experience to anybody.***

With conservation and environmental issues such a priority, many organisations, large and small, are involved in protecting the magnificent wildlife and landscapes of Africa. A good starting point for locating interesting organisations is the website africanconservation.org which has a searchable database of organisations and vacancies in the field.

It may be possible to offer your services on a voluntary basis to any hospital, school or mission you come across in your travels, though acceptance is not guaranteed. Travellers who have found themselves in the vicinity of a famine crisis have often expressed shock when their offer of help has been turned down. Passers-by cannot easily be incorporated into ongoing aid projects.

If you have a useful skill and the addresses of some suitable projects, you are well on the way to fixing something up. Mary Hall had both, so wrote to a mission clinic in Uganda offering her services as a nurse:

> ***There wasn't a doctor so the work was very stressful for me. After a couple of weeks I was helping to run the clinic, see and examine patients, prescribe drugs and set up a teaching programme for the unqualified Ugandan nurses.***
>
> ***We had no running water, intermittent electricity and a lack of such niceties as cheese and chocolate. Obviously adaptability has to be one of the main qualities. Initially I worked on my visitor's visa which wasn't a problem, but when it became apparent that I would be staying for longer, the clinic applied for a work permit for me. Quite an expensive venture (£100) and I think very difficult without a local sponsor. The local bishop wrote a beautiful letter on my behalf, so I got one. A white person is considered to be the be-all and end-all of everyone's problems, and I found it difficult to live with this image. I'd like to say that the novelty of having a white foreigner around wore off but it never did. Stare, stare and stare again, never a moment to yourself. Still it was a fantastic experience. I've learnt an awful lot, and don't think I could ever do nursing in Britain again. My whole idea of Africa and aid in particular has been turned on its head. Idealism at an end.***

This professed disillusionment with aid work has not prevented Mary from pursuing a career in development in Africa and the Middle East.

A myriad of specialist programmes exists to encourage volunteer exchanges. For example volunteer sports coaches, phys ed teachers, recreation leaders and sports organisers are placed by an organisation called SCORE International with offices in Cape Town and Amsterdam (☎ 021 461 0466; info.nl@score.org.za; score.org.za). The work includes coaching, establishing sports clubs and organising tournaments and festivals in rural or urban settings. Suitable candidates over 20 must be interested in hands-on development work and willing to live with a host family. The work period is six months or a year starting in January or July. Participants pay a fee of €2,500 for six months (which includes living expenses and travel within Africa) and €3,500 for 12 months; coaches also receive a nominal monthly stipend.

Paul Edmunds signed up with Sussex-based Travellers Worldwide (☎ 01903 502595; travellersworldwide.com) to join a cricket-coaching project on the outskirts of Accra in Ghana. He enjoyed the experience enormously and felt that it was extremely beneficial to the children to experience the structured framework of a sport. As well as bringing them pleasure, it also taught them discipline.

Sending Organisations

Azafady: London W10; ☎ 020 8960 6629; mark@azafady.org; madagascar.co.uk; 10-week Pioneer Madagascar programme allows volunteers to work on a grassroots level trying to combat deforestation and extreme poverty in Madagascar; fundraising target is £2,000 excluding flights; they also offer short-term volunteering and lemur conservation projects.

Blue Ventures: London N6; ☎ 020 3176 0548; enquiries@blueventures.org; blueventures.org; volunteers are needed for at least six weeks to carry out marine research, coral reef conservation and day-to-day management of field camps in South Western Madagascar; fee for 6 weeks is £2,100 for non-divers, slightly less for PADI divers.

BUNAC: London EC1; ☎ 020 7251 3472; africa@bunac.org.uk; 2–3 month Volunteer Ghana programme (£749–£849); and Volunteer South Africa programme, lasting 5–33 weeks (£969–£2,299).

Cross-Cultural Solutions: Brighton; ☎ 0845 458 2781; crossculturalsolutions.org; volunteer vacations in Ghana and Tanzania, Morocco and South Africa, to teach English, provide skills training or enhance recreation programmes; programme fees cover expenses but not airfares: from £1,449 for 2 weeks (minimum) to about £3,249 for 12 weeks off-season.

EIL: Malvern; ☎ 0800 018 4015; eiluk.org; founded in 1937, EIL offers teaching and intern programmes in Nigeria, Morocco and South Africa; details on volunteering18–30.org.uk and overseasvolunteering.org.uk.

Frontier: London EC2; ☎ 020 7613 2422; frontier.ac.uk; tropical research training, field experience and conservation volunteering in Madagascar's forests and sea, Tanzania's savannah or reefs, Mozambique and Uganda. Volunteers carry out biological surveys and socio-economic research for 3–20 weeks; participation fees are £1,395–£2,800 for ten weeks, £3,000–£3,595 for 20 weeks.

Global Vision International (GVI): St. Albans, Herts; ☎ 01727 250250; gvi.co.uk; projects in about a dozen African countries.

Greenforce: London SW6; ☎ 020 7384 3343; greenforce.org; recruits volunteer researchers to join biodiversity conservation aid projects in Tanzania for 3–10 weeks; fieldwork assistants study endangered species and habitats; no previous experience needed as training is provided; £2,600 for 10 weeks plus flight; also penguin projects and shark monitoring in South Africa from £1,200 for six weeks.

Madventurer: Newcastle-upon-Tyne; ☎ 0845 121 1996; madventurer.com; charity that arranges summer and 3-month expeditions to Ghana, Tanzania, Kenya, South Africa and Uganda that combine development work and adventurous overland travel; the fee for a 6-week project at the time of writing was £999 plus possible add-ons.

Reefdoctor.org Ltd: London SW15; ☎ 07866 250740; ReefDoctor.org; hands-on conservation programme in Madagascar, working with the local fishing communities of the Bay of Ranobe, part of the third largest coral reef system in the world; open to gap year, university students and enthusiastic volunteers who work in small groups of 4–8 people on expeditions lasting 4, 6, 8 or 12 weeks; sample fee of £950 for 4 weeks, £1,400 for 6-week programme (2009) including free PADI dive training and certification.

It is always sensible to do as much research as possible about a project and an organisation to which you intend to commit considerable time and money. We are grateful to Amelia Cook who alerted us to serious problems encountered with a Scandinavian-based organisation Humana-Tvind which aggressively recruits volunteers for Angola, Mozambique, Zimbabwe, etc. under different names. The internet site at tvindalert.com warns people that the extensive training promised by the organisation never materialises and that, amongst other dubious practices, volunteers may be placed in dangerous situations in Africa and elsewhere and subjected to psychological pressure. Invariably the organisation requires volunteers to pay large upfront fees for training and placement and then expects them to meet huge fundraising targets after that. The Danish directors have been involved in legal battles for years charged with corruption and tax evasion. This organisation operates under many names worldwide including DAPP (Development Aid from People to People), One World Volunteer Institute, Humana and in the US the Institute for International Co-operation and Development (IICD).

Short-term Projects

Thousands of small charities and NGOs accept volunteers to participate in rural and community development for varying periods. Invariably you have to finance your own travel and pay a registration fee to cover food and lodging, typically for three to six weeks. The work may consist of building, installing water supplies, conservation or assisting in homes for disabled or underprivileged children and adults.

In some cases, a national organisation fields applications from international volunteers who want to join a voluntary workcamp. For example VOLU is the acronym for the Voluntary Workcamps Association of Ghana (☎ +233 21 663486; voluntaryworkcamps.org); their summer and winter workcamps last three to four weeks conducting AIDS awareness campaigns, building schools and community centres, planting trees in deforested areas, etc. The registration fee is €200 for one camp, €300 for two or more. For links to other national workcamp agencies in Africa check the website of Service Civil International (sciint.org), though participation in these projects is normally arranged through the workcamp sending agency in your home country like IVS or Concordia in the UK.The listing from Volunteers for Peace (see VFP in Volunteering chapter) for example contains information on workcamps in 21 African nations from Tunisia to Togo. In recent years many African organisations have acquired internet access which makes communication infinitely cheaper and easier.

If you decide to join a project once you are in an African capital like Maputo, Accra, Addis Ababa or Kampala, it should not be hard to track down the co-ordinating office. Foreign embassies might also be in a position to offer useful advice. They may have a Community Liaison Office which holds information about local charities and aid projects needing volunteers. It might also be worth asking at the British Council office (especially if teaching interests you), the YMCA or in prominent churches.

ROGER BLAKE DID EXACTLY THAT WHEN HE TRAVELLED TO ETHIOPIA AND UGANDA:

I had contemplated a 'voluntary' placement fixed up through an agency at home but I find the modern concept of paying to volunteer your services a crazy idea. So I decided that I would go it alone. I was in Ethiopia for almost two months and had a great time. On my return to Addis Ababa, I decided to ask around for any English teaching possibilities and was recommended to a charity who invited me to spend a short time supporting their qualified local teacher in the classroom with physically disabled children. I did not get paid but they did make it worth my while by giving me three excellent meals a day and I got to stay in a wonderful house in an idyllic countryside location with magnificent gardens. My 'employment' was unofficial, thus the short stay. I have ascertained that there are casual opportunities to teach here in Addis but you must search hard to find them.

Continuing his trans-African journey, Roger next enquired about working possibilities in Kampala where he had already encountered the huge expatriate community and their attendant recreations – cinema, pubs, gyms, supermarkets:

> *On the notice board of the Red Chilli Hideaway, a backpackers' hostel and campsite, Kabira School had an advert for a youth worker at their youth centre. Nothing ventured, nothing gained, so I applied and got the job (for a trial period). I worked evenings and weekends with expat teenagers, in the same environment as a youth club at home. They would have been willing to arrange a work permit for me and pay me a very reasonable salary equivalent to $250 a month – enough to live on as I was staying in my tent at the hostel. I was tempted but I decided to move on with the African trip, mainly because I didn't want to lose my non-refundable onward air ticket to Australia.*

Grassroots Organisations

Till Bruckner is another veteran world traveller who shares Roger Blake's fondness for fixing up teaching and voluntary placements independently rather than with the help of an intermediary:

> ***My advice to anyone who wants to volunteer in Africa (or anywhere else) is to go first and volunteer second. That way you can travel until you've found a place you genuinely like and where you think you might be able to make a difference. You can also check out the work and accommodation for yourself before you settle down. If you're willing to work for free, you don't need a nanny to tell you where to go. Just go.***

However for those who find this prospect daunting (and unless you are a mature and seasoned traveller you probably will), you might like to pursue the middle way which is to make contact with small local organisations in Africa which actively look for volunteers abroad, though make sure you do some research to avoid signing up with an organisation like the one described by American travel writer Lies Ouwerkerk who wrote to the editor of the online magazine *Transitions Abroad* at the end of 2008:

> ***I would like to share a worry about a local Senegalese enterprise. It's just a one-man 'organization' with a cell phone as office. The 'director' is simply a money-driven crook and liar who promises gold, but does not deliver and rips people off. He is definitely bad news for supporters of small (and sincere) local volunteer organizations and their prospective users. Apparently there were already warnings against him on Responsible Travel, but his website, links, and names of organizations looked so convincing, that I went in it without any suspicion. Responsible Travel removed him from their site already years ago, but he is still carrying their logo on his website. I would hate to see other, innocent people, especially young kids, getting stuck with this con-artist!***

The following organisations have received no such bad reports as far as this book is aware:

STAESA (Students Travel And Exposure South Africa): ☎ +27 73 651 8203; info@staesa.org, staesa.org; provides volunteers with work placements in a range of community projects and small-scale industries throughout sub-Saharan Africa; costs are from \$395 for two weeks in Ghana including host family accommodation to \$5,000+ for one year in any of the 15 countries in which STAESA has partners.

The following is a sample of the range of active organisations, listed in alphabetical order by country:

ICEYOM (International Centre for Education Youth Orientation and Mobilization): c/o Society for Women Empowerment Education & Training (SWEET) Africa, South West Province, Cameroon; ☎ +237 958 0292; iceyom@yahoo.co.uk or rosembone@yahoo.com; placements for all types of voluntary service including hospitality, conservation, teaching, water and sanitation, community and fundraising throughout Africa, especially Liberia, Ghana, Cameroon and Nigeria; placement fee €400.

Robbooker Voluntary Organization: Kumasi, Ghana; ☎ 233 51 47596; robbookervoluntary_organization@yahoo.com; robborg.org); service/volunteer projects in Ghana lasting 2–12 weeks or longer; prices from \$350 for 1 month to \$950 for 6 months include homestay accommodation with meals.

Volunteer in Africa: Accra, Ghana; ☎ +233 244 761050; ghanaprograms@yahoo.com; volunteeringinafrica.org; placements in Ghana for volunteers and unpaid interns in teaching, orphanages, HIV education, conservation, etc. Varying periods; private accommodation and meals are provided; the contribution to expenses is \$477 for 2 weeks, \$677 for 4 weeks and \$77 a week thereafter.

WWOOF/FIOH Ghana: ☎ +233 21 716091; kingzeeh@yahoo.co.uk; places volunteers on traditional farms, as assistants in schools, in bicycle workshops, and with workcamps in Ghana; membership fee $25, plus three international reply coupons.

Kenya Voluntary & Community Development Project: PO Box 554, Bondo, Kenya (with office in Nairobi International Youth Hostel); kvcdp.org; accepts everyone over 18 to work with children, teaching in sustainable agriculture, conservation, etc. in Wagusu/Abimbo village in Bondo District, Nyanza province, Western Kenya; placement fees from $350 for 2 weeks to $950 for 2 months.

Project Volunteer Ghana: Accra; projectvolunteerghana.com; places paying volunteers in psychiatric hospitals, orphanages, and environmental and educational projects; structured placements lasting up to three months cost from £1050 for the minimum stay of 4 weeks.

RIPPLE Africa: 18 Eden Way, Pages Industrial Park, Leighton Buzzard, Beds LU7 4TZ; rippleafrica.org; a charity working in Malawi, started in 2003 by a British couple, based at Mwaya Beach on the northern shores of Lake Malawi; the charity recruits volunteers to assist in the local nursery, schools, health centre, etc. Variable start dates and lengths of stay; sample price is £1,350 for 12 weeks which includes accommodation but not local transport or food.

Health Action Promotion Association (HAPA): Derbyshire; volunteerafrica.org; NGO in Tanzania that works with village projects in the Singida Region of Tanzania; volunteers may join the project for four, seven or ten or more weeks for fees (respectively) of £1,050, £1,380 and £1,710, a large proportion of which is given as a donation to the host programme.

Soft Power Education: Jinja, Uganda; ☎ +256 774 162541; softpowereducation.com; British-registered charity and Ugandan NGO refurbishing government primary schools in Uganda, among other projects; self-funding volunteers stay for 1 day to 12 months (paying £75 per week).

WWOOF Uganda: PO Box 2001, Kampala, Uganda; ☎ +256 346856; bob_kasule@yahoo.com; subscription for printed list of 20 member farms is £20 by bank draft.

Throughout Africa there are a great many volunteer workers with the mainstream aid agencies like VSO and the Peace Corps in hospitals, schools and agricultural projects who are sometimes willing to assist travellers. Probably the more remote and cut-off the volunteers are, the more welcoming they will be, but be careful not to abuse or presume on their hospitality. Always offer to pay your way, or go armed with treats.

Conservation and Wildlife

A number of wildlife reserves in southern Africa have introduced programmes for paying volunteers, especially gap year students, to get close to the animals by monitoring them and protecting their environment. The costs, which are usually substantial, are used to support the conservation of the reserve, many of which are privately owned. Programmes like the Modgaji Conservation and Rehabilitation Project in the Eastern Cape of South Africa (modgaji.co.za) offer working holidays at almost tourist prices, e.g. R3,300 per week.

Some overseas agencies involved with conservation in Africa have already been mentioned. African Conservation Experience with an office in Gloucestershire (☎ 0845 5200 888; conservationAfrica.net) arranges conservation work placements lasting 4–12 weeks on game reserves in Southern Africa including South Africa, Botswana and Zimbabwe. Tasks may include darting rhino for relocation or elephant for fitting tracking collars, game capture, tagging, assisting with veterinary work, game counts, etc. Alien plant control and the re-introduction of indigenous plants is often involved. The average cost for 12 weeks is £5,270 including flights from London, transfers, accommodation and all meals.

One of the projects to which volunteer-sourcing agencies like Aviva (mentioned earlier in this chapter) and Enkosini Eco Experience (enkosiniecoexperience.com) send foreign volunteers is the seabird conservation organisation, the South African National Foundation for the Conservation of Coastal Birds. SANCCOB requires volunteers to help with the cleaning and rehabilitation of oil-soaked birds (mainly penguins) since oil pollution is a major problem in the coastal waters of South Africa. Volunteers must pay a joining fee of R800 and fund their own living expenses for at least six weeks. Details are available from SANCCOB based in Cape Town (☎ 021 557 6155; sanccob.co.za).

Wild at Heart in Kwazulu Natal (wah.co.za) offers up to 2,500 conservation opportunities annually, with cheetahs, elephants, equine care, monkeys and other animals; and hands-on opportunities to work with species such as cheetah at wildlife rehabilitation centres in South Africa and Namibia.

A well publicised survey asked people to rank the 50 things they wanted to do before they died. Well over half of these dream trips involved contact with wildlife, particularly African big game. Chris Giles and his wife Christine worked at Kwando Safari Camp in Botswana, arranged through The Leap Overseas Ltd in Berkshire (☎ 01672 519922; theleap.co.uk), where they did mainly menial work in the kitchen and the grounds but had plenty of thrilling brushes with the wildlife:

> ***Our jobs were not strenuous or difficult but extremely important because it made us feel part of the team running the safari camp. Christine has been in the kitchen and I have been a waiter, scullery (washing up) and helped mend a walkway when an elephant wandered through during the middle of the night! As I have absolutely no practical skills, this was quite an achievement, although I'm not sure the maintenance manager, who showed great patience, was impressed with how long it took me.***
>
> ***The scenery and wildlife in this remote part of northern Botswana are stunning so things that are normally mundane and routine suddenly become exciting. I was quite happy clearing plates, washing glasses, making fruit salad, serving drinks and chatting to guests from all around the world.***

Many high-profile conservation charities like the Born Free Foundation, which works with endangered colobus monkeys in Kenya among other projects, refer potential volunteers to voluntourism agencies like Worldwide Experience in Surrey (☎ 01483 860560; worldwideexperience.com) or the British Trust for Conservation Volunteers (btcv.org.uk).

Other conservation volunteer opportunities are offered by the following:

African Impact: Gweru, Zimbabwe; tel/fax +263 4 252710; UK: ☎ 0800 520 0926; info@africanimpact.com; africanimpact.com; conservation projects in a dozen countries including Botswana, Kenya, Mozambique, Zambia, Zimbabwe and South Africa; sample price for volunteer programme at lion breeding centre in Zimbabwe is £2,245 for 6 weeks; or 4 weeks on a whale shark and turtle research programme in Mozambique for £1,695 including 5-day PADI diving course.

In Defense of Animals (IDA) Africa: Oregon; ☎ 503 643 8302; ida-africa.org; sends volunteers who are able to communicate in French to a chimpanzee sanctuary in Yaounde, Cameroon, for a minimum of six months.

Limbe Wildlife Centre: Limbe, Cameroon; ☎ +237 998 2503; limbewildlife.org or the information blog site http://limbewildlifecentre.wildlifedirect.org; runs a programme working with endangered Cameroonian wildlife including chimpanzees, gorillas, monkeys and various bird and reptile species; volunteers stay 1–3 months and pay €650 a month.

Shumba Experience: Brighton; ☎ 0845 257 3205; shumbaexperience.co.uk; conservation and community projects in South Africa, Kenya and Namibia; 2, 4, 8 or 12 weeks; sample prices £1,400 for 4 weeks, £2,100 for 8 weeks.

ISRAEL AND THE PALESTINIAN TERRITORIES

Israel is not a happy country. In the wake of the Israeli offensive in Gaza in early 2009 that led to so much civilian bloodshed, the conflict between the Israelis and Palestinians often seems beyond resolution. As the situation has worsened, Israel has lost much of its appeal for travellers, and the number of young people choosing to head for what was a generation ago a favourite travellers' destination is drastically down. At present few if any opportunities exist in the Palestinian-governed Territories and many projects such as archaeological digs have been curtailed or cancelled. But behind all the shocking violence and retaliation in the headlines, thousands of individuals and groups are working towards a peaceful two-state solution. Spending time in this troubled region will enable people from outside to gain more insight into one of the world's most bedevilled trouble spots. Personal security is bound to be a consideration in a country where indiscriminate terrorist attacks are at times a real threat.

The prospects for finding paid work are much gloomier than they once were, partly because of very high unemployment (up to 11%), a large resident population of cheap labour from Thailand, etc. and because of a radical clampdown on foreigners working without official work permits. Employers caught employing illegal workers are heavily fined, so the managers of restaurants, hostels and other tourist establishments that at one time would have hired backpackers without a thought are now extremely reluctant to do so.

Fortunately it is still possible to enter Israel as a volunteer. Most people associate working in Israel with staying on a kibbutz, an opportunity of which many thousands of international travellers have taken advantage over the years but which is now in severe decline.

REGULATIONS

For anyone without an Israeli passport who wishes to volunteer on a kibbutz or archaeological dig, it is obligatory for your sponsor to obtain a B4 Volunteer Visa from the Ministry of the Interior within 15 days of your joining a volunteer scheme. The visa will be valid for up to six months and cost NIS75 ($18/£13).

It is virtually impossible to obtain a work permit for the kind of casual work travellers tend to do in Israel and, as mentioned, it is increasingly risky working on a tourist visa.

KIBBUTZIM

From the 1960s to the 1990s, every self-respecting backpacker would at least have heard of the possibility of spending a few months on an Israeli kibbutz, exchanging his or her work for free living. But nowadays, the concept is not widely known among the travelling community, though the possibility still exists and thousands of volunteers continue to spend between two and six expense-free months on one of the 250+ kibbutzim in Israel.

Originally a kibbutz was a communal society, usually based on agriculture, in which the means of production were owned and shared by the community as a whole. But this utopian concept has rather faded from view, and many kibbutzim have been partly or wholly privatised. A further change is that kibbutzim have increasingly become based on tourism and light industry rather than agriculture. But after a period of crisis, there seem to be signs (in 2008/9) of a slight upturn in the fortunes of the movement. The majority of kibbutzim still accept volunteers and some recruit online e.g. Kibbutz Ketura (ketura.org.il).

The unofficial site kibbutzvolunteer.com has links to about 25 kibbutzim with their own websites and continues to be maintained by John Carson, a kibbutz enthusiast who as of 2009 still receives lots of emails from potential volunteers seeking advice. He feels that '*whatever form the kibbutz takes, there will still be volunteers*' (kibbutzvolunteer@gmail.com).

Arranging a Job

The demand for volunteers fluctuates according to many factors including national politics, the time of year, competition from new Jewish settlers and so on though, in the present circumstances, demand for volunteers is likely to outstrip supply.

All foreign volunteers should make arrangements through the official Kibbutz Program Center which represents kibbutzim throughout the country and is authorised to apply for a volunteer visa on your behalf (Volunteer Department, KPC, 6 Frishman St, Corner of Hayarkon St, Tel Aviv 61030; ☎ +972 3 524 6154/6; fax 3 523 9966; kpc@volunteer.co.il; kibbutz.org.il/eng/welcome.htm). The office is open Sunday to Thursday 8am–2pm. The buses needed to reach the office are: number 475 from the airport, 10 from the railway station and 4 from the Central Bus Station.

In order to be eligible for a visa through the Kibbutz Program Center, you must take your passport, medical certificate and registration fee of $90. This one-off fee covers you for a year, including if you move to another kibbutz. They will also want to see proof of funds ($250). The KPC sells specialised health insurance for about $90, which provides cover for up to 12 months. A returnable deposit of $50–$100 is payable to guarantee that you stay for the minimum period of eight weeks.

If you are clued up, it is possible to request a certain kind of kibbutz – big or small, politically left or centre, well established or new – and in a certain location, though usually the KPC assigns you to the first available vacancy. The vast majority of kibbutzim are located in the fertile lands of northern and southern Israel. It is best to be prepared for the climate; for example the north can be cold and rainy in winter, whereas the Jordan Rift Valley can be one of the hottest and driest places in the world.

For contact details of representative offices in other countries, see kibbutz.org.il/eng/welcome.htm. American applicants should contact the Kibbutz Program Center, 114 West 26th St, Suite

1004, New York, NY 10001 (☎ 212 462 2764; kibbutzprogramcenter.org) which acts as a clearinghouse for American volunteers. The registration fee is $360.

South Africans can book kibbutz volunteer placements through one of 23 Overseas Visitors Club offices throughout South Africa (ovc.co.za).

Life on a Kibbutz

In return for their labour, volunteers receive free room and board and a small amount of pocket money, perhaps $65–$100 a month. Most volunteers enjoy their stay, and find that some kibbutzim make considerable efforts to welcome volunteers. For example the majority of kibbutzim try to provide occasional organised sightseeing tours for volunteers, sometimes every month. Yet kibbutzim expect volunteers to work hard for their keep. The average working week is 42–48 hours though hours may be reduced in the hot summer or extended at busy times. You are entitled to a day off for every six hours of overtime you put in. Many kibbutzim give an extra two or three days off per month to allow their volunteers to travel (since travel is difficult on the sabbath when there is no public transport).

Jimmy Hill describes the variety of jobs he did in just two months at a small kibbutz south of Jericho: '*dining hall duties, chopping date trees, a lot of gardening, working in a vineyard, electrician, turkey chaser and guest house cleaner*'. New volunteers are often assigned the undesirable jobs though most volunteer organisers are willing to transfer a dissatisfied volunteer to a different job. Catherine Revell claims that if you are assertive and show willingness to work hard, you can find yourself doing more interesting work; among the jobs she did on three different kibbutzim were kitchen manager, shepherdess and a sculptor's assistant. Increasingly, work is in factories or of an industrial nature, though it is impossible to generalise and interesting options crop up. For example Allan Kirkpatrick from Glasgow spent an enjoyable six weeks at a kibbutz in northern Israel cleaning a theatre where a classical music festival was taking place. (What made his stay more interesting but less relaxing was that a town three kilometres away was being bombed by the Lebanese Army at the time, and he spent three days in the bomb shelter.) Agricultural jobs are still available at some kibbutzim. One unexpected hazard in the fields is the wildlife. The only job John Mallon was reluctant to do was to carry bunches of bananas since they housed rats and spiders. And although in most respects Deborah Hunter's kibbutz was no Garden of Eden, she recalls several shrieks and hasty descents of the ladder when volunteers encountered snakes in the fruit trees.

Facilities can differ radically from one kibbutz to the next as Kevin Boyd discovered when he moved from a kibbutz 2km from the Gaza Strip fence to another recommended by a woman he had met: '*My first kibbutz was very poor. Our rooms consisted of two pre-fab concrete huts with very thin plastic walls which meant that there was very little privacy in the rooms.*' Although his second kibbutz had a swimming pool, barbecues, volunteers' pub, etc., these were all closed for the winter, and Kevin was made to feel that by arriving in the autumn, he had come just as the party was over. He was told that the best time to join a kibbutz is March, so that you can be well established by the time numbers swell in May/June.

Julee Wyld from Canada is in a long line of volunteers who have ended up raving about kibbutz life:

> ***I had an incredible experience on the kibbutz, one of the best things I ever did. I adapted well, loved my job (working in the zoo), got along very well with my volunteer leader, made friends from all over the world (many from Europe whom I will visit next month) and even made many kibbutznik friends. I also learned quite a lot of Hebrew, which is exciting to me. The volunteers on my kibbutz***

(approximately 30) were like family to me. We spent a lot of time together, looked out for each other, took care of each other and these people will be friends for life.

TOURISM

The current situation in Israel and the Middle East generally has crippled the tourist industry, so work is not very plentiful. In general the best places for finding work in tourism are Eilat, Tel Aviv, Herzliya (a wealthy resort north of Tel Aviv) and, to a lesser extent, Haifa and Jerusalem. Many cheap hostels around Israel employ two or three travellers to spend a few hours a day cleaning or manning the desk in exchange for a free bed and some meals. If you prove yourself a hard worker, you may be moved to a better job or even paid some pocket money. Heather McCulloch worked for a hostel in Tiberias, the main resort on the Sea of Galilee (where at that time it was easy to find restaurant, beach or hotel work).

Casual jobs in cafés, restaurants, bars and hotels can be unearthed with difficulty. As in Greece, these jobs are much easier to get if you're female. The pay is usually low and sometimes non-existent, but you will get free food and drink, and tips. As throughout Israel, the price of a day's work has to be negotiated. Most working travellers recommend collecting your wages (and paying your own hostel bills) on a daily basis to prevent aggravation later. Also be aware that many travellers have had their money stolen from hostels including one group who lost money entrusted to the hostel 'safe'.

The tourist season in Eilat lasts from late October to March, so it might be possible to fill a temporary vacancy in a hotel or cruise business. Because Eilat is an important yachting and diving centre, you can check for job notices posted on the gates to the Marina or on the Marina noticeboard, or talked about in the Yacht Pub. Work as crew or kitchen staff, cleaners or au pairs is usually found by asking boat to boat. Sarah Jane Smith landed a job as a deckhand and hostess on a private charter yacht for scuba divers:

I was taken on cruises lasting between a week and a month to the Red Sea, Gulf of Suez, etc. to some of the best diving spots in the world. I was taught how to scuba dive and also did lots of snorkelling. I saw some of the most amazing sights of my life – the sun rising over Saudi Arabia as the moon sank into Egypt, coral reefs, sharks, dolphins, and so on. The social life on the marina was better than the kibbutz with hundreds of other travellers working on boats or in Eilat. Every night was a party and I hardly know how I survived it. The only bad thing is the low wages (if you get paid at all) and the hard work. But the harder you work and longer you stay, the better the wages and perks become.

Over the years, thousands of travellers have spent some time working in the modern city of Tel Aviv doing everything from bouncing in clubs to au pairing. Work has been offered in bars, restaurants and beach cafés, especially to women. If you are considering doing a tips-only job, try to have a private conversation with the staff before accepting.

The hostels along Hayarkon Street were once valuable sources of job information or jobs themselves though it must be reiterated that the employment situation is much tighter now and in fact many of the hostels that used to maintain Work Lists have closed. At last report this system was still being used at Momo's Hostel at 28 Ben Yehuda St (☎ 03 629 7421; momoshostel.com) to which veteran traveller Jane Harris and her boyfriend Pete moved: *'Momo's had loads of work coming in, using a work list system. Pete got work loading and unloading containers, dishwashing and cleaning. I worked for Momo in the hostel. I'd recommend this hostel for work.'*

The Kibbutz Program Center recommends several hostels on its website including The Hayarkon 48 Hostel at 48 Hayarkon St (☎ 03 516 8989; info@hayarkon48.com) and Sky Hostel at 34 Hayarkon St (☎ 03 620 0044; skyhostel@walla.com).

Buskers and sellers of handicrafts such as home-made jewellery report good profits in Jerusalem. For example Leda Meredith sold woven string bracelets on Ben Yehuda Street.

OTHER PAID WORK

Professional and other vacancies are listed at janglo.net/index.php/taanglo which calls itself the largest online community for English speakers in Israel. Although the demand for live-in childcare is strong, the visa issue makes it next to impossible to work for longer than three months. Whereas there used to be several agencies actively placing foreign au pairs and nannies, now there are none.

Farms can be tracked down (with difficulty) inland from Eilat though again those without permits will find it difficult to join the transient labour force picking and packing melons, tomatoes and other produce. The Golan Heights is a prolific fruit-growing area of apples, pears, plums, cherries and berries. A visit to the Golan Fruit Sorting Center in Merom HaGolan (off Route 959) might provide leads, although here the sorting is mainly done by robots.

Teaching

Because of the large number of English-speaking Jews who have settled in Israel from the US, South Africa, etc. many native speakers of English are employed in the state education system and there is little active recruitment of foreign teachers. Wall Street International has several franchises in Israel including Tel Aviv, Ra'anona, Beer Sheba and Haifa. They pay NIS25 (£4.25) an hour. The British Council maintains a presence in Israel and has Teaching Centres in Tel Aviv and Jerusalem which recruit qualified EFL teachers mainly from the local English-speaking population.

Shortly after reacquainting himself with a girl he knew in Tel Aviv, Tom Balfour started discovering possibilities:

> ***I sent emails with my CV to various English schools, mostly branches of the two big companies Berlitz and Wall Street Institute, explaining my situation – that I would be leaving Israel in a week to return to England for my summer job, but that I wanted to come back in September and teach English in Tel Aviv. Most of the schools simply sent me a reply saying 'get back to us when you return' but Wall Street Institute Tel Aviv invited me for an interview. In the interview I was asked various questions about teaching, and then the director pretended to be a low level student and asked me to explain various words to her. When she asked me what a model was, I said 'Naomi Campbell, Kate Moss' and then got up and did a pretend cat-walk round the room. Although I'm sure that my qualifications helped, I think that might be what got me the job: knowing how to keep explanations simple, and being prepared to look silly if it helped. She told me that if I came back I would be offered a contract. I think that my Trinity TEFL qualification and my planned work at the summer school made me stand out from the native candidates, some of whom were hoping for a job simply on the strength of being English speakers.***

Tom Balfour has no regrets about choosing Israel: '*Israel is an amazing country and Tel Aviv is a great, cosmopolitan city with a good beach and fantastic nightlife.*'

One difficulty that native speakers may run into is getting a visa. Even if you are an English speaker and experienced teacher, there is no guarantee that you will get one, unless you improve your chances by being in a relationship with an Israeli (or Jewish).

VOLUNTARY OPPORTUNITIES

The Tel Aviv based volunteer agency Go Eco (goeco.org.il) registers humanitarian and conservation volunteer openings in Israel as well as worldwide, for the benefit of international travellers. Examples include a sea turtle rescue centre in Michmoret and an eco-tourism project in Nazareth. The Friends of Israel Educational Trust in London (☎ 020 8444 0777; foi-asg.org) have long run a gap year programme called the Bridge Programme for 12 British school leavers who are sent to Israeli cities to help on gardening, English teaching and other projects for six months from January. After being chosen at interview (in July), participants' expenses are covered apart from spending money.

The Christian Information Centre at Jaffa Gate in Jerusalem keeps a frequently updated list of schools and charitable institutes that may take on volunteers. From cicts.org follow links to 'Christian Charitable Organizations'.

The Jewish/Arab village of Neve Shalom/Wahat al-Salaam between Tel Aviv and Jerusalem accepts five or six volunteers to work in the guesthouse, kitchen, school or gardens attached to the community's School for Peace for six or twelve months. In addition to board and lodging, volunteers receive $50 a month pocket money. Details are available on the website or from the Volunteer Co-ordinator, 99761 Doar Na Shimshon (☎ 02 991 5621 ext. 101; nswas.org/rubrique7.html).

Palestinian Projects

The political situation has made it impossible for projects to continue in Gaza and even in the other Palestinian territories. The educational charity Unipal (Universities' Trust for Educational Exchange with Palestinians; unipal.org.uk) runs a summer programme of teaching English to teenagers in refugee camps. Volunteers spend five weeks in refugee camps in Lebanon or in any territory deemed safe for foreigners to enter. Volunteers pay £500 to cover flights, food, accommodation and insurance. The deadline for applications is the end of February, interviews are in March and training is provided.

Friends of Birzeit University, a UK-based charity that supports Palestinian education, has assisted this University near Ramallah in the Occupied West Bank to recruit international volunteers for summer work camps since the 1970s. Volunteers work alongside Palestinian students, on two-week summer workcamps. Participants pay living expenses, flight and a £35 admin fee. Further details and an application form are available from Friends of Birzeit University in London (☎ 020 7832 1340; fobzu@fobzu.org; fobzu.org).

The British Council have withdrawn from the Palestinian Territories and their educational activities in Nablus, Ramallah, Gaza and East Jerusalem have been halted.

Jewish Projects

To search for opportunities open to visitors, go to Volunteering in Israel at ivolunteer.org.il/eng for a list of charities and organisations that accept volunteers.

A two-year Teach and Study Program (TASP) in Tel Aviv enables students to combine 15 hours a week of interning in schools with study for an MA in Teaching English as a Foreign Language, as well as Hebrew language classes. Details are available in Israel from TASP in Kadima (☎ 9 899 5644; tasp.org.il) and in the USA from the Jewish Federation of Greater Los Angeles (TScharlin@JewishLA.org). The fees are from $11,000 per year.

Archaeology

Volunteers are needed to do the mundane work of digging and sifting. In the majority of cases, volunteers must pay a daily fee of $35–$40 to cover food and accommodation (often on a nearby kibbutz) plus a registration fee (typically $50–$75). Most camps take place during university holidays between May and September when temperatures soar. Volunteers must be in good physical condition and able to work long hours in hot weather. Valid health insurance is required.

Information on volunteering at archaeological digs in Israel is most easily accessed via the Israeli Ministry of Foreign Affairs every January (mfa.gov.il, search 'Excavations'). After choosing an excavation of interest, you make contact directly with the person in charge of the research, some of them in the Department of Classical Studies at Tel Aviv University and others at universities elsewhere in Israel or abroad. Prices are posted on the website and are mostly about $50 a day for two or more weeks. A longstanding project is at the ancient port site of Yavneh Yam (tau.ac.il/~yavneyam); the participation fee is $450 per week.

Long-term excavations are taking place in Tiberias, in a region rich in antiquities, most recently to expose the Roman basilica and other buildings in use between the 2nd and 10th centuries CE. If interested in joining the excavations in March or November, contact the Volunteer Co-ordinator via the website tiberiasexcavation.com/volunteering.html. The all-in cost for five days is a steep $370 if you share a room, though it may be possible to camp for much less.

JENNIFER MCKIBBEN, WHO WORKED ON A KIBBUTZ, IN AN EILAT HOTEL AND ON A DIG IN THE NEGEV DESERT, WAXED MOST ENTHUSIASTIC ABOUT THE LATTER EXPERIENCE:

Actually the work was often enjoyable but not usually before the sun had risen (it gets incredibly cold at nights in the desert). It did seem madness at times when a Land Rover would take a team of us out to an unremarkable spot in the desert marked only by a wooden peg, and we would be told to start digging. I think the romance of excavations quickly fades once the blisters begin to appear and that long term camps are suitable only for the initiated or fanatic.

However despite the difficulties I really enjoyed the camp. Group relations were good – there were people of all nationalities – and there was normally a camp fire going with a couple of musicians. It was wonderful just to spend time in such a beautiful desert, to go off wandering over footprintless dunes, over great red hills to look and see no sign of civilisation.

ASIA

For a continent as vast as Asia, this chapter may seem disproportionately short. That is simply because there are not many kinds of work open to the traveller in developing countries, as has already been noted in the chapters on Africa and Latin America. The kinds of job which travellers get in the developed world (seasonal farm work, tourist resorts, as nannies, etc.) are not available in most of Asia.

The main exception is provided by those countries with a Western style economy, principally Japan, Singapore and increasingly China (including Hong Kong), Taiwan and Korea. One of the most surprising economic miracles has been taking place in India, where Europeans are being recruited to work alongside Indian professionals in business and other roles.

Having made your fortune in an industrialised country, you should be able to finance many months of leisurely travel in the inexpensive countries of Asia. In most of Asia it is better to concentrate on travelling for its own sake rather than for the sake of working. The climate is another factor. Although Robert Abblett had carefully planned his trip to India and had the addresses of organic farms where he intended to work, he had not counted on the debilitating heat and decided to enjoy a holiday instead.

However, described below are a number of ways to boost your budget between enjoying the temples of Thailand and beaches of Turkey. Note that a working holiday visa scheme operates for young Britons going to Japan, plus young Australians are eligible for a WH visa for Hong Kong, Korea, Taiwan and Thailand, while New Zealanders can choose any of those countries plus Malaysia and Singapore.

TEACHING

Although the English language is not a universal passport to employment, it can certainly be put to good use in many Asian countries especially China, Japan, Taiwan, Korea, Thailand, Vietnam and Turkey (dealt with in the next chapter). Thousands of people of all ages are eager for tuition in English and native English speakers with a university degree or just a degree of enthusiasm have been cashing in for a generation.

Working as a self-employed freelance tutor is more lucrative but hard to set up until you have been settled in one place for a while and have decent premises from which to work. By putting up small adverts in universities, colleges, coffee shops, bookshops, etc., you should gradually build up a clientele of paying students.

Extensive detailed information on teaching English in the countries of Asia is contained in the 2009/10 edition of *Teaching English Abroad* by Susan Griffith (Crimson, Vacation-Work Publications, £14.99/$24.95). For a list of useful TEFL websites see the introductory chapter on Teaching in this book.

Japan

Teaching English in Japan is one of the classic jobs for working travellers. In times of economic downturn, schools tend to become more selective, and competition for decent jobs can be fierce. The basic monthly salary of 250,000 yen for full-time EFL teachers has remained static for many years, but it is still considerably more than can be earned in most other countries. Wages are of course meaningless without balancing them against the local cost of living which in Japan is notoriously high.

A prerequisite for success is a university degree. Ideally, a job can be arranged before leaving home, for example with the government's prestigious JET programme or with one of the major chains of schools that recruits internationally. Otherwise you will have to join the fray of job-seekers already in Japan, answering ads, checking job websites and following up leads.

The most common means of recruitment is online (e.g. via sites like jobseekjapan.com), by word-of-mouth among expat teachers and by advertising your services. The free weekly English language magazine *Metropolis* (metropolis.co.jp) has a good classifieds section which is worth checking for jobs.

Another useful free publication is *Tokyo Notice Board* (tokyonoticeboard.co.jp). The twice-monthly free electronic newsletter *O-Hayo Sensei* (which means 'Good Morning Teacher') has pages of teaching positions across Japan at ohayosensei.com. Many of these are open only to candidates who are already in Japan. To find private students try findateacher.net which, according to Joseph Tame, really works. Simply enter your details (what you teach, what area of Japan you teach in, how much you charge, etc.), and the students will make contact. Joseph was also impressed with gaijinpot.com when he was looking for bits and pieces of teaching work (the word *gaijin* is Japanese for 'foreigner').

In order to shine over the competition, dress as impeccably and conservatively as possible, and carry a respectable briefcase. Inside you should have any education certificates you have earned, preferably the originals since schools are catching on that forgery is a widespread practice. Also have a typed resumé which does not err on the side of modesty. Increasingly prospective employers ask interviewees to teach a demonstration lesson so it is well to arrive prepared for this. Always speak slowly and clearly.

One of the most often recommended places to start the job hunt in Tokyo is the Kimi Information Center in Tokyo (☎ 03 3986 1604; kimiwillbe.com) which offers a fax and telephone answering service as well as advising on visas and cheap accommodation including at the Kimi Ryokan, their affiliated Japanese-style guest house, and reasonable apartments in and around Tokyo. For job-seekers, vacancies are listed on the web page kimiwillbe.com/joboppo.htm, though you have to register before applying. Another office recommended for accommodation referrals in Tokyo is Fontana (☎ 03 3382 0151; fontana-apt.co.jp).

Note that a pub called Mickey House near Takadanobaba Station (☎ 03 3209 9686; mickey-house.jp) holds regular social evenings when English speakers meet up with Japanese people, which could be a good way to meet potential students.

RED TAPE

Britons, Canadians, Australians and New Zealanders are eligible for a working holiday visa for Japan. Candidates must be aged 18–30. The quota of working holiday visas for Britons has been raised to 1000 from 2009. Visa holders may accept paid work in Japan for up to 12 months, provided it is incidental to their travels. Applicants must show that they have sufficient financial backing, i.e. savings of £2,500. Note that applications are accepted from April and once the allocation has been filled, no more visas will be granted until April of the following year. Further details are available by ringing 020 7465 6565 or on the embassy webpage at uk.emb-japan.go.jp/en/visa/work_hol.html.

Most participants make use of the services of the non-profit Japan Association for Working Holiday Makers (jawhm.or.jp) whose principal offices are in Tokyo, Osaka and Fukuoka. A large proportion of the jobs notified to the JAWHM are as English teachers. Note that membership in the Association costs a modest 1,000 yen and you must show your working holiday visa stamp to be eligible for their assistance.

For those ineligible for a working holiday visa, the key to obtaining a work visa for Japan is to have a university degree and a Japanese sponsor. This can be a private citizen but most teachers are sponsored by their employers. Not many schools are willing to sponsor their teachers since they can safely rely on a stream of native speakers who already possess a visa that allows them to work. Documents that will help you to find a sponsor are the original or notarised copy of your BA or other degree and resumé.

The UK and US have a visa exemption arrangement with Japan (uk.emb-japan.go.jp/en/visa/visa-exempt.html). British citizens can stay for up to six months without a visa, US citizens can stay for up to 90 days. It is possible to enter Japan, look for work and then apply for a work visa from outside Japan. Those found to be overstaying as tourists can be deported. Furthermore, employers caught employing illegal aliens as well as the foreign workers themselves are subject to huge fines, and both parties risk imprisonment.

PLACEMENT FROM ABROAD

If you want to arrange a teaching job in advance, the best bet is the government's JET (Japan Exchange and Teaching) Programme. Anyone with a BA who is under 39 and from the US, UK, Ireland, Canada, Australia or New Zealand (plus a number of other countries) is eligible to apply. In Britain contact the JET Desk, Embassy of Japan, 101–104 Piccadilly, London W1J 7JT (☎ 020 7465 6668; jet-uk.org) to apply for one of the 200 positions each year. Applications in Britain are due by the last Friday of November for one-year placements beginning in August. The annual salary is 3,600,000 yen (equivalent to about £28,000/$40,000).

Non-British applicants should contact the Japanese Embassy in their country of origin for information and application forms. US applicants can obtain details from any of the 16 Consulates of Japan in the US or from the Embassy in Washington (2520 Massachusetts Avenue NW, DC 20008; ☎ 202 238 6772/3; us.emb-japan.go.jp/JETProgram/homepage.html).

A number of the largest language training organisations recruit graduates abroad as well as in Japan. Some chains have been described as factory English schools, where teachers are handed a course book and told not to deviate from the formula. They depend on a steady supply of fresh graduates who want the chance to spend a year in Japan. Often new recruits do not have much say in where they are sent and in their first year may be sent to the least desirable locations. The main employers include:

AEON Corp: Recruitment office in El Segundo, California; ☎ 310 662 4706; aeonet.com; interviews in various American and Canadian cities, plus Sydney and London between February and April; places 800 native English-speaking teachers with a BA/BSc in their 300+ branch schools in Japan.

Berlitz: hr@lc.berlitz.co.jp; http://careers.berlitz.com; more than 1,000 teachers but must be already residing in Japan with a work visa.

ECC Foreign Language Institute: with regional offices in Osaka, Tokyo and Nagoya; recruitment website for job applicants is http://recruiting.ecc.co.jp/index.html; 600 teachers for 150 schools throughout Japan.

GEOS Corporation: geoscareer.com; currently interviewing and hiring only in Japan.

Interac Co Ltd: Tokyo; ☎ 03 3234 7840; interac.co.jp/recruit; 1,500 full-time Assistant Language Teachers; overseas recruitment offices located in USA, Australia, etc.

Taiwan

The hiring policy is virtually universal in Taiwan: almost anyone with a BA can land a job. The country remains a magnet for English teachers of all backgrounds. Hundreds of private language institutes or *buhsibans* continue to teach young children, cram high school students for university entrance examinations and generally service the seemingly insatiable demand for English conversation and English tuition.

Many well-established language schools are prepared to sponsor foreign teachers for a resident visa, provided the teacher is willing to work for at least a year. Only teachers with a university degree are eligible. Many people arrive on spec to look for work. It is usually easy to find a *buhsiban* willing to hire you but not so easy to find a good one. If possible, try to sit in on one or two classes before signing a contract. (If a school is unwilling to permit this, it doesn't bode well.) The majority of schools pay NT$500–$600 (roughly $15–$18) per hour.

After arrival check the Positions Vacant column of the English language *China Post* and *China News* though work tends to result from personal referrals more than from advertising. One of the best notice boards is located in the student lounge on the sixth floor of the Mandarin Training Center of National Taiwan Normal University at 129 Hoping East Road. You might also make useful expat contacts in Taipei at the Community Services Centre, 25 Lane 290 Chung Shan North Rd, Sec. 6, Tien Mu (☎ 02 2836 8134) or at the Gateway Community Centre, 7Fl, 248 Chung Shan North Rd, Sec. 6, Tien Mu (☎ 02 2836 8134; community.com.tw).

The following language schools hire on a large scale:

Hess Educational Organization: Taipei City; ☎ 02 2592 3929; hesswork@hess.com.tw; specialise in teaching children including kindergarten age; 500 Native Speaking Teachers (NSTs) in more than 150 branches; very structured teaching programme and curriculum.

International Avenue Consulting Company: Taichung City; ☎ 04 2285 5139; iacc.com.tw.

Kojen ELS: Taipei; fax 02 2581 0947; kojenenglish.com. Employs 200–300 teachers at 21 schools, mostly in Taipei but also Kaohsiung and Taichung; minimum starting wage of NT$580–590 per hour.

VISAS

Tourists who arrive without any visa are allowed to stay in Taiwan no more than 14 days. People who intend to look for work can apply for the resident visa after arrival; however they will need to enter the country on a Visitor Visa valid for 60 days (an extension may be granted, but this isn't easy). To apply for this visa you need proof of a return air ticket and a document verifying the purpose of your visit, or a recent bank statement. During those 60 days, you must find a job and organise all the paperwork for a work visa. If time runs out you will have to leave the country.

Once you sign a one-year contract with an employer, the school will apply to the local education authority for a working permit which entitles you to obtain an Alien Resident Certificate (A.R.C.). Australians and New Zealanders aged up to 30 should note that they are eligible for a 12-month working holiday visa to Taiwan.

Having discovered the joys of world travel at age 30, Stephanie Fuccio from the US took the plunge and fixed up a teaching job with Todd's English School in Tainan via the internet (toddsenglishschool.com). She found that good money could be earned and the cost of living was really low, which had the disadvantage that many of the foreigners there were focussed on money to the exclusion of everything else. Her low overheads included $200 a month for a small apartment all to herself and a used scooter bought for $250. Meanwhile she was earning $17 an hour despite having no teaching certificate or experience. She concluded that '*the whole country is simply gone mad with learning English*'.

Korea

Although South Korea does not immediately come to mind as a likely destination for British TEFLers, it has been long known in North America as a country which can absorb an enormous number of native speaker teachers, including fresh graduates with no TEFL training or experience.

Hundreds of language institutes (*hogwons*) can be found in Seoul the capital, Pusan (Korea's second city, five hours south of Seoul, sometimes transliterated Busan) and in smaller cities. The majority of these are run as businesses where profit takes precedence over education. Certificates and even degrees are in many cases superfluous, though a university degree will be needed in order to obtain the right visa. The English Program in Korea (EPIK) is a scheme run by the Ministry of Education, and administered through Korean embassies in the US, Canada, Britain and Australia, to place about 2,000 native speakers in schools and education offices throughout the country each year. The annual salary offered is 1.8 to 2.5 million won per month (depending on qualifications) plus accommodation, round trip airfare, visa sponsorship and medical insurance. Current information should be obtained from the EPIK website (http://epik.knue.ac.kr) or by contacting the local Korean government representative, e.g. in the UK the Education Director, Korean Embassy, 60 Buckingham Gate, London SW1E 6AJ (☎ 020 7227 5547; fax 020 7227 5503; education-uk@mofat.go.kr).

In the UK, jobs in Korea can be fixed up in advance with huntesl.com and Flying Cows Consulting Ltd based at Nottingham Trent University (flying-cows.com) who are willing to consider anyone with a degree. Since the visa rules changed, it is preferable to arrange a job before arrival. Under new visa regulations (Dec 15th 2007) any person who arrives in Korea to teach English must get their final visa processing completed in their country of residence. This means that entering on a tourist visa for job hunting is simply not possible, at least this is the official line. There are all kinds of interesting conversations happening in Korea as to whether this regulation is really necessary.

In North America and Korea a range of brokers and agents acts on behalf of institutes or groups of institutes to recruit teachers. Typically, advertisements placed by such intermediaries request only native-speaker fluency and a BA/BSc. Some charge a fee though these should be avoided. Identifying the good ones who are interested in more than collecting their commission from schools is tricky. Check out peoplerecruit.com based in Pusan and englishwork.com in Seoul.

Dozens of agents in North America recruit EFL teachers, particularly in Canada. To name just one of the longest-standing: Russell Recruiting based in Vancouver, Canada (russellrecruiting.com) recruits only for schools whose practices they can vouch for, mostly with big companies like YBM, Wonderland and Pagoda. Also try Canadian Connection Consulting Agency in Toronto (canconx.com). After doing a two-week evening course on TESL teaching in her final term of university, Jessie Cox from Ontario and her boyfriend scoured the job forums at daveseslcafe.com to find some decent recruiters for Korea who would not renege on their agreements. They sent their resumés (including the compulsory photo) to five different recruiters, and soon began receiving job offers, including some with split shifts, long working weeks, mean holiday entitlements and/or low wages. The best offer came from Canadian Connections in Toronto.

JESSIE COX DESCRIBES HER YEAR OF TEACHING IN PROVINCIAL KOREA:

A few weeks after applying, we received a job offer we were very interested in, teaching at two middle schools in nearby towns, which would allow us to share an apartment. We each did an interview with the recruiter over the phone and were offered contracts shortly after. To sign our contracts we met with one of the recruiters at their office in Toronto, a Canadian with eight years' experience teaching in Korea who was extremely helpful and answered all our questions.

I taught at the only middle school in a small farming town, and the biggest problem I encountered was the extremely low English level of most of the students. Even simple directions were hard for me to give, so we had to spend some time learning simple instructions like 'Open your book to page 22' or 'Re-

peat after me'. The language barrier also made discipline more of a challenge for me. If a student was misbehaving, I was pretty much limited to 'Stop that' 'No!' and 'Be quiet please'. I was mostly responsible for leading pronunciation and speaking exercises, along with conducting memory tests in which the students had to recite a passage from the text book. The teaching was mostly textbook based.

The best feature of working in a public school as the only non-Korean teacher was the chance to be completely immersed in Korean culture in a way that would never be possible as a tourist. Once a week we spent an evening with a Korean family living in our apartment building. They taught us Korean and we taught them English, and we had many good meals and discussions together.

The wages at public schools in Korea are quite good. They can vary from province to province and even slightly from school to school, but the pay of 1.8 million won per month was more than enough to cover our expenses. During the school holidays (I had eight weeks off altogether which was twice as much as my contract stated), we travelled further afield within Korea, to places like Seoul, the DMZ and Jeju island. I was able to climb mountains, visit Buddhist temples, visit the border between North and South Korea, explore ancient palaces, and even eat a live octopus!

YBM Education employ about 250 native English teachers for English Conversation Centers (ECCs) and other kinds of institute throughout Korea. The headquarters are in Chongno-gu, Seoul (☎ 2 2267 0532; eccmain@ybmsisa.co.kr; ybmecc.co.kr).

Despite contract language promising good salaries, furnished apartments and other amenities, many teachers find they actually receive much less than they were promised; some do not even receive benefits required by Korean law, such as health insurance and severance pay. Teachers' complaints range from simple contract violations to non-payment of salary for months at a time. Teachers are advised to keep their passports in their possession after the visa processing has taken place.

If you wait until you get to Korea, it may be possible to fix up a job by making a personal approach to language schools, though the visa question will remain. Every day adverts for teachers appear in the English language newspapers like the *Korean Herald* and *Korea Times*. Often new arrivals stay in one of the popular yogwons (hostels) and visit internet cafés to link up with the grapevine and learn about the English teaching scene. The Chongro area of Seoul contains a high concentration of both hostels and language schools and is a suitable area for a door-to-door job search.

China

Recruitment of teachers for the People's Republic of China is absolutely booming in the private sector. (For information about teaching opportunities in the Hong Kong Special Administrative Region, see the section below.) The internet is a prolific source of possibilities and is expanding all the time. Any web search or a trawl of the major ELT job sites is bound to turn up plenty of contacts, such as jobchina.net with long lists of jobs, all dated and described in detail. Another to try is teach-in-china.cn based in Shenyang City but with vacancies throughout the country.

Round-the-world American traveller, Bradwell Jackson, landed a job with ease last year and is more than satisfied with his conditions of work:

> ***In March of 2008, I was offered a job with Aston in China on the basis of a telephone interview and I am very happy with this. Aston is good to me, and my co-workers scramble to help me whenever I have even a mild matter that needs attention. For example, when I told them I was looking for a***

kung-fu school, they took this as a very important issue and had many long discussions-cum-negotiations with each other in order to come up with the best option for me. I think it might be hard to convince a Westerner to come and stay in an out-of-the-way city like Tangshan.

Really, I'm living the life of Reilly here. I've got nothing to complain about. The school has given me a free apartment complete with cable TV, washing machine, toaster oven, microwave, and refrigerator. Whenever I'm hungry, I just mosey on down to the street vendors and get some proper Chinese food for a friendly budget price. Who can ask for more?

Some of the tried and tested old schemes are still in place and still work. The British Council places language assistants (who must be university graduates) to work with classes of 50 in secondary schools across China from September to June. Preliminary training is provided on a two-week expenses-paid induction course in Shanghai. Participants receive free accommodation, a one-way flight back to the UK and an expert's salary which is normally in the range of 2,500–3,500 Renminbi yuan per month. Details of the application procedure and the registration fee (£48 in 2009) can be obtained from the Assistants Department at the British Council (London SW1A; ☎ 020 7389 4955; britishcouncil.org/languageassistants-china.htm).

IST Plus Ltd in the UK (☎ 020 8939 9057; info@istplus.com; istplus.com) runs Teach in China for graduates from the UK while CIEE in the USA places Americans in the same programme. Placements in secondary and tertiary institutions last five months from February or ten months from August. The programme fee starts at £775 with the possibility of reimbursement of the flight home at the end of a 10-month contract. BUNAC also has a choice of China programmes (summer, 20 weeks or 40 weeks) operated in conjunction with TTC (Teach and Travel China based in Beijing); the cost for a six-month stay including a four-week TEFL Certificate course is £1,999.

With an invitation letter or fax from an official Chinese employer, you will be able to obtain a Z-visa (valid in the first instance for three months) or an F (business or cultural exchange) visa. Since the Beijing Olympics, it has become more difficult to obtain the proper residence and work documents. An official health check and registration with the police are now compulsory in many places. Bradwell Jackson was struck by how discretionary the granting of visas is, and concluded that the lack of either a degree or relevant experience was not necessarily an impediment, even in Hebei province, whose officials have a reputation for being strict about visas.

Thailand

Despite political unrest in the country that led to the shut-down of the airport in late 2008, demand for English courses is holding up and plenty of opportunities exist for teachers, especially in schools that teach English to children. Bangkok and other Thai cities are a good bet for the casual teacher. Finding a list of language schools to approach on spec should present few difficulties. The best place to start is around Siam Square where numerous schools and the British Council are located or the *Yellow Pages* which lists dozens of language school addresses.

One of the best all-round sources of information about teaching in Thailand with an emphasis on Bangkok and on inside information about the main hiring companies is the website ajarn.com with stories and tips as well as many job vacancies (teflasia.com/ajarn). The site is run and constantly updated by a teacher who has been in Thailand for many years. The English language *Bangkok Post* also carries job advertisements (jobjob.co.th/en). The noisy Khao San Road is lined with expat pubs and budget accommodation, many with notice boards offering teaching work and populated with other foreigners (known as *farangs*) well acquainted with the possibilities. They will also be able to warn you of the dubious schools which are known to exploit their teachers. As usual, it may be necessary to start with part-time and occasional work with several employers, aiming to build up a decent number of hours in the same area to minimise travelling in the appalling traffic.

Teaching opportunities crop up in branches of the big companies like ECC (eccthai.com) with 50 branches around Thailand, and AUA (auathailand.org) which employs 200 teachers for four branches in Bangkok and 11 upcountry, mainly at universities.

Tourist destinations like Chiang Mai are very attractive to job-hunting teachers and opportunities crop up in branches of the big companies and in smaller schools. A good source of leads is Eagle Guest House which is run by a long-time expat who knows everything about local opportunities.

Outside Bangkok and tourist magnets like Chiang Mai and Phuket, there is far less competition from *farangs* for work, particularly in lesser-known cities like Nakhon Sawan, Khon Kaen, Udon Thani and Ubon Ratchathani. For a job in a university you will definitely have to show a degree or teaching certificate. Among the best places are Hat Yai (the booming industrial city in the south) and Songkhla. Hotels are always worth asking, since many hotel workers are keen to improve their English. If you find a place which suits and you decide to stay for a while, ask the family who runs your guesthouse about the local teaching opportunities.

The wages for *farang* teachers are uniformly low. The basic hourly rate has risen only slightly over the past six years to B250–B300 an hour though some professional schools and company work can pay considerably more. The norm is for schools to keep their staff on as part-time freelancers while giving them full-time hours; this is primarily to avoid taxes. Jobs that pay better often involve a lot of travelling, which in Bangkok is so time-consuming that it is necessary to work fewer hours. Most teachers conclude that it is just as lucrative and much less stressful to work at a single institute for the basic wage.

Alternatively, it is possible to work for no money at all. A number of volunteer schemes are heavily promoted at present, for example by a company called Thai Dragonfly in Nakhon Ratchasima in Northeast Thailand (dan@thai-dragonfly.com) which accepts 150 volunteers a year. A choice of programmes involves a short intensive TEFL training course (programme fee £395) or a 120-hour TEFL course with volunteer placement, which is much more expensive. Another new programme worth investigation is Volunteer Teacher Thailand (volunteerteacherthailand.org).

The Thai authorities keep changing the visa goalposts and the situation is very complicated. The relevant pages on ajarn.com convey the current picture. For those staying for an extended period on a tourist visa, they must leave the country every 15 days (recently reduced from 30) to renew their visa. Some schools will help their teachers to obtain the Thai teacher's licence (for which you need a university degree), work permit and Non-Immigrant B visa for which you will need multiple documents (including a police clearance from your home country).

Indonesia

Most language schools in Indonesia (and Singapore as well) recruit only trained EFL teachers who are willing to stay for at least a year. Salaries paid by the schools that hire native speakers provide for a comfortable lifestyle including travel within Indonesia during the vacations and the possibility of saving. Most schools pay 8,000,000–10,000,000 rupiah per month, after Indonesian tax of 10% has been subtracted. If you plan to complete a one or two-year contract, enquire about reimbursement for airfares and a possible tax rebate. EF mounts a huge operation in the country hiring more than 700 teachers for 68 schools.

The most lucrative employment is in the oil company cities but opportunities exist in small towns too. At local schools unused to employing native speaker teachers, teaching materials may be in short supply. One of the problems faced by those who undertake casual work of this kind is that there is usually little chance of obtaining a work permit.Travellers have stumbled across friendly little schools up rickety staircases throughout the islands of Indonesia, as the German round-the-world traveller Gerhard Flaig describes:

> ***In Yogyakarta you can find language schools listed in the telephone book or you just walk through streets to look for them. Most of them are interested in having new teachers. I got an offering to teach German and also English since my English was better than some of the language school managers. All of them didn't bother about work permits. The wages aren't very high, but it is fairly easy to cover the costs of board and lodging since the cost of living is very low.***

Vietnam, Cambodia and Laos

Vietnam is chronically short of language teachers due to its dizzying rate of economic growth (second only to China). One of the main reasons for this growth is the booming oil industry, which operates largely in English, as well as the growth of a young middle class, who invest in electronic goods, luxury items and English. It is therefore relatively easy for native speakers to get a job in Hanoi or Ho Chi Minh City (HCMC) on the basis of a telephone interview. Schools will snap you up, especially if you have a bachelor's degree and a CELTA or Trinity certificate (or equivalent).

Furthermore, Vietnam has low living costs and high salaries, e.g as much as US$20 an hour at the quality schools like ILA (discovereltvietnam.com), RMIT International University, Apollo and Language Link, while $10–$15 is the going rate at the more cheap and cheerful establishments. Stephanie Fuccio had no trouble getting work in Hanoi with Language Link after doing the CELTA course with them.

Cambodia is a relatively stable country, emerging from the shadow of its past and of its neighbours. The ELT market has been wide open to private enterprise in Cambodia ever since the UN ceased to be in charge in the 1990s. Wages for casual teachers are about $8 an hour in a country where you can live comfortably on $20 a day. Qualified EFL teachers can earn double or even treble that amount. Visa extensions are relatively easy to get and schools usually organise them for their teachers. Tourists are given one-month visas which are extendable. Those who want to work should get a business visa at the airport which are easier to renew than tourist visas.

One of the longest established schools in Phnom Penh is the Australian Centre for Education or ACE (☎ 23 724204; info@acecambodia.org) which employs upwards of 60 teachers in Phnom Penh and 14 in Siem Reap. Teachers must have a degree and the CELTA or Trinity TESOL. In addition there are many other commercial institutes like ELT (elt.edu.kh), New World Institute (nwi.edu.kh) and Home of English in Phnom Penh.

HONG KONG

With the birth of the Hong Kong Special Administrative Region (HKSAR) of the People's Republic of China on June 30th 1997, Britons lost their preferential status. Like all nationalities (except New Zealanders and Australians who can obtain a one-year working holiday visa), Britons must now obtain a work visa prior to arrival if they wish to take up legal employment in Hong Kong.

Regulations

British citizens may visit the HKSAR without a visa for up to 180 days provided they can satisfy the immigration officer on arrival that they are entering as bona fide visitors with enough funds to cover the duration of their stay without working and, unless in transit to the Mainland of China or the region of Macau, hold onward or return tickets. USA citizens are given 90 days. The visa requirements are posted at immd.gov.hk/ehtml/hkvisas_4.htm. Visitors are not normally allowed to change their status (e.g. from visitor to employment) after arrival except in special circumstances.

Normally it will take about six weeks to process an application for a work visa, assuming all accompanying documents are in order including the nomination of a local sponsor (usually the employer). Applicants should complete application form ID-990A. The HKSAR Immigration Department is located on the 2nd Floor of Immigration Tower, 7 Gloucester Road, Wan Chai; ☎ 2824 6111; fax 2824 1133; enquiry@immd.gov.hk.

Teaching

The Hong Kong government has an official scheme by which hundreds of English speakers are employed to teach in the Chinese-medium state education system. The NET scheme is administered by the Hong Kong Education Bureau (netrecruit@edb.gov.hk; edb.gov.hk). Foreign teachers known as 'Netters' are assigned randomly and singly to government schools (primary and secondary) across Hong Kong and working conditions can be tough especially in a Band 5 school with low-achieving pupils. On the other hand salaries and benefits are generous. The salary range for primary NET is HK$21,830 to HK$38,265 per month and for secondary NET, HK$21,830 to HK$45,970, depending on experience and qualifications.

The Chatteris Educational Foundation (33 Sycamore Street, Tai Kok Tsui, Kowloon; ☎ 2520 5736; chatteris.org.hk) offers recent university graduates from English-speaking countries the opportunity to teach in Hong Kong. Tom Grundy completed the nine-month programme before he became a Netter:

> ***The wages were just enough to live on and save some for travel. I travelled for three months in total, bought two laptops and cameras and still was able to pay off my student overdraft, though I saved hard. Chatteris has its problems and its 'charitable' status is questionable, but they support and train you. You'll be placed with another British, Canadian, Australian or American in a primary or secondary school, there'll be several dozen others who you'll train with and so you'll immediately have a big social network. With Chatteris, your emphasis will be on oral English with a 'non-formal' approach, i.e. games, crafts and other 'fun' activities.***

Film Extras

Although Hong Kong's film industry has been ailing of late (for which video piracy is partly responsible), foreign and local film crews do continue to crank out Chinese language movies. While the stars are invariably Chinese, *gweilos* (pale-skinned foreigners or ghosts) are sometimes taken on as extras, often to portray villains, fall guys or amazed onlookers.

One round-the-world traveller en route to New Zealand in 2006 described his experiences on his travelpod blog when he was staying at the Travellers Hostel in Chungking Mansions, a warren of backpackers' accommodation:

> ***Before I left for Macau, I was approached by Michael, who works for an agency recruiting actors. He needed a few Caucasian people to work for two nights. I said yes and when I came back we went straight to the shooting location in Central HK. The film has the English title of 'Confessions of Pain' which will be released in mainland China in December 2006. It was a new and interesting experience to work as an extra in the movie industry. One of the main characters is the famous Japanese***

actor Takeshi Kaneshiro and women everywhere ran to him to get autographs or took pictures with their mobile phones. We worked from about 7pm until 2am shooting street or restaurant scenes celebrating Christmas. This involved many repeat shootings of the same scene depicting us shouting 'Merry Christmas' and hugging each other and Santa on the street. We also got real beer to drink while playing the scenes. The company fed and clothed us and we got paid HK$400 for each day. This was welcome money as HK is not the cheapest place to hang out as a backpacker.

Casual Opportunities

The entrance to the Star Ferry and the corridors of the Mass Transit Railway stations are favourite locations for buskers. Official hassle should be minimal as long as you don't block thoroughfares. Kim Falkingham recommends being able to sing some songs in Chinese. She looks back fondly on one listener who dropped the equivalent of £80 in her cap, but also remembers long days when nobody contributed anything.

Each spring the rugby sevens tournament draws huge crowds and many temporary bar staff are needed for a weekend before Easter. You get a commission for every jug of beer you sell and can drink as much as you like. Call the headquarters of the major breweries (Fosters, San Miguel, etc.) before the event. People are also hired to sell commemorative shirts and souvenirs on the streets.

Disneyland Hong Kong employs several thousand staff but in almost all cases a good standard of Cantonese is required; hongkongdisneyland.com carries detailed recruitment information.

ENTERTAINMENT

Many of the opportunities for film extras, buskers and models pertain to other countries in Asia as well as Hong Kong. Here are some other scattered suggestions.

Hollywood does not have the world monopoly on film-making. There is an enormous film industry in the Hindi, Chinese and Japanese speaking worlds and it is just possible your services will be required, especially if you're blonde. Foreign travellers hanging around the Salvation Army Red Shield Hostel on Mereweather Road in Mumbai, Broadlands Lodge in Chennai, the main travellers' hotels in Goa, the Banglamphu area of Bangkok, or Bencoolen St in Singapore may be invited by a film agent to become an extra. Danny Jacobson and his girlfriend Marion might have had a chance to be in a Thai movie a couple of years ago but never quite managed it:

Early on in my time in Bangkok, I met an Australian guy who told me about possible work as an extra in Thai films. He gave me a cell number; i called, and a guy said come to such and such a café – 'plenty of work'. After a few calls on the cell-phone he sat down at our table and explained there was a war film going to be shot up near Chiang Mai and they needed Westerners as extras. Food and accommodation plus 500 Baht per day was the take. Not a lot of money, about $11US. But in Thailand that was enough to live very well on as a tourist for a day. We waited around while he made sporadic and seemingly non-pointless calls on his phone. He was the picture of what I assumed a casting agent would be like. Quick, up and down 'assessment' glances greeted all who approached him. Later the Dutch guy with us whispered to me that Mr. Agent had been talking into a switched-off cell-phone. So we hopped out of the taxi.

It is likely that agents like this do occasionally find work for extras but can't predict when or where until the very last minute. They keep their young hopefuls hanging around so that if the summons does come, they will be ready to supply the right kind of extras and collect their commission.

Without the services of an agent, you will simply have to find yourself in the right place at the right time, which can happen to anyone. Even the author of this book, while travelling in the Swat Valley of Northern Pakistan, had to disappoint a Pakistani film director also staying at the Heaven Breeze Hotel who wanted her to mount a horse and impersonate a colonel's daughter.

Mumbai is probably the most promising destination for aspiring 'crowd artists' since every year hundreds of films are made in 'Bollywood'. Fast-talking agents with mobile phones lurk around the Salvation Army Hostel (☎ 22 284 1824) signing up prospective extras. If signed up, you must take a rickshaw to the state-run Film City or wherever else in the vast city of Mumbai shooting is taking place. First-time extras are typically paid 500 rupees (£7) plus expenses. Expect to be kept hanging around much longer than originally told, often into the wee small hours.

Mimes, guitarists, dancers and musicians should go to Ginza in Tokyo or any Japanese city, especially in the evening. Once a few people gather, the Japanese herd instinct guarantees that the street will become all but impassable. Old Beatles and Simon and Garfunkel songs do well.

Hostessing

A reasonably reliable way for a western woman to make money in Japanese cities is to work as a hostess. Catherine Quinn, a freelance journalist, enjoyed her stint as a hostess in Tokyo several years ago and has kindly provided this description of how it works. According to Catherine, hostesses and hostess bars are widely misinterpreted in the west. Most accounts suffer in the translation, and are rendered at worst as a method to lure unsuspecting girls into prostitution, and at best as a dubious activity to be approached with great caution. This was highlighted in press coverage of Lucie Blackman, the English hostess who was murdered in Tokyo in 2000. Her tragic death was mistakenly reported in the western media as a direct consequence of hostessing.

Hostess bars rely on a drinking culture completely alien to the west, where overworked salarymen pay for the company and attention of lively women. The preference is for European women, and prejudices can make it more difficult for 'non-Aryan' looking women. Generally, two types of hostess bar can be found. More traditional style bars open from about 8pm until midnight, pay around 2,500 yen an hour, and serve a small number of Japanese-speaking clientele. These bars are more often the choice of women with full-time English teaching jobs in the day, and often offer good chances to learn Japanese by talking with customers.

The second type of hostess bar is more in the style of a western nightclub. These bars attract groups of Japanese businessmen on high incomes, in search of a night on the town – although they also attract a steady flow of single regulars. Many clubs run shorter hours (10pm–2am for example) if customers are scarce. Most clubs run a *dohan* (dinner date) reward system, which hostesses have to meet to earn serious money. Pressure to go on regular *dohan* has increased with economic necessity, with the strictest clubs operating fines for girls who don't make enough. Depending on the club, bonuses can be earned by drinking many drinks (these are charged to the customer) and persuading the customer to buy champagne. Many techniques abound for diluting the inordinate flow of alcohol, including the famous 'Lady's Special' (bar code for water), or the well-positioned pot plant in which to tip your drink.

Working hostesses are expected to wear nightclub style clothing which is glamorous rather than revealing, and to be well groomed. Appearance issues vary from club to club, with the top-end establishments often demanding a dizzying level of personal maintenance. Generally, work involves conversing with men who arrive at the bar, and acting as a drinking companion. Some clubs also like girls to sing karaoke with customers. For many hostesses, the major advantages of the job are the social company it provides and the unlimited drinks, a particular perk in a city where alcohol is so expensive. Although there is no guarantee that customers won't be tedious, to some extent your interest in the clientele will determine your enjoyment of the profession. Hours of speaking slowly can become tiring but, for some women, hostessing is an unrivalled method of earning money whilst experiencing another culture. Note that this kind of employment is forbidden under the terms of the working holiday visa scheme, as is bar work.

In Tokyo hostess clubs are scattered throughout Roppongi and Ginza, and can be difficult to distinguish from normal bars, nightclubs and strip-joints. Traditional hostess bars are virtually impossible to track down without a knowledge of written Japanese.You should be able to find out the names of clubs by word of mouth, so put your best dress on and ask at the door. In Roppongi, some of the clubs along the main strip (Minato-ku) are strip clubs and lap dancing clubs, so tread carefully.

Modelling

Caucasian faces are sought after in the advertising industries of Singapore, Thailand, Japan, China, etc. Interested people should get some photos taken back home rather than risk being ripped off by agencies which charge you to put together a portfolio and then don't hire you. When you arrive, register with one of the numerous modelling agencies. Earnings are good if you average more than one or two assignments per week. Jaime Burnell couldn't believe how easy it was:

> ***When I was in Thailand, I was approached by an American scouting for white/blonde girls to have their photos taken for adverts. White faces sell in Thailand so even me who is not model material usually got paid for one day's work at a rate of 5,000 baht. It was all done very professionally and the photos are kept in a photo library for future use. As long as you don't mind it being used two years later in a soap commercial then go for it. That money let me travel for over two months with some left over.***

Apparently scouts hang around hostels on the Khao San Road. Try to track down modelling agencies such as Carrie Models and the Pikanake Group to find work as a magazine model and a film extra.

Similar opportunities exist in Japan. Again, you don't have to be particularly stunning, though obvious tattoos will probably disqualify you since these have connotations of gangster status. There are big agencies in Tokyo and Osaka; otherwise occasional jobs are passed on by word of mouth. The routine is you give them a call, go for an interview, they take your measurements, take a few photos and get you to sign a contract. Then they call you when they have work.

TOURISM AND BUSINESS

Some travellers find opportunities teaching scuba diving in Thailand or working as a croupier in Japan. Thailand affords the best chances as Vaughan Temby discovered:

> ***We spent a great Christmas on the islands and although we weren't looking for work, we did come across some opportunities. On Koh Samui several bars along Chaweng beach needed staff during the peak season. The huge Reggae Bar Complex a little further inland hires some foreign staff. On Koh Pha'Ngan a friend of mine worked as a DJ and another as a waitress/kitchen helper in the excellent German-style bakery.***

Throughout Asia, especially in China, there are many ex-pat run restaurants and hotels. Often these are the most popular places to stay since they are tuned into providing what westerners want. Anyone who can obtain a long-term visa through local loopholes or by marrying a local, might try to capitalise on this situation.

Japanese ski resorts provide openings for people with a 'basic understanding of the Japanese language'. Young foreigners are employed to operate the ski lifts, as waitresses, golf caddies and in fast food restaurants. Food and accommodation are normally provided in addition to a good salary. Snowjapan.com has links to current job vacancies with companies such as Ski Japan Holidays (japanspecialists.com).

AUSTRALIAN REBECCA BARBER SUGGESTS VOLUNTEERING TO ASSIST WITH ONE OF THE MULTITUDE OF RAFTING TRIPS WHICH MANY COMPANIES RUN IN NEPAL:

When I went on a rafting trip (which are fantastic but expensive by Nepali standards – minimum $200 for ten days), I met a guy who had just done two free trips as 'safety kayaker'. No qualifications were needed apart from being confident of your ability to paddle the river. When in Kathmandu, simply walk into every agency you see and offer to work. You would be unlikely to get full-time or long-term work but as a way of getting a few free trips, living at no expense and getting some great paddling experience, not to mention the chance of future employment, it's ideal.

The Cotswold-based specialist upmarket tour operator to Mongolia, Panoramic Journeys (panoramicjourneys.com), offers a classic working holiday: people who are willing to work behind the scenes to help run the tour can join it for free.

As has been well publicised, many major European companies have outsourced their call centres en masse to India, creating many training jobs for British and European citizens. One company that specialises in recruitment in this field is Konduco Ltd (konduco.com) with offices in London and Faridabad (Haryana state). It places graduates in a variety of roles and candidates with call centre experience on assignments throughout India among other countries. Some packages include return airfares, accommodation and a local salary.

VOLUNTEERING

Many people who have travelled in Asia or perhaps seen the film *Slumdog Millionaire* are dissatisfied with the role of tourist and would like to find a way of making a contribution. In very many cases this is laudable but naïve. It may be worth quoting Dominique Lapierre, author of *The City of Joy*, which movingly describes life in a Calcutta slum. Although he is talking specifically about India, a similar situation exists in all poor countries:

> ***Many of you have offered to go to Calcutta to help. This is most generous but I am afraid not very realistic. Firstly because Indian authorities only give tourist visas of limited duration to foreign visitors. This is much too short a period for anyone to achieve anything really useful. Secondly because only very specialised help could really be useful. Unless you are a doctor or an experienced paramedic in the fields of leprosy, tropical diseases, malnutrition, bone tuberculosis, polio, rehabilitation of physically handicapped, I think your generous will to help could be more of a burden for the locals in charge than anything else. Moreover, you have to realise that living and working conditions on our various projects are extremely hard for unaccustomed foreigners.***

It must be stressed that Westerners invariably have to make a financial contribution to cover food and accommodation as well as their travel and insurance. Some grassroots programmes will seem to Western eyes almost completely unstructured, so volunteers should be able to create tasks for themselves. If you have not travelled widely in the developing world you may not be prepared for the scruffiness and level of disorganisation to be found in some places. If this is potentially alarming, try to find an organisation with an office abroad which can provide briefing materials beforehand, though this means that you will end up paying a sizeable arrangement fee.

India and Bangladesh

Many volunteer companies and organisations in the UK and US send volunteers to teach English or undertake other voluntary work in India (contact details in introductory chapter *Volunteering*). At an opposite extreme from a cushy attachment to an English-medium private school is working for Mother Teresa's Missionaries of Charity in Calcutta. It is possible to become a part-time volunteer at Mother Teresa's children's home in Calcutta and other charitable houses, but no accommodation can be offered. The work may consist of caring for and feeding orphaned children, the sick and dying, mentally or physically disabled adults and children or the elderly. To register, visit the Mother House at 54A A.J.C. Bose Road, Calcutta 700 016.

As mentioned above, the visa problem can prove a difficult one for people who want to commit themselves to stay longer-term in India. If you do want to stay longer than the standard 180 days for tourists, you will have to leave the country and apply for a business or employment visa with an official letter of invitation from your Indian sponsor (see Indian Embassy website hcilondon.org). Note that from 2008, the visa process has been outsourced to VF Services Ltd (http://in.vfsglobal.co.uk) with several offices in London, while the Indian Consulate General in Birmingham and Edinburgh are still issuing visas.

Development in Action based in central London (☎ 07813 395957; developmentinaction.org) arranges attachments to various Indian NGOs for volunteers to spend the summer or five months from September. Fees are £700 for July/August and £1,290 for the 5-month placement.

Dakshinayan (dakshinayan.org) works with tribal peoples in the hills of Rajmahal and nearby plains. Volunteers join grassroots development projects every month and contribute $300 per month.

GEOFFROY GROLEAU IS AN ECONOMIST AND CONSULTANT FROM MONTREAL WHO FOUND HIS WAY TO DAKSHINAYAN VIA THE INTERNET:

The application process is simple and can be conducted fully over the internet. The registration fee which must be provided before setting out for the project is the primary source of revenues for Dakshinayan. So there I was in early March stepping onto a train from New Delhi heading to Jharkhand. The project provides an opportunity to acquire a better understanding of the myths and realities surrounding poverty in the developing world, and specifically about the realities of rural India. The tribal people of these villages do not need or want fancy houses or televisions, but simply an education for their children and basic healthcare in order to improve the life they have been leading in relative isolation for centuries. It was interesting for me to see that they lead a quiet and simple life based on the rhythm of harvests and seasons, in marked contrast to most westerners. The primary role for volunteers is to teach English for a few hours every day to the kids attending the three Dakshinayan-run schools. I should also mention the numerous unforgettable football games with enthusiastic kids at the end of another sunny afternoon. One should be aware that Dakshinayan is an Indian NGO fully run by local people, which in my view is another positive aspect. But it also means that volunteers will have to adapt to Indian ways.

The Calcutta-based SMILE Society (smilengo.org) arranges workcamps and internships in teaching, health, rural development, etc. for students from abroad. Volunteers pay no fee but only cover their basic living costs of €100 per week for stays of up to three weeks, and €80 for stays of 4–24 weeks.

Many travellers to India stay at monasteries, temples or ashrams, which are communities for meditation, yoga, etc. There may be no official charge or at least a very small one, but it may be assumed that you are a genuine seeker after enlightenment. The residential non-formal school Samanway Ashram (Bodh-Gaya 824 231, Bihar; ☎ 0631 400223) has links with various educational and sanitation projects in the state to which it sends volunteers. WWOOF India (wwoofindia.org) lists nearly 60 contacts in India and costs $20 to join.

Twenty-three year old Jenna Bonistalli wanted a complete change from her life as a student in New York so fixed up two voluntary placements in India, the first at a school in the Himalayas through Help-Education (listed below under 'Nepal') and later for an NGO, Full Circle (fullcircle.org.uk) that organises health and education outreach to a number of villages in rural Rajasthan.

> ***After some travelling, a friend and I began our placement with the Veerni Project in Jodhpur, Rajasthan. Our role was as teachers in their Creative Literacy Programme, teaching remedial English through the Arts. This has been a very interesting placement, but also very difficult because the girls know very little English and most of them have been married off as children, so do not have much hope of continuing their studies past 15 or 16. The reason we chose this project was for its creative opportunities. The current fee for participation is $200 for placement plus 5000–7000 Rupees per month for living costs and a $100 donation to the project's funding.***

A community organisation in the Himalayan foothills with the charming acronym ROSE (Rural Organization on Social Elevation), in the state of Uttarakhand (jlverma_rosekanda@hotmail.com; rosekanda.org) can assist volunteers wishing to work with poor villagers, teaching children, carrying out environmental work and organic farming in this village. Volunteers pay Rs500 a day for board and lodging and a Rs3500 registration fee.

The Bangladesh Work Camps Association in Dhaka (fax 02 956 5506; mybwca.org) will try to place you on two-week community development camps between October and March for a fee of $250. They publish detailed camp information in English. BWCA can also accommodate foreign volunteers on a medium-term basis (one to three months) and longer term.

Sri Lanka

Volunteers are engaged in post tsunami reconstruction, welfare service, education, and other projects including information technology. For example Samasevaya Sri Lanka is an established NGO that has been doing excellent post-tsunami work, particularly in the Muslim area of Kinniya. The National Secretariat in Talawa (samasev@sltnet.lk) invites volunteers to help in rural locations. Volunteers can be used rather loosely for their educational and development programmes, though it is more akin to a cultural exchange. If the volunteer wants to stay past the initial month of their tourist visa, it is sometimes possible to arrange a renewal. The organisation provides simple accommodation in their office complex in Talawa or with local families. They expect a contribution of about $100 a month for meals.

The charity VESL in Edinburgh (vesl.org) provides rural Sri Lankan schools with exposure to enthusiastic and creative native English speakers. VESL sends volunteers to the South and Central Provinces of Sri Lanka (and India) on four to six week summer programmes or longer programmes throughout the year to teach English or science. The cost is £400 for a short summer placement and £850–£950 for three to six months. Fiona Passey describes herself as a young-at-heart 38 year old who wrote from a rural village in Andhra Pradesh, India (and had to retype it on the computer three times because of the frequent power cuts):

> ***I decided to volunteer for four months during the summer of 2008. I found VESL on the web and liked what I read about them. The selection day in London helped me make up my mind as Tom and Ian, VESL's co-founders, strike the right balance between the serious issues that volunteers face (poverty, AIDS, disease) with an acknowledgement that you are a volunteer who wants a great experience.***
>
> ***For the first month, my volunteer partner Avni and I ran a summer school for local children teaching spoken English and arts and crafts. For the next three months we taught English in local primary and secondary schools. We teach at four schools in the village which are desperately poor and short of teachers so we are much in demand (you could send a busload of volunteers here). I am sure I will look back on this time in years to come as a special time in my life, when status and possessions were irrelevant, when kindness and being able to give to others made you richer than you ever felt possible.***

Internships for people 18–25 are arranged by a company in Colombo called Volunteer International (148/1B Kynsey Road, Colombo 7; ☎ 74 720658; volunteerinternational.com). They offer a structured programme in the hospitality industry, journalism, business, conservation, teaching and so on. Participants pay £1,495 for three months and £2,395 for six months (plus travel). Some internship placements are available in the Maldive Islands for people who can speak a language in addition to English.

Nepal

After a decade long campaign against the constitutional monarchy, the Maoist rebels have secured its abolition and formed the government. In June 2008, King Gyanendra and his family quietly moved out of the royal palace which was turned into a museum in 2009. It is now to be hoped that Nepal's political problems will dissipate and the country can concentrate on improving the lives of its people, 100,000 of whom were displaced during the violence.

So once again Nepal is a promising destination for short-term volunteers and casual English teachers. However people who find voluntary openings in Nepal will be faced with a visa problem. Tourist visas (which can be purchased on arrival for $30 cash) are valid for 60 days and can be extended for up to 120 days from the Department of Immigration in Kathmandu and Pokhara Immigration Office on request (for $30). An additional 30 days can be requested from the Department of Immigration, but that's the maximum. Note that a $4,000 fine or up to a ten-year prison sentence can be imposed on foreigners found overstaying their visas.

A range of organisations makes it possible for self-funding volunteers to teach. Of course living expenses are very low by western standards, though the fees charged by mediating or gap year organisations like i-to-i and Africa & Asia Venture as well as by Nepali agencies (some listed below) can increase the cost significantly. If you want to avoid an agency fee you can make direct contact with schools on arrival.

Relevant organisations include:

Cultural Destination Nepal: Kathmandu; ☎ 01 437 7623; volunteernepal.org.np; volunteer Nepal, a service work programme; fee of €650 includes 2-week pre-service orientation and homestay throughout; placements last 2–4 months starting February, April, June, August and October.

HELP (Himalayan Education Lifeline Programme): Kent; tel/fax 01227 263055; help-education.org; volunteer teachers, nurses and child-carers work in needy schools in Himalayan India (Sikkim, West Bengal, Ladakh and Himachal Pradesh) and Nepal (Kathmandu Valley, Pokhara and Chitwan); cost includes admin fee of £150 plus donation of £100 (students) or £250 (non-students) plus about £70 per month for accommodation with host families or in school hostel.

Hope And Home Volunteer Program: Kathmandu; ☎ 1 441 5393; hopenhome.org; volunteer opportunities in the fields of teaching English as well as community, health and environmental programmes in the Kathmandu Valley, Pokhara, Chitwan and Nawalparasi; programme fees cover homestay accommodation and food: $250 for 2 weeks, to $800 for 3 months.

Insight Nepal: Pokhara; insight@fewanet.com.np; insightnepal.org.np; 7-week and 3-month placements for all post A-level and high-school graduate native speakers of English; participation fee of $990 for 3 months and $650 for 7 weeks.

KEEP (Kathmandu Environmental Education Project): Thamel, Kathmandu; ☎ 01 421 6775; keepnepal.org; opportunities for volunteers to teach English in trekking villages, government schools, etc.; volunteers stay with a host family and must be self-funding.

New International Friendship Club: Maharajgunj, Kathmandu; ☎ 01 442 7406; geocities.com/nifcnepal; 40 English-speaking university graduates placed in schools or colleges; volunteer teachers should contribute $100 per month for their keep plus a $150 registration fee; also runs programme of 15-day workcamps; fee 15,000 Nepalese rupees (€165); basic Nepalese standard accommodation is provided and Nepali (rice-based) meals.

RCDP Nepal: Kathmandu; ☎ 1 427 8305; rcdpnepal.com; paying volunteers work on various programmes lasting 2 weeks to 5 months, including teaching English; volunteers stay with families in villages; also have volunteer programmes in India, Sri Lanka and Tibet.

Volunteer Service and Support Program Nepal (VSSP): Sinamangal, Kathmandu; ☎ 1 6219343; vnepal@wlink.com.np; volunteer-nepal.org; summer programme involves teaching two hours a day; fee is €380 for 4 weeks, €38 for each extra week.

Volunteer Nepal National Group: c/o Anish Neupane, Bhaktapur; ☎ 1 6613724; volnepal.np.org; workcamps in Kathmandu Valley and volunteer placements in schools, colleges and universities; $500 fee includes pre-service training, language instruction, homestay and meals, trekking, rafting, jungle safari and volunteering; reps abroad, e.g. in Reading, UK; (shekharbhattarai@volnepal.np.org).

WWOOF Nepal is run by an energetic coordinator who has links with other NGOs and charities in Nepal (☎ 01 436 3418; fdregmi@gmail.com; wwoofnepal.org). The WWOOF membership fee is $30 ($40 for a couple) which gives access to contact details for the organic farmers in Nepal. Since few have email, the WWOOF director will try to find willing volunteers a suitable volunteer placement from the list.

Southeast Asia

The mainstream London-based conservation expedition organisers all run projects in Asia. These expeditions are normally open to anyone reasonably fit who can raise the cost of joining (typically £2,500–£3,500 for three months excluding flights):

Coral Cay Conservation Ltd: London; ☎ 020 76201411; coralcay.org; recruits paying volunteers, expedition leaders, scuba instructors, etc. for its marine and forest conservation projects in the Philippines and Cambodia.

Gapforce: ☎ 020 7384 3343; gapforce.org; sends paying volunteers to join biodiversity conservation projects among others including English teaching in a range of countries including Thailand, Borneo, India, Nepal, China, and Fiji; prices range from £1500 for three weeks to £2600 for 10 weeks.

The Orangutan Foundation: ☎ 020 7724 2912; orangutan.org.uk; arranges for volunteers to be based in the Tanjung Puting National Park in Kalimantan, Indonesian Borneo for six weeks at a cost of £700; tasks range from carrying out infrastructure repairs, trail cutting and constructing guardposts, but involves no direct work with orangutans.

Starfish Ventures: tel/fax 0800 197 4817; starfishventures.co.uk; places volunteers and gap year students of all nationalities in development projects in Thailand, especially Surin Province, including teaching, community development, construction and conservation; sample fees are £1,200 for 8–12 weeks which include insurance, travel within Thailand, homestay accommodation and (if appropriate) preparatory TEFL training weekend.

Most of the activities of NGOs providing educational and other assistance to displaced persons in Thailand are located at the Thai/Burmese border. In the Burma Volunteer Program (Thailand), volunteers teach English to groups of Burmese refugees for at least 12 weeks near Mae Sot near the western Thai-Burma border (maesotel@gmail.com; burmavolunteers.org).

Near Phuket at the other end of Thailand, conservationists are working to protect marine turtles, mangrove forest and coral reef on the island of Phra Thong. Though projects in this area were badly hit by the 2004 Tsunami, Naucrates has resumed its programme and recruits volunteers to help with rebuilding and education. The volunteer contribution is €325 per week (minimum two weeks). Prospective volunteers and student conservationists can obtain more details from the Italian NGO Naucrates in Italy (☎ +39 3334 306643; naucrates.org).

Far East

Japan and Korea have WWOOF organisations, both of them web-based. It costs 5,500 yen to join WWOOF Japan (Sapporo; fax 011 780 4908; wwoofjapan.com) whose list of member farms has expanded hugely to nearly 350; and 50,000 won ($50) for the Korean list from WWOOF Korea (koreawwoof.com).

WHILE DOING HIS YEAR ABROAD OF A DEGREE IN JAPANESE AT SHEFFIELD UNIVERSITY AND ON PREVIOUS TRIPS, JOSEPH TAME HAS HAD A WONDERFUL TIME WWOOFING:

I spent a few weeks in a beautiful little seaside village on the southern island of Shikoku, working as a volunteer for an organic tangerine co-operative. We would be picked up by local farmers at about 6am, work with them on the tangerine terraces until 11am when the heat got to be too much to bear. One particularly memorable day was when an Australian Wwoofer and I were given the job of picking caterpillars off the leaves of a huge field of organic Japanese potatoes. Over the course of 3 hours we collected two huge sacks of creepy crawlies, but at the end of the day forgot to tie the sacks up – when we returned to the field the following day we found the caterpillars had all escaped and returned to their former homes!

WWOOF Japan is a good way to meet Japanese people, as it is popular among city dwellers eager to experience a quiet rural lifestyle. The WWOOF list also includes some paid employment since a few of their hosts run hostels, campsites or little schools (for which a working visa would be necessary).

More and more workcamp organisations are being established; links to all of them can be found at nvda-asiapacific.org, the Network for Voluntary Development in Asia. Joining a short-term volunteer project can be a good way to visit an exotic place like Mongolia (contact the Mongolian Workcamps Exchange ☎ +976 99131777; mce-mn@magicnet.mn) with partner agencies abroad. The fee for joining a two-week camp is €160. An NGO in Ulaanbaatar that places international volunteers is the New Choice Mongolian Volunteer Organization (tel/fax 011 314577; volunteer.org.mn/new/index.html). It arranges short- and long-term placements for volunteers to teach English, renovate buildings, etc. for a fee of $495–$1,950.

THE MIDDLE EAST

With bitter anti-Western feelings running higher than ever in the wake of the 22-day Israeli offensive in Gaza in January 2009 and ongoing tensions elsewhere in the region, the taste for travel and employment in the Middle East has been suppressed. Many prospective travellers have been put off by fear for their personal security. One optimistic note is that Australia has just signed a Work and Holiday visa agreement with Iran whereby tertiary educated people aged 18–30 can stay up to a year and pick up temporary paid jobs.

The areas of employment to consider throughout the Middle East are English teaching, nannying/nursing or a position in the petro-chemical or construction industries if you happen to have superior qualifications and relevant managerial experience. A hopeful sign in post-war Iraq is that a university in Kurdistan was seen advertising in 2009 for TEFL teachers (http://uod.ac).

Countries in the Middle East vary greatly in degree of Islamic restrictiveness. Bahrain, Oman and the United Arab Emirates, for example, have a relatively relaxed atmosphere. On the one hand, the wealthy countries of Saudi Arabia, Bahrain, Oman and the Gulf states generally employ teachers with top qualifications such as an MA in TESOL or Applied Linguistics with at least three years of experience, preferably at university level. On the other hand, countries like Syria and Jordan may have more casual opportunities. Anyone interested in teaching English to the Palestinians scattered throughout the Arab World is likely to be working on a voluntary basis or for accommodation and a local stipend, rather than for expatriate salaries. Accepting a TEFL contract in an oil state usually means first-class accommodation in a luxury apartment complex, cheap shopping, etc.

ELS Language Centers Middle East is a group of 12 centres in the region which employ a number of full-time teachers and many part-time teachers to teach American English; the regional office is in Abu Dhabi (02 642 6640; jobs@elsmea.com). Possible leads may be available from Amideast headquartered in Washington DC (☎ 202 776 9600; amideast.org) which teaches American English at its field offices in Kuwait, Syria, Yemen plus North Africa.

The Israeli bombing of Lebanon in the summer of 2006 smashed much of the transport infrastructure, wrecked the reviving tourist industry and destroyed hope in a prosperous future. This may force Lebanon to lean even more strongly towards the west, and some demand for English teachers will persist. Similar opportunities exist in neighbouring Syria where there's an enthusiastic demand for private tuition in English. The American Language Center, part of the Amideast network runs American English courses for adults, and anyone with a TEFL background already in Damascus has a chance of getting some part-time hours with them.

Many people consider Yemen to be the most beautiful and interesting of all Middle Eastern states although the kidnapping and murder of foreign aid workers in 2009 caused international consternation. Enthusiastic and adaptable university graduates could try for teaching work at the Modern American Language Institute (MALI) in the capital Sana'a (☎ 01 441036; arabicinyemen.com/employment.com) with centres also in Aden and Mukalla.

Palestinian schools struggle on and anyone who supports their cause might be prepared to become a volunteer teacher. The Shepherd School in Beit Sahour (shepherdschoolesol@yahoo.com) took on volunteers (in September 2008) to establish a programme of evening classes for residents of the Bethlehem area, in collaboration with the British Council and Cambridge University. Volunteer teachers taught English up to 20 hours a week in exchange for housing near the school and a monthly stipend.

The educational charity UNIPAL (Universities Trust for Educational Exchange with Palestinians) organises summer schools for children aged 12–15 in Palestinian refugee camps, provided it is safe for volunteers to enter. Volunteers must be native English speakers, based in the UK and at least 20 years old. The approximate cost is £500 including airfares. Applications must be submitted to Unipal (unipal.org.uk) by the end of February in time for interviews at the end of March and two training days in the spring and summer.

TURKEY

Teaching English

Turkey's ambition to join the European Union, together with a remarkable expansion in tourism during the last two decades, means that Turkey's prosperous classes are more eager than ever to learn English. It also means that they may have the money to pay for it because 'pre-accession assistance' alone was worth €500 million (earmarked by the EU in 2007).

Expat teachers routinely earn good money for private English lessons. The boom in English is not confined to private language schools (*dershane*) that cram students for university entrance, but there are dozens of private secondary schools (*lises*) and a few universities where English is the medium of instruction. This has meant that Turkey has been an attractive destination for fledgling teachers with a university degree who could be fairly sure of finding employment.

Most of the mainstream schools will expect to see a TEFL Certificate of some kind, preferably the Cambridge (CELTA) or Trinity (TESOL) Certificate, in addition to a BA. This may apply to the established chains, but there are still dodgy operators and swashbuckling employers willing to hire (and exploit) others. One British teacher sets out what you should look for when choosing an employer: *'I worked at four different schools in Istanbul. You'll want a school that's professional (with good resources, support and teacher development), offers a good package (salary, accommodation, holiday entitlement) and has a timetable to suit you.'*

Although Istanbul is not the capital, it is the commercial, financial and cultural centre of Turkey, so this is where most of the EFL teaching goes on. On the negative side, there may be more competition from other travelling teachers here and also in Izmir than in Ankara or less obvious cities like Mersin and Bursa. Among the main language teaching organisations in Istanbul are Dialogue, Dilko English, Kent School of English, English First and English Time (addresses below). Without a degree and a TEFL certificate it will not be possible for English teachers to get a work permit and virtually impossible to get a residence permit. If you can show that you have means to support yourself, you might be eligible for a residence permit (which costs over 605 YTL or £250).

Many casual teachers work on a tourist visa which means that they must renew it every three months, either at the immigration office (by showing that they have the means to support themselves; for example having a Turkish friend undertake to support them) or more usually by leaving the country and obtaining a fresh tourist visa, which costs £10 or $20 in cash at the point of entry.

For short-term opportunities, the Education Department of the youth travel and exchange organisation, Genctur, in Galatasaray, Istanbul (☎ 212 244 62 30; genctur.com) organises summer camps for children where English, German and French are taught by native speakers who work for two weeks in exchange for free board and lodging. Pocket money may also be given according to experience and skills. Applicants must have some experience of working with children.

Among the main indigenous language teaching organisations in Turkey are:

Best English: Kizilay, Ankara; ☎ 312 417 1819; bestenglish.com.tr.

Dilko English: Bakirköy, Istanbul; ☎ 212 570 1270; dilkoenglish.com; franchise schools also in Kadiköy, Besiktas, Izmit, Canakkale and Adapazari, employing up to 60 teachers altogether.

English First: Istanbul branches in Suadiye, Levent, Beyoglu and Bakirköy, among others; efdilokulu.com.

English Time: Esentepe, Istanbul; ☎ 212 273 2868; esljob@englishtime.com; englishtime.com; employ about 125 times for their branches; most teachers are paid 20–26 YTL an hour which allows teachers to live comfortably.

Kent English (Ankara): Kizilay, Ankara; ☎ 312 433 6010; kentenglish.org; monthly wage £600 plus subsidised accommodation.

Childcare

Demand is steady for English-speaking au pairs and also among wealthy Turkish families for professional nannies who have studied childcare and child development. The following agencies make placements in Turkey:

Anglo Nannies London: Wimbledon; ☎ 020 8944 6677; anglonannies.com; specialises in placing professional English-speaking nannies and teachers in Turkey; support provided by Istanbul office.

ICEP (International Cultural Exchange Programs): icep@icep.org.tr; au pair in Turkey programme for 3–12 months; icep.org.tr/english/aupairturkey.asp; minimum pocket money $200 a month; interns with Turkish companies receive accommodation, meals and $150 a month; ICEP also places qualified English teachers who earn $500 a month.

ATS International: Wood Green, London; ☎ Mob 077 9520 5649; anglo-turkishservices.com; specialises in placing Turkish au pairs with British families but also places some Britons in Turkey.

The high salaries quoted for nannies sound very attractive, though the life of a nanny can be frustrating because of cultural differences. Some nannies have had to get used to having their freedom and independence curtailed, and also the extent to which Turkish children tend to be spoilt and babied. But despite this, many have thoroughly enjoyed their stint in Turkey.

Tourism

There is a large population of seasonal travellers looking for casual employment, and many succeed. The main Aegean resorts of Marmaris, Kusadasi and Bodrum absorb a number of foreign travellers as workers. Other places firmly on the travellers' trail like Antalya on the south coast and Goreme in Cappadocia are also promising. Antalya hostels regularly pay travellers $200 a month on top of a bed and one or two meals to man the desk or do other hostel chores. The best time to look is March or early April. Danny Jacobson met lots of foreign workers when he travelled in Turkey:

> ***I would say Turkey is a hot spot. I met loads of travellers working in the south and even in Selcuk. In Fethiye, Oludenez, definitely in Olympos, it was like an Aussie/Kiwi resort complex. There are so many of them working and travelling down there, the Turkish people have started talking English with an Australian accent.***

As in Athens, Istanbul hostels enlist the help of touts to fill their beds, of whom Roger Blake was one:

> ***I found myself a job 'touting' for a new hostel. For this I got my accommodation and not much else (US$1 per person per night and 5% of trips and tours booked by them). I have been here for a month and have earned about $80. This is not much considering the early start and long hours. In the mornings I'm at the tram stop; afternoons I go out to the airport and evenings are spent at the bus or train station. Whilst trying to entice potential customers, I was once picked up by the police who gave me a ride in their car. 'Work. Visa. Problem' they chanted. I insisted I had a visa. They drove me to my hostel and let me out, no questions asked.***

Proprietors of bars, shops, travel agencies, etc. aim to use native English speakers to attract more customers to buy their souvenirs or stay at their hotels. In the majority of cases, this sort of work finds you once you make known your willingness to undertake such jobs.

Major Turkish yachting resorts are excellent places to look for work, not just related to boats but in hotels, bars, shops and excursions. (See section on Cyprus for information about Turkish Cyprus.) A good time to check harbourside notice boards and to ask captains if they need anyone to clean or repair their boats is in the lead-up to the summer season and the Turkish Yacht Charter Show in Marmaris in May. Laura O'Connor describes what she found in Marmaris:

> ***There's a large British community living there, retired and fed-up Brits who have sold their houses, bought a boat and are whooping it up. There's plenty of work opportunities in the Marina, especially for painting and varnishing in April. Also girls can do hostessing on the boats. I was cleaning boats with a friend for enough money to cover my accommodation and evenings in the pub. Just walk around the Marina and ask.***

If you can handle long hours, rich demanding guests and the politics of living and working with the same people for the four-month season, doing a season on a charter yacht is a good way to save a lot of money and see the Turkish coast.

Some UK tour operators hire childcare staff, watersports instructors, yacht crew, etc. for Turkey. For example Setsail Holidays in Suffolk (01787 310445; setsail.co.uk) are a specialist tour operator providing flotilla sailing and bareboat charter holidays in Turkey and the eastern Mediterranean. Sunsail Ltd based in Hampshire (sunsail.co.uk/hr) has many openings for skippers, hostesses, mechanics/bosuns, dinghy sailors, cooks, bar staff and nannies to work in the watersports centres at Club Javelin on the Gulf of Bodrum, Perili near Datca and Phokaia near Foça north of Izmir. Applications for the summer season should be submitted by March. Try also

Goldtrail Holidays in Surrey (☎ 020 8287 2999; goldtrail.co.uk) which in February 2009 were advertising on the job site traveljobsearch.com for 'new entrants' to work as reps.

Voluntary Opportunities

The youth travel bureau Genctur mentioned above (workcamps.in@genctur.com; genctur.com/kp/yike/guide.php) runs international workcamps for manual and social projects as well as acting as a youth and student travel bureau and co-ordinating summer camps. GSM Youth Services Ctr in Ankara (☎ 312 417 1124; gsm-youth.org) is another workcamp organiser in Ankara with links to projects in Anatolia and throughout Turkey. Recruitment of volunteers for the fortnight long camps takes place through all the major workcamp organisations in the UK and worldwide.

An impressive WWOOF exchange has been inaugurated by the Bugday Association in Istanbul (info@tatuta.org; bugday.org). At present there are about 70 member farms, and applications should be sent via Genctur (as above).

Paid internships in Turkey and the Turkish Republic of Northern Cyprus are arranged by USEH which in addition to two offices in Turkish cities, has offices in Atlanta in the US (☎ 770 618 8450) and Australia (useh.org). University students and recent graduates with relevant training may be placed in positions in finance/banking, human resources, tourism management, etc.

IN EXTREMIS

The best protection against getting into serious difficulties is to have a good travel insurance policy (see *Introduction*). This is an expense that should not be shrugged off given the possible repercussions of not having cover. One of the benefits of the International Student Identity Card and International Youth Travel Card (for young people under 26) is access to a toll-free emergency helpline on which medical, legal or financial advice can be sought in a crisis. The ISIC and IYTC cards cost £9 and do not in any way replace the need for insurance. Details are available from any branch of STA Travel.

If you do end up in dire financial straits and for some reason do not have or cannot use a credit card, you should contact someone at home, if possible, who is in a position to send money.

TRANSFERRING MONEY

Ideally your account at home will remain in credit and you can access it via any ATM. If your card is lost, stolen or damaged, you should ring your bank's emergency number to request a replacement which will be sent to your home address, so you will have to ask someone to forward it to you securely. This of course will take some days, so you will need money in the interim. Your bank can wire money to a nominated bank in your destination. This will be easier if you have set up a telephone or internet bank account before leaving home since they will then have the correct security checks in place to authorise a transfer without having to receive something from you in writing with your signature.

Various products are on the market that aim to get round the problem, in the form of prepaid, reloadable cards that can be used at ATMs and in outlets worldwide. See the section on Money in the Introduction for a description of the Travel Money Card (from the Post Office), the Travellers Cashcard (MasterCard) and Cash Passport (Travelex), though transaction fees and exchange rates can be punitive on these.

If both you and your family or friends have a MasterCard, they could use the MoneySend system in a crisis to send cash from their MasterCard or Maestro to yours via an ATM.

Western Union offers an international money transfer service whereby cash deposited at one branch can be withdrawn almost immediately by you from any other branch or agency, which your benefactor need not specify. Western Union agents – there are 260,000 of them in 200 countries – come in all shapes and sizes, e.g. travel agencies, stationers, chemists. Unfortunately it is not well represented outside the developed world. The person sending money to you simply turns up at a Western Union counter, pays in the desired sum plus the fee, which is £14 for up to £100 transferred, £21 for £100–200, £37 for £500 and so on. For an extra £8 your benefactor can do this over the phone with a credit card. In the UK, ring 0800 833833 for further details or calculate fees on ukmoneytransfer.com. The website westernunion.com allows you to search for the nearest outlet.

Thomas Cook and the UK Post Office offer a similar service called Moneygram. Cash deposited at one of their foreign exchange counters is available within ten minutes at the named destination or can be collected up to 45 days later at one of 176,000 co-operating agents in 190 countries. The fees are very slightly less than Western Union's. The Post Office website postoffice.co.uk explains how it works.

US citizens can ring Overseas Citizens Services (☎ 1 888 407 4747), part of the State Department, which can arrange for money wired (e.g. via Western Union) to a US Embassy abroad to be given to a named citizen for a fee of $30; personal cheques are not accepted.

Despite the popularity of online banking, you may still find it necessary to open a local account for example if your employer pays by cheque. One way of simplifying this procedure is to set the wheels in motion before you leave home. Before setting off, you open an account at a large bank in your destination city, which may have a branch in London. Most won't allow you to open a chequing account so instant overdrafts are not a possibility. But knowing you have a nest egg waiting for you in Sydney, San Francisco or Singapore is a great morale booster if you are planning to be abroad for a long period.

EMBASSIES AND CONSULATES

With luck you will never have to visit your consulate while travelling. But it is still a good idea to have the contact details handy especially if you are travelling in an unstable country where an incident might incline you to register with the consular officials. This can now be done quickly and easily via the FCO website (fco.gov.uk). The majority of people who do end up in consular waiting rooms are there because they have had their passports stolen. Note that it is much easier to arrange replacement documents if you have a record of the passport number and date and place of issue; even better is a photocopy or scanned email of the relevant pages.

In an emergency, your consulate can help you get in touch with friends and relations if necessary, normally by arranging a reverse charge call. Consulates have the authority to cash a personal cheque to the value of £100 supported by a valid banker's card. But do not pin too much faith in your consulate. When Jane Roberts turned to the British Consulate in Toronto after having all her money stolen, they just preached at her about how she should have thought about all this before she left home.

If you are really desperate and can find no one at home or among your fellow travellers willing to lend you some money, you may ask your consulate to repatriate you. If they do this your passport will be invalidated until the money is repaid. In fact permission is very rarely granted these days because of the thousands of unpaid debts incurred by indigent travellers; for example these days there are fewer than 100 repatriations to the UK a year. A British consular official advised that in the 18 months she worked in India, only two repatriations were approved, despite the queues of desperate people.

The Foreign and Commonwealth Office of the UK government provides updated travel information and cautions for every country in the world and additional risk assessment of current trouble spots and advice on how to find consular help and legal advice. You can contact the Travel Advice Unit by phone on ☎ 0845 850 2829 (£0.04 per minute from BT phones) though you will be told only what is already posted on their excellent website fco.gov.uk/travel.

In the US, the Department of State publishes its country-by-country travel warnings on its website travel.state.gov, highlighting any potential dangers to American travellers such as coups or terrorist activity. The office of American Citizens Services and Crisis Management can be contacted by phone on ☎ 202 647 5225.

LEGAL PROBLEMS

Everyone has heard hair-raising stories about conditions in foreign prisons, so think very carefully before engaging in illegal activities. Several thousand Britons are held in foreign prisons, at least half on drugs charges. If you do have trouble with the law in foreign countries, remain calm and polite, and insist on an immediate visit from a consular official. He or she can at least recommend a local lawyer and interpreter if necessary. Britons should contact the charity Prisoners Abroad (London N4 ☎ 020 7561 6820; prisonersabroad.org.uk) including travellers who would like to visit prisoners since many prisoners go years without a visit. The local consulate will have a list.

DIRE STRAITS

Try not to be too downcast if destitution strikes. Elma Grey had been looking forward to leaving Greece and rejoining her old kibbutz, but she was unexpectedly turned away from the ferry because of her dire shortage of funds. She describes the 'worst down' of her travels:

> ***Back to the Athens hotel where I'd spent the previous evening, feeling utter despair. But I found that other people's problems have an incredible way of bringing out the best in total strangers. Everyone I came into contact with was full of sympathy, advice and practical suggestions regarding possible sources of work. And quite apart from this, the feeling of much needed moral support was probably what got me through the whole thing without my degenerating into a miserable heap. Although I'd never want to feel so stranded and desperate again, in a way it was all worth it just to experience the unique feeling of just how good fellow travellers can be in a crisis.***

Several travellers have insisted that when you get down to your last few dollars/pesos/euros, it is much wiser to spend them in a pub buying drinks for the locals who might then offer useful assistance than it is to spend the money on accommodation or food. David Irvine found himself in Tasmania with just $10 in his pocket. He walked into a pub and bet two men $20 each that he could drink a yard of ale, a feat he was fairly confident that he could accomplish.

Less than 24 hours after Ilka Cave from South Africa arrived in Tel Aviv, all her luggage, money and documents were stolen. One of the girls in the hostel suggested that she contact an au pair agency and soon she was living with a nice family and earning a salary. Michel Falardeau wanted to live rent-free in Sydney, so he offered his assistance to a number of charities, one of which gave him a place to live. Mark Horobin was down to his bottom dollar in San Diego and queued up outside the Rescue Mission. Several days later he had signed on as a kitchen helper and stayed for some time free of charge.

It is to be hoped that you will avoid the kind of disaster that will require the services of a lawyer, doctor or consul abroad. If you find yourself merely running short of funds, you might be interested in some of the following tidbits of information, intended for entertainment as much as for practical advice.

HELP. Look out for churches that conduct services in English: the priest or vicar should be able to give you useful advice and often practical help. But be cautious about accepting help from fringe religious groups.

NIGHT SHELTERS. Most large towns and some railway stations in Western Europe and North America have a night shelter run by the Catholic organisation Caritas, the Salvation Army or similar which provides basic but free food and accommodation. They want to help genuine vagrants, not freeloading tourists, so you should be genuinely impoverished or a potential convert. You can find out where to find these hostels by asking around – any policeman on the night beat should be able to help you. Be warned that many of these organisations are run by religious movements, and you may be expected to show your gratitude by joining in worship.

MONASTERIES and NUNNERIES. Monastic communities often extend hospitality to indigent wayfarers. Sometimes it is freely given but try to be sensitive as to whether or not a small donation is expected. Greek Orthodox monasteries are normally open to males only.

JAIL. Travellers have on occasion found a free bed for the night by asking at police stations if there are any spare cells, though with the British prisons scandalously full to bursting at present, this is not a very promising possibility. According to US law, all people (including non-citizens) have the right to demand protective custody. You are most likely to be successful (and escape unharmed) in peaceful country towns.

SLEEPING OUT. It is illegal to sleep out on private property without the landowner's permission (except in Sweden); most farmers will grant their permission if you ask politely and look trustworthy. In cities try public parks and also railway or coach stations, though some are cleared by security after the last train or bus or you may be asked for an onward ticket. Anna Ling felt safe sleeping in fenced parks in Seville (going to bed after dark) and also on a theatre porch with an overhanging roof, where there was a community of street people and young punks mainly from France. Some kind locals offered food and coffee. Many people try to camp discreetly near a proper campsite so that they can make use of the toilet and shower block. Ian Moody tried to avoid sleeping out on private property in Spain and one night chose a seemingly ideal shelter, a concrete covered ditch. At about 5am he was rudely awakened by a torrent of water which swept away his gear and nearly drowned him. Many people sleep on beaches; beware of early morning visits from the local constabulary and also large vacuum machines. Jonathan Galpin recommends taking a mosquito net, not only as protection against biting insects but (when doubled over) from falling dew.

SQUATTING. Every city has a selection of abandoned buildings, many of which have been colonised by squatters. Finding a welcoming squat is a hit-and-miss business; some are more exclusive than others. Squatters are tough people who will not tolerate freeloaders, so you have to show that you can contribute something (cleaning, decorating, maintenance, etc.). And be prepared for confrontation with the authorities. It is not unknown for long-stay squatters to make contact with the owner of the empty building and negotiate to stay there legitimately.

FREE KIPPING. Half-finished buildings usually provide enough shelter for a comfortable, uninterrupted kip. Robin Gray recommends garden huts in large garden centres which are often left open and provide a good night's shelter. Your luggage can be safely stowed in a locker at the station during the day. Elma Grey (the very same whose dire straits are described above) now lives in Utrecht and is registered with an anti-squatting agency. Their remit is to protect empty buildings which are liable to attract squatters. By getting someone to live in the building it's no longer a squattable option. It's a great way of having a huge place to live in very cheaply.

PSYCHIATRIC HOSPITALS. A most unexpected piece of advice came from a reader calling himself 'Superbean' who professes to have a borderline personality disorder and is schizo-affective:

> ***At one time I would frequently visit another UK town and their psychiatric unit for free sleeps. UK nuthouses are best hit out of hours. In Cornwall I would not have got in if I went via A&E. As it was, I was looking for a night shelter so I hit the homeless day centre and they did the rest. Police can get you assessed just about anywhere. Muteness and hiding away will get you a longer stay (free food and lodging) if that is your wish. Not eating/drinking will also cause alarms. All tried and tested. Should go in the next edition because your book is a survival bible and I'm a survivor (and a skint one at that).***

Apparently, psychiatric hospitals in most countries will admit a patient in a crisis or if deemed suicidal, but will still ask to see a European Health Card. I have censored some of his more distasteful hints concerning self-harm but pass on that the best 'nuthouse' Superbean ever stayed in was in Copenhagen.

FREE MEALS. Sometimes charities such as the Red Cross and Caritas give out free food, as David Bamford discovered when he was stranded in Villefranche unable to find a grape-picking job, along with scores of North Africans.

Restaurants may be willing to give you a free meal if you promise to recommend them to a guidebook or to correct the spelling on their menu (depriving future travellers of the delights of 'miscellaneous pork bowel', 'grilled chicken with swing' and 'vegetable craps'). It may also be possible to do an hour's work in exchange for a meal by going to the back door, possibly at fast food outlets. Some will even give a hand-out if you are brazen enough to request one.

SKIPPING. Also known as skip-diving, dumpster-diving or freeganism, this refers to retrieving from skips decent food that has been discarded by supermarkets and shops. The 'freecycle' culture is well established in most European cities and, once you become plugged into the network, you will discover the best places and times (e.g. Tuesdays after 10pm in Rotterdam). Beware of police looking for trespassers. There is even a website for British Freegans (freegan.org.uk).

BUFFET RESTAURANTS. In some countries like Sweden, the USA and Australia, reasonable restaurants offer all-you-can-eat buffets. Diners have been known to share their second and third helpings with friends who have merely bought a soft drink.

FREE WINE. You may come across free tastings at the roadside in wine producing areas from California to France (where these tastings are called *dégustations*). There will sometimes be something to eat – perhaps bread and cheese, or a local speciality.

FACTORY TOURS. Ask tourist offices if there are any food or drink factories nearby that offer free guided tours; these tours normally end with the gift of free samples of whatever is being produced. For example, distilleries in Scotland may hand out miniature bottles of whisky, and chocolate factories may dispense free treats. Note that some of the big mainstream factories now charge admission for their tours.

HAPPY HOURS. To attract customers at off-peak times, bars and pubs sometimes offer free snacks as well as cut-price drinks.

FAIRS AND FESTIVALS. Watch for giveaways at annual fairs and festivals. To take just one example in Italy, there are often free snacks at *sagra* (fairs).

SCAVENGING FOOD. If you are not too fussy about what you eat you can look for stale or sub-standard food that has been discarded by shops, bakeries at the end of the day, market stalls or even restaurants. Fancy resort hotels are also prone to throw out good food on a regular basis.

RAIDING FRIDGES. When Roger Blake was broke in Brisbane, he became semi-reliant on the communal fridge at the backpackers hostel. Most hostels have a communal shelf for well meaning travellers to leave behind unwanted and perishable items. Apparently it is possible to live off unwanted food, especially in city hostels where there is a major departure airport.

WASHING UP. In hostels, everyone is expected to wash and dry his or her own dishes. If you make it known that you are willing to take over this chore in exchange for a small contribution, you may find lots of willing takers. Never underestimate the laziness of travellers. One night Roger Blake made $8 in 'tips' by doing this. He then asked the hostel owners whether he could set up as a 'dishy' for tips only. But they didn't welcome the idea as it went against their philosophy of getting everyone to muck in together.

SELF-SERVICE RESTAURANTS. The original publisher of this book had an odd experience in a huge New York self-service restaurant. Having eaten his Waldorf salad he went to the water fountain for a drink. On returning to his table to conclude his repast he found a tramp-like character, who had obviously assumed the customer had left for good, busily wolfing down the much anticipated apple pie: the unwanted guest promptly fled. On leaving the self-service emporium the victim spotted the culprit peering through the plate glass window with several pals, in search of customers who left their tables leaving uneaten remains still on the table.

CASINOS. Large casinos often put on a lavish spread in the staff canteen. Assuming the staff is large and changeable enough, it may be possible to infiltrate it on an occasional basis for a good binge. Paul Edwards has happy memories of the seven cuisines served to staff at the Crown Casino in Melbourne. Casinos from Istanbul to Las Vegas are also known to hand round free snacks to punters who may not be required to spend money gambling.

FREELOADING. It might be possible to follow in the footsteps of the penniless young Dutch traveller, Ramon Stoppelenburg, who set up a website letmestayforaday.com. He claims that he received 2,784 offers of free hospitality on his two-year tour. More recently, journalist Paul Smith from Newcastle, aka the Twitch-hiker, set off to test whether social networking could possibly get a person round the world on the good will of people contacted solely through twitter. Amazingly he got close to his destination, but in April 2009 had to abandon his attempt to find a boat going to remote and uninhabited Campbell Island near Antarctica.

PUBLICITY TRADING. Just as the Twitch-hiker exploited international publicity of his quest, so an enterprising Canadian called Kyle MacDonald accomplished an incredible feat. Starting with a red paper clip, he used the internet to offer to trade up, and in 14 trades he had a house in a nondescript town in Saskatchewan. You can read how he did it at http://oneredpaperclip.blogspot.com.

BEGGING. Straightforward begging is normally humiliating, boring, unprofitable and illegal. The best way of achieving results is to make yourself so unbearable that people will pay you to go away – for example two people impersonating a lunatic and his keeper around the cafés of Paris, would be soon bribed to go away by pleasure-seeking Parisians and tourists.

IMPERSONATING PROPERTY BUYERS: Timeshare companies sometimes offer attractive sweeteners to potential investors simply to tour a property and sit through a sales spiel. While in Bali Jennifer and Eric decided to go for it:

> ***We've earned several free week stays in 5-star hotels by pretending we were going to buy a timeshare. On crowded streets in tourist resorts, locals are employed to find western tourist couples and offer them a free taxi ride to the complex. One guy that picked us up told us what the qualifications are so we could get our prizes and he a commission. One in the couple has to be over 30 and fully employed; you must have been living together more than three years and your holiday on Bali no longer than four weeks. We pretended we were staying at a more expensive hotel than we actually were. You fill in your ID and agree to listen for 90 minutes to their blah blah (careful, very tricky talk). And you get your prize, whether you buy their timeshare or not. I felt a little nervous though, in my disguise covering tattoos and dreadlocks, but we managed. We got the holiday, parasailing tickets and ugly white T-shirts. A week later we did it again for another company and have collected holidays in India and Aussie. Too bad you have to pay a $50 administration fee but you're still getting a week's stay worth $800.***

CLAIMING DEPOSITS. In Denmark, Sweden, Norway, Mexico, France, Spain, Italy, Australia, the US and many other countries you can earn some small change by taking wine, beer and coke bottles or aluminium cans for recycling back to shops for a refund of the deposit. It is best to look for bottles or cans after a beach party, a special event such as a festival or in the dustbins outside holiday villas early in the mornings.

AIRPORT TROLLEYS. In some airports, you have to insert a coin in order to have the use of a trolley. Many luggage-laden travellers do not bother returning their trolley to the trolley park for the return of their coin, and dump them by the taxi or bus stands. While waiting for a flight out of Toronto Airport, Hugh Hardie once made $15 by gathering up abandoned trolleys and retrieving a quarter for each one, though this practice has now been banned.

TRICKS AND SKILLS. If you know that you can drink a yard of ale, juggle four plates or smoke 27 cigars simultaneously, you might find people willing to have a sporting bet with you. We have heard of a traveller who erected a sign on the pavements 'Jokes – 25 Cents Each' and another who actually set up a Kissing Booth in London while waiting to find a proper job.

MEDICAL RESEARCH. Private companies providing clinical trials to the pharmaceutical industry often pay volunteers handsomely to test new drugs and techniques. Biotrax International maintains a free directory listing hundreds of such places worldwide that pay healthy volunteers to take part in drug trials. To access the Biotrax database you have to complete a short questionnaire (biotrax.com). Also check centerwatch.com or clinicaltrials.gov for US studies. You might also enquire at university psychology departments, where there may be a need for participants for perception tests, etc. More information can be found in the chapter on the UK.

SELLING BLOOD. Many countries pay blood and plasma donors handsomely, especially the USA and Middle East. Even if you donate your blood free of charge, you are always given a free drink and a snack.

SPERM DONATION. In many countries, fertility clinics pay (typically £25) for sperm samples. Men should be aware that they will only be invited to donate after screening and analysis of potential fertility (which might be traumatic). In the UK, donors can no longer maintain anonymity (so that any children born subsequently can trace their genetic fathers) which has resulted in a sharp drop in the number of donors and sperm shortages for couples seeking assisted fertilisation. Men should take seriously the decision to take part and not focus merely on the immediate financial gain.

EGG DONATION. Egg donation is a much more serious business and is against the law in the UK. Private fertility clinics in the US have been offering upwards of $5,000 for donated eggs which involves hormone treatment and surgery. Donors are paid 'compensation' starting at £600. According to another press report, Jewish donors can automatically expect $10,000–$15,000 and Oxbridge students are also in great demand. A simple web search reveals sites with names like eggdonor.com.

SELLING BELONGINGS. By the end of your trip many of your belongings may have become expendable. You can try selling them to fellow travellers in hostels, to second-hand shops or in markets. Be ruthless about what you do and do not need: you have taken your photos, so you don't need your camera, and you can transfer your belongings from your expensive backpack to a cheaper bag. Be prepared to spend some time haggling.

THE LAST RESORT. Sell this book – but memorise the contents first! Peter McGuire sold this book's sister publication *Teaching English Abroad* for 5,000 won in Korea to someone who was immediately offered double that amount by someone else. He in turn made copies of the relevant chapters and doubled his money.

APPENDIX 1

SOME USEFUL PHRASES

English: Do you need a helper/temporary assistant?
French: Avez-vous besoin d'un aide/assistant intérimaire?
German: Brauchen Sie eine Hilfe/einen Assistenten für eine begenzte Zeit?
Dutch: Kunt U een helper/tijdelijke assistent gebruiken?
Italian: Ha bisogno d'un aiutante/d'un assistente provvisorio?
Greek: Khryázeste kanénan ypálliyo/prosorynó voythó?

GB: Do you know if there is any work in the neighbourhood?
F: Savez-vous s'il y a du travail dans les environs?
D: Wissen Sie, ob es in der Nachbarschaft irgendwelche Arbeit gibt?
NL: Weet u of werk is in de buurt?
S: ¿Sabe usted si hay trabajo por aquí?
I: Lo sa si c'e lavoro nel vicinato?
GR: Xérete an yaprkhy dhoulyá styn peryokhý?

GB: Where is the employment office?
F: Où se trouve le bureau de placement?
D: Wo ist das Arbeitsamt?
NL: Waar is het kantoor voor arbeidsvoorziening?
S: ¿Donde esta la Oficina de Empleos?
I: Dove sta l'agenzia di collocamento?
GR: Poú ýno to grafýo (evréseos) ergasýas?

GB: What is the wage? Will it be taxed?
F: Quel est le salaire? Sera-t-il imposable?
D: Wie hoch ist der Lohn? Ist er steuerpflichtig?
NL: Hoe hoog is het loon? Is het belastbaar?
S: ¿Cuanto es el salario? ¿Esta sujeto al pago de impuestos?
I: Che e la paga? Sara tassata?
GR: Poso ýne to ymeromýsthyo? Tha forologhiyhý?

GB: Where can I stay? Will there be a charge for accommodation/food?
F: Où pourrais-je me loger? L'hébergement/les repas seront-ils payants?
D: Wo kann ich wohnen? Muss für Unterkunft und Verpflegung selb gezahlt werden?
NL: Waar kan ik onderdak vinden? Moet ik betalen voor huisvesting en maaltijden?
S: ¿Donde puedo alojar? ¿Hay que pagar por el alojamiento/la comida?
I: Dove posso stare? Avra una spesa per l'alloggio/il cibo?
GR: Pou boró na mýno? Tha khreothó ya ty dhyamoný/to fagytó

GB: Are there any cooking/washing facilities?
F: Est-ce qu'il y a des aménagements pour faire la cuisine/la lessive?
D: Gibt es Koch/Waschgelegenheiten?
NL: Is er kook/wasgelegenheid?
S: ¿Se puede cocinar/lavar la ropa?

I: Ci stanno dei mezzi per cucinare/lavorare?
GR: Ypárkhoun efkolýes ya mag#aayrema/pl#aaysymo?

GB: When will the harvest/job begin? How long will it last?
F: Quand commencera la moisson/le travail? Combien de temps dure-t'il?
D: Wann beginnt die Ernte/Arbeit? Wie lange wird sie dauren?
NL: Wanneer begint de oogst/job? Hoe lang zal het werk duren?
S: ¿Cuando comenzara la cosecha/el trabajo? ¿Cuanto durara?
I: Quando incomincia la messe/il lavoro? Per quanto tempo durera?
GR: Poté tharkhýsy o theryzmos/y dhoulyá? Póso tha dhyarkésy?

GB: What will be the hours of work?
F: Quelles seront les heures de travail?
D: Wie lange ist die Arbeitszeit?
NL: Wat zijn de werkuren?
S: ¿Cual sera el horario de trabajo?
I: Che saranno le ore del lavoro?
GR: Pyéz tha ý ne y órez ergasýas?

GB: Thank you for your help.
F: Merci de votre aide.
D: Danke für Ihre Hilfe.
NL: Dank U voor Uw hulp.
S: Gracias por su ayuda.
GR: Sas efkharystó ya tyn vóythýa sas.

APPENDIX 2

ANNA LING'S SHOESTRING TRAVELS

Cambridge
Departs home after A levels
↓
Morocco
Lived on a daily budget of €4
↓
Granada, Spain
Squatted and busked
↓
Beneficio, Spain
Worked and lived free in a community in the hills
↓
West Country, England
12-hour shifts in an egg-packing factory
↓
Bought a van with boyfriend Andy
↓
Rotterdam, Holland
Stayed in a squat (July 2008)
↓
Epernay, France
Champagne harvest (September 2008)
↓
Paris
Fire poi busker
↓
Cambridge
Worked in theatre bar to save for transatlantic flight
↓
Guatemala
Worked in hostel on Lake Atitlan (March 2009 – present)

BRADWELL JACKSON'S TEACHING TRAVELS

Tampa, Florida
Left job as a drug abuse counsellor to work his way around the world
↓
Registered with Servas and Hospitality Club for free accommodation
↓
Mexico City
Found a teaching job at the second institute he approached and stayed for 6+ months
↓
England
Stayed free with various hosts via Servas

Marseilles
Got responses after advertising as a private English tutor in free ads papers

↓

Registered with Couchsurfing for free accommodation

↓

Mauritania
Teacher at the English Language Center in the capital, Nouakchott (Mar-Dec 2007)

↓

Bamako, Mali
Stayed for 2 months with a couchsurfing host who paid him for English lessons (Jan-Feb 2008)

↓

Hebei Province, China
Teaching contract with Aston English Schools (Apr 08 - summer 09)

↓

Planning to move on to look for work in Southeast Asia

RICHARD FERGUSON'S ADVENTURES

New Zealand
Started from home in Auckland

↓

Lisbon, Portugal
Worked in 2 pizzerias while living in the Bairro Alto (old district)

↓

Buenos Aires, Argentina
Freelance English tutor @ 30 pesos per hour

↓

Barcelona, Spain
Unsuccessful job hunt due to visa problems

↓

Palma de Mallorca
Pub job (June-July 2008)

↓

Faliraki, Rhodes
Barman in nightclub, with accommodation provided

↓

Obtained 1-Year Working Holiday Visa for Sweden

↓

Brussels, Belgium
Hostel cleaner and barman in exchange for bed, food and €100 a week (Oct 2008)

↓

Stockholm, Sweden
Working in Galway Irish pub
(Jan 09 – present)

↓

Planning to go to Goa later in 2009 to look for bar work

APPENDIX 3

CURRENCY CONVERSION CHART

COUNTRY	£1	US$1
Argentina	5.3 peso	3.6 peso
Australia	A$2.06	A$1.41
Brazil	3.2 real	2.2 real
Bulgaria	2.1 lev	1.5 lev
Canada	C$1.80	C$1.24
Chile	850 peso	580 peso
China	10 renminbi	6.8 renminbi
Colombia	3,500 peso	2,400 peso
Czech Republic	29 koruna	20 koruna
Denmark	8.2 kroner	5.6 kroner
Ecuador	US$1.46	1
Egypt	8.2 Egyptian pound	5.6 Egyptian pound
Eurozone	1.10 euro	75 euro
Hong Kong	11.2 HK dollar	7.8 HK dollar
Hungary	327 forint	223 forint
India	73 rupee	50 rupee
Indonesia	17,000 rupiah	11,600 rupiah
Israel	6.1 New Shekel	4.1 New Shekel
Japan	146 yen	100 yen
Kenya	117 Kenya shilling	80 Kenya shilling
Korea	1,929 won	1,300 won
Malaysia	5.2 ringgit	3.6 ringgit
Mexico	20 peso	13.7 peso
Morocco	12.3 dirham	8.4 dirham
Nepal	117 rupee	80 rupee
New Zealand	NZ$2.50	NZ$1.73
Norway	9.7 krone	6.6 krone
Peru	4.5 new sol	3.1 new sol
Poland	4.9 zloty	3.3 zloty
Russia	49 rouble	33 rouble
Saudi Arabia	5.5 riyal	3.75 riyal
Singapore	2.20 Singapore dollar	1.51 Singapore dollar
Slovakia	33 koruna	22 koruna
South Africa	13.3 rand	9.1 rand
Sweden	12 krona	8.2 krona
Switzerland	1.6 Swiss franc	1.14 Swiss franc
Taiwan	49 Taiwan new dollar	33 Taiwan new dollar
Thailand	51 baht	35 baht
Turkey	2.35 lira	1.60 lira
USA	1.65 dollar	–

Current exchange rates are printed every Monday in the *Financial Times* and are available on the *FT* site as well as at other sites such as the Universal Currency Converter at xe.com/ucc.

Nicole Gluckstern (American free spirit writing from Africa): *Hi there, how nice to find mail from a cult hero while in Burkina Faso, it's almost surreal! Love the book.*

Roger Blake from Harrogate: *Last summer I picked up the new edition of* WYWATW *and found my name in the Acknowledgements – what more inspiration do I need to head off again? Thank you for your support in publishing such an interesting and informative read... In the closing passage of your Preface you say that your book tries to renew optimism and spark the imagination; well Susan, it certainly does just that!*

Hillary Chura (*New York Times* journalist): *Work your Way around the World was a great book and actually encouraged several of my friends and me to take off after college. I was abroad for 2.5 years in London, Spain and Cairo... We all talk about what a great experience it was.*

Charlie Wetherall (runs a website 'The Runaway Trader'): *I first met with Susan Griffith's work in the early 1980s when I... was attracted to the title because it offered a glimmer of hope that – someday – I could scrape up enough courage to escape the drudgery of my own existence and see some of the world, earning my way as I moved along... If you' ve got any kind of yen to get away from it all, check out Griffith's book. She may just plant a seed in your mind to make the Great Getaway, like she did in mine those many years ago.*

Catherine Howard, Irish woman who worked at Disneyworld, Florida. *I'd like to commend you on your excellent publication, Work Your Way Around the World. I received a copy of it for Christmas last year and my only complaint is that after reading it you can't decide what you want to do because there's so much choice. Thanks again for your wonderfully informative book!*

Joseph Tame, between studying in Japan and taking the Trans-Siberian train home to the UK: *I remain grateful to you and WYWATW – if it wasn't for the inspiration I got from that I wouldn't be here today! Thank you!*

Caity Williams (Special Programmes Director, CCUSA): *Work Your Way was my bible in my younger days when I was traveling – so I got this strange sort of star-struck feeling when I got an email from you.*

Richard Ferguson (New Zealander working his way around the world): *I just want to say your book is great. Before leaving NZ I was full of apprehension. But after reading about so many people landing jobs all over, I was put at ease. I've been working in Lisbon for almost two months now.*

Carisa Fey (from Stuttgart): *Thanks for your books, they helped me so much, especially the psychological effect. Everyone first told me that I was crazy and cannot do it, but so I knew, many others have done it before and so can I.*

Michael Jaczynski, London: *Learned Oracle: I have been in possession of WYW for less than 24 hrs but am already a fan. I just couldn't put it down last night and today feel much more confident about my impending adventure.*

Karen Martin from Grimsby who worked in the Netherlands, on a French farm and a winter season in the Alps: *I do feel that my time travelling – even if I didn't get to half as many places as I would like (still time though!!) – touched me in many ways and changed my life, confidence and outlook for the best.....and I will not forget the influence your book had on me!!*

Indu Shakya, Know Nepal: *We appreciate your hard work to bring people around the world together.*